Caribbeana.

BEING

Miscellaneous Papers

RELATING TO THE

History, Genealogy, Topography, and Antiquities

OF THE

BRITISH WEST INDIES.

EDITED BY

VERE LANGFORD OLIVER, M.R.C.S., F.S.A.
MEMBER OF THE AMERICAN ANTIQUARIAN SOCIETY.
CORRESPONDING MEMBER OF THE NEW ENGLAND HISTORIC GENEALOGICAL SOCIETY

Vol. 5

VOLUME V.

LONDON:
MITCHELL HUGHES AND CLARKE,
11 & 13, BREAM'S BUILDINGS, CHANCERY LANE, E.C.4.

1919.

Holborn (or Fontabelle) House, Bridgetown, Barbados.

PREFACE.

WITH the completion of this volume has come the armistice, and with the advent of peace we may now look forward to an amelioration of the difficult condition of the printing trade.

In spite of shortage of workmen, high prices and scarcity of paper, this magazine has been carried on without a break, for which our thanks are due to Messrs. Mitchell Hughes and Clarke.

To meet partly the increased charges and wages it has been found advisable to raise the amount of subscription from 10*s*. to 15*s*. per annum, and even with that increase the Editor will be out of pocket £100 a year.

Among several subscribers who have passed away, we have to deplore more especially the loss of Sir Alfred Scott-Gatty, "Garter," who was, on his mother's side, great-grandson of a planter in Dominica, and grandson of the Rev. A. J. Scott, who resided in Antigua 1772-76 with Sir Ralph Payne, and was later Chaplain of H.M.S. *Victory*. Another old contributor was the late Lieut.-Col. H. W. Pook, who was interested in St. Kitts, and was an active member of the Society of Genealogists of London.

During the past year the list of wills in Barbados to 1800 has been concluded, and P.C.C. Administrations brought down to 1666.

West Indian Grantees of Arms have been reprinted from the Harleian Society's volumes. Mr. Reginald Glencross has been able to resume his abstracts of Nevis Wills for which we are grateful. West Indian M.I. in this country have appeared regularly, and there is very little material left.

Numerous short pedigrees continue to be printed, and of these there are hundreds more in MS. They must of necessity be often sketchy and doubtful, until a search in the island record offices has been made, but they nevertheless afford a basis for future research and correction.

A supplement to the Book-plates has increased the collection to 806, and it is now very difficult to discover additional plates, though Mr. Frederic Cattle is ever on the watch.

V. L. OLIVER.

LIST OF SUBSCRIBERS.

Athill, Chas. H., Richmond Herald, College of Arms, Queen Victoria Street, E.C. 4.
Baun, William W. van, M.D., 1404 Spruce Street, Philadelphia.
Bosanquet, N. E. T., Arthur's, St. James's Street, S.W. 1.
Bowen and Sons, 20 Broad Street, Bridgetown, Barbados (2 copies).
Bromley, Mrs. John, 30 Manchester Street, W. 1.
Calder, J. V., Worthy Park, Ewarton, Jamaica.
Cattle, F., Ravenswood, Heanor, Derbyshire.
Chambers, Bertram, Rear-Admiral R.N. On active service.
Cornish, J. E., 16 St. Ann's Square, Manchester.
Da Costa, Dr. G. F., 14 Duke Street, Kingston, Jamaica.
Douglas, R. Langton, 2 Hill Street, Piccadilly, W. 1.
Dyett, R. H. Kortright, St. John's, Antigua.
Ferguson, T. Colyer-, Ightham Mote, Sevenoaks.
Firebrace, C. W., Frensham Place, Farnham, Surrey.
Ford, H. A., British Consulate General, Philadelphia, U.S.A.
Fry, George S., The Grove, Nether Street, Finchley, Middlesex.
Gibson, Mrs. Wm., Shady Avenue, Squirrel Hill, Pittsburgh, U.S.A.
Gillespie, W., 82 Fenchurch Street, E.C. 3.
Glencross, R. M., 176 Worple Road, Wimbledon, S.W. 19.
Grant, Capt. Percy, C.B., R.N. On active service.
Hay, Miss G. C., Fort William Estate, Petersfield, Jamaica.
Haynes, Hon. A. P., Bissex Hill, Barbados.
Hillman, E. H., 4 Somers Place, Hyde Park, W.
Kenneway, Mrs., Stephens Plot, Spetisbury, Dorset.
Lawrence, W. F., Cowesfield House, Salisbury, Wilts.
Leigh, R. A. Austen-, The Froyles, Lindfield, Sussex.
Livingston, Noel B., 63 Harbour Street, Kingston, Jamaica.
Lyons, W. D. W., 80 St. George's Road, S.W. 1.
Murray, Keith W., 37 Cheniston Gardens, W. 8.
Nembhard, Miss M., Hotel Somerset, Orchard Street, W. 1.
Oliver, Tho. L., Oakhill, Bursledon, Hants.
Ottley, Sir Chas., Rear Admiral R.N., 17 Queen's Gate Gardens, S.W. 1.
Pedder, J. L. K., Heywoods, St. Peter's, Barbados.
Phipps, H. R., Col. R.F.A., Innellan, Cavendish Road, Sutton.
Sainthill, Mrs. A., 104 Sloane Street, S.W.
Scarlett, Mrs. B. F., Penenden House, Boxley, Kent.

Sinckler, E. G., Douglas, St. Peter's, Barbados.
Skeete, E. L., Whitehaven, St. Philips, Barbados.
Stechert, G. E. and Co., 2 Star Yard, Carey Street, W.C. 2 (2 copies).
Taylor-Watson, J.A., Wellington Club, Grosvenor Place, S.W. 1.
Trollope, Sir W. H., Bart., 5 Montagu Square, Marylebone, W. 1.
West, E. E., Shoyswell, Highfield Road, Dublin.
Woodruff, C., M.D., Hyattsville, Maryland.
Yearwood, H. G., Friendly Hall, St. Michael's, Barbados.

LIBRARIES AND INSTITUTIONS.

American Antiquarian Society, Worcester, Mass.
Baltimore, Maryland—Peabody Institute.
Barbados—Free Public Library.
Boston, Mass.—Boston Athenæum.
Cambridge—University Library.
Cambridge, Mass.—Harvard College.
Dominica—Free Public Library.
Dublin—Trinity College Library.
Edinburgh—Advocates' Library.
Jamaica—The Institute, Kingston.
London—British Museum.
Royal College of Arms.
Royal Colonial Institute.
New England Historic Genealogical Society, 18 Somerset Street, Boston, U.S.A.
New York Historical Society, 170 Central Park West, New York, U.S.A.
New York Public Library.
Oxford. The Bodleian Library.
Pennsylvania Historical Society, 1300 Locust Street, Philadelphia, U.S.A.
St. Kitts, Administrator's Office.
West India Committee, 15 Seething Lane, E.C. 3.

CONTENTS.

LIST OF ILLUSTRATIONS.

ADDITIONS AND CORRECTIONS.

Page 2.

Mrs. Henrietta Tobin was Capt. Tobin's sister not wife, who married 9 Dec. 1736 Samuel Clarke, Jr. Her sister Sarah Tobin married Maurice Berkeley, Jr., and died 23 Aug. 1755, aged 53. Another sister, Mary, b. 1696, married John Symonds, b. 1686, B.A. Oxf. 1708, speaker 1712. She was buried 10 Dec. 1762, aged 66. Further notes will appear in Vol. VI.

Page 17.

1687, March. Lieut. John Hill then a Member of the Assembly.

1672, Nov. Petition of John Rodney & Frances his wife to the King that Stephen Mall d. seized of an est. in N. worth £500 a year. Pet^{r} Frances his dau. & h. mar. Wm. Richardson, merch^{t}, after whose death petitioners intermarried & returned for England. In their absence Tho. Cole, pretending a debt of 60,000 lbs. of sugar (about £300), s^{d} pl^{n} was sold by outcry in 1670, & Cole bought it for 60,000 lbs., turned out their servants, seized their stock & goods & felled timber.

Inventory appended: 33 negroes & Indians, 4 w. servants, 9 cattle, 2 sugar mills, 7 coppers with stills & coolers, besides houses & near 100 acres of canes.

Gov. Sir Jas. Russell replied that the estate was greatly encumbered with debts & Cæsar Rodney, Capt. R.'s brother, wasted the stock (Col. Cal., p. 429). On 23 June 1673 a special commission was ordered to be held in Nevis. (*Ibid*, p. 502.)

Hon. James Symonds of Nevis. Will dated 21 July 1758. To Eliz. & Henriotta Richardson, daus. of John Richardson, Esq., by my niece Eliz. his wife, 10,000 lbs. each at 21.

Page 35.

See p. 306 for the will of Jonathan Netheway, sen. It was his son who died in 1726.

Letter from John Netheway, Dep.-Gov. at Nevis, 24 Sept. 1689. ... My old age & infirmities ... desire to go to New England, where I have a son & dau. (America & W.I., vol. 550, p. 118.)

Page 41.

In Gillingham Church is a tablet recording the death at Nevis of Mrs. Christiana Broome, widow of Richard (*sic*) B., on 1 Nov. 1720, aged 68. On her tombstone the date of her birth is given as 25 Feb. 1657, but the 7 may be 1. She was evidently baptised 21 March 1652-3. Some additional notes will appear later.

Page 57.

Susanna Temple was dau. of Robert not Thomas Temple according to her M.I. Eliz. widow of James Lawes died 15 & was buried 23 Jan. 1784, aged 80, in Westminster Abbey, & by her will, dated 19 Nov. 1783, bequeathed to her relation Wm. Gale son of the late Henry Gale of St. Eliz., Jamaica, then at Westminster School, her house in Portman Sq. and her estate in the said island.

Page 128.

11th line. For "Cooke" read "Tooke."

P. 138.

In the Sloane MSS. are four letters from Dr. Rose Fuller, 1733-39 at Jamaica.

Page 168.

St. George's, Basseterre, St. Kitts. 1776, Feb. 12. Henry Morton Willis, s. of Mark & Ann Arabella Dyer, b. 20 Oct. 1775, bapt.

St. Anne's, Sandy Point, St. Kitts. 1748, Oct. 10. The Honourable Charles Morton, Esq., & Anne Louisa Georges.

Page 173.

St. George's, Basseterre, St. Kitts. 1762, . . . John Spratt & Mary Roberdeau p. Lycence.

Page 186.

Newton Walker was only child & heir of Alex. Walker of Barbados, Esq., and died 1772. Wm. Walker, attorney-gen., was of Mount Wilton plantation in 1722.

Page 197.

St. John's, Antigua.

1810 June 13 William Sinclair Cathcart, Infant son of L[t] Col. George Mackie, 3[d] Batt[n] 60th Reg. and Catherine Culy his wife, bapt.

Page 211.

James Smith of St. Thomas Lowland, Nevis, Esq. Will dated 29 Oct. 1778. To Roger Pemberton Bridgwater, son of Thadeus M[c]Carty B., by his late deceased wife Hannah, £800 at 14, & to Bridget Pemberton B. his sister £600. (Warburton, 323.)

St. George's, Basseterre, St. Kitts.

1762 Nov. 3 Rich[d] s. of Rich[d] & Susan Bridgwater, bapt.

1763 Aug. 17 Henrietta dau. of Rich[d] & Susannah Bridgwater, b. 11 June ult. bapt.

1764 Dec. 1 Sarah Bridgwater, buried.

Page 227.

On the 24th Dec. 1918 at 20 Gloucester-terr., Hyde Park, Magnus Forbes Morton-Herbert, late Capt. 48th Northamptonshire Regt. & Exon of the Yeomen of the Guard in his 93rd year. (West Indian papers please copy.) ("Morning Post" of 30 Dec.)

Page 288.

Luffman writing in 1786 describes a tumulus to the south of Parham, as oblong in shape, very regular, lessening gradually from its base to the top, which was flat, 5-600 feet long and from 40-50 feet high.

Page 328.

To the Campbell coat add :—*a bordure gobony Ermine and Vert*, but this may have been omitted from the book plate by the designer. Peter Campbell Scarlett was left his grandfather's watch, chain and seal.

The following names were unfortunately omitted from the Index :—

Caribbeana.

Tobin of Nevis.

James Tobin, the Elder, of Nevis, Esq. Will dated 13 Oct. 1767. My son James and dau. Eliz. Cross £10 each. (All estate to several coloured children. A black woman called Sophy Tobin named.) Sworn 31 March 1770. (Nevis Deeds, Book of Wills, p. 258.)

Geo. Webbe, the Elder, of Redland in Westbury-upon-Trym, co. Gloucester. Esq. Will dated 31 Dec. 1788. My dau. Eliz., wife of James Tobin, Esq., £1100 and £100 a year (316, Bishop).

1707-8. Census of Nevis. Walter Tobin 4 w. males, 4 w. females, 42 slaves,

1713. Walter T. appraises goods. (Nevis Records, p. 33.)

1724. Deposition of Mr. John Tobin of Nevis that his sister Symonds had not had an illegitimate child.

1727. Census of Nevis. Tho. and John Tobin.

1728, Nov. 21. Ind're between the Hon. Chas. Bridgewater, Senior, Esq., and Eliz. his now wife, Chas. B. his son and heir by Eliz. his wife, and Eliz. Tobin, dau. of Walter T., planter, dec[d], and John T., planter, and Sarah T., widow of Walter. A marriage to be solemnized between Cha. B., J[r], and Eliz. T. Walter T. by his will made 10 April 1719 gave his dau. Eliz. £200 st. and £500 c. (Nevis Deeds, ii., 65.)

1731, Nov. About the middle of Oct. last some persons arm'd broke into the House of M[r] Spike at Cove in Ireland, where lodg'd M[r] Maurice Berkley, jun. his Wife, Wife's Sister, & a Servant Maid, Passengers in the Apollo, Cap[t] Tobin for Nevis.

They went up into the Chamber, where M[rs] Henrietta Tobin lay, took her out of Bed, & carry'd her off with only her Shift on. The Principal in this Fact was one William Power, who had lately been several Times in her company. M[r] Berkley took his Sword, engaged & wounded a Person who stood Centinel at the Door; then pursu'd them to the Strand, where he was again oppos'd by three Men armed with Swords & Pistols. Upon which he cry'd out Murder, etc., two or three coming to his assistance, they follow'd them to the Waterside, took Boat, & coming up with them, rescued her amidst all their Fire. The account she gave of their Usage was, that they forced her on Horseback before William Power, which with struggling, she had quitted several Times, & was as often remounted by his assistants. ("G.M.," 498.)

1761, April 30. James Tobin, the Elder, of Nevis, Esq., conveys to James Smith, Esq., his plantation in the p. of St. Thomas of 200 acres in Trust. (Nevis Deeds, vol. K., p. 325.)

1766, July 7. Ja: Tobin of Salisbury, Esq; to Miss Webbe of Stradford, with 10,000 l. ("G.M.," 342.)

See *ante* for several close rolls recorded in 1760, 1774, 1792, 1795 and 1797.

1776, Dec. 3. James Tobin recommended for the Council of Nevis.

ARMS.—*Or, three (? holly) leaves.*
CREST.—*A dove, in its beak a sprig.* (From W.I. Bookplate No. 605.)

Walter Tobin of Nevis 1707-8.=Sarah . . . ., a widow 1728; bur. at St. John's 17 April 1749. Will dated 10 April 1719.

John Tobin, born 1693; bur. at St. John's, Figtree, 19 Oct. 1757, aged 64.

James Tobin, born 1698; ? a ship master and of the "Apollo" 1731; bur. at St. John's 31 March 1770, aged 72. Will dated 13 Oct. 1767; sworn 31 March 1770. Conveyed to T. in 1761 his plantation in St. Thomas of 200 acres.=[? Henrietta 1731.]

Elizabeth Tobin, mar. Cha. Bridgewater, Jun.; settlement dated 21 Nov. 1728. She remar. . . . . Thomson. Her will dated 1765.

A

James Tobin, born 1737; articled 1753 as a solicitor; of Salisbury 1777; of Berkley Square, Bristol, 1798; died 6 Oct. 1817, aged 80. M.I. in Clifton Burial-ground (*ante*, II., 378). Wrote political pamphlets in defence of slave owners. ("D.N.B.;" W.I. Bookplate No. 605.)=Eliz. Webbe, dau. of Geo. Webbe of Nevis and Bristol; mar. at Stratford-sub-Castra, co. Wilts, 30 June 1766; died 8 July 1821, aged 80. M.I. in Clifton.

Eliz. Tobin, mar. . . . . Crosse. John Tobin Crosse, ? their son, mar. 1790 Mary Burke. (*Ante*, II., 168, 325.)

B

James Webbe Tobin of Bristol and Nevis, born 1767; of Wadham Coll., Oxford, matric. 9 Nov. 1787, aged 20, B.A. 1791; died 30 Oct. 1814 in Nevis.=. . . .

George Webbe Tobin, born 13 Dec. 1768 at Salisbury; Rear-Admiral R.N., C.B.; died 10 April 1838, aged 69, at Teignmouth. M.I. there with his arms (*ante*, IV., 85).=Dorothy, dau. of Capt. Gordon Skelly, R.N., and widow of Major Duff, 26 Foot; mar. 13 June 1804; died 30 Aug. 1840, aged 72. M.I. at Weston, Bath.

Walter Tobin, admitted to St. Paul's School 1 June 1821, aged 9.

Henry Hope Tobin, admitted to St. Paul's School 5 Feb. 1822, aged 8; drowned at Heidelburg 5 June 1831, aged 17.

Frederick Tobin, went to California; last heard of 1840.

George Webbe Tobin, at Eton 1821; Capt. Q. Bays; died 21 Sept. 1840, aged 33. M.I. at St. Paul's, Bristol, and at Weston. (*Ante*, I., 181; II., 305.)=Susannah Christian, dau. of John Cobham, Esq., of Barbados and Bristol; first-cousin to her husband; died 2 Jan. 1840. M.I. at St. Paul's, Bristol. (*Ante*, II., 305.)

Eliza Lucy Hope Tobin, only dau., born 25 Nov. 1810; died 11 March 1834, aged 23. M.I. at Weston. (*Ante*, I., 181.)

C

O'Hara John Tobin, born 1848; Lieut. R.M.=Lillian May, mar. 1890.

James Tobin, born 1849; died 1855.

Margaret Anne, mar. Surg.-Major Trouh (?); died 1888.

1776, Sept. 23. Power of Attorney by Lydia Thomas Tobin, late of Nevis, now of Bristol, spr., to Jas. Tobin of Salisbury, who intends soon to embark to Nevis .... mentions slaves and other property as joint owner with her sister Anne Tobin.

1791. Jas. Tobin of Bristol, Esq., power of Attorney to Geo. Webbe, the Yr, and Edwd Brazier of Nevis. (Nevis Deeds.)

1798, Nov. 9. Jas. Tobin of Berkley Sq., Bristol, Esq., power of Attorney to John Taylor of Nevis to manage his plantation, etc. (*Ibid.*)

1798, Oct. 29. Ind're of sale of a slave by Jas. Williams as attorney for Jas. Tobin, Azariah Pinney and Henry Hope Tobin of Bristol, merchants.

1798. Sarah Tobin, widow, ex'trix of the will of Walter Tobin, deceased, release to Y. S. Symonds in the presence of John Tobin.

1801, June 13. Capt. Tobin R.N. to Mrs. Duff, of Richmond co. York, widow of the late Major D. of the 26th foot. ("G.M.," 595.)

A

Henrietta Tobin, mar. 9 Dec. 1736 Sam. Clarke, Jun.

Lydia Thomas Tobin and Anne Tobin, their power of attorney 1776.

B

Henry Hope Tobin of Bristol, merchant, dead 1812. = Lucy, dau. of Tho. Oliver, Lieut.-Gov. of Mass., and of Antigua and Bristol; mar. 22 Nov. 1798 at St. Augustine's; died 16 Jan. 1857, aged 85. M.I. at Clifton. (*Ante*, III., 90.)

John Tobin, born 26 Jan. 1770 at Salisbury; of Lincoln's Inn 1784, play-writer; died Dec. 1804. M.I. at Cove, co. Cork.

Eliz. Tobin, born 1772; mar. 4 Jan. 1808, at St. Augustine's, John Cobham of Bristol and Barbados. He died 26 Oct. 1811, aged 48. She died 20 May 1824, aged 52. M.I. at St. Paul's, Bristol. (*Ante*, II., 804.)

D

Jas. Webbe Tobin, born 1801; 2nd Lieut. R.A.; died 1821.

Cha. Meadows Tobin, born 1802; Lieut. 58th Regt.; died 1826.

Mary Theodosia, youngest dau. of Major O'Hara Baynes, R.A.; mar. at Dawlish. = John Tobin, born 1804; Capt. 11th Foot; died 1873. = Mary, widow of Major Good. s.p.

E

Tho. Geo. Webbe Tobin, born 1847; Ensign 6th Foot; died 1891. = Alice Maud Mary, dau. of Capt. Atwood, 27th Foot.

Cha. J. Villiers Tobin, born 1849; died at Cape Town 20 Dec. 1869, aged 20.

Wm. Henry John Tobin, born 1850. = Laura Brown, mar. 1878; in New Zealand.

C

Charles Tobin, born 1879.

Geo. Hen. Webbe Tobin.

William Tobin.

Laura Tobin.

Frederica Tobin.

Constance Tobin.

Eleanor Tobin.

1808, Jan. 4. At Bristol, John Cobham, Esq. of that city, to Miss Tobin, dau. of Jas. T. esq. ("G.M.," 85.)

1811. The Hon. Jas. Weekes of Nevis wrote that Mr. J. W. Tobin was first met by John Peterson 25 years ago, and that the former's mother's family was connected with the latter.

1811. See an extract of Mr. Jas. Tobin's letter in Southey's "West Indies," p. 498.

1814, Oct. 30. Died at his father's estate in Nevis, of a fever, James Webbe Tobin, esq., etc. Long notice. ("G.M.," 1815, p. 178.)

1815, Dec. 8. Capt. Geo. Tobin, R.N. to be a C.B. (*Ibid.*, 629.)

1821, June 1. Walter Tobin, aged 9, s. of James Webb T., 17 Ratcliffe Terrace.

1822, Feb. 5. Henry Hope Tobin, aged 8, s. of James Webbe Tobin, 1 Little Carter Lane. ("Register of St. Paul's School," pp. 264, 265.)

1831, June 5. While bathing at Heidelburg, in his 18th year, Henry-Hope, youngest son of the late Jas. Webbe T. esq. of the I. of Nevis and of Bristol. ("G.M.," 561.)

1834, March 11. At Bath, aged 23, Eliza Lucy Hope, only dau. of Capt. Tobin, R.N., C.B. (*Ibid.*, 566.)

1838, April 10. At Teignmouth, Devonshire, aged 69, Rear-Adm. Geo. Tobin, C.B. Long notice. (*Ibid.*, 101.)

1840, Jan. 2. At Clifton, Susanna-Christian, wife of Geo. Webbe Tobin esq. only dau. of the late John Cobham, esq. of Barbadoes. (*Ibid.*, 218.)

B

- Chas. Meadows Tobin, born 1775; matric. from Wadham College, Oxford, 9 Nov. 1792, aged 17, B.A. 1797.
- Joseph Webbe Tobin, born 1776; Gen. R.A.; died at Exmouth 21 Feb. 1863, aged 86. M.I. at Littleham, co. Devon. (*Ante*, IV., 83.) = Harriet Baynes, mar. 1799; died 29 April 1863, aged 83.
- Frances Tobin, mar. 3 May 1804, at St. Augustine's, Bristol, Rob. Bush of Clifton.

D

- Eliz. Margaret Tobin, died 21 Dec. 1879, aged 72. M.I.
- Henry Tobin, born 1808; mar.
- Geo. Edw. Alex. Tobin, Capt. 2 Queen's, born 1815; died 29 June 1892, aged 77. M.I. at Littleham, co. Devon. = Louisa, only dau. of Capt. Williams, R.N., D.L., of Sowdon, co. Devon; mar. 2 Nov. 1846; died 16 April 1909, aged 89.
- Edward Tobin.

E

- Edw. O'Hara Tobin, born 1852; R.N.; in New Zealand.
- Fred. John Tobin, born 1856; Major R.I. Rifles. = Clare Edith Georgie, dau. of T. Waters of Parsons Town; died 1897.
- Rev. Cecil Alex. Tobin, born 1856, in New Zealand. = Sarah Eliz., dau. of Capt. Brown, 8th Foot.
- Fra. Alfred Tobin, born 1863; died 1864.

The last two are the children of Rev. Cecil Alex. Tobin and Sarah Eliz.:

- Jas. Fethard Tobin.
- Kathleen Tobin, born 1891.

1846, Nov. 2. At Lympstone, George Tobin, esq. Queen's Royal Regt. to Louisa, only dau. of Thos. Williams, esq. Commander R.N. a magistrate for Devon. ("G.M.," 1847, p. 194.)

1847, Sept. 23. At Dawlish, Capt. John Tobin, late of the 11th Regt. eldest son of Lieut.-Gen. Tobin, Royal Art. to Mary-Theodosia, youngest dau. of Major O'Hara Baynes h. p. Royal Art. (*Ibid.*, 632.)

1863, Feb. 21. At Exmouth, aged 86, Gen. G. W. Tobin, Commanding 3rd Brigade R.A. entered the service in 1794, etc. (*Ibid.*) Also Harriet his widow.

COVE, IRELAND.

M.I. to John Tobin esq. of Linc. Inn who d. at sea Dec. 1804. ("G.M." for 1815, p. 178.)

There is a good account of him in Hoare's "Wilts," vi., 653.

STRATFORD-SUB-CASTLE, CO. WILTS.

1766, June 30. James Tobin, esq., and Eliz. Webbe; sp. lic.

James Tobin wrote several pamphlets in favour of the planters. The Rev. James Ramsay, sometime Rector in St. Kitts, wrote in favour of the slaves. The two thus became antagonists, and numerous letters, replies and rejoinders passed between them.

I have "A letter to James Tobin Esq. late M. of H.M. Council in Nevis from James Ramsay A.M. Vicar of Teston pp. 40, 8vo, published in 1787." This was written after the publication of "A short Rejoinder to the Rev. Mr. Ramsay's Reply by James Tobin Esq." Mr. Ramsay states that he knew a ship-master of Nevis called Tobin, whose son was sent to England and placed with an attorney. About 1760-1 this son visited Nevis, but soon returned to England. On the death of his father about 1768-9 he made another short visit to Nevis, and in 1779 came out a third time and remained two or three years.

In another volume of pamphlets, formerly Jas. Tobin's own copy with his bookplate, is bound "A plain man's thoughts on the present price of Sugar pp. 22, 8°, 1792." Signed in ink: "James Tobin."

Some few years ago a gentleman interested in the Tobins corresponded with me, and as a result printed "Notes on the Tobin Family," pp. 6, 8vo, with a folding tabular pedigree.

The Case of Henry Willoughby, Esq;

Claiming the title, honour, and dignity of

WILLOUGHBY OF PARHAM.

To be heard at the bar at the House of Lords on the .... Day of .... 1767.

The Petition ſets forth, That Sir *William Willoughby*, Knight, was, by Letters Patent dated 16th *February*, 1ſt *Edward* 6th, created Lord *Willoughby of Parham*, to hold to him, and the Heirs Male of his Body.

That he was ſucceeded in the ſaid Honor by his Son Lord *Charles*, who had Iſſue Five Sons; namely, *William*, Sir *Ambroſe*, *Edward*, *Charles*, and Sir *Thomas*; and was ſucceeded in the Honor by his Grandſon Lord *William*, the Son and Heir of *William* his eldeſt Son.

That the Heirs Male of the ſaid *William*, Firſt Son of Lord *Charles*, enjoyed the ſaid Honor, ſucceſſively, till the Year 1680, when Lord *Charles*, the laſt ſurviving Heir Male of *that* Line, died without Iſſue Male; and thereby the Line of the ſaid *William*, Firſt Son of Lord *Charles*, became extinct.

That thereupon the Petitioner's Grandfather *Henry*, the only Son and Heir of *Edward*, who was the only Son and Heir of the ſaid Sir *Ambroſe*, *Second* Son of the firſt-named Lord *Charles*, became rightfully intitled to the Honor of

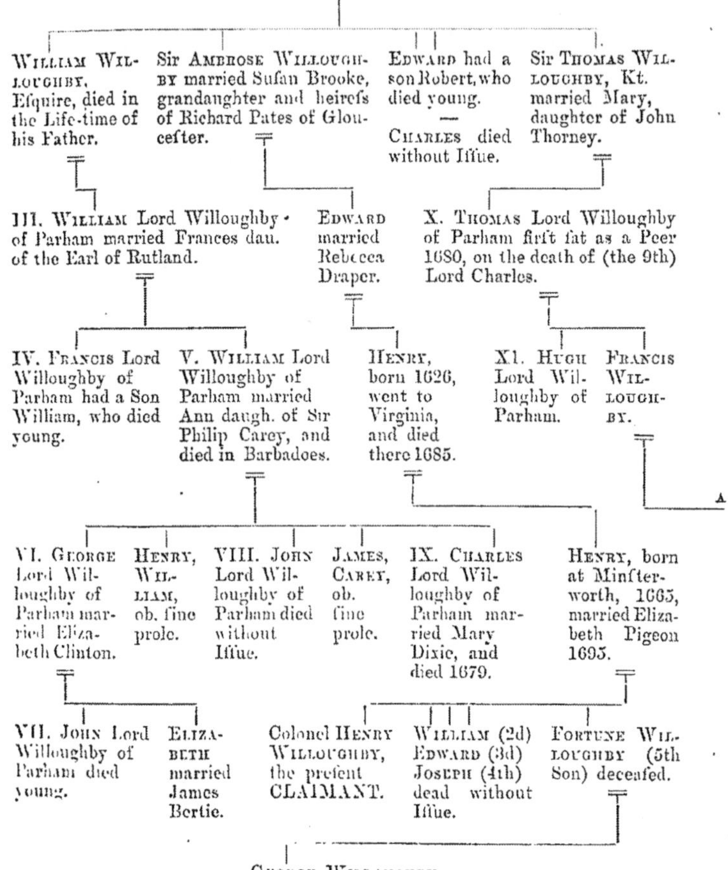

Reſolv'd that the Petr has fully made out his Claim. (Written in ink.)

Willoughby of Parham; but that in 1680, and for fome Years before, the Petitioner's Grandfather was fettled in *Virginia*, and died there in 1685, ignorant of the Failure of the Iffue Male of the *elder* Branch, defcended from the *firft* named Lord *Charles*, and left Iffue the Petitioner's Father his only Son, then an Infant.

That the Petitioner's Grandfather and his Infant Son being, in 1680, the only Male Defcendants of the faid Sir *Ambrofe Willoughby*, *Second* Son of Lord *Charles*, and the Petitioner's Grandfather not appearing to claim the faid Honor; and *Edward* and *Charles*, the Third and Fourth Sons of Lord *Charles*, being long before dead without Iffue, *Thomas Willoughby*, the only Son of Sir *Thomas Willoughby*, the *youngeft* Son of Lord *Charles*, claimed the faid Honor, and took his Seat in Parliament on the 21ft of *October* 1680; and the Defcendants of the faid *Thomas* fat in Parliament until the laft *Hugh*, who fat in Parliament by that Title, and died without Iffue in *January* 1765; by whofe Death the Iffue Male of Sir *Thomas Willoughby*, the *Fifth* Son of the *firft* named *Charles*, became extinct.

That the Petitioner is *Heir Male* of the Body of Sir *William Willoughby*, Knight, the Firft Grantee of the Honor; being a *Lineal* Defcendant from the faid Sir *Ambrofe*, the Second Son of the firft named *Charles* Lord *Willoughby*, in the following Manner:

Sir *Ambrofe Willoughby*, by his Wife *Sufan Brooke*, the Grandaughter and Heirefs of *Richard Pates*, had Iffue *Edward*, their only Son, who, by *Rebecca* his Wife, had Iffue *Henry* (who was in *Virginia* at the Time of the Failure of the Iffue Male of the eldeft Son of the firft named *Charles* Lord *Willoughby*) who, by *Mary* his Wife, had Iffue *Henry*, who, by *Elizabeth* his Wife, had Iffue the *Petitioner*.

His Majefty having been gracioufly pleafed to refer this Petition to the Right Honourable the Houfe of Peers, to examine the Allegations thereof, as to what relates to the Petitioner's Title, the Cafe made by the Petition (it is humbly fubmitted) will be fully made out, if the following Propofitions are proved, after fhewing the Creation of Sir *William Willoughby* a Baron in Tail Male, by the Title of Lord *Willoughby of Parham*, and that he was fucceeded by his Son Lord *Charles*, who had Iffue *William*, his eldeft Son.

Firft, That the Heirs Male of *William*, the *eldeft* Son of *Charles* Lord *Willoughby*, became extinct in 1680.

A

XII. Edward Lord Willoughby fat in Parliament in 1712, died in 1713 without Iffue.

XIII. Charles Lord Willoughby fat in Parliament in 1713.

XIV. Hugh Lord Willoughby of Parham fat in 17 . ., died without Iffue January 1765.

Second, That the prefent Claimant is the *Lineal Defcendant*, and *Heir Male* of the Body of Sir *Ambrofe Willoughby*, the *Second* Son of the faid Lord *Charles*, and, in confequence, the Heir Male of the Body of Sir *William Willoughby*, the Firft Grantee of the Honor.

William Willoughby, Efq; the eldeft Son of *Charles* Lord *Willoughby*, had Iffue *William*, who fucceeded Lord *Charles* in the Honor.

William Lord *Willoughby*, Grandfon of *Charles*, had Iffue two Sons, *Francis* his eldeft, and *William* his youngeft Son; and *Francis* fucceeded his Father in the Honor.

The faid *Francis* Lord *Willoughby* afterwards died, without Iffue Male; upon whofe Death the faid *William Willoughby*, his Brother, became intitled to the Honor, who died, leaving *George* his eldeft Son, and *John* and *Charles*, his younger Sons; and upon the Death of the faid *William* Lord *Willoughby* (Brother of the

ſaid *Francis*) the ſaid *George*, his eldeſt Son, ſucceeded to the ſaid Title, and died, leaving *John*, his eldeſt Son, an Infant, who ſucceeded to the ſaid Honor, and died without Iſſue Male; upon whoſe Death the Honor deſcended to the before named *John*, the Uncle of the ſaid *John* laſt named; and upon the Death of the ſaid *John* the Uncle without Iſſue Male, the Honor deſcended to *Charles*, the youngeſt Brother of the ſaid *George*, and *John*; who likewiſe died without Iſſue Male in 1680, leaving *Elizabeth Willoughby*, afterwards *Elizabeth Bertie*, his Niece and Heir at Law; and thereby the *Male Line* of *William Willoughby*, Eſq; the *eldeſt* Son of the *firſt* named *Charles* Lord *Willoughby*, became extinct.

The Male Line of the ſaid *William, eldeſt Son of the firſt named* Lord *Charles*, being thus become extinct in 1680, the Claimant's Grandfather *Henry Willoughby* became then intitled to the Honor; he being the Son and Heir of *Edward Willoughby*, who was the *only* Son and Heir of Sir *Ambroſe Willoughby*, the *Second* Son of the *firſt* named Lord *Charles*.

But it appears, That in 1680, and for ſome Years before, the ſaid *Henry*, the *Grandfather*, was ſettled in *Virginia*, and died there in 1685, ignorant of the Extinction of ſuch Iſſue Male of the Firſt Line, leaving *Henry Willoughby*, the Claimant's Father, his only Son, then an Infant.

In 1680, during the Abſence of the *real Heir*, in a foreign Country, *Thomas Willoughby*, the Son of Sir *Thomas*, the *Fifth* Son of the *firſt* named Lord *Charles*, was ſummoned to Parliament, by the Title of Lord *Willoughby of Parham*, and took his Seat accordingly, upon a Preſumption, that Sir *Ambroſe*, and his Two Brothers, *Edward* and *Charles*, were all dead, without Iſſue Male; and the Deſcendants of *Thomas* continued to enjoy the Honor, until the Death of *Hugh*, the *laſt* Lord *Willoughby of Parham*, who died, unmarried, in *January* 1765.

The *Firſt* Line being *extinct*, the preſent Claimant's Title, it is humbly ſubmitted, is clear; he being the *Lineal Deſcendant*, and *Heir Male* of the Body of Sir *Ambroſe Willoughby*, the *Second* Son of the ſaid *firſt* named *Charles* Lord *Willoughby*, and, in conſequence, the *Heir Male* of the Body of Sir *William Willoughby*, the *Firſt Grantee* of the Honor.

Ambroſe, (afterwards Sir *Ambroſe Willoughby*) was *Second* Son of the *Firſt Charles* Lord *Willoughby*, and married *Suſan Brooke*, the Grandaughter, and Heireſs of *Richard Pates* of *Matſon*, in the County of *Glouceſter*, Eſquire.

Sir *Ambroſe Willoughby*, and Dame *Suſan*, had Iſſue *Edward Willoughby*, Eſquire, their only Son, who married *Rebecca Draper*, and Sir *Ambroſe Willoughby* dying, Dame *Suſan*, his Widow, afterwards intermarried with Sir *Robert Lovett* of *Sulbury*, in the County of *Bucks*, Knt.

Edward Willoughby, and *Rebecca* his Wife, had Iſſue *Henry*, their eldeſt Son, baptized at *Steukeley*, in *Bucks*, 14th *November* 1626.

Henry Willoughby married *Mary*, and had Iſſue *Henry* (the Claimant's Father) and lived at *Minſterworth*, in the County of *Glouceſter*.

In 1675, *Henry Willoughby* (the Claimant's Grandfather) by the Advice of *George Hudſon*, to whom he had ſold his Eſtate, went to *Virginia*, taking with him a Daughter named *Rebecca*, who afterwards married *Richard Hull*, and leaving behind him, at *Minſterworth*, *Mary* his Wife, *Henry* (the Claimant's Father) his eldeſt Son, and *Sarah* his Daughter.

In 1680, (being the Year in which the Iſſue Male of the *eldeſt Son* of the *Firſt* Lord *Charles* became extinct) *Henry* (the Claimant's Father) was of the Age of Fifteen Years; and on the 26th of *November* 1685, *Henry*, the Claimant's Grandfather, died at *Hull's Creek*, in *Virginia*.

Henry Willoughby, the Claimant's Father, married *Elizabeth Pigeon*, 28th *July* 1693.

Henry and *Elizabeth* had Iſſue the preſent *Claimant*, their eldeſt Son, and *William*, *Edward* and *Joſeph* (who are all dead without Iſſue) and *Fortune*, their youngeſt Son, who is alſo dead, leaving *George*, his only Son and Heir.

C. YORKE.
AL. WEDDERBURN.
JOHN MADOCKS.

List of Wills recorded in Barbados down to the year 1800.*

Year.	Names of Testators.
1762	Lopess, Moses
"	Lindsay, Dorothy
1763	Lindo, Abraham
"	Long, Christopher
"	Lettoab, Leah Gabay
1764	Lavine, Isaac
"	Lucumb, John
"	Lashley, James
"	Lawson, John
"	Lampyne, Nicholas
1765	Long, George
"	Lewis, Sarah
"	Lynch, Andrew
1766	Lashley, Mary
"	Lynch, Anthony
"	Lindsey, Joseph
"	Lewis, Francis
"	Lewis, George Taylor
"	Leman, John
1767	Lyte, John
"	Lacey, Henry
"	Lewis, "Pelelion," Mary
"	Lanahan, John
"	Lewis, Richard
1768	Leslie, Mercy
"	La Roque, Anthony
"	Lashley, Thomas
"	Lake, Thomas
"	Lake, Elizabeth
"	Lake, John
"	Lanahan, John
"	Lindsay, George
"	Leslie, Richard
"	Lawrence, Henry
"	Leary, Elizabeth
"	Leader, Jane
1769	Lawrence, William
"	Lucous, Jacob
"	Lewis, Ann
"	Luke, Rebecca
1770	La Rogue, Francis
"	Leslie, Catherine
"	Leslie, Charles
"	Lewis, Joseph
"	Lewis, Francis
1771	Lindsay, Sarah
"	Lucas, Nathan
1771	Littlewood, Elizabeth
"	Lavine, Isaac
"	Lamb, William
1772	Leach, Anne Ross
"	Leach, Benony
"	Lockman, Finslia
"	Lucomb, Thomas
"	Laming, Edward
"	Lynton, John
"	Lashley, Ralph
1773	Lavington, Mary
"	Lucomb, Thomas
"	Lane, Richard
"	Lynch, Robert
"	Linton, John
"	Leslie, John
1774	Leach, Samuel
"	Lucas, Sarah
"	Lewis, Snr., Philip
1775	Laverick, William
"	Lynch, Harrett
"	Lynch, Johnny
1776	Lewis, Mary
1777	Long, Thomas
"	Lowe, William
"	Lewis, James
1778	Lamprey, Samuel Giles
"	Luke, Elias
"	Lopez, Moses
"	Lynch, Elizabeth
1779	Letts, Jnr., William
"	Letts, William
"	Lewis, Samuel
"	Lewis, John
1780	Leacock, John
"	Lawson, Mary
"	Lewis, Philip
"	Lamplu, Alexander
"	Lion, Mathias
1781	Lock, John
"	Levis, Sarah
"	Laming, Dymock
"	Leacock, Susanna
"	Lewis, Charles
"	Lyte, William
1782	Limessurier, Nicholas
"	Lynch, Elizabeth

* Continued from Vol. IV., p. 358.

Year.	Names of Testators.
1782	Lamming, Mary
1783	Lindsay, Susanna
,,	Leary, Christopher
,,	Law, Upton
,,	Leslie, Katherine
,,	Leacock, Joseph
,,	Leacock, Joseph
,,	Littlewood, George
,,	Lyder, Thomas
1784	Lavine, Mary
,,	Love, Nathaniel
,,	Lindo, Jnr., Abraham
,,	Lashley, Susanna Cooper
,,	Lewis, Jacob
,,	Lascelles, Daniel
1785	Leeds, Mary
,,	Lewis, Margaret
,,	Lewis, Mary
1786	Leath, John
,,	Leslie, Bowman
,,	Luke, John
,,	Loyd, Agnes
,,	Lovell, Joseph
,,	Lucomb, John
1787	Lowe, Richard
,,	Lee, Joseph
,,	Lynch, Michael
,,	Leach, Elizabeth
,,	Legay, Jane
1788	Lovell, Jnr., Edward
,,	Leath, Ann
,,	Luke, Joshua
,,	Leacock, Hamble
,,	Leader, Henry
1789	Lashley, Sarah
,,	Lanahan, Ruthe
,,	Lyder, Joseph
,,	Lopez, Sarah
,,	Lanahan, Jnr., Dengill
1790	Lamprey, Richard Giles
1791	Lovell, Philip
,,	Lowe, Mary
,,	Leslie, Jane
,,	Leach, Benony
,,	Lawson, James
,,	Lewis, Katherine
1792	Lavine, Laurentia Trent
,,	Lawrence, William
,,	Leeth, Arthur
,,	Lewis, Dr. Peers
,,	Lloyd, Francis
,,	Leacock, Mary
,,	Lewis, Nathanil
,,	Linton, Elizabeth
,,	Long, John
,,	Leach, Sarah

Year.	Names of Testators.
1793	Lewis, James
1794	Le Messurier, John
,,	Lynch, Robert
,,	Leslie, Margaret Applewaite
,,	Lynch, Patricia
,,	Lord, John
,,	Leslie, John
,,	Langford, John
,,	Leslie, Tomasin
1795	Lang, Elizabeth
,,	Lawson, Samuel Husband
,,	Lewelling, Josiah
,,	Lascelles, Edwin
,,	Lewis, Nathan
,,	Lindsey, James
,,	Leach, Elizabeth
,,	Lloyd, Robert
1797	Lovell, Margaret
,,	Lynch, Elizabeth
,,	Long, George
1798	Lynch, Thomas
,,	Lewis, Jane
,,	Lewis, Sarah
,,	Lane, Andrew Jack
,,	Lynch, Mary Elizabeth
1799	Littlewood, Mary
,,	Lindsey, Francis
,,	Liman, John
,,	Lynch, Sarah Eleanor
,,	Leslie, John Bowman
,,	Lord, Richard Sargeant
,,	Lord, John
1650	Mephelomic, Cormock
,,	Morris, John
,,	Meade, James
,,	Martin, James
1651	Mills, Mrs. Mary
,,	Marshall, William
1652	Morgan, William
,,	Mott, Steven
,,	Morewood, Andrew
,,	Miller, Henry
1653	Malpas, George
,,	Morgan, Edward
,,	Morgan, Capt. Francis
,,	Mann, Richard
1654	Marsh, George
,,	Morris, Gordan
,,	Miller, Thomas
1656	Miller, William
,,	Masters, Joseph
1657	Malpas, Mary
,,	Macumbe, Calib
,,	Morris, William

Year.	Names of Testators.
1658	Mayo, Edward
,,	Morgan, Roger
,,	Mersam, Timothy
,,	Maior, Robert
,,	Morris, Peter
,,	Mackrall, Andrew
1659	Morse, John
,,	Maibbye *alias* John Wilkins
,,	May, John
,,	Mackerness, John
,,	Maning, Patrick
1660	Mayne, Lewis
,,	MacSwain, Evan
,,	Minitt, Thomas
,,	Murihie, Dirmott
,,	Maine, William
,,	Moore, Charles
1662	Maxfield, Hugh
,,	Martin, Thomas
,,	Morgan, John
,,	Mills, Richard
1664	Mitchell, Athinatius
,,	Marlohen, Farrell
,,	Morris, Owen
,,	Morrison, Gay
,,	Morris, William
1665	Mills, John
,,	Minor, John
,,	Mills, Robert
,,	Millard, Robert
,,	Mullan, John
,,	Moore, Thomas
1666	Morris, Christopher
,,	Murray, William
1667	Marsh, William
,,	Mullins, Alexander
,,	Matkins, Henry
,,	Marsh, William
,,	Murphey, Daniel
,,	Mills, George
,,	Marcle, John
,,	Martin, John
1668	Mackney, Daniel
,,	Murrey, Robert
,,	Melloy, Charles
,,	Mackvada, Dermont
,,	Martindale, John
,,	Murley, Darby
1669	Mosside, Judith
,,	Mullen, Teague
,,	Moody, John
,,	Marcy, William
1670	Middleton, Miles
,,	McCracher, John
,,	Morris, Thomas
,,	Mapletopp, Margery

Year.	Names of Testators.
1671	Morgan, Rees
,,	Morser, Christopher
,,	Merrick, Thomas
,,	Morrell, William
,,	Meredith, Thomas
,,	Mansell, Robert
1672	Maccallester, Charles
,,	Moure, Ferchird
,,	Marshall, William
,,	Morgan, John
,,	Middleton, Thomas
1673	Morgain, Evan
,,	Maverick, Nathaniel
1674	Monrow, Daniel
,,	Malozar, Nicholas
,,	Morgan, Thomas
,,	Morrison, William
,,	Muntrons, Roger
,,	Mullinax, John
1675	Martindale, John
,,	Murphey, Edmond
,,	Mascoll, Timothy
,,	Montermack, William
,,	Murrow, William
,,	Mindis, John
,,	Martin, Andrew
,,	Maxwell, James
,,	Murphey, Edmond
,,	Murfey, Thomas
1676	Macoy, John
,,	Mosse, Thomas
,,	Mitchell, James
1677	Manning, Edward
,,	Maggs, George
,,	Macrumarrow, Daniel
1678	Maidwell, Philip
,,	Moor, John
,,	Milles, Henry
,,	Machahall, Dennis
,,	Munyon, Josias
,,	Moore, Richard
1679	Mills, Thomas
,,	Mocoy, John
,,	Macartie, Daniel
,,	Morrell, Nicholas
,,	Maccleif, Dennis
,,	Morgan, Evan
,,	McIntosh, Henry
,,	Morrell, Nicholas
,,	Munrow, Andrew
,,	Mayr, John
1680	Millar, Andrew
,,	Munrow, John
,,	Morris, William
,,	MacGuin, Archibold
,,	Morris, Nicholas

Year.	Names of Testators.
1680	Matthews, William
„	Mackcloud, Anguist
„	Mann, John
„	Martin, John
1681	Miles, Richard
„	Mackenny, Alexander
„	Mirrell, Thomas
„	Mills, Andrew
„	Malony, Derman
„	Manson, Thomas
1682	Miles, Andrew
„	Mattha, Farrell
„	MacDowell, John
„	Moraine, Matthew
„	Martyn, John
„	Moyor, Samuel
„	Maycocke, Thomas
„	Mannack, Andrew
„	Mannack, Elinor
1683	Madden, Daniel
„	Moggs, Anna
„	Mears, John
„	Mackill, Daniell
„	Maddison, Robert
1684	Merricke, Humphry
„	Morrell, Jane
„	Moore, Susannah
„	Makbernes, William
„	Moore, Susannah
„	Mackerwhoe, Thomas
„	Moore, John
„	Marson, Edward
„	Mason, George
„	Mackahall, Jone
„	Marke, Mary
„	MacHolland, James
„	Mackellister, Thomas
1685	Murcoft, John
„	Mercado, David, de Raphel
„	Middleton, William
„	Meazy, William
„	Murcott, George
„	Mills, Henry
„	Meade, Robert
„	Morgan, Joan
1686	Morgan, William
„	Marane, Margaret
„	Monereiffe, Robert
„	Malloney, Cornelius
„	Murray, Henry
„	Morphey, Cornelius
„	Mynard, Samuel
1687	Morgan, Thomas
„	Matson, Matthew
„	Murford, Richard
„	McLeod, Philip
1687	Murphey, Dirmonte
„	Murfie, Teague
„	Murfey, Hugh
„	Marshall, William
„	Moore, John
„	Mathews, William
1688	Man, Bernard
„	Mausfield, John
„	Meare, Roger
„	Millesant, William
„	M'Carine, Abraham, Governor of Tobago
„	Monroe, John
„	Mercer, James
„	Melandins, Byran
1689	Manby, Joan
„	Maycock, Thomas
„	Miller, William
„	Murrah, Jannes
„	Mitchill, Richard
„	Mill, Thomas
1690	Markclare, Elizabeth
„	Mings, James
„	Morgan, Paul
„	Mackbombes, John
„	Murphey, Richard
„	Mackerness, William
„	Moore, Thomas
„	Meade, George
„	McGuett, William
1691	Martin, William
„	Morris, Patrick
1692	Munyon, Ann
„	Mirray, John
„	Morrison, George
„	Mord, Francis
„	Mercer, Richard
„	Mountstephen, David
„	Malone, Mathew
1693	Middleton, Richard
„	Mayllam, Jonathan
„	Murrill, William
„	Meade, William
„	Mead, Marcellus
„	Maccolister, Eleonor
„	Mills, Henry
„	Maccalister, Ellinor
„	Moncrief, Nathaniel
„	Maddock, Thomas
„	Maycock, Margaret
„	Mills, John
„	Mille or Wil'e, Raleigh
„	Mills, Joseph
„	Manfell, Robert
„	Maddox, Peter
1694	Markland, Henry

Year.	Names of Testators.
1694	Morfey, Edward
"	Mellows, Elisha
"	Messar, James
"	Middleton, Nathanil
"	Morrow, Christian
"	Menzies, John
"	Miller, John
"	Mason, Mitchell
1695	Mountstephens, Thomas
"	Morris, Richard
"	Marcris, Mary
"	Murphy, Alice
"	Marshall, Thomas
"	Maloney, Owen
"	Martin, Elizabeth
"	Moloan, Edward
"	Morgan, David
"	Makalley, Thomas
"	Morris, Thomas
"	Morris, Elizabeth
1696	Manning, John
"	Martholin, Joseph
"	McKowine, David
"	Mead, Samuel
"	Moore, John
"	Morris, Thomas
"	Morrey, William Loring
"	McMahon, Roger
"	Murphy, Dennis
1697	Metcalfe, James
"	Marshall, John
"	Maynard, Charles
"	Metcalfe, James
1698	Morgan, Walter
"	Massey, George
"	Monck, Henry
1700	Mansell, Samuel
"	Murrell, William
"	Moyle, Randolf
"	Miller, Edward
"	Mayre, John
"	Mayre, Elizabeth
"	Macey, Elizabeth
"	Morgan, Benjamin
"	Macey, Elizabeth
1701	Murphy, Peter
"	Maverick, Nathaniel
"	Moody, Anna
"	Morgan, Edward
"	McKale, Markman
"	Martin, Nicholas
"	May, Mary
"	Makernes, William
"	Monk, Robert and Mary
"	Maddocks, William
"	Meza, de Fonseca

Year	Names of Testators.
1702	Merchant, Mary
"	Mashart, James
"	Macoy, Daniel
1703	Markland, John
"	Moore, John
"	Mills, Alexander
"	Mackneal, Laughlin
1704	Mason, William
"	Maxwell, Momas
"	Molton, Humphry
"	Merrick, John
"	Martin, William
"	Milles, Benjamin
"	Millward, John
"	Mascott, James
"	Mitchell, John
"	Moore, Richard
1705	Moody, George and Anne
"	Markland, Henry
"	Marder, John
"	Mathew, Lewis
"	MacBrudy, Bryan
"	Musgrave, Mary
1706	Meare, Dennis
"	Murroe, William
"	Muckleston, David
"	Mackswain, Cornilius
"	Mitchell, David
"	Mehem, Teage
"	Murry, John
1707	Merricke, Ellinor
"	Minuett. Robert
1709	Muffy, Patrick
"	Martin, Sarah
"	McCondline, Daniel
"	Mackbassell, Mary
"	McKarty, Joan
"	Mings, John
1710	Martin, Gabriel
"	Mackcollin, Alexander
"	Murray, John
"	Mings, Ann
"	Mackaskill, Daniel
"	Morris, Nicholas
1711	Morris, John
"	Marriner, Cornelius
"	Mackaskill, Norman
"	McKenzie, George
"	Mein, Patrick
1712	Malloney, Ann
"	Moore, Benjamin
"	Matson, Benjamin
"	Middleton, Richard
"	Mountstephen, Sarah
1713	Mitchell, William
"	Mayns, Robert

Year.	Names of Testators.
1713	Moody, George
1714	Middleton, Benjamin
"	Martindale, Mary
"	Maverick, Nathaniel
"	Markland, Sarah
"	Miller, Nathan
1715	Mackdaniell, Anguish
"	Murry, John
"	Mellado, Teague Henrique
"	Mapp, Samuel
"	Morrell, Nicholas
"	Mings, Elizabeth
"	Matson, Matthew
"	Maccollock, David
1716	Mason, Richard
"	Mellowes, Elisha
"	Murphey, William
"	Madox, Edward
"	Maynard, Nicholas
"	Martin, Elizabeth
1717	McCarty, Daniel
"	Markland, Samuel
"	Moore, Alexander
"	Mounter, John
"	Marshall, George
"	Maddison, May
"	Macdaniel, Forker
"	Maverick, John
1718	Milles, Joseph
"	Mackay, Malcom
"	Mendez, Moses, de Soloman
"	Moore, Robert
"	Morphey, Edward
"	Melles, John
"	Martin, Adrain
"	Martin, Gabriel
"	Morris, Richard
"	Mofford, Thomas
"	Mitchell, Frizwith
"	Miller, Momas
1719	Man, Mary
"	Martin, John
"	Mangles, Abraham
"	Murphey, William
1720	Marriner, Cornelius
"	Mordrick, Samuel
"	Manson, Alice
"	Mayers, John
1721	Mellechamp, Francis
"	MacGoune, Stafford
"	Mansell, Samuel
"	Magrow, Daniel
1722	Mescamp, John
"	Milles, Jane
"	Messon, George
"	Munrow, Elizabeth
1722	Maynard, Samuel
"	McCannon, Neil
"	Murphey, Pingston
1723	Miller, John
"	Mountstephen, Lucy
"	Macksield, Susannah
"	Marlton, Ceaser
"	Maskall, Thomas
"	Moore, Constance
"	Mosely, Henry
1724	Mackandrew, James
"	Marlow, Katherin
"	Martin, Mary
"	McFirson, Daniel
"	Morris, Francis
"	Mead, Edward
"	Mackluer, William
"	Macoy, John
"	Middleton, Thomas
1725	Martin, Robert
"	Mears, Mary
"	Maynard, Christian
"	Marquez, Jacob
1726	Milward, William
"	Magown, Ann
"	Morgan, Richard
"	Mickey, John
"	Milward, William
"	Mulliner, Elizabeth
"	Macfarson, Richard
1727	Moody, James
"	Muschamp, William
"	Mason, Elizabeth
"	Maxwell, Thomas
"	Miller, John
1728	Murrell, Francis
"	Moore, John
"	Moore, Susannah
"	Martindale, John
"	Martindale, Jane
"	Moore, Archibald
"	Morris, Elizabeth
1729	Maycoye, Patrick
"	Millons, Martha
"	Molins, John
"	Maude, Martha
"	Meyer, Herman Angus
"	Mills, John
"	Mackswceney, Ursula
1730	Miller, Jonah
"	Moin, Jane
"	Mitchell, John
"	Macallister, John
"	Mear, James
"	McCall, John
"	Mount, Richard

Year.	Names of Testators.	Year.	Names of Testators.
1730	Marshall, Abraham	1739	Marlton, Abraham
1731	Milles, John	,,	Mathewes, Joyce
,,	Mills, Elizabeth	,,	Mason, Joseph
,,	McKegan, Susanna	,,	Moore, Peter
,,	Maycock, Thomas	,,	Mendez, Rachael
,,	Maynard, Samuel	1740	Mashart, James
1732	Martin, Richard	,,	Millington, John
,,	McCarty, Martha	,,	Mascoll, Stephen
,,	McCarty, Charles	,,	Mitchell, John
,,	Mings, James	,,	Mason, Sarah
,,	Moseley, Mary	,,	Miller, John
,,	Massett, William	1741	Mascoll, Ann
,,	Manning, Charles	,,	Mascoll, Robert
1733	Murphey, Thomas	,,	Malloney, Mary
,,	Murrey, Alice	1742	Masterson, James
,,	Morris, Elizabeth	,,	Manning, Ann
,,	Miller, Henry	,,	Manning, Joseph
,,	McDonnell, Richard	,,	Morecroft, Richard
,,	Mackleur, Anthony	,,	Moore, Mary
,,	Murrey, Elizabeth	,,	Massiah, Daniel
1734	Miller, Francis	,,	McKill, James
,,	Moore, William	,,	Marshall, William
,,	Merrick, John	,,	Mellowes, Francis
,,	Moore, Edward	1743	McCollock, Thomas
,,	McDonnald, Alexander	,,	Maddocks, William
,,	McKeorer, Norman	,,	McDonnell, Randle
,,	Moore, Sarah	,,	Mordin, Edward
,,	Monsanto, Jacob Nunez	,,	Morris, John
1735	Mayhew, Marmaduke	,,	McClair, Elizabeth
,,	Marshaw, Law	,,	Minviello, David
,,	Matthews, William	,,	Mill, Patrick
,,	Middleton, Richard	,,	MacCollin, John
,,	Mitchell, John	1744	Murray, Alexander
,,	Milles, William	,,	Mingham, Mary
1736	Mounter, John	,,	Maddey, Mary
,,	Marshall, Robert	,,	Morrison, George
,,	Magraw, Mercy	,,	McMachon, Gilasius
,,	Mitchell, Archibald	,,	McDonnell, Randle
,,	Marshall, George	,,	Murray, Andrew
,,	Marshart, Philip	,,	Mason, William
1737	Milward, Ann	,,	McCloud, John
,,	Maycock, Thomas	,,	Morris, Sarah
,,	Mottley, John	,,	Mayers, Joseph
,,	Mackelawlin, Elizabeth	,,	McKaskill, Daniel
,,	Morris, Edward	,,	Mahon, Michael
1738	Mapp, Thomas	,,	Mallard, James
,,	Mitchell, James	,,	Maddey, Thomas
,,	Moore, Arthur	,,	Murrell, Nicholas
,,	Mafford, John	1745	Munrow, John
,,	Mackaskill, Daniel	,,	Mahawn, John
,,	Merry, Richard	,,	McDermott, Roger
,,	McBrudye, Terrence	,,	Maycock, John
,,	Meares, Thomas	,,	Miller, Theadorah
,,	Medford, Elizabeth	,,	Matthews, Edward
,,	Mallard, Thomas	,,	Middleton, Nathaniel
,,	McCarty, Carala	,,	Maddocks, Thomas

Year.	Names of Testators.
1745	Munday, Joseph
,,	Mayers, Honner
,,	Moore, Elishia
,,	Milward, William
1746	Mayhew, Richard
,,	Miller, Matthew
,,	McChullum, Alexander
,,	Morris, William
,,	Millward, James
,,	Maxwell, Thomas
,,	Marlin, Francis
,,	McMurray, Evar
1747	Munrow, John
,,	Moore, Francis
,,	Morrison, Thomas
,,	Mackeeon, Simon
,,	McKashell, Ruth Holder
,,	Moore, Joseph
,,	Morgan, William
,,	Meare, James
,,	Miller, Habbuckah
1748	Mayers, Margaret
,,	Milles, Damaris
,,	Merrick, Joseph
,,	Merrick, Mary
,,	Melm, Margaret
,,	Millward, John
1749	Malsworth, Nicholas
,,	Menvielle, David
,,	McBrudy, Thomas
,,	Michler, Conrad
,,	Massiah, Judith
,,	Murray, Martha
,,	Mead, Charles
,,	Murrell, William
,,	Mapp, Samuel
,,	Milles, Joseph
,,	Morris, Robert
1750	Miller, Henry
,,	Maloney, Daniel
,,	Maverick, Catherine
,,	Maxwell, Elizabeth
,,	Mapp, Robert
,,	Matthew, Humphry
,,	Mann, Michael
,,	Maynard, Mary
,,	Morreson, Charity
,,	Martin, Sarah
1751	Morris, John
,,	Mapp, Robert
,,	Meller, George
,,	Morris, Thomas
1751	Massett, Mary
,,	Martin, Sarah
,,	Miller, Ann
1752	Martin, Sarah
,,	Moore, Archibold
1753	Meares, John
,,	Malloney, Benjamin
,,	Mellowes, Samuel
,,	Menvielle, Susannah
,,	Maycock, Mary
,,	Mendes, Isaac Jeosherin
,,	Moore, John
,,	Moore, Thomas
,,	Matthews, Ephraim
1754	McMahon, Thomas
,,	Maddock, Ann
,,	Mitchell, Elinor
,,	Minge, James
,,	Mears, Roger
,,	Millward, William
,,	Morgan, Mary
,,	Meckneal, James
,,	McBrudy, Mary
,,	Mottley, Henry
1755	Moore, Ann
,,	Massiah, Jacob
,,	Mountford, Lord Henry
,,	Moseley, Richard
1756	Malone, James
,,	McConchy, Robert
,,	Mosley, Richard
,,	Mascoll, James
,,	Manning, John
,,	Mower, Anne
,,	Mcfarguhar, Kenneth
,,	Mayers, Jane
,,	Mayers, Robert John
,,	Miller, Ruth
1757	Mahon, Edward
,,	McDonald, Allan
,,	Mamsfield, Elizabeth
,,	Martin, John
,,	Mapp, James
,,	Mayran, Thomas
,,	Moses, John
,,	Morris, John
,,	Maxwell, Dorothy
,,	MacDonold, Jane
,,	Morgan, John
,,	Moseley, John
,,	Magrath, Henry Owen
1758	Malsworth, Nicholas

(To be continued.)

VIEW OF LORD'S CASTLE, BARBADOS.

From an old lithograph, lent by Sir W. H. Trollope, Bart., the owner of the estate. The original drawing was by his mother Frances, only child of John Lord, who died in 1862.

Richardson of Nevis.

. . . . Richardson of London, gent., dead 1751. = Jane Netherway, sister to Col. John Netherway, Lieut.-Govr. of Nevis. She died in London.

Joseph Hill of Morning Star plantation. His estate passed to his four daus. and coheiresses. =

John Richardson, Esq., President 1724; dead 1751. =	Elizabeth Hill, dead 1731 and left a will; coheiress of John Hill and Joseph Hill.	Mary Hill, mar. Wm. Pym Burt, Chief Justice. See his petition of 1715.	Ann Hill, mar. in or before 1711 John Dasent, Chief Justice of Nevis. He was born 4 March 1691-2 and died 7 March 1752. She died 1724—35.	Frances Hill, mar. Col. Rd. Brodbelt. She died 27 Aug. 1725, aged 37. M.I. at St. John's.

John Richardson of Nevis, Esq., 1751; son and heir, æt. 17 in 1731; born 1714; M. of C. 1749; of Morning Star in St. John's Figtree; Chancery Petition 1751. =	Elizabeth, mar. before 1755.	Ann Richardson, mar. Wm. Huggins, Esq. He died intestate, adm'on 25 March 1752.	Mary Richardson.

Henrietta P. (? Paris or Pemberton), mar. 13 Dec. 1783. = Hon. John Richardson, born 1756; died 6 Sept. 1816, aged 60. M.I. at St. Paul's, Charlestown. = Grace, remar. 29 May 1828 Col. J. F. Browne. of 28th Regt.

1717. "We John Richardson Esq. and Elizabeth his wife, William Pym Burt gentleman Frances Hill spinster, all of the Island of Nevis . . . .

Three or more debentures made out in the names of Elizabeth Robinson (? Richardson—Ed.), Mary Hill afterwards the wife of the said William Pym Burt and since deceased, Anne Hill now the wife of John Dasent of Nevis Esq., and Frances Hill . . . . 22 May 1717." (*Re* Invasion of the French in 1706. John Dasent, attorney.)—Note by Lieut.-Col. Pook from P.R.O. Exchequer Receipts, Miss. Book No. 206.

1724. John Richardson then President of Nevis.

John Richardson aged 17 in pursuance of the will of his late Mother Eliz. R. disclaims to his 2 sisters Ann Huggins now wife of Wm H. and Mary R. all rights to his said mother's est. as one of the coheirs of John Hill and Joseph Hill dec^d. His mother and her 3 sisters Mary Burt dec^d wife of Wm. Pym B., Frances Brodbelt dec^d late wife of Richd B. esq. and Anne Dasent the present wife of John D. esq. Recorded 31 May 1731. (Nevis deeds, II., 137.)

1739, May 8. John Richardson of N. esq. and Eliz. his wife for love for their brother and sister Wm. Huggins esq. and Anne his wife convey Morning Star of 13½ acres to them. Recorded 6 Sept. 1755. (*Ibid.*, V., 84.)

1748-9, Feb. 3. John Richardson to be of the Council.

1828, May 29. Col. J. F. Browne, Bristol, 28th Reg. to Grace, relict of the late Hon. John Richardson of the I. of N. ("G.M.," 640.)

See Petition of John Richardson in 1750. (*Ante*, III., 31.)

Pollard of Barbados.

(*Ante*, III., 237.)

Add. MS. 35.635 in the British Museum, from which the following notes are taken, contains 371 folios, and comprises the correspondence of Walter Pollard, son of Dr. Tho. Pollard of Barbados. The explanatory notes in square brackets and footnotes are by the Editor.

Fo. 7. Eton, June 23, 1771. John Pollard* to his brother Walter Pollard at Harrow.

15. Oct. 3, 1771. John about to go that term to Oxford.

17. Jan. 4, 1772. John at Queen's College, Oxford. Walter's departure for Cambridge.

27. Nov. 29, 1772. Walter is at Emmanuel Coll., Cambridge.

71. Nov. 10, 1775. D. Ottley† to Walter Pollard, Esq., Chandos Street. I must cross the Atlantic, shall be absent 12 months and study law on my return.

80. Barbados, June 7, 1777. Thos. Pollard, J^r. to Walter P., Golden Square. Dear Brother. Our sister Mrs. Mayers' death after lying in on 20 April, has left a fine little boy.‡

82. Cove of Cork. Jan. 16, 1778. Walter P. to the Hon. Philip Yorke.§

89. Amsterdam, Nov. 20, 1779. Yo^r Excellency [? a relative of P. Yorke].

102. Basseterre, July 31, 1781. Walter P. to his father Dr P. at Bridgetown, Barbados. Mr. Gardiner his wife and dau. My mother, my sister.

106. Barbados, Oct. 8, 1781. W. G. H. to Walter P., Esq., at Warner's,‖ Esq., M.D., Hatton Street. Mr. Mayers has married Con. Adams' daughter.¶

114. Barbados, Nov. 22, 1781. Dear Wally. Your affectionate Car. Hen Pollard.

143. Barbados, April 21, 1782. Dr. Thomas P. [Junior] to Walter P. at Joseph Warner's. My sister's lung complaint. My father has sold his furniture and will retire to England and settle at Bath.

155. Barbados, July 19, 1782. From W. G. [?] Holder.** Your cousin Carrington Eliza Willing†† is now Mrs. Alleyne. Jack Forster is the happy man.

161. Barbados, Aug. 28, 1782. Dr. Thomas P. to his son Walter. Your sister has hæmorrhage from the lungs as the fate of your two brothers. Your mother's failing health.

* John, entered Eton 7 Sept. 1761, and left in 1771 (MS. list by R. A. Austen Leigh). He matriculated from Queen's College, Oxford, 7 June 1771, aged 18 (Foster), and apparently died young of consumption. His brother Walter also entered Eton 7 Sept. 1761, but evidently removed to Harrow.

† Drewry Ottley of St Kitts, great-grandson 1759 of Drewry O. George O., probably a brother, was bapt. 1758 as son of Drewry and Eliz. O.

‡ John Pollard Mayers, bencher of the Middle Temple, late Agent for Barbados, died at Brasted, co. Kent, 30 Dec. 1853, aged 76. ("G M." for 1854, p. 221.)

§ Philip Yorke, son of Charles, Lord High Chancellor, succeeded his uncle in 1796 as 3rd Earl of Hardwicke. He was probably a college friend of Walter Pollard, whom he befriended in many ways, offering him a room in his town house.

‖ Joseph Warner, son of Ashton W., Attorney Gen. of Antigua, born 1717, was educated at Guy's Hospital, M.R.C.S. and F.R.S., and was sometime of 35 Hatton Street. He owned Hatton Garden estate in Dominica, and died in 1801, aged 83. He was a very popular surgeon with West Indians.

¶ This must be the second wife. The Hon. Conrad Adams died 2 Aug. and was bur. 3 Aug. 1788 at Christ Church. (*Ante*, III., 312.)

** Probably William Philip Holder, eldest son and heir of Wm. Thorpe H. of Hilloby plantation and of Grosvenor Place, died bachelor 1797.

†† In the Gibbes enclosure, in the churchyard of St. James, Hole Town, is a stone to Mrs. Eliz. Hannah, relict of Cha. Willing, Esq., late of Philadelphia. She was born 12 March 1739 and died 12 Oct. 1795. The Hon. John Forster Alleyne of Porters mar. Eliz. Gibbes Willing, spinster, of Philadelphia, but this letter corrects her names. He was President 1807, and died 29 Sept. 1823, aged 63. His wife predeceased him 12 Feb. 1820, aged 55, having nine sons and seven daus.

201. Hatton Street, Nov. 21, 1783. Joseph Warner, Jr, to Dr. P., Post Office, Bath. Your son has gone to Carolina.

205. Charlestown, Carolina, Feb. 14, 1784. Walter P. writes.

282. April 1, 1786. R. [Ruth] P. to her brother Walter P. Our dear father died 26 March. Yesterday he was buried with my brothers in Clifton churchyard. By his will he left Mama and myself the little remains of his fortune giving you a legacy of £20.

294. Copy of the will: Thos. Pollard of Bath, doctor of physic, March 1786. To my wife Caroline Henrietta* all her jewels. Whereas I have by deed given my son Walter P., Esq., my moiety of two parcels of land in Virginia drawn in the lottery of Colonel Byrd I confirm it and give him £20. I have received and used considerable sums the property of my wife I leave all my estate to her and my dau. Ruth P. and appoint them Ex'trices.

301. Barbados, Oct. 12, 1786. Tho. Græme to Walter P., Esq., at Philadelphia. Your father and my uncle were bosom friends. My grandfather was for many years one of ye masters at William and Mary College in Virginia (where my father was educated) and he had ye care of Governor Spotiswood's affairs, a distant relative. On leaving America to settle in this Island he left behind him a tract of land. £500 was still due in 1773. My uncle Stevenson's death. I was a minor under the guardianship of my mother. Mrs. Græme. My mother, my brother, my sister Jones.

312. The second Mrs. Pollard was a Bostonian woman.

327. Walter P. to his sister. A long undated letter breaking off all correspondence. He was bitterly opposed to his stepmother.

355. May 18, 1788. Philip Yorke, M.P. for co. Camb., to Walter P. at Bridge Town.

363. Oct. 4, 1788. Ph. Yorke at Hamels [co. Herts] to Walter P. Good advice as to the bar. Sir Philip Gibbes is going to the W.I. to visit his estate. His son who was at St. John's Coll. and his two daus.

368. The last dated letter was on 26 Nov. 1788.

The last letter of all is addressed to Walter P., Esq., 27 Southampton Buildings, and is sealed with the Yorke arms.

In St. Michael's Churchyard is a tomb recording the deaths of Emlin Pollard, died 21 June 1712, aged 78, also Mrs. Mary, wife of Dr. John Pollard, died 26 May 1733, aged 45, and several of their children.

1779 (? Oct.). At Barbadoes, Mrs. M. Pollard, aged 115. ("G.M.," 566.)

Dwarris of Jamaica.

1709, Aug. 23. Died, Herman Dwaris, kinsman of Mr Barnard of St. Mary Woolchurch Haw, bur. Aug. 28. (Par. Reg. of St. Mary Woolnoth, London.)

1748. Fortunatus Dwarris, son of Tho D., "Militum Tribuni," America; born in the I. of J., schools first Uxbridge, then Eton (Mr. Cook); adm. fell. com. tutor and surety Dr. Rutherforth 23 June æt. past 20. (St. John's Coll., Camb. Admissions, p. 126.)

A note quotes M.I. from Archer. He was not a graduate of Camb. (p. 579.)

1750, Sept. 28. Fortunatus D., Anglo-Americanus. (Leyden Students.)

There is no entrance-book at Eton before 1754. Dwarris' name does not occur in any extant school list. It is not in the list of 1745 or 1748 and none survives between those two years. (R. A. Austen-Leigh.)

* 1808, Nov. 11. In Burlington-str. Bath, Mrs. Pollard, relict of Dr. P. of the island of Barbados. ("Dorchester and Sherborne Journal," and "Gent. Mag.," 1128.)

ARMS.—*Argent, on a chevron gules three roses between as many griffins' heads erased.*

Col. Thomas Dwarris of Jamaica. ? Will proved there in 1738. Owned Golden Grove of 600 acres and Cherry Garden of 300 acres, both in St. George's. =┬= . . . . died 1 Jan. 1782. She had 9 negros and dower of £100 a year charged on her son's estate. =┬= . . . ., survived his wife and inherited her £5000. 2nd husband. s.p.

A

John Dunston, mar. 6 Nov. 1752; dead 1770. 1st husband. =┬= Frances, dau. of Tho. and Anne Harris of St. Thomas-in-the-East; living 1810. =┬= Hon. Fortunatus Dwarris, 1st son and heir, born 1727 in Jamaica; inherited Golden Grove; educated at Eton; Fell. C. of St. John's, Camb., 1745; M.D. of Leyden 1750; M. for St. Geo. 1754; Custos 1784; died 5 Feb. 1790, aged 63. M.I. Kingston (Archer, 85). Will (683, Loveday). s.p.

Herman Atkins Dwarris, inherited Cherry Garden, late of Greenwich, then of Worksop, co. Notts. 1751. =┬= . . . .

George Pinnock Dunston. =┬= . . . ., mar. Jan. 1783.

Ann Dunston, born 1758; mar. . . . . Neufville; spent 14 months in England, returned to Jamaica June and died 15 Aug. 1782, aged 24. M.I. in Kingston (Archer, 85).

William Dwarris, born 1753; educated at Harrow; succeeded his uncle at Golden Grove; attorney-at-law; went out first in 1771; died 4 Oct. 1813, aged 60, at Stanmore. M.I. in St. James, Cheltenham (*ante*, IV., 136). Will (493, Heathfield). =┬= Sarah Smith, dau. of Lilley Smith of Coventry; born 1760; went out in 1781 with her husband; died at Cheltenham 17 and bur. at Stanmore, co. Middlesex, 24 Nov. 1846, aged 86.

B

Ann Margaret Dwarris Dunston, bapt. May 1786; died Jan. 1787, aged 8 months.

Frances Dwarris Dunston.

Sarah Taylor Dwarris Dunston.

Fortunatus Dwarris, born 5 March and died July 1785.

Sir Fortunatus Wm. Lilley Dwarris, F.R.S., Knt., born at Kingston 23 Oct., bapt. 3 Dec. 1786; entered Rugby in 1801, aged 14; of Univ. Coll., Oxford, matric. 23 Mar. 1804, aged 17; B.A. 1808; barrister-at-law, Middle Temple, 1811; knighted 2 May 1837; Bencher 1850; Recorder of Newcastle-under-Lyme; Master of Queen's Bench; died 20 May 1860. =┬= Charlotte Augusta, youngest dau. of Rev. Alex. Sterky; mar. at Pimlico 19 July 1815.

Rev. Brereton Edward Dwarris, at Eton 1832; Fellow and Tutor of Durham, Vicar of Bywell St. Peter's, Northumberland. =┬= Georgiana, youngest dau. of Capt. Ponsonby, R.N., of Springfield, co. Cumberland; died at Brighton 4 March 1853, aged 28.

This Ind're made the 27 April 24 Geo. 2d 1751 Between Herman Atkins Dwarris l. of Greenwich co. Kent but now of Worksop co. Nott. gt. of the one part and W. Welby of the Middle T. gt. of the other Wit. that for barring all est. tail and for 10s. H. A. D. sells all that his pln adjoining Fort Stewart in the p. of St George I. of J'ca. called Cherry Garden heretofore belonging to Col. Thos. D. father of the sd H. A. D. of 300 a. with the houses negroe slaves and stock on trust to reconvey to T. H. D. Lease of 26 April. (Close Roll 5867.)

A

Mary Atkins Dwarris, mar. 1st John McLean of Kingston, merchant (his will dated 1764), and had a dau. Mrs. Eliz. Hayes. Mar. 2ndly Dr. John Martin Butt. (See Mann v. Dwarris in Livingston's "Sketch Pedigrees," 55.)

Honoria Dwarris, mar. about 1760 Robt. Brereton, Esq. He mar. 3rdly Sept. 1782, then aged 58. His son by his 1st wife studying law 1786.

Janet, died Oct. 1796. = Dr. Grant, 1782. Letter 8.

. . . . = Dr. David Grant. Letter 57. Only surviving child = ...

David Grant, Junr., 1789.

Two sons and a dau. 1788.

This Ind're made the 28 March 24 Geo. 2d 1751 Between Fortunatus Dwarris late of St John's College Camb. but now of St George's in the I. of Jamaica Esq. of the one part and Jonathan Ewer of L. Mt of the other Wit. that for barring

B B

Will. Henry Dwarris, born 1791; entered Rugby in 1803, aged 12, and the Navy 1808; Lieut. 1817; on half-pay 1849. = Eliz. . . . ., died 24 Oct. 1858, aged 54. M.I. at St. Mary's.

Edward John Dwarris, born 1797; entered Rugby in 1806, aged 9.

all est. tail and for 10s. F. D. grants to J. E. all that pln of his abutting on Fort Stewart in the p. of St George called Golden Grove formerly in the possession of Col. Tho. D. his father of 600 acres with the buildings mills negroe slaves stock on T. to reconvey. (Close Roll 5871.)

1790, Lately. At J., Fortunatus D'Warris, M.D., custos of the parish of St. George. ("G.M.," 476.)

1796, Oct. Mrs. Janet Grant, mother of Doctor David Grant. ("Columbian Mag.," *ante*, IV., 206.)

1813, Oct. 4. At Stanmore, in his 61st year, William Dwarris, esq. of Southampton-street, Bloomsbury, and Golden-grove, St. George's, I. of J. ("G.M.," 505.)

1820, Dec. 28. Wm. Gibney, M.D. of Cheltenham, to Frances, dau. of the late Wm. Dwarris, esq. of Great Stanmore, Middlesex. ("G.M.," 634.)

1823. Letters patent to Henry Maddock and Fortunatus Dwarris to inquire into the admon. of criminal justice in the Windward and Leeward Islands.

The West India Question, etc., by F. Dwarris. 8vo. 1828.

1830, June. At Everton vicarage, Hunts, the Rev. Charles Augustus Dwarris, M.A. of Eman. coll. Camb. ("G.M.," 560.)

The Rev. C. A. Dwarris (who died March 20, 1830) was the youngest son of the late Wm. D., esq. of Golden-grove plantation, in the p. of St. Geo., J'ca. (*Ibid.*, 1831, 652.)

1843, Nov. 16. At Cheltenham, Henry Adolphus Shuckburgh, Capt. 40th Bengal Nat. Inf. yst. s. of the l. Sir Stewkley S. Bt. (and bro. of the present Sir Fra.) of S. park, Warwickshire, to Sarah-Eliz. dau. of the l. Wm. D. of Golden-grove, J. (*Ibid.*, 1844, 88.)

1845, July 19. At Pimlico, Fortunatus Wm. D. to Charlotte-Augusta, yst. dau. of the l. Rev. Alex. Sterky. (*Ibid.*, 417.)

1846, Sep. 9. At Keswick, the Rev. Brereton E. D., M.A., V. of Bywell St. Peter's Northumberland to Georgiana, yst. dau. of the l. Capt. John Ponsonby, R.N. f. of Springfield, Cumb. (*Ibid.*, 643.)

1846, Nov. 17. At Cheltenham, a. 86, Sarah, rel. of Wm. D. of J. (*Ibid.*, 1847, 105.)

1853, March 4. At Brighton, aged 28, Georgina, wife of the Rev. Brereton E. Dwarris, Vicar of Bywell St. Peter's, Northumberland (son of Sir Fortunatus Dwarris), and youngest dau. of the l. Capt. Ponsonby, R.N. of Springfield, Cumberland. (*Ibid.*, 455.)

1801. Fortunatus Dwarris, s. of W. D. Esq. Warwick, a. 14, Oct. 23 (p. 86). Barr.-at-l. Author of various legal works. Knighted. A Master of the Court of Q. B. Recorder of Newcastle. D. 1860. (Rugby School List.)

1803. Wm. Henry D. 2[d] s. of W. D. Esq. Warwick, a. 12, Jan. 4. Comm[r] R.N. Served as Mid[n] of the Loire, 38 guns. Silver War medal, 2 clasps. Present at the capture of the Islands of Martinique and Guadaloupe. (*Ibid.*, p. 89.)

B

Rev. Cha. Augustus Dwarris, born 1801; entered Rugby in 1815, aged 14; of Eman. Coll., Camb., matric. Nov. 1819; moved to Christ Coll., B.A. 1823, M.A. 1826; died 20 March 1830 at Everton Vicarage, co. Hunts.	Caroline Matilda Dwarris, died at Bath 12 April 1867, aged 71. M.I. — Frances McKeand Dwarris, mar. 28 Dec. 1820 Wm. Gibney, M.D., of Cheltenham.	Sarah Eliz. Dwarris, mar. 16 Nov. 1843, at Cheltenham, Capt. Henry A. Shuckburgh.

1806. Edw. J. D. 3[d] s. of W. D. Esq. Warwick, a. 9, Jan. 15 (p. 93); re-admitted in 1810 (*Ibid.*, p. 105).

1815. Chas. D. s. of W. D. Esq. Warwick, a. 14, Aug. 9 (p. 123).

Sir Fortunatus William Lilley Dwarris, son of William Dwarris, of the I. of Jamaica, Esq., matriculated from University College, Oxford, 23 March 1804, aged 17; B.A. 1808, barrister-at-law of the Middle Temple 1811, a bencher 1850, recorder of Newcastle-under-Lyme, one of the municipal corporation commissioners, a master of the Court of Queen's Bench, F.R.S.; Knighted 2 May 1837, d. 20 May 1860. (Foster.)

The following grant of arms to Dwarris of London is given by Rowlandson:— ARMS: *Argent, on a fesse Gules between three eagles' heads erased Sable as many roses Or.* CREST: *A demi-lion rampant Argent, pelletée, in its paws a battle-axe Or.*

John Dwarris of East Greenwich, co. Kent, gent. Will dated 20 Aug. 1642. My son John D. £20. My dau. Ann D. 12d. All residue to my wife Judith. Proved 1655. (25, Aylett.)

Fortunatus Dwarris of Kingston, Jamaica, dr. of phy. Will dated 17 June 1789. Neph. Wm D. £200 c. Friend Dr David Grant £50 c. My wife Fra., furn., plate, carriages and horses, and house negroes. I am entit. in her right by the sett. made by Geo. Pinnock Dunston, Esq., on 29 Nov. 1784 to £4371 for arrears of a rent charge of £300 c., payable to my wife by the will of her l. husb^d^ John Dunston, Esq., I give her that sum. To Rob. Brereton, Esq., who was the husb^d^ of my l. sister Honoria, £20. My niece Eliz. Hayes, dau. of l. sister Mary Maclean by her husb^d^ John M., Esq., dec^d^, £100. To my neph. W. D. 3 negros. To my wife my house in K'ston for life, then to be sold and the proceeds for my 2 goddaus. and granddaus.-in-l. Fra. Dwarris Dunston and Sarah Taylor D. D. at 21, in default to my s.-in.-l. Geo. P. D. All r. and pers. est. and slaves to Tho. Stoakes Harris, Tho. Bell, Cha. Mitchell, and Geo. P. D., Esq^rs^, in T., to pay to my wife £800 c. a yr. out of the rents of my pl^n^ called Golden Grove in the p'sh of St Geo. A mortg. I gave of it to Hilton and Biscoe, M^ts^ in L., in 1764, to be discharged now £720 only due. Trustees to purch. negroes, and after death of my wife to pay my niece Eliz. Hayes £140 c. a yr., to my neph. Rob. Brereton, J^r^, £300 c. a yr., grand-nephew David Grant, J^r^, £1000 c. at 21. All res. of est. to my neph. Wm Dwarris. Tho. Bell, Esq., to be acting Ex'or and manager of est., and in case of his death or leaving Cha. Mitchell, Esq., Tho. Stoakes Harris, my neph. Wm D., and my wife Fra., Ex'ors. Witnessed by Will Mitchell, Tho. Williams, Tho. Lowry. Proved 28 Sept. 1809 by Wm D., Esq., the neph., p. r. to Fra. D. the rel., the other surv. substituted Ex'or. (683, Loveday.)

Wm. Dwarris of No. 3 Southampton Str., Bloomsbury, Esq. Will dated 16 Feb. 1810. My wife Sarah. My s. Fortunatus Wm. Lilley D. My wife's father Lilley Smith's will. My ch^rn^ Wm Henry, Sarah-Eliz., Caroline Matilda, Edw.-John, Fanny M^c^Keand D. and Chas.-Aug., £2000 each. My aunt D. in J. My l uncle D.'s will. Proved 1813. (493, Heathfield.)

DWARRIS LETTERS.

The following 57 letters were written by William Dwarris and his wife from Jamaica to her father Lilley Smith, Esq., of Coventry. Some of them are very long and uninteresting, but I have made abstracts of all items of local interest. The letters were sold to me by a dealer.

1. 1781, May 14. On board the Vere and approaching the Downs. Yesterday we scaled our Guns, as did two other armed ships.

2. 1781, July 20. St Lucia. We left p^tsmth^ the 20th May in company with the Newfoundland Fleet &c. with which we parted on the 5th of June, & proceeded on our passage towards Barbadoes, with two Frigates & 19 Sail of

Merchantmen . . . . We arrived last Monday at Barbadoes, which place we found under arms at our approach—& was informed of the taking of Tobago by the French—here we found only three Men-of-Warr, Two Admirals having sailed from thence two days before our arrival, having left orders for our Fleet to proceed to this place on arrival, & take other ships from hence to join for Jamaica. We left that unfortunate Island Barbadoes on Tuesday night & arrived here yesterday. But not before I had taken Sally on shore, to see the Dismal ruins of a once flourishing Town. 'Tis impossible to describe the dreadful effects of the Hurricane,* not a single house but what was somewhat Damaged & whole Streets in ruins. The Church which was a very Elegant one Level'd & some hundreds yet lay buried in the ruins. Three bells out of six are safe & placed up near a Temporary Church . . . . every article of Produce is very scarce, particularly fruit, all the Trees in the Island having been blown up by the roots. St Lucia is about 25 Leagues from Barbadoes so we soon run it here, but to our disappointment saw Ad^ml Drake coming out as we made the Island, going to St Kitts (Xoph^rs) . . . . The French made an attack on this place last May & landed some Thousand Troops, seven Ships of the Line anchored, none of ours being here, but the Battery on the Hill soon drove them out & they were obliged to get their Men off in great confusion. A Lieu^t Mills of the Navy resides on shore & had about 200 Men on the Hills, with which he accomplished his Defence . . . . [Sketch of Pigeon Island with its guns given.]

Love & Duty to Mother, Brother, Sisters, Aunt, etc., Villers's, Mr Little, Mr Sherwood. Addressed to "Mr Lilley Smith, Coventry, Warwicks^hire."

3. 1781, July 30, St Kitts . . . . two days from St Lucia, Sir George Rodney sent two line of Battle ships from hence to convoy us up from S^t L^a. On our arrival here yesterday we found Sir Geo. R. squadron & Adm. Drake's with a convoy ready to sail for England . . . . Sir Geo. Rodney is just sailed for St Eustatia to which place we are to sail tomorrow.

4. 1781, Nov. 19, Jamaica, Kingston. The late dreadful season the worst & most fatal to all kinds, both Europeans & old standers that ever was known. Last Wednesday the 15th Nov. the Thermometer was up so high as 92. The Morn^gs are cool & pleasant as the North Wind now begins to come in. Yo^r daur. & myself ride round the Race Course every morn^g at day break . . . . I am sorry to inform you of the Death of a very worthy & promising young Man—poor Dawson died the 31st Octr of a putrid Fever. A lock of his hair I now enclose for his poor Mother. Mr. Craven his uncle Mr Mayo's partner. My cousin Dr. Grant. Flour in Barrels which contained about 200 w^t has for some time sold at Publick Vendue for £16 p^r Bar. but is now down to £8 owing to two large Prizes having come in a few days ago loaded with that article . . . .

The ham which my aunt Gascoigne was so kind as to give Sarah . . . . money due to me from my name being on the Bristols Books about 8 Months . . . . you can learn at the Navy Office, when I came the Bristol was gone home & the Captn was dead . . . . When the Æolus left Jamaica I sold my pay to Captn Atkins. Decr 23. The Cork Fleet are arrived at Barbadoes & compleatly blocked up by 36 Sail of the Line . . . . Our Governor leaves us in a few days which we are all heartily happy at, altho' we have reason to fear, we shall not have a better in Genl Campbell. Dalling has been treating the Council & Assembly this fortnight so they are studying elegant Addresses for him to carry home . . . .

5. 1782, Jan. 14. Cheese 3 shillings p^r pound & hams D^o as to flour a loaf like a halfpenny roll with you for 7½^d . . . . The Death of my Grandmother on New Years Day after a few days illness, her estate being Personal her Husband comes in for it, indeed one half was spent before she died. My Uncle gets 9 Negroes which she had for life & saves a £100 p^r ann. which was paid out of

* Of 10 Oct. 1780, when there was a loss of life exceeding 3000 and of property over one million sterling.

his Estate . . . . tis unfortunate for me she had not died before she married, as she was worth £5000 & by will left it to myself & Robt Brereton but when she married she made all over to the longest liver . . . . We are under the greatest apprehensions of the Spaniards & French attacking us . . . . the few Regiments we have have not half their Complements of Men & but four Ships of the Line however it must be a great force that can carry Port Royal. Genl Campbell our present Lt Govr is acting with the utmost Diligence to get all the Ports in Order & the Militia daily exercising likewise the Engineers, we have booms ready to lay across the channell on their approach. We do not expect them to come with less than 25,000 soldiers . . . . They make little or no secret at the Havannah that Jamaica will soon be theirs . . . . As Mr Harrison did not make myself or Sally a present of Mourning I had almost resolved not to go into it neither did my uncle but my aunt prevailed upon us . . . . Potatoes has sold lately at £4 pr hundred I suppose they did not cost above 4 shillings at home.

6. 1782, Feb. 10. About two o'clock in the Morning of the 3d Inst. a fire broke out at a small dwelling house tenanted by a Free Mulatto Woman (but how we cannot learn for certain yet think t'was set on fire by some of the French Prisoners who to the Scandal of our Police go at large here) & was so very rapid in its communication to the adjoining houses that the neighbours had scarcely time to save their lives, it soon made its way into Port Royal Street which is the most capital tho' not largest street in Town, as all the Merchants Stores are there & the place of Business . . . . four or five streets & as many lanes were all at one time on fire . . . . our houses have all Balconies joining each other & tops of the houses shingled with wood (wood split & made like your Tiles) . . . . The Fire continued burning till Six in the Morning, by which time one hundred houses were consumed & nine wharfs with all their stores & goods. I have an acquaintance who poor fellow, the day before was a man of easy Fortune, he lost on one wharf 2500 Barrels of Beef & Pork, 1500 firkins of Butter & 70 Pipes of fine Madeira wine, & is not now worth £500. One Liverpool house has lost £25,000 which is the most that has befell one concern, scarcely a house that is burnt that rented for less than £80 per ann' & some so high as £200, the loss is computed at about a Million & a half . . . . My uncle has sent us a cook & waiting boy which came to him from his Mother's death. Tea before the fire was at 22/6 & is now at the enormous price of forty shillings pr pd. I am informed there are not now four chests in Town. I wish I had all here from your shop in Coventry.

7. 1782, March 5. My uncle yesterday gave me a sight of all the Private Intelligence of our spies to the Governor. The French & Spaniards should land 10,000 at Port Antonio which has a noble harbour for their Fleet . . . . 10,000 at Morant Bay about 30 miles to windward of Kingston—10,000 at Carlisle Bay about 40 miles to leeward of Kingston & where I am sorry to say there is not a gun mounted & a fine open country to march thro' to Spanish Town, 10,000 to be kept on board the ships as a reserve, a feint to be made on Port Royal by the whole fleet . . . . Our Assembly found it absolutely necessary to consent to the laying on Martial Law . . . . We have only one Frigate out at this critical juncture & abt 18 Pendants flying here in Harbour instead of at least one half being out on observation . . . . My cousin Mrs Grant has offered to take Sally in the mountains with her family, she will either go with her or my aunt Dwarris. I believe I must now go & take my old post as first Lieutt of the 12 Apostle Battery opposite Pt Royal (42 Pounders & a blockhouse with 8 six Do) . . . . there are certain Mountains laid out for the reception of women & children well fortified & where all the live stock is to be drove . . . . Ham 5/ pr pound cheese Do butter 3/9d & that very indifferent.

[Mrs. Sarah Dwarris his wife adds:] We shall be obliged to my Uncle V. for the ale as also to my Mother for cheese & bacon.

8. 1782, April 16. We have the park of artillery next our house & stands on some of our vacant ground .... there has been about £250,000 expended already .... Two of the best companys of one of the Kingston battalions of Militia lately ground their arms & refuse duty to act under a certain Major only because he did not know his duty so well as these martinets .... The London fleet is at S[t] Lucia. My uncle Dr. Grant.

9. 1782, May 6. Our minds are perfectly easy now as to the French & Spaniards from the glorious victory obtained over the French on the 12th April by S[r] Geo: Rodney, we have six sail of French line of battle ships here amongst which is the Ville de Paris of 110 guns & had 1500 men on board, with their Admiral Compte De Grasse who is develish surly in Spanish Town, a house being provided for him there, as it is tho[t] he is a man of too much penetration & observation to go at large. My old friend Viscount D'Escan commanded the Glorieux & behaved like an hero every mast & stick being carried away, he nailed his colours to the stump of the main mast, he had about 400 killed on board as was hisself fine fellow. S[r] Geo: is here .... Adm[l] Hood is cruizing off Hispaniola & Rowley is ordered out in a few days with 5 fresh sail of the line to recruit them, as to Greaves you may order him home & hang him if you please .... I think my mother [in law] cannot do otherwise than like Killingworth, for tis the most pleasant village I ever saw.

10. 1782, May 18. [Mrs. S. D. to her father:] When you write to Birmingham remember me to my Grandfather & Aunt Wheeler.

11. 1782, June 26. The London fleet is safe arrived after only a passage of 8 weeks one of which they stayed at S[t] Lucia. In the fleet came M[rs] Neufville & M[r] & M[rs] Wallace from Notting' the first my uncle's dau'r in law who went off ab[t] 14 months since for her health & has spent my uncle 100 guineas a month in England, having kept a coach 2 footmen &c. this he told me hisself. Beef when we came was at its old price 7½, soon after at 10, no one complained as everything was rising, lately on S[r] Geo: fleet coming in it got up to a shilling & is now at the price of 2 bitts 1[s] 3[d] pork has this week past got up to [blot] mutton now at 1. 10½ 3 bitts, flour indeed is now low £5 p[r] barrell, fish of which we have every day great plenty has made a quicker progress than anything else from a bitt to 2. Jack Keyworth is always with us when on shore .... he is gone out with Drake's squadron .... he belongs to the Conqueror 74.

12. 1782, July 8. M[r] M[rs] & Miss Wallace & two children, the family we went to visit in Nottinghamshire .... the death of a sister who died a few weeks before their arrival .... the death of cousin Keyworth in his ship after only 14 hours sickness of a putrid fever.

13. 1782, Sept. 13. Poor Wallace* is dead, also his son a fine boy about 5 years old, & this day month died M[rs] Neufville† .... her jealousy of us. M[r] Brereton has lately taken unto himself a young wife of twenty .... he is 58 & he has a son older than his mother in law. We have not at present any naval force here having sent them all to New York. We have above 4000 regulars.

14. 1783, April 6. Peace being established it was proclaimed here a few days since & the people shewed every possible mark of disapprobation .... the American loyalists, several of whom are here in the greatest distress. I believe there has been about £3000 distributed amongst the poorer sort, most of them are

* Peter Wallace, Esq., died 15 July, aged 28, and his son Tho. Stoakes Wallace died the following day, aged 4 years and 5 months; bur. in Kingston Churchyard. (Archer, 152.)

† Mrs. Ann Neufville, dau. of Mrs. Frances Dwarris by her first husband John Dunston, Esq., died 15 Aug., aged 25. (*Ibid.*, 85.)

going back to America .... The late additional duty on sugars .... I believe Mr Conway your present Member was at school with me at Harrow as there were three of them there & boarded at Mrs Underwoods when I was at Mrs Reeves's .... Mr Ellis* who was unfortunately lost in his passage home last year held 12,000 acres under different patents from the Crown, out of which he had about 1800 settled & would neither lease or sell the rest & why? because we in this Island only pay a farthing an acre quit rent. But if an Act was to pass the Assembly to lay on 6d in the pound on all uncultivated land the owners would have it at their option either to pay it or give up the surplusage land, by which means several Americans who are come here with numbers of negroes would immediately begin to patent those lands ....

15. 1783, April 17. The Prince is here as also Lord Hoods fleet of 18 sail of the line .... he is still only a midshipman & always appears in that uniform with his star & garter.

16. 1783, May 11. [Mrs. S. D. to her father.] We have not heard from my uncle Keyworth .... the captain had sent my cousin John's clothes to Plymouth. My sister Nancy.

17. 1783, June 27. [Mrs. S. Dwarris to her father.] Mr. Waugh a distant relation of Mr Dwarris's sails for England in a few days & who as (*sic*) ever treated us with the greatest kindness for after my many illnesses in Kingston I have allways gone to his house at Port Royal for change of air .... he is a plain & honest man & never was in England before. Mr Dwarris writes about Mr & Mrs Gascoignes affairs. In my last I mentioned having gone twice on board the Formidable to visit Adl Pigot .... Sr Charles Douglass his first Captain. Mr Benton the present ordnance store keeper is a Lincolnshire man & his sister was married to a gentleman that lives near Market Rason. My uncle will make about 170 large shipping h'ds & abt 110 puncheons of rum .... his relation Mr Maclean.

18. 1783, July 1. Letter of introduction for Mr Waugh to Lilley Smith, Esq.

19. 1783, Aug. 31. The thermometer up as high as 92 .... we have lost several gentleman of this town from the heat & amongst the rest one of our members & Mr Brereton who married an aunt of mine now stands as candidate for the ensuing election. Lord Montague who raised a regiment in America & who has been here some time, sailed yesterday with most of his officers & men for Nova Scotia. Mr Waugh a very worthy young man who has by his industry acquired about £5000. We expect Admiral Gambier out to relieve Admiral Rowley† in whom we shall not have the least loss as he is a very proud & illiterate man. Mrs S. D. writes of Nancy & Billy [her sister and brother].

20. 1783, Oct. 10. On Thursday last the 6th Oct. the thermometer was up at 102. I have known it twice at 97 but never felt the heat equal to this last week.

21. 1784, Jan. 18. Admiral Rowley sails tomorrow for England. We have been feasting & carousing from one house to another these three weeks past .... a dance at my uncles .... he was as young as any one in company & pushed about claret & champaigne very briskly, the latter article is very dear in this

* John Ellis was lost at sea with his wife and niece. He was father of Lord Seaford.

† Sir Joshua Rowley, Vice-Admiral, succeeded Sir Peter Parker as Naval C. in C. in 1782. He was created a baronet in 1786 and died 26 Feb. 1790, aged 70. ("D.N.B.")

island £10 per dozen the other £5, but he can very well afford it, as he is out of debt & has no children to save for. Mr Harris & Mrs. Wallace . . . . his estate about 50 miles out of town . . . . he has been appointed one of the judges.

[Mrs. S. D. adds:] "As my father used to be very much troubled with the rumatics if he will follow this receipt he will find it do him a great deal of good but he must take it for a long time. Take two ounces of lignumvitæ add a quart of haff rum half brandy shake it well together & take a teaspoonful of it night & morning in a wine glass of water."

22. 1781, March 20. Mrs S. D. Five weeks visit to Mr Harris's family & Mrs Wallace. Mr Harris & Mrs. Wallace leave Jamaica in May next for England where she is going to stay two or three years with her children which she left there, she means to reside at Notingham. Mr. H. will not stay with her in England as she cannot prevail upon her mother to leave this country.

23. 1781, May 3. Mrs Wallace & her father . . . . the little girl which she brought out is to stay here with the grandmother. Miss Wallace Mr Wallaces sister who came out at the same time is very happily married, she has got a fine little girl . . . . Mrs. Brereton too has a little girl.

24. 1781, June 28. Altho' youth is frequently sent from here to England for improvement it must be recollected that they are in general youth of fortune or great expectations t'is therefore thot most advisable to send them to the first schools such as Eaton or Westminster where they may form connections with the first familys in the kingdom.

Mr Harris is a very genteel man, but rich & prodigious stingey.

25. 1781, July 20. Poor Mr Thomas Maclean is dead, & we are in mourning for him; my uncle, who has always refused honours, has been at length tempted to accept from Governor Campbell before he left us the appointment of Custos Rotulorum of St Georges, the parish where his estate lies, so that he is the Honble F. D. . . . . Remember us to my uncle & aunt Keyworth grandfather Cowlys cousins &c.

26. 1781, Aug. 11. We have experienced a very dreadful hurricane on this side of the country it continued its course about 90 miles, all the estates 60 miles to windward of this town are destroyed—all the ships but two here were either sunk run on ground or dismasted, & several of their crews totally lost—all the brick walls & fences down & several houses unroofed. A vessell coming round the island is lost & 11 passengers in it amongst which is the collector of Port Antonio. If my father can now ask Ld B. or any other acquaintce to apply to the commissioners for it for me it will be a greater matter to me than any other person for although the salary is only £120 per ann yet the profits make it about 400 currency, & I could carry on my business at Port Antonio the only atty that practised there lately having died.

27. 1781, Aug. 29. Mr Sam. Cator who from his great extravagance has for I may say a 3d time ruined himself is now in goal for life . . . . he will lose two places which he enjoys comptroller of Port Antonio & Deputy Register of the Court of Vice Admiralty . . . . a new appointment lays with a Mr Owsley Rowley* of London the patentee. I served my time 5 years with Mr Hinton East the former Dep. Regt. The judge is an old school fellow of mine Mr Ricketts† a counsellor at our bar . . . . [details about applying for the post].

* 1781, Dec. Owsley Rowley, esq; to be register of the vice-admiralty court in J. vice John Morse, esq dec. ("G.M," 595.)

† William Henry Ricketts, born 1740, barrister-at-law of Gray's Inn 1765, bencher 1769, M. of C., of Longwood, Hants, died in Jamaica 5 Oct. 1798. Geo. Crawford Ricketts, his nephew, was Attorney-Gen. in 1796, and died 6 April 1811.

28. 1784, Oct. 1. At Mr Breretons. His neighbour Mr Clarke & Dr Pugh of Spanish Town were rivals the lady being on a visit at Mr Clarkes. The doctor calling at Mr Clarkes asked for a glass of water alighted from his horse & told Mr C. he had something to say to him in private & went in a field at the back of the house, when he pulled out a surgical knife & stabbed him twice in the left breast. Mr Clarke run a few yards called out he was a dead man fell & expired. The wretch then plunged the same bloody instrumt into his own breast 4 times & expired . . . . I run to the place where they both lay 10 yards of each other . . . . both amiable young men . . . . his corpse was buried in the highway.

29. 1784, Nov. 14. We have in the course of this last week catched 3 desperate pirates & murderers who murdered a whole crew & brought the vessell in here & sold the same with her cargoe (consisting of lumber from America) they have spent all the money in rioting.

30. 1784, Dec. 12. I believe this packet carries home our Assemblies Petition to have the duties lately laid on sugar taken off & to allow the Americans to trade with us in their own bottoms . . . . Since our late hurricane 1st Aug. the Governor with the advice of his Counsel allowed the Americans to bring us supplies in their own vessells.

31. 1785, Jan. 23. The death of the land & tide surveyor of this port a Mr Fenton. My aunt Dwarris has been out of town these five weeks at her sons wedding. Mr Stoakes Harris is dayly expected. [Example of his stinginess.]

32. 1785, March 20. My dear Sally was safely delivered of a clever little boy on the 5th inst. We are hourly expecting to hear of some dust being kicked up between the Spaniards & our people on the Mosquito Shore our ships of warr are all under sailing orders at Port Royal . . . . we have had 300 men sent to the defence of that place by different detachments in small vessells & without any noise. Mr Lewis* the oracle of the barr is dead he made the year he died £8000. [On the back is a letter from W. D. Smith, Coventry, 20 May 1785, to his father.]

33. 1785, April 24. Mr & Mrs Dunston at my uncle Dwarris's. I was there the night before last to pay a formal visit to her.

34. 1785, July 17. Mrs. S. D. to her Mother:—The death of our beloved child—so much the greater was our loss after having been married so many years without a child. Mrs. Brereton was brought to bed a few days since of another girl. Mrs Hayes a cousin of Mr D. was very kind when my little Fortunatus was sick. I wrote to my sister Mrs Ellis.

[Mr. W. D. writes:] I have been this morning sent for to the goal by a gentleman who calls himself The Honble Cap. Manners . . . . what or who he is no person here knows. He knows everybody in Lincoln & my friends the Bolderos in Yorkshire . . . . he has been but illiterately brought up at Beverly in Yorkshire, he came here about 5 months since & brought a great quantity of cash with him which is all gone.

35. 1785, Sept. 11. On Sat. the 27th Aug. about 4 o'clock it began to blow very hard . . . . the hurricane increased dreadfully till about 8 o'clock . . . . many more houses blown down than in the last one in July 84 . . . . there were about

* Hugh Lewis, born 3 Aug. 1753, barrister-at-law and Advocate-Gen., died 23 Jan. 1785. (Archer, 56.)

300 poor souls lost in this harbour. My uncle's estate has suffered much, part of his own dwelling house unshingled, his overseers house down all the negroe houses gone, his canes lodged &c. however his damage does not exceed £3000.

36. 1785, Sept. 25. My uncle has been all his life hitherto contented with a cattle mill on his estate. But now he is out of debt & declining in life, he wants to clear 200 more acres of land for canes, & make a large waterwork—the water he is to carry 3 miles in a stone guttering to his wheel, he has laid out a plan to run in debt to the amount of about £10,000 & he is then to make 300 hogsheads of sugar a year. I think him much to blame. He has no children is out of debt & makes about 150 hds now & ab[t] 90 puncheons of rum—he was 59 yesterday. He has ordered Sally to leave off eating suppers. When first I came over to this island every family had regularly cloth laid at night, & now I scarce know 4 familys that do, persons in general finding they enjoy better health by leaving off that meal.

37. 1785, Dec. 11. M[r] Harris has been extremely ill up at Stoaksfield* his country house.

38. 1786, March 27. We have nothing stirring here but seizing the poor American vessells & condemning them for not being navigated agreeable to law.

39. 1786, June 26. Mrs. Dunstons little girl was christened about a month ago .... the child's name is Ann Margaret Dwarris. Having some time since been requested by my uncle Keyworth to send him home some rum (60 gallons) .... it is distilled with cocoa nuts & civil (*sic*) oranges & I shall put in the juice of about 20 large pines. I am to have it at 2/8 p[r] gallon which is the price my uncle's factor sold 15 puncheons at last week in town .... to prevent its being touched by sailors it is to be cased in another large cask & will cost £14 st.

40 and 41. 1786, July 3. The death of the Hon. Tho. Davison the collector of this port. Mr. Papley the collector at Port Antonio may succeed to it .... one of the commissioners of the customs being married to his sister.

42. 1786, July 16. M[r] Brereton & his wife have given up their house in town & are gone to live at their penn .... she is his third wife his first was Miss Dwarris my uncle's sister & by whom he has a son now living who is learning the profession of the law. M[r] B. has two children by his present wife.

43. 1786, July 25. The puncheon of rum properly cased is shipped on board the Justina for want of the opportunity of a droguer coming round was obliged to ship it at Annotto Bay.

44. 1786, Oct. 13. M[rs] S. D. My brother William in L. My little niece.

45. 1786, Nov. 6. We have experienced another hurricane which happened in the morning of the 20th of last month but has had less dreadful effects on this side of the island than any storm has had these five years. By accounts from the windward parts, we learn that they have suffered very much & will lose about one third of their next sugar crop. But the Leeward accounts are dreadful they have suffered but little less than in the year 1780 when the whole town of Savannah La Mar was destroyed scarcely a house or set of works in two of their parishes but what are half down & their canes blown up by the roots. My uncle had just got 40 hhds. on board a ship at the Bay near his estate & the ship has rode out the storm. The 23[d] Sally brought a fine little boy.

* See description of this old mansion in Cundall's "Historic Jamaica," p. 242.

46. 1786, Nov. 10. The windward part of the island have been provident enough to put in a great quantity of ground provisions such as sweet potatoes.

47. 1786, Dec. 9. Our dear little fellow was christend the third of this month at my uncles . . . . we had a very genteel supper & sat down about twenty we have called him Fortunatus William Lilley. Mr Dwarris stood for you & Mrs. Davidson for my aunt Mary. My uncle and aunt Dwarris both stood for themselves & a Mrs. Betts. Mrs. Brereton was brought to bed about a month before me of another girl she has now three & the eldest not four years old.

Mr & Mrs. Davidson talk of going home in the spring. You will I dare say see them as they will be a good deal with her sister in Nottingham.

48. 1787, Jan. 21. We are going this week to inoculate our dear boy as the small pox is in town & of a very favourable kind.

This island will be all in flames in a few weeks if the Lieut Govr does not dissolve our rascally Assembly. Just before they were prorogued they passed bills giving their Speaker £1500 their messenger £500 st. & to an old broken member a Sir Chas Price Bart £5000 by way of mortgage.* Our Speaker never had any sallary before.

The death of Mrs. Dunstons child 8 months old.

49. 1787, Feb. 18. Mr. Cousins who is arrived informed me that he had seen my aunt Cowley & my grandfather . . . . Most Europeans die here from imprudence & excess on first coming over. Here is a club held in honour of Rodneys victory every 12th April by old veterans, who meet & spend the day jovially. To be a member a person must have been 30 years here, an honorary member 25 years, & there generally dines from forty to fifty, all from within the vicinity of this town. My uncle's paternal & family estate which has been in this country above 100 years in our possession. Mrs. Hayes a cousin of Mr. Dwarris has been staying with me.

50. 1787, July 15. I was very happy to hear that your son was married to so agreeable a young lady.

51. 1787, Aug. 11. My uncle has lately made a purchase of a house in town which he gave £2000 for. They do not dine till near five & never eat suppers. I cannot say I am fond of such very late hours. I think three o'clock a very good hour if you are alone, & if you have company half past.

52. 1787, Sept. 30. I am just come from a jaunt to the north side of the island, but the roads to that part are always bad, and particularly so this time of the year. I was under the necessity of swimming my horse over one river three times, the precipices & road are very dangerous, in many places not above a foot wide—A man who made an immense fortune here in former days ust to say—make me your executor & I dont care who is made your heir.

53. 1788, Jan. 27. My dear little Fortune is very well. Mr. Brereton is at present very much involved.

54. 1788, April 22. My uncle had in company with my aunt the misfortune to be over turned in his chariot this day 3 weeks by which she was much bruised & he had his left arm broke . . . . he lives so very low . . . . I think

* This was rescinded by the next Assembly as being unconstitutional. (Cundall's "Historic Jamaica," 205.)

a man at his time of life (63) should drink as usual his half pint of Madeira (it being our common wine here) . . . . To my certain knowledge he advanced £500 three months since to keep her son out of goal, who with his wife & child lives in his house & upon his generosity. My 17 years residence in this island.

55. 1788, June 1. Notwithstanding all our frugality we dont spend less than £500 a year.

56. 1788, Sept. 6. I send early intelligence of the vacancy of the comptrollers place of Port Antonio of this island by the death of a very particular old friend a M[r] Cator, who has a brother of prodigious fortune 14 or 15 £1000 p[r] ann. in London . . . . the place or salary is either 80 or £100 p[r] ann. besides a few perquisites & entirely a sinecure . . . . about 20 barristers & above 100 attorneys here. My uncle Keyworth's loss of a son . . . . his other son & Sukey. It would amuse you & my mother to hear little Fortune talk half negroe like, which is the worst thing attending children here, but as they are always playing with the negroe children they learn their ways & language, notwithstanding my being very particular.

57. 1788, Nov. 9. D[r] Grant* has been exceedingly ill—he has a very fine boy in England by his first wife, & by the present one three, two boys & a girl the youngest is not above two months old . . . . poor old M[rs] Grant was really miserable at the thoughts of losing her son, as he is the only child she has left. The fire my uncle had at his estate . . . . the great house was on fire two or three times but it was put out . . . . My aunt has not been there these eighteen years.

Nov. 15. Prince William Henry has just entered Port Royal harbour . . . . he is come to winter here.

Patent for a French plantation in St. Kitts to Dame Ann Stapleton and Sir William Stapleton of Nevis, Baronet, A° 1696.

William by the Grace of God of England Scotland France and Ireland King and soveraign Lord of S[t] Christophers and all other his Majesty's American Plantations and Colonies Defender of the Faith &c[a] To all to whome these Prefents shall com Greeting. Whereas in the Reigne of our Royall Predeceſsors there has bin ſeverall conſiderable Colonies settled as well on the Islands as Maine Lands of America by our Subjects which has bin found very advantageous to the propagation of the Christian Faith the Enlargement of our Dominions the Avancement of our Royall Dignity the Encreaſe of our Revenue and the trade of our Kingdom of England and to the comfortable Support of many of our Loving subjects. And whereas Wee of our Royall Goodneſs are Deſirous to promote and encourage what has bin found productive of so many good effects to which nothing can tend more then to grant shuch Lands as now are or hereafter shall be undiſposed of in any of our said Colonies to shuch Diſcreet and Industrious Perſons who will improve the ſame for the Ends aforeſaid. And whereas it hath pleaſed the Allmighty Goodneſs to bleſs our Armes whith succeſs aginst the

* 1817, May 1. Died at Portsmouth on the 18th inst. Lieut. Sam. Grant, royal navy, youngest son of Dr. Grant of Jamaica.

1817, Sept. 25. Died on the 29th June at Kingston, Jamaica, as universally and deeply lamented as he was justly respected and beloved, David Grant, M.D. ("Bath Chronicle.")

Subjects of the French King our Declared Enemy in the aforefaid Island of St Christophers whereby We have not only regained that part to us formerly belonging but made an abfolute and Entire Conquest of the whole Island and thereby become wholy seiz^d thereof in the Right of our Crown. And whereas it is greatly our Interest to Encourage a thorow: and speedy Settlement of the said Island by shuch of our Loving Subjects as shall repair thereto or who are in Circcumstances effectually to settle which will tend much to the prefent Strenthening and Security of the Island During the Warr and to ye making of the Settlement thereof in a much greater forwardnefs and in a fairer Prospect on the Conclufion of a Peace then Can otherwife be hoped for greatly to the promoting and advancement of the afore mentioned Ends. Now know Yee that in Confideration of the Premyses Wee of our Special grace certain knowledge and Meer Motion by and with the Advice of our trufty and Well beloved Christopher Codrington Esqr our Captain General and Governour in Chief of our said Island of St Christophers and all other our Caribbe Islands from the Leeward of Guardeloupe to the Island of St John de porto Rico in America have given granted and Confirm'd and by Thefe Prefents for ous our Heirs and succefsors do give grant and Confirme unto our Trufty and Wellbeloved Subjects Dame Ann Stapleton and Sr William Stapleton of our Island of Nevis Baronet and to there Heirs and Afsignes for ever the Plantation formerly belonging to the Father Hermit Lying in Cayan Quarter Containing Two hundred and Forty Acres beginning at the Mouth of Kayan River and extending by the several Angles of the River to the interfection of the Common Path, Northwesterly Twenty Degrees one Chain and a half, Northwesterly Seaventy two Degrees two Chains, Northwesterly sixty two Degrees two Chains to Davies Line; Thence Northwesterly two Degrees twenty Six Chains and a half; Thence West five Chains Forty Links to the Common Path; Thence Northesterly two Degrees Three Chain and a half Northesterly six Degrees seven Chain sixty Five Links Northesterly seven Degrees two Chains Eighty six Links Northesterly Three Degrees Eleven Chains Northwesterly Thirteen Degrees two Chain and a half Northwesterly twenty seven Degrees three Chains and a half Thence over the Path by the Interfection of the Chains Southwesterly Eighty Degrees two Chains Northwesterly Eighty two Degrees Fouer Chains and a half Southwesterly Eighty Degrees Three Chain Northwesterly Eight Degrees Forty Five Chains to the Sea side. Thence by The Several Angles of the fea side to the Mouth of the River which was the first station Bounded to the North E^{a}st with the fea To the south East with Kayan River to the West with the Land of Davies Deceafed the Common Path and part of Durres Together With all and finguler Mefsuages Houfes Edifices Buildings Structures Mills Suger Works Orchards Gardens Lands Tenements Pastures Foodings Mountain Lands Marfhis Timber Trees Wood Underwoods Cains Cornes with the soyl and ground of the same Waters Water Courfes Fifhings and Fifhing Places with all other Profits Com^{m}odities Emoluments and Appurtenances Whatsoever unto the said Plantations and Tract of Land in any wife belonging or appurtaining. And of our Spaciall Grace Certain Knowledg and Meer Motion we Do by thefe Prefents for Us our Heirs and Succefsors give grant and Confirme Unto the said Dame Ann Stapleton and Sr William Stapleton Baronet their Heairs and Afsignes for ever the said Land and Plantation with all and singular The Rights Members and Appurtenances by thefe prefents before given granted and Confirmed or Mentioned or intended to be given granted and Confirmed and all our Right Title and Enterest of in and To the Premifes and every part and parcell Thereof as fully freely abfolutely and Intirely and in as Large and beneficial Manner the same came to our hands by vertue of the Conquest of the said Island or by any other good Right or Title Whatfoever and in as full Free Ample, Large and beneficial Manner as any of the former Proprietors Pofefsors or occupyers of the premyses have heretofore held and enjoyd the sam To have and to hold all and singuler the said lands and premifses with their & every of their appurtenances of the said Dame Ann Stapleton and Sr William Stapleton

Baronet their heirs and afsignes for ever to the only proper ufe and behalf of the said Dame ANN STAPLETON and Sr WILLIAM STAPLETON Baronet there heirs and Afsignes for evermore to be holden of Us our Heirs and succefsors as of our Fort of Charles Fort by F^ealty only in Free and Common soccage Yelding and paying for the said Lands and premifses hereby granted or Mentioned To be granted unto Us our Heirs and Succefsers that is to say to the hands of such officers as shall by us or our Commander in Chief of our said Island of St Chriftophers for the time being be Conftituted and Appointed for the Receiving of the same and at such place within our faid Island as shall be for that purpofe by us or our said Commander Nominated and Appointed there Yearly sum of Twelvepence Currant and Lawfull mony of our faid Island to be paid yearly at the Feast of Chriftmafs and alfo yielding and paying such further Rents and performing such services and Conditions for our Benefit and the thorow and Speedy Settlement of our said Island in proportion according to the Quantity of Land as shall hereafter be Establifht by Us as a Standing and General Rule in all our Grants of the Lands and Plantations of our faid Island AND farther of our Like Special grace certain Knowledge and meer motion by the Advice and Confent aforefaid We well and by thefe Prefents for Us our Heirs and succefsors do grant unto the said Dame ANN STAPLETON and Sr WILLIAM STAPLETON Baronet there Heirs and Afsignes that thefe our Letters Patents or the Enrollment Thereof shall be in all things firme good strong sufficient effectuall and available in the Law against Us our Heirs and succefsors as well in all our Courts as elfewhere without any farther Confirmation Lycenfe or toleration from Us our Heirs and succefsores hereafter by the said Dame ANN STAPLETON and Sr WILLIAM STAPLETON Baronet there Heirs and Afsignes in that behalf to be procured or obteined: NOTWITHSTANDING any misnaming or not naming Mifreciting or not reciting any part or parcell of the aforefaid Lands and Premifses or the Quantity thereof or the exact and true Limits and Bounds thereof. AND NOTWITHSTANDING the Not naming or ill naming the not reciting or ill reciting of any of the places Parifh or Divifions or Precincts wherein or in which the Premifsis or or any parcell of them are or do lye AND NOTWITHSTANDING any Defects of the certainty Computation, or Declaration of the true Yearly Value of the Premifis or of any part or parcell thereof AND NOTWITHSTANDING the Statute or Act of perlement made and Establefhed in our Kingdom of England in the Eighteenth Year of the Reign of our Noble Progenitor King Henry the Sixth AND NOTWITHSTANDING that our Writs ad Quod Damnum were not Issued forth to Inquire of the Premifsis or any part or parcell thereof before the Making of thefe our Letters Patent AND NOTWITHSTANDING any other Defect in not rightly naming the Nature Kinds sorts Quantities or Qualities of the premifsis or any Part or Parcell thereof. AND NOTWITHSTANDING the not Naming or ill Naming the not reciting or ill reciting of any of the former Proprietors Pofsefsors or Occuppyers of the Premifsis or any part or parcell thereof AND NOTWITHSTANDING any Statute Act Ordinance Prohibition Restraint or Provifion whatfoever to the Contrary AND NOTWITHSTANDING any other Matter Caufe or thing whatfoever for the avoyding Annulling or Weakening thefe our Letters Patents In Witnefs whereof wee have Caufed thefe our Letters to be made Patents Wittnefs our faid Captain General at Nevis the First Day of May 1696 and In The Eighth year of our Reign.

CHRISTOPHER CODRINGTON.

Endorsed: The within Patent Recorded the 8 Day May 1696 In the Book of Records for Inhabitants In folio 660-661-662.

Jno Smargin Jun.
D. Sec.

See *ante*, III., 225, for a lease of this estate in 1749, and *ante*, I., 23, for another lease in 1756.

Nethway of Nevis.

Thos. Neathway of Bristol, mariner. Will dated 7 Feb. 1595; proved 26 Feb. 1595 (15, Drake). = Eliz. ....

Children:

- George Nethway of Bristol, Merchant. Will dated 27 Sept. 1628; proved 14 Dec. 1628 (110, Barrington). = Mary, dau. of Mr John Gonning. s.p.
- Thomas Nethway, living 1628; of Bristol, Merchant; bur. at St. Walburg. Adm'on 8 Nov. 1639 to Sarah, the relict. = Sarah .... Will dated 11 Jan. 1640; proved 18 June 1641 (74, Evelyn).
- Richard Nethway of Bristol, brewer, 1640—53.
- Roger Nethway of Barbadoes 1651—62.

Children of Thomas and Sarah:

- 1. Thomas Nethway, eldest son, living 1628.
- George Nethway.
- John Nethway.
- Sarah Nethway.
- Eliz. Nethway.

.... = ... Netheway. = Margaret. ? 2nd wife.

Children:

- Jane Netheway, mar. .... Richardson of London, gent., dead 1751.
- Col. John Netheway of Nevis, Merchт. and M. of A. 1668; Govr. 1691; died 12 Feb. 1691-2; Will dated 25 July 1691. (171, Fane.) = Mary ...., party to deed of 1720; died 1727. Adm'on to Ph. De Witt 1728. s.p.
- Edward Netheway of London, Merchт., 1683.

John Clarke of Hogsdon, co. Middlesex, Merchant, 1682. =

Sam. Clarke = Ann ....

Children of John Clarke:

- Mary Clarke, æt. 22 in 1681 at marriage. = Jonathan Netheway of London, Merchant, born 1657; æt. 24 in 1681; kinsman 1691; nephew of Col. John; died in 1726, prisoner for debt. Will dated 21 Oct. 1720; proved 9 Oct. 1722 (200, Marlboro').
- Wm. Clarke of London, Merchant, 1751.

... Netheway, cousin of Jonathan, died about 1736.

Thomas Nethwaie of Bristoll, co. Som., maryner. Will dated 7 Feb. 1595. To my yst s. Tho. N. £100 at 21 years; my good freind John Younge of B. to have the putting forth of it; if he die under age, then to my eldest s. George N. Whereas I was part victualer at the time of my hurt in the good ship the Swan of B. in the sum of £45, I give this to my sd s. Thos. Rob. Trippett my apprentice my sea chest and instruments. My wife Eliz. and Geo. N. my eldest s. to be Ex'ors and John Young overseer, in the p. of Barth. Hogget, Tho. Greves, John Chesses, F. Armarer. Proved 26 Feb. 1595

by Tho. Lovell, n. p., the attorney of Eliz. the relict; p. r. to G. N. (15, Drake.)

Geo. Neathway of Bristol, Mercht. Will dated 27 Sept. 1628. My wife Mary 1500l. Bro. Tho. N. 1100l and to him after my wife's death all the lds. I purch. of Mr John Tomlinson. To my nephew Tho. N., s. of my sd bro., 100l. My f. in l. Mr John Gonninge my mare. My bro.-in-l. John G. 50l. Cosen Abr. Lyne. Gyles Elbridge (and others) overseers. Proved 4 Dec. 1628 by M. N. the relict. (110, Barrington.)

1639, Nov., fo. 84. Tho. Nethway. On 8th adm'on to Sarah N. the relict of T. N., late of the city of Bristol, decd.

Sarah Nethway of Bristol, widow of Tho. N., mercht., decd. Her will made 11 Jan. 1640 with a Codicil dated 27 Feb. 1640, and a later Codicil dated 7 March 1640. To be buried in the church of St Walburgh near l. husbd. My brother Mr. Geo. Lane, mercht, Ex'or. Friends Mr. Giles Elbridge and Mr. Joseph Jackson, merchts, overseers. Children under age. My sister Lawrence. My sister Butler and her 3 children she had by John Hurston, viz.: Lawrence, John and Anne H. My brother-in-law Wm. Holman. Whereas my brother-in-l. Mr. Edw. Pitt, now one of the Sheriffs, and Mr. John Goning, mercht, became bound to my decd husbd for £250 after the death of my sister-in-l. Mrs. Pitts, sd bond to my eldest s. Tho. N. My 5 chn Tho., Geo., John, Sarah and Eliz. My sister Butler's husbd. My husbd died without a will. Geo. and Rd, sons of my brother Geo. Lane. Rd Nethway, brewer. My cousin Hall her . . . . My sister Jone Lane. My sister Anne Butler. To my dau. Sarah N. the 4 pictures of her grandmother, father and mother. Proved 18 June 1641. (74, Evelyn.) (Waters' "Gen. Gleanings," p. 1009.)

Nevis. Collo John Netheway of this Island, Governor. Will dated 25 July 1691. My sister-in-law Anne Hanscombe, widow, living in L., £300 c., her former husband Mr Mathew H., deceased. My sister-in-law Eliz. Smith in L. £300 c. My mother-in-law Mrs Margaret Netheway, widow, living in Bristoll, £100 st. My kinswoman Mrs Sarah Gurney's eldest child 8000 lbs. of sugar at 14. My cousin John Richardson 8000 lbs. at 18. My wife's kinsman's son Phillip Dewitt, son of Phillip Dewit, 40,000 lbs. in 4 years at 18, if he die then to the next son. My godson John Huffam 5000 lbs. at 18. My godson Wm Chisurs 3000 lbs. at 18. My godson Simon Brown, son of Simon Brown, deceased, 3000 lbs. at 18 to buy a young negro boy. Mary Thompson 4000 lbs. and to Eliz. Thompson 2000 lbs. at 14. Tho. Thorne 2000 lbs. for writing my will. All residue to my wife Mary and to my kinsman Mr Jonathan Netheway of L., gent., and his heirs, and at her death all to him, she to charge by will £500 st. on the estate. My loving friends Cap. Walter Simonds, Esq., Cap. Wm Helmes, Cap. John Standley, Cap. Daniel Smith and Lieut. Philip Dewitt, overseers, and 1000 lbs. each. Witnessed by John Smargin, Tho. Belman, Tho. Thorne, Wm Marden, Jas. Rawleigh.

Nevis. 16 April 1692. A letter to Mr Jonathan Netheway saying that the Governor died 12 Feb. last past, signed by John Stanley, Phil. Dewitt, Danll Smith.

On 17 Sept. 1692 appeared Jonathan Netheway of L., gent. On 15 Sept. 1692 appeared Joseph Martyn of L., mercht, who swore to the signatures of above letter, and said that Philip Dewitt was formerly his servant and now corresponds with him. Proved 17 Sept. 1692 by Jonath. N., power reserved to Mary N. the relict. (171, Fane.)

Jonathan Netheway, late of L., merch^t. To Sarah Waxham, S^r, £100. My cousins Mary, Thomas, Eliz. and Sarah W., Junr, Judith, Ann, Henrietta and Wm W., and Lucy Ashwood and Benj. Ashwood £100 apiece. My aunt Eliz. Cudsden and her son John C. £100. My uncle Mr Samuel Clarke and his wife Ann £50 apiece. My cousins, W^m, Sam. John and Mary Clark £20 each. My cousin Netheway Smith and his wife £50 each. Cousin Ann Warren £10. Marg^t Haynes, Mary Warren, 40s. ea. Cousin Edwd Nelson £5 and his wife 40s. Kinsman Peter James one g^a. Cousin John Tucker 1 g^a. All residue to Mr Samuel Clark and Mr Tho. Waxham equally and Ex'ors, 21 Oct. 1720. In the presence of Margaret Battry and others. Proved 9 Oct. 1722 by Sam. Clarke, Esq., and Tho. Waxham (200 Marlboro'.)

1653, Sept. 24. Licence to Richard Netherway of Bristol to transport from Ireland to Virginia 100 Irish tories. (Col. Cal., p. 409.)

1668. John Netheway, then M. of the Assembly of Nevis. ("Antigua," i., xli.)

On 10 Jan. he signed the petition of the merchants to Wm., Lord Willoughby. (Col. Cal., p. 538.)

1677-8. Census of Nevis. Capt. John Nethway's Company.

Capt. Nethway's family: 7 w. men, 2 w., 8 ch^n, 57 negroes. (*Ante*, III., 80.)

1683. Petition of the merchants in L. trading to the Leeward Islands signed by Edwd Netheway. (49, Colonial, Leeward Islands.)

1689. Letter from John Netheway describing the Irish attack on St. Chr. Seal of arms: *A tun (?) between three pheons.* (America and W. I., vol. 52.)

1698, June 17. James Vernon, Esq., Sec. of State, recommends Mr. Jonathan Netheway, to whom a good estate in Nevis has descended, for a seat in the Council there. (B. T. Leeward Islands, vol. 5.)

1720, Dec. 29. Mary Netherway of Nevis, widow of John N., late of Nevis, Esq., who made his will on 25 July 1691, and gave his nephew Philip De Witt of Nevis, planter, £500. (Nevis Records, i., 617.)

1728, July 10. Philip De Witt, administrator of the estate of Mary Netheway. (*Ibid.*, ii., p. 57.)

1751. Chancery suit at Antigua. Richardson, Netheway and Clarke.

ST. MICHAEL, BARBADOS.

1651	Oct.	5	Robt ye s. of Roger Nothway, buried.
1662	Aug.	15	Alice the D^a of Mr Rog^r Netherway, buried.
1691	Oct.	4	Mr John Netherway, buried.

BARROW GURNEY, CO. SOM. (Phillimore, ii., 143.)

1676 May 13 William Netheway and Mary Terry, both of Yatton.

1682, Dec. 29. Jonathan Netheway of Throckmorton Str., L., Gent., B., ab^t 24, and Mrs Mary Clarke of Hogsdon, Midd., Sp^r, ab^t 22, with consent of her father Mr. John C. of the same, Merch^t, at St Leonard, Shoreditch, Midd., or All Hallows in the Wall, L. (Mar. Alleg. Vic. Gen. of Archb. of C., p. 118.)

Davies of Jamaica.

Arms used, those of Davies of Marsh, co. Salop.

Rev. . . . . Davies of co. Brecon. Supposed to have had 21 children, of whom the names of six only are known.

. . . . 1st wife. = David Byron Davies, born 27 March 1765; Brevet Lieut.-Col. in the Army 12 Aug. 1819, 99th Regt. of Foot; 1st Com. 19 Oct. 1791, 16th Buckinghamshire Regt. of Foot; purchased New Battle, St. David's (? a coffee estate); Grand Master of Royal Sussex Lodge; died at River Head 11 Jan. 1822; bur. at New Battle. Estate had 69 slaves and 8 stock. See "W.I. Bookplates," No. 768. = Cath. Robinson, dau. of Tho. Lancaster of Eccleston, St. David's; mar. there 22 Dec. 1795. Wrote in 1833 from Orchard St. James.

Thomas Davies, born 30 Jan. 1767.

A

Eliz. Dillon Rosina Davies, mar. Edw. Croasdaile, M.D. Edin., of River Head estate, St. David's. He was bur. at Boulogne, France, 30 Dec. 1856, aged 77. She died 3 June 1864. His 1st wife, dau. of . . . . Despard of Golden Square, died s.p. 1819.

Tho. Lancaster Davies, matric. from Magdalen Hall, Oxford, 4 June 1818, aged 19; Ensign 3 March 1814 100th Regt. of Foot (renumbered in 1816 99th); A.D.C to George, 8th Marquis of Tweedale; Lieut., later Surgeon 99th Regt.; bur. at New Battle 10 Oct. 1838, aged 40. = Isabella, dau. of Geo. McGowan of Galloway Hill, Jamaica; born at Garliston, Wigtonshire, 4 Jan. 1815; mar. at Port Royal 8 Nov. 1832; remar. 16 May 1844 Robert Chevallier Cream, M.D. Edin., who died 6 May 1897. She died 3 Aug. 1885.

Lancaster Byron James Davies, born 1 Dec. 1834; Ensign 13 Feb. 1853 11th N. I.; Capt. Bengal Staff Corps; died at Jumalpore, Suffrabad, India, 24 Sept. 1867, aged 33. = Harriett Marianne, dau. of Lieut.-Col. Ralph Thorpe, E.I.C.S.; born 9 March 1839; mar. at Dinapore 16 May 1860; died 29 Nov. 1884, aged 45.

Decima Isabella Kath. Davies, born 27 Jan. 1836; mar. 15 Sept. 1853 Cha. Inman of Old Hall, Spital, Birkenhead, great-grandson of Cha. Inman of Kingston, merchant (Archer, 88, and Burke's "Landed Gentry"). He was born 11 Oct. 1823. She died 1871.

LANCASTER OF JAMAICA.

Thos. Lancaster of Eccleston in St. David's, died there April 1800. Besides a dau. Cath. Robinson, who mar. 22 Dec. 1795 Lieut.-Col. David Byron Davies, he left a son Tho. Farrar Lancaster of Content and Eccleston, who matriculated from Trinity College, Oxford, 10 Dec. 1806, aged 20. In the "Jamaica Magazine" is the following obituary notice:—

1812, July. At Content, in St. Davids, on the 14th inst. Caroline, wife of Thomas F. Lancaster, Esq. of that property: This highly accomplished and much respected Lady survived her sister Mrs. Tait, but five weeks, whose early fate but

too severely operated on her affectionate mind; she was buried the following day at Mount-Charles in the same parish by the side of her beloved sister attended to her grave by many who knew her worth and who testified by their sorrow the loss society had sustained by her premature death: She died as she had lived an exalted pattern for imitation. ("Jamaica Mag.," i., 358.)

A

William Davies, born 9 March 1769.	John Davies, = born 28 Mar. 1771; died 15 Oct. 1819.	= Mary Seaman, remar. William S. Paine, Esq., Solicitor, of Furnival's Inn. She died 1 Feb. 1851.	Margaret Davies, born 9 Aug. 1775; died 30 Sept. 1790.	Henry Davies, born 25 May 1782; died 1 March 1800.

Henry Byron Davies, = born 10 Feb. 1802; died 14 March 1883.	= Anne, dau. of Abel Ashford and his wife Susannah (*née* Seaman) of Kenton Hall, Debenham, co. Suffolk. She died 4 Dec. 1884.	Will. Seaman Davies, born 24 March 1804; died 29 Oct. 1808.

Blanche Isabella Davies.	Son and dau., died young.

In the "Almanac" of 1822 he is given as deceased, and Eccleston then contained 81 slaves and 7 stock.

McGOWAN OF JAMAICA.

George McGowan of Garliston, Wigtonshire, Scotland, born there 7 June 1774, after the death of his wife removed with his family to Jamaica. He had four daus:—

1. Margaret, born 3 May 1812; mar. before 1833 James McFadyen, M.D. Glasgow 1837, born 1799, Island botanist of Jamaica, where he died of cholera 24 Nov. 1850 (*ante*, IV., 80). She died 21 June 1843, M.I. in Kingston Churchyard. (Archer, 143.)
2. Isabella, born at Garliston 4 Jan. 1815; mar. 8 Nov. 1832 at Port Royal, Tho. L. Davies of New Battle estate.
3. Elizabeth, mar. 4—6 July 1833 John White Cater, sometime of Kingston, Jamaica, where two of their children were buried in 1834 and 1840 (Archer, 143). He was later of Lyston Hall, co. Essex, then of West Lodge, East Barnet, co. Herts, J.P. Bucks and Herts, Director of the Bank of England and of Lombard Street, banker.
4. Caroline, mar. in Jamaica.

There were probably also some sons sent to school in England in 1833. The above George died in Jamaica June 1821. His brother James owned Galloway Hill estate, and was presumably father of Isabella, wife of Alex. Miller of Kingston (Archer, 143). W. W. McGowan, J.P., of St. Thomas, is given in the "Handbook" of 1890.

Further particulars of the above families are desired.

Helme of Nevis.

Arms.—*On a bend . . . . three pheons.*

Alice . . . ., bur. 2 June 1643. = Robert Helme of Gillingham, co. Dorset. = Mary Card, dau. of Tho. Card, mar. 7 Nov. 1643; bur. 10 Aug. 1683. 2nd wife.

A

1. Robert Helme, bapt. 21 May 1643; ? mar. and had 12 children.

2. Thos. Helme, Gent., of Gillingham, bapt. 17 July 1644; only brother and heir-at-law of Robert in 1705. = Mary Sutor, mar. 12 Feb. 1670-1.

Robert Helme of Nevis, Merchant 1676; æt. 30 in 1680; Agent for R. African Co. until 1685. Made a will, now lost. = Sarah Baxter, dau. of John Baxter of St. Dionys Backchurch, clothworker; bapt. 31 May 1655; mar. lic. dated 1680, then æt. 23. Will dated 4 Oct. 1687; proved 17 May 1690 (72, Dyke). s.p.

Robert Helme, bapt. 26 Oct. 1673.

Thos. Helme, bapt. 6 June 1675.

William Helme, bapt. 8 Feb. 1679-80; bur. 25 April 1680.

Mary Helme, bapt. 3 Jan. 1671-2; ? mar. 1 Oct. 1720 Jos. Osboldstone of Sarum.

Christiana Helme, bapt. 3 Feb. 1677-8; bur. 11 Jan. 1679-80.

Anna Helme, bapt. 11 Nov. 1688.

William Helme, bapt. 14 Jan. 1682-3.

Sarah Helmes of Nevis, sole Ex'trix of Robert H. of Nevis, deceased. Will dated 4 Oct. 1687. The £300 st. demised by my late husband to my sister Christian H., for which Cap. Philip Lee hath on my behalf entered into an obligation to her, is to be paid him out of such sums due to me by Mr John Maryon of Breuntree, co. Essex. To my sister Eliz. wife of Cap. Wm Freeman all my clothes, jewels, plate, linen and household stuff and £200 st., for which I have obliged myself in the penal sum of £400 st. to Mr Joseph Little of Montserrat to be paid him. To Silvanus Taylor of Nevis, merchant, £20. My 3 servants Humphrey Edwards, Eliz. Hughes and Eliz. Hatchfeild, £10 each. To my friend Cap. Philip Lee my large silver tankard. To my friend Mrs Jane Masculine of L. my wrought bed in England. To Mrs Mary Maryon, dau. of the said John M., my silver bason. To my aunts Mrs Mary Baxter of L. and Mrs Mary Little of Alsebury, co. Bucks, £25 each. To my dear brother Cap. Wm Freeman £100, also £50 to Mr Henry F. his brother. All residue to my neece Mrs Eliz. Baxter of L., only dau. and sole heir of my dear brother Wm Baxter of L., lately deceased, and Ex'trix. James Houblin, Esq., and my brother Cap. Wm Freeman of L., and Philip Lee and Henry Carpenter of Nevis, Esquires, overseers. To Jas. Houblon and Henry Carpenter each a hogshead of claret.

Witnessed by Arch. Hutcheson, Ra. Lomax, Silvanus Taylor, Wm Harrington. Proved 17 May 1690. Commission to Jas. Houblon, Esq., guardian of Eliz. Baxter, a minor. Proved 25 June 1701 by Eliz. Baxter, now of full age. (72, Dyke.) ("Antigua," i., 271.)

Eliz. Helme of Gillingham, co. D'set, spr. Will dated 12 May 1787. To my niece Mary Cox the close called Thorngrove of 2 acres. To my servant Eliz. Pavett my house near the common mead called the Chauntry House and £60. My niece Grace Cox my moiety of the plantations, negroes, etc., in the Island of Nevis and all residue, and sole Ex'trix. Proved 7 Sept. 1792 by G. C., spr. (470, Fountain.)

A

Christopher Helme, bapt. 17 Mar. 1647-8; mar. and had 7 children.

Richard Helme, bapt. 17 Oct., bur. 18 Oct. 1662.

Mary Helme, bapt. 25 June 1646.

Christiana Helme, bapt. 21 Mar. 1652-3.

Christiana Helme, born 25 Feb. 1657; named 1687 in the will of Mrs. Sarah Helme; mar. 1st Aron Chapman, Merchant, of Nevis, who died 15 March 1693, æt. 40; 2ndly, Philip Brome of Nevis, Esq., who died 15 Dec. 1705, aged 52. His will dated 8 Dec. 1705; proved 25 Sept. 1708, s.p. (196, Barrett). M.I. to all three at St. Thomas, Nevis.

Major William Helme of Antigua, born 25 Feb. 1657-8; M. of Gen. Council 1691. = Mary . . . . , died in Hatton Garden. Will dated 3 May and proved 10 May 1703 (138, Degg). = Henry Traveis, Junr., died intestate in 1703 at Nevis. s.p.

William Helme, son and heir 1703; apparently dead 1707.

Maria Helme, only dau. and heiress; mar. 1708. = John Pinney of Nevis, born 3 May 1686; of Pembroke College, Oxford, 1703; of the Middle Temple 1710; died 11 Dec. 1720. M.I. in St. John's, with his wife's arms on a shield of pretence.

1680, Oct. 10. Robert Helme of S[t] Andrew's, Holborn, Bach., 30, and Sarah Baxter, Spr., 23, of S[t] Dionis Backchurch; consent of parents; at S[t] Andrew's, Holborn, or elsewhere in diocese. (Mar. Lic. of Bp. of L.)

1682. Capt. Helmes's ship. (Jeaffreson Papers, i., 300, 321, 324; ii., 90.)

1685, Dec. Tho. Belchamber and Henry Carpenter appointed by the R. African Co. as Agents at Nevis in the room of M[r] Robert Helme. ("Antigua," ii., 250, 258.)

1705, July 8. Mr. Thomas Helme of Gillingham, co. Dorset, Gent., only brother and heir-at-law of Robert Helme, late of Nevis. Letter of Attorney to Mr. Philip Brome of Nevis, Gent., and Mr. Robert Helme of Nevis, Merchant, to recover all sums owing at the Leeward Islands. ("Antigua," i., 272.)

1736, Nov. 15. Christian H. of Gillingham, co. Dorset, now residing in L., power of attorney. (Nevis Records, ii., p. 335.)

1740, Nov. 13. Tho. H. of Gillingham, butcher, power of attorney to John Fred. Pinney, Esq., etc., for taking possession of certain lands in A. (*Ibid.*, p. 455.)

GILLINGHAM, CO. DORSET.*

1643 Vicesimo primo die Maij Rob'tus Elmes filius Rob'ti Elmes baptizatus erat.

1643 Secundus die Junij Alicia Elmes uxor Roberti Elmes sepulta erat.

1643 Septimo die Novembris Rob'tus Helme duxit Mariam Card filia' Thome Carde.

1644 Decimo septimo die Julij Thomas Helme filia (*sic*) Rob'ti Helme baptizatus erat.

1646 Vicesimo quinto die Junij Maria Helms filia Rob'ti Helms baptizata erat.

1647-8 Decimo septimo die Martij Xpopherus Helmes filius Rob'ti Helmes baptizatus erat.

1652-3 Vicesimo primo die Martij Christiana Helmes filia Robti Helmes baptizata erat.

1657-8 William Helme sonne of Robert Helme was borne the xxvth day of February, 1657.

1662 Decimo septimo die Octobris Ric'us Helmes filius Rob'ti Helmes baptizatus erat.

1662 Decimo octavo die Octobris Ric'us Helmes filius Roberti Helmes sepultus erat.

1670-1 Duodecimo die Februarij Thomas Elmes duxit uxore' Mariam Sutor.

1671-2 Tertio die Januarij Maria Elmes filia Thomæ Elmes baptizata fuit.

1673 Vicesimo sexto die Octobris Robertus Helmes filius Thomæ Helmes baptizatus erat.

1675 Thomas Elmes filius Thomæ Elmes baptizatus erat eodem die [sexto die Junij].

1677 Robertus Elmes de Cloverd duxit uxorem Doritheam Alford filiam Dorítheæ Clarke vid: septimo die Maij.

1677-8 Christiana Elmes filia Thomæ Elmes baptizata erat tertio die Februarij.

1679-80 Christiana Elmes filia Thomæ Elmes sepulta erat undecimo die Jannarij.

1679-80 Gulielmus Elmes filius Thomæ Elmes baptizatus erat octavo die Februarij.

1680 Gulielmus Elmes filius Thomæ Elmes sepultus erat vicesimo quinto die Aprilis.

1682-3 Gulielmus filius Thomæ Helme baptizatus fuit decimo quarto die Januarij.

1683 Maria Elmes vidua sepult. decimo Augusti.

1684 Gulielmus Helme fil' Rob'ti Helme sep^{tus} vic^{o} 3° Maij.

1688 Anna fil^{a} Tho. Helme bap^{s} 11° Novem.

1696 Xpoferus Helms 7° Septembris sepultus.

Children of Robert Helme.

1677-8 Maria filia Roberti Elmes baptizata erat sexto die Januarij.

1679 Johannes Elmes filius Roberti Elmes baptizatus erat tertiodie Julij.

1680-1 Robertus Helme filius Roberti Helme baptizatus erat vicesimo septimo Februarij.

1682 Gulielmus filius Roberti Helme baptizatus fuit decimo quarto die Novembris.

1684 Thomas Helme fil^{us} Rob^{ti} Helme bap^{us} Dec^{o} 9° Maij.

1686 Carolus Helms fil^{us} Rob'ti Helms vicesimo die Junij bap^{s} erat.

1688 Sarah fil^{a} Roberti Elms bapt^{a} 21° Octobris.

1690 Elizabetha fil^{a} Roberti Helme bapt^{a} 30° Novemb.

1692 Dorothea Helme fil^{a} Roberti Helme 25° Septembris baptizata.

1693-4 Ricardus Helmes fil^{us} Roberti Helmes de Newbery† 11° Feb. baptizatus.

1695-6 Jana fil^{a} Roberti Helme 11° Feb. bap^{a}.

* Forwarded by Canon Mayo, co-editor of "Somerset and Dorset Notes and Queries."

† In Gillingham.

1696 Richardus fil^{us} Roberti Helms 21° Dec. Sep^{us}.
1696 Jana filia Rob'ti Helms 24 Dec^{bris} sepulta.
1696-7 Thos. fil^{us} Annæ Helms 12° Jan. sep^{us}.
1697 Jeana Elmes filia Roberti Elmes baptizata erat 11mo die Septembris.
1698-9 Robertus filius Roberti Elmes sepultus 1mo Februarij.

Children of Chr. Helme.

1683 Robertus filius Christopheri Helme fuit baptizatus vicesimo quinto die Martij.
1684-5 Arthur Helmes fil^{us} X^{to}pheri Helmes bap^{us} 2° Feb^{rij}.
1686 Guiel fil. Christ^{i} Helme vic. sept. Decemb. bap^{us} erat.
1689 Xtopherus fils Xtopheri Helme bap^{tus} 28 Julij.
1691 Maria fil^{a} Xtopheri Helme bap^{a} 14° Aprilis.
1693 Thomas Helmes fil^{us} Xtopheri Helmes 3 Septembris baptizatus.
1695-6 Eodem die (2 Feb.) Xtiana Helms fil^{a} Xtopheri Helmes bap^{a}.

MERE, CO. WILTS. (Phillimore, vol. i., 43.)

1720 Oct. 1 Joseph Osboldstone of Sarum and Mary Helme of Gillingham.

Baxter.

. . . . Baxter.=

John Baxter of St. Dionys Backchurch, London, clothworker, bur. 12 Sept. 1662. = Ann . . . ., bur. 8 Mar. 1682-3.

Mrs. Mary Baxter of London 1687.

Mrs. Mary Little of Aylesbury 1687.

Children of John Baxter and Ann:

Sarah Baxter, bapt. 31 May 1655; mar. 1680 Robert Helme of Nevis.

Wm. Baxter of London, Merchant, of St. Dionys 1685. = Jemima . . . ., bur. 10 Dec. 1685.

Anna Baxter, bapt. 31 Dec. 1657.

Eliz. Baxter, mar. Capt. Wm. Freeman of St. Kitts and of Fawley, co. Bucks. He died 11 Oct. 1707, aged 62. M.I. Will (199, Poley).

Daughter of Wm. Baxter and Jemima:

Eliz. Baxter, bapt. 29 Jan. 1678-9, only dau. and heiress; proved will of her aunt Mrs. Sarah Helme in 1701.

Wm. Baxter, sen., of London, Merchant. Will dated 31 March 1686, 2 Jas. II. ½ of my estate to my wife Alice, ¼ to my dau. Anne B. at 21, ¼ to my son Wm. at 21. If both die their shares to my wife, my sister Abigail Tumbling, my sister Dorothy Skinner, my sister Martha Proud, my cozen Wm. Baxter, M^{t}, and cozen John Skinner. My sister Mary Baxter. My wife sole Ex'trix. My kinsmen Mr John Hind, Capt Wm. Freeman and Wm Baxter, overseers. Proved 26 July 1686 by Alice B. the relict. (92, Lloyd.)

Monumental Inscriptions in England relating to West Indians.*

EWELL, CO. SURREY.

On a ledger-stone in the floor of the old church tower (the only remaining portion of the former church):—

SACRED
To the Memory of
THO: HERCY BARRITT
Died Febry 3rd 1804
Aged 18 Months and 3 days
Alſo
LOUISA ANN BARRITT
Died Febry 16th 1812
Aged 12 Years
Alſo
T. H. BARRITT *Esqr:*
Died Octr 28th 1817
Aged 79 Years.

Mr. Leonard C. Price of Essex Lodge, Ewell, writes that there is a much worn stone with "Barritt Vault" on it, in the pathway leading up to the tower from Church Street.

1796, March 24. Thomas Hercey Barritt, Esq., W., and Ann Mellas, Spr; Lic. (St. George's, Hanover Square.) His will was dated 17 March 1817. He came of an old Jamaican family (Archer, 29 and 33). His first wife was Eleanor, dau. of Sam. Booth of Vere, and I think Geo. Booth Barritt of Lewisham in 1807 was their son.

GARBRAND HALL, EWELL.

A lofty arched gateway on the west side of the street leads to the mansion. It is in the Adams style, a large talbot standing on the top and the usual sphinxes lower down at the sides of the arch. There is a rough-looking shield with many coats of paint on it, which render the identification of the arms difficult, but they are Barritt and Garbrand quarterly. Edmondson's "Heraldry" gives grants of both, viz.:—

BARRITT: *Azure, on a chevron Ermine between three griffins' heads erased Or, two serpents in saltier, as part of a caduceus proper.* Crest: *A talbot's head per fess Argent and Ermine, collared Or, eared Sable.* Granted to Thomas Hercy Barritt of Jamaica Oct. 28, 1768.

GARBRAND: *Or, a battle-axe in bend sinister, surmounted of a launce in bend dexter, and in chief a dart barwise pheoned and flighted, all proper.* Granted to Joshua Garbrand of Jamaica Oct. 28, 1768.

---

* Continued from Vol. IV., p. 331.

WORPLESDON, CO. SURREY.

On a stone slab over brick grave in the north portion of churchyard:—

Here lies the Body of
MR ROWLAND BRYAN of
the Parifh of CLARENDON
in JAMAICA
who departed this life
April 25th 1791,
Aged . 1 Years.

Wm. Bryan was a merchant of Port Royal in 1793, and Richard Bryan a M. of Assembly for Liguania in 1663. (Feurtado).

There is a stone in Kingston churchyard to Mrs. Susanna Bryan, died 17 Oct. 1804, aged 20. (Archer, p. 137.)

MICKLEHAM, CO. SURREY.

In the churchyard, south-east of chancel, is a low brick vault surmounted by a stone slab and enclosed by iron railing, rusty and broken:—

In this Vault
are Depofited the Remains
of JONATHAN WORRELL Efqr
of Juniper Hall in this Parifh
Who Departed this Life
the 26th January 1814
Aged 79 Years
ALSO
the remains of BRIDGETTA
Daughter of the above
and Wife of HENRY KNIGHT Efqr
who died at Brighthelmftone
19th Novr 1815
Aged 43 Years.
ALSO
the Remains of
Mrs CATHERINE WORRELL
Relict of the above
JONATHAN WORRELL EsqRE
Died September 1st 1835
Aged 87 Years.

1814, Jan. 26. At Juniper-hall, Mickleham, Surrey, in his 80th year, Jonathan Worrell, esq. ("G.M.," 300.)

1835, Sept. 1. In Albemarle-str., aged 87, Catherine, widow of Jonathan Worrell, esq. of Juniper Hall, Mickleham. (*Ibid.*, 442.)

In his will, dated 19 Nov. 1811, proved 22 March 1814 (191, Bridport), he names his wife Cath., 5 sons, Wm. Bryant, Jonathan, Charles, Edward and Septimus, and 3 daus., Harriet, Bridget and Celia Maria. He owned Sedge Pond, Neels, The Spring and The Hill in Barbados, and 44,000 acres in Prince Edward's Island. See *ante*, II., 81, 308.

BATH ABBEY, CO. SOMERSET.

North aisle. A Chippendale shield-shaped tablet.

On a small shield above: Arms.—*Barry of six Argent and Sable* (perhaps *Azure*):—

In Memory
Of
EDWARD JESUP *Esqr.*
of *Writtle Park* in *Essex*
A Man
of strict Honour & Probity
who Died 24 March 1770
Aged 76.

1770 Mar. 2. (*sic*) Edward Jesup, Esq. (Burial Register.)

1770, March 29. Friday died in this city, Edward Jesup, Esq. ("Bath Chronicle.")

Edward Jesup of Writtle Park, co. Essex, Esq. Will dated 20 Feb. 1769. To my wife Eleanor a rent charge of £400 st. charged on my real estate in Nevis, all my furniture and plate, etc., in G. B., also my stock and corn on my farm together with the lease. To my dau. Isabella J. a rent charge of £10. To Mrs. Margaret Short, now living at Brussells, and to Mrs. Peregrina Short, now residing at Louvain in Brabant, each a rent charge of £5. To John Vaniel, now of Lincoln, gent., the son of my niece Fra. V., his late mother, dec^d, at 21 £500. To Fra. Gostling of Norwich, merch^t, the interest of £1500 for the maintenance of his 3 children by his present wife and the capital to them at 21. To Edward Jesup Toulman, s. of Mary Naylor of Kingston in Jamaica, at 21 £500. To my wife £200. To Emma Walgrave of Stapleford Tanny, co. Essex, spr., £100. To my servants one year's wages. Richd Maitland of L., Merch^t, and Geo. Irwin and Fra. Phillips, both of St Chr., Esq^{res}, my wife and her brother John Ede, Esq., to be Ex'ors and £50 each. All residue in Nevis or elsewhere I give to the said John Ede. Proved 9 April 1770 by John Ede, Esq., power reserved to the others. (149, Jenner.)

The above will was recorded in Nevis in Book of Wills, p. 292.

Job Ede, apparently son of John Ede, seems to have inherited the estate in Nevis. (See *ante*, III., 325.)

1752, March 25. Edwd Jesup, late of Nevis, now at L., esq., and Eleanor his wife and Wm. Woodley, late of Little Parndon, co. Essex, but now of Rougham, co. Suff., esq. E. J. mortgages his pl^n in St Tho. called *Dewits* of 300 a. for £1740. (Nevis Deeds, iv., p. 498.)

1759, June 19. Edwd J., late of Nevis, now of Writtle Park, co. Essex. In a later deed he was described as of co. Norfolk. (*Ibid.*, K., p. 89.)

(*To be continued.*

Notes and Queries.

FENWICK OF THE WEST INDIES.

I am engaged in the work of tracing the family of Fenwick, both in Northumberland, England, the county of their origin, and the original thirteen states of the United States. In some instances the Fenwicks came direct to the Coast line of North America, but apparently in other cases, as in the case of my great-grandfather, John Fenwick of South Carolina, they came from the Islands, particularly Barbados, and unquestionably Jamaica, possibly Antigua. I am to-day tracing, through Mr. Lopez of Spanish Town, the record of the Fenwicks in Jamaica, commencing with Henry Fenwick, who was a member of the Assembly for St. Catherine in 1678.

I have a large amount of information regarding the Fenwicks of Rhode Island, Connecticut, New Jersey, Delaware, Maryland and South Carolina, they apparently being all members of the family, who came direct, with the exception of those in South Carolina, who were represented by two distinct family heads, John Fenwick of Charleston and London, formerly of Barbados, and Robert Fenwick, who came from the West Indies to Charleston in about 1690, on the ship "Loyal Jamaica," a so-called privateer. With this Robert Fenwick, the first arrival (whose relationship to John Fenwick is not established), came some of the leading family progenitors of Charleston and vicinity.

Any information would be greatly appreciated.

WILLIAM B. GOODWIN,
(State Agent, Ætna Insurance Co.)

309 Hartman Building,
Columbus, Ohio.

GARDNER OF NEVIS. (II., 236.)

Lieut. George Gardyner of Nevis was sent in 1656 by Governor L. Stokes to Jamaica. (Thurloe's "State Papers," v., 48.)

Anne, who mar. 1733 Richard Gardiner, was probably a dau. of Roger Pemberton.

Ind're of 5 parts made 2 and 3 March 1760 between David Gardner eldest son and heir of Richard Gardner the Elder Esq., who was eldest son and heir of Samuel Gardner Esq. his late grandfather deceased, who was eldest son and heir of Samuel Gardner the Elder of Nevis Esq. his great-grandfather; Richard Gardner the Younger Esq. the other son of Richard Gardner the Elder and brother of the said David G.; and Ann G., widow of the said Richard G. the Elder and Mother of David and Richard. Sale for £1000 to Tho. Cottle of *Roundhill* plantation of 40 acres. (Nevis Deeds, K. 217—227.)

Ind're made 3 May 1769 between Anne G. of Nevis widow and relict of Richard G. late of the said island Esq. and David G. of ditto Esq. eldest son and heir of Richard G. of the one part; Alex[r] Houstoun, John Clerk, Wm. Crichton and Wm. Macdowall of London merchants of the other. The Gardners in consideration of 5s. sell to the latter a plantation called *Rawlins Land* in the parish of St. James containing 58 acres and 43 negroes. Signed by Anne G. and David G. Armorial seal. ARMS.—*Vert, a lion rampant between three crosses-crosslet fitchy.* CREST.—*A sinister arm couped, embowed, in the hand a sword.*

1772, Dec. 22. Petition of Margaret G., aged 19½, for her brothers-in-law David G. and Wm. Sanders, Esquires, who married her two sisters, to be her Guardians. Granted. (Nevis Book of Wills, p. 319.)

1775, Jan. 14. Petition of David G. of Nevis, Esq., that Ann his wife is dead and a legacy is due under the will of his father James G., deceased. Granted. (*Ibid.*, p. 369.)

David G. of Nevis, Esq. Will dated 5 June 1779. My nephews and niece Edward, Thomas and Richard, and Ann, sons and dau. of my brother Roger G., gent. Sworn 9 Aug. 1785. Inventory £655. (*Ibid.*, 667.)

James Smith, Esq. Will proved 1779. The lands called Greenland or the Middle Work plantation, which I lately purchased of David G., Esq. (323, Warburton.)

The Gardners appear to have mortgaged or sold all their lands and perhaps removed elsewhere. Roger is referred to in 1799 in the parish register of St. Peter, Basseterre, St. Kitts.

NORTON OF TORTOLA.

I visited the churchyard of Trinity (Episcopal) Church on Broadway, opposite Wall Street in this City, last Saturday, August 26, 1916, and copied the following inscription on a brown tombstone, in the south side of the churchyard, a few feet from Broadway:—

Here lies the body of Iohn Norton
Merchant from Tortolah One
of the Virgin Islands who
Departed this life the 7th
Day of February 17$\frac{4}{5}$ (*sic*)
Aged 20 years.

Treasury Department, Wm. M. Sweeny.
U.S. Customs Service, New York.

A Colonel James Norton was Deputy-Governor of St. Kitts 1697 until his dismissal in 1700, when he settled down as a planter. I cannot say if he was connected with the above. (Editor.)

WEST INDIAN MEMBERS OF THE HIGHLAND SOCIETY.

I was looking over some papers of the Highland Society, and found the following among the signatories to the "Act for the Incorporation of the Highland Society of London 21 May 1816."

William Murray, Esquire, Barbadoes.
Gilbert Salfoun, Esquire, Bermuda.
Alexander Macrae, Esquire, of Demerara.
Charles Grant of the Island of Jamaica, Esquire.
Peter Grant of the Island of Jamaica, Esquire.
William Hoseason of the Island of Jamaica, Esquire.
John Macintyre of Jamaica, Esquire.
Hector Mackay of Jamaica, Esquire.
Alexander Macrae, Esquire, of Clarendon, Jamaica.

27 Gilbert Street, W. Mabel Nembhard.

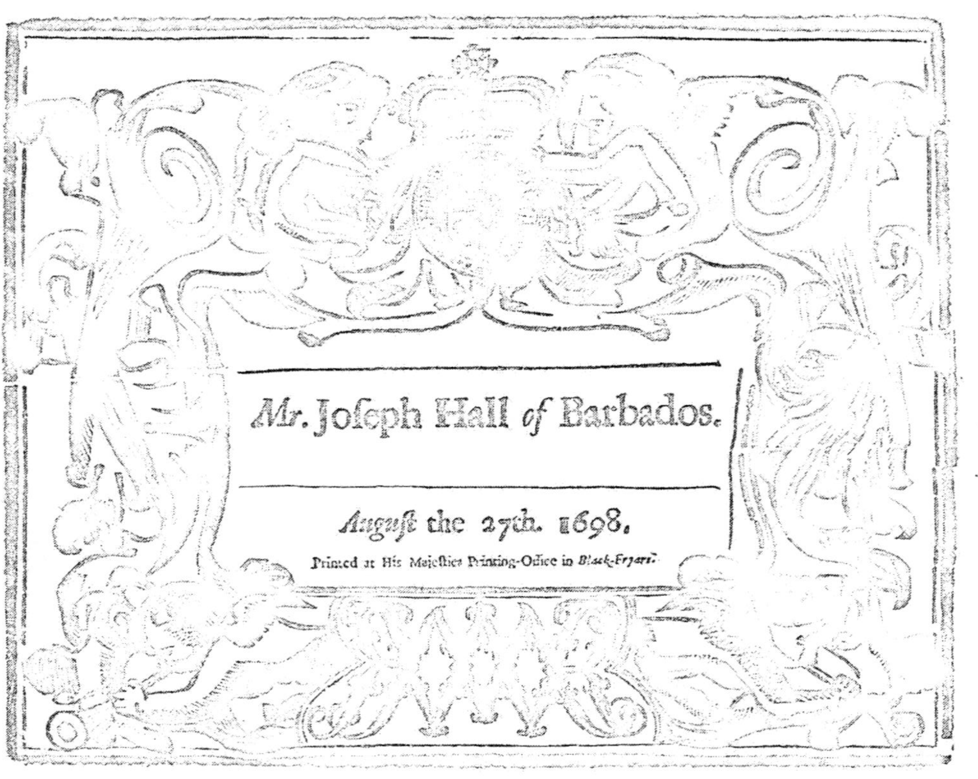
Mr. Joseph Hall of Barbados.

August the 27th. 1698.

Printed at His Majesties Printing-Office in Black-Fryars.

Greatheed of St. Kitts.

Governor Wm Matthew, in his will dated 1752, refers to an Indenture of 22 and 23 Jan. 1716 between testator of the 1st part, his son Wm Matthew of the 2^d part, and John Willett and John Greatheed of the 3rd. ("Antigua," ii., 254.)

Richd Wilson of St. Chr., Esq. Will dated 23 July 1755. To my dau. Ann Greatheed £100 c. a year; my two grandsons Richd Greatheed and John Douglas Greatheed and four granddaus. Eliz., Ann, Mary Bertie and Jane Greatheed £300 each at 21. Sworn 11 July 1760. (409, Lynch.)

Sam. Greatheed of St Geo., Hanover Sq., Esq. Will dated 21 April 1756. To my wife Lady Mary gold and silver plate and furn. in Eng., coach and horses. Whereas by our Mar. sett. I have charged my plantation in St Chr. with the payment of an annuity of £600 and £10,000, part of her mar. portion is assigned after my death for her use and £5000 part of that we have agreed to be laid out in the purchase of the Mansion house wherein we reside called Guys Cliff near Warwick, and the remainder in the purchase of other lands, I give my s^d plant^n to my friends Tho. Truman and Jas. Geo. Douglas of L., M^ts, on Trust to pay my wife the further annuity of £150, and to pay my brother Marmaduke G. £100 c. yearly and the like to my brother Richard G., they to release all claims, and to levy £5000 for any younger ch^n. To my brother Craister G. £100. My sister Mary G. £100. All res. to any eldest s. or dau. If no ch^n to my right heirs. All slaves to belong to plantations and not to pers. est. My bro. Craister to manage pl. and be p^d £200 a yr. My wife and s^d Trustees to be Ex'ors for pers. est. in England and bro. Craister for St Chr.

Codicil dated 12 June 1762. Whereas my bro. Marm. is dead leaving issue one son R^d Wilson G. and several daus., the ann^ty to s^d nephew. Proved 3 March 1766 by Lady Mary G.; power reserved to J. G. D., T. T. ren. (101, Tyndall.)

Rt. Hon. Lady Mary Greatheed, widow and relict of Samuel Greatheed, late of Guy's Cliff, co. Warwick, Esq. Will dated 19 Aug. 1767. My only surviving child Bertie Greatheed. Craister G. of St. Chr., Esq., brother of my late husband. Richd G., son of Marmaduke G., Esq., brother of my late husband. My sister the R^t Hon. Lady Jane Mathew the interest of £5000 and after her death to her children. Witness, Mary Greatheed.

Adm'on 15 April 1782 to Bertie Greatheed the son, now 21. On 19 Dec. 1774 appeared R^t Hon. Lord Brownlow, the uncle and guardian of Bertie Greatheed, a minor. Testatrix was late of St. George's, Bloomsbury. (437, Bargrave.)

John White, late of St. Chr., now of Chichester, Esq. Will dated 2 March 1775. My cousin Craister Greatheed of St. Chr., Esq., £1000. (104, Bellas.)

Mary Greatheed, late of Guyscliff, but now of the borough of Warwick, spinster. Will dated 28 April 1784. To be buried in the vault of my late brother Sam. G., Esq., deceased, in the parish church of St Mary, Warwick. To my nephew Dr Richd G. £300. To each of my 3 nieces Eliz. G., Ann the wife of Bertie G., Esq., and Mary Bertie G., the daus. of my late brother Marmaduke G., Esq., dec^d, £500. My plate and furniture to my said niece Eliz. G. All residue of estate to my nephew Bertie G. My nephews Dr R^d G. and Bertie G. and Wm Manning of L., Merch^t, and my niece Eliz. G., Ex'ors. Proved 29 May 1790 by Dr R^d G. and B. G. (241, Bishop.)

ARMS.—. . . . *A saltire between four fleurs-de-lis.*

John Greatheed of St. Mary Cayon, St. Kitts, party to a deed of 1716; appointed Chief Justice in 1722, and removed by Gov. Mathew in 1727. = Frances . . . .

A

. . . . 1st wife. = Samuel Greatheed, Whig M.P. for Coventry 1747—61; purchased Guy's Cliff, co. Warwick; died 2 Aug. 1765; bur. in St. Mary's, Warwick. Will dated 21 April 1756; codicil 12 June 1762; proved 3 March 1766 (101, Tyndall). = Lady Mary Bertie, 1st dau. of Peregrine, 3rd Duke of Ancaster; mar. 21 Feb. 1747 at St. George, Hanover Square; died 23 April 1774. Will dated 19 Aug. 1767; proved 19 Dec. 1774 (437, Bargrave).

Richard Greatheed, born 1725; matric. from University Coll., Oxford, 13 May 1742, aged 17; died 23 Dec. 1763. = Pricilla, dau. of Col. James Weatherill of Antigua and St. Kitts; died intestate. s.p.

B

Peregrine Francis Greatheed, admitted to Eton 22 April 1761, left 1765.

Bertie Greatheed, born 1760; only surviving child 1767; died 16 Jan. 1826 at Guy's Cliff, aged 66. = Anne.

Richard Wilson Greatheed, born 14 and bapt. 28 March 1748-9; only surviving son 1762; M.D. before 1784; living 1792.

John Douglas Greatheed.

Eliz. — Mary Bertie. — Jane.

Bertie Greatheed, jun., at Eton 1791—3; died at Vicenza, Italy, 8 Oct. 1804, aged 23. = ..., mar. in France.

Anne Caroline Greatheed, born 1805, only child and heir; mar. 20 March 1822; died 8 June 1882, aged 77. = Lord Chas. Percy, 8th son of Algernon, Earl of Beverley; born 4 March 1794; had a grant of arms in 1826 on assuming the names of Greatheed and Bertie; died 11 Oct. 1870.

Mary Greatheed of Croydon, co. Surrey, widow. Will dated 2 Jan. 1792. Whereas I am seized of a plantation called Arnos Vale in the parish of St. George, I. of S[t] Vincent, and the negroes and stock subject to the undivided moiety thereof, heretofore the estate of my late husband Craister G., Esq., deceased, charged with a certain rent charge which, by the Ind're of release made on the marriage of my son Samuel G. with Mary his wife, late Mary Wilson, spr., were secured to her by way of jointure, I give the moiety to my said son. The other moiety which formerly belonged to Wm. Crooke, Esq., deceased, to the use of my said son for his life, and after the determination of the said estate to Richard Wilson, Esq., of Baker str., and Rich[d] Wilson Greatheed, Esq., nephew of my late husband in T. for him, and after his death for any of his children he shall direct, and in default to his eldest son in tail male, then to daus., then to my

nephew Milward Crooke, Esq., of St Chr. All residue to my s. Sam. and sole Ex'or. In the presence of Fran^{s} Fisher, I.^{e} Auber, J^{r}, Eliz. Greatheed of Croydon. Proved 29 Jan. 1793 by Sam. G., Esq., the son. (24, Rodwell.)

A

- Marmaduke Greatheed of St. George Basseterre, died 1756—62. ═ Anne Wilson, dau. of Richard Wilson of St. Kitts; named in his will 1755.
- Craister Greatheed, Chief Judge of St. Kitts 1766; President 1775 until his death 26 Feb. 1780; bur. 27 Feb. at St. George; owned Arnos Vale, St. Vincent. ═ Mary Crooke, dau. of Sam. Crooke; bapt. 31 Dec. 1726; sole heir to her son John; died 6 Oct. 1792, aged 66. M.I. Will dated 2 Jan. 1792, then of Croydon, co. Surrey; proved 29 Jan. 1793 (24, Rodwell).
- Mary Greatheed, late of Guy's Cliff, then of Warwick. Will dated 28 April 1784; proved 29 May 1790 (241, Bishop).

B

- John Greatheed, at Eton 1764—67, and as son and heir admitted to Inner Temple 20 Jan. 1768; owner of Arnos Vale, St. Vincent. Will dated 18 Sept. 1786; codicil 25 May 1790.
- Mary Wilson, died 1796. ═ Samuel Greatheed, born 2 July 1752 and bapt. 3 May 1753 at St. George Basseterre; purchased Landford Lodge, Salisbury; died there 10 July 1829, aged 77; owned Arnos Vale, St. Vincent. Will dated 26 May 1823. ═ Sophia White, mar. 2 Aug. 1797; living 1838.
- Wm. Greatheed, matric. from Christ Church, Oxford, 17 Jan. 1774, aged 18; ? died 25 June 1781.
- Mary Greatheed, born 21 May and bapt. 25 Sept. 1748 at St. George Basseterre.

Children of Samuel Greatheed (born 1752):

- Samuel Greatheed of Landford Lodge and Arnos Vale, St. Vincent, æt. 21 in 1830; died at Southampton 4 April 1847. ═ . . . .
- John Greatheed.
- Sophia Greatheed, mar. Rev. Rich. Burgess.
- Mary Greatheed, mar. Barnard Trollope.

Children of Samuel Greatheed (died 1847):

- Wm. Sam. Greatheed of Landford Lodge, at Eton 1841; late of 41st Regt. and Capt. Hants Militia; living at Arnos Vale 1850—53. ═ Amelia Frances, dau. of Hugh Jas. Baillie; born *circa* 1820.
- Matilda Margt. Greatheed, 1st dau., born 1827; died 1 Feb. 1909, aged 82.

Children of Wm. Sam. Greatheed:

- Hugh Bertie Greatheed.
- Jas. Percy Greatheed.

Frances Crooke of King Str., Portman Sq. Will dated 1797. My neph. Sam. Greatheed £500, his ample fortune. (765, Walpole.)

Brownlow, Duke of Ancaster. Will dated 6 Jan. 1808. My nephews Bertie Greathead and Brownlow Matthew, Esq^res, etc., est. on Trust for my grandson Colyear, and in case of his death to them. (160, Loveday.)

LANDFORD LODGE, CO. WILTS.

This mansion was formerly denominated Breach House, and belonged, with the estate attached to it, to Dodington Egerton, Esq. In 1776 Sir William Heathcote of Hursley in Hampshire, Bart., purchased the property; and, having taken down the greater part of the former residence, rebuilt nearly the whole of the present mansion house in a style of architecture somewhat corresponding with Hursley Lodge. He, however, sold it in 1787 to . . . . Spooner, Esq., and in 1792 Mr. Spooner again disposed of it with the adjacent lands to Samuel Greathead, Esq., who made it his permanent residence.

On his death the estate descended to his eldest son and heir of the same name, who also resides here, and has made considerable improvements in the premises. (Hoare's "Wilts," v., 87.)

On a mural tablet in the north chapel of the Church :—

"Near this place are deposited the remains of Mrs MARY GREATHEED, widow of CRAISTER GREATHEED, Esq. who died 6th Oct. 1792, aged 66 years."

In the churchyard :—

"Here are deposited the remains of SAMUEL GREATHEED, Esquire, of Landford Lodge, who died July 10, 1827,* aged 77 years."

WEST INDIAN INCUMBERED ESTATES COURT.

March 27—30, 1858. *Re* Greatheed.

A petition for the sale of the Arnos Vale Estate in St. Vincent. The estate is charged as to one moiety with a jointure to Mrs. Sophia G., the widow of the late Sam. G., Esq. (who d. in 1827), and the entirety is charged by his will with a sum of £24,000 for his three younger children John G., Esq., Sophia the wife of the Rev. Richard Burgess, and Mary the wife of Barnard Trollope, Esq., in equal shares. Reference to Chancery suits of G. *v.* G. and G. *v.* Elliott. £2000 arrears of jointure are due to the widow and £3,276 principal due to each of the younger children with interest. The estate has been unproductive since 1854, when the jointress distrained on the crops and stock. Conditional order for sale made absolute.

Nov. 1, 1858. The first sale by auction of this Court took place on 1 Nov., and was of the above estate of 454 acres, and it was knocked down to the Rev. F. R. Braithwaite for £10,050.

* The year 1827 is an error for 1829.

May 12, 1859. The following claims on the proceeds of sale were settled, viz.: Mr. Tho. Chapman, consignee from 1850—55, £734—allowed; Messrs. Davis and Boddington about £3.286, balance of account current—allowed. In April 1843 Sam. G., owing the firm £5,261, executed a mortgage. Mr. Wm. Sam. G. on coming of age inherited an insolvent estate, sold his commission in the army, and from 1850—53 acted as manager and receiver and conducted the estate successfully until Mrs. Sophia G. distrained in 1855 on the mules, etc., and threw the estate out of cultivation.

May 27, 1859. John G., by his will dated 18 Sept. 1786, devised a moiety of the estate in question to his mother Mary G. in tail and devised all the residue to her. and by a codicil dated 25 May 1790 gave a rent charge of £40 c. to Anne McDowal, which has been paid her for 60 years. Claim with 6 years' arrears allowed.

June 24, 1859. The claims of Mr. Wm. Sam. G., the owner, and Mr. John G. disallowed. (Cust's "W. I. Estates and Reports," pp. 207—215.)

In the Privy Council on appeal. Feb. 7—March 29, 1860. As to the manager's claim. In 1823 Sam. G. was tenant in fee simple of a moiety of the estate subject to a charge of £600 a year jointure to his wife Sophia. He was tenant-in-tail of the other moiety. He had two sons Sam. and John and two daus. Mary and Sophia, and on 26 May 1823 made his will and charged his estate with £24,000 for his younger children, and devised the whole estate to his eldest son and appointed his two sons Sam. and John Ex'ors. Testator died 10 July 1829 leaving his wife and four children surviving. On the death of his father, Samuel the eldest son became tenant-in-tail, and in 1830. having attained 21, barred the entail. In Hilary term 1833 a suit was instituted in the Court of Chancery, Eng., by John G. *v.* his brother Sam., and on 14 Dec. 1833 a decree was made. £10,000, part of the £24,000, was then paid, and the balance due eventually reduced to £9,500. On 22 June 1843 Sam. G. mortgaged the plantation to Messrs. Davis and Boddington to secure £5,261. Sam. G. died 4 April 1847 intestate as to his real estate in the W.I., which descended to W. S. G. his eldest son. £1,800 claim by the Ex'or of Grant the manager allowed. (*Ibid.*, pp. 246—261.)

In 1805 on Arno's Vale, St. George's Parish, there were 337 negroes, and the crop made 615 hhds. of sugar, 184 pun. of rum and 92 of molasses. For the 14 years 1800—14 the average crop was 456 hhds. of sugar.

1763, Dec. 23. Rich. Greathead, Esq, and his lady, of the island of St. Kits. ("G.M.," 619.)

1765, Aug. 2. Sam. Greathead, Esq; at Guy's-Cliff, in Warwickshire; he was member in the two last parliaments for Coventry. (*Ibid.*, 395.)

1766, May 29. London. Craster Greatheed, Judge of the Vice-Admiralty Court of the Island of St. Christopher's, is appointed Chief Justice of the said Island. ("Bath Chronicle.")

1766. Warwick. Peregrine Greatheed nephew of the Duke of Ancaster. ("London Mag.," 53.)

1768, Feb. 1. James Greathead, Esq; in Charles-street, Berkley-square. ("G.M.," 94.)

1774, April 23. In Charlotte-street, Bloomsbury, the Rt Hon. Lady Mary Greathead, sister to his Grace the Duke of Ancaster. (*Ibid.*, 239.)

1780, April. The Hon. Craister Greatheed, president of his majesty's council, and comptroller of the customs, in Antigua. ("Town and Country Mag.," 223.)

1790, May 10. At Warwick, Mrs. Mary Greatheed. ("G.M.," 478.)

1792. As to a work by Bertie Greathed. (*Ibid.*, 691.)

1796, Lately. At Landford-lodge, near Salisbury, Mrs. Greatheed, wife of Samuel G. esq. (*Ibid.*, 356.)

1797, Aug. 2. Samuel Greathead, esq. of Langford-lodge, Wilts, to Miss Sophia White, of George-street, Manchester-square. (*Ibid.*, 710.)

1804, Oct. 8. At Vicenza in Italy, a. 23 . . Bertie only s. of Sam. G. &c. (Long obituary notice, 1073 and 1236.)

1819. By the death of the Hon. B. C. Colyear, son of Viscount Milsintown & grandson of Brownlow late Duke of Ancaster . . . £300,000 now goes equally to Samuel Greathead esq. of Guy's-court & General Montagu Mathew. (*Ibid.*, 280.)

1822, March 20. Hon. Charles Percy, son of the Earl of Beverley, to Miss Greathed, the rich heiress. (*Ibid.*, 369.)

1826, Jan. 16. Long obituary notice of Bertie G., aged 66. (*Ibid.*, 367.)

1829, July 10. At Landford Lodge Wilts. a. 77, Sam. Greatheed. (*Ibid.*, 93.)

1847, Lately. May. At Southampton, Sam. Greathead, of Landford Lodge, Wilts. (*Ibid.*, 563.)

1909, Feb. 2. On the 1st inst., at 24, Pembridge-road, after an operation, aged 82, Matilda Margaret, eldest daughter of the late Samuel Greatheed, Esqre., of Landford Lodge, in the county of Wilts, and of Arnos Vale, St. Vincent.

1724. Hon. John Greathead, Esq., party to a deed. (Vol. A. No. 1, Series No. 26.)

1727. Petition of John Greatheed of St. Chr., Esq., that Gov. Wm. Mathew had removed him from his office of Chief Justice to which he was appointed by Letters Patent in 1722. (C.O., 152.)

1753. Sam. Greatheed, esq. one plantation in St Peter Basseterre. (Baker's map.)

1771, March 23. Attached to an affidavit sworn before Craister Greatheed, Chief Justice of St. Kitt's, is a seal with Arms: *A saltire between four fleurs-de-lis.* Crest: *A fleur-de-lis.* (B.T. Leeward I., vol. 34.) In 1776, as President, he was acting as Governor. (*Ibid.*, vol. 36.) See Burke's "Armory" for the coat granted in 1826.

Abbott Hamilton Greatheed: admitted (after one term at Trinity) pensioner under Mr. Ash 13 Jan. 1834.

B.A. (26th jun. opt.) 1837, M.A. 1841. Admitted scholar (Somerset) 30 Oct. 1834. Youngest son of the Rev. Sam. G. of Bishops Hull, near Taunton. Died in Piccadilly 26 April 1842, aged 27. (Register of Christ's Coll., Camb., ii., 449.)

The above may have been of the St. Kitts family. The Mills's of that island resided many years at Bishops Hull.

ST. GEORGE BASSETERRE, ST. KITTS.

Burial.

1780 Feb. 27 Craister Greatheed Commander in Chief & President.

Baptisms.

1747-8 Mar. 9 Frances, D. of Marmaduke & Ann Greatheed, b. 29th Febr 1747-8.

1748 Sept. 25 Mary, D. of Craister & Mary Greatheed, b. 21st May 1748.

(There are several more.)

1748-9 Mar. 28 Richard Wilson S. of Marmaduke & Anne Greatheed, b. 14th March 1748-9.
1752 Mar. 7 John Douglas S. of Marmaduke & Anne Greatheed, b. 27th Febry 1752.
1753 May 3 Samuel, S. of Craister & Mary Greatheed, b. 2d July 1752.

ST. MARY CAYON, ST. KITTS.

Baptisms.

1721-2 Mar. 10 Richard Son of John and Franses Greathead.
1722-3 Feb. 4 Richard Son of John and Franses Greathead.
1723-4 Mar. 18 Richard Son of John and Franses Greathead.

ST. THOMAS, MIDDLE ISLAND, ST. KITTS.

Burial.

1763 Oct. 12 Richard Greathead & Priscilla (? a child of).

ST. GEORGE, HANOVER SQUARE.

1747 Feb. 21 Samuel Greatheed, Esqr, & the Rt Hon. the Lady Mary Bertie, Spinster. Special Lic.

Lawes of Jamaica.

Sir Nicholas Lawes. Will dated 1 Aug. 1730. Late of Isleworth, now of Jamaica: Born in 165* of honest and loyal parents, who suffered for their loyalty to the Royal Family in the late Grand Rebellion. Confirm indenture of 1 Oct. 1720 between myself and James Lawes, Esq., my eldest son and heir, made on his marriage with Eliz. Gibbons, spinster, only dau. and heiress of Wm. G., late of Vere, deceased. My plantation called Snow Hill in St Andrews and Penn, Mount James plantation, a moiety of Swallowfield and Penn, and a moiety of Temple Hall and tract on New River to my said son. The other moieties and 50 acres Savannah in Liguanea and 2 lots in Orange Street, Kingston, to my son Temple Lawes, and to both my sons equally my moiety of Townwell Plantation, formerly purchased from the heirs of Daniel Clicho (?). £50 per annum in the South Sea annuities to my dau. Judith Maria Lawes, and the said stock to be made up to £2000 according to the settlement I made with her mother before marriage. My granddau. Eliz. Hammerton £20 per annum. My sister-in-law Lady Ann Cheshire† and Sir John Cheshire £50. My dau.-in-law Grace Beeston, widow, £40 per annum. My cousin Mary Jennings £20 per annum. My kinsman Henry Archbould, Esq., £25. (Add. MS. 27,968, fos. 6 and 179.)

* Blot here.
† A short pedigree is given of Sir Tho. Lawley, father of Eliz. Cotton and of Lady Ann Cheshire.

James Lawes in his will says:—My cousin Sir Tho. Littleton of Hagley, co. Worc., Bart. Kinswoman M[rs] Christian Pitt, eldest dau. of the said Sir Tho. Littleton, Bart., and wife of Tho. Pitt, Esq., of Swallowfield, co. Berks. Richard Littleton, 3[d] son of Sir Tho. L., residuary devisee. Legacy to niece Susannah Bernard, sister of Wm. Henry B. Mrs. Susannah Dickens £100 c. Lucretia wife of D[r] Mathew Gregory £50. Mary dau. of the said Mathew and Lucretia Gregory. (*Ibid.*, fo. 6.)

(Add. MS. 27,968, fos. 7, 84, 132, 181.)

Nicholas Lawes of co. Wilts, yeoman. = Amy, bur. 1689 at St. Jas. = Col. Gregory Tom, arrived in J. 1663 with his wife Amy; died 1665. = Capt. Henry Archbould, mar. 1668 at St. Andrew.

1. Eliz. Potter, mar. at St. Andrew's 20 May 1680; bur. 10 Feb. 1684-5 at Half Way Tree. = Sir Nicholas Lawes, Kt., born 1652; went to J. 1663, then aged 11; returned to England 1703; resided at Isleworth 14 years; knighted 1717 and Gov. till 1722; arrived at J. 26 April 1718; died in J. 17 June 1731, aged 79, after living there 54 years. Will dated 1 Aug. 1730, late of Isleworth; proved in J. = 2. Frances, dau. of Paul Godwyn Carter, s. of Fra., Bp. of Hereford; mar. 23 May 1684; bur. 7 March 1692-3. M.I. at St. Andrew's (Archer, 247). s.p. = 3. Elizth. (See opposite page.)

Amy Lawes, bapt. 18 Nov. 1681; mar. 26 July 1699 Chas. Long. She died Nov. 1702.

Frances Lawes, bapt. 22 Nov. and bur. 8 Dec. 1684.

Tho. Bernard of St. Cath., J., Esq. Will dated 11 June 1728. Brother Jas. Lawes £50. S[r] Nich. L. £20. Brother Temple L. £20.

Nicholas Lawes of Compton Chamberlen (co. Wilts). Will dated 6 June 1646. Very impotent by reason of owld age. To be bur. at C. C. near my dec[d] wife. I dispose of my est. as by art. of agreement between myself and my grandchild John Bushell, gent., made the 8 May 1644. Edward Pile my great-grandson 40*s*. Poor 20*s*. Church 20*s* All residue to my s[d] grandson J. B. and Ex'or. Proved 30 Dec. 1647 by J. B. (234, Fines.)

1655-6, March. John Lawes. On the 21st adm'on to Eliz. L., relict of J. L. of Broadchalke, co. Wilts. (fo. 59.)

ENTRIES FROM REGISTER OF HALF WAY TREE, PARISH OF ST. ANDREW.

Taken 23 July 1787 by John Roberts (Add. MS. 27,968, fo. 129).

Baptisms.

1681	Nov. 10	Amey als. Ayme Daur. of Nicholas & Eliz[th] Law.
1684	Nov. 22	(*blank*) Daur. of Nicholas & Eliz[th] Law.
1697	June 11	James S. of Colonel Nic' Laws.
1699	Dec. 26	Temple S. of Nic' & (*blank*) Laws.
1738	Sept. 18	Eliz[th] Butler, Daur. of Temple & Mary Laws.

Marriages.

1680	May 20	Nic' Laws & Eliz[th] Potter.*
1684	May 23	Nic' Laws & Frances Carter.
1693	July 2	Nic' Laws & Eliz[th] Barry.

Sir Nicholas Lawes, Kt. (See opposite page.) = 3. Elizth., only dau. of Sir Tho. Modyford, Bart., and widow of Col. Sam. Barry; born 1660; mar. 2 July 1693; died 11 Nov. 1694 in J. — s.p.

= 4. Susanna Temple, 5th dau. of Tho. T. of Franckton, co. Warw., and widow of Sam. Barnard, son of Dr. Sam. B., S.T.P., Rector of Croydon; mar. 11 June 1696; died 20 April 1707, aged 46. M.I. Isleworth. Her arms on the chandelier in St. Andrew's Church, Jamaica.

= 5. Eliz., dau. of Sir Tho. Lawley, 3rd Bart., of Spoonhill, co. Salop, and rel. of Tho. Cotton of co. Warw.; died 26 Oct. 1725, aged 35. M.I. in Bath Abbey.

Children (by 4th wife):

- James Lawes, born in J. 26 Feb. and bapt. 11 June 1697; M. of A. 1721-2; M. of C. 1725; Lieut.-Gov.; bur. 29 Dec. 1733. M.I. at St. Andrew's (Archer, 240). = Eliz., only dau. and h. of Wm. Gibbons of Vere; mar. 20 Oct. 1720. She remar. 1742 Wm., 8th Earl of Home. Granddau. of John Favell of Vere 1720. Bookplate. — s.p.
- Temple Lawes, bapt. 26 Feb. 1699; died at Bath June 1754. Bookplate. = Mary, dau. of Col. Butler; mar. 6 Jan. 1730.
  - Eliz., born 6 months after her father left J.; bapt. 18 Sept. 1738; mar. a son of Mark Hall Butler of J.

Child (by 5th wife):

- Judith Maria, only child, mar. 1737 Simon Luttrell, Lord Irnham, and later Earl of Carhampton.

Burials.

1684	Dec. 8	Francis Law, Jun[r].
1684-5	Feb. 10	Eliz[th] Law.
1692-3	Mar. 7	Francis Law.
1733	Dec. 29	James Laws.

* As Eliz. Coale mar. 18 Jan. 1675-6 John Potter, who was bur. 7 Nov. 1676.

ST. CATHERINE'S. (*Ibid.*, fo. 29.)

1696 June 11 Coll. Nicholas Lawes & Susannah Barnard.
1699 July 26 Charles Long & Amy Laws.
1720 Oct. 20 James Laws, Esq., & Elizabeth Gibbons.

CLARENDON. (*Ibid.*, fo. 30.)

1730 Jan. 6 Temple Laws & Mary Butler.

1624. Obiit apud Milstone, co. Wilts, Nicholas Lawes, etc.
1630. Nich. Lawes, living at Compton Chamberlain.
1656. Tho. Lawes, then of Sarum.
The M.I. and trick of arms of Susa. L. at Isleworth are given on fo. 182.

1717, July 25. The King conferr'd the Honour of Knighthood on Nicholas L., Esq., and appointed him Gov. of J. in the Room of the Lord Archibald Hamilton. (Historical Register. p. 33.)
1720. His speech to the Assly. (*Ibid.*, 258—265.)
1734, April 16. James Laws, Esq; of J. ("G.M.," 330.)
See the W.I. Committee Circular for 29 July 1913 for an illustration of Cheere's monument to James Lawes in St. Andrew's Church at Halfway-Tree. Mr. Cundall gives a translation of the Latin inscription, and describes the arms painted thereon as:—*Or, on a chief Azure three estoiles of eight points of the first.* On an escutcheon of pretence:—*Or, a lion rampant Sable debruised of a bend Gules charged with three escallops of the field.*

Browne of Antigua.

Antigua, January 20, 1817.

Sir,
I would have had the pleasure of writing you long ere this on the subject of the Family Queries you confided to my attention, but the hope I have had of affording you very satisfactory information respecting your Ancestors induced me to defer communicating such as I obtained soon after my arrival from England.

The knowledge I have as yet gained of your Family is principally from the Records of the Register's Office, which I took every pains to search, and began with the Establishment of the Records as early as the year 1668. I beg leave therefore to inform you that in the year 1668 there was living in this Island Anthony Browne, to whom Lord Willoughby of Parham, the Governor in Chief of Barbados and the rest of the Charibbee Islands, in that year, made a Grant of a Plantation in Willoughby bay Division. Between 1668 and 1699 there were several Transfers of Property to Anthony Browne, and in the latter year I find Anthony Browne and *Elizabeth* his Wife began conveying away Property. In 1703 a Deposition was made by Anthony Browne, who swore he was then *forty years of age*, which circumstance proves that he was not the same Anthony

Browne to whom the Grant of the plantation was made, and induces me to believe that he to whom the Grant was made, so early as in the year 1668, was one of the first settlers in the Island, the same Person with *Elizabeth* his wife conveying away property, and the Father of the Anthony Browne who swore he was *forty years* of age in 1703; although it is not improbable that the latter also might have been a settler, since he appears to have been born in 1663. During the years 1703 and until 1708 several Transfers of Property principally in Nonsuch Division were made and recorded to Anthony Browne; and in the latter year Anthony Browne and *Mary* his Wife sold and conveyed property in that Division. This circumstance made me again strongly suppose that the latter Anthony Browne was either the Son of, or a different Person from, the first mentioned Anthony Browne, who in 1699 had a Wife named *Elizabeth*, and in 1708, supposing him to have become a settler before 1668, when he obtained a Grant of a Plantation, he must have been a very old man. During the years 1708 and 1720 several Deeds and Conveyances relating to Lands in Nonsuch Division and Willoughby bay are recorded to and from Anthony Browne and *Mary* his Wife. In 1726 the Will of Anthony Browne, dated January 1723, was proved and recorded, in which his Wife *Mary* is mentioned, and his Sons and Daughters, viz., Anthony Browne, to whom *his Estate at Point Cagoway and all the Residue of his Estates,* Thomas Browne, Nicholas Browne, George Browne, Barbara Cary, Sarah Browne, and Mary Browne, and also his Grand Daughter Mary Cary. In 1730 Anthony Browne, *Son of Anthony Browne*, conveyed his *Estate, &c., mentioned in the Will of his Father Anthony Browne*, to George Skerrett, and soon after that George Skerrett married *Mary Browne* the widow; for in the same year he and his Wife Mary, *late Mary Browne, Widow*, made a Deed of Gift to *Sarah Browne* Daughter of the said Mary Skerrett. George Skerrett died in about 1734, in which year his Will is dated, and in 1735 his Executors conveyed Slaves to his Widow *Mary Skerrett.* Nicholas Browne, one of the Brothers of the third mentioned Anthony Browne, made his Will and died in 1740, at which time it appears he left living two of his Brothers, Anthony Browne and Thomas Browne; three Nephews Will[m] Howard Browne, Anthony Browne and Francis Browne, and one Niece Mary Browne; but it was not mentioned whose Children were those Nephews and the Niece. You observe however a fourth Anthony Browne is introduced! In 1759 Mary Skerrett made her Will which was proved and recorded in 1760, and therein she also mentioned her Grandsons William Browne, Anthony Browne and Francis Browne, and her Great Grand Daughter Sarah Browne, Daughter of her Grand Son Anthony Browne. This Grand Son I have taken to be your Father, who must have died before the year 1773 before your Mother, since in that year I find by the Will of Mary Bladen, late Browne, and your Father's Sister,* some devises to her Nephew *Anthony Browne*, Son of Sarah Browne, Widow.

Upon finding out the foregoing particulars, I applied to the Rector of the Parish of Saint Philip in the Division of Willoughby bay, in which it appears the Family of Browne resided and possessed considerable property almost from the earliest Settlement of the Island; but I regret to inform you that I was much disappointed in finding only your marriage inserted in the Parish Record of Marriages, without being able to ascertain from any of the Parish Books the Baptism, Marriage, or Death of any other Browne, except the Death of your Brother, which happened not many years ago, notwithstanding there is a Family Vault in the Church yard, which has arisen from the unpardonable negligence and carelessness of former Rectors and Clerks of the Parish; since I had the mortification to observe that the Records in the possession of the present Rector, The Reverend George Collins, are not older in date than a few years previous to your Marriage, and it is only at the present time that they are correctly kept. On my ride to Willoughby bay, which you know is very far from Saint John's, to ascertain the particular dates of Baptisms, Marriages and Deaths in the Family,

* The letter writer has made a slip here—for sister read aunt.

and procure the necessary Certificates to substantiate them, I was informed, upon making particular inquiries, that many very aged Persons were living in that Division of the Island, and some of them upon Lands or Estates which were your ancestors, who could give me some useful information; but I have not been able from unavoidable causes to take the necessary rides to Willoughby bay. I beg leave to inform you there is also a Natural Daughter of your Father, before his Marriage, who is rather advanced in age, and who has sent to inform me that she recollected your Grand Father, and would give me all the Information in her power. You will, I hope, excuse this part of my Letter, and be assured I shall use her Information only as far as it may lead to Facts, which other Persons may be able to prove.

Having your Instructions now before me, in which the first Information particularly wanted is to ascertain who Anthony Browne your Grandfather was, whether a native of the Island, or if not, from whence he came; I think on this head I need only call your attention to the statement I have made of the Family in the forepart of my Letter, founded upon Records in the Register's Office; and from that statement there can be no doubt but that your Grand father was a Native of this Island, and the Son of Mary Skerrett, who was the Widow of one Anthony Browne, whose birth place cannot be traced with so much probability as that of his Son, for as I said before he might have been the Son of the Anthony Browne whose Wife was *Elizabeth*, or like him might have come to this Island soon after it's Settlement. It is unfortunate for the chain of circumstances so well connected from the time of Anthony Browne the Great Grand Father and Husband of Mary Skerrett to your time, that before the former period I could find no Record of a Will or any Deeds to shew the Relationship, if any, between your Great Grand Father and the Anthony Browne who had a Grant in 1668. The only hope I have is in finding the Petition of that Anthony Browne which is mentioned in the Grant to have been presented to the Council and Assembly, in which there may be a description of the Person. I have made repeated searches in the Secretary's Office for that purpose, but on account of the Records to which I must refer being so ancient, it is very difficult to find out anything. You may however rely on my continued exertions.

I have not procured any of the Certificates of Marriages, Baptisms, &c., mentioned in your Instructions, for the reasons I have given respecting the Parish Records of Saint Philip—there being no Entries made in them; and I could not find any after making regular searches in the Parish Books of Saint John's; but it is my intention to search the Books of all the Parishes, to the Rectors of some of which I have already applied for leave.

A copy of M[rs] Skerrett's will, and that of her first Husband Anthony Browne, I have seen and have deferr'd obtaining them till I hear from you—but I could not find the Will of your Father or Mother in the Register's Office; neither could I find any Will of your Grandfather; but in that of his Brother Nicholas Browne there are no allusions made to Relations before settled in the Island.

I have agreeably to your directions endeavoured to ascertain whether any Family of the name of Malbranke ever resided in or owned any Estates in the Island, but I have not been able to find out any Person of that name among the Records which I searched for the purpose from 1668.

It may be necessary Sir for me to observe that I have sometimes found the name spell'd without an *e*; but more often with it.

I now beg leave to assure you that I shall use my best endeavours to find out the particulars you wish, and I will not fail to make the necessary Extracts, and secure the proof of every circumstance I think necessary to the cause; and I hope by the next packet to give you more interesting intelligence; at the same time I wish you to be informed that my motive for making enquiries and searches relating to the affair you have confided to me I endeavour to keep as much as possible to myself.

As I have been at some expence in procuring the Information which I have given you, and other expences will necessarily be incurred, I have taken the liberty of draws upon you for £30 Sterling at thirty days Sight, which I beg you will pay, and which Sum I shall hold to your Credit, and apply it towards defraying the Expenses incurred in your business, of which I shall furnish you with a correct account. I have preferred drawing on you as you desired, to calling upon Mr Athill or any other Person for money, as it would be unpleasant to do so as often as small expenses are incurred.

I remain with great Respect,
Sir,
Your most obedient
humble servant
RICHARD WILSON.
St. John's.

Anthony Browne, Esq.,
M.P.,
Montagu Place, Russel Sq.,
London.

NOTES BY THE EDITOR.

In the Book of Claims dating from 1667 there is an entry under Willoughby Bay of a claim by *Richard* Brown to 45 acres (as administrator of George Mould in right of his wife Barbery Mould, sister of deceased), also 60 acres by purchase, total 105 acres.

In the Book of Patents, transcribed in 1678 from an earlier book, is the record of a grant in 1668 at Willoughby Bay to Anthony Browne of 105 acres, but there is no patent to Richard. John Cox of Nonsuch, by his will dated 1675, bequeathed all residue (13,000 lbs.) and his 50 acres to Anthony Brown, a child, his son-in-law (? stepson). The will of Darby Noonan of Nonsuch, dated 1691, was witnessed by Anthony Browne. In a petition in 1716 for a patent Anthony Browne stated that he owned 50 acres in Nonsuch, also parcels of 20, 10, 10 and 75 acres. The 50 acres may have been derived from John Cox. In the pedigree printed in "Antigua," i., 74, I erroneously took it for granted that Anthony II., the testator of 1723, was identical with Anthony I., the patentee of 1668, but there is no doubt that there were two generations. The first settlers were nearly always dead by 1700, or if octogenarians by 1710. I do not know which register books Mr. Wilson saw in 1817, but in 1888-9 I found baptisms commenced in 1767, marriages in 1683 and burials in 1685. Anthony Browne V. was M.P. for Hedon in 1806 and nearly fifty years agent for Antigua, dying in Kensington 6 March 1840, aged 72. ("G.M.," p. 442.) He was a partner of Browne, Cobbe and Co. of 67 Lombard Street, Bankers. His wife Dorothy was a dau. of the Hon. Samuel Harman of Harmans in St. Philip's parish, but there were no children. The extraordinary conservatism among West Indians in retaining the same christian name is here exemplified, there being five generations of Anthony. In my own family there have been six generations of Thomas. It is most confusing for the genealogist.

List of Wills recorded in Barbados down to the year 1800.*

Year.	Names of Testators.
1758	Murray, Dorcas
,,	Marshall, William
,,	Maloney, Elizabeth
,,	Mascoll, Clayborne
,,	Miller, Israel
,,	Mashart, Prudence
,,	Mahon, John
1759	Moore, John
,,	Moore, Abraham
,,	Maycock, John
,,	Morgan, Richard
1760	McMahon, Elizabeth
,,	Mahew, Susan
,,	Marshall, Thomas
,,	Mapp, Thomas
1761	Morris, John
,,	Miller, Joseph
,,	Miggett, John
,,	Matthews, John
,,	Miller, John
1762	Miller, Francis
,,	Mower, Thomas
,,	Miller, Matthew
,,	Mackeluer, Affleck
,,	Maud, Susannah
1763	Miln, David
,,	Martin, Edward
,,	Mosceley, Henry
,,	Manderfield, Emanuel
,,	Mayers, Edward Lascelles
,,	McConnehe, John
,,	Moore, Francis Grant
1764	McDonald, William
,,	Moores, John
,,	McCavouck, Patrick
,,	Mandewell, Emanuel Francis
1765	McBrudy, snr, James
,,	Maloney, Thomas
,,	Marshall, William
,,	Marshall, Thomas
,,	McCragh, Alexander
,,	Murray, Gilligan
,,	Mawson, Jeremiah
,,	Malsworth, George
,,	Martindale, John
,,	McDonold, Anguish
1765	Maynard, William
,,	Marshart, Elizabeth
,,	McDonold, Anguish
,,	Mascoll, Peter
,,	Miller, Margaret
1766	Mathes, John
,,	Mayers, John
,,	Martindale, Elizabeth
,,	McCluer, Elizabeth
,,	Maddock, Samuel
,,	Menzies, Gilbert
,,	Matthews, Thomas
,,	Mayhew, Thomasin
,,	Miller, William
,,	Miller, Margaret
,,	Marshall, Samuel
,,	Minvielle, Mary
,,	Manning, Richard
,,	Murphey, Basil
1767	Mayhew, Jane
,,	Malloney, William
,,	Mahon, James
,,	Marshall, William
,,	Morris, Mary
,,	Munson, Ann
,,	Merry, Richard
,,	Misson, George
1768	Murray, Richard
,,	Morphey, Trente
,,	Murphey, Trusto (*sic*)
,,	McKaskell, Samuel Gollop
1769	Malloney, William
,,	McBrudy, Benjamin
,,	Meare, John
,,	Mapp, Mary
,,	Murray, Mary
,,	Mashart, James
,,	Mashart, Mary
1770	McCarty, William
,,	Martindale, Jehodden
,,	Merritt, John
,,	Morris, Barnard
,,	Malloney, John
,,	Mascall, Mathew
,,	Millward, John
,,	Millward, Edward

* Continued from p. 16.

Year.	Names of Testators.
1770	Millward, Thomas
"	McCave, Elizabeth
"	McConckey, Mary
"	Middleward, John
"	McNiel, Lachlan
"	Milvin, Francis
1771	Morphey, Elizabeth
"	Millor, Augustus
"	Miller, Maynard
"	Morrison, Sarah
"	Mayers, Elizabeth
"	Mose, Nicholas
1772	Mayers, Ann
"	Matthews, Elizabeth
"	Moll, William
"	Murray, Margaret Quinton
"	Murray, Mary
"	Miller, Elizabeth
"	Martindale, William
1773	Mose, Francis
"	Mose, James
"	McCarty, William
"	Millington, John
"	Moore, Benjamin
"	Masters, Philip
"	Martindale, Mascoll
"	Mole, Sarah
1774	Morrison, Morris
"	Mascoll, James
"	Miller, George
"	Marshall, Robert Johnson
"	Mineville, Thomas
"	Maynard, Margaret
"	Mattison, James
"	Morris, Robert
"	Moore, Mary Ann
"	McCollin, Alexander
"	Mascoll, Mary Baldrick
"	Millons, Sarah
1775	Mayers, John
"	Mason, Richard
"	Malloney, Elizabeth
"	Moore, Benjamin
"	Martin, Jnr., William
"	Mitcham, John
"	Morrison, Rev. Kenneth
"	Moore, Elizabeth
"	Maverick, Lydia
"	Martin, Mary
"	Millward, Sarah
"	McDaniell, James
1776	Moore, Henry
"	Martindale, Ann
"	Meade, Garritt
"	Marshall, Henry
"	Morris, John
1776	Maycock, James
"	Massiah, Simeon
"	McKerse, Elizabeth
1777	Morris, Katherin
"	Morris, John
"	Milward, William
"	Merritt, Martha
"	Mercer, James
"	Mann, Sarah
1778	Morris, Margaret
"	Mapp, Rebecca
"	McBrudy, John
"	Murray, Thomasin
"	Moore, Jnr., William
"	Moseley, Joseph
1779	Mings, John
1780	Mashart, Ann
"	Maloney, Ann
"	Meade, Mary
"	Mathews, Richard
"	Mings, William
"	Moore, Alexander
"	Morphey, Joseph
"	Marshall, Robert
"	Morphey, Edward
1781	Moody, William
"	Morphey, Mary
"	Marshart, Mary
"	Morrison, Niel
"	Moore, John
"	McCloud, Rowland
"	McCarthey, Daniel
"	Manderfield, Philip
"	Martin, John
"	Maynard, Jonas
1782	Mose, Mary
"	Massiah, Esther
"	McPherson, Daniel
1783	Maggee, Henry
"	Moore, Joseph
"	Martin, William
"	McClean, Alexander
"	Meller, Lydia
"	Misson, George
"	Miller, Jacob
"	Matthews, Abel
"	Mascoll, Sarah
"	Marshall, Robert
"	Moody, Mary
1784	Marshall, James
"	Matthews, Edward
"	Mellowes, Benjamin
"	Mose, Ann
"	Martindale, Jonathan
1785	Miller, Aaron
"	Martin, Francis

Year.	Names of Testators.
1785	Morrison, Lydia
"	Moe, Irinaues
"	Miller, Ann
"	Mascoll, Timothy
"	Mashart, Michael
"	Martin, Sarah
"	McDonold, John
"	Mullineux, Maribah
1786	Millward, Mary
"	Massiah, Benjamin
"	Middleton, Thomas
"	McMurdo, James
"	Moll, Elizabeth Barnadiston
"	McCarthy, Elizabeth
"	Moore, William
1787	Morris, Jasper
"	Morphey, Thomas
"	Moore, James
"	Mashart, Samuel
"	Morris, John
"	Mackay, Anthoney
"	Mayers, William
"	Mashart, Conrade
"	Mings, Mary
"	Massiah, Simeon
"	Mandeville, Thomas
"	Mings, Olive
1788	Moore, Richard
"	Matthews, Jeremiah
"	Massiah, David
"	Murphey, Alias
"	Murphey, Mary
"	Maher, Alice
"	Miller, John
"	Moseley, Henry
"	Miller, Sarah Willy
"	Morphey, Benjamin
"	Moore, Betty
"	Mackgarry, Mary
"	Murray, Andrew, Manasser
"	Moore, James
1789	Mortimer, Francis
"	McCarthey, Wilkinson
"	Mears, Daniel
"	Morris, Edward Harttle
"	Murrell, Nicholas John
"	Miller, Henry
"	McDuglin, John
1790	Millowes, Elisha
"	Massiah, William
"	Mahon, John
"	Mahon, Elizabeth
"	Mansey, William
"	Marshall, Thomas
"	Mascoll, Snr., William
1791	Massiah, Isaac

Year.	Names of Testators.
1791	Macourt, Anthoney
"	Malloney, Matthew
"	Maynard, Thomas
"	Milbourne, Mary
"	Morris, John Henry
1792	Manning, Robert Howton
"	Moseley, Mary
"	McClure, William
"	Milward, Prudence
"	Mascoll, Elizabeth
"	Millor, Ann
1793	Makins, George
"	Morris, Michael
"	Mahon, Elizabeth
"	Maycock, Dottin
"	Murrill, Nathaniel
"	Masline, Richard
"	Mascoll, Francis Forde
"	Moore, William
"	Musroon, Brock
1794	Maynard, Sarah
"	Moe, Christopher
"	McClure, Elizabeth
"	Morgan, Stephen
"	Morris, John
"	Mashart, Elizabeth
"	McNiel, Christian
"	Moore, William
1795	Maycock, Sarah
"	Morrison, Mary
"	Morgan, Richard
"	Martindale, Abigail
"	McBrudy, Terrence
"	Miller, Robert
"	Miller, Andrew
"	Massiah, Esther
1796	Mosley, Henry
"	Massiah, Sarah
"	Mapp, James
"	Manning, John
"	Morris, William
"	Manning, William
"	Moll, Nicholas
"	Morris, Jane
"	Maloney, Thomas
"	Marr, John
1797	Mitchell, Samuel
"	McConney, Henry James
"	Miller, Margaret Sarah
"	Manderfield, Mary Ann
"	Mower, Ann
"	McGueen, Archibald
"	Malloney, Thomas Spuen (?)
"	Mascoll, Alexander
"	Manning, Joseph
1798	Martindale, Elizabeth

Year.	Names of Testators.
1798	Malet, Alexander
,,	Morris, Richard
,,	Marshall, Robert
,,	Moore, Isaac Massiah
,,	Mascoll, Christianity
,,	Mottley, Henry
,,	Murphey, John
,,	May, John
1799	Massiah, Jacob
,,	Mascoll, Robert
,,	Mitchell, Samuel
,,	Marshall, John
,,	Moore, Sarah
,,	McAlpine, Agnes
,,	Moore, Thomas
,,	Mastin, John
,,	McAndrew, John
,,	McDonold, John
,,	McPherson, William
1651	Nelson, Thomas
1654	Nicholas, Thomas
,,	Nock, Thomas
,,	Nunn, William
1659	Neavis, Francis
,,	Nyell, Ambrose
,,	Norwood, William
,,	Norris, Magdaline
1660	Nelson, Henry
,,	Nunn, John
1661	Neilsome, James
,,	Norris, John
1662	Norman, Peter
1664	Norris, Jeremiah
1665	Norton, Dennis
,,	Nealan, William
,,	Norton, George
1667	Nutt, Robert
1668	Nightingale, Edward
1671	Newbold, Richard
,,	Nop, Richard
1673	Neale, Patrick
1674	Norton, Thomas
,,	Nevinson, John
1676	Nightingale, Pricilla
1678	Nowell, John
,,	Nore, George
,,	Nelson, Dennis
,,	Nelle, Ambrose
1680	Nightingale, Grenado
,,	Nelson, Julian
1681	Nicholas, John
,,	Nicholas, Joyce
1683	Newton, Edmond
,,	Nelson, Arichibold (*sic*)

Year.	Names of Testators.
1683	Neckson, Edmond
1684	Northey, John
,,	Newton, George
,,	Newton, Samuel
,,	Nowell, Abraham
1685	Nugent, Patrick
,,	Northeast, John
,,	Navarro, Aaron
,,	Nickson, James
,,	Neweman, Valentine
1686	Noble, Marke
,,	Nickolls, George
,,	Nyles, John
1687	Nelson, Anthoney
,,	Nelson, Ann
,,	Nielson, Thomas
,,	Norgrove, Ann
1688	Nelson, Priscilla
1690	Neckson, Mary
,,	Norvell, Thomas
1691	Noell, Sir Martin
1692	Nighton, Samuel
1693	Nellson, Peter
1694	Nyle, Ambrose
,,	Newton, Barbara
1695	Norris, Elizabeth
1696	Nore, George
1698	Nelson, John
,,	Newman, James
1700	Newsum, Richard
1701	Nowell, Robert
,,	Nicholes, Brise
1702	Newton, Ann
,,	Nore, Lucy
,,	Nickels, Richard
1703	Nurse, Robert
,,	Niccolls, Margaret
1705	Newland, John
,,	Nickson, Thomas
,,	Newton, Basal
1711	Niccolls, William
,,	Needham, Allin
,,	Neale, Daniel
1712	Northey, Samuel
,,	Nicholls, Robert
1713	Northey, Isabella
1714	Namias, Manull
,,	Nelson, Rebeccak
1715	Nuson, Katherine
,,	Nusum, Edward
1716	Nixon, Penelope
,,	Nowell, Francis
,,	Neblitt, William
,,	Nickolls, Darcas
1717	Nesfield, William
1718	Nicholson, Thomas

Year.	Names of Testators.
1719	Newman, Grace
,,	Newton, Robert
1720	Nimmo, John
,,	Newsam, Somers
1721	Neale, Thomas
,,	Nusam, Samuel
1722	Nevison, Ann
1723	Newton, Chomley
,,	Nicholls, Robert
,,	Newton, John
1724	Neblitt, Lydia
1725	Newton, John
,,	Nurse, Robert
,,	Nurse, John
,,	New, Jonathan
,,	Newsum, Christopher
1727	Nicholas, Robert
,,	Nusum, William
1729	Neal, Newman
1730	Neale, William
,,	Nurse, George
1731	Newsum, Richard
1732	Northey, Jane
1733	Needham, Susanna
1734	Noell, Abraham
,,	Nelson, William
1735	Nicholls, Christopher
,,	Neblitt, John
1736	Nightingale, Nathanil
,,	Nunez, Abraham
1737	Nurse, Fearnot
,,	Norman, Thomas
1738	Neblitt, Jane
,,	Nusum, Arthur
1740	Nanfan, Richard
,,	Nusum, Susannah
,,	Nessfield, John
1741	Neel, John
1742	New, Jonathan
,,	Nurse, Richard
,,	Neblitt, William
1743	Newgent, William
,,	Niccolls, Marmaduke
1744	Niles, John
,,	Nelson, John
1745	Newton, Bassil
,,	Nunes, Abraham Israel
,,	Niccolls, Edward
,,	Neblitt, Henry
1746	Nunes, Benjamin
1747	Nurse, Robert
,,	Nurse, John
1748	Neblitt, Samuel
,,	Newton, Thomas
,,	Nicolls, William
,,	Newton, Samuel
1749	Newland, Elizabeth
,,	Newport, George
1750	Neale, William
1751	Nicholson, Edward
1752	Newbold, Ann
,,	Needtors, John Frederick
1754	Needham, Thomas
1755	Neblitt, Samuel
1756	Neell, Eleanor
,,	Neblitt, Thomas
,,	Neblitt, Benjamin
1757	Nutt, Edward
,,	Newton, Abraham
1758	Norley, Mary
1759	Neblitt, John
,,	Nurse, Samuel
1762	Neblitt, Lydia
,,	Nutt, William
,,	Newton, Isaac
1764	Nurse, James
1765	Niles, Ambrose
,,	Nurse, Richard
1766	Neblitt, Samuel
1767	Navarro, Daniel Lopes
1768	Niles, John
1769	Norris, Robert
,,	Nutt, Eleanor
1770	Nightingale, Grando
,,	Nutt, Hannah
,,	Niccolls, George
,,	Nurse, William
1771	Niles, Francis
1772	Nurse, Alexander
,,	Nurse, Joseph
1773	Nurse, Ann
,,	Neblitt, Elizabeth
1774	Newbold, Samuel
,,	Napleton, Rebecca
,,	Nurse, Thomas
,,	Nunez, Judith
1775	Neblitt, Christian
,,	Neblitt, Thomas
,,	Newton, George
,,	Nunez, Rebecca
1776	Neate, William
,,	Nightingale, Grinado
,,	Newton, Jonah
,,	Nash, Richard
1777	Niles, Joseph
,,	Norris, Richard
,,	Nusum, Arthur
1778	Norris, Rachael
1779	Nurse, Mary
1780	Neblitt, Jane
,,	Nash, William
,,	Norville, Ann

Year.	Names of Testators.
1781	Neblitt, Henry
„	Nurse, James
„	Norris, John
„	Nehill, Daniel
„	Nurse, Elizabeth
1782	Nissfield, John Peter
1783	Norville, Elizabeth
„	Neblitt, Lydia
„	Nowill, John Henry
1784	Nurse, George
„	Newton, John
„	Nurse, Mary
1785	Niles, Michael
„	Nurse, Samuel
„	Nelson, William
„	Nightingale, Gamaliel
„	Napleton, Neale
1787	Niles, Jane
1788	Nusum, John
„	Neblitt, Walter Scott
„	Nicholls, Richard
1789	Neblitt, John
„	Niles, Joseph
„	Niles, Thomas
1790	Nicholas *alias* Clarke, Elizabeth
1791	Nurse, William
„	Newton, William
„	Nicolls, Benjamin
1792	Newsum, Samuel
„	Niles, Ann
„	Niles, Michael
„	Newby, William
1793	Neblitt, Ann
„	Nurse, Eliza, *alias* Miller
„	Nehill, Thomas
1794	Neblitt, Elizabeth
„	Niccolls, Robert John
„	Niles, Francis
1795	Norris, William Robert
„	Nusum, Ann
„	Neafield, Ann Carlton
1796	Nisfield, William John
„	Nisfield, Elizabeth
„	Nunez, William
„	Niles, Jane
1797	Nunes, Jacob Israel
„	Nurse, William Lynch
1798	Nunegan, John
„	Nusum, Samuel Christopher
1799	Nehill, Michail
„	Norvill, Rebecca
1650	Ohaine, Connell
„	Ogle, Cuthbert
1653	Oshia, Richard

Year.	Names of Testators.
1653	O'Gary, Daniel
„	Osborne, John
1659	Oursloth, William
„	O'Gary, Daniell
1662	Orchard, George
„	Osler, Richard
1663	Oatley, Gilbert
1664	Orrick, John
1668	Odonoghon, Hugh
1670	Oistine, Edward
„	Osmond, Thomas
1671	Ocanly, Teage
1677	Owen, Roger
1678	Owen, David
„	Oresbid, Thomas
1679	O'Carnye, Patrick
1681	Occurrant, Jenkins
1682	Ohaley, Thomas
„	Osborne, Samuel
„	Oharah, Hugh
1684	Ormond, Richard
1685	Ormunt, Rebecca
„	O'Canty, Dennis
„	O'Canty, Cornelius
1687	O'Canty, Darby
„	Osborne, Mary
1689	Overton, Jonathan
„	Osborne, Jonathan
1690	Oker, George
„	Oates, George
1695	Oestine, James
„	Osborne, Alexander
1696	Oately, John
1701	Outtram, William
1702	Owing, Mary
„	Owins, Richard
1706	Ostreham, Thomas
„	Odiarne, Thomas
1709	Owens, Thomas
1710	Osborne, Ellinor
1715	Osborne, Robert
1716	Olton, Ralph
„	Osborne, Jonathan
1725	Oatly, John
„	Odell, Andrew
1728	Oateley, Gilbert
„	Odiarne, Elizabeth
1731	Outtram, John
„	Oneal, Dennis
1734	Odwin, Thomas
„	Oxnard, Edward
1735	Olton, Moses
„	Olton, Gira
„	Odwin, Samuel
1736	Osborne, Samuel
„	Osborne, Robert Jonathan

Year.	Names of Testators.
1741	Orderson, John
„	Odwin, John
1742	Osborne, Agnes
„	Oxnard, Thomas
1743	Oxley, John
1745	Oatley, Gilbert
1746	Odwin, Thomas
„	Odiarne, John
1747	Osborne, Thomas
„	Ostrehan, John
1748	Osborne, Richard
„	Oxnard, Agnes
„	Odiarne, Nathaniel
1749	Osborne, James
„	Otrehan, Thomas
„	Osborne, Robert
„	Ogden, Joseph
1752	Orne, John
„	Ostrehan, Katherine
1753	Outram, Elizabeth
1756	Oxnard, Edward
„	Odell, Thomas
„	Osborne, Samuel
1757	Owen, Henry
„	Oxley, Sarah
1758	Olton, Nathan
1761	Odwin, Cornelia
1763	Osborne, Elizabeth
„	O'Brian, John
1765	Osborne, Robert
1766	Outtram, Chomley
1767	Oxley, John
„	Odwin, John
„	Order in ordinary reprocrity Institute
1768	Osborne, James
1769	Odell, Mary
1772	Olton, Thomas
„	Olton, Ralph
1773	Owen, Abel
„	Ovelton, Elizabeth
1775	Ostrehan, Sarah
1778	Olton, Moses
1779	Olton, Elizabeth
„	Ogden, John
„	Odwin, Samuel Agard
1781	O'Donnell, George
„	Ostrehan, Thomas
1783	Odwin, Mary Ann
„	Osborne, Catherine
1784	Osborne, Samuel
1785	Oxley, William
1787	Olton, Benjamin

Year.	Names of Testators.
1790	Oneale, James
„	Odle, Hannah
„	Odwin *alias* Knight, Horatia
1792	Oatley, John
1793	O'Neale, Phillip
„	Odell, Joseph Rawlins
1794	Odell, Edward
„	Odell, Thomas
1795	Olton, Josias
1796	Odwin, Thomas
„	O'Bryan, Nathaniel
„	O'Mira, Jane Maria
1798	Owens, Mary
1799	O'Bryan, William

Year.	Names of Testators.
1648	Powell, William
„	Palmer, Peter
1650	Peasly, Elizabeth
1652	Parker, Robert
„	Parsons, Michael
„	Parker, James
„	Patterson, John
„	Potter, George
„	Powell, Morgan
„	Phumpher, Isaac
1653	Patrick, Fenyn
„	Paley, William
„	Pitts, George
„	Poskoske, John
„	Parlett, Richard
„	Peade, William
„	Price, Philip
1654	Petty, Richard
„	Priest, James
„	Price, Thomas
1655	Payne, Launclott
1656	Powell, Edward
„	Parker, James
„	Powell, Richard
„	Pellis, John
„	Powell, Daniel
1657	Parke, Daniel
„	Parker, Richard
„	Phillips, Edward
„	Pigot, Francis
„	Pinney, Anthoney
1658	Pyett, Mary
„	Price, Edward
„	Pooly, Robert
1659	Pope, Robert
„	Parker, Daniel

(*To be continued.*)

Watkins of Antigua.

A copy of the following suit has been sent me by Mr. Dyett, the Registrar. The bill of complaint covers 12 fo. pages, and of this I give an abstract:—

'Antigua. In Chancery. . To H. E. Geo. Thomas, Esq., Capt.-Gen., etc.

Humbly complaining sheweth your oratrix Ann Watkins of the said island widow of John W. late of the s[d] island Esq. dec[d] and sole acting Extrix of his will and Rowland Oliver late of the said island but now of the island of Nevis Esq. That upon your oratrix intermarriage with John Watkins an Indre. trip. made 29 Jan. 1741 between the said John Watkins of the 1st part; John Murray Esq. now dec[d] and your orator of the 2[d] part; yo[r] oratrix as Ann Oliver spr. dau. of Rich[d] O. of this island dec[d] and sister of Rowl[d] O. of the 3[d] part; by which £1000 c. was to be paid by the s[d] Rowl[d] O. being a fortune left her by her father did give to John Murray and Rowl[d] O. one rent charge of £150 c. to be issuing out of all that plantation in the Body Division of 30 acres bounded E. with land of Abr. Redwood called the Cassada Garden, W. with lands late of Lucy Parke then of Cha. Dunbar, S. with the broad path called Long Lane and N. with lands of Walter Nugent Esq. and lands late of Jas. Langford with the houses etc. also that parcel of land in the Division of Dickinsons Bay containing 10 acres bounded E. and N. with lands of Wm. Mackinen Esq., S. with lands of Wm. Hillhouse and W. with the sea, also all those 24 slaves boys and girls the annuity payable after the death of J. W. and J. W. and your orator sold to Walter Nugent Esq. dec[d] the s[d] parcels of land by Indre. of 7 Sept. 1742 and J. W. made his will 27 Feb. 1762 and appointed your oratrix, Fra. Farley Esq., Tho. Oliver Esq., Wm. Smith Esq. and yo[r] orator his Exors. and gave her the residue and she hath taken on the execution thereof and testator died Aug. 1762 seized of four messuages in the town of St. John and of the slaves which are chargeable with the annuity and she hath sold the houses for £800 c., £380 c., £400 c. and £345 c. and sold the slaves and goods as in schedule A. so that the whole of testator's real and personal est. amounted to £10,900 c. All sums in his possession as Master in Chancery were paid over to Edw[d] Gamble Esq. his successor as per schedule B. and John Watkins did upon the 29 May 1756 mortgage to your orator the 4 messuages and divers slaves and she hath paid £883 in discharge thereof and testator died indebted much more than his est. will pay and judgments have been obtained against your oratrix by Rich[d] Oliver the Elder now dec[d], Rich[d] Oliver the Y[r], W[m] Smith Esq. and W[m] Lessly and Tho. Tew mariners as in schedule C. and a certain Indre. was made 2 Jan. 1740 between Judith Liott widow of the one part and John Liott planter of the other [*gap here*] and that Fra. Moore, John Pyne and Wm. Roth merchants and partners did bring an action in the Court of C. P. on 20 May for £30, Sam. Clapham on 31 May for £37, Elias Ferris and Rob. Malloun merchants and partners on 1 June 1763 for £81, John Yeamans and W. Atkinson Exors. of the will of Wm. Wardsworth dec[d] for £120, W. Shaw and Chas. . . . . adm'ors of Tho . . . . for £36, Joseph Buckley carpenter for £280, W. Buckley and Joseph Buckley adm'ors of R[d] B. dec[d] for £235 and for rent £495, Jas. Tate and David Roberts merchants and partners for £59, Geo. Green £21, and plaintiffs threaten to levy upon the whole of houses slaves and goods sold by your oratrix and refuse to permit your oratrix to keep as much of the money as will be sufficient to pay her rent charge of £150 and Judith Liott her rent charge of £90 and W. Smith, Fra. Farley and Tho. Oliver combine with the s[d] plaintiffs and your oratrix claims to have £2500 c. laid out to secure her rent charge she could not have sold the est. except free from the annuity. The two parcels of land had been charged with £300 c. to Mary Watkins afterwards wife of Isaac Anderson payable in four years after the death of Giles Watkins and Eliz. his wife and with £300 c. to Alice wife of Henry

Knight another of the daus. of Giles Watkins and Eliz. his wife in two years and £15 c. a year to Eliz. Thibou late Charles the other dau. of Giles Watkins and Eliz. his wife and your oratrix discharged all incumbrances and Judith Liott in consideration of a rentcharge of £90 a year conveyed to John Liott 35 acres in the Road Division in the parish of St Mary with the building and 4 slaves by Indre. of 2 Jan. 1740 and by Indre. of 12 Feb. 1745 John Liott and Mary his wife for £500 c. sold to John Watkins the said 35 acres with 11 slaves and 7 cattle and the said John Watkins and your oratrix by Indre. of 12 Oct. 1747 in consideration of [*blank*] £ conveyed the plantation to John Ellyatt discharged of the annuity, and Benj. Steele planter as surviving partner of Sam Sanderson l. of A. Esq. on 29 May 1763 brought an action in the court of C. P. against your oratrix for £240 c. for the use of 30 acres in the parish of St John . . . . Tho. Rainy mercht for £50, W. Mackinen, Fra. Farley and W. Warner Exors. of the will of John le Sprainger Spencer Rossington for £25, John Morison and W. Mackintosh merchts for £35, W. Miller, John Muir and Hugh Ferguson merchants and partners for £200, Kenneth McDonald [*gap here*] Pray for an Injunction and writs of subpœna to W. Smith, Tho. Oliver, Fra. Farley, Ben. Steel, John Grice, Tho. Rainy, Wm Mackinen, Wm Warner, John Morison, Wm Mackintosh, Wm Millar, John Muir, Hugh Ferguson, Kenneth McDonald, Fra. Moore, John Pyne, Wm Roth, Sam. Clappam, Elias Ferris, Rob. Malone, John Yearmans, Wm Atkinson, Wm Shaw, Cha. Crouch, Jos. Buckley, Wm Buckley, Jas. Tate and David Roberts, John Ross and Geo. Green and Sam. Clapham.

Signed by "Thomas Warner."

Schedule "A" mentioned in and referred to by the foregoing Bill. Account of Sales of the Goods and Chattels and effects of John Watkins, Esqr, deceased.

Purchasers' Names.	What Sold.				£	s.	d.
Neil Campbell	Ned				150	0	0
John Yearman	Tom				40	0	0
Galbraith Patterson	Old Johnny				6	15	0
Baptist Looby, Esqr.	Quamino				51	0	0
Isaac Thibou, Esqr.	Cranky				50	0	0
Samuel Martin, Esqr.	Does				100	0	0
Edward Horne, Esqr.	Cæsar				90	0	0
Samuel Martin, Esqr.	Humphray				80	0	0
Samuel Martin, Esqr.	Sherborn				102	0	0
Thomas Oliver, Esqr.	Lydia				95	10	0
Mrs. Ann Watkins	Molly with her children Sally and Quamino				80	0	0
Thomas Oliver, Esqr.	Philis				60	0	0
Robert Malloun	Silence, Beaty and Mischief				90	0	0
Robert Malloun	Sabina				70	0	0
Edward Horne, Esqr.	Cudjoe				91	0	0
Samuel Martin, Esqr.	Old Susanna (past labour)				1	0	0
William Mackinen, Esqr.	Beneba				70	0	0
William Mackinen, Esqr.	Tack and Pear				100	0	0
Robert Malloun	Belinda				50	0	0
Robert Malloun	Obba				85	0	0
Robert Malloun	Chloe				40	0	0
Robert Malloun	Cudjoe				66	0	0
John Warren	Adjah with her children Ned, Quaco and Hagar				184	0	0
His Excellency General Thomas	Old Toney	£50	0	0			
	Friday	110	0	0			
	Samford	110	0	0			
	Tom Jones	110	0	0			

Purchasers' Names.	What Sold.				£	s.	d.
His Excellency General Thomas	Tack Day	£110	0	0			
	Halliday	80	0	0			
	Quashey	90	0	0			
	Winter	80	0	0			
	George Walker	50	0	0			
	Will Pitt	65	0	0			
	Good Luck	50	0	0			
	Halifax	50	0	0			
	Leg	70	0	0			
	Cook Daniel	50	0	0			
	Guy	80	0	0			
	Sammy	70	0	0			
His Excellency General Thomas	Esau	100	0	0			
	Tomau	90	0	0	2405	0	0
	Toney	80	0	0			
	Occum	70	0	0			
	Hamlet	60	0	0			
	Ham	70	0	0			
	Stephen	70	0	0			
	Billy	80	0	0			
	Duncomb	90	0	0			
	Warner	70	0	0			
	Terry	70	0	0			
	King	80	0	0			
	Sackey	80	0	0			
	Nannet	90	0	0			
	Stephen	70	0	0			
	Tacks	50	0	0			
Thos. Oliver, Esqr.	Glascow	60	0	0			
	Brutus	45	0	0			
	Cajsuis	50	0	0			
	Sambo	70	0	0			
	Beef	50	0	0			
	Coomba	35	0	0			
Thos. Oliver, Esqr.	Gatley	60	0	0			
	Natty	50	0	0	800	0	0
	Cyrus	50	0	0			
	Symon	40	0	0			
	Peter	50	0	0			
	Bob	50	0	0			
	Quammy	70	0	0			
William Smith, Esqr.	Sam				120	0	0
Docr. John Muir	Pontac				70	0	0
John Lyons, Esqr.	Philip				62	0	0
John Lyons, Esqr.	Trim				53	0	0
Baptist Looby, Esqr.	Fanny				51	0	0
William Jarvis, Esqr.	Billy				165	0	0
William Jarvis, Esqr.	Tom				165	0	0
Mr. Cæsar Roach	Handel				132	0	0
Richard Donovan	Femmy				92	0	0
Robert Malloun	Sance				0	1	0
Mr. Cæsar Roach	Daniel				111	0	0
John Smith, Junr.	A Cœdar Book case with Sach Doors				15	10	0
Mr. Gamble	A parcel of Paper				4	10	0
John Yearman and		9	0	0			

Purchasers' Names.	What Sold.	£	s.	d.
Thomas Oliver	A parcel of Books £9 0 0	18	5	0
Francis Farley, Esqr. . .	Nine yards and p. cloth and 100 yards lace	8	19	6
William Alexander . . .	A silver mounted Sword . .	7	6	0
John Gatley	A ditto	1	11	0
Mitchell	An Old Muskett	1	10	4
James Brebner, Esqr. . .	Two Cutlasses for Watchmen .	0	6	0
Captain Ockley	Two Oval Mahogany Dinning Tables	5	5	0
Doctor Coakley	Two Square Mahogany Dining Tables	8	0	0
John Weir	One ditto	4	11	0
John Smith, Junr. . . .	One Card Table	5	3	0
Doctor Malcolm . . .	A Mahogany Tea Table . .	2	19	0
Benjamin Bannerman . .	A Japan'd Tea Table . . .	1	5	0
William Jarvis, Esqr. . .	A Dozen Mahogany Chairs .	21	0	0
Captain Ockley	Six old ditto	6	18	0
John Gattley	Two Elbow Chairs . . .	2	0	0
Mrs. Watkins	Half a doz. Chairs with Straw Bottoms	6	0	0
Ann Boudinet	Half a doz. Chairs with Covers and one easy Do. . . .	11	10	0
Thomas Oliver, Esqr. . .	A pair of Silver mounted Pistells	6	12	0
Doctor Coakley . . .	A pair of Brass mounted Do. .	6	14	0
Lawrence McLintocke . .	A Close Stool Chair . . .	3	14	0
Edward Byam, Esqr. . .	Eight Windsor Chairs . .	7	0	0
Captain Ockley	Ten small Chairs . . .	6	2	6
Mrs. Hurst	A marble Slab or stand . .	5	10	0
Doctor Coakley . . .	A Beaufett	6	2	0
Benjamin Bannerman . .	A Tutelar and Glass	7	12	0
George Bingham . . .	A Rum Case	6	1	0
Thomas Oliver, Esqr. . .	A Carpet	1	16	0
Roach	A Flour Clouth	1	0	0
Doctor Mckittrick . . .	A Do.	2	16	0
Revd. Mr. Lovely . . .	A Feather Bed, Bedstead, Matrass and Pavilion . . .	21	0	0
Samuel Henry Warner, Esqr. .	A Do.	6	1	4
William Atkinson . . .	A Do.	8	1	1
Charles Weathril, Esqr. . .	Some Landscapes . . .	17	14	0
Benjamin Bannerman . .	Ditto	5	2	0
Thomas Oliver, Esqr. . .	Ditto	3	18	0
Mr. Alexander Campbell . .	A Sedan	4	10	0
William Smith, Esqr. . .	A parcel of Old Pewter . .	1	4	0
Edward Byam, Esqr. . .	A Gun	1	12	0
. . . . . .	. . . .	1	1	0
Gattley	A Tack and Appurtenances .	3	0	0
Mr. Roach	A Fish Kettle	2	0	0
Mr. Roach	Two Gridirons, a pair of Dogs and Cullendar	2	0	0
Mr. Roach	A Bell metal Pott	0	10	0
Mrs. Watkins	A Feather Bed, Bedstead, Matrass and Pavilion . . .	7	0	0
Doctor Coakley . . .	A Ditto	9	0	0
Mrs. Watkins	A Large square Dinning Table .	2	0	0
Mrs. Watkins	A round small	1	0	0
Mrs.	A round tea Table . . .	1	0	0

Purchasers' Names.	What Sold.	£	s.	d.
Mrs. Watkins	A Sideboard Table of red Launders	3	0	0
Mrs. Watkins	Twelve Mahogany Chairs, different sorts	12	0	0
Mrs. Watkins	A Close Stool Chair	1	10	0
John Yearmans	A Large Rum Case full of Brandy	24	10	0
Mrs. Watkins	A Small Rum Case, old	1	0	0
Mrs. Watkins	An iron Chest	15	0	0
Francis Farley, Esqr.	A Chest of Drawers	13	15	0
Mrs. Watkins	An old wainscoat Beaureau	0	7	6
John Gatley	A Mahogany Slab	5	5	0
Henry Vassell, Esqr.	A Mahogany Shaving Stand	4	18	0
Mrs. Watkins	A Small Lamp Stand	0	15	0
John Gatley	Two Large Looking Glasses, one of them broken	5	6	0
Mrs. Watkins	A Dressing Glass	0	15	0
Mrs. Watkins	A Carpet and two flour Matts	1	10	0
Francis Farley, Esqr.	Two Trays and a Bread Baskett	4	0	0
John Smith, Junr.	A Silver mounted Hanger	8	2	0
Mr. William Byam	Two Mourning Swords	0	10	0
John Smith, Junr.	A Carbine and Bayonet	4	1	0
Mrs. Barton	An old Glass Lanthorn	0	7	6
Edward Horne, Esqr.	A Blue and white China Taureen and two Dishes	3	10	0
John Yearmans	2 Doz. Enamled China Plates and 10 Dishes	8	5	0
John Weir	1 Doz. and 11 Blue and white China Plates, 1 Doz. soup Do., and large soup Dish and three other Dishes	5	5	0
Edward Horne, Esqr.	1 Doz. Burnt tea Cups and saucers, 6 Blue and White			
Denbow Sawcolt	Twelve Chocolate Couloured Basons	1	5	0
John Smith, Junr.	Twelve red and white Basons and 12 plates	6	2	0
John Lyons, Esqr.	Two China Pint and one Quart Mug	1	14	0
Captain Ockley	Two Quarts, two pints and one Gallon Decanter, and one Dozen Glasses	2	0	0
John Smith, Junr.	1 Large red and white, 1 Blue, and 2 red China Bowls	2	15	0
Mrs. Watkins	A Cœdar			
Thomas Oliver, Esqr.	A Silver Tea Kettle			
Thomas Oliver, Esqr.	A Coffee Pot, 38/15 at 13*s.*	25	3	0
William Smith, Esqr.	A Candle Cup, 72 17 at 13*s.*	47	7	0¾
Doctor Mckittrick	A Tankard, 33 oz. at 11*s.* 1*d.*	18	5	9
Thomas Oliver, Esqr.	Two Half pint Cups, 10 11 at 8*s.* 6*d.*	4	9	8
W. Roach	Two pint Cans, 24 12 at 9*s.*	11	1	4
William Smith, Esqr.	One pint and a half pint Can, 19 oz. at 9*s.*	8	11	0
Charles Payne Sharpe, Esqr.	Two Sauce Boats, 18 16 at 11*s.* 6*d.*	10	15	9

Purchasers' Names.	What Sold.	£	s.	d.
John Gatley	One Sauce Boat, plain, 9 6 at 10s. 3d.	4	15	0
Edward Horne, Esqr. . .	Two embossed Salvers, 61 oz. at 12s. 6d.	38	2	6
William Smith, Esqr. . .	Four Pillar'd fluted Candlesticks	62	0	0
Francis Farley, Esqr. : .	Four Hall Candlesticks, 77 10 at 10s. 6d.	40	13	9
Mr. Roach	A Pair Chamber Candlesticks, 20 16 at 9s.	9	6	10
William Smith, Esqr. . .	A Set Silver Castors, 28 5 at 10s.	14	2	6
	Another Set Castors, 33 19 at 12s.	20	7	5
James Brebner, Esqr. . .	A Soup Spoon, 6 18 at 8s. 10d. .	3	0	11½
Francis Farley, Esqr. . .	A Soup Laddle, 8 oz. at 10s. 3d.	4	2	0
Charles Payne Sharpe, Esqr. .	A punch Laddle	2	1	0
John Smith, Junr. . . .	A Doz. Table Spoons, 24 oz. at 10s. 8d.	12	16	0
Thomas Oliver, Esqr. . .	One Doz. Desert Spoons, 11 11 at 10s. 10d.	6	6	1
Charles Payne Sharpe, Esqr. .	A Doz. Desert Spoons, 12 10 at 10s. 10d.	6	15	5
Doctor Mckittrick . . .	Eleven Table Spoons, old, 22 10 at 8s. 6d.	9	11	3
Edward Horne, Esqr. . .	Four Scollopt Salt and Spoons, 15 18 at 11s. 6d.	9	2	10
John Smith, Junr. . . .	Four plain Salt and 2 Spoons, 10 8 at 8s. 6d.	4	9	3½
Mrs. Watkins	A pair Chambers Candlesticks, 20 16 at 9s.	9	6	10
Mrs. Watkins	A Taureen Ladle, 7 15 at 8s.	3	2	0
Mrs. Watkins	A punch Ladle, 2 oz. at 10s.	1	0	0
Ditto	A Doz. Silver Spoons, 23 oz. at 10s.	11	10	0
Ditto	Six old Desert Spoons, 6 oz. at 7s. 6d.	2	15	0
Ditto	A Dozen tea Spoons, Tongs, in a case, 8 oz. at 10s. . . .	4	0	0
Ditto	Eight old Tea spoons, 3 10 at 7s. 6d.	1	6	3
Ditto	A silver Peper Box, 2 oz. at 7s. 6d.	0	15	0
Ditto	A silver Cream pot, 3 oz. at 7s. 6d.	1	2	6
Ditto	A silver Sugar Dish, 9 oz. at 8s.	3	12	0
Thomas Oliver, Esqr. . .	A silver Sugar Dish and Cream pot, 17 11 at 13s.	11	8	1
Edward Horne, Esqr. . .	Three Skewers and a Marrow Spoon, 9 19 at 9s. 6d. . . .	4	14	6
Charles Payne Sharpe, Esqr. .	Two Tortoise shell Cups and stands, silver rims and pedistals	12	15	0

Purchasers' Names.	What Sold.	£	s.	d.
John Weir	Two cases silver handled Knives and Forks and 12 spoons	28	10	0
John Gatley	Two Cases silver handled Knives and Forks	8	10	0
Edward Horne, Esqr.	Two cases China handled Knives and Forks	27	0	0
Mrs. Watkins	A parcel of linen	2	0	0
Doctor Gloster	A post Chariot and two horses	165	0	0
Mrs. Watkins	A single horse Chaise and a Mare	50	0	0
Wm. Atkinson	An old Chaise	11	0	0
Baptist Looby, Esqr.	An old axletrere to a Chaise	1	10	0
Samuel Martin, Esqr.	5096 feet Boards at £10	50	19	2¼
Edward Gamble	8770 feet Boards at Do.	87	14	0¾
Elizabeth Carnega	500 Do. Do.	5	0	0
A Free Negro	1000 Do. Do.	10	0	0
Edward Gamble, Esqr.	2402 feet Toit at £8 pm	19	4	3¾
Edward Horne, Esqr.	1580 Staves at £7 5s.	11	9	1
William Snaip	7952 Shingles at 35s. pm	13	18	3¼
Mrs. Gamble	A parcel of rough Stone	20	0	0
Mr. Roach	Three Hogshead Lime	6	0	0
Mr. Roach	Four Small Casks Terras	1	10	0
John Gatley	Seven Wheelbarrows	2	12	6
Joseph Manwaring	A Cart and Harness	20	0	0
William Atkinson	A parcel old rotten Harness	0	7	6
Doctor John Muir	4 Empty oil Tugs	1	1	0
John Smith	Ten Keggs of Paint	16	19	0
Edward Reed	Six Tuggs of Oil	9	0	0
John Smith	168 30 Nails at 9½	6	9	6
Edward Reed	500 20 Nails	4	3	9
Lawrence Mclintock	A Cask 4 Nails 57	12	16	6
John Smith	A Cask 6 oz. Nails 24	7	18	7
John Smith	A Cask 20			
Baptist Looby, Esqr.	A pair of Shades	2	0	0
John Gatley	1050 of old Iron at 10s. 6d.	5	10	3
Edward Reed	An old Trucks	0	10	0
Edward Reed	Two Boxes of Window Glass	6	2	0
Mr. Roach	Cow Sarah	10	0	0
Robert Browne, Esqr.	Cow St. John	11	0	0
Robert Browne, Esqr.	Another Cow and Calf	13	0	0
Robert Browne, Esqr.	Another Cow and Calf	12	0	0
Doctor John Muir	A Black Cow	11	15	0
Doctor John Muir	Cow Lydia and her Calf	10	0	0
Robert Browne, Esqr.	A Black Cow	11	0	0
Robert Browne, Esqr.	Cow Lee and her Bull Calf	13	10	0
Baptist Looby, Esqr.	Cow Suly and Calf	9	5	0
Benjamin Bannerman	Cow Franky and Calf	14	15	0
Robert Browne, Esqr.	Cow Hannah and Calf	10	15	0
Robert Browne, Esqr.	Cow Marote and her Bull Calf	20	0	0
Robert Browne, Esqr.	Cow Cherry	11	0	0
Mrs. Lawford	An old Cow, very poor	3	0	0
Baptist Looby, Esqr.	Cow Sally	10	0	0
Baptist Looby, Esqr.	Cow Marote and Calf	17	0	0
Benjamin Bannerman	Cow Cherry	10	5	0
John Richardson	A Cow and Calf	16	0	0
John Weir	A Cow	12	0	0

Purchasers' Names.	What Sold.	£	s.	d.
Robert Browne, Esqr. . .	A Steer	15	15	0
Robert Browne, Esqr. . .	A Ditto	22	15	0
Robert Browne, Esqr. . .	A Ditto	8	10	0
Doctor John Muir . . .	A Young Bull	13	0	0
Doctor John Muir . . .	A Young Bull	7	10	0
Doctor John Muir . . .	A Ditto	7	10	0
Doctor John Muir . . .	A Ditto	8	0	0
Henry Vassal, Esqr. . . .	Horse Hulton	20	0	0
Tate	Horse Buckhunter	20	0	0
Edward Horne, Esqr. . .	Eleven Weather Sheep at £3 3*s*. 6*d*.	36	0	0
Revd. David Hopkins . .	Eleven do. at do.	36	0	0
Baptist Looby, Esqr. . . .	Ten do. at do. and one Ewe at £1 0*s*. 0*d*.	32	15	0
John Yearmans	Six Lambs	6	0	0
Robert Browne, Esqr. . .	Six Ewes and a Ram at £1 10*s*. 6*d*.	10	13	0
Ditto . .	Seven Ewes at £1 5*s*. 6*d*. . .	8	18	6
Ditto . .	Fifteen do. at 45*s*. 6*d*. . .	11	12	6
John Weir	Four Kids and two Rams . .	6	6	0
Samuel Martin, Esqr. . .	Four Kids	9	10	0
Thomas Oliver, Esqr. . .	Four Ewe Goats	6	0	0
Mrs. Watkins	A parcel of Law Books . . .	81	0	0
John Gatley	A Cœdar Press	7	5	0
John Lyons, Esqr. . . .	A parcel of Paper	5	5	0
Mr. Roach	A Mahogany Cabinet	4	2	0
Charles Payne Sharpe, Esqr. .	Six Windsor Chairs, two old Chairs, and stool	6	18	0
Mr. Roach	A Writing Deske	3	11	0
Edward Gamble, Esqr. . .	An old paper Press	1	10	0
John Galway	An old Desk	0	13	0
William Atkinson . . .	A sideboard	1	10	0
William Atkinson . . .	An old Saddle	1	0	0
John Gatley	12500 of Bricks at £4 10*s*. pm .	56	5	0
Edward Horne, Esqr. . .	1000 Do. at Do. .	4	10	0
Mrs. Gamble	6000 Do. at Do. .	27	0	0
Mr. Roach	1500 Do. at Do. .	6	15	0
Thomas Tew	2000 Do. at Do. .	9	0	0
Edward Bull	1000 Do. at Do. .	4	10	0
William Hillhouse . . .	5000 Do. at Do. .	22	10	0
Walter Burke	A Negro man, Scipio . . .	31	10	0
Piggott	A Negro Woman, Grace . .	70	0	0
Charles Winstone . . .	Negro Woman Rachel and her child Sarah	120	0	0
Oliver	Negro Wrench or Gruffy . .	40	0	0
Richard Oliver, Esqr. . .	Boy Lorenso	45	0	0
William Smith, Esqr. . .	The Testator's Watch, a Legacy appraised	40	0	0
Jeremiah Nibbs . . .	A parcel of Bermudas Stone .	25	0	0
Ann Watkins	Three silver	21	15	0
. . . .	A Carpet	2	0	0
. . . .	A sedan Chair	16	10	0
. . . .	An old Mare	10	0	0
William Atkinson . . .	Testator's wearing Apparel, Legacy to Atkinson, appraised of	48	10	0
Joseph Buckley . . .	6275 feet Lumber at £12 pm .	75	5	6

Purchasors' Names.	What Sold.				£	s.	d.
Richard Oliver	A Kitchen Jacke .	£5	0	0			
Ditto	Eight Doz. Maderia Wine . . .	12	0	0			
Ditto	Allocke . . .	10	0	0			
					27	0	0
. . . .	A cask of Nails				30	13	1
. . . .	A sett of Books				21	17	3
John Atkinson	2050 Shingles at 50s. pm . .				5	2	6
					£8975	2	3½

Schedule "B" mentioned in and referred to by the foregoing Bill.

Account of the Estate of John Watkins, Esq., deceased, containing the amount of money and securities for money found in the House, the amount of what his lands, Tenements, Slaves, Household furniture and other effects sold for, and also an Account of the debts due to him at his death, for and how the money's arising by such Sale have been paid and applied by Ann Watkins his Widow and only acting Executrix, viz. :—

The Estate of John Watkins, Esq., deceased. *Contra.*

1762.			£	s.	d.	£	s.	d.
Aug.	5	To Cash paid the General for Licence to bury the Testator in his own family burying Ground £1 10s. 4d., and for proving the Will and Codicils 75s. . .	5	5	4			
		To Do. paid several Portors into the Country funeral		2	3			
		To Do. paid Thomas Bogte for the Coffin and attending to the Grave . . .	4	11	0			
		To Do. paid the Grave Diggers . . .		7	6			
						10	6	1
	9	To Do. paid Lawerence McLintock for 39 Bushels of Indian Corn to feed the Negroes				12	12	6
	12	To Do. paid for Mourning for the Ex'trix .	20	18	6			
		To Do. paid Lucy Reynolds what she laid out for stock meat and the week the Testator died	2	5	0			
						23	3	6
	15	To Ditto paid for a of Rice for the Negroes	4	19	2			
	16	To Ditto paid Thomas Beech recording Clerk in the Regist. Office . . .	16	10	0			
	17	To Ditto paid the Bell-ringer . . .		3	0			
		To Ditto paid the Ordinary for Warrant of Appraisement		15	0			
	18	To Ditto paid the printer advertising the Effects to be sold		7	6			
	30	To Ditto paid for a tierce of Rice for the Negroes	6	0	8			
		To Ditto paid the printer for a second advertisement		7	6			

1762			£	s.	d.	£	s.	d.
Sep.	4	To Ditto paid Williams and Co. for a Barrell of Beef for the Negroes . .	1	13	0			
						30	16	7
	6	To Ditto paid Thomas Warner, Esqr., retaining	16	10	0			
	11	To Ditto pd. the Farrier curing the Mare of a Lamenal	1	10	4			
		To Ditto pd. the printer for a third advertisement		7	6			
		To Do. pd. the Register's fee for Recording the Testator's Will		9	0			
		To Do. pd. the secretary for the same .		15	0			
		To Do. pd. three weeks allowance to 36 negroes they were sold @ £2 10*s*. 3*d*. per week	7	10	9			
Oct.	9	To Do. pd. the smith for shoeing the Horse Buckhunter		3	9			
		To Do. pd. for keeping 67 days @ 1/6 (he being lame)	5	0	6			
	13	To Do. pd. a Portor to General Thomas's to appoint a day for executing Conveyance of Slaves to him		1	6			
						32	8	4
	19	To Do. pd. advertising the lands and tenements		7	6			
		To Do. pd. Francis Elliott Rent of the Chambers	37	3	11			
	23	To Do. pd. Judith Liott a Quarter's Annuity due 13th instant	22	10	0			
		To Do. pd. the Parson and Clerk's Fees for the Interment	4	14	10			
		To amount of Warner and Gloster's Bill discounted with Gloster	120	16	1½			
						185	12	4½
	7	To cash paid the Midewife delivering Rachel a Negro Woman	3	6	0			
		To Ditto paid the Barber shaving Mr. Watkins when dead	1	10	4			
		To Do. pd. Edward Horne, Esqr., retaining	16	10	0			
		To Do. Pd. for a half a Quire of Bands and Judgments		3	9			
Nov.	16	To Do. pd. for an advertisement . .		7	6			
		To Do. pd. William Wordsworth on account	3	6	0			
		To Do. pd. Doctor Warner . . .	7	10	0			
	24	To do. pd. for Taxes	6	18	9			
Dec.	1	To Do. pd. the adjutant of Blue regt. for Clerks non appearance	1	16	0			
	5	To Do. pd. William Wordsworth on Account	3	6	0			
	7	To Do. pd. his housekeeper to get the necessary's for Funeral	9	6	9			
	8	To Do. pd. George Freeman on Account .	11	16	0			
1763.								
Jan.	17	To Do. pd. Wm. Atkinson	16	10	0			
		To Do. pd. Thos. Beech	6	12	0			

1763		£ s. d.	£ s. d.
Jan. 24	To Do. pd. Do.	7 14 6	
			57 1 3
	To this sum discounted with Ferris and Malloun on the Testator's Bond Account .	330 18 0	
	To Cash pd. Judith Liott a Quarter's Annuity due 13th instant . . .	22 10 0	
29	To Do. pd. Robert Killingly for several surveys of Land and for horsehire . .	10 4 0	
	To Ann Watkins for the Board and of George Freeman	25 0 0	
	To Cash paid Wm. Atkinson on Account .	13 10 0	
Mar. 1	To Do. pd. the printer for two advertisements	15 0	
Apr. 13	To Do. pd. Lawyer's Judge . . .	9 18 10	
	To Do. pd. Judith Liott her Annuity due this day	22 10 0	
			445 16 2
18	To Cash pd. Edward Gamble Master in Chancery on Account of the Testator's Debt to the Suitors in Chancery . .	6790 0 0	
	To Walter Tullideph his two bonds up to Edward Gamble in full of the said Debt to the Suitors in Chancery . . .	1500 0 0	
			8290 0 10½
	To Cash paid Wm. Atkinson . . .	19 16 0	
	To Cash paid Caesar Roach his vendor Account	211 8 1½	
	To so much discounted with Caesar Roach in full of his Account against the Testator	227 19 11½	
	To Cash pd. the Executors of Daniel Warner, Esqr., in full of Testator's Bond . .	64 18 0	
	To Do. pd. Andrew Lessly, senr., in full of Testator's Bond	151 6 3	
	To Do. pd. George Bingham Do . .	312 2 0	
			987 10 4
	To cash paid Blizard and Warner in Full Testator's Bond	648 12 11	
	To Ditto paid John Halliday Ditto .	366 2 9	
	To Ditto paid Alexander Crawford Ditto .	157 4 5	
	To Ditto paid Isaac Anderson for his claim	382 11 0	
	To Ditto paid Elizabeth Clarke Do .	66 0 0	
			1520 11 1
	To Ditto paid Freeman on Account	8 0 0	
Nov. 2	To Ditto paid Do. due 13th instant . .	22 10 0	
			53 0 0
	To the following sums allowed Thomas Oliver in his Account, the same having been paid by him to the undermentioned Creditors of the Testator, Vizt.—		
	Samuel Simpson the amount of his account	53 4 0	
	John Atkinson for Robert Donnison . .	17 16 3	
	Hart and Hillhouse	2 6 0	
	Thomas Martin	20 0 0	

1763		£	s.	d.	£	s.	d.
Nov. 2	William Beaty	61	3	2			
	John Smith Bond	121	15	4			
	Walker and Weir	39	6	11¾			
					315	11	8¾
	To this sum discounted with Alexander Willock, being the amount of his accot. .	265	10	4¾			
	To this sum credited in this account for Ord and Lyms Bond a verdict being found for the Deft. when the bond was put in suit	166	0	0			
	To the like for Aron Lyms Bond, the same having been satisfied to in the Testator's life	160	0	0			
	To this Sum credited for Edward Green's Bond, the testator being indebted to said Green in a larger Sum for monies received of Hans Mackens to Green's use and for Bussiness done 66 @ 150 Exchge. . .	99	0	0			
	To so much credited for Doctor Muire Bond, the same being discounted age, his account of Medicines and for Goods sold	200	0	0			
	To so much credited for Jane Lyons's Bond, the same having been allowed to the estate in passing the Accot. with the suitors in chan.	200	0	0			
	To a Loss on Andrew Irwin's Debt, he being not to be found	7	4	2			
	To the like on Pierce Murphy's . . .	96	19	0½			
	To the like on Thomas Woolward's . .	12	3	3			
	To this sum credited for Andrew Lessly's Note, the same having been paid the Testator in his life	71	19	10½			
	To this sum credited as due from John Monteigue, he being Dead . . .	1	16	0			
	To cash paid Ann Watkins, her Annuity to 4th August 1763 being one year . .	150	0	0			
	To Ditto paid Ditto a Fund to secure her Annuity settled on her	2500	0	0			
	To Ditto paid Rowland Oliver, Esqr., his Mortgage account	883	8	6			
	To this sum supposed necessary to answer the Annuity of Judith Liott of £90 pd. and granted her by the Testator . .	270	0	0			
	To Richard and Richard Oliver Ditto .	1179	9	7			
	To Richard Oliver the Elder being so much received by the Testator for the use of Oliver of the Estate of Robert Patterson and for which Judgments .	2224	14	5			
	To this sum credited in this Account as due from Richard and Richard Oliver, the same being allowed to the estate before the last Judgment was granted . .	104	1	10			
	To William Smith, Esqr., on Judgment .	42	14	1			
	To Thomas Tew on Judgment	229	7	7			
	To Wm. Lessly on Judgment . . .	60	17	4½			

1763		£	s.	d.
Nov. 2	To this sum supposed necessary to answer Lawyer's Bills and Office fees . . .	150	0	0
	To Clerks hire and	100	0	0
		21,942	18	2¼
	To this sum paid James Athill, Attorney to Richard and Richard Oliver, being so much received of Nathaniel Knight by the Testator a few days before he dyed for the said Knight's Debt to the said R. and R. Oliver and	550	0	0

1762, August 5. By Cash found in Iron Chest; amount of Sales of the Testator's Slaves, House and furniture; Cash of Thomas Tew in full of his Bond; Richard Donavan his Bond with interest; Samuel Nibbs his Bond. Interest thereon to 17th November 1763. By Mansfield Ord and Aron Lym their joint Bond for £166; Aron Lym's Bond £160; Edward Green Bond for £66 sterling Exch. at £150, £99; James Dealy's Bond £12; John Muire Bond £200; John Martin £107; Jane Lyons's Bond £200; Richard Donavan and Patrick Byrne their joint Bond; Interest thereon; Alexander Willocks Bond; James Athill's Bond and interest; Thomas Sawcolts Bond; John Wand; Anthony Browne's Note; Pierce Murphy; Thomas Woolward; Andrew Lessly's Note; John Monteigue Do.; Thomas Nicholas Bond £22; John Patterson's note; Walter Tullideph's Five Bonds £1501; a brick house sold for ; a wooden House sold for ; a Do.; a Do.

By the following sums due to the Testator for Law Business Task Work. By Ceasar Roach for self and Hill Huggins, Henry Blizard, Saml. Nibbs, Eare Daniel, Baptist Looby, Patrick Byrne, John Bird, William Sheriff, Harry Alexander, Estate John Tomlinson, John Otto Bayer, Robert Christian, Francis Elliott, Thomas Elmes, Thomas Burton, Main Sweet Walrond, Bernard Salwarve, George Hurst, William Mackinen, John Gilchrist, Charles Wm. Mackinen, John Halliday, Byam Freeman, Ex'ors of Oliver Burke, Estate Valentine Browne, Richard and Richard Oliver, Cash paid Ann Watkins in Silver.

N.B.—The following persons appear by the Testator's Books to be indebted to him in the sums after mentioned. But as they deny the , Executrix cannot sufficiently prove them. They are therefrom:—

Alexander Fraser, Heyns and Sawcolt, Doctor John Muir, Thomas Stevenson, William Jarvis, Day and Gloster.

Schedule "C," mentioned and referred to by the foregoing Bill.

William Lessly, Mariner, obtained a Verdict upon the day of 1763 for the sum of £60 17*s*. 4½*d*. Currency ags. the Complt. Ann Watkins in an Action upon the case for goods sold and delivered and Judgments thereon Entered on the day of 1763. 5th April 1763 Ann Watkins confessed a Judgment when assetts to Richard Oliver the Elder for

£60 17*s*. 4½*d*. Currency.

5th April 1763. Ann Watkins confessed a Judgment when Assetts to Richard and Richard Oliver of the City of London, Merchants, for the sum of £714 16*s*. 9*d*. lawfull money of Great Britain with five Pounds Currency for Costs of suit in an Action upon the case for money lent, laid out and expended for the use of the said John Watkins. £714 16*s*. 9*d*. Sterling.

3rd April. Ann Watkins confessed a Judgment when Assetts to William Smith, Esqr., for the sum of £40 14s. 1d. Gold and Silver Current money of the Island of Antigua with five pounds Currency for Costs of suit in an Action upon the case for money's had and recd. by the said John Watkins to the use of the said Wm. Smith. £40 14s. 1d. Currency.

2nd May 1763. Ann Watkins confessed a Judgment when Assetts to Richard Oliver the Elder of the City of London, Merchant, for the sum of £2224 14s. 5d. Gold and Silver money of Antigua with five pounds Currency for costs of suit in an Action upon the case for money had and recd. to the use of the said Richard Oliver the Elder. £2224 14s. 5d. Currency.

Ann Watkins confessed a Judgment when Assetts to Thomas Tew of the Island of Antigua, Mariner, for the sum of £220 currency with pounds Currency for Costs of suit an Action and upon an accepted order and for the use and occupation of two Chambers. Currency.

Grant of Arms to William Beckford.

(British Museum, Add. MS. 14,293, fo. 24.)

To all and singular to whom these presents shall come Sr William Dugdale Knt garter principall King of armes and Sr henrey St Gorge (*sic*) Clarenceux King of armes send greeting whereas (*blank*) son & heir of Sr Tho. Beckford Knt late alderman of ye citty of London deceased haveing made application to his grace Henry Duck (*sic*) of Norfolk Earl marshall of England touching a coat of armes and crest to be granted to him and his desendents the said Earl marshall being well satisfied of ye loyalty and worthiness of ye said (*blank*) did thereupon by his warrant bearing date ye 28 day of January last past order and appoint us to devyse grant and assign unto ye said [William Beckford*] and his descendents such armes & crest as he and thay may lawfully bear Know ye that we the said Garter and Clarenceux [King*] of armes by authority of the letters patents of our offices under ye great seal of England to us respectively granted and in pursuance of ye said Earl Marshalls warrant have devysed and do by these presents grant and assigne unto ye said [William Beckford*] ye armes and crest here after mentioned viz. party per pale gules and azure on a cheveron argent between three martlets or an eagle displayed sable and for the crest, on a wreath argent and gules a cranes head erased or holding in ye beak a fish argent, as in ye margin here of more plainly appeareth to be borne and used for ever hereafter by him ye said [William Beckford*] & ye heirs and others descendents of his body lawfully begotten in shield coat armore penon seal or otherwise according to ye law of armes without ye lett or interruption of any person or persons whatsoever.

In witness whereof we ye said Garter and Clarenceux (*blank*) of armes have to these presents subscribed our names and affix ye seale of our respective offices this second day of february in ye first year of ye reign of our sovereign lord James ye second by ye grace of god (*blank*) of England Scotland france and Ireland defender of the faith etca: annoq dni millesimo sexcentesimo quinto.

William Dugdale, garter.
Hen. St George, Clarenceux.

[The arms and crest are sketched in pencil preparatory to being painted. This volume is a collection of copies of grants of arms. Only the first 23 folios have the arms painted in the shields, in the remainder of the volume the latter are blank and unfinished. I have omitted using the numerous capital letters.—Ed.]

* In pencil.

Administrations (P.C.C.) relating to West Indians.

In the early Administration Act books the entries are in contracted Latin. In the margin is noted the diocese, but if the person died abroad "in partibus" is written. The great majority of such were of course mariners, and they are usually noted as having died "in partibus ultramarinis" or "transmarinis" or "super alto mare," the name of the ship not as a rule being given. Occasionally persons are recorded as having died in Scotland, Ireland, East India, Persia, Muscovy, Spain, France, Germany, Holland, etc. Entries of Virginia appear in 1627.

Commencing my search in 1623, I found no entry of the W. I. previous to 1630, when the first one occurs relating, as one would expect, to St Christopher, which was founded shortly before Barbados. This entry is given as a specimen in full:—

"1630, June. Daniel Gulliford. Octavo die emanavit Comiſſio Bridgitte Gulliford relce Danielis Gulliford nup̄ infra Inſulam ſc̄ti Chriſtoferi in ptibus ultramarinis def hēntis etc. ad adminiſtrand̄ bona jura et Cred̄ dc̄i dēf de bene etc. Coram Richo Knight Clico vigore Com̄ etc. Jurat 12^li 6^s 10^d." fo. 174.

folio.

1632, Feb. Marcus Marshall. *6, to Robert Marshall, the brother of M. M., "nup̄ intra Insulam vocat Le Barbadoes," with consent of Mary M. the relict. 148

1633, Dec. 9, to Roger North,† Esq., creditor of—

William Arrundell,
Francis Acton,
Edward Bradford,
Thomas Beeton,
Robert Balard,
William Bud al's Gowen,
Francis Bolton,
Amer Bickliffe,
Henry Burdet,
Roger Carpenter,
Phillip Curtis,
Robert Crosse,
Jonathan Downer,
Henry Dillam,
William Flud,
Nathaniel Gold,
Raphe Moore,
Philip Mackerna,
Edward Lacy,
Richard Robinson,
Richard Sparke,
Thomas Thornebury,
James Williams,
Robert Wake,
all of Amazonia, deceased. 206

1636, Oct. Roger Lymbrey. 29, to Mary L., the relict of R. L., "nup̄ in Infula Barbathoes," deceased. 24

1636, Oct. Anthony Hilton.‡ 21, to George Griffith, principal creditor of A. H., in foreign parts, bach., deceased. 25

* The words "Adm'on on the" in each entry for the saving of space I omit.

† Captain Roger North, brother to Lord North, had accompanied Sir Walter Raleigh on the latter's last voyage to Guiana. After his return a company was formed in 1618, and with other adventurers to the number of 120 he secretly sailed from Plymouth the last of April 1620, settled 100 leagues up the Amazon, and returned with a cargo of tobacco, but through Spanish opposition was committed to the Tower. Mr. Tho. Warner, John Rhodes, and Robert Bims, after living two years on the Amazon, sailed for England, went thence to Virginia, and then settled the Island of St. Christopher in 1623-24. Captain North in 1628 dispatched a reinforcement of four ships with 200 men: "the first ship with 112 men not one miscarried." The administration of the goods of the above 24 men in 1633 leads one to suspect that a ship was lost, or these settlers were carried off by an epidemic. ("John Smith's Travels," II., 188. Colonial Cal. of State Papers.)

‡ "Capt Anthony Hylton, President of Mevis," signed the Treaty of Peace 5 Sept. and 8 Nov. 1628 at St. Christopher. He became about 1631 Governor of Tortuga, where the English Governor (probably Hylton) was killed at the Spanish attack in Dec. 1634. (See *ante*, II., 5.)

folio.

1637, June. Sam. Lymbrey. 2, to Jonas Hopkins, a creditor of S. L., bach., in pts., dec^{d}. 84

1638, Oct. D^{ns} William Tufton, Kn^{t}.* 16, to George Hawle, creditor of Sr W. T., in foreign parts, bach., deceased. 216

1638, Jan. Thomas Barton. 24, to Anne Barton, now wife of Lewis Morris,† "in partibus Barbadus remanen," relict of T. B., late of Barbadus, deceased. 2

1638, March. Robert Baylie. 31, to Henry Pitt and Nath. Bacheler, of the town of Southampton, merchants, to administer the goods of R. B., late of Antiego in America, bach., deceased. 21

1639, Feb. Sam. Linaker. 26, to Peter Cole of St Michael, Cornhill, citizen and staconer, one of the creditors of S. L., late in the Island of St Christofer, wid^{r}, deceased. 20^{li}. 105

1642, Feb. Ralph Batson. 6, to Edmund Batson, clerk, the brother of R. B., late deceased in Le Barbadoes. 8

1643, May. Michael Wilkinson. 20, to Tho. Townsend, creditor of M. W., late of the Island of St Christofer but in London, deceased. 24

[There is a hiatus from Aug. 1643 to Nov. 1644.]

1648, March. William Davies. 9, to Richard Davies, the father of W. D., in le Barbados, deceased. 28

1649, April. Thomas Browne. 21, to Mathew Edwards, principal creditor of T. B., bach., late in le Barbadoes, deceased. 57

1649, June. John Richardson. 9, to Stephen Richardson, gen., the brother of J. R., late of Carron Hill in the Island of Barbadoes, bach., deceased. 66

1649, Sept. Thomas Willoughby. 12, to Edward W., the son of T. W., late of Southwark, but in the Island of Le Barbados, deceased. Eliz. W. the relict. 109

1649, Oct. Edmund Fraser. 5, to John Cooke, a mother's brother, principal creditor of E. F., in the Island of Barbados, bach., deceased. Also John Frazer. (The like adm'on.) 128

1649, Nov. Thomas Powell. 17, to Peirce P., brother of T. P., late of the Island of St Xpofer, deceased. 134

1649, Dec. John Latter. 21, to Jane L., relict of J. L., late of the Island of Barbadoes, deceased. 3^{l} 10^{s}. 161

1649, Dec. Edward Cranfield. 5, to Mary Peisly al's Cranfeild, the mother of E. C., late in the Island of Barbadoes, deceased, during the minority of Francis, William and Edward C., the children. See also April 1653 and July 1663. 170

1649, Feb. John Bradford. 26, to Anne B., relict of J. B., late of Barbadoes, deceased.. 18

1649, March. George Hartlett. 8, to Richard H., the brother of G. H., late in "India Occidentali," bach., deceased. 37

1649, March. Derman Harrowe. 29, to Mary H., widow, the relict of D. H., late of the Island of Sr Christofer and there deceased. Inv. 36^{l} 16^{s}. 44

1649, Oct. Edward Asforby. 25, to Chr. Porrell and Anne P. al's Asforby, his wife, the mother of E. A., l. in foreign parts, deceased. 117

1650, April. John Olver. 9, to Eliz. Levericke, widow, principal creditor of J. O., bach., late of the Island of Barbados, deceased. 53

* Sir William Tufton, commissioned as Governor of Barbados by the Earl of Carlisle, arrived on 21 Dec. 1629, but was superseded in June 1630 by Capt. Henry Hawley. In May 1631 Tufton was found guilty of treason by a packed tribunal and shot. Schomburgh incorrectly styled him a baronet.

† Col. Lewis Morris, a Cromwellian who had captured Chepstow Castle, became a prominent planter in St. Joseph's in 1657.

folio.

1650, May. Jasper Emrey. 30, to Richard E., the brother of J. E., late of the Island of S[t] Christofer, deceased. 69

1650, May. Edward Asfordby. 8, to Charles A., the brother of E. A., late of le Barbadoes, deceased, the adm'on granted in Oct. 1649 to Christopher Purrell and Anne his wife being revoked. 81

1650, Oct. Joseph Weekes. 19, to Lewis W., the brother of J. W., late of Chimley, co. Devon, but in the Island of S[t] Christopher, deceased. 150

1650, Nov. Richard Robotham. 1, to Elianor Roberts, the mother and attorney of R. R., late of the Island Barbadoes, deceased. 162

1650, Feb. David Hewett. 17, to Henry H., the brother of D. H., late in the Island of Barbadoes, bach., deceased. 18

1650, March. Isaac Greene. 15, to Mary G., widow, the relict of I. G., late of the Island of Mevis in pts., deceased. 34

[In 1651 the entries are no longer in Latin but in English.]

1651, Aug. Philipp Strangeway. 1, to Wm. S., the father of P. S., late deceased in the Barbadoes, during y[e] minority and to y[e] use of Cath S., his dau. 129

1651, Feb. John Read. 18, to Burnell R., the brother of J. R., late of Barbadoes, widdower, deceased, during y[e] minority and to y[e] use of Eliz. and Mary R., y[e] daus. 28

1652, June. Wm. Trevis. 24, to Tho. T., the brother of W. T., late of y[e] barbadoes, deceased. 99

1652, June. Chr. Dinghurst. 25, to Frances Hobbs al's Dinghurst, the sister of C. D., late of Bristol but dyed at the Isle of S[t] Christophers. 100

1652, July. Rob. Cox. 17, to Mary Cox, widow, the relict of R. C., late of the Island of the Barbadoes but dieing in y[e] city of Westm[r]. 140

1652, Sept. Tho. North. 2, to Alice Westwood, wife of David W., creditor of T. N., late dyeing at the Barbadoes. 171

1652, Oct. Vincent Large. 1, to Eliz. L., wid., y[e] relict of V. L., late deceased at ye Barbados. 183

1652, Oct. John Brasyer (Pauper). 14, to Mary B., wid., y[e] Mother of J. B., bach., in y[e] service of y[e] State at y[e] Barbadoes, dec[d]. 184

1652, Oct. W[m] Pope. 19, to John Stephens, the nephew by the brother of W. P., late of Stepney but dying at Barbadoes abord the ship Ruth. 186

1653, April.* Edward Cranfeild. 26, to Tho. Payne, curator of Francis C. and Edward C., minors, the sons of E. C., late in y[e] Barbadoes, Esq., dec[d], of est. left unadministered by Mary Peasely al's C., since dec[d]. Adm'on de bono in April 1658. Adm'on de bono non July 1663. The 1st adm'on in Dec. 1649. 3

†1653, May. Henry Hainsworth. 9, to Henry H. (*sic*), the father of Rob. H. (*sic*), late at Antiguo, dec[d]. 5

1653, July. W[m] Howell. 20, to Anne H., the sister of W. H., late in y[e] Barbadoes, bach., dec[d]. 19

1653, July. Rich[d] Butler. 20, to W[m] Rudd, creditor of R. B., late of the Barbadoes, dec[d]. 22

1653, Sept. Tho. Porter. 26, to Tho. Batson, creditor to T. P., late in y[e] West Indyes, dec[d]. 33

1653, Jan. Robert Hinderson. 6, to Ellinor H., wid., the relict of R. H., late in the Barbadoes, dec[d]. 44

* In this volume occur the names of many men in the States service, the ships being also given.

† The first 78 folios of the volume, 1653 and 1654, relate to "pt[s]. beyond the seas." Then follows London, and the other administrations are all arranged under counties.

folio.

1653-4, Feb. Francis Browne. 17, to Edward B., the brother of F. B., l. of yᵉ Isle of Sᵗ Christopher, W.I., batch., decᵈ. 51
1653-4, Feb. Wᵐ Burch. 14, to Patience Ashfeild al's B., the relict of W. B., l. in the Barbadoes, decᵈ. 52
1654, May. Richard Morris. 24, to Prescilla M., the relict of R. M., l. of the p. of Sᵗ Martin Legran, L., but in the Barbadoes, decᵈ. 60
1654, June. Wᵐ Kilbee. 13, to John K., only brother of W. K., l. in the Barbadoes, decᵈ. 63
1654, Aug. Sam. Waad. 26, to Sam. W., father of S. W., l. in the Caribda Ilands (*sic*), batch., decᵈ. 68
1654-5, Jan. Nich. Pulsever. 30, to Joyce P., widow, the mother of N. P., l. in Barbadoes, batch. 17
1654-5, Feb. Wᵐ Weston. 27, to John W., the brother of W. W., l. in yᵉ Barbadoes. 40
1655, May. James Radley. 2, to Tho. R., the brother of J. R., l. in yᵉ Barbadoes. 105
1655, May. John Harborne. 24, to Fra. Brooker, yᵉ G. and Curator of Wᵐ H., a minor, yᵉ nephew by yᵉ brother of J. H., l. in the Barbadoes, batch., decᵈ. 107
1655, May. Tobias Cooper. 18, to Eliz. C., widow, the mother of T. C., l. in the Barbadoes, batch. 107
1655, June. John Dunn. 26, to Eliz. Okeram al's Dunn, yᵉ sister of J. D., l. of yᵉ Isle of Barbadoes, decᵈ, paup. 122
1655, Sept. Jeffery Cransack. 26, to Jane C., wid., yᵉ rel. of J. C., in yᵉ W.I., at sea, decᵈ. 181
1655, Oct. Robert Curtis. The last day, to Wᵐ Corbold, G. of John C., a minor, the only brother of R. C., l. of Jamaica, batch. 198
1655, Nov. Anne Maddrin. 3, to Kath. Sparke, wife of Archibald S., yᵉ only sister of A. M., l. of yᵉ I. of Barbadoes, widow. 217
1655, Nov. Mark Vincent. 6, to Ester V., wid., yᵉ rel. of M. V., l. of Sᵗ Buttolph without Aldgate, but in yᵉ Barbadoes. 217
1655, Nov. Geo. Upcott. 8, to Dorothy U., wid., yᵉ rel. of G. U., l. of Nevis in the Caribda Islands in the W. I. 218
1655, Nov. John Parsonson. 16, to Robert P., the only brother of J. P., l. of Nevis, batch. 226
1655, Nov. Josiah Gardner. 19, to Timothy G., the brother of J. G., l. of yᵉ I. of Barbadoes, batch. 226
1655, Nov. Tho. Goodcheape. 29, to John G., yᵉ brother of T. G., in yᵉ States Service in yᵉ W. I. 227
1655, Dec. Tho. Meggs. 15, to Susan Rock, wife of Wᵐ R., pr. cr. of T. M., l. of White Chappell, but in the Barbadoes. 251
1655, Dec. Wᵐ Fryer. 15, to Roger Price, pr. cr. of W. F., l. of White Chappell, but in yᵉ Barbadoes. 251

Monumental Inscriptions in England relating to West Indians.*

BATH ABBEY, CO. SOMERSET.

South transept, west wall. On a white marble tablet shaped like a sarcophagus:—

Sacred to the Memory of CHARLOTTE,
Widow of the late ASCANIUS WILLIAM SENIOR Efq[r]
and Daughter of JOHN ABEL WALTER Efq[r]
by his Wife JANE Daughter of
GEORGE, *Lord Abergavenny* Premier Baron of *England*,
she died the 10th of Novr. 1811, Aged 75.
(4 lines omitted.)

(*Ante*, IV., 282.) (Copied 24 April 1916.)

1811, Nov. 14. Saturday died, at her house in Brock-street, Mrs. Senior, relict of A. W. Senior, esq. ("Bath Chronicle.")

1786, June 29. Friday died, at his house in Upper Church-street, Nassau Thomas Senior, esq. (*Ibid.*) I found no tablet to him in Walcot Church. Upper Church Street runs north out of Brock Street at the back of the Royal Crescent.

ST. DUNSTAN-IN-THE-EAST, LONDON.

Nave. On a blue stone in the floor of central passage:—

Here Lies the Body of
M[r] DENSIE ALLEYNE Son of the
Hon[ble] Brigad[r] THOMAS ALLEYNE Efq[r]
of the Ifland of *Barbadocs* in
AMERICA who Departed this Life
the 5th Day of March 17$\frac{1}{3}$$\frac{2}{3}$
In the 16th Year of his Age.
Here ALSO LIES The Body of
M[R] THOMAS ALLEYNE Another
Son of The SAID HONOURABLE
BrigADIER THOMAS ALLEYNE ESqr
who DEPArtED this LIFE The 20th
OF DeceMBer 1715 AgeD 20 YeArs.
Alfo the Body of M[R] ROBERT JOHNSTOUN
Son of ROBERT IOHNSTOUN Esq[r] of the
Ifland of *Barbadoes* who departed this
life the 3[d] of March 1720 Ætatis Svæ 19.

(Transcribed 10 May 1916.)

Lettering all of same size except capitals, and curiously mixed up.

The Brigadier was eldest son of the Hon. Abel Alleyne, Lt.-Gen., by Eliz. Denzy. He m. Judith dau. of Sir Timothy Thornhill, Bart. (marriage articles dated 30 June 1688), and made his will 1 June 1713. "To my son Thomas my Four Hill plantation at the age of 21 which will be on 27 Oct. 1716." Four other sons survived, viz.: Col. Abel Alleyne, Timothy Alleyne, born 1691, Reynold, who came of age on 23 Jan. 1720, and Col. John Alleyne, who came of age on 1 Jan. 1722.

* Continued from p. 46.

ROSTHERNE, CHESHIRE.

On a tablet:—

SACRED TO THE MEMORY OF
ELIZABETH BROOKE
WIFE OF THE LATE PETER BROOKE ESQ
OF MERE-HALL, IN THIS COUNTY
DAUGHTER AND HEIRESS OF JONAS LANGFORD ESQ.
OF THE ISLAND OF ANTIGUA
SHE DIED THE 15TH DECEMBER ANNO DOMINI 1809
AGED 75 YEARS.

There are other memorials to Jonas Langford-Brooke 1784, Tho. Langford-Brooke 1815 and Maria Langford-Brooke 1811. Mrs. Brooke was born 2 and bapt. 28 March 1734-5 at St. John's Town. Her will was proved P.C.C., 121, Collingwood. Her eldest son Jonas took the name and arms of Langford, on succeeding to the estate of his grandfather Jonas Langford.

Transcribed by T. L. Oliver Aug. 1913.

WALTHAMSTOW. (Lysons' "Environs of London," iv., 212.)

Mr Archer Martin of Jamaica, merchant, d. 1707.

ST. CATHERINE, JAMAICA. (Archer, 64.)

Mary wife of David Pugh, Esq., died 1710 in her 29th year. Her mother Mary Watson died 1691, aged 33.

Also the body of Mary Martin, beside Archer Martin, Esq., her former husband, who died 1703.

Arms: *A lion passant between three fleurs-de-lys* (PUGH); impaling: *On a cross between four fleurs-de-lys a crescent.*

Crest: *A demi-lion, in its jamb a fleur-de-lys.*

Archer Martin of the parish of St. Tho. in the Vale, I. of Jamaica, Esq. Will dated 11 May 1706. To my wife Mary M. £500 c. a year for her life in lieu of dower. My cozen Kath. Gregory, 1st dau. of Mathew G. of sd parish, Esq., £100 c. To each of the chn of the said M. G. £50 c. My gods. Edw. Winter, s. of Edw. W. of sd p., 3 cows. Gods. Edwyn Savage, s. of Dr Edwin S. of sd p., the like. Gods. Mathew Cosens, s. of Chas. C. of sd p., the like. To my wife 5 house negroes. My plantation at Sixteen Mile Walk with the negroes, houses and land at Passage Fort in case I die s.p. to my sisters Jane Risby and Dorothy Smith. ⅔ of the produce to Jane and ⅓ to Dorothy, and after my wife's death to them absolutely. All residue to my wife, but if I with my wife shd perish at sea in our intended voyage to Eng., then I give to Mrs Martha Watson, sister of my wife, £500, to Mr Fra. W. her brother £300, Mrs Kath. Gregory, dau. of Mathew G., Esq., £200, and all debts owing to me in J'ca and all money in Eng. to the chn of my uncle Mathew Gregory. My wife sole Ex'trix. Witnessed by Hu. Totterdell, Robt Nedham, Jno Ellis.

Codicil. 20 Feb. 1706. At St. Jago de la Vega. J'ca, about to take a voyage to Eng. for the recovery of my health. My sisters to enter into bonds of £2000 for the punctual payment of the £500 a year to my wife. Witnessed by Wm Brodrick, James Hurst, Benj. Burton. Proved 13 Jan. 1707 by Mary M. (16, Barrett.)

Testator was son of Gabriel Martyn of Jamaica (will proved there in 1688) by Cath. Gallimore. Her sister Jane mar. Mathew Gregory.

(To be continued.)

See "West Indian Bookplates," No. 243.
The date of this plate is about the year 1800.

Burt of Nevis.

The family of Burt occupied from early days a very prominent position in the Leeward Islands. A short pedigree appeared in Vol. I. of "Antigua" in 1894, since which date additional information has accumulated, many notes being contributed by Lieut.-Col. H. W. Pook. The following revised pedigree is believed to be fairly accurate. It corrects the Pym one which appeared *ante*, Vol. III.

DEEDS FROM THE NEVIS AND ST. KITTS RECORD OFFICES.

Jane Lanhather of Nevis, widow. Will dated 23 Oct. 1693. To my grandchⁿ Mary Pike, Penelope Pike, John Pike and Cath. Pike, ch[n] of my dau. Barbary P., 10,000 lbs. each. My granddau. Eliz. Burt and her dau. Eliza 10,000 lbs. each. To Eliz. Rolt dau. of James R., dec[d], l. of A., 20,000 lbs. All est. to my grand dau. Jane Pym, widow of Tho. Pym, l. of N., and Tho. P. son of Eliz. P. at 16 (his father Chas. Pym) equally. Sworn 14 Feb. 1695-6. Recorded at Nevis in 1738.

1694, Nov. 13. Chas. Pym, S[r], of Nevis, in consideration that a moiety of a plantation belonging to M[rs] Jane Lanhather is given by her will to my s. Tho. P., I release all claim to the other moiety. (Nevis Court of Ordinary Records, p. 536.)

Deposition of Ann Brodbelt as to the will of M[rs] Jane Lanhather, who left 10,000 lbs. to Eliz. wife of Wm. Burt, Esq., formerly President of N., and to Eliz. dau. of the said Wm. Burt and Eliz. his wife. Sworn 28 March 1726. Recorded 1 Feb. 1743-4. (Nevis Records, iii., p. 35.)

1715, Dec. 23. Indre made between Wm. Pym Burt of N., planter, and John Dasent and others. W. P. B. owns ¼ of Morning Star pl[n] and negros, w[h] were the estate and inheritance of Mary B., dec[d], his late wife, as she was one of the daus. and coheirs of Joseph Hill, late of N., planter, dec[d], and gives this to Eliz. B. and Frances B., his 2 daus. and only ch[n] by her. Lease of the said ¼ for 60 years in T. for them. (Nevis Deeds, i., p. 589.)

1719, Aug. 4. Antigua. Wm. Pym Burt of Nevis, gent., states that Sir Wm. Stapleton granted a patent to his grandf. Wm. B., esq., of an I. called Dog Island, to the leeward of Anguilla. The patent was burnt or lost in the late French invasion; prays for a new one, w[h] is granted on 2 April 1719. (*Ibid.*, i., p. 445.)

1730, Sept. 8. Wm. Weekes of N., pl[r]. Whereas Wm. B. of N., esq., made his will and gave to Mary his dau., now wife of me, 40,000 lbs., and made his eldest s. Wm. Pym B., then of N., now of S[t] Chr., Esq., sole Ex'or. Release. (*Ibid.*, ii., p. 129.)

1752, April 22. Abednego Vanlamput Burt of N., esq., and the Hon. W[m] Mathew B. of S[t] Chr., Esq., sale of a moiety of 2 plantations of 250 a. and 60 a. (*Ibid.*, iv., p. 450.)

1753, Feb. 9. The Hon. Wm. Mathew Burt of S[t] Chr., Esq., confirms to Chas. Pym Burt of N., esq., that plant[n] l. of Abednego V. B., dec[d], of 250 a. Whereas the Hon. Wm. Pym B., l. Chief Justice of S[t] Chr., dec[d], father of Wm. Mathew B. and of Chas. P. B., by his will, made 21 Nov. 1748, gave his est. in N. to his two sons Chas. P. B. and Abed. V. B., and d. 4 Ap. 1750. His 3 sons Wm. M. B., Chas. P. B. and Abed. V. B. survived, and Abed. V. B. d. long since intestate and s.p. (*Ibid.*, v., p. 109.)

ARMS.—*Argent, on a chevron Gules between three bugle-horns stringed Sable, as many crosses crosslet of the first* (BURT).

(? Lieut. Daniel Lanhather, M. of C. 1660 and 1676.) = Jane . . . . Will dated 23 Oct. 1693, then of Nevis, widow; sworn 14 Feb. 1695-6.

- Col. Wm. Burt of Nevis, Planter 1670; M. of C. 1678; Deputy Governor 1685; died 1686. = ...
- Eliz. Lanhather, dau. and coheir. = Col. Charles Pym, Senr., President of Nevis, died 1699. (See *ante*, III., 50.)

- Col. Wm. Burt of Nevis, M. of C. 1692-3; President 1699 until his death in 1707. Will dated 15 Oct. and recorded 4 Nov. 1707. = Elizabeth Pym, granddau. of Mrs. Jane Lanhather 1693.
- Charles Pym of Nevis. Will dated 13 Dec. 1739; proved 16 April 1741 (132, Spurway); uncle of Wm. Pym Burt and Mrs. Eliz. Fox.

A

Mary Hill, one of the four daus. and coheirs of Joseph Hill of Morning Star plantation, Nevis; dead 1715. = Col. Wm. Pym Burt, eldest son, sole ex'or of his father's will; nephew of Chas. Pym of Nevis, planter, 1715; M. of C. 1722; removed to St. Kitts 1725; Chief Justice there; died 4 April 1750. Will dated 21 Nov. 1748; recorded at St. Kitts. = Louisa Mathew, youngest dau. of Gov. Sir Wm. Mathew; a minor 1704; living 1756.

B

Children by Mary Hill:

- Eliz. Burt, mar. 19 April 1730 at St. Thomas, Middle Island, St. Christopher, Wm. Eldrington Markham.
- Frances Burt, mar. 28 Aug. 1730 at Sandy Point, St. Christopher, Benj. Markham, Junr.

Child by Louisa Mathew:

- Wm. Mathew Burt, 1st son, M.P. Great Marlow 1761; Gov. of the Leeward Islands 1776; bur. at St. John's, Antigua, 28 Jan. 1781. Will dated 30 Dec. 1776; proved 27 Mar. 1781 (118, Webster). = Sarah Foster, dau. of Col. John Foster of Jamaica; born 1727; mar. at St. George, Hanover Square, 29 Aug. 1754; died at Bath June 1781. Will dated 18 Mar. and proved 13 Sept. 1781 (572, Webster).

C

- Chas. Pym Burt, son and heir, a minor 1781; died a bachelor.
- Eliz. Burt, a minor 1776.
- Louisa Burt, a minor 1776; mar. before 1789 Major Rich. Massey Hansard of Miskin, co. Glamorgan.
- Wm. Pym Burt, named 1756 in will of his aunt Mrs. Anne Gunthorpe.
- Chas. Pym Burt, born 29 and bur. 30 April 1751.

D

- John Morgan Burt, died at Bognor 27 Sept. 1799, aged 10.
- Robert Gascoigne Burt, posthumous son, born 1792; of Exeter College, Oxford; matric. 7 Dec. 1810, aged 18; B.A. 1814; M.A. 1818; Rector of St. Mary's, Hoo, 1816 until his death 18 Feb. 1875. = Joannah Smart, 3rd dau. of Mrs. Smart of the Strand; mar. April 1829 at St. Clement Danes.
- Third child.

1753, Aug. 14. Chas. Pym Burt and Kath. his wife. He was 2[d] s. of the late Hon. Wm. Pym B., Chief Justice. Recites Indre of Lease and Release of 3 Aug. 1750 between Chas. P. B., then of Grays Inn, and Kath B. his wife, then Kath. Wood, late of Red Lion Sq., then of Richmond, co. Surrey, spinster, whose marriage was to be solemnised. Her parents Robert Wood and Jane his wife. Kath Wood was entitled to ¼ of £10,000 at her mother's death. (Very long deed.) (*Ibid.*, v., pp. 205 to 225.)

John Burt of Nevis, Chirurgeon, ? father of Thomas Burt, M. of C. of Nevis 1737. = Jane Abram, mar. at St. John, Antigua, 1701.

Mary Burt, born 1688; mar. Wm. Weekes of Nevis, Esq., before 1730. He was Gunner of Fort Charles 1748. She died 2 April 1784, aged 96. M.I. at Charlestown, Nevis.

Eliz. Burt, widow of Capt. Anthony Fox and niece of Chas. Pym 1739. The will of Wm. Fox (probably her son) was dated 1749.

Cath. Wood, dau. and coheir of Robt. Wood, Doctor of Laws, and Jane his wife; mar. sett. dated 14 Aug. 1753. 1st wife. = Chas. Pym Burt, 2nd son, bapt. 22 Nov. 1726; M. of C., Nevis, 1753; sold his Tower Hill plantation there in 1769; resided for several years in St. Eustatius and St. Croix; later of Albemarle St.; died 30 June 1788; bur. at Isleworth. Will dated 1772; proved 1788 (385, Calvert). His arms in the Dutch Church impale four quartered coats. s.p. = Hester Duport, mar. 1762 at St. George Basseterre. 2nd wife. = Petronella Heyliger, dau. of John Heyliger, Governor of St. Eustatius; born 1742; bur. 11 June 1770, aged 28, in the Dutch Church, Austin Friars. M.I. Arms. 3rd wife. = Anna van Hemert, only dau. of John van Hemert of London, merchant; born 12 and bapt. 29 June 1748 at St. Dionys Backchurch; mar. 21 Sept. 1770; named 1778 in the will of her mother and 1782 of her uncle; sole heir 1802 of her son Wolfert.

Robert Burt, born 1760; of Trin. Coll., Camb.; LL.D., Vicar of Twickenham, where he died 17 Oct. 1791, aged 30. = Sarah Gascoyne, mar. at St. George, Hanover Square, 7 June 1786.

Charles Burt, born 1755 in the West Indies; Mid. R.N. and aged 18 in 1773; died 10 Nov. 1776.

Cath. Mathew Burt.

Jane Wood Burt, bapt. 20 Nov. 1753.

Ernestine von Staffeldt. 1st wife. = John Heyliger Burt, died 1856. = Augusta Margaretha Caroline Moltke, mar. 1831.

John Heyliger Burt, born 22 Oct. 1822.

Jeannetta Burt, born 3 May 1824; mar. Baron Cai von Brockdorff.

Maria Bertha Helena Burt, born 5 April 1826; mar. Helmuth Karl Barnardt von Moltke, Field-Marshal and Count; s.p.

Ernestine Burt, born 2 July 1839; mar. Wolfgang Knudson.

Henry Victor von Burt, born 15 Jan. 1841.

William Pym Burt, Chief Justice. Will dated 21 Nov. 1748. My wife Louisa £1000 and £300 a year. My est. in Nevis to my two sons Chas. Pym B. and Abednego Vanlemput B. My dau. Pen. Verchild £680. My dau. Ann Gunthorp £1000 c. My dau. Louise Frazier £200. My dau. Sus[a] Phipps £1000. My dau. Mary B. £1000. My son Daniel Mathew B. £1000. My dau. Margaret B. £1000. All residue to my eldest s. Wm. Mathew B. My 2[d] s. Cha.

A — A

Chas. Pym Burt of St. John's, Nevis. = Rebekah Wooley, named in the will of her mother Mrs. Eliz. Wooley dated 22 Nov. and proved 1 Dec. 1762; bur. 19 Feb. 1785, aged 83.

- James Burt, born 17 and bapt. 26 July 1732; named 1762 in the will of his grandmother.
- Child, bapt. 1733.
- Eliz. Burt, born 24 and bapt. 30 Oct. 1734.

B — B

- Abednego Burt, 3rd son, died 25 June 1730, aged 1½. M.I. at Sandy Point.
- Abednego Valemput Burt of Nevis, born 1730; died 2 Dec. 1752, aged 22, intestate. M.I. at Sandy Point.
- Daniel Mathew Burt, witness 1756 to will of his sister Mrs. Anne Gunthorpe.
- Edward Blake Burt, died 27 March 1739, aged 4. M.I.
- Penelope Burt, mar. 26 June 1735 Hon. James Verchild, and had 13 children bapt. 1736—57. President 1750 until his death in North America Sept. 1769.
- Mary Burt, mar. 9 March 1761 at St. Thomas, St. Kitts, Chas. Spooner. He died 1790. Will (352, Bishop), *ante*, I., 1.

F — F

E

John Heyliger Burt of Colton House, Lichfield, J.P., mar. 1796; died at sea June 1817. = Judith, dau. of Wm. Robinson of Hill Ridware, co. Staff.; died 1837. She mar. 1stly John Holden, Jun., of Sheepy Hall, co. Leic., who died 1 Dec. 1789; 2ndly, 30 May 1791, Rowland Farmer Okeover of Oldbury, co. Warwick (as his 2nd wife).

Louisa Burt, mar. 1stly, 12 June 1788 at St. George, Hanover Square, John Morgan of Tredegar, M.P.; 2ndly, 2 Oct. 1794, Geo. Tho. Smith, Capt. 2nd Life Guards, born 14 Jan. 1775; Sheriff of Carnarvon 1812. She died March 1815. He died 9 Sept. 1843.

G — H

- Wm. Pym Burt. = . . .
- Edward Burt.
- Henry Burt, 4th son, born 1802; of Worc. Coll., Oxford; matric. 2 April 1821, aged 19.
- Charlotte Eliza Burt, 1st dau., mar. at Freshford, co. Som., 19 April 1838, Luke Henry Wray, Com. R.N.

Children of Wm. Pym Burt:

- Wm. Burt.
- Henry Burt.
- Louisa Burt.
- Emma Burt.

Pym B. My s.-in-l. Col. John Gunthorp of A. a'n Ex'or. Ind. of 3 Sept. 1740, between me and my wife of the one part and His Exc^y Genl Mathew of the other. Sworn 6 June 1750. Cod. 28 March 1750. (St. Kitts Deeds, No. 4335.)

1762, Jan. 20. Chas. Pym B. of N., esq., sells to Cha. Spooner of St Chr., esq., Tower Hill plantation of 240 a. C. P. B. married Cath. his late wife, one of the daus. and coh. of Robert Wood of L., Dr. of Laws. (*Ibid.*, vol. l.)

A

Codrington Burt of St. Mary Cayon, owner of vessel 1736. = Mary, dau. of James Bisse, Senr.; deed of 1768.

Kemp Burt, posthumous son, bur. 8 Jan. 1742.

Eliz. Burt, born 16 May 1726; mar. 20 Dec. 1745 John Earle; living 1702. He was born 14 May 1722 and died 10 Nov. 1771, aged 49. M.I.

Mary Burt, bapt. 20 May 1726; died 1768.

Ann Burt, born 8 and bapt. 11 May 1728; mar. ? Jas. Friend, who died 1759.

B

Anne Mathew Burt, mar. 1stly Benj. Hutchinson; 2ndly Hon. Col. John Gunthorpe of Antigua. He died 26 Nov. 1754. Will sworn Dec. Her will dated 22 May 1756; sworn 18 May 1757.

Cath. Mathew Burt, born 1720; mar. 8 May 1741 Hon. Jas. Emra of Nevis. She died 11 Nov. 1745, aged 25. M.I. He mar. 2ndly, 13 July 1749, Rachel Yeamans of Antigua. He died 28 Dec. 1759, aged 37. M.I. at St. Peter's, Antigua.

Louisa Burt, mar. Alexr. Fraser, Surgeon of Dalzell's regt. at Antigua; three children bur. 1745—47. She and two daus. living 1756.

Susannah Burt, 5th dau., born 1724; mar. Francis Phipps. She died 17 Dec. 1748, aged 24. His will dated 5 June 1762. Recorded 27 Nov., No. 6933. M.I. *Ante*, II., 361.

Margt. Burt, born 16 April 1736; died 25 March 1739. M.I.

A 2nd Margaret living 1748.

F

Wolfert van Hemert Burt, died in Portman Sq. Dec. 1802. Will (669, Kenyon).

Nath. Burt.

Edward Burt, born at Abergavenny 1778; entered R.N. in 1795, aged 17; Comr. 1808; died at Worthing 18 Nov. 1859, aged 79 (*sic*). = Charlotte . . . ., died at Littlehampton 11 Jan. 1831.

Eliz. Burt, 1st dau. 1779; mar. 10 May 1800 Rear-Admiral Wm. Cumberland. He died 15 Nov. 1832, aged 67. M.I. in Cheltenham parish churchyard.

Anna Burt.

H

Anna Burt, 2nd dau., mar. 28 Feb. 1842 John Lewis of the Madras Army.

Sophia Cumberland Burt, 3rd dau., mar. at Freshford 19 April 1838 Walter Ettrick.

Evelina Pym Burt, 9th dau., died at Brixham 1 Jan. 1851.

A dau., mar. at Freshford 23 Feb. 1832 John Manning of London.

Wm. Burt of Nevis, Esq. Will dated 15 Oct. 1707. To my daus. Eliz. wife of Anthony Fox, Anne Burt, Frances B., Mary B. and Jane B. 40,000 lbs. of sugar each. Wife with child, if a boy, 50,000, if a girl, 40,000 lbs. To my sons Codrington B. and Cha. Pym B. 50,000 lbs. each. My wife Eliz. ⅓ of my estate in lieu of dower, plate during life, and a negro woman. All residue to my s. Wm. B. and sole Ex'or. Col. Rich[d] Abbott, Col. Tho. Butler and Mr. James Symonds of Nevis, and Col. Anthony Hodges and Cap. Geo. Weekes of S[t] Chr., Ex'ors in Trust and G.

Witnessed by Rich[d] Abbott, Jn[o] Norwood, Mich[l] Nowell, Carew Brodbelt, Eliz. Pym, Jane Isaacks. Sworn 4 Nov. 1707. From a copy in the P.R.O., B.T., Nevis, 12, p. 233. (Lt.-Col. H. W. Pook.)

Ann Gunthorpe the Y[r] of Antigua, widow and relict of John G. of A., Esq., deceased. Will dated 22 May 1756. M[rs] Cath. Warner, wife of M[r] Edward W., £10. My mother Louisa Burt £50. My sister Louisa Fraser £50. All residue to my s. Benj. Hutchinson at 21, and in default to my nephew Wm. Pym Burt s. of my brother Chas. Pym B. My l. husb[d] Benj. H. If my said nephew W. P. B. come into my est., then he to pay to my sister Louisa Fraser £300 c., and £100 a yr. to my mother Louisa Burt, and £100 to Ann Verchild dau. of Jas. V. of S[t] Chr., Esq., and £100 to Mathew Phipps dau. (*sic*) of Susannah P., dec[d], and £100 to Cath. Mathew Burt dau. of Cha. Pym B., and £100 c. each to each of my nieces Louisa Fraser and Ann Gunthorpe F., daus. of my sister Louisa F. Stephen Blizard, Alex. Fraser, and Tho. Warner, Esq., Ex'ors. Wit. by Daniel Mathew Burt, Jer. Blizard, Cha. W. Mann. By Gov. Thomas was sworn Ch. Wager Man, 18 May 1757. Recorded 14 July 1757 at Antigua.

Eliz. Woolley, l. of Nevis. n. of S[t] Chr., widow. Will dated 22 Nov. 1762. My granddaus. Mary King, Rebecca King, and Eliz. Burt dau. of Rebecca Burt. My godson Benj. King s. of my dau. Eliz. King. My godson James Burt. Sworn 1 Dec. 1762. (Lt.-Col. H. W. Pook.)

We, Chas. Pym Burt and Anna Burt his wife of Argyle Str., co. Mid[x], 3 Sep. 1772. Whereas I by Ind. dated 21 Sep. 1769 have settled £2000 S. Sea annuities on my four children by my 1st marr. with Cath. Wood, viz., W[m] Pym B., Rob[t] B., Chas. B. and Cath[n] Mathew B., and have also settled £3500 for them charged on the moiety of the plant[n] called S[t] Johns in the I. of S[t] Croix, I do confirm the same to be in lieu of legacies given them by the will of my l. wife Petronella B. and myself, dated 17 May 1768. She died of smallpox. My two ch[n] by my s[d] wife Petronella are John Heyleger B. and Louisa B. Whereas since her death I have married with Anna Van Hemert and previously settled £200 a year on her charged on my s[d] plant[n]. To my dau. Louisa B. £2000 at 21. Danish Church at S[t] Croix and the Hospital 50 rix dollars each. My s[d] plant[n] and all est. to my son John Heyliger B. in tail. John Jacob Dewindt and Ab. Heyliger Johnson at S[t] Eustatius, Tho. Lillie at S[t] Croix, Cha. Spooner and Dan[l] Mathew at London, and Messrs. Lewer and De Bruine, M[ts] at Amsterdam, T. and Ex. Translated from the Danish 13 Aug. 1788. *Cod.*, n. of Albemarle Str., Esq. I appoint Messrs. Hope and Co., M[ts] in Amsterdam, Sam. Thompson of S[t] Croix, my son John Heyliger B. of Albemarle Str., and my wife Anna B. T. and Ex, instead of those named in my will. I went to the W. I. in 1770 and left a will there with my bro.-in-l. by marriage, John Jacob de Windt at S[t] Eustatius, which I cancel. I have four ch[n] by my wife Anna, on whom is settled their mother's fortune, and they have also had legacies from their aunt Cath. Skricke and uncle Wolfert van Hemert. To my wife all furn., etc., coach and 2 coach horses. 11 May 1786. Codicils also 20 May and 19 July 1788. Proved 21 August 1788 by Anna B. the rel., and 24 Oct. by J. H. B., Esq., the son. (385, Calvert.)

Wolfert Van Hemert Burt of Crosby Square in the city of London, merchant. Will dated 16 Sept. 1802. To my mother Anna Burt all my estate and sole Ex'trix. Proved 23 Sept. 1802. (669, Kenyon.)

EXTRACTS FROM THE "GENTLEMAN'S MAGAZINE."

1786, June 7. Rev. Robert Burt, Chaplain in ordinary to the Prince of Wales, to Miss Gascoyne of Sunbury.

1789, Dec. 1. At Birmingham, John Holden Jun[r] esq. of Sheepy Hall co. Leicester.

1791, May 30. At Sheepy co. Leicester, Rowland Farmer Okeover esq. of Oldbury to Mrs. Holden of Sheepy.

1791, Oct. 17. At Twickenham, Rev. Robert Burt, Chaplain to the Prince of Wales, and vicar of that parish. He was in good health on the 14th inst. and had not then completed his 31st year. He has left two children and a pregnant widow to increase the general regret for his death.

1794, Oct. 2. George Thomas Smith esq. of the 2nd Reg. of Life Guards to M[rs] Morgan, widow of John Morgan esq. of Tredegar.

1799, Sept. 27. At Bognor Rocks aged 10, John Morgan Burt, eldest son of the late Rev. Robert Burt, vicar of Twickenham, Mid. who died 1791.

1815. At Tuxford, Louisa wife of George T. Smith Esq. of Pendyffryn, co. Carnarvon.

1816, April 3. At Bath, the lady* of Admiral Sir Henry Trollope.

1817, June. On his passage to England, J. H. Burt Esq. of Colton co. Stafford, and one of the County magistrates.

1829, April. At S[t] Clement Danes, the Rev. R. G. Burt, of S[t] Mary Rochester, to Joannah, third dau. of Mrs. Smart of the Strand.

1831, Jan. 11. At Little Hampton, Charlotte wife of Capt. Edward Burt, R.N.

1832, Feb. 23. At Freshford near Bath, John Manning Esq. of London, to Miss Burt, niece of Adm. Sir H. Trollope.

1838, Ap. 19. At Freshford, L. H. Wray, esq. Capt. R.N. to Charlotte Eliza; and at the same time, Walter Ettrick, esq. s. of the Rev. W. E., of High Barnes Park, Durham, to Sophia, eldest and third dau. of Capt. Edw. Burt, R.N. surviving nephew of his late Excellency W. Mathew Burt, esq. M.P. for Berks, and Gov.-gen. of the West Indies. (655.)

Adm. Sir Henry Trollope G.C.B. d. 2 Nov. 1839 a. 83. M.I. in S[t] James Bath. (1840, p. 320.)

1851, Jan. 1. At Brixham, Evelina Pym, ninth dau. of Capt. Edward Burt, R.N. (216.)

NOTES.

Sir Tho. Rich, Bart., Vice-Admiral of the Blue, in his will dated 2 June 1798, mentions his six natural children by Eliz. Burt. Proved 3 May 1803. (469, Marriott.)

Eliz. Burt, late of Stonehouse, co. Devon, now of Sonning, co. Berks, in her will dated 3 May 1804, after naming her six children by her late much beloved friend Sir Tho. Rich, states that she is entitled to £3500 charged upon her late father's estate in the W. I. by his will, and to £210 from the estate of her late brother. Proved 4 March 1805. (147, Nelson.) Sir Thomas had been married at S[t] George's, Hanover Sq., 15 July 1774, to Anne Willis, who survived him.

* In the Baronetage she is called "Fanny Burt." The Trollope family history gives no information about her.

This Eliz. Burt has not been identified. Chas. Pym Burt in his will of 1772 refers to £3500, but does not name a dau. Elizabeth. His brother Gov. W. M. Burt had a dau. Eliz., a minor in 1776.

Charles Burt, entered in the muster book of the "Seahorse" 8 Oct. 1773, born in the W. I., aged 18, Midshipman, died 10 Nov. 1776.

Edward Burt, born at Abergavenny, is half-brother of the late Lieut. Charles Burt, R.N. Entered the R.N. as a 1st class volunteer 12 Aug. 1795, aged 17; Midshipman 2 Sept. 1796; Lieut. 28 Dec. 1802; Commander 23 Jan. 1808; invalided June 1810; pensioner of Greenwich Hospital 25 June 1842; on the reserved list July 1851. He has an eldest dau. Charlotte Eliz., m. to Commander L. H. Wray, R.N.; and a second dau. Anna, m. 28 Feb. 1842 to John Lewis, Esq., of the Madras Army, s. of the late Rear-Adm. J. M. Lewis. (O'Byrne's "Naval Biog. Dict.," 1849, and "Naval Records.")

ST. THOMAS, MIDDLE ISLAND, ST. KITTS.

*1730 Apr. 19 Mr William Eldrington Markham and Elizabeth dau. of Judge Burt, both of Sandy Point.

†1730 Sept. 24 Mr Benjn Markham, junr, and Miss Frances Burt dau. of Wm Pym Burt, Esq.

1761 Mar. 9 Mary Burt and Charles Spooner.

ST. GEORGE'S, BASSETERRE, ST. KITTS.

1762 — Charles Pym Burt and Hester Duport, jr. Lyc.

ST. JOHN'S, FIGTREE, NEVIS.

1732 July 26 James s. of Charles Pym Burt and Rebekah his wife, b. ye 17 July, bapt.

1733 — . . . . ym Burt & Rebekah . . . ., bapt.

ST. GEORGE'S, HANOVER SQUARE, CO. MIDDX.

1786 June 7 The Rev. Robert Burt, Clerk, of this p., and Sarah Gascoyne of Sunbury. Wit.: Chas Pym Burt, John G. Fanshaw, John Morgan.

ISLEWORTH, CO. MIDDX.

According to a plan made at the restoration of the church about 1866 the vault No. 32 of Charles Pym Burt was filled in. There appears to be no tablet to him.

* Also in the register at Sandy Point.

† Also in the register at Sandy Point, where the month is 28 August. (Lt.-Col. H. W. Pook.)

Rawlins of St. Kitts.

Henry Rawlins late of St Chr., now of Lower Grosvenor Street, Esq., 1782. My wife Mary Hill R., plate, furniture, horses and £700 a year. Benj. Markham Brotherson of St Chr., Esq., and Lewis Brotherston now of G^t^ B., Esq., trustees. Proved 1782. (149, Gostling.)

Fra. Degen of Hammersmith, 19 March 1783. My friend Mrs. Hartman, dau. to Mr. Joseph Rawlins of St. Kitts, £500. (*Ante*, I., 292.) (507, Cornwallis.)

Stedman Rawlins of St Chr., Esq., 1793. My wife Eliz. Taylor R. £600 a year. Estate to sons Stedman and William. My brothers John, Henry, Rich^d^ and Joseph R. My sisters Mary Satterthwaite, Eliz. Young. and Ann Akers. My late father Stedman R. Testator died Dec. 1793 at St Andrew's, Holborn. (A long will.) (526, Harris.)

Joseph Rawlins late of the I. of St Chr., now of the Town of Baltimore in Maryland. Will dated 13 Sept. 1793. All my plantation to my sons-in-law J. H. Wallwyn and Edmund Fleming Akers, my nephew Stedman R. and my friend William Manning, M^t^ in L., Esq^res^ on trust to pay my son Joseph R. £200 a year, and the residue to be divided into 7 parts. 5 shares to my 5 daus. Ann Hutchinson Wallwin, Mary Estridge Hartman, Eliz. van Wych, Rebecca Hutchinson Thomas and Frances Akers, 1/7 to my s^d^ son Joseph R. and 1/7 to my two grandchildren Maria R. and Henry R., children of my late son Henry R. Codicil, 3 Feb. 1794. Baltimore, 13 Apr. 1795, sworn. Proved 5 Apr. 1797. (Very short abstract.) (269, Exeter.)

Will of Henry Rawlins. Mentions his wife Eliz^th^ (*née* Wilkes), sons Stedman, Henry, Worthington and John, and daus. Ann Maynard, Caroline Galpine, Fra. E. Tyson, Rose R. and Reb^ca^ R. He died 1823. (Nevis Records.)

ST. THOMAS, MIDDLE ISLAND.

Baptisms.

1731	May 30	Joseph s. of Mr Henry Rawlins and Ann his Wife; b. 25.
1768	Nov. 19	Richard s. of Stedman and Mary Rawlins; b. Oct. 15, 1764.
1769	July 16	Henry s. of Stedman and Mary Rawlins; b. July 7, 1761.
		Joseph s. of Stedman and Mary Rawlins; b. Apr. 2, 1768.
		Eliz^th^ dau. of Stedman and Mary Rawlins; b. Nov. 12, 1762.
		Ann dau. of Stedman and Mary Rawlins; b. Oct. 15, 1764.
1784	July 2*	Henry s. of Henry and Eliz^th^ Rawlins; b. Nov. 9, '84.
1784	Sept. 10	Stedman s. of Henry and Eliz^th^ Rawlins; b. Aug. 24, '82.
1790	Oct. 8	Stedman s. of Rich^d^ and Eliz^th^ Rawlins; b. June 20, 1789. Sponsors: Robt Spence and Stedman Rawlins, Esq., Mrs Frances Spence and Miss Rebecca Walters.

* There must be an error in this entry.

ARMS.—*Azure, three swords barwise, the points to dexter.*
CREST.—*An arm in armour embowed, couped, in the hand a dagger.*
MOTTO.—STRIKE HOME. [Seal of John Hart Rawlins of *circa* 1820—30 and bookplate.]

Elizabeth . . . ., bur. at Christ Church 7 Nov. 1722. ═ Henry Rawlins of Christ Church, Nichola Town, St. Kitts. ═ Ann . . . .

Eliz., bapt. at Christ Church 4 Aug. 1722; bur. there 10 March 1722-3.

Henry Rawlins, bapt. at Christ Church 17 Oct. 1724; of Lower Grosvenor St., Esq. Will proved 1782 (149, Gostling). ═ Mary Hill Brotherson, dau. of Lewis Brotherson of St. Christopher, Esq.; single in 1775. s.p.

Steadman Rawlins, bapt. at Christ Church 21 Dec. 1725; dead 1793; named in his son's will; died 6 June 1788, aged 63. ═ Mary Johnson, dau. of John Johnson; born 24 Jan. 1733; mar. 31 Dec. 1752; died in England 18 Nov. 1797.

A

B

Steadman Rawlins of St. Kitts and St. Andrew's, Holborn, Esq., died 12 Dec. 1793 (526, Harris). ═ Eliz. Taylor.

John Rawlins, born 5 April 1757; died 25 May 1800 in England. ═ Sarah Johnson Hart, 3rd dau. of Wm. Hart; mar. 5 April (? 1784); died Aug. 1837, aged 76.

C

Steadman Rawlins, born 1784; President 1817—1821; named 1793 in the will of his uncle Joseph; matric. from Christ Church, Oxford, 22 Oct. 1801, aged 17; Acting Govr. of the Leeward Islands in 1817; living 1840. ═ Gertrude Tyson, mar. 28 March 1805.

Mary, born 1 Dec. 1789; bapt. 5 Jan. 1791.

Henry Rawlins, born 21 Feb., bapt. 2 March 1791.

Joseph Rawlins, born 23 and bapt. 25 July 1792.

Anne Taylor Rawlins, mar. 22 Aug. 1803, at Eltham, Capt. Rawlins of the 30th Foot.

William Wharton Rawlins, M. of C.; Speaker 1821; died 9 Dec. 1840 at St. Kitts. ═

James Tyson Rawlins, bapt. 1 Jan. 1814.

William Wharton Rawlins, bapt. 1 Jan. 1814.

John Rawlins, died Oct. 1839 at Sandy Point.

Louisa Frances, 3rd dau., mar. 12 Dec. 1844, at St. Kitts, Rob. Murray Rumsey, Col. Sec.

This pedigree is believed to be fairly accurate. It has been checked with one in the possession of Mr. John Bromley. There must be many deeds in the Record Office at St. Kitts relating to Rawlins.

1790 Nov. 14 William Henry s. of Hy and Elizth Rawlins; b. Jan. 27, 1788. Sponsors: Mr Wilkes, Mr Henry Sprott, Mrs Wilkes and Mrs Garnett.

1790 Nov. 14 John s. of Henry and Elizth Rawlins; b. Apr. 18, 1789. Sponsors: John Rawlins and James Akers, jun., Esq., Miss Hart.

1790 Nov. 14 Worthington s. of Henry and Elizth Rawlins; b. Oct. 15, 1790. Sponsors: Stedman Rawlins and Joseph Rawlins, Esqrs, Mrs S. Rawlins.

A

Joseph Rawlins, bapt. at Christ Church 30 June 1727; bur. there 25 Aug. 1729.

Charles Rawlins.

Ruth Rawlins, dau. of Henry Rawlins; mar. Chas. Lowndes, who removed to South Carolina and died March 1736, leaving three sons.

Mary, mar. .... Satterthwaite.

Eliz., born 12 Nov. 1762; mar. at St. Kitts, 21 June 1787, Capt. Anthony Young.

Ann, born 15 Oct. 1764; twin with Richard; mar. 9 Sept. 1784 James Akers.

B

Henry Rawlins, born 7 July 1761. See Pedigree A.

Richard Rawlins, born 15 Oct. 1764; twin with Ann. = Eliz. Maillard, mar. 4 Sept. 1788.

Joseph Rawlins, born 2 April 1768. See Pedigree B.

C

Rev. William Henry Rawlins, born 1785; died 14 Jan. 1840, aged 55, leaving 8 children. = Eliz. ....

Anthony Rawlins, Barrister.

John Hart Rawlins, born April 1795; M. of A. for Trinity, St. Kitts, 1821; Lieut. of 13th Regt.; died 1840. See his seal. = Martha Hart Wilson, dau. of Wm. Ponsonby Wilson of Glasgow; born 1803; mar. 1820; died 18 Feb. 1833.

Stedman Rawlins, born 20 June 1789; bapt. 8 Oct. 1790.

Mary Ann, born 24 Aug. 1791; bapt. 29 July 1793.

John Rawlins, born 5 Sept., bapt. 27 Dec. 1790.

Richard Rawlins, born 21 Oct. 1792; bapt. 12 May 1793.

Frances, bapt. at St. John's, Nevis, 28 Dec. 1835.

Alice Hart Rawlins, born 3 Jan. 1828; died 23 Feb. 1906 in London; mar. 26 May 1846, at St. George, Basseterre, Tho. B. Hardtman-Berkeley of St. Kitts, later President and C.M.G. He died 6 Nov. 1881. Clock Tower in Basseterre and Reredos in St. Peter's, Basseterre, to his memory.

1790 Dec. 27 John s. of Richd and Elizth Rawlins; b. Sept. 5, 1790. Sponsors: Adam Sprott and Peter Maillard, Esqrs, Mrs Mary Sprott and Mrs Mary Bryan Webb.

PEDIGREE A.

Henry Rawlins of Nevis. Will recorded there. Born 1760; Acting Govr. of the Leeward Islands in 1815; bur. at St. Geo.* 24 Oct. 1823, aged 63. = Eliz., dau. of .... Wilkes; bur. at St. Geo., Nevis, 23 Aug. 1826, aged 64.

- Stedman Rawlins of St. George's, Nevis, Esq., born 24 Aug. 1782; bapt. 10 Sept. 1784. =
- Henry Rawlins, born 9 Nov. 1784. — William Henry Rawlins, born 27 Jan. 1788; bapt. 14 Nov. 1790. — John Rawlins, born 18 April 1789; bapt. 14 Nov. 1790.
- Worthington Rawlins, born 15 Oct. and bapt. 14 Nov. 1790; ? M. of A. for Trinity, St. Kitts, 1821.
- Anna Margaret, 3rd dau., born 15 April 1792; bapt. 17 Feb. 1793; mar. 27 Oct. 1814, at St. John's, Wm. Maynard, Esq.
- Caroline Galpine. — Frances, mar. E. Tyson. — Rose. — Rebecca.

Children of Stedman Rawlins:

- Richard Johnson Rawlins, bapt. at St. Geo. 10 and bur. 25 Sept. 1820.
- Stedman Akers Rawlins, died 28 Aug. 1850, aged 43. M.I. at St. Geo., Nevis. = Eliz. Maynard, born 1815; mar. at St. Geo. 20 Nov. 1834; died 23 March 1891, aged 76.

Anna Rawlins, mar. at St. John's, Nevis, 18 Dec. 1855, Sholto Tho. Pemberton, Chief Justice of Dominica. He was bur. at St. Tho., Nevis, 30 June 1889. (*Ante*, I., 271.)

1791 Jan. 5 Mary dau. of Stedman and Eliz[th] Rawlins; b. Dec. 1, 1789. Sponsors: Joseph Rawlins, Esq., the brother of the above Stedman Rawlins, Esq., Miss Rittah Garnett.

1791 Mar. 2 Henry s. of Stedman and Eliz[th] Rawlins; b. the 21st ...., 1791. Sp[rs]: Joseph Rawlins, Esq. (brother of S.), Miss Rittah Garnett.

1792 July 25 Joseph s. of Stedman and Eliz[th] Rawlins; b. 23 inst.

1793 Feb. 17 Ann Marg[t] dau. of Henry and Eliz[th] Rawlins; b. Ap[l] 15th. Sponsors: Adam Sprott, Esq., Miss Sarah Wilkes and Miss Mary Johnson Rawlins.

1793 May 12 Rich[d] s. of Rich[d] and Eliz[th] Rawlins; b. Oct. 21, 1792. Adam Sprott, Joseph Rawlins, jun[r], Mich[l] Maillard, Esq[rs], M[rs] Mary Maillard.

1793 July 29 Mary Ann dau. of Rich[d] and Eliz[th] Rawlins; b. Aug[t] 24, 1791. Henry Rawlins and Joseph Rawlins, jun., Esq., M[rs] Eliz[th] Young and M[rs] Eliz[th] Rawlins, Sen.

1794 Apr. 4 Sarah dau. of Henry and Eliz[th] Rawlins; b. Nov. 20, 1793. Henry Hart, Anthony Young, Rich[d] Rawlins, Esq[rs], M[rs] Hart, M[rs] Young and M[rs] Rawlins.

* I have a note that President Henry Rawlins died 18 Nov. 1815. One of his daus. mar. 12 June 1806 James Davoren.

Pedigree B.

Joseph Rawlins, late of St. Kitts, then of Baltimore. See Close Roll dated 1761. Died 31 Jan. 1795. Will dated 13 Sept. 1793; proved 5 April 1797 (269, Exeter). ═ . . . ., died in U.S.A. July 1792.

Children:

- Joseph Rawlins, Junr., to have £200 a year; ? mar. 29 May 1806 Eliz. Caines; dead 1817. His miniature *penes* Dr. F. H. Markoe of New York. ═ Frances Ann, 1st dau. of Wm. Payne Georges of St. Chr. and Manchester Square; named in her father's will of 1800.
- Henry Rawlins, died v.p. ═
- Ann Hutchinson, mar. J. H. Wallwin.
- Mary Estridge, mar. Isaac Hartman. They had 6 children; 1st child born 1777. She was named 1783 in will of Fra. Degen.
- Eliz., mar. . . . . van Wych.
- Rebecca Hutchinson, mar. . . . . Thomas.
- Frances, mar. Edm. Fleming Akers, later of Berrymead Priory, Acton, co. Middlesex. She died 31 Dec. 1811. He mar. 2ndly, in Feb. 1816, Miss Cath. Dewhurst of Baker Street, and died 16 Feb. 1821 at Brussels.

Child of Joseph Rawlins, Junr.:

- Frances George, mar. Lieut. J. Rawlins Thomas, R.N. She died at St. Kitts 10 June 1817.

Children of Henry Rawlins:

- Henry Rawlins.
- Maria.

Both named in the will of their grandfather Joseph.

1795	July	2	Elizth Frances dau. of Henry and Elizth Rawlins; May 7, '95. John Rawlins, Adam Sprott, Esq^{rs}, Mrs Sarah J. Rawlins, Miss Rebecca Walters.
1795	July	26	Henry s. of Rich^{d} and Elizth Rawlins; b. Feb. 22, '94. Henry Rawlins, Esq., by his friend Adam Sprott, Esq., and Joseph Rawlins, Esq., Mrs Mary Satterthwaite and Mrs Elizth Rawlins, W. of Hy. Rawlins, Esq.
	—		Elizth dau. of Rich^{d} and Elizth Rawlins; b. July '95. John Rawlins and Henry Hart, Esq^{rs}, Mrs Sarah J. Rawlins and Mrs Elizth Young.
1795	July	30	Elizth dau. of Rich^{d} and Elizth Rawlins; b. July 1, '95. Godf^{rs}: John Rawlins and Henry Hart, Esq^{rs}. G^{mns}: Mrs Sarah J. Rawlins, M^{rs} . . . . Young.
1814	Jan.	1	James Tyson s. Honble Stedman Rawlins and his wife Gertrude. Sponsors: the Hon. John Julius, Thomas Tyson, Esq., Miss Sarah Tyson and Miss Christian Tyson.
1814	Jan.	1	William Wharton s. of Hon. Stedman Rawlins and his wife Gertrude. Spou^{s}: Hon. John Garnett, David Elliot, Clement Challenger, Esq^{rs}, Mrs Elliot and Mrs Stedman Rawlins.
1814	Jan.	1	Thos Charles Corry, s. of above. Richd Rawlins and Thos Charles Stewart Corry, Esq^{rs}, Mrs Richd Rawlins and Mrs Rebecca Walters.

BURIALS.

1733 Aug. 12 Mr Henry Rawlins.
1768 Oct. 31 Mary R.
1788 Feb. 17 Miss Sally R.
1791 Jan. 7 Mary infant dau. of Stedman and Eliz. R.
1791 Mar. 2 Henry s. of Stedman and Elizth R., from the Estate called The Walk.
1792 Aug. 3 Joseph infant s. of Stedman and Elizth R.
1793 Oct. 26 Mary Ann dau. of Rich. and Elizth R.
1797 Feb. 3 Eliz. dau. Richard and Elizth R., from his Estate called Somarsalls, Sandy Pt.
1800 Dec. 16 William s. of Richard and Elizth R., from his Estate called Somarsalls (Sandy Point).
1802 Dec. 19 Mary infant dau. of Rich. and Eliz. R., from his Estate called Newtons.

MARRIAGES.

1738 Sept. 21 Joseph Peets and Mary Rawlins, spin.
1777 June 15 John Satterthwaite and Mary Rawlins.
1784 Sept. 9 James Akers and Ann Rawlins; by Lic.
1788 Sept. 4 Richd Rawlins and Elizth Maillard, spin.; by Lic.
1822 Nov. 14 Under Licence, Revd William Henry Rawlins, curate of St Ann's, Sandy Point, bachelor, and Elizabeth Rawlins Maillard, eldest daughter of Peter Maillard, Esq., spinster. At Old Road, by the Revd J. H. Walwyn, minister of St Ann's, Sandy Point, and St Paul's, Capisterre.
1828 May 15 Wm Bryan P. Point and Frances Rawlins of Middle Isld.
1832 Mar. 22 Howard Maillard Clifton, M.D., widower, St Geo. Basseterre, and Harriet Elizth Rawlins of M. Ild.

CHRIST CHURCH, NICHOLA TOWN, ST. CHRISTOPHER.

BAPTISMS.

1722 Eliz. D. of Henry and Eliz. Rawlings, Augst 4th.
1724 Henry S. of Henry and Ann Rawlings, 8ber 17th.
1725 Steadman S. of Henry and Ann Rawlings, xber 21st.
1727 Joseph S. of Henry and Ann Rawlings, June 30th.
1729 Charles S. of Henry and Ann Rawlings, April 26th.

BURIALS.

1722 Buried Eliz. wife of Henry Rawlings, 9ber 7th.
— Eliz. Daugtr of Henry Rawlings, March 10th, 1722/3.
1729 Joseph S. of Henry and Ann Rawlings, Augst 25th.

(*Ante*, I., 37, 38.)

ST. JOHN'S FIGTREE, NEVIS.*

1835 Dec. 28 Frances d. of William Henry and Elizabeth Rawlins (clerk). Bap.
1855 Dec. 18 Sholto Thomas Pemberton and Ann Rawlins. Mar.

* I think these entries were sent me by the late Maj.-Gen. R. B. Pemberton.

1814 Oct. 27 Wm Maynard, Esq., and Anna Margaret 3rd d. of Henry Rawlins, Esq.* Mar.
1856 Oct. 16 Stedman Bayford Rawlins of St Kitts, Bach., and Mary Woodley Caines of St. John's, Spr. Mar. Lic.

ST. GEORGE'S, GINGERLAND, NEVIS.

1820 Sep. 10 Richard Johnson s. of Stedman Rawlins, Esq., and his wife. Bap.
1834 Nov. 20 Stedman Akers Rawlins, Bach., and Elizabeth Maynard, Spr, both of St George's Parish. Mar.
1820 Sep. 25 Richard Johnson inf. s. of Mr and Mrs Stedman Rawlins. Bur.
1823 Oct. 24 Henry Rawlins, Esq., æt. 63. Bur.
1826 Aug. 23 Mrs Elizabeth Rawlins, æt. 64, wid. of Henry Rawlins, Esq. Bur.

1771. Mr Rawlins then in St Kitts and his children in England. "Mr Joe Rawlins has taken a house within 3 miles of Exeter." (Lt.-Col. H. R. Phipps.)

1787, June 21. At St. Kitts, Capt. Anth. Young, to Miss Rawling, dau. of Stidman (*sic*) R. esq. ("G.M.," 738.)

1803, Aug. 22. At Eltham, Kent, Capt. Rawlins, of the 30th foot, to Miss Anne Taylor R. dau. of the late Stedman R. esq. of St. Kitts. (*Ibid.*, 788.)

1815. The Hon. Henry Rawlins then acting Gov. of the Leeward Islands ("Antigua," i., cxlix) and Stedman Rawlins in 1817.

1817, June 10. At the estate of her late father, Joseph Rawlins, esq. at St. Christopher, where she went for the recovery of her health, Frances George, wife of Lieut. J. Rawlins Thomas, R.N. great niece of Gen. Sir William Payne, bart. and of the late Lord Lavington. And Sept. 7, at Stonehouse, Devon, aged 8 months, Frances Anne, infant dau. of the above. ("G.M.," 282.)

1821. Stedman Rawlins, President.
Hon. Wm. W. Rawlins, J.P., M. for St Tho., Middle I., and Speaker.
Stedman Rawlins, M. for St John's, Cabbesterre.
John H. Rawlins and Worthington Rawlins, M's for Trinity P. pt.

1839, Oct. 22. At Sandy Point on Thursday last Mr. John Rawlins, a son of Stedman R., Senr, Esq. ("St. Chr. Advertiser.")

1840, Jan. 3. On Saturday morning at Rawlins Mornes Estate, Mr. William R. a son of Stedman R., Esq., sen. ("St. Chr. Gazette.")

1840, Jan. 14. At Nevis, on Tuesday last the Rev. W. H. R. aged 55 years, leaving eight children to lament their irreparable loss. ("St. Chr. Advertiser.")

1840, Dec. 9. At St. Chr. Wm. Wharton R. ("G.M.," 1841, 558.)

1844, Dec. 12. At St. Chr. Robert Murray Rumsey, Colonial Secretary, to Louisa-Frances, 3d dau. of the late Hon. Wm. Wharton R. member of H.M. Council in that island. (*Ibid.*, 1845, 311.)

There are Close Rolls of the years 1761, 1764 and 1794 noted *ante*, I.

Charles Lowndes, bap. 6 Dec. 1658, by Sarah his wife had a son Charles, who settled at St Kitts and later removed to Charlestown, S. Carolina. He m. Ruth dau. of Henry Rawlins, and died March 1736, leaving 3 sons. (See pedigree of Lowndes in Burke's "Landed Gentry," 7 Ed., p. 1145, and *ante*, I., 333.) Ruth's mother is supposed to have been Ruth Garner, a widow, of St. Kitts. (E. H. Hillman.)

---

* This marriage is also recorded at St. George's. He is there styled "Hon."

Hussey of Montserrat.

This Ind're made 10 Dec. 21 Geo. II. 1747 Between Tho. Lee of the I. of Montserrat but now residing in the parish of S[t] George the Martyr Esq. of the one part and Peter Hussey of L. M[t] of the other part Wit. that T. L. for £500 p[d] by P. H. sells all that capital messuage in the Town of Plymouth in s[d] I. bounded S. with the great street, E. with the house and ground of Wm. Chambers, W. with the house and grounds of Tho. Meade, N. with the lands of John Cooper and D[r] Jas. Schaw. Lease of 9 Dec. precedes the above. (Close Roll, 5878.)

This Ind're made the 18 Jan. 23 Geo. II. 1749 Between Peter Hussey of L. Merch[t] of the one p[t] and Jas. Davenport of L. wharfinger of the other Whereas by Ind'res of L. and R. dated 9 and 10 Dec. 1747 Tho. Lee of the I. of Montserratt but then residing in the parish of S[t] Geo. the Martyr Esq. for £500 st. sold to Peter Hussey the capital messuage of him T. L. in the town of Plymouth now P. H. for £600 p[d] by Jas. D. sells the same by way of mortgage for a year to the use of Peter Hussey and Bridget his wife.

The lease of 17 Jan. precedes the above. (Close Roll, 5872.)

This Ind're made 1 Feb. 24 Geo. II. 1750 Between Walter Lawrence of Lissregan co. Galway Esq. of the one part and James Hussey of Montserat Esq. of the other Whereas John Scott late of Greenish co. Gallway g[t] dec[d] being seized of a pl[n] in the Windward Div[n] called the Mountain pl[n] in Little Garden Hill did by his will dated 13 July 1746 bequeath to his dau. Mary Scott (then an inf't.) at 18 £500 st. and the residue to his s. Rob. Scott (then also an inf.) and appointed his brother Marcus ffrench, his brother John ff. and others Ex'ors and d. soon after and Rob. S. the inf. d. before 21, and the fee became vested in Mary S. as h. at l. and sole dau. and she m. John Lawrence Esq. by whom she had issue only the s[d] W[r] L. and Whereas by Ind'res of L. and Rel. of 17 and 18 Ap. 1747 between s[d] John ffrench of Rahashane co. Galway Esq. the Ex'or Edmond Kelly of Balygarty co. G. gt. and Anstace K. otherwise Scott otherwise ffrench wife of s[d] Edm[d] K. then lately the widow of John Scott of the one part and Peter Hussey of M. merch[t] of the other reciting that J. S. was seized of s[d] pl[n] in the possession of P. H. by art. of sett. previous to the m. of s[d] J. S. and Anstace did settle £60 a yr. on her as jointure and Peter H. owed £600 st. arrears of rent J. F., Edm[d] K. and A. his wife agreed to sell the said pl. to P. H. for £1000 st. they in consideration of £1600 conveyed est. to P. H. Mary Scott to confirm when of age of 21 and the considered sum was p[d] to Cha. Hamilton l. of Grays Inn Esq. (since dec[d]) by a p. of att[y] to which John L. was a witness and whereas John L. and Mary his wife d. long since and Mary having d. before 21 and Peter H. is dead and Jas. is his eldest s. and h. at l. and disputes having arisen they were submitted to Augustin Boyd of L. M[t] and Jas. Egan of St. Geo. the Martyr Esq. as arbitrators they on 29 Nov. last past awarded that W. L. sh[d] execute a good title to J. H. and J. H. sh[d] pay £875, £75 to be abated. Release of all claims. W. L. now conveys s[d] pl[n] of 44 acres with the mills negroes and stock. (On skins 36, 37 and 38.) Skin 35 is the lease for one year made the 31 Jan. (Close Roll, 5836.)

Peter Hussey of Montserrat, merchant, lessee of the = Mountain plantation 1747; dead 1750.

James Hussey, Esq., eldest son and heir 1750, when he purchased the Mountain plantation (Close Roll, 5856); executed bonds in 1757 and 1768; dead 1774. =

Peter Hussey of L., mercht. 1747; abroad in 1758; of Guadeloupe 1764. = Bridget ...., releases her dower 1758.

Bridget Hussey, mar. 10 Nov. 1724 Patrick Roche, Esq. His will dated at Bath 22 Nov. 1763; proved 16 Aug. 1764 (325, Simpson.)

Mary Hussey, mar. 23 June 1724 Tho. Meade, Esq., who died about 1763. His will dated 9 Oct. 1758 (455, Pakenham).

James Hussey, son of Peter Hussey 1764.

James Hussey the younger of M., son and heir, mortgaged in 1768 Hamonds, Dyers and Germans Bay plantations; died abroad insolvent before 1800.

Catherine Hussey, mar. about 1757 Daniel McNamara of Lincoln's Inn Fields, barrister. His will dated 29 Nov. 1793; proved 13 Feb. 1800 (128, Adderley). He died at Streatham 20 Jan. 1800, aged 88.

Walter Hussey of Montserrat, Esq., 1794.

Tho. Hussey of Antigua. Will dated 1778 in M. = Martha ...., sister of Cath. Murphy; mar. sett. dated 13 June 1766. In 1793 had £3000 secured on Chateau Belair, St. Vincent.

Tho. Hussey of Essequibo. Will dated 4 May 1802; proved 3 March 1803 (210, Marriott). *Vide ante*, II., 383.

Mary Hussey of Baker Street, widow, 1801. = Michael White of Chateau Belair, St. Vincent, ? 2nd son of Hon. Mich. W. of Antigua.

Catherine, living 1807. — Antoinetta.

Martha. — Eliz.

Michael White, eldest son and heir, sole heir 1802 to his uncle Tho. H.; of Baker Street 1807.

John White.

Lydia.

Eliz.

Bridget Hussey wife of Peter H. send greeting Whereas by the within deed of release the s[d] P. H. doth covenant with Jas. Davenport that he P. H. and Bridget his wife will next Hilary term levy a fine and execute such other act as by the law of Montserrat is tantamount to a fine to assure to J. D. the house and lands and Whereas P. H. is beyond the seas now B. H. to bar all dower and for 10*s*. release to J. D. all my dower 14 Dec. 32 Geo. II., 1758. She appeared on 19 Dec. and acknowledged the above deed poll. (Close Roll, 6023.)

This Ind're made the 8 Dec. 5 Geo. III. 1764 Between James Hussey of L. gt. s. of Peter H. late of L. M[t] now of Guadeloupe of the one part and Jas. Doran of the p. of Allhallows Barkin mariner of the other. Whereas Mary Farrill wife of R[d] F. of the I. of M. Esq. by her Will dated the 19 Jan. 1764 did by virtue of the power reserved in her m. sett. bequeath to Jas. Hussey n. or l. of L. gt. s. of Peter H. l. of L. M[t] now or late of G. all her lands and real est. comprized in the s[d] sett. to s[d] Jas. H. now he for £400 st. p[d] by Jas. D. sells him the land called the Wash as mortgage and J. H. appoints Chas. Mollineux and W[m] Irish of M. his attornies. (Close Roll, 6161.)

This Ind're made the 14 Nov. 15 Geo. III. 1774 Between John Dyer late of the I. of M. but at present of the p. of S[t] George Hanover Sq. Esq. of the one part and Jas. Hussey of M. Esq. s. and h. of Jas. H. l. of M. Esq. dec[d] of the other Whereas by Ind'res of 27 and 28 Feb. 1748 made between s[d] John Dyer and Mary his wife since dec[d] of the one part and s[d] Jas. H. the father since dec[d] of the other in consideration of £2700 p[d] by J. H. to J. D. and M. they conveyed to J. H. all that pl[n] in the parish of S[t] Anthony bounded N. and W. with R[d] Cooke Esq. formerly the lands of W[m] Finch gt. bounded E. with Nineteen Gutt S. with lands called Symes pl[n] at the head with the Mountain containing 100 a. also that parcel of land in S[t] Geo. bounded S. with above land E. and N. with l'ds of Tho. Cross dec[d] then l. in the poss. of Peter H. dec[d] W. with lds. lately Martin Frenches c. 22 a. called Dogleap also Allers's pl[n] in S[t] Geo. c. 60 a. except the house where Daniel Allers then lived and 4 a N. with Brian M[c]Mahon dec[d] S. the River c. Col. Geo. Wykes's River E. Edw. Parson Esq. called Cross's Land W. Col. R[d] Cooke dec[d] and Whereas Jas. H. the father d. leaving Jas. H. his s. and h. and Mary Dyer is also dead and doubts having arisen to confirm the title J. D. confirms. (Close Roll, 6380.)

Daniel Macnamara of Stretham, co. Surrey (Esq. in margin). Will dated 29 Nov. 1793. All estate to my wife Catherine and appoint her sole Ex'trix. In the presence of Maria Macnamara, Henry Thomas, Thos. Meade. Proved 13 Feb. 1800 by C. M., widow, the relict. (128, Adderley.)

1800, Jan. 20. Aged 88, John (*sic*) Macnamara, esq. of Streatham, Surrey. ("G.M.," 184.)

ST. GEORGE'S, MONTSERRAT.

1724 June 23 Thomas Mead & Mary Hussy, by L.
1724 Nov. 10 M[r] Patrick Roch & Bridget Hussy, by L.

Robert Hussey of London had sons Edward, George, Robert, Peter and Joseph, all in Barbados in 1666. (Berry's "Sussex and Surrey.")

Oliver and Royall of Massachusetts and Antigua.

Col. Robert Oliver, second son of the Hon. Col. Richard Oliver of St. John's, Antigua, was born in 1700, but his baptism is not on record there. At his father's death in 1716 he received a legacy of £1500 c., and then purchased "Graers" of 56 acres for £1500 c., and "Duggans" of 40 acres for £360 c., and with other lands formed a plantation of 120 acres in Nonsuch, N. of St. Philip's Church, about 12 miles from St. John's. In 1726, on the death of the widow of his uncle Robert Oliver, he succeeded to a plantation of 80 acres in New North Sound, on the N. side of Gunthorpes, but this being neglected and ruinous he obtained a private Act in 1731 for the sale of it to Lt.-Gov. Edw. Byam for £1127 c., which sum was then charged on his estate at Nonsuch.

He had married in 1721-22 Anne Brown, only child and heiress of James Brown, deceased. Her mother, Mrs. Elizabeth Brown, had remarried in 1707 Isaac Royall of Dorchester, Mass., and of Popeshead, Antigua, by whom she had a son Isaac Royall, Jr., and a dau. Penelope, who m. Col. Henry Vassall of Boston and Jamaica.

On account of this family connection Robert Oliver forsook the Island in 1738 and removed to Dorchester, where he purchased lands and built a house, dying there in 1762, aged 62. In the memoir of the Royalls by E. D. Harris, Boston, it is stated that in 1747 Isaac Royall, Jr., and Henry Vassall leased for 7 years of Robert Oliver a plantation of 148 acres in Popeshead, but I cannot identify this estate. Col. Robert Oliver had five sons, of whom the second, Thomas, was Lt.-Gov. of Mass. 1774-76, removing the latter year to England on account of the rebellion. His first wife, Eliz. Vassall, d. in England, but when or where is not known. The Lt.-Governor's estate in Mass. having been confiscated, he might have been ruined like other Loyalists, but visiting Antigua, where he still owned his Nonsuch plantation, he there m. in 1781 Harriet, only child and h. of the Hon. Byam Freeman, deceased, and so acquired "Byam Freemans" plantation in Popeshead (afterwards called Fryers Hill), besides a good fortune. He then seems to have turned planter, and in 1790 purchased Morgans of 74 acres for £3000, and Watkin's of 93 acres for £2500. In 1791 he leased Mrs. Vassall's moiety of Royalls, and purchased the late Isaac Royall's moiety. In 1793 he sold his father's plantation in Nonsuch, then of 104 acres, for £4400, and in 1806 purchased Mrs. Vassall's moiety of Royalls for about £6000. He retired to Bristol, where he d. in 1815 at the age of 83, leaving no sons but four daus. by his 1st wife and two by his 2nd one. Byam Freemans, otherwise Fryers Hill estate, descended by the intail to Harriet Watkins O., the elder dau. by the 2nd wife, who m. Capt. Henry Haynes, R.N., of the Barbados family, and had two children, Freeman Oliver Haynes, Fellow of Caius C., Camb., and Thomasina Oliver Haynes, who m. the late Sir W. S. Thomas, Bart., and their heirs appear to have sold the estate. I have inquired in several likely quarters for any colonial papers and historic documents that may have been the Lt.-Governor's, but without success.

Mr. Edmund Haynes of 9 New Square, grands. of the above F. O. H., possesses a miniature of the Lt.-Governor and a fine portrait of "Uncle Isaac Oliver," a yr. brother, b. 1738, killed in a duel, probably at Boston, at the age of about 25. Sir George Thomas, Bart., also lent me a plan of Fryers Hill and Dunbars. The Lt.-Gov. had a nephew, Richd. O., a planter in Antigua, who m. at St. John's in 1805 Eliz. Isles, spr., and d. in 1809. His widow made her will in 1823, and left her few slaves and small property to her nephews Isles, so presumably she left no children. If there are any male descendants of this branch in U.S.A. I shall be glad if they will communicate with me.

The following abstracts were made by me in 1914 from deeds on record at Antigua:—

This Ind're made the 17 Dec. 1791 between Penelope Vassall late of Antigua widow now of Boston Mass. on the one part and Tho. O. of Bristol Esq. of the other Witnesseth that for the rent she leases to him her moiety of an estate in the parish of St. John and Division of Popeshead bounded etc. for 9 years at £350 rent. Schedule of slaves. The growing crops slaves and stock are appraised at £5167. (Lib. V., vol. 5, fo. 86.)

This Ind're made the 9 Dec. 1791 between Sir Wm. Pepperell of Marylebone Baronet Joseph Royall of ditto Esq. and Tho. Palmer of S[t] George's Hanover Sq. of the one part and Tho. O. of the parish of S[t] Augustine Bristol Esq. of the other Witnesseth that they sell to T. O. that plantation formerly belonging to Isaac Royall in the parish of St. John and Division of Popeshead as by writ of partition in 1765 and that parcel of land of Isaac R. in his own right whereon the Works are, bounded N. on the Sea and Chr. Hodge Esq. dec[d], W. and S.W. on land of Tho. Jarvis Esq. purchased of said T. O., S. on the road to S[t] John's, E. on lands set off on the said writ of partition to Henry Vassall in right of his wife Penelope Vassall, containing 59 acres 2 r. 35 p. also 2 small pieces C. and B. in the plan of partition bounded N. on Henry Vassall, S. on Henry Vassall and Tho. Jarvis purchased of T. O., E. on T. J. containing 4 a. 2 r. 20 p. also part of a piece E. whereon the negro houses are containing 3 a. 7 p. the whole amounting to 67 a. 1 r. 22 p. with the windmill, houses and slaves (about 40) and stock for one year.

Release of 10 Dec. 1791. Isaac Royall formerly of Medford, Mass., late of Kensington Esq. dec[d] by his will made 26 May 1778 ordered his estate in Antigua to be sold. Will proved P.C.C. and legacies to be paid. The Ex'ors now in consideration of £5000 st. paid by Tho. Oliver convey the said plantation of 67 a. to him. (Lib. W., vol. 5, fos. 222 to 229.)

This Ind're of three parts made 24 Feb. 1795 Between Geo. Lee of Lombard Street Banker, Geo. Erving of George Street Hanover Sq. Esq. and Tho. Latham of Tower Street M[t] assignees of estate of John Lane, Tho. Fraser and Tho. Boylston late of Nicholas Lane L. M[t] and co-partners as Lane Son and Frazer of the 1st part, said J. Lane and T. F. surviving co-partners of Tho. Lane dec[d] of 2[d] part and Tho. Oliver of Bristol Esq. of the 3[d] part.

Whereas by an Ind're of 28 Feb. 1765 Henry Vassall late of Camb. co. Essex Mass. now dec[d] and Penelope his wife now his widow conveyed to John Rowe of Boston Esq. William V. of B. Esq. s[d] Tho. O. and John V. of Camb. their moiety of a plantation in the Division of Popes Head and parish of S[t] John's formerly the estate of Isaac Royall of Medford Mass. Esq. dec[d] and then held by Henry V. in right of Pen. his wife and by Isaac R. s of s[d] Isaac Royall as tenants in common bounded 1 parcel N. sea and lands of Chr. Hodge, W. on s[d] Tho. O., S. on high road E. on Tho. Jarvis and s[d] Tho. O. and the other parcel N. on Tho. O., W. on Tho. Turner S. and E. on T. Jarvis c. in the whole 115 a. and their moiety of 64 slaves and 25 slaves purchased by Henry V. and I. R. as tenants in common and 7 in Henry V. of her own, and also 17 slaves of Penelope V. given her by her father subject to payment by said Henry V. to John Rowe of £966 with Interest at 6 per cent., to William V. of £800, and to Tho. O. of £266 and £250, and to John V. £241, and by another Indenture of 6 parts of 15 July 1778 between John Rowe of 1st part, s[d] William V. of 2nd, s[d] Tho. O. of 3[d], John V. of 4th, and Penelope V. widow of Henry V. of 5th, and Tho. Lane, John Lane and Tho. Fraser of

6th recites that Henry V. did not pay J. Rowe the £966 and £800, but paid Tho. O. on 12 Jan. 1768 £266 and £250, and John V. £241, and on the £966 a balance of £657 and £261 Interest making £922 c. or £691 st. to 1771 is now due to John Rowe, and £800 with £641 Interest or £1441 is due to William V. and Penelope V. applied to Lanes to pay off said sums and they paid off £1773 st., all said Henry and Penelope V's moiety of said plantation was released to Lanes and the slaves to John R, William V., Tho. O. and John V. as mortg. and default was made and the Lanes became bankrupt in 1793 and Geo. Lee etc. were trustees for creditors and £707 was due to them which Tho. O. now paying they convey to him the moiety of said plantation and slaves. (Lib. O., vol. 7, 1793 to 18(? 0)4, fos. 87 to 92 inclusive. This volume has index.)

This Ind're made the 18 Nov. 1806 between Penelope Russell and Catherine Russell spinsters and David Pearce merchant and Rebecca Pearce his wife (late Rebecca Russell spr.) all of Boston Mass. which said Pen. Russell, Cath. Russell, and Rebecca Pearce, with Eliz. Vassall Degen wife of Chas. Furlong Degen of Leghorn merch[t] are the 4 daus. and coheiresses of Eliz. Russell late of Boston widow of Cha. Russell of Antigua Esq. and which said Eliz. Russell was the only child and heiress and universal devisee and executrix named in the will of Penelope Vassall late of Antigua but afterward of Boston Mass. widow deceased of the one part and Tho. Oliver of Bristol Esq. of the other Whereas Penelope Vassall by her will recorded in America gave all her estate to her dau. Eliz. Russell who proved it there and Eliz. Russell hath lately died intestate leaving the above 4 daus. and only children and by an appraisement pursuant to a Lease granted by Pen. Vassall to Tho. O. dated 17 Dec. 1791 he is entitled to receive £2000 c. and Pen. Russell, Cath. Russell and David Pearce and Rebecca Pearce in consideration of Tho. Oliver releasing them of £1500 c. and in consideration of the sum of £3300 st. sell to him their ¾ shares of their land and slaves in the p. of S[t] John and division of Popeshead which were set off to Pen. Vassall on a writ of partition made the 6 Aug. 1765 one parcel bounded N. and E. on Chr. Hodge Esq., S. and W. on lands formerly of Isaac Royall Esq. but now of the said Tho. Oliver containing 17 acres and marked IIII.; one other parcel bounded N. on the hill and quarry f. of Isaac Royall now of Tho. O., E. on land of T. Jarvis purchased of Tho. O., S. on the high road and W. on land f. of Isaac R. now of Tho. O. containing 8 acres and marked VII.; one other parcel bounded N. on T. Jarvis purchased by Tho. O., E. on T. Jarvis, S. on T. Jarvis, W. on Eliz. Turner containing 30 a. and marked VIII. IX. X.; and one small parcel with negro houses of 1 a. with sugar and boiling houses and slaves 28 men 36 women, children and cattle all now vested in Tho. O. by lease of 18 Aug. 1800 for 7 years at the rent of £350 st. and the sellers appoint Sam. Warner and Rich[d] Oliver gentlemen and O. Y. Ash Esq. all of A. their Attornies. Various Powers of Attorney and affidavits follow. Sworn 3 Feb. 1809 by Sam. Warner, Rich[d] Oliver and O. Y. Ash. (Lib. F., vol. 7, pp. 203 to 214 inclusive.)

There is also a separate conveyance from the Degens of their ¼ share which I did not take.

This Ind're made the 9 Dec. 1790 Between Godschal Johnson of London Esq. and Samuel Eliot of Antigua now in Harley St. Esq. surviving devisees in trust by the will of William Gunthorpe formerly of Antigua afterwards of Paddington Esq. deceased of the one part and Tho. Oliver of Bristol Esq. of the other Witnesseth they sell to Tho. O. *Morgans* of 74 a. bounded E. with high road and Jonas Langford deceased W. with high road and Jonas L. and William Mackinnen and heirs of John Lindsay, N. with the centre division of Morgans allotted by a writ of division to Byam Freeman and Ann his wife both deceased, S. with

land of J. Lindsay, formerly in tenure of Tho. Jarvis Esq. also *Watkins's* of 93 a. bounded E. with Edward French deceased now of Hon. Row. Burton, W. with centre division of Morgans allotted to Byam F. and Ann his wife and the high road; N. with the centre division of Watkins also allotted to Byam F. and Ann his wife and high road; S. with lands of late Jonas Langford deceased late in tenure of John Dunbar Esq. in division of Dickinsons Bay and parish of S[t] John, which plantations are now in the occupation of Tho. O., and also about 20 slaves for 1 year..

Release of 10 Dec. 1790. William G. made his will 8 July 1777 and gave his 2 plantations called Morgans and Watkins to trustees to sell and Tho. O. hath agreed to buy them for £5500 st. exclusive of the slaves and Langford Lovell purchased for Tho. O. and paid for Morgans £3000 and for Watkins £2500 by auction—reference to a decree by the Court of Chancery in London. (Lib. W., vol. 5, fos. 4 to 15.)

Tho. Oliver Esq. to John Elliott Esq. conveyance and assignment; and John Elliott Esq. and Catherine his wife to Tho. Oliver Esq. mortgage.

This Ind're made the 2 March 1793 Between Tho. O. late of the City of Bristol but at present in Antigua Esq. of the one part and John Elliott of Antigua Esq. and Catherine his wife of the other.

Whereas Tho. O. being seized as of fee of a plantation in the division of Nonsuch by Ind're of 20 Dec. 1781 between him and Sam. Athill Esq. of the other in consideration of the rent payable by said Sam. A. he Tho. O. leased to Sam. A. his Tho. O.'s plantation of 104 a. bounded N. on lands of Sam. Harman, William Wickham Harman late Murrays and said Sam. A. late Lynch's; E. on lands Tho. Elmes's and lands of Sam. A. late Lynch's; S. on lands of Ben. March[t], Sam. Harman and Sam. A. late Lynch's; W. on the High R[d] and lands of Sam. Harman, with the windmill houses from the 10 Oct. for 12 years paying the yearly rent of £250 st. Plan of estate referred to—details of lease as to guinea corn, canes and trash, blast or cricketts, 2 baskets of dung to each hole, and Whereas by Articles of Agreement of 21 Jan[y] present 1793 between Tho. O. of Bristol of the one part and John Elliott of Antigua Esq. of the other Tho. O. in consideration of £4400 st. conveyed to John E. all the plantation of 104 a. then in the tenure of the Hon. Sam. A. as tenant and John E. was to execute to said Tho. O. a mortgage thereof also of 35 slaves for securing £4400 with interest at 6 per cent. to be paid in 7 years and Tho. O. should assign the Lease which will expire on 10 Oct. next. Tho. O. now sells and conveys said plantation free of dower of Harriet wife of Tho. O. Schedule of Slaves.

John Elliot is bound in £8800, 2 March 1793. (Lib. X., vol. 5, fos. 200—213.)

Tho. Oliver of Bristol Esq. Power of Att[y] to Sam. Warner of Antigua gent. to carry on the plantation business of all my several estates and in case of his death the power to my nephew Rich[d] O. of Antigua gent. 9 Sept. 1806. (Lib. O., vol. 7, p. 133.)

Ind're made the 24 Jan. 1811 between Tho. Oliver of Bristol Esq. recites the Ind're of 22 March 1793 between Tho. O. and John Elliott of Antigua Esq. and Catherine his wife by which Tho. O. sold a plantation in Nonsuch subject to redemption on payment of £4400 st. and the said plantation was afterwards purchased of the Elliotts by Rob. Burnthorn and by deed of 15 and 16 Feb. 1810 was conveyed to Rob. Hyndman on Trust to sell. Tho. O. releases all claim. (Lib. G., vol. 7, fo. 151.)

Isaac Royal of Charlestown New England. Will dated 27 Dec. 1738. My dau.-in-law Ann wife of Robert Oliver of Antigua now in New England 2 negros and their 10 children. Estate there ½ to dau. Penelope and ½ to son Isaac. Wife Elizabeth etc. Recorded 5 Nov. 1739 at Antigua. (See full abstract in "Antigua," iii., 56.)

Elizabeth Royall of Charlestown co. of Middlesex gentlewoman. Will dated 4 April 1747. I give to my four grandsons Doctor James Oliver, Thomas Oliver, Isaac Oliver and Richard Oliver at 21 £500 apiece. Mrs Eliz. Hewes of Cambridge singlewoman £300. My sister Mary Dunton £100. To my granddaus. and goddaus. Eliz. Royall, Eliz. Oliver, and Eliz. Vassall I bequeath as follows: To Eliz. Royall at m. or 21 £1000. To Eliz. Oliver £1000 now lying in debts owing from her father Robert O. Esq. of Dorchester upon two bonds one dated 16 Apr. 1743 for £150 and the other 11 Feb. 1744-5 for 242 oz. of silver. To Eliz. Vassall at 21 or m. £1000 lying in debts owing from her father Henry Vassall upon 2 bonds one dated 22 Oct. 1744 for 375 oz. of silver the other 1 Dec. 1744 for 250 oz. To my granddau. Mary Royall at 21 or m. £500. A suit of mourning and a ring to my son Isaac and his wife, my son-in-law Robert Oliver and his wife, son-in-law Henry Vassall and his wife, Jacob Royall Esq. and his wife, my eldest grandson James Oliver, Mrs. Eliz. Hewes and Mr. Chr. Minot one of my Ex'ors. A ring and a pair of gloves for each other Ex'or and my sister Dunton. I appoint Wm. Brattle Esq. of Cambridge, Mr. Joseph Dowse and Mr. Chr. Minot both of Boston merchants and Jonas Langford of the I. of Antigua Esq. to be Ex'ors. Legacies to be paid when due with interest. All residue in trust to Ex'ors to give one half of the interest to my dau. Ann Oliver and if she survive her husband to her absolutely but if he survive her then to their 5 children. The other one half to my dau. Penelope Vassall (in like manner but no children named). Witnessed by Francis Whitmore, John Mitchell, Joseph Skinnar. Middlesex Registry of Probate.

5 May 1747 Joseph Dowse refused. 18 May 1747 Letter of Chr. Minot.

Inventory taken 1 Aug. 1747. £9719. Sworn 10 Oct. 1747 by Mr Chr. Minot the only acting Ex'or.

On 8 Oct. 1747 Isaac Royall Esq. the only son and Col. Rob. Oliver appealed alledging testatrix was weak in mind .... her large fortune—the improper control of one of her Ex'ors. 4 May 1747 Col. Brattle refused the trust.

The parties being represented by Council the Hon. Sam. Danforth, Judge of Probate, found for the will on 8 June 1747.

(Copy of will and other documents on 33 quarto sheets procured in 1912 by the late Mr. Lothrop Withington.)

Isaac Royall late of Medford co. Middx Mass. New England now of Kensington. Will dated 26 May 1778. Dau. Mary McIntosh Erving wife of the Hon. Geo. Erving Esq., son-in-law Sir Wm. Pepperell. Sister Penelope Vassall. My nephews his Honour Tho. Oliver and Richd Oliver Esquires. Late dau. Lady Pepperell. Estate in Antigua to be sold. (Long will.) (553, Webster.) Will also recorded in co. Middx, Mass.

Meade of Montserrat.

Tho. Meade of Montserratt, but late of Ougerhill in the parish of Chertsey, co. Surry, Esq. Will dated 9 Oct. 1758. To my wife Mary £200 a year and the use of plate and furniture in Great Britain, my coach and four horses and my title I now have to the house and lands that belonged to the late Randolph Greenway during the minority of his nephew John G. To my son Peter and my five daus. Bridget M., Cath. M., Mary M., Eleanor M. and Sarah M. £3000 at 21. To my son James M. 5s., having already paid him his portion. To my Ex'ors £2000 in Trust, the interest to be p[d] to my dau. Judith Lynch and at her death to her ch[n]. My pl[n] called the Water Work in the parish of S[t] Peter in M. which I lately purchased from W[m] Fenton, now in lease to Tho. Caines, I give to my son Dominick M. and his heirs male, and in default to my son Peter M., my son Thos. M., my daus. and granddaus. as tenants in common. All other lands in the West Indies and Great Britain to my son Thos. and in default to my son Dom. and my son Peter. £200 annuity due to W[m] Fenton, now or late of Maidstone, and Juliana his wife. My dau. Ann M. £10 a year. Poor of S[t] Geo. £20 a year for 7 years. All residue of personal estate to Ex'ors for son Thos. at 21. By articles of 15 April 1756 I have agreed with Mary Newton, Spr., and Randolph Horne, two of the devisees of Randolph Greenway, gt., dec[d], for the purchase of ⅔ of a house at Onger Hill, but by reason of the minority of John G., son and heir of the late Rob. G., who has ⅓, the purchase cannot be completed, it shall be carried out. My friends Rob. Freeman of Weston, Derbyshire, Dom. Trant, late of M., now in Great Britain, Constantine Phipps, late of S[t] Chr., now in Great Britain, W[m] Irish, Jas. Hussey the Elder, Cha. O'Gara, all of M., and my nephew Edmund Morphy, Esquires, Ex'ors and G. Witnessed by John Piper, Robert Dyelt, W[m] Beach. If any child become religious my heir to pay only the portion of the house and £10 a year as my dau. Anne is paid. On 7 Aug. 1815 adm'on of estate of testator, late of M., Esq., dec[d], granted to Tho. Hill, Esq., one of the Ex'ors of Bridget M., Spr., dec[d], the dau. and a legatee. The Ex'ors died without taking probate of the goods of dec[d], and Tho. M. the son died a bach. intestate, Dom. Meade the brother, Mary M., Bridget M. and Eleanor or Helena M., sprs., the sisters and only next of kin of Tho. M. the son, with Cath. Lynch, spr., and Eleanor Dutoit his nieces by a dec[d] sister having died. On 19 May 1829 adm'on of Tho. M., late of Onger Hill, etc., left unad. by Tho. Hill, was granted to John Hopton Forbes the adm'or of Tho. M. the son. (455, Pakenham.)

Dominick Meade. Will dated 20 March 1805. All my property in Montserrat to my sisters Bridget Meade and Mary Meade, they to settle £200 a year on my son Stanislar Meade. Wm. Sheldon of Gray's Inn, Esq., guardian of my son, and £200. To each Ex'or £50. W[m] Sheldon, Nicholas Hill, Wm. Furlong, J[r], and Henry Hamilton of M., Esquires, Ex'ors, recommending my nephews and nieces to my sisters. £20 a year to my sister Eleonora Meade. All residue to my said son.

Codicil. My son to take the name of S[t] Hilair instead of Meade.

Proved 16 May 1805 by Wm. Sheldon. (371, Nelson.)

Helena Meade of Spetisbury Ho., co. D'set, Spr. Will dated 24 Feb. 1806. All my real and personal estate unto my sisters Bridget M. and Mary M. of Duke Str., Manch[r] Sq., sprs. Witnessed by Rev. Ja[s] Newsham, Spetisbury, Rev. Ralph Southworth of Spetisbury Ho. On 5 Aug. 1815 adm'on of the goods of Eleanor otherwise Helena M. granted to Tho. Hill, Esq., one of the Ex'ors of the will of Bridget M., Spr., dec[d], the sister; Mary M. the other sister died without proving. (455, Pakenham.)

Bridget Meade, late of Duke Str., Manchester Sq., now residing in Edward Str., Portman Sq. Will dated 26 May 1813. All real estate to W[m] Sheldon of Gray's Inn, Esq., Nich. Selby of Acton, Esq., and Tho. Hill of the I. of Montserrat, Esq., upon Trust to sell to pay debts as well my own as those of my late sister Mary, dec[d]. To Stanislaus the son of my late brother Dominick M., now residing in France, £2000. My nephew Tho. Lynch the interest of £1500 for his life, and at his death to his 4 daus., his present wife. My nephew Isidore L. £500. My niece Cath. L. £500. My niece Eleanora Dutoit £500. Louisa Farrell, spr., now residing in Paris, who resided with M[rs] Macnamara, dec[d], £50. Madame Charboniere (late Liddy Farrell), wife of M[r] C., £100. M[rs] Stonor of Spetisbury Ho. £180 due to her by my late sister Helena M., also £200. W[m] Sheldon, Nich. Selby and Tho. Hill £50 each. All residue to Stanislaus Tho. L., Isidore L, Cath. L. and Eleanora Dutoit. Trustees to be Ex'ors.

Codicil. 31 Oct. 1813. Leg. to servants. Proved 7 Aug. 1815 by W. S. and T. H., Esq[res]; power reserved to Nich. Selby, Esq. On 4 Nov. 1837 adm'on of estate left unad. by W. S. and T. H., dec[d], granted to Tho. Hopton Forbes, the Ex'or of Eleonora Mary Du Toit, wid., dec[d], the niece. Nich. Tuite (written Nich. Selby) having renounced and is dead, Tho. Henry L., Cath L., spr., and s[d] El. Mary Du Toit survived, but died, and Isidore L., Esq., not appearing. (455, Pakenham.)

Mary Meade, late of Duke Str., S[t] Marylebone, Spr. Will dated 26 March 1809. All my real and personal estate to my sister Bridget M., late also of Duke Str., spr. On 27 Sept. 1815 adm'on of testatrix, late of King's Bench Prison, spr., granted to Tho. Hill, Esq., Ex'or of B. M. On 18 May 1829 adm'on of estate left unad. by T. H. granted to John Hopton Forbes, the adm'or of goods of s[d] T. Hill. (510, Pakenham.)

Sarah Meade, Spr. Will dated 15 April 1789. All estate to my 2 sisters Bridget M. and Mary M., Sprs. On 23 Sept. 1815 test., late of Portman Str., granted to Tho. Hill, Esq., Ex'or of Bridget M., dec[d]. (510, Pakenham)

Close Roll 5920.

This Ind're made the 9 May 26 Geo. II. 1753 Between W[m] Fenton of Maidstone co. Kent Esq. and Juliana his wife of the one p[t] and Tho. Meade of Isleworth co. Midd[x] Esq. of the other Wit. that for £6500 W. F. and J. sell all that pl[n] called Waterwork in the p. of S[t] Peter and S[t] Anthony in the I. of Montserat containing 5 or 600 a. and all buildings negroes stock heretofore the est. of W[m] F. l. of Monts[t] dec[d] the father of W[m] F. (subject to a lease made by W. F. the father to Tho. Canes for a term of years).

Lease of 8 May for one year precedes the above.

Close Roll 5909.

This Ind're made the 10 May 26 Geo. II. 1753 Between Tho. Meade l. of the I. of Montserat but at present of Isleworth co. Midd[x] Esq. and Mary his wife of the one part and Peter Leheup the Elder of Steeple Morden co. Camb. of the other Wit. that for 5*s.* paid by P. L. they sell to him all that pl[n] of him T. M. in the p. of S[t] Geo. called his Windward est. bounded at the foot with the sea at the head with dry gutt, N. with Sharps River and S. with the land of Col. John Daly, containing 200 a. with the buildings 160 negroe slaves mules horses cattle mills also all that other pl[n] in the s[d] p. called the New Windward est. bounded at the foot with the sea at the head with the lands of W[m] Beach or John Joyce;

Nicholas Meade of Montserrat, Capt. in the one Regt. of foot 1678; M. of C. 1680—88.

Sergeant Dominick Meade of Montserrat 1678.

Tho. Meade of Montserrat, planter. 1729; purchased in 1753 the Waterwork plantation in the parish of St. Peter of Wm. Fenton; owned the Windward plantation in St. George of 200 acres and the New Windward of 140 acres; died in M. in 1763. Will dated 9 Oct. 1758; adm'on 7 Aug. 1815 (455, Pakenham). = Mary, dau. of Peter Hussey of M., Merchant; mar. 23 June 1724; living 1758.

Dominick Meade, 1st son and heir, died s.p.l. Will dated 20 March and proved 16 May 1805 (371, Nelson).	Thomas Meade of St. George, Hanover Square, and residuary devisee May 1763; purchased the Hussey plantation 1779; ex'or 1785 of Michael White; arrived in England 1793; died intestate a bachelor before 1805.	Peter Meade. — James Meade.	Bridget of Marylebone. Will dated 26 May 1813; proved 7 Aug. 1815 (455, Pakenham).

Stanislaus St. Hilair, in France 1813.

N. with the lands of John Beach and John Joyce; S. with Pelican Gutt cont. 140 a. n. in possession of Rob. Hixon at the yearly rent of £450 st. and all houses windmills cattle mills with 40 negroe slaves and stock also those 140 negroo slaves which he hath placed upon the pl^n he l. held by lease from the l. Sir Wm. Gage and stock also all that pl^n l. of Wm Fenton called Waterwork pl^n in the p. of St Peter cont. 5 or 600 a. and all slaves and stock for one year.

Release. This Ind're made the 11 May, 1753 (as in the lease). Tho. Meade has an estate and 340 slaves and hath entered into a treaty with Wm. Fenton Esq. for the purchase of his est. and pursuant thereto by Ind'res of the 8 and 9 inst. made between Wm. Fenton of Maidstone co. Kent Esq. and Juliana his wife of the one part and Tho. Meade of the other they sell to him all that the Water Work pl^n formerly the est. of Wm F. l. of Montserat dec^d the father of s^d Wm F. and whereas Tho. Meade applied to Peter Leheup for an advance of £5000 on the security of all his estates and T. M. hath not any of his title deeds or lists of slaves Nich. Tuite of Lyme Str. merch^t and Isidore Lynch* of Jefferys Square St Mary Axe (who is the son in law of s^d T. M.) will become security and join in bonds now in consideration of £8000 W. F. and J. convey all est. to P. Leheup interest to be at 5 per cent. and they appoint Dominick Trant, James Farrill and Wm. Ryan all of M. Esquires their attorneys. On 10 skins.

Chancery Proceedings, 1714—58, Bundle 1886. Phipps *v.* Oliver.

16 June 1766. Bill by Constantine Phipps, William Irish and Charles O'Gara, Esquires, surviving Ex'ors of Will of Thomas Meade late of . . . . ? Hill, Surrey, Esq., dec., and Thomas Meade of St. George's, Hanover Square, Middx., Esq., one of the sons and legatees of aforesaid Thomas Meade, *v.* Richard Oliver, Thomas Oliver and John Piper. Thomas Truman, George Douglas and Richard

* 1776. July 15. Isidore Lynch, Esq; one of the oldest merchants in London. ("G. M.," 336.)

Neave, merchants of London, bought in 1755 certain plantations, etc., in St. George's, Montserrat, from Dominick Farrill of M. and Mary his wife. The Bill is longer and the answer voluminous. Nothing more *re* Phipps, who acted only as Ex'or of Thomas Meade.

[pr. Lt.-Col. Phipps, R.A.]

The Editor applied at the P.R.O. for the above suit, but it could not be found in the bundle.

A

Judith = Isidore Lynch of Jefferys Sq., St. Mary Axe, Merchant 1753; ? died 15 July 1776.	Catherine.	Mary, died in the King's Bench prison. Will dated 26 March 1809 (510, Pakenham). — Helena, or Eleanor, of Spetisbury, co. Dorset. Will dated 24 Feb. 1806 (455, Pakenham).	Sarah, of Marylebone. Will dated 15 April 1789 (510, Pakenham). — Ann, entered a religious house.

Stanislaus Tho. Lynch, mar. and had four daus.	Isidore Lynch, Esq.	Cath. Lynch.	Eleanora Mary Lynch, mar. . . . . Dutoit.

General George Gordon Meade of Gettysburg fame was descended from a family in Montserrat. ("N. Y. Nation" for 4 Feb. 1909.)

In 1780 Tho. Meade of M. was godfather to a grandson of Robert Meade of Philadelphia, which last-named emigrated from Limerick in 1742.

In St. Botolph's, Aldersgate, is a tablet at the west end to a wife of Robert Meade of Philadelphia.

ST. GEORGE'S, MONTSERRAT.

1723	Nov. 24	Terence Hart & Eleanor Mead, by L.
1724	June 23	Thomas Mead & Mary Hussy, by L.
1728	Oct. 1	Redmond Theige & Elizabeth Mead, by L.
1723	Oct. 4	George, S. of Wm Mead & Mary his wife (also at St Anthony); bap.
1725	April 17	John S. of Wm Mead & Mary his wife (May 17 at St Peter's); bap.
1726	Mar. 6	Judith Mead, Widdow; bur.

ST. ANTHONY'S, MONTSERRAT.

1726-7 Jan. 7 Anne D. of Wm Mead & Mary his wife; bap.

In the census of this parish in 1729 he is styled a waiter (of customs).

List of Wills recorded in Barbados down to the year 1800.*

Year.	Names of Testators.
1659	Peake, Lyonell
"	Peppercorne, William
"	Perry, Francis
"	Perry, Jane
"	Pinnell, John
"	Pope, George
1660	Pilgrim, Elias
"	Parris, John
"	Pitfold, Thomas
"	Pawley, John
1661	Peers, Richard
"	Padmore, Thomas
1662	Pate, Ann
"	Pate, Thomas
"	Pearde, George
"	Partridge, Nathaniel
"	Powney, Richard
1663	Phillips, George
1664	Pullein, Alexander
"	Plening, George
"	Padmore, Thomas
"	Pearse, John
1665	Peers, Edward
"	Phillips, William
"	Palmer, William
"	Porte, Jeffrey
"	Pickering, Joseph
1666	Parris, Henry
"	Parker, James
1667	Purle, Richard
"	Pickering, William
"	Price, John
"	Paynter, Elizabeth
"	Phillips, William
1668	Peelle, Roger
"	Pearse, James
"	Price, Thomas
"	Peal, Thomas
"	Pinnington, Robert
1669	Powdrell, Thomas
"	Parry, Samuel
"	Pile, Theophilus
1670	Pickering, Joseph
"	Piggott, Francis
"	Powell, Andrew
1671	Pargeter, Thomas
"	Powell, Hugh
"	Pinckett, Daniel
1671	Pottiu, William
"	Pinkitt, Richard
"	Proberts, John
"	Pugh, Edward
"	Pilham, Edward
"	Prichard, Thomas
1672	Ponfritt, Abraham
"	Phillips, Ambrose
"	Powrey, John
"	Priddith, James
"	Pearce, William
1673	Price, Lawrence
"	Parris, Thomas
"	Pearson, Francis
1674	Pallmer, Samuel
"	Pitt, John
"	Purver, George
1675	Phillips, Humphry
1676	Price, John
"	Povey, Joan
"	Pyne, Thomas
"	Piporcorne, John
"	Pickford, Robert
"	Phumley, William
"	Powell, Edward
1677	Pollard, Thomas
"	Pickering, Elizabeth
"	Powlitt, William
1678	Plowman, William
"	Parsons, William
"	Price, Richard
1679	Power, Pierce
"	Parris, Edward
"	Peterson, John
"	Pearce, Richard
"	Porter, John
1680	Polgrun, Thomas
"	Peak, Thomas
"	Parnell, Thamar
"	Puddiford, John
"	Parkins, Thomas
"	Pinnestone, Thomas
"	Perry, Samuel
"	Pinn, Richard
"	Portall, Nicholas
"	Pinckett, Matthew
"	Perriman, John
"	Pinell, Thomas

* Continued from p. 68.

Year.	Names of Testators.	Year.	Names of Testators.
1681	Powell, William	1688	Plunkett, Robert
„	Pile, Theophulus	„	Proverb, Thomas
„	Pillfield, Sebastin	1689	Prothers, Thomas
„	Purse, Daniel	„	Pearce, Thomas
„	Payne, William	„	Preswell, Mary
„	Preston or Prison, Mary	„	Peters, Thomas
„	Prince, Anthony	1690	Patridge, Nathanil
„	Powell, Daniel	„	Peers, John
„	Poake, James	„	Paterson, Dunkin
„	Pinkette, Mary Elizabeth	„	Pargiter, Thomas
„	Pady, Roger	„	Perfect, Augustin
„	Paliotozus,* Fardinand	„	Perwedgh, Elizabeth
1682	Palmer, Samuel	„	Phillips, John
„	Pollard, Richard	„	Parrott, Mary
„	Poyne, Patrick	1691	Prince, Edward
„	Prim, Martha	„	Potter, Col. Cuthbert
„	Parrott, John	„	Price, William
„	Perfitt, Augustin	1692	Prout, Thomas
„	Palmer, Thomas	„	Pearnell, John
„	Pollard, James	„	Page, Thomas
„	Parker, Snr., Richard	„	Parrish, William
„	Pathscoe, Jacob	„	Pratt, George
„	Potticary, Christopher	„	Pope, Charles
1683	Purson, Richard	„	Payne, Adam
„	Palmer, Adam	„	Parkes, Thomas
1684	Pearchhouse, Elizabeth	1693	Ponys, John
„	Pierce, William	„	Prigg, Charles
„	Parker, Ambrose	„	Phillpott, Thomas
„	Price, Henry	„	Pickett, Adam
„	Pritchett, Mary	„	Pyke, William
„	Perrin, John	„	Phillips, William
1685	Phillicott, Thomas	„	Prining, Teage
„	Pickering, Alice and Joseph	1694	Poore, Michael
„	Phillicott, Richard	„	Plinkett, Thomas
1686	Price, Elizabeth	„	Phillips, Thomas
„	Pritchard, John	„	Price, Philip
„	Powell, Humphry	„	Porteous, William
„	Parker, John	„	Price, Philip
„	Payne, Sampson	„	Pounders, Garrett
„	Phillips, Thomas	1695	Palmer, William
„	Paynter, Paul	„	Piddock, Tobias
„	Pinchback, Thomas	„	Porter, Richard
„	Phenton, Samuel	„	Porter, Elizabeth
„	Phenton, Elizabeth	1696	Pollard, James
„	Proverbs, John	„	Pecke, Thomas
1687	Pollard, John	„	Parsons, Richard
„	Piggott, John	„	Pearce, Thomas
„	Perkins, Nathaniel	1697	Padmore, Thomas
„	Parris, George	„	Pinder, Richard
„	Pichford, Honnor	1698	Pryor, Mary Ann
„	Powell, Mary	„	Parsons, Edward
„	Phillicott, Jane	„	Peers, John
„	Price, John	1700	Payne, George
„	Pooler, Thomas	„	Phillips, John
1688	Pollard, George	„	Pasfield, Samuel

* ? Paleologus.

Year.	Names of Testators.
1700	Phillips, William
„	Parsons, Edward
1701	Pegge, Edward
„	Pooler, William
„	Polgrun, John
„	Poor, John
„	Pococke, Richard
„	Parsons, Edward
„	Perrin, Robert
„	Pinckett, Daniel
„	Parr, George
„	Parr, Elizabeth
„	Parry, Edward
„	Pierce, John
„	Penberton, James
„	Price, Lawrence
„	Peach, Thomas
„	Parker, Ann
„	Prince, Edward
„	Pym, Thomas
„	Povery, Ann
1702	Prideaux, Nicholas
„	Parris, Morgan
„	Pond, William
„	Parker, Malachi
„	Parker, William
„	Pearne, Thomas
1703	Peters, Thomas
„	Pile, Sarah
„	Polgrun, Jean
„	Porter, Richard
„	Pineston, Thomas
„	Parsons, Francis
„	Parris, Evan
1705	Ponard, Edward
„	Pilgrim, Dorathea
„	Pickering or Picker, Sir Henry, "Bart."
„	Phillips, Mary
„	Prothers, John
1706	Pryer, William
1709	Piggott, Roger
„	Pearce, John
„	Pope, Nicholas
1710	Puckering, John
„	Prish, Samuel
1711	Pare, Edward
„	Phillips, John
„	Piggott, Jane
„	Pulling, Mary
„	Perry, Samuel
„	Perrin, John
1712	Payne, Richard
„	Perryman, Richard
„	Parkinson, Daniel
1713	Prior, Mary

Year.	Names of Testators.
1713	Prideaux, Damaris
„	Parsons, Edward
1714	Pemberton, Charles
„	Parris, Alexander
„	Peacock, Susan
1715	Pickering, Joseph
„	Payne, Benjamin
„	Platt, Nathaniel
„	Penny, Humphry
„	Penney, William
„	Phillips, William
„	Pilgrim, John
1716	Proverbs, Ambrose
„	Poyer, Thomas
„	Passalargne, Peter
„	Panton, John
„	Pilgrim, Thomas
1717	Pinder, John
„	Poor, John
„	Park, John
„	Pannizzar, John Matthew
„	Pilgrim, Richard
1718	Poor, Richard
„	Pacheco, Ester
„	Price, Richard
„	Perrin, Mary
„	Poyer, Abel
„	Price, John
„	Pearce, John
„	Porter, Thomas
„	Parsons, Richard
1719	Peyton, Charles
„	Poore, Benjamin
„	Pond, Margaret or Mary
„	Paterson, John
„	Preston, Robert
1720	Peyton, Elizabeth
„	Perkins, Ann
1721	Potts, William
„	Pegg, Robert
„	Punnet, Christopher
„	Prescott, Moses
„	Parsons, Jean
„	Poor, Thomas
„	Peters, Olive
1722	Pollard, Anne
1723	Pubbles, John
„	Parris, Elizabeth
„	Palmer, William
„	Pearcey, Israel
„	Phillips, Josias
„	Pinder, Timothy
„	Parsons, William
„	Perrin, Alexander
„	Parris, Elizabeth
1724	Phillips, Ann

Year.	Names of Testators.
1724	Payne, Charles
,,	Price, William
,,	Pulling, James
,,	Peacock, William
1725	Power, Richard
,,	Peltzer, Mary
,,	Parkes, John
,,	Payne, Peter
1726	Proverbs, John
1727	Palmer, Mary
,,	Pare, Edward
,,	Pemberton, Joseph
,,	Pile, Theophilus
,,	Pear, Edward
,,	Peisotto, Rachael
1728	Pinkett, Mary
,,	Pocket, William
,,	Palmer, Thomas
,,	Priest, Ann
,,	Perryman, Francis
,,	Polgrun, James
,,	Phillips, Renn
1729	Pirratt, John
,,	Poor, Benjamin
,,	Popel, John
,,	Pleston, John
,,	Pickering, Ann
,,	Poor, Thomas
,,	Pooler, Mary
1730	Platt, Elizabeth
,,	Polgrun, John
,,	Porter, Robert
,,	Paine, John
,,	Popell, John
,,	Pollard, William
,,	Polgrun, Henry
1731	Pile, Francis
,,	Perkins, Thomas
,,	Phillips, Thomas
,,	Parker, Samuel
,,	Pinder, John
,,	Padmore, Thomas
,,	Perryman, John
,,	Phillips, Edward
1732	Podd, William
,,	Phillips, James
1733	Paultress, John
,,	Parsons, Daniel
,,	Pritchard, John
,,	Palmer, Ann
,,	Paine, Dorothy
,,	Piggott, Thomas
,,	Price, Rebecca
,,	Phillips, Edward
,,	Phillips, Mary
,,	Palmer, Elizabeth

Year.	Names of Testators.
1734	Petterkin, Robert
,,	Popell, Elizabeth
,,	Pile, Michael
1735	Pile, Francis
,,	Parsons, John
,,	Ping, Joseph
,,	Pead, Mary
,,	Pinkett, Richard
,,	Payne, Nicholas
,,	Phillips, John
1736	Pollard, John
,,	Payne, Hannah
,,	Pilgrim, Thomas
,,	Pilgrim, John
1737	Pollard, Margorey
,,	Pinder, Richard
1738	Parkes, John
,,	Poyer, John
,,	Poore, James
,,	Pegg, Robert
,,	Peele, Mary
,,	Pollard, Benjamin
1739	Perkins, Thomas
,,	Pilgrim, Mary
,,	Pinder, Ruth
1740	Pollard, John
,,	Peers, Henry
,,	Pegg, Sarah
,,	Part, John
,,	Palmer, Robert
,,	Padmore, John
,,	Pereira, Aaron
,,	Parsons, Edward
1741	Pile, Francis
,,	Paulsworth, Richard
,,	Pearcey, Thomas
,,	Peters, Thomas
,,	Payne, Grace
1742	Puckering, Dorothy
,,	Porter, Thomas
,,	Padmore, Elizabeth
,,	Poole, Thomas
,,	Pemberton, Elizabeth
,,	Pilgrim, Edward
,,	Phillips, Bushell
,,	Palmer, Rebecca
,,	Parsons, Richard
1743	Polgrun, Thomas
,,	Pinder, William
,,	Piggott, Roger
,,	Phillips, George
,,	Percefull, Edward
,,	Palmer, John
,,	Punnett, Henry
,,	Pollard, Pollard
,,	Pile, Mary

Year.	Names of Testators.
1743	Piggott, Robert
1744	Pile, Francis
„	Perkins, David
„	Pegg, Stephen
„	Pollard, Sarah
„	Piercy, Benony
„	Pollard, John
„	Perryman, Richard
1745	Poyer, Abell
„	Parr, Margaret
„	Peters, John
„	Polgrun, Katherine
„	Peers, John
„	Price, Wiliam
1746	Pooler, Sarah
„	Perrieza, Rynia
„	Palmer, Joseph
„	Pickering, John
„	Pearcy, Elizabeth
1747	Paine, John
„	Perratt, John
„	Pile, Ann
„	Parsons, Margaret
„	Punnett, Sarah
„	Pulman, William
1748	Parsons, Sarah
„	Phillips, Joseph
„	Palmer, Samuel
„	Phillips, Thomas
1749	Phillips, Ann
„	Palmer, Eliakim
„	Phillips, Josias
„	Pool, Thomas
1750	Peake, John
„	Prichard, Clement
„	Prentis, John
„	Pinder, Timothy
„	Pegg, Ann
„	Parratt, Richard
„	Payne, John
„	Peters, Dorothy
„	Parfitt, James
„	Perkins, Hannah
1751	Pickering, John
„	Partridge, Sarah
„	Pratt, Henry
„	Pinkett, Matthew
„	Pearce, Thomas
„	Partridge, Samuel
„	Poor, Thomas
1752	Paterson, Ann
„	Pile, Conrad
„	Pile, Francis
1752	Purcell, Henry
„	Poore, Elizabeth
„	Poyer, George
1753	Pockett, Esther
„	Price, Philip
„	Phillips, Elizabeth
„	Pinder, Edward
„	Pinder, Sarah
„	Perkins, Thomas
„	Phillips, Wilkerson
„	Porter, Samuel
„	Porter, John
„	Pilgrim, Rachael
„	Pritchard, John
„	Poyer, George
„	Parkinson, John
1754	Proverbs, Mary
„	Petree, George John
„	Patterson, William
„	Parks, Thomas
„	Platt, Edward
1755	Peterkins, John
„	Pinheiro, Abraham
„	Pinder, Ann
„	Pollard, William
„	Pollard, Elizabeth
„	Pearce, Hannah
1756	Peters, John
„	Page, Dorothy
„	Polgrun, Thomas
„	Popel, Ann
„	Phillips, John
1757	Paine, John
„	Price, John
„	Perry, Samuel
„	Pemberton, Agnes
„	Price, John
„	Pare, Edward
„	Phillips *alias* Hopkins, Peter
„	Packer, Charles
„	Pearce, Francis
1758	Pollard, John
„	Parfit, Augustus
„	Polegrun, Jane
„	Pockett, Ann
„	Phillips, Elizabeth
„	Perry, Widmor
„	Parks, George
„	Popel, Stephen
„	Payne, Benjamin
1759	Pullinger, Love Fearnot
„	Pullinger, George
„	Poyer, Phillip

(To be continued.)

Rawdon of Barbados.

The following notes have been made from Add. MS. 15,556, British Museum. which is labelled "Abstracts of Titles, 1687—1800":—

By deed poll dated 3 April 1652 and recorded at Barbados 31 March 1653, James Holdip of the said Island, esq., sold to Dame Eliz. Rawdon, Tho. Rawdon, esq., Eliz. Forster, widow, and Robert Swinnerton, merchant, all of London, a moiety of that plantation called Fisher's Pond, containing 350 acres; also that parcel of 300 acres part called Rawdon plantations in the parish of S[t] Michael.

It appears that between 1653 and 1666 the 300 a. was leased out by Col. Tho. Rawdon without M[r] Swinnerton, who d. 1674, being consulted. Fisher's Pond (the other moiety having been conveyed to Col. Tho. Rawdon by John Waldoe of the said Island, esq., by deed of 8 Sept. 1653) was in consideration of £13,000 st. conveyed by Col. Rawdon to Edward Thornburgh. The present claimant, Joseph Keeling, esq., married Hester, only child of Marmaduke Rawdon, esq., the last heir male, who by lease and release of 14 and 15 Oct. 1750, recorded 30 April 1762, conveyed Rawdons Rents, otherwise Rawdons plantation, to the said Joseph Keeling and Esther and to the longest liver now devolved on M[r] Keeling by survivorship. (fo. 111.)

Schedule of Ind'res granted by Col. Tho. Rawdon, 1654 to 1665, taken from the Sec. Office at Barbadoes in 1762. 22 names are given. (fo. 110.)

Appended (fo. 109) is a short tabular pedigree of 5 generations down to M[rs] Hester Keeling.

Marriage Licences.

1610-11, March 16. Marmaduke Rawdon, Clothworker, of All Hallows Barking, Bach., 29, and Elizabeth Thorogood, of Hodsden, Herts, Maiden, 19; consent of father Thomas Thorowgood of same, Gent.; at Broxborne, Herts. (Bishop of London.)

1672, Sep. 17. Christopher Sparke of Inner Temple, Gent., Bach., about 30, and Elizabeth Rawdon, of Hoddesdon, Herts, Sp[r], about 18; her mother's consent; at Hoddesdon afs[d]. (Vicar-Gen. of Archb. of Canterbury.)

1672, Dec. 16. Marmaduke Rawdon, of Broxbourne, Herts, Esq., Bach., about 25, and Hester Corsellis, of Stepney, Midd., sp[r], about 24, her parents dead; at S[t] Cath. Coleman, S[t] Dunstan in the E., or S[t] Olave, Hart Str., London. (Faculty Office.)

1681, July 19. Nathaniel Brent, of Hodsdon, Herts, Bach., 30, and Eliz. Roydon, Spr., 18, dau. of Marmaduke R. of same, who consents; alleged by Henry Crew, of S[t] Olave's, Hart Str., L.; at Hertford, Stapleford or Amwell, co. Herts. (Faculty Office.)

1689, Dec. 9. Marmaduke Rawdon, of S[t] Mary Magdalen, Bermondsey, Surrey, Mariner, Bach., about 35, and M[rs] Margaret Peverell, of the same, spr., about 20, at own disposal, no parents or guardians; at S[t] Mary Magd. afs[d]. (Vicar-Gen. of Archb. of Canterbury.)

ALL HALLOWS' BARKING.

Baptisms.

1612 Mar. 29 Tho[s] Rawdon s. of Marmaduke Rawdon and Elizabeth his wife.
1618 Apr. 9 Elizabeth dau[r] of Marmaduke Rawdon and Eliz[h] his wife.

Arms.—*Argent, a fess between three pheons, all Sable.*
Crest.—*On a mural coronet a pheon with a laurel branch issuing thereout.*

Rafe Rawdon of Stearsby in Yorkshire 1568. He heads the pedigree in the Visitation of London of 1633—5. = Jane, dau. of John Brice of Sullington, Yorkshire.

A

Laurence Rawdon of York, born at Bransby; freeman and grocer 1593; Sheriff 1615; Alderman 1624; bur. in Crux Church 6 July 1626, aged 58. Arms on bluestone. Will dated 6 and proved 21 July 1626 at York. = Margery, dau. of Wm. Barton of Cawton Hall; died 17 April 1641, aged 74.

Robert Rawdon, citizen and fishmonger of London, died 15 Sept. 1644. Will (204, Fines). = Katherine, dau. of Tho. Hacker of London.

Roger Rawdon.

Robert Rawdon of Mitcham, co. Surrey, died 1644 and left issue.

Marmaduke Rawdon, bapt. at Crux 18 March 1609-10; merchant in the Canaries; died bachelor 6 Feb. 1668. M.I. at Broxbourne. Will (22, Coke). See his Life and "D.N.B."

Margery, mar. Sir Roger Jaques of Elvington, Knt.

Mary, and a 3rd dau.

B

Marmaduke Rawdon of Hoddesdon, 1st son and heir; died 30 Oct. 1681, aged 35. = Hester, 4th and youngest dau. of Abraham Corsellis of London, brewer; mar. lic. dated 16 Dec. 1672, then aged 24; died 7 July 1719, aged 75. M.I. at Broxbourne. Will (169, Browning).

Thomas Rawdon, 2nd son, 1666.

Charles Rawdon, died young.

Dorothy, dau. of John Freeman of Colchester, co. Essex; mar. 3 Feb. 1705; living 1712. 1st wife. = Marmaduke Rawdon of Hoddesdon, only son and heir, attorney-at-law of Colchester; purchased Fingringhoe manor in 1707; had claims to Fisher's Pond and Rawdon's Rents in Barbados; died 31 Oct. 1752, aged 72. M.I. at Broxbourne. Will (286, Bettesworth). Last heir male. = Rebecca . . . . 2nd wife. s.p.

C

Dorothy, died young.

Robert Plumer of Great Amwell, High Sheriff of Herts; died 11 Jan. 1740, aged 52. M.I. at Great Amwell (Cussans, ii., 128). = Hester Rawdon, only surviving child and heir, died at Fingringhoe, near Colchester, 5 Sept. 1756. Will (18, Herring). s.p. = Joseph Keeling of Barking, Esq., bapt. at St. James, Clerkenwell, 4 July 1724; mar. 25 July 1744; J.P. Essex and Middlesex; Collector of Customs at Barbados; owned Rawdon's plantation; died 9 Aug. 1792. Will (436, Fountain). See W.I. Bookplates, No. 208. s.p. = Alice Slaney, sister of John Slaney of Norwich, Esq. His will (405, Bevor).

Joseph Keeling. John Keeling. William Keeling. Mary, mar. . . . . Tooke.

1621 Aug. 29 Marmaduke sonne of Marm[ke] Roydon and Eliz[h] his wife.
1622 Dec. 19 Martha dau[r] of Marmaduke Roydon and Eliz[h] his wife.
1624 Apr. 25 Katherine dau[r] of Marmaduke Roydon and Eliz[h] his wife.

(A long notice of Sir Marmaduke is given in the History of the parish, pp. 66-67.)

A

Sir Marmaduke Rawdon, Knt., bapt. at Brandsbie 20 March 1582, aged 29 in 1610-11, of All Hallows Barking; a great merchant adventurer; M.P. Aldborough 1627; Lieut.-Col. of City Bands 1629; Master of Clothworkers' Co.; owner of plantations in Barbados 1627; fined for Alderman 1639; raised a regiment for the King 1643; Govr. of Farringdon, where he died 28 April 1646, and was buried.
= Eliz., only dau. and heir of Tho. Thorogood of Hoddesdon in Broxbourne, co. Herts; mar. 7 April 1611; lic. dated 16 March 1610-11, then aged 19; her fortune was £10,000; sole ex'trix 1646 of her stepmother Mrs. Martha Molesworth. Had 10 sons and 6 daus. Will dated 27 Feb. 1666; proved 5 March 1668 (36, Coke).

William Rawdon, 4th son.

James Rawdon, 5th son.

D

B

Col. Thomas Rawdon of Barbados, born 20 and bapt. 29 March 1612 at Barking; F.C. Trin. Coll., Camb., 1624; resided in Portugal 1630—8; Envoy there and Col. of Horse 1644; retired to Canaries for two years; resided in Barbados until 1662; bur. 3 Aug. 1666 and M.I. at Broxbourne. Will (136, Mico).
= Magdalen, dau. of Randolph Crew of Hatham Barne, co. Kent, Esq.; mar. 21 April 1642, aged 15. Will dated 3 Nov. and proved 2 Dec. 1675 (130, Dycer).

Marmaduke Rawdon, 2nd son, born 16 and bapt. 29 Aug. 1621 at Barking; F.C. of Jesus Coll., Camb.; a merchant; heir and ex'or 1668 of his cousin Marmaduke.
= Sarah, 2nd dau. and coheir of Hugh North of Tewin, co. Herts. (Cussans, ii., 13).

George Rawdon, 3rd son, 1666.

Eliz., 1st dau., mar. Chr. Sparke of the Inner Temple; mar. lic. dated 17 Sept. 1672, he aged 30 and she 18.

Magdalene.

Martha.

Katherine.

C

Magdalen, mar. Geo. Lysons of Gray's Inn.

Hester, proved her mother's will in 1719.

Elizabeth, mar. Sam. Bagnal of London, salter. She died 11 Dec. 1712, aged 34. M.I. at Broxbourne.

Marmaduke Rawdon and Edmond Foster were two of those London merchants, who obtained from the Earl of Carlisle a grant of 10,000 acres in Barbados in 1627-28. This company sent out a ship the Marygold, John Jones master, with Capt. Charles Wolferstone and Capt. John Swan as their agents, which arrived in Carlisle Bay on 5 July 1628. ("Memorials of St. Lucia," p. 474.) The 10,000 acres are shewn in Lygon's map of about 1650.

1686, Sept. 2. Ind're between Tho. Rawdon of Hoddesden Hartfordshire Esq. and Capt. Wm. Mott of Barbados gent. concerning certain lands near the Indian Bridge in St. Michael's parish belonging to Dame Elizabeth Rawdon widow of Sir Marmaduke Rawdon. (New Eng. Reg. for 1911, p. 181.)

1756, Sept. 5. Mrs. Hesther Keeling, Colchester, Essex. ("London Mag.," 452.)

1756, Sept. 13. Wife of Jo. Keeling, Esq.; at Fingringhoe, Essex. ("G.M.," 451.)

1792, Aug. 9. At Barking, Essex, Joseph Keeling, esq. collector of the customs for Bridgetown, Barbadoes, and in the commission of the peace for Essex and Middlesex. (*Ibid.*, 774.)

The manor of Westbury in Barking was owned by Blackburne Poulton, attorney at law, who died 1749, leaving it to his nephew Poulton Alleyne, from whom it descended to Joseph Keeling, Esq. (Wright's "Essex," ii., 481.) A pedigree of Keeling was entered in the Visitations of London and Staffordshire.

For other authorities see Clutterbuck's "Herts," ii., 64, 74; Cussans' "Herts," ii., 190; Wotton's "Baronetage," iv., 470; Wright's "Essex," ii., 734; "Mis. Gen. et Her.," 5 S., i., 19; the "Life of Marmaduke Rawdon of York," Camden Soc. Pub., 1863; "Visitation of York"; Calendar of State Papers, Domestic, 1628-29; Illustration of Rawdon book-plates in Ex Libris Soc. Pub., vol. vii., 10.

Robert Rawdon, citizen and fishmonger of L. Will dated 7 Aug. 1644. £700 I owe my son-in-law Nich. Raynsford by bond of £1000 to be first paid.

D ——————————————————————— D

Bevell Rawdon, 3rd son, a merchant at Surinam 1666.	Robert Rawdon, 9th son, godson 1614 of his uncle Robert; died a bachelor in the Canaries.	Elizabeth, 1st dau., bapt. 9 April 1618 at Barking; mar. Edmond Forster, partner of Col. Tho. Rawdon, and a grantee of land in Barbados 1628; Capt. of City Bands 1633. She living 1666.	Martha, 2nd dau., bapt. 19 Dec. 1622 at Barking; mar. Tho. Williams of Layton, co. Essex; a widow 1666.

Katheren my wife shall have ⅓ of my personal estate. My s^{d} son-in-law N. R. and Eleanor his wife and my s. Wm R. shall have ⅓, and the testators ⅓. I will as following. To my s. W^{m} £20. To my bro. Marmaduke R. my best cloke and £3 for a ring. Rob. R. my godson, his son, £5 at 21. My cozen Raphe Trattle £3. Cosen Mary Trattle £3 at marriage. My part of the good ship the "Marmaduke" to my 4 grandch^{n} Rob., Edwd, Marm. and Nich. Raynsford. My grandchild Kathtryne Raynsford £20. Poor of Magnus parish 40*s*. Poor of Magd. Bermondsey £3. All residue to Katheryne my wife and my said son-in-law N. Raynsford and Ex'ors. To my wife the house on the baucksyde which I purchased of Mr Edwd Gryffen in St Saviour's, Southwark, for her life, then to s^{d} son-in-law. To my dau. El^{r} Raynsford those 3 tenements I lately bought of John Pope in Mitcham, co. Surrey. I give that house I bought of Harryson Eatlaffe in Burnham, co. Essex, to my 2 Ex'ors. My brother Marm. and cosen Raphe Trattle to be overseers. Proved 8 Oct. 1647 by Kath. R. the relict and Nich^{s} Raynford. (204, Fines.)

Martha Molesworth of Hoddesdon, co. Hartford, widow. My l. husband Pryn's gods. Wm P. of Lincoln's Inn, Esq. I give unto Marmaduke Rowdon son of my Ex'trix £100. To Bevill Rowdon her son £200. Rob. R. her son £200. To Marm. R. s. of Tho. R. £200 at the age of 7. Cozen Anne Forster. Widow Martha R. dau. of my Ex'trix £1000. To the 2 daus. of my grandson Edward (*sic*) Forster of L., march^{t}, to Eliz. the eldest £150, and Martha 2^{d} dau. £150, in discharge of all promises bills made unto the s^{d} Edmond (*sic*) F. To Edmond F. s. of s^{d} Edmond F. £200. My dau.-in-law Eliz. Lucey my gold ring with 5 diamonds. Martha her dau. a gold chain. To my s^{d} grandsons Edmond F., Wm Bowyer

and Henry Crowe £10 each. All residue to my dau.-in-law Dame Eliz. Rowdon al's Rawdon al's Thorowgood and sole Ex'trix. Tho. Thorowgood, my late dec^{d} husband and father of the s^{d} Dame E. R., left me a plentiful estate. I do love her and her children. 19 July 1646. Proved 26 Oct. 1646 by Dame Eliz. Rowdon al's Rawdon al's Thorowgood. (148, Twisse.)

Testator's 3^{d} husband was Bevile Molesworth, whose will was proved in 1636. (Vivian's "Visitation of Cornwall," i., 327.)

1653-4, Jan. St Roger Jaques, Kn^{t}. Adm'on on the 21st to Dame Mary Jaques, relict of Sr R. J. of the city of York, alderman. fo. 623.

Tho. Rawdon of Hoddesdon, co. Hertford, Esq. Will dated 1 April 1664. All my estate in the Isle of Barbadoes to my six younger children, viz., Thos., Geo., Eliz., Magdalen, Martha and Kath., equally at 21 or day of marriage; to be educated and brought up by their mother. To my s. Thos. all suger and sums due to me from my brother Bevill R. which I sent him towards the setling of his plantation in Surrinam. All residue to Magdalen my wife and sole Ex'trix. My trusty friends Sr John Colleton, B^{t}, and Benj. Sheppard, scriveno^{r}, overseers, and £10 apeece. In the p. of Wm Rawdon, etc. Proved 25 Sept. 1666 by M. R. the relict. (136, Mico.)

D

Katherine, 3rd dau., bapt. 25 April 1624 at Barking; mar. Wm. Gamble *alias* Bowyer of Laytonstone, Esq. He died 22 Sept. 1658, aged 43. M.I. at Broxbourne. (Cussans, ii., 183.) She living 1668.	Jane, mar. Ralph Trattle of Greenwich.	. . . ., dau., mar. Henry Crewe of Bristol, Surveyor of Customs. He died 4 March 1685, aged 69. M.I. at Broxbourne. (Cussans, ii., 196.)

Marmaduke Raudon of L., merch^{t}, s. of Lawrence R. late of the city of York, alderman. If I die near York to be buried in Crux church in the chancel where my dear father and mother and most of my family have been buried. If I die at Hodsden to be buried in the chancel of Broxborne church near my cossen Bowyer. To the sons and dau. of Sr Roger Jaques, viz., Roger, Henry, W^{m}, Robert and Grace, 20*s.* each. To my aunt the Lady Raudon £10. To Coll. Tho. R., to his son Marmaduke, his dau. Eliz., and to his wife £30, and to his son Marmaduke my emerald ring with the R.'s arms. My cossen Bevill R. my great ring of diamonds with the King's picture in it and one of my Spanish rapers. My cossen Mrs Kath. Bowyer my cup of pure gold and great cup of mother of pearl set in silver and £10. Mrs Eliz. Forster £10. Mrs Jane Crew and her husb^{d} £20. Mrs Martha Williams £50 and £10. Her son Mr David W. £10. Cossen Allington and his wife £10, and his sister Kate and other brothers £5 apiece. Cossen Mr Wm Bowyer £5. Mr Tho. Boycott and Mr Nath. Fen his brother £5 each. Cossen Wm Rawdon and his wife £20, and to her £100, and each of his sons £50 only. To my godson Lawrence £100, and to each of his daus. £20. Cossen Raphe Trattle and his wife £10 each. Cossen Mrs Mary Fellowes £5. Cossen Mrs Jane Tice £5. Cossens Chr. Hebden, Wm Hebden and Tho. White each a silver tankard with my arms to be engraven thereon, and to every of their children 20*s.* Cozen Mrs Ann Brice, wife to Mr Fra. B., my ring with 5 diamonds. To the eldest child of Mr John Harrison of Bransbie £5, for the love I had for their uncle my Stuart [*sic* ? steward] Marmaduke Harrison. Cossen Mrs Eliz. Templer my oriental emerald ring. My Lady Hewley, wife unto Sr John Hewley, my great jewel of gold with K. David his picture. To the parish of Crux, York, where I was born, £100, to be imployed in land and penny loaves given every Sunday to the poor. £60 to the citty of York for a gold chain to be

worn by the Lady Maioress, and £100 for buying those houses which belonged to Mr Scott next Allhallows to be pulled down and to widen the pavement and to make a cross or shelter for the market people that sell meal and corn, also a cup of pure gold of £100 with the citty's and my arms engraven on it, also a silver chamber pot of £10 for the Ld Mayor. To the poor of Bransby and Stersbie where my dear father was born, and parish of Canton where my good mother was born, £5 each, to be disposed by my cossens Hebdens of Stersbie and cosen Barton of Canton. To Mary How, once servant to my sister the Lady Jaques, £5. Towards repairing the chapel in the town of Hodsden £10. Gods. Marmaduke R. s. of Rob. Raudon of York Pinner £10 and £50 at 21. My nephew Mr Wm Jaques and Mrs Margt. Brown £10 each. Cossen Raphe Trattle the Elder my fur coat with 4 doz. pure gold buttons upon it. £100 upon a monument in Broxborne church in that E. window where Mr Baily lieth buried, which may correspond with the monument of Sr Rob. Cock on the other side, which I give in memory of my ever honored Unckle Sr Marmaduke Rawdon; also hard by the great window in the chancel, to correspond with my cossen Bowyer's monument, £20 or £30 in a small monument in memory of me and recording my travels in Holland, Flanders, France and Spain. All residue to my loving cossen Marmaduke R., 2d son of Sr Marmaduke R. of Hodsden, Knt, and sole Ex'or.

In London this 19 June 1665. Mr Hugh Hassall my plain gold ring with the King's picture and £5. Proved 9 Feb. 1668 by M. R. (22, Coke.)

Magdalen Rawden of Hoddesden, co. Hartford, widow. Will dated 3 Nov. 1675. To my dau. Magd. R. £900. My son Geo. R. £700. My son Thos. R., having advanced, I give only £10. My household goods in the house at H. to my son Marm. My brother and sister Crew and sister Price £10 each. My children Marm., Eliz. Sparke and her husbd Geo.,* Magd., and to my son Marmaduke's wife £10 each. Magd. dau. of my son Marm. £10. My negro Frances £10. To my dau. Magd. all arrears of rent for my joynture. Whereas I have granted to my son Sparke rents in Hartfordshire of £15 2s. 6d. for £200, this sum to be repaid. To my son Marm. £5 to buy 2 silver trencher plates. My son Geo. R. and my dau. Magd. R. Ex'ors and the residue of personal estate. To be buried in the parish church of Broxborne near my late husbd. Proved 2 Dec. 1675 by Geo. R., the son and surviving Ex'or. (130, Dycer.)

Dame Eliz. Rawdon of Hodsdon in the parish of Broxbourne, co. Hertford, widow. To be interred in the parish church of Broxbourne. To my grandson Marmaduke R., eldest son of my son Tho. R., decd, all my messuages, lands in the parish of St Antholin's within the walls of the city of L., also my messuage the white hinde and the messuage and toft adjoining in the town of Hodsdon, also my copyhold messuage called the upper house in the parish of Waer, co. Hertford, and 5 acres, also my copyhold land and tenemt within the manor of Nasingbury, co. Essex. My said houses in St Antholin's was burnt by the late great fire I give £500 towards the rebuilding of them. To Marm. R., my 2d son, my messuage in Hodsdon, the Cock with the 2 other decayed tofts adjoining, and 7 acres and 1 acre of meadow lying in Dutch meade, 2 acres called Chadwell meade. To Berell R., my 3d son, my messuages in the parish of St Mary Matfellon al's Whitechappell, co. Middx, for his life, and at his death to return to my sd grandson Marm. R., and failing him to my grandson Geo. R., 3d son of my eldest son Tho., decd. To my dau. Martha William, widow, £600, to be laid out by my dau. Kath. Bowyer in land for an annuity, and at her death to my sd grandson Marm. R. To my godson (*sic*) Tho. R., 2d son of my eldest son Tho., decd, £50 at 21. Geo. R., the youngest son of my 1st son Tho. R., decd, £50 at 21. To each of my sons and daus. £5 for mourning, vizt, my dau. Magdalen R., son Marm. and Sarah his wife, Eliz. Foster my dau., Henry Crew my son-in-

* His name was Christopher.

law and Jane his wife, Martha Williams my dau. Gifts to servants. Poor £10. Forgive debts due from my dau. Martha W. or her husb[d] Tho. W., dec[d]. I have left in writing several legacies to my sons and daus. not incerted in this will. All residue of lands and goods to my son Bevell R., at present on the plantation of Surenam beyond the seas, and my right in that plantation called Barbados. My s[d] son and dau. Kath. Bowyer, widow, joynt Ex'ors. 27 Feb. 1666, 19 Chas. 2[d], in the presence of Henry Alington, W[m] Bowyear, W[m] Turner. Proved 5 March 1668 by K. Bowyer the dau.; power reserved to B. R. (36, Coke.)

Hester Rawdon of Hodsdon, co. Hertford, widow. Will dated 17 Dec. 1712. To be buried in Broxbourne Church. To my s. Marmaduke R. and my dau. Hester R. all my household goods (except all such as were my sister Anne Williamson's which I give my s[d] dau.). To my s. Marm. all family pictures and £800, but if he die before me the s[d] sum to my cousins Nich. Corsellis of Layer Marney, co. Essex, Esq., and Marm. Allington of Linc. Inn, Esq., and my s[d] dau. upon T. to invest with the approbation of my dau. Dorothy R., wife of my s[d] son for the use of my granddau. Hester R. his dau. and any other dau. To my granddau. Anne Lysons 20 gs. she having a very plentiful est. Of the residue ⅓ to my s. Marm. R., ⅓ to my dau. Hester R., ⅓ to my s. Sam. Bagnall of L., salter, and my dau. Hester R. on trust for my 3 grandchildren Sam. B., Eliz. B., and Hester B. Whereas my sister Anne Williamson, dec[d], by her will dated 27 Oct. 1709 gave me and my s. Marm. £800 in trust for the use of my dau. Eliz. Bagnall and her children, and my dau. is dead leaving 3 children. No accounts to be demanded for my s[d] sisters boarding with me. My s. Marm. Rawdon and dau. Hester Rawdon Ex'ors. In the p. of Nic. Corsellis, Tho. Bagnall. Proved 26 Sept. 1719 by both Ex'ors (169, Browning).

Marmaduke Rawdon, late of Hodesdon in the p. of Broxborne, co. Herts, now of Kentish-Town, p. of Pancrass, co. Middx., Esq. Will dated 17 Oct. 1750. To be buried in the Church of B. where my Father and Mother were laid. To my dau. Esther, wife of Joseph Keeling of Barking, co. Essex, Esq., all my lands in the I. of Barbadoes or Eng. and all moneys yet in arrear for the purchase of one pl[n] in B'oes called Fisher's Pond, which was sold by my grandf. Tho. R. shortly before his death, and for which a judgment was obtained as by my box of writings relating to the est, and to one other called Rawdon's Rents or pl[n], which last I have conveyed to my son-in-law Joseph K. and Esther his wife my dau., to be delivered to her also the picture of my Father and grandf. To my wife Rebecca plate and arrears of rent and one annuity from the Exchequer, all furn. and personal est. My son-in-law Joseph K. and my wife Ex'ors. Proved 4 Nov. 1752 by Joseph K.; power reserved to Rebecca R., the relict (286, Bettesworth).

John Keeling of the parish of St. James, Clerkenwell,* co. Middx., brewer. Will dated 21 March 1753. To be interred in my family vault in Leigh, co. Stafford. M[r] Jas. Reynolds late of S[t] Jas., C., butcher, £100. My brother Joseph K., Esq., £250. Bro.-in-l. Tho. Hughes £100. My wife Ann £100 and ½ my furniture. All residue of personal estate in trust to pay £200 a year to her and to carry on the business of brewing until my son John K. be 21, then all to him, if he die ½ to my brother Joseph and ½ for my wife. All real estate to son John and in default to my s[d] brother.

Codicil. Cousin Mary wife of R[d] Prerst £50. 9 Jan. 1755. On 28 May 1759 appoints Jos. K. of S[t] Jas., C., Esq. Proved 30 May 1759 by Ann K., wid., etc. (174, Arran.)

Hester the now wife of Joseph Keeling of Fingringhoe, co. Essex, Esq., late Hester Rawdon, spr. Will dated 21 Aug. 1756. All my real estate in England

* Testator, 2nd son of John and Mary Keeling, was bapt. 25 May 1721.

or elsewhere to my loving husband Joseph Keeling and his heirs absolutely, also all personal estate and sole Ex'or. Proved 20 Jan. 1757 by J. K. (18, Herring.)

John Slany of the city of Norwich, Esq. Will dated 3 Sept. 1787. To Trustees £3000 bank stock, £1600 3 per cent. bank annuities, £54 per ann. bank long annuities, £100 short annuities and £500 5 per cent. annuities to pay the interest to my s[d] sister Alice Keeling for her life, and at her death the interest of ⅓ for her husb[d] Joseph K. for his life.

Codicil. 4 Oct. 1790. Plate, linen, china and glass to my s[d] sister.

Proved 30 Aug. 1791. (405, Bevor.)

No Slanys are named, only nieces Kath. Hunt and Mary Cooke.

Joseph Keeling of Westbury House in the parish of Barking, co. Essex. Will dated 6 Jan. 1792. Infirm of body. To my wife Alice all my farms and lands in Great Britain, bank stock and consols, plate, furniture, horses, chariot for her life, to be disposed of by her by will to such of her ch[n] as she thinks proper. My snuff box and gold watch to my dau. Mary Tooke. The new gold watch to my dear son Capt. John K. with the seal of arms of K., Rawdon and Slaney. Whereas my son has been most cruelly treated and neglected by his late uncle John Slaney, Esq., who has taken no notice of him in his will, and I am entitled to a moiety of a mortgage of £1000 from Lord Cahir of Irel[d], the interest being payable to my wife and at her death to go to her son and dau., and my son having disposed of the post obit to M[r] Playters for £100, w[h] I purchased, I bequeath it to him. I give him my claim on my lands in the parish of S[t] Michael, I. of B'oes, conveyed to me by my late F.-in-l. Marm. Rawdon, Esq., for which I have expended large sums endeavouring the recovery thereof without effect, but have recovered part which I have called Rawdon Place, consisting of 3 houses and lands adjoining the fort called Greenwill fort to the Leeward of Bridge Town. My wife Alice sole Ex'trix. If I die in Barking to be interred in that part of the ancient symmetry (*sic*) w[h] I have ordered to be enclosed and set apart as a burial place for myself and family next the chy[d] of Barking, the wall of w[h] I shall break a gateway fronting the N. door. If I die at Buxton or near Leigh in Staffordshire, in w[h] chy[d] I have a family vault, to be interred there with my ancestors.

1 Aug. 1792. *Codicil.* Whereas I have £500 stock of the Bank of England worth £1000, my wife to have it, but sh[d] my son succeed in his application for the Harwich packet, the stock to be applied towards fitting that out and having £1300 or £1400 at my bankers, let that be applied towards the annuities of my nephew John Keeling and his wife, and the copyhold malthouses in the manor of Canonbury, Kingston, may be sold.

Proved 20 Aug. 1792 by Alice K., wid., the relict. (436, Fountain.)

TOBIN OF NEVIS. (*Ante*, 1.)

Maurice Berkeley, Jun., had married in London, in or before 1731, Sarah, dau. of Walter Tobin. Henrietta Tobin, spinster, was her sister, and afterwards married in 1736 Samuel Clarke, Jun.

In the Nevis Records (vol. ii., 55) I noted an indenture dated 29 May 1725, by which Sarah Tobin, widow and executrix of Walter Tobin, deceased, quits claim against Mary Symonds, widow and relict of John Symonds, and her son Edward Symonds. This John Symonds was born 1686, B.A. Oxford 1708 and Speaker 1712. His wife Mary was probably the "Sister Symonds" of John Tobin in 1724.

Stoney Grove, the property of Messrs. Gillespie Brothers, and the residence of the late Hon. J. S. Hollings, is a fine old mansion. The Tobins formerly owned it, and Mrs. Bromley writes that the original plan of the estate with their coat of arms on it is preserved there.

Lears, in the parish of St. Michael, Barbados.

Lears, St. Michael's.

This old house is a few miles from Bridgetown. The basement and ground floor are of the usual eighteenth century style, the stonework being very strong and thick. The gables are also probably original, but not the roof, which is now of ugly galvanized iron. The oblong wooden panel in the east or right-hand gable has:—

"R. 1651 H.
JAN. 28 E. 1758."

R. H. was doubtless the builder of the mansion and the second date may record a reconstruction. The shield on the panel in the west gable has suffered damage, but there are traces of arms, viz., *two bends and a canton.* Some charges which may have been affixed are now missing. In a grove adjoining is a brick vault surmounted by a stone slab recording the burial of "M^(IS) ALCE LEAR," wife of Thomas Lear, who died 24 Oct. 1688. On a mantled shield are his Arms: .... *a fesse ragulé between three unicorns' heads couped.* Crest: *A demi-unicorn rampant couped, in its paws a spear—over wreath and helmet.*

Peter Lear was appointed by Penn and Venables one of the commissioners of the Prize Office in Barbados in 1655. He became a wealthy planter, and was created a Baronet on 2 July 1660, having then retired to London, and died s.p. in 1684. At Allhallows Barking, was baptized—

1660 March 1 Thomas sonne of Sir Thos Leare.

In the census of the island in 1680 under St. George's Parish are entered:—

Sr Peter Leare	336 acres,	8 white servants,	123 negroes.	
Mr Thomas Leare	127 „	1 „	75 „	

Sir Peter was succeeded by his nephew and heir Sir Thomas of Lindridge, co. Devon, M.P. for Ashburton 13 Will. III. and 1 Anne, who died s.p. 1705, having married Isabella, third dau. of Sir William Courtenay, Knt., of Powderham Castle (who was bapt. 18 Dec. 1660). Sir Thomas was succeeded by his next brother Sir John, who died about 1740, when the title became extinct. By his wife, a dau. of Christopher Wolston, he left Mary, an only child, who mar. Sir Thomas Tipping, Bart.

1700, May 7. It was ordered that the Council meet at the house of Wm. Davis, joining upon Lears plantation near Henleys in St. Michael's parish.

Col. John Lear of Nancymond co., Virgin'a, was sworn a M. of C. 22 May 1683, was collector of Lower James River, and died in 1696, having married the widow of Seth Sothell, Gov. of Carolina. (Col. Cal.)

David Lear was of the same county in 1677.

Col. James Lear was M. of A. for the said county in 1683 and Tho. Lear in 1693. It is not known if this Virginian family was related to the Barbadian one, as no search has been made.

The illustration is from an enlargement of a photograph taken in 1914 by Mrs. Vere Oliver.

Francis Ford, Esq., of St. Michael's, by his will dated 1772, devised Lears to his dau. Anne. "I do also give my daus. their residence in my dwelling house on my plantation called Lears, each to have the sole use of a chamber to herself." (*Ante*, III., 372.)

Rose of Jamaica.

Anthony Swymmer of Bristol and Jamaica, Esq. Will dated 11 Oct. 1684. My brother and sister Fulke Rose of St Jago de la Vega, Esq., and his wife. (141, Exton.) (*Ante*, IV., 229.)

Fulke Rose of the parish of St. Katherine and Island of Jamaica. Will dated 27 Oct., 5 Wm. and Mary, 1693. I bequeath the marble at my storehouse in town and at the *Angells* and at *Sixteen Mile Walkes* at my plantation to pave the chancel of the church now to be erected at Sixteen Mile Walkes. To my eldest dau. Eliz. Rose my plantation and negroes in St Thomas in the Vale called *Knollis*, and my farm at Oxney, near Deale in Kent, lately in the occupation of Mr Wood. To my 2d dau. Anne Rose my other plantation in the said parish called *Mickleton* with the negroes, also my land at Maggatty called *Warrens* and *Hipperslys* and negroes, and to them all my houses and lands in the town of St Jago de Laviega, my lands over the river and at the Red hills, both in St Katherines. To my youngest dau. Mary Rose, Nonnington farm, near Canterbury, and £1500 now in the hands of my brother Mr Wm Rose of London, apothecary, also my lands on the North side of this Island in St Maries and St George. To my sister Eliz. Milner £30 a year. My aunt Margaret Tudor a suit and the continuation of the allowance my brother Wm. has paid her. To my brother Wm Rose and his wife, my brother John Rose and his wife, my brother Fra. Rose and his wife, my brother Norgrove and his wife, and my sister Milner each £20. My brother-in-law Andrew Langley and sister Martha Langley £10 each. My sister-in-law Martha Langley £100. My goddau. Kath. Feake £20 a year till 16. My godsons Cha. Reid and Ellis Langford at 10 a good bible. Philip Wheeler £30 when free of his apprenticeship to me at 21. If all my daus. die without heirs then to Fulke Rose, 2d son of my brother Wm. Rose, Knollis plantation and Oxney farm, he paying my sister Milner £200 a year. To my brother Francis Rose, Mickletons plantation, etc., he paying to my sister Norgrove £150 a year. To my brother John Rose, Nonnington farm, etc. If my wife have a son all my estate to him, then to my dau. Eliz. £2000 at 17, my daus. Anne and Mary £1500 each. My children to be paid £60 a year till 10. My wife Eliz. sole Ex'trix, her thirds and £2000, all plate, jewells and household stuff. My friends Sam. Bernard, Esq., Mathew Gregory, Esq., Edward Broughton, Esq., my brother Capt Fra. Rose and Mr Rob. Nedham Trustees and overseers and £10 each. All residue for my daus. Witnessed by Leonard Claiborne, Henry Lowe, Mich. Houldsworth, Wm Lavers, Jas. Whitchurch, Sam. Jones.

Codicil, 8 Nov. 1693. In case my wife have a son I give to my dau. Eliz. the further sum of £2000 and my daus. Anne and Mary £1500 each. Witnessed by John Smith, Sam. Lewis, Henry Sanders. Proved 24 March 1693 by Eliz. Rose the relict. (97, Box.)

Tho. Hals of Clarendon, J'ca, Esq. Will dated 21 Aug. 1702. Wife Mary. Capt. John Rose and his wife. Tho. Rose, son of Capt. John Rose of London, merchant. (69, Degge.)

Eliz. Rose of the I. of J'ca in America, but now in L., widow and relict of the Hon. Fra. R., late of J., Esq., decd. Will dated 20 Dec. 1725. My nephew Fra. Sadler £600 st. at 21. My nephew Tho. Bush £300 at 21. My sister Eliz. Bush £100. My sister Ann Norgrove £100. My negro woman Margt £4 a year. My negro woman Amimba and her 2 chn £12 a year. Whereas my late husbd by his will dated 18 Nov. 1720 gave to our late son Tho. Rose all the residue of his estate, and for default of issue to me for my life, then to his

nephew John Rose, subject to the payment of £3000 c. to such persons as I sh[d] appoint, and Tho. Rose is since dead without issue, I hereby appoint the £3000 to be paid to my 2 neices Mary Fuller, wife of Tho. F. of J'ca, Esq., and Christian Forbes, wife of Alex. F. of J., Esq. To Fra. Oldfield of Bloomsbury Sq., Esq., and M[r] John Serocold of L., merch[t], £50 apiece. All residue to my said two neices and sole Executrixes for J'ca and F. O. and J. S. for G. B. Witnessed by Ann Modyford, John Halton, Tisa Bernard, Rob. Hobbs. Proved 11 Dec. 1727 by F. O. and J. S. (306, Farrant.)

Sam. Heming of S[t] Annes, J., Esq. Will dated 3 June 1720. My M. in law Eliz. Rose now residing in L. £20 a year. My couzen Tho. Rose, Esq.

Tho. Rose, late of the parish of S[t] Cath. and I. of J., but now of G[t] B Will dated 7 Nov. 1724. To my Mother £2000 st., my plate, chariot and 2 coach horses. My aunt Eliz. Bush £50 yearly, and to her son, my cousen, Francis B. £200. My cousen Eliz. Snell £25 yearly. Cousen Christian Price £500 c. To Mrs. Ann Beckford, dau. of Peter B. of J., Esq., £2000 c. Henry Byndloss, son of Polnitz B. of J., £1000 c. at 21. To Jane Byndloss, dau. of said P. B., £500 c. at 21. My friend Wm. Cockburn £500. Cap[t] Digby Dent £500. Col. Twogood £200 and release claims I have as his attorney. John Gregory's bond to be cancelled, also W[m] Aikenhead's bond. Churchwardens of S[t] Cath. £100 c. yearly for 10 years for maintenance of poor children and apprenticing them. I manumise my slaves Molly and Grace and give them £6 a year. I free my negro Sasoe and give him £12 a year and free his wife Cœlia. I free Mimba, Scotland and Abba. All monies to be remitted to M[r] Sam. Bernard and M[r] John Serocold of L., merchants, to be laid out in the purchase of land for my cousens Cha. Price and Tho. Price, sons of my uncle Chas. Price of the parish of S[t] Johns, J., Esq. I devise my plantan walk and land at the Magotty in the parish of S[t] Thomas in the Vale adjoining any of my 3 plantations or sugar works, my land in the parish of S[t] Mary called Bagnall Ticket, my pen and pen land at Cut Woath Gully in the parish of S[t] Cath. to such persons as shall enjoy my 3 sugar estates in the parish of S[t] Tho. in the Vale called the Old plantation, Burtons, and the New Works.* All residue to my said 2 cousens equally at 21. Sam. Bernard and John Serocold to be Ex'ors for G[t] B. and my uncle Cha. Price for J. and £20 apiece. In the presence of Tho. Barrow, Tho. Pickhaver, Tho. Clarke.

Abstracted from an ancient copy on seven sheets of folio paper in the Editor's possession. It is also recorded P.C.C., 253, Bolton

---

John Rose of Cotterstock, co. N'ton, Esq. Will dated 24 Nov. 1736. Cousin Rob. Fotherby and Fra. his wife £25 apiece. Cousen Mary Stileman £20. Cousin Martha Milner £20. Cousin Tho. Bush £15. Cousin Tho. Pain the Elder of Oundle £35 for himself, his wife and 2 sons. My sister Eliz. Pate and her 2 daus. Eliz. P. and Anne P. £20 apiece. Elmes Spincks of Allwinckle, co. N'ton, Esq., £10. Chr. Bainbrig, clk., V. of Cotterstock and Glapthorn, £10. Mary Buzzard of Oundle, spr., £10, all for mourning. To Eliz. Pate and Anne Pate £500 apiece. Fra. wife of Rob. Fotherby £400. Mary Stileman £400. Mary Buzzard £100. Tho. Cooper £100. W[m] Ward of C. £10. Cousins John Paine and Tho. Paine, the younger sons of s[d] Tho. P. the Elder, £100 apiece at 21. Tho. Bush £300 at 21. £100 for the poor. My sister Eliz. Pate £25 a year. Martha Milner £15 a year. My effects from J'ca. My cousin Rose Fuller of J'ca, Esq., £50 c. Cousin Francis Sadler of J., gt., £20 c. and £2000 c. when he shall have

* These estates were called "Rose Hall" when in the possession later of the Prices.

remitted the whole of my personal estate from J. All my real estate in Cotterstock, Glapthorn, Oundle, Tansor, Brigstock, and Ringstead to my nephew John Pate, inf., and in default to my cousin Fra. Sadler, cousin Rose Fuller, s[d] nephew to change his name to Rose. £6 a year for poor ch[n] of C. to be apprenticed. Elmes Spincks and Chr. Bainbridg G. and T. and 100 gs. apiece. Joseph Billcars of Bristol £12. Cousin Mary Smith of Leic[r], wid., £12. To John Pain, 1 s. of Tho. P. the Elder, £100. Mary Dodgson, dau. of Rev. Master Jas. D., Vicar of S[t] Ives, co. Hunt., 50 gs. £50 c. to the 2 sons of Tho. King, late of Spanish Town, J., dancing master, dec[d]. Fra. Sadler £1000 c. £6 a year for poor ch[n] of Glapthorn. 5½ a. to the Vic. of C. All residue to s[d] nephew John Pate and sole Ex'or. M[r] Tho. Bush £10 a year. On 13 Jan. 1736 appeared Elias Micklethwait of S[t] Marg[t], Westm[r], gt. On 15 Jan. 1736 adm'on to Eliz. Pate, the M. of J. P. the nephew by the brother (*sic*). Proved 13 Dec. 1740 by J. P. the nephew, he having attained the age of 17. (12, Wake.)

John Rose of Northill, co. Bedford, Esq. Will dated 17 Aug. 1758. All my estate real and personal in the I. of J'ca and Eng. to the use of Tho. Wentworth of Brittons in the p. of Silkston, co. York, Esq., and Joseph Letch of the Mid. T., gent., upon Trust. To my brother-in-law M[r] John Serocold £30 and my brother-in-law M[r] James Esdaile. My aunt M[rs] Sarah Kitchen, wife of M[r] John K., and my uncle M[r] Tho. Nickless each £20. M[rs] Martha Henn, now living with me, £50. To each of my trustees £50. Rev. Rich[d] Price of Cotterstock, co. N'ton, £50. M[r] Henry Clark of Chas. Str., Westm[r], and Dominick Pile of Westm[r], apothecary, and John Shickle of J'ca, Esq., each £20. To the Hon. Cha. Price, Esq., and his son Chas. P., Esq., both of J'ca, each £50. Tho. Wentworth and Jos. Letch and Cha. Price the father and Cha. Price the son to have each £50 a year if they will take on the trusts. Trustees to pay to Martha Henn £30 a year and £120 a year, and maintain and educate my two daus. Lætitia Rose and Sophia Rose. L. b. 28 Ap. 1751 and bapt. on 7 May following in the p. of S[t] James, Westm[r], and S. b. 10 May 1752 and bapt. 12 May in the s[d] parish. If Martha Henn shall have any other child, to be also maintained, and at 21 all residuary estate to my children. If they die all to Martha Henn for her life, then to my nephew Peter Esdail, the son of s[d] Jas. E., and in default of issue to all the ch[n] of my late sister Eliz. E., and in default to Jas. E., Joseph E., Mary E. and W[m] E., the ch[n] of my s[d] bro.-in-law Jas. E., then to Kingsmill Clark in Figtree Court, Inner T., and the son Sir Simon C. of J'ca. My plantations to be kept well stocked with slaves, etc. Tho. Wentworth and Jos. Letch Ex'ors for G. B. and Cha. Price, s[r] and j[r], for J'ca. Proved 28 Nov. 1758 by T. W., Esq., and J. L. (346, Hutton.)

John Serocold of L., merch[t]. Will dated 13 Oct. 1743. My copyhold messuages in Ruislipp, co. Midd[x], to my son John S. and his heirs, then to my son Tho. S., my sister Eliz. S., my cousin Tho. S., grocer, and his son Walter S., if latter inherit he shall pay £1000 to his sister Marg[t] S. ⅓ of my personal estate to my 2 ch[n] John and Thos. S. I am a freeman of L. of the c[o] of mercers. Of the other ⅓ I give to my friends Col. Chas. Price and John Hudson Guy, Esq., both of J'ca, my sister Eliz. S., my sons and friends M[r] Slingsby Bethell and M[r] Harding Tomkins £20 each. Debts to me in J'ca. To Eliz. Trewhella my serv[t] £50. All residue to my sister Eliz. S. in Trust for my s[d] ch[n] at 21. She to be sole Ex'trix and G. Proved 20 July 1744. (179, Anstis.)

John Serocold, late of Love Lane, L., merch[t], now residing in Q. Ann Str., East. Will dated 3 Nov. 1788. All residue to my dau. Eliz. Jackson, wife of M[r] John J., Sir Jas. Esdaile, Kn[t], Ald[n] of L., W[m] Jones, late of Love Lane,

now of Grange Walk in Southwark, gt., and John Roebuck of S[t] Mary at Hill, grocer, upon Trust to invest in the funds. I give them 20 gs. each for a ring and to pay the interest to my s[d] daus. Children of my bro. Tho. S. T. to be Ex'ors. Proved 11 Dec. 1788 by Eliz. Jackson the dau.; power reserved to the others. (621, Calvert.)

This Ind're tripartite made the 15 July 1703 2 Anne between Eliz. Rose of the parish of S[t] Gyles in the ffeilds co. Middx. spinster 1st dau. of ffulke R., l. of the parish of S[t] Katharines in the I. of Jamaica in parts beyond the Sea Esq. deceased of the 1st part; John Fuller J[r] of Waldron co. Sussex Esq. of the 2[d]; and H [*rubbed here by fold*] of the parish of S[t] Gyles in the ffeilds doctor in physick and Eliz. his wife (l. wife of the said ffulke Rose) and John Heathcott of London Merchant of the 3[d] part. Whereas ffulk Rose by his will dated 27 Oct. 1693 devised to Eliz. his eldest dau. all that his plantation in S[t] Thomas in the Vale called Knollis Plantation with the negros stock houses and also that farme at Oxney co. Kent then or l. in the tenure of M[r] Wood and further devised to Eliz. and Anne her sister all his houses in the Town of S[t] Jagoe de Lariega his lands over the River and at the Red hills in S[t] Katharines parish with all buildings negros and stock and to each of his children 60[l] per annum till the age of 10 and after that age 80[l] per annum and constituted his wife Eliz. sole Ex'trix and devised to her the third part of the profitts also the money owing him by his brother Francis R. and as much more out of the estate as w[d] make up 2000[l] and devised all residue as trust for all his daus. and appointed Sam. Bernard Esq., Matthew Gregory Esq., Edw. Braughton Esq., his brother Capt. Fra. Rose and M[r] Rob. Needham Trustees and Overseers and Whereas Eliz. Rose the relict proved the will and married Hans Sloane and the Trustees preferred their Bill in Chancery against the said Hans Sloane and Eliz. his wife and against Eliz. R., Ann R., Mary R. and Philippa R. the 4 daus. and it was ordered that defendants D[r] Sloan and Eliz. his wife should produce accounts before a Master of the Court and they have done so before Tho. Pitt Esq. and Eliz. Rose the eldest dau. being now 21 applied for her share and by an order made the 25 June last it is decreed that one third be let out for D[r] Sloan and Eliz. his wife and that the residue (subject to a charge to one Eliz. Milner) be divided equally among the 4 daus. and the Master made his Report dated the 12 instant July and reported due to Eliz. R. 489[l] for her fourth share and there is further due to her one fourth of 1493[l] debts outstanding and for her share of the produce of the estate 611[l], 225[l], and 1650[l] and for her share of the produce of the plantations to her devised 1012[l], and for interest 105[l] making a total of 4125[l] and Whereas a marriage is intended between John Fuller and the said Eliz. Rose she doth acknowledge to have received the said 4125[l] and discharges all parties.

Signed by "Eliz. Rose." Lozenge-shaped seal:—Arms: . . . . *on a bend three roses* . . . . In the presence of Oliver Marton, John Butler, Sam[ll] Osborn.

On two skins formerly in the Editor's possession. [Mem. 22 June 1911. I sold this deed to the Rev. A. Fuller of The Lodge, Sydenham Hill, S.E., who writes that he has now the Releases of Eliz., Philippa and Mary Rose.]

This Indenture made the 17 June 1709 8 Anne Between Hans Sloane of the p'sh of S[t] Giles in the ffeilds co. Middx. D[r] in Physick and Eliz. Sloane (formerly Eliz. Rose wife of ffulke Rose Esq. deceased) n. wife of s[d] Hans S. of the one part and John Heathcott of L. Merch[t] of the other. Whereas by an Ind're trip. dat. 9 May 1695 betw. Hans Sloane of the 1st part; Eliz. his wife (then Eliz. Rose) of S[t] James within the Liberty of Westminster widow of the 2[d] part; and John Heathcott and John Bernard cit. and upholster of L. of the 3[d] part after reciting that a marriage was then intended betw. H. S. and Eliz. Rose and that

Fulke Rose Esq. had been seized of several plantations and houses in Jamaica and of divers messuages in England and of a considerable pers. est. made his will on 27 Oct. 1693 and gave his said wife in lieu of her dower one third of the neat profits of all his est. both real and personal for her life as also the money his brother Fra. R. owed him and as much more money within 2 years as w[d] make up £2000 and gave the residue to trustees for his daus. and made her sole Ex'trix and she did accordingly assign to John Heathcott and John Bernard her said one third share for 99 years upon trust to place out the said £2000 and pay one third the interest thereof and of her said share to her for her sole use and the residue or ⅔ to Hans Sloane and Whereas John Bernard is dead now this Ind're Witnesseth that Hans Sloane and Eliz. his wife acknowledge they have received their shares and acquit John Heathcott and Whereas by Ind're dated 14 Feb. 1708 made between Mary Rose (one of the 4 daus. of the said ffulke Rose) of S[t] Giles in the ffeilds spinster one of the daus. of said F. R. of the parish of S[t] Katherines in J. Esq. dec[d] of the 1st part, Tho. Green of S[t] Margarett Westminster Esq. of the 2[d] part and Hans Sloane and Eliz. his wife of the 3[d] part reciting a marriage shortly intended and since solemnized between Tho. Green and Mary Rose and that there was due £10 11s. to Eliz. Sloane for life being the interest on £489 and £143, the £632 being the share of Mary Rose in the partible est. of F. R. thitherto received and Hans Sloan and Eliz. his wife had agreed for £85 to sell their interest in the £10 11s. charge Tho. Green hath paid that and they acquit him and it was also recited that by an Ind're dat. 18 Jan. 1708 which is a marriage settlement of 6 parts it was agreed that Mary Rose should as soon as she attained the age of 21 convey Nunnington ffarme near Canterbury her share of her father's est. (wherein Eliz. Sloane was intitled to ⅓) to Tho. Cross and Wm. Green and it was agreed that if the latter paid £258, Hans Sloane and Eliz. his wife would release her claim and they appoint the said sum to be paid to ffrancis Annesly of the Inner Temple Esq. in trust for them and appoint John Heathcott after such payment to convey and assure the farm.

Signed	Hans Sloane	L.S.	Crest.—*A hound sejant.*
	Eliz: Sloane	L.S.	" "
	[*blank*]	L.S.	" "

In the presence of Edw[d] Clifton, Tho. Page, Edw. Wood.

The following is endorsed on the 2nd skin:—

To all People Sir Hans Sloane of S[t] Gyles in the ffeilds Baronett and Dame Eliz. his wife send greeting. Whereas since making the within Ind're John Heathcott acted some years and dyed and made his will and constituted Sir Gilbert Heathcote (*sic*) of L. Kn[t] and Wm. Heathcott l. of L. Merchant (now dec[d]) Ex'ors who acted in the Trusts until the death of Wm. H. and he having made his will constituted Sir Gilbert Heathcott Ex'or who hath acted . . . . They quit claim against the Heathcotts this 8 March 1719 6 George.

Signed by Hans Sloane and Eliz. Sloane. Seals not heraldic.

In the presence of Tho. Isted, Philippa Rose, John Eccles.

On the 1st skin is endorsed:—

"17 Junij 1709 Doctor Sloane and his Lady to M[r] John Heathcott one of the two Releases touching the Estate late of ffulke Rose Esq[r] deceased and other matters."

[On 3 skins sent by Colemans 2 June 1911 in error and returned to Rev. A. Fuller.]

ST. CATHERINE'S, JAMAICA.

1670 Oct. 4 William May and Margaret Rose. (*Ante*, I., 13.)
1678 July 11 Fulke Rose and Elizabeth Langley (at Porte Royall). (*Ibid.*, 61.)

ST. PETER'S, CORNHILL,* LONDON.

1687 April 21 Fulke Rose son of Fulke Rose, in the Chancell.
1694 Mar. 29 ffoulke Rose, Marchant, in the Chancell, North side.

ST. OLAVE'S, HART STREET.

1695-6 Mar. 18 Fulke Rose, buried att Barkin, in London.

FACULTY LIC. OF THE ARCHB. OF CANTERBURY.

1695, May 9. Hans Sloan, D[r] of Physic, of S[t] Giles in the Fields, Middx., Bach. 30, and Elizabeth Rose of S[t] James in the Fields, Middx., Widow; at S[t] James afs[d] or— (Harl. Soc. Pub., p. 215.)

1703, July 19. John Fuller, J[r], of Waldron, co. Sussex, Esq., Bach. 23, and Elizabeth Rose of S[t] Giles in the Fields, Middx., Sp[r] 22, dau. of M[rs] Sloan, wife of D[r] Sloan, who consents; at S[t] Giles afs[d] or—

1703, July 19. Thomas Isted of the Middle Temple, Esq., Bach[r] 25, and Anne Rose of S[t] Giles in the Fields, Middx., Sp[r] 19, dau. of M[rs] Sloan, wife of Dr. Sloan, who consents; at S[s] Giles afs[d] or— (*Ibid.*, p. 216.)

EXTRACTS FROM THE CALENDAR OF STATE PAPERS, W.I.

1670. St. Katherine's parish. Fulke Rose. 380 acres.

As M. of A. for St. Tho. in the Vale he was elected in 1675 (then styled Capt.), 1677, 1678, 1679 (J.P. 1680), 1682, 1683 (as D[r]).

1684, Feb. 25. A List of the fittest men in J. to be Councillors:—

Dr. Fulke Rose, a surgeon bred, and a very discreet and virtuous man. His plantations render him over 4000*l.* per annum and his practice about 600*l.* A member of Assembly.

1693, March 23. Lt.-Gov. Sir Wm. Beeston recommends Fulke Rose, a man of integrity, ability and estate, for the Council.

1693, May 4. He was elected M. of A. for S[t] Johns and Francis R. for St. Tho. in the Vale.

1693, June 30. Order of the Queen in Council. Fulke Rose to be of the Council.

1694, Feb. 12. The Lt.-Gov. writes that M[r] Fulke Rose was gone to England when the warrant for his appointment arrived.

* The Langleys lived in this parish, which was probably why Dr. F. Rose was buried there.

1694, March 5. Journal of the Lords of Trade. Col. Rose from J. was heard and his Memorial about J. read.

1695. Col. John Bourden's Reg. of Foot. Major Fra. R's company.

1700, Feb. 1. Major Fra. R. of S[t] Tho. in the V. of good interest and a settled family recommended for the Council.

1701, July 1. Major Rose, then M. of A.

1702, Aug. 6. Francis Rose returned as M. for S[t] Catherines.

1702, Dec. 10. Lt.-Gov. to the Earl of Nottingham :—

I beg your Lordship would be pleased to put in as Councellor Lt.-Col. Francis Rose, a man that is faithful and zealous for H. M. service, and one of a very good estate in this Island.

1703, Jan. 28. Francis Rose sworn a M. of A. for St. Georges.

1703, March 9. Col. Francis Rose, M. of A., granted leave of absence.

1703, Sept. 10. Petition of . . . . and Francis Rose of the Council.

1655. A Capt. Stephen Rose was at the capture of J. (Venables Narrative.)

Lond[n], May 2[d], 1721. L'res from S[t] Iago in Jamaica, say the Hon[ble] Francis Rose, Esq[r], president of his Majesties Council there, is dead. ("Mawson's Obits" in Genealogist, New S., iii., 140.)

1724, Nov. 12. Dy'd Major Kose (*sic*), an eminent Jamaica Merchant, and formerly one of his Majesty's Council in that Island. (Historical Register, 48.)

1735, Oct. 8. The Revd. Mr. Stanley, to Miss Rose Daughter to the late Fulk Rose, of Jamaica, Esq ; by Dame Elizabeth afterwards Marry'd to Sir Hans Sloan, Bart. ("G.M.," 619.)

1825, April 27. At St. Dunstan's Church, Fleet-st., John Parson, of Bottesdale, Suffolk, to Eliz.-Georgiana, only dau. & h. of the l. Fred. Geo. Rose, of Black River, J., & niece of Lady Davidson, with a fortune of 30,000l. & 1000l. per annum in pin money. ("G.M.," 462.)

Cotterstock Vicarage,
Oundle.

Sir, *Oct.* 17*th*, 1916.

Mr. Rose was the owner of Cotterstock Hall and Impropriator of the Rectorial Tithes. He is, I believe, buried in the chancel of the Church of Cotterstock. I do not know how he became the owner of nearly the whole of Cotterstock, I suppose by purchase, but I do not know the name. The only one near his time was a Mr. John Norton, whose name I can find.

I know nothing of the bequest of £6 yearly for apprenticing poor children. We have another called Bellamy's Charity for that purpose. Bellamy lived during the Commonwealth days, and was contemporary with Mr. Norton aforesaid. He and his son lived at different times in Cotterstock and Tansor, I believe.

I do not know anything of the 5½ acres left to the Vicar. There is no such property belonging now to the Vicar, only the vicarage and a small meadow given in lieu of common rights when the parish was enclosed.

Mr. Pate Rose gave £200 which was met by a grant from Queen Anne's Bounty Board of a similar sum, £80 of which was given for the vicarage, there having been no vicarage before. I believe the vicarage had been his property.

In the Terrier it is called the house and orchard and the extent ½ an acre. The remaining £120 was expended on leasehold land in the parish of Warmington; in the Terrier it is described as 57¾ acres, and was in little strips in various parts of the parish. At the Enclosure 30¼ acres were given instead. The measurements must have been very bad, as that I was told by the churchwarden and overseer of Warmington was the case with all the lands. He described it as 7 roods to the acre.

I believe Mr. Pate Rose was buried in the family vault. He left two daughters; one Letitia married Rev. Sir Richard Booth, and both she and her husband are buried in the vault. There is a large mural tablet to Sir R. Booth, and the burial of the others is mentioned on it. I forget the other daughter's name. The property was left to them, and they sold it to the Countess of Westmoreland, who left it to her sister's son Viscount Melville, whose nephew is the present Viscount.

I think this is all that I can tell you.

Yours faithfully,

FRANCIS BRETTANSHAW.

ST. CATHERINE'S, JAMAICA.

On the floor of the nave, white marble with blue veins:—

ARMS.—*On a bend three roses.*

Here lyes the Body of the Honble | FRANCIS ROSE, Esq | late President of the Council of | this ISLAND, who departed this Life | ye 20th of November 1720 in the | 67th year of his age. (Roby, p. 32.)

On the floor of the north transept, white marble with blue veins:—

ARMS.—*On a bend three roses;* impaling *Barry of six, a canton.*

Here lyeth the body of | Mrs ELIZABETH ROSE | late wife of | the Honble THOMAS ROSE Esq | who departed this life | the 8th day of October | 1722. Aged 25 years. (*Ibid.*, 47.)

On the east wall of the north transept, a marble monument with Arms: *Sable, on a bend argent three roses gules;* impaling *Barry of six argent and gules, a canton of the second:*—

Near this place | lyes Interred ye body of | THOMAS ROSE Esq: | who departed | this life | ye 12th of Nov. 1724 | Aged 35 years. (*Ibid.*, 44.)

John Langley, Alderman of London, born 17 March 1612, and bapt. at St. Peter's, Cornhill, 28 March 1613. Had 8 sons and 5 daus. (See his pedigree in "Misc. Gen. et Her.," 2nd S., iii., 170.) = Eliz. Middleton, dau. and coheir of Rich. M., Alderman of L.; mar. 14 Sep. 1640.

A

Jane Langley,* 5th dau., mar. Anthony Swymmer of Jamaica, merchant, 1681, later of Bristol, Esq. Will dated 1684 (141, Exton), names his brother Fulke Rose of J.

Andrew Langley of J'ca 1684.

Sir Hans Sloane,† Bart., M.D., P.R.S. and R.C.P., mar. lic. and settlement 9 May 1695; died 11 Jan. 1753, aged 91; bur. in old Chelsea churchyard. M.I. in "G.M." for 1808, p. 670, and pedigree in 1810, p. 207. = Eliz. Langley, dau. and coheir, died 27 Sep. 1724, aged 66; bur. in Chelsea churchyard. M.I. = Dr. Fulke Rose of St. Thomas in the Vale, Jamaica, mercht. and Col., owned 380 a. in St. Cath. in 1670; M. of A. for St. Thomas in the Vale 1675; mar. at St. Cath. 11 July 1678; M. of A. 1682; named 1692 in will of Esther Cope and in that of his brother-in-law Sam. Langley; M. of C. 30 June 1693; bur. at St. Peter's, Cornhill, 29 March 1694. Will (97, Box).

Fulke Rose, bur. at St. Peter's, Cornhill, 21 April 1687.

Eliz. Rose, born 1681, 1st dau. and coheir; inherited Knollis in St. Thomas in the Vale; mar. lic. 19 July 1703, aged 22. She died 18 and bur. 26 Feb. 1727-8, and M.I. at Waldron, æt. 46. = John Fuller of Brightling, co. Sussex, J.P., bapt. at Waldron 28 July 1680; bur. there 10 Aug. 1745, aged 66. Will (223, Seymer).

Anne Rose, 2nd dau. and coheir, born 1684; mar. lic. 19 July 1703, aged 19, to mar. Tho. Isted of the Middle Temple, Esq.

Mary Rose, 3rd dau. and coheir, mar. Tho. Greene of Northland Ho., Chelsea, brewer; mar. sett. dated 14 Feb. 1708. She died 23 July 1724-5. Both bur. at Weston Favell.‡

Philippa Rose, youngest dau., witness to deed of 1719.

John Fuller of Rose Hill, co. Sussex, 1st son. Will (42, Paul).

Hon. Rose Fuller, 2nd son, Graduate of Leyden 1729; Dr. of Physic 1736; M. of C. of Jamaica; of Brightling; M.P. for Rye. His father settled the estate in Jamaica on him. Bur. at Waldron 15 May 1777. Will (211, Collier). = Ithamar, only dau. and heiress of Hon. Richd. Mill of St. Cath.; died 22 April 1738, aged 17. M.I. at St. Catherine's, Jamaica.

s.p.

Stephen Fuller, 8th son, agent of Jamaica; mar. and left four daus.

* A Major Andrew Langley, perhaps her brother, was a J.P. in J. Aug. 1687 (W.I. Cal., p. 416), and M. of A. for St. Mary's 1688 (*Ibid.*, p. 509).

† Sir Hans Sloane left two daus. and coheiresses: 1, Eliz., who mar. 1717 Chas., Lord Cadogan; 2, Sarah, mar. Geo. Stanley of Poultons, co. Hants.

‡ See pedigree in Hutchins' Dorset, i., 122.

ARMS.—*Sable, on a bend Argent three roses Gules* (ROSE).

John Rose of London.

A

Hon. Major Francis Rose, born 1654; of St. Thomas in the Vale, J.; M. of A. 1693; Speaker 1702; M. of C. 1703; died 20 Nov. 1720, aged 66. M.I. at St. Cath. with his arms (Roby, p. 32). Will dated 18 Nov. 1720; ? recorded in J. = Eliz. Price, dau. of Capt. Fra. Price of J. Will dated 20 Dec. 1725 in L. (306, Farrant).

Capt. John Rose of L., merchant, 1702.

William Rose of L., apothecary. = … → Fulke Rose, 2nd son.

Eliz. Rose, mar. . . . . Milner. — Ann Rose, mar. . . . . Norgrove.

Mary Rose, mar. 1st, Major Tho. Hals, who died 1702; 2ndly, Col. Cha. Sadler. Both of Jamaica.

Tho. Rose of St. Cath., J., M. of C. 1722; died 12 Nov. 1724, aged 35. M.I. (Roby, p. 44). Will dated in Eng. 7 Nov. 1724 (253, Bolton). Left his three plantations to his cousins Cha. and Tho. Price. = Elizabeth Fuller (? dau. of Chas. F., who died 1705-6), died 8 Oct. 1722, aged 25. M.I. at St. Cath. (Roby, 47). Arms.—*Barry of six argent and Gules, a canton of second.* s.p.

John Rose of Cotterstock, co. Northants, Esq. Will dated 24 Nov. 1736; nephew and heir of Francis Rose 1720.

Eliz. Rose. = ... Pate.

Eliz. Pate. 1st wife. = Sir James Esdaile, Knt., Alderman of L., Lord Mayor 1778. Of Upminster, co. Essex; died 6 April 1793 in Bunhill Row. Will dated 29 Oct. 1790; proved 9 April 1793 (198, Dodwell). = Mary . . . . 2nd wife.

Ann Pate, mar. John Scrocold of L., mercht. His will was dated 3 Nov., proved 11 Dec. 1788 (621, Calvert).

John Pate, nephew and heir of John Rose, whose surname he assumed, and whose will he proved 13 Dec. 1740, then aged 17. Will dated 17 Aug. 1758, then of Northill, co. Bedford, and proved 28 Nov. 1758 (346, Hutton); died s.p.l.; bur. at Cotterstock.

Letitia Rose, born 28 April 1751; bapt. 7 May at St. James', Westminster. = Rev. Sir Richd. Booth. M.I. at Cotterstock.

Sophia Rose, born 10 and bapt. 12 May 1752 at St. James', Westminster.

Fuller of Jamaica.

John Fuller of Brightling, co. Sussex, Esq. Will dated 21 Feb. 1743. To be bur. in the parish church of Waldron near my late wife. Whereas by my mar. sett. dated 15 July 1703 £6000 is charged upon my est. for such of my younger chn as I appoint. Whereas my son Rose F. is now in Jamaica and I have by Ind're of 31 Dec. 1736 between me and Rose F., Dr in Phys., my 2d son, of the 1st part; Sir John Lade of Southwark, Bt, of the 2d, and John Serocold of L., mercht, and John Kent of S., druggist, of the 3rd, settled my est. in J'ca upon my son Rose, I give him £2000. My s.-in-l. Wm. Sloane, Esq., and my dau. Eliz. his wife £20 each. My cousin Tho. Fuller of Mayfield, gent., and to Tho. F. my son, sugar baker, of L. my advowson of the Rectory and parish church of Mottisfont, East Dean and Lockerly, co. Southampton, upon T., to present my son Henry and convey the inheritance to him. If he do not be in orders my son Stephen to be presented, and in default to my eldest son John. To my son Henry £5000 and £1000 more if he do not take orders. Whereas I have advanced to my son Thos. £4000, I give him £2000 more. My son Stephen £5000, and if he do not take orders £1000 more. Whereas I am possessed of the next presentation of the parish church of N. Stoneham, co. S'ton, I give it to Tho. F. of Mayfield and Tho. F. my son of L.. sugar baker, upon T. to present my son Henry or Stephen. My founders, miners, colliers, furnace men and wood cutters. All residue of personal estate to my eldest son John, and I bequeath unto him all my manors, lands, etc. Witnessed by Lawrence Noakes, etc.

Codicil. 12 July 1744. My son Stephen is now m. to Mrs Eliz. Noakes and by his mar. sett. of 7 July inst. I paid over £4000 and give him £1000 more. My coz. Tho. F. of Mayfield is now decd.

Proved 13 Aug. 1745 by John F., Esq., the son. (223, Seymer.)

John Fuller of Rose-hill, co. Sussex, Esq. I confirm my mar. sett. and give my wife £300. To my brother Rose F. and his heirs male all my manors and lands, remainder to my brothers Henry, Thos., Stephen. Bro. Henry £1000. Bro. Tho. £1000. Bro. Stephen £1500, and £200 a year more until my bro. Rose take possession for his trouble in collecting rents and managing the furnace foundery and iron works. To my sister Sloanes chn £100 each. Gods. the son of John Fuller of Heathfield, Esq , £100. (Other godchn.) All residue to my bro. Rose, and with Henry, Tho., and Stephen, Ex'ors. Will dated 17 Jan. 1755. In the presence of Richd Beckford and others.

Codicil. 17 Jan. 1755. Bro.-in-l. Wm Sloane and his wife £100 each.

Proved 5 Feb. 1755 by Henry, Tho., and Stephen F., Esquires; power reserved to Rose F., Esq. (42, Paul.)

Rose Fuller of Brightling, co. Sussex, Esq. Will dated 4 Dec. 1774. To be buried in the chancel of the church of Waldron. Whereas by Ind'res dated 6 and 7 May 1771 made previous to the m. of John F., Esq., eldest son of my brother Tho. F. of L., mercht, with Eliz. F., since decd, one of the daus. of my brother Stephen F. of St Geo., Bloomsbury, Esq., to which I was a party, I confirmed to Godfrey Webster and Henry Hunter, Esqres, the manor and farm of Oxney, co. Kent, on trust for them. All my manors in G. B. and plantations or sugar works in Jamaica with the slaves and stock to Henry Hunter of Beach Hill, co. Berks, Esq., and James Dalrymple of Mayfield, co. Sussex, Esq., to the use of my brother Tho. F. and his 2 sons John F. and Rose F., my brother Stephen F. and my nephews Hans Sloane and Wm. Dickinson for 500 years, to the use of my nephew John F., only son of my late brother Henry F., for his life, then to his sons in tail, remainder to my brother Tho. F. and his sons, my brother

Stephen F. and his sons, then ⅓ to my nephew Hans Sloane and ⅔ to my nieces Eliz. F. and Fra. F., daus. of late bro. Henry F.; if my nieces die before me rem^r to my nieces Philippa wife of Wm Dickinson and Sarah wife of s^d Hans Sloane. An inventory of my estate in J. to be enrolled in the Secretary's Office. Whereas I am seized of an estate tail with remainder to Rose Herring May of J., Esq. (nephew of my late wife Ithamar) in a pl^n called Hog Hole in St Thos. in the Vale by virtue of an Ind're quadrupartite dated 26 April 1737 made between the Hon. R^d Mill of St Cath., Esq., of the 1st part, Rose Fuller, doctor in physick, and Ithamar F. his wife, late I. Mill, the only dau. and h. of s^d R^d Mill, of the 2^d p^t; Joan Mill and Ithamar Mill, sisters of the s^d R^d Mill, of the 3^d part; Edmund Hyde of St Andrew, Esq., and Wm May, clerk, R. of Kingston, of the 4th p^t, my trustees to settle accounts with Rose Herring May. Whereas I am seized of a pl^n called Gregorys pl^n or Fullers Hall in St Thomas in the Vale adjoining Hog Hole, and have worked the two together and have but one water mill, my trustees to purchase Hog Hole. My brother Tho. F. £200, bro. Stephen F. £300, 2 nieces Eliz. and Fra. F., daus. of bro. Henry, £1000 each. My nephew John F., son of my late brother Henry, £300 a year for his education. My nephews John F. and Rose F., sons of my brother Tho. F., and nephews Hans Sloane and Henry Hunter and friend Jas. Dalrymple £50 each. My sister Fra. F., widow of late bro. Henry F., nephew Wm Dickinson, niece Philippa his wife and niece Sarah wife of my nephew Hans Sloane, nephew Nash Mason, Esq., niece Eliz. his wife, nephew Capt. R^d Hughes, niece Jane his wife, niece Mary wife of my nephew Henry Hunter, nieces Hester Sloane, Eliz. Southerby, Ann Southeby, Rose Southeby and Philippa Sloane, nephews Wm Southeby and Tho. Southeby and nephew Rose Hering May £10 each. To Mary Johnson Rose of J'ca a free mulatto woman formerly my housekeeper, £100 c. a year; legacies to other blacks. All residue to nephew John F. son of Henry. T. to be Ex'ors.

Codicil. 3 Dec. 1776. S^d term of 500 years to cease when John is 21. Bro. Tho. F. £100 more.

2nd Codicil. 27 April 1777. Estate to be put under the C^t of Ch^y. Sworn 9 May 1777, testator late of Rose hill in Brightling, but of St Ann, Westm^r, dec^d.

Proved 15 May 1777 by Tho. F., Esq., the brother, John F., Esq. (son of H. F., dec^d), the nephew, and Stephen F., Esq., the brother; power reserved to the others. (211, Collier.)

Frances Fuller. Will dated at Offham 22 March 1766. To my daus. Eliz. F. and Frances F. jewels except my dear husbands diamond hart to my son John. All residue to my s^d 3 ch^n. My brother Rose F., Esq., of Rose Hill in Sussex and brother John F., Esq., of Parkgate in Sussex to manage their estate and to be G. To be buried by my husb^d Henry F. at Northstoneham, Hampshire.

Codicil. 22 Jan. 1768. S^d brothers to be Ex'ors in T.

Proved 6 June 1780 by John F., Esq., the surviving Ex'or. (312, Collins.)

Geo. Wenham Lewis of Westerham, co. Kent, gent. My nephew John Fuller of Rosehill, co. Sussex, Esq. My brother John Fuller of Catsfield, co. Sussex, Esq. Proved 1797. (607, Exeter.)

See pedigree in Berry's Sussex, 278, Burke's "Landed Gentry," Crisp's Visitation of England Notes, vol. ix., p. 39.

1711. Tho. F., b. at Waldron (near Hurst Green), Sussex, s. of Stephen F. gt; school Merch^t T. (Mr. Parsell); adm. pensioner, tutor and surety Mr. Anstey, 14 June æt. 18. (St. John's C. Cam., p. 201.)

There was another family of Fuller in Jamaica from Norfolk not connected with the Sussex one.

1720, April 26. Rosius Fuller, Londinensis. (Leyden students.)

1745, Aug. 4. John F. Esq; at Rose-hill in Sussex, who represented that county in 1713. ("G.M.," 444.)

1777, May 7. Rose F. Esq; member for Rye, in Sussex. (*Ibid.*, 247.)

1789. Stephen and Rose Fuller, merchants, 4 Church-co., Clements-lane, Lombard-st. (Kent's Directory.)

1812. Nov. 6. At Beccles, Suffolk, John Tho. F., esq., royal horse artillery, of Catsfield Ho., Sussex, to Emily, youngest dau. of the late Tho. Carthew of Woodbridge, Suffolk. (Dorchester Journal.)

1821, Nov. 16. In York-st. Portman-sq., aged 78, Rose F. Esq. ("G.M.," 178.)

1833, Nov. 15. In Montague-sq. the lady of Capt. Rose H. F., R.N. a son. (*Ibid.*, 462.)

1834, April 11. In Devonshire pl. aged 77, John F. of Rose Hill, Sussex, &c. (Long notice. *Ibid.*, 106, 660.)

1835, Feb. 24. At Ashdown Ho. Sussex, at an advanced age, the Hon. Anne, widow of John Trayton F, &c. (*Ibid.*, 445.)

Sir Geo. Wm Tapps, 2d Bart. M.P. m. 26 Sep. 1826, Clara 1st dau. of Augustus Elliott F. of Ashdown Ho., Sussex. (1835, I., 659.)

1837, Jan. 19. At Naples, a. 66, Wm. Dickinson, of Kingweston, Som. barr.-at-l. f. M.P. for that co. He was the s. & h. of Wm. D., M.P. for Som. from 1796 to 1806, by Philippa eldest dau. of Stephen F. of J. &c. (429.)

1837, April 23. At Rosehill, Farnham, in her 63d year, Eliz. wid. of Tho. F. (669.)

1840, Aug. 29. At Dover, Eliz. Anna, wife of John Hamilton, eldest dau. of the l. John Trayton F. of Ashdowne Ho. Sussex, & sister to A. Eliott F. (443.)

1842. Lately, March. At St. Jas., Piccadilly, Townsend Ince, Chrisleton, Cheshire, to Lucy, dau. of Aug. Eliot F., M.P. of Rosehill, Sussex. (322.)

1845, May 2. At Hall Lands, Nutfield, Sarah-Maria, dau. of the l. John Trayton F. (90.)

1847, July 13. At Brighton, Jas. Harwood, to Charlotte, yst dau. of the l. John Trayton F. of Ashdown Ho. Sussex. (422.)

ST. CATHERINE, JAMAICA.

Here lyeth interr'd the body of ITHAMAR the wife of the Honble ROSE FULLER Esq. who d. t. l. the 22d day of April 1738, aged 17 years. (Archer, p. 14.)

List of Wills recorded in Barbados down to the year 1800.*

Year.	Names of Testators.
1759	Phillip, Mary
„	Proverbs, John
„	Parks, Mary
„	Pinder, Daniel
„	Phillips, Rachael
„	Pullinger, George
„	Perryman, William
1760	Phillips, James
1761	Parris, Edward
„	Phillips, Margaret
„	Phillips, Josias
„	Palmer, Fidelia
„	Popple, Magnes
„	Preston, Thomas
„	Phillips, Deliverance
1762	Proverbs, Mary
„	Phillips, John
„	Prideaux, James
1763	Phillips, Mary
„	Proverbs, John
„	Perry, Thomas
1764	Pilgrim, Robert
„	Parson, John
„	Port, John
„	Pearce, Elizabeth
1765	Poyer, John
„	Parris, Richard
„	Perkins, Jonathan
„	Phillips, Nathaniel
„	Pierce, Thomas
„	Pile, Ann
„	Phillips, Richard
1766	Payne, Thomas Abel
„	Pemberton, Rachael
„	Poor, Katherin
„	Parr, George
„	Pearce, Katherine
„	Parris, George
1767	Pollard, Robert Jeffrey
„	Payne, Richard
„	Prosser, Eleanor
„	Pinder, Francis
„	Phillips, Benjamin
„	Payne, Richard
„	Power, Richard
„	Parris, Alexander
1768	Pemberton, Benjamin
„	Palmer, Mary
1768	Perkins, Gooding
„	Prentis, Jemima
„	Payne, Mary
„	Polgrun, Cooper
„	Perry, Jacob
1769	Porter, Charles Thomas
„	Pile, Thomas
1770	Payne, Agnes
„	Parris, Martin
„	Pickett, Francis
„	Pinheiro, Lunah
„	Padmore, Robert Jones
„	Price, Edward
„	Porter, Thomas Oxnard
„	Phillip, John
1771	Phillips, Sarah
„	Pinder, George Lake
„	Parris, Richard Stanton
„	Perry, John
„	Padmore, Thomas
„	Puckerin, Elizabeth
1772	Proverbs, Sarah
„	Pemberton, Charles
„	Phillips, John
„	Petchard, Clement Bowcher
„	Preston, John
„	Peters, Thomas
„	Payne, Richard
„	Perry, William
1773	Phillips, John Randall
„	Pile, Theophilus
„	Power, Charles
1774	Price, Edward
„	Pooler, Nathanil
„	Payne, Joseph
1775	Poyer, Price
„	Phillips, Samuel
„	Phillips, Renn
„	Pearen, David
„	Phillips, Thomas
1776	Palmer, George
„	Parkinson, James
„	Poole, William
„	Payne, Thomas
„	Piggott, John
„	Purchase, Elizabeth
„	Polegrun, Thomas
„	Payne, Richard

* Continued from p. 120.

Year.	Names of Testators.
1776	Payne, Hearn
1777	Perry, Mary
,,	Polgrun, John
,,	Payne, Edward
,,	Phillips, John
,,	Port, Snr., Joseph
1778	Pollard, John
,,	Piggott, Mary
,,	Pilgrim, John
,,	Peters, William
,,	Phillips, Ann
1779	Pearn, Ann
,,	Perkins, William
,,	Piggott, James
,,	Pollard, Jared
,,	Payne, Samuel Mapp
,,	Perry, Ambrose
,,	Parsons, Elizabeth
1780	Priddu, Sarah
,,	Pierce, Emlin
1781	Pare, Edward
,,	Payne, Thomas
,,	Payne, Katherin
,,	Pare, Jane
,,	Payne, Elizabeth
,,	Phillips, Josias
,,	Pinheiro, David
1782	Pinheiro, Jael
,,	Pullinger, George
,,	Porter, Thomas Wesbury
,,	Prince, Frank
,,	Parris, Sarah
1783	Penny, Thomas Woodin
,,	Polgrun, Nicholas
,,	Page, Mary
,,	Piggott, Thomas
,,	Parris, John
1784	Parris, Rachael
,,	Phillips, Jnr., Evan
,,	Polgrun, Mary
1785	Payne, Eleanor
,,	Power, Michael
,,	Pickering, William
,,	Parris, Edward
1786	Porter, William
,,	Phillips, Susanna
,,	Phillips, Josias
,,	Pollard, Thomas
,,	Parris, Elizabeth
,,	Payne, Abel
,,	Peispotto, Abraham
1787	Power, Sarah
,,	Penny, Thomas
,,	Phillips, Joseph
,,	Perry, William
,,	Perry, Hugh

Year.	Names of Testators.
1787	Payne, John
,,	Pooler, Jonathan
,,	Price, William
,,	Phillips, John
1788	Phillips, Thomas
,,	Pile, Francis
,,	Platts, Edward
,,	Payne, Sarah
,,	Parris, Francis Butcher
,,	Pinder, Thomas
,,	Paterson, William
,,	Peters, Mary
1789	Pollard, Richard
,,	Perkins, Thomas
,,	Piggott, Snr., Thomas
,,	Poore, Betty Buck
1790	Pollard, James
,,	Porter, Edward Harris
,,	Paul, John
,,	Parr, Samuel Henry
,,	Payne, Michael
,,	Peacocke, William
1791	Payne, Richard
,,	Pispotto, Judith
,,	Phillips, Joseph
,,	Polgrun, Rachael Pringle
,,	Pickett, Sarah
1792	Phillips, Ann
,,	Packer, Eburn
1793	Payne, Agnes
,,	Pierce, Thomas
,,	Polgrun, Cooper
1794	Proverbs, Isaac
,,	Payne, Hannah Maria
1795	Padmore, Charles
,,	Pinheiro, Aaron
,,	Penny, Marry
1796	Porter, John
,,	Parris, David
,,	Payne, Joseph
,,	Porter, Alice
,,	Payne, John
,,	Port, James
,,	Phillips, Samuel
,,	Payne, Sarah Rushworth
,,	Prixty, Richard
,,	Pinheiro, Isaac
1797	Parks, Edward
,,	Parks, Robert
,,	Peck, Ann
,,	Poyer, Abel
,,	Polgrun, James
1798	Penny, William
,,	Penny, Mary
,,	Pearce, Mary
,,	Pearson, Priscilla

Year.	Names of Testators.
1798	Part, John
"	Payne, Elizabeth Ann
"	Proverbs, John
"	Payne, George
"	Perry, Hugh
"	Pollard, Thomas
"	Pile, Peter
"	Pickering, Tobias
"	Perkins, Philip
"	Pounder, Daniel
"	Payne, Mary
1799	Power, Richard Dela
"	Pickering, Mary
"	Pollard, James Shepherd
"	Packer, Joseph
"	Poyer, Thomas
"	Price, Sarah
1681	Quile, Hugh
1685	Quin, Jeffrey
1687	Queen, Honor
1693	Quintyne, Mary
1695	Quintyne, Thomas
1727	Quintyne, Sarah
1731	Quarless, William
1739	Quintyne, Thomas
1750	Quintyne, Henry
1753	Quintyne, Edward
1767	Quintyne, Alleyne
"	Quintyne, Elizabeth
1769	Quintyne, Ann
1771	Quarless, George William
1772	Quintyne, Elizabeth
1781	Quoys, William
1792	Quoys, Mary
1650	Read, John
"	Richardson, William
"	Rennett, Elizabeth
1651	Rickford, Peter
1653	Robinson, John
1654	Radley, James
"	Reade, Richard
"	Reynold, Robert
1655	Richardson, Samuel
"	Reynolds, John
1656	Rippon, Ralph
"	Roberts, Evan
"	Rogerman, Adam
1657	Rutlidge, Richard
"	Rooper, Thomas
"	Rimgam, William
1658	Regaime, Charles

Year.	Names of Testators.
1658	Rowly, Priscilla
1659	Ross, Daniel
"	Rich, Charles
"	Ross, John
"	Randall, John
1660	Robinson, David
"	Rootsey, Thomas
"	Risley, Peter
"	Rumball, Robert
"	Reade, Thomas
"	Rawlings, Henry
"	Ryley, Hugh
"	Raylson, Richard
1661	Redway, John
"	Rice, Thomas
"	Russin, Richard
"	Runnick, Robert
1662	Roach, John
"	Robinson, Joseph
"	Ruder, Eaven
"	Runsbury, Francis
"	Rice, Griffin
"	Ryder, Peter
"	Robinson, Robert
1663	Roberts, Susanna
"	Ruce, Morgan
"	Ryalton, Richard
"	Rayeson, Richard
1665	Rudderford, John
"	Rainsbury, Francis
"	Royley, Edmond
"	Rous, Anthony
1667	Risley, Mary
"	Roberts, Richard
"	Russell, John
"	Redwood, Johanis
1668	Revell, Thomas
1669	Russell, Abraham
"	Rouse, Anthony
"	Roberts, William
"	Rosewell, William
1670	Rene, Thomas
"	Rogers, Oliver
"	Rainsbury, Joane
"	Robson, John
"	Read, John
"	Rous, Anthony
"	Richardson, John
"	Rainsford, Jonathan
"	Rogers, Oleon
1671	Read, George
"	Reinolds, Henry
"	Read, Edmund
"	Robertson, David
"	Rice, Marcus
"	Rosse, Walter

Year.	Names of Testators.
1671	Reece, Morgan
1672	Richardson, Richard
"	Rockeby, John
"	Robbin, William
"	Rolleston, Simon
1673	Ridge, Roger
"	Rows, Elizabeth
"	Read, John
1674	Riley, Dennis
"	Ree, Martin
"	Reynold, John
"	Richards, Margaret
1675	Richards, Isaacs
"	Ramsey, George and John
1676	Rawden, Magdalin
"	Roberts, John
"	Ramsey, David
1677	Rice, Nicholas
"	Rycroft, Ellis
"	Raleigh, David
"	Renny, Teage
"	Rootsey, John
"	Ramsey, Robert
1678	Ross, Robert
"	Ramsey, Robert
1679	Reynolds, Simon
"	Rolstone, Alexander
"	Richardson, Anthony
"	Rous, Thomas
1680	Raynes, Francis
"	Rich, Robert
"	Rider, Pheby
"	Rossin, John
"	Rulsing, Grace
"	Renney, John
1681	Ranton, James
"	Rose, Robert
"	Rean, Martha
"	Rice, Maria
"	Rawham, Daniel
"	Roach, William
"	Read, Thomas
"	Richards, John
1682	Richardson, John
"	Ruske, Andrew
"	Robinson, Richard
"	Riddock, Alexander
"	Robinson, Manus
"	Riley, Hugh
"	Ross, Philip
"	Rosse, William
1683	Richball, Robert
"	Roper, William
"	Roe, Richard
"	Robinson, William
1684	Rollstone, Samuel

Year.	Names of Testators.
1684	Richards, Robert
"	Roberts, William
"	Rees, Lawrence
"	Rollins, William
"	Revers, Mary
"	Richardson, Robert
1685	Reed, James
"	Rhenolds, Thomas
"	Reece, Bartholomew
"	Reynell, Edward
1686	Ramsey, George
"	Roberts, James
"	Read, Phillip
"	Rice, George
"	Rash, Edward
"	Ross, William
"	Redman, John
"	Read, John
"	Reaper, Grace
1687	Roebucke, Edward
"	Rogers, John
"	Richardson, Nicholas
"	Roderico, Symon
"	Rondell, Richard
"	Rectis, John
1688	Randell, Edward
"	Roberts, Edward
"	Ross, Alexander
"	Rainsford, Edward
"	Reavell, Claud
"	Rosse, Daniel
"	Richards, Susanna
"	Rugg, William
1689	Rinney, Tige
"	Richeson, David
"	Robuck, Edward
1691	Roach, Richard
"	Raven, Capt. John
1692	Roach, Edmund
"	Ridgway, John
"	Rous, Ambros
"	Rope, John
"	Reynold, David
1693	Rouse, Thomas
"	Robeuse, Thomas
"	Reed (Read), John
"	Rows, Ann
"	Rootsey, James
1694	Rogers, William
"	Reed, John
"	Robinson, George
"	Rumballs, Deposition of Geo. Robinson *re* Geo. Robinson
"	Rudyard, Thomas
"	Robinson, George
"	Read, Philip

Year.	Names of Testators.
1695	Rardon, Ellinor
"	Ridley, Foster
"	Richardson, William
"	Rees, Sarah
"	Rice, Walter
"	Rous, John
"	Rose, Anne
"	Robinson, John
"	Read, George
1696	Robinson, Thomas
"	Randall, Edward
1697	Robertson, Charles
"	Rushbrooke, Henry
1700	Raa, James
"	Reed, John
"	Ramsden, Henry
"	Ruck, John
"	Ramsey, Buller
1701	Ridgway, Susannah
"	Russell, Richard
"	Russell, James
"	Rogers, John
"	Richmond, Bartholomew
1702	Robinson, Thomas
"	Relfe, John
"	Richards, Latimer
"	Ridgway, Jonathan
"	Rice, Richard
"	Raynsford, Solomon
1703	Reede, John
1704	Randolph, Ann
"	Reynolds, Thomas
"	Roach, David
"	Ruch, John
1705	Russel, Andrew
"	Reimer, Dr. Isaac
"	Richardson, Richard
1706	Ramsey, David
"	Roy, John
"	Reirton, Philip
1709	Roebuck, Edward
"	Robertson, James
"	Rickford, John
1710	Redman, Thomas
"	Read, John
1711	Rawlins, Thomas
1712	Reeves, John
"	Rushworth, John
1713	Richards, Robert
"	Roach, Elizabeth
"	Rawlins, Mary
"	Roach, John
1714	Rocquitte, James
"	Row, Elizabeth
1715	Ravin, Ann
"	Rogers, Joseph

Year.	Names of Testators.
1715	Russell, Patrick
"	Round, Samuel
"	Relfe, John
"	Ridgway, John
"	Roberts, William
"	Rogers, William
1716	Robinson, Benjamin
"	Richardson, Phillis
"	Rudder, Charles
"	Ruston, Bartholomew
"	Rice, Edward
"	Reed, Robert
"	Reeve, George
"	Richardson, George
"	Richardson, John
1717	Reed, William
"	Ridgway, Philadelphia
"	Redwar, John
"	Reynoldson, Susanna
"	Rawlins, Benjamin
"	Raper, Henry
1718	Rose, John
"	Reyley, Ann
"	Roberts, William
"	Redwar, Ann
"	Richardson, Mary
"	Reeve, Dorothy
"	Ring, Susanna
"	Raylie, Mary
1719	Read, Elizabeth
"	Roach, Richard
"	Richardson, John
"	Roberts, Henry
"	Ruck, Thomas
"	Robinson, William
1720	Read, William
"	Rowe, Thomas
"	Rider, John
"	Redwar, John
"	Ridley, John
"	Rose, Martha
"	Roke, Thomas
1721	Roberts, Timothy
"	Roberts, John
"	Redwar, Elizabeth
"	Robertson, Duncan
1722	Robinson, David
"	Rawlins, James
"	Ross, Alexander
1723	Robinson, Elizabeth
"	Roberts, Samuel
"	Rawlins, Edward
"	Roffe, Mary
1724	Robinson, William
"	Russell, John
1725	Ragg, Edward

Year.	Names of Testators.
1725	Robertson, Robert
1726	Rider, Judith
„	Rollick, Andrew
„	Ryley, Oliver
„	Roach, Martha
„	Rollock, William
1727	Ross, Nicholas
„	Read, Elizabeth
„	Rogers, John
„	Rous, Daniel
„	Roberts, Samuel
1728	Reeve, Rachael
„	Riley, John
„	Rosell, William
„	Randoll, John
„	Rudd, Ann
„	Ramsay, Gilbert
1729	Rollstone, Thomas
„	Russell, William
„	Rice, Nicholas
„	Russell, William
„	Ridgway, John
1730	Rawlins, Charles
„	Robinson, Ruth
„	Rice, Nicholas
„	Rycroft, David
1731	Ramsay, Chamberlain
„	Richards, Henry
1733	Robinson, Snr., Edward
„	Rucastle, Adam
„	Roby, Thomas
„	Roome, Charles
„	Reede, William
1734	Robinson, Daniel
„	Robinson, Mary
„	Reese, John
„	Rushworth, Rachael
„	Ridley, John
„	Rudder, Richard
„	Robson, Mary
1735	Riste, Philip
„	Rowe, Thomas
„	Robe, John
„	Robinson, Charles
„	Roach, William
„	Righton, Peter
1736	Reece, Sarah
„	Ross, John
„	Ruddock, Noblet
„	Richardson, Robert
1737	Robinson, Daniel
„	Robinson, John
„	Rundell, Edward
„	Rous, John
1738	Rayner, Ruth
„	Roberts, William

Year.	Names of Testators.
1738	Roberts, Mary
„	Rawlins, Edward
„	Reynold, John
1739	Rudder, Philip
„	Rollstone, John
„	Ross, Rebecca
1740	Rundell, Elizabeth
„	Rice, Francis
„	Roach, John
„	Roberts, William
„	Roach, Edward
„	Reece, Katherine
1741	Russel, William
„	Robson, James
„	Richards, Ann
„	Rice, Thomas
1742	Rice, Edward
„	Rider, Benjamin
„	Rollstone, John
„	Reede, Jean
„	Ramsay, John
„	Russell, Jonothan
„	Rugg, Anne
„	Rosbotham, Cornileus
„	Rawlins, Thomas
„	Robinson, Richard
1743	Ross, John
„	Ray, Abraham
„	Redwar, John
„	Roach, Rose
„	Richards, Samuel
„	Rawlins, Charles
„	Rycroft, Richard
„	Russel, William
„	Robinson, Peter
1744	Richardson, John
„	Ramsay, Alexander
„	Robson, Elizabeth
1745	Richardson, John
„	Richards, Thomas
„	Roach, Henry
„	Ramsay, Elizabeth
„	Robarts, Sarah
„	Robson, Ann
1746	Robinson, Richard
„	Rawlins, John
„	Ruck, John
„	Rosbotham, Deborah
1747	Rawlins, Thomas
„	Rudduck, Andrew
„	Ridley, Richard
„	Robinson, John
„	Rawlin, William
1748	Roberts, Humphry
„	Rowe, Hilary
„	Rous, Thomas

Year.	Names of Testators.
1748	Rash, Sarah
"	Ross, Alexander
"	Rudder, Charles
"	Reeves, Susannah
1749	Rutherford, Thomas
"	Rider, Elisha
"	Russell, Mary
1750	Richey, Richard
"	Rous, Margaret
"	Rycroft, Mary
"	Reed, Robert
"	Reynolds, Mary
"	Ruck, Elizabeth
"	Ridaway, John
"	Ross, John
"	Richards, Catherin
1751	Renood, John
"	Reed, John
"	Rose, John
1752	Riley, William
"	Rogers, Henry
"	Rawlins, Mary
"	Rawlins, Charles
"	Robinson, Barbara
"	Rudder, Thomas
1753	Robertson, Elinor
"	Roberts, Edward
"	Rose, Richard
"	Rudder, David
"	Rudder, Philip
"	Robinson, Elizabeth
1754	Reed, Jennitt
"	Reed, Margaret
"	Roe, Littler
"	Rudder, Philip
"	Reed, Grace
1755	Richards, Latimore
"	Richards, William
"	Reeves, Elizabeth
"	Revill, Richard
"	Ross, Alexander
"	Russell, Thomas
1756	Reeves, Joseph
"	Redwar, Ann
"	Robson, Thomas
"	Ross, Daniel
"	Ridley, Margret
"	Reece, Alice
1757	Rose, Ro. Patrick
"	Richards, Robert
"	Ridgway, John
"	Robinson, John
"	Ramsey, Thomas
"	Riley, Thomas
"	Rider, George
1758	Rolstone, Eleanor
1758	Ridley, John
"	Richards, Alice
"	Rist, Dorothy
"	Richards, Richard
1759	Russell, Ann
"	Rice, John
"	Robinson, Alexander
"	Robinson, Samuel
"	Robinson, William
"	Robinson, John
1760	Ridgway, Samuel
"	Redaway, Sarah
"	Rowe, Hilary
1761	Ramsey, Titus
"	Richards, John
"	Rushbrook, John Pead
"	Rous, Mary
"	Rawlins, John
1762	Robinson, Thomas
"	Robinson, Samuel
"	Ramsey, Henry
"	Rose, William
1763	Redwar, John Salman
"	Rowe, Philip
1764	Reece, John
"	Richardson, John
"	Reece, Thomas
"	Rudder, Philip
"	Rawlins, John
1765	Roach, Snr., Richard
"	Richardson, Courtney
"	Roberts, William
"	Redwar, Margaret
"	Robinson, James
"	Reed, Thomas
1766	Rosell, Thomas
"	Ross, William
"	Rice, Nicholas
"	Rachill, Joseph
1767	Rayne, Sarah
"	Ruck, Jepthath
"	Robertson, James
"	Rider, Joseph
"	Rayne, Sarah
"	Ruck, Jepthath
"	Robertson, James
1768	Ricorft, Sarah
"	Rolstone, Thomas
"	Rous, Rachael
"	Rawlins, Mary
1769	Russel, Francis
"	Ross, William
"	Reece, William
"	Rosbotham, Robert
"	Richards, Susannah
"	Rous, William John

Year.	Names of Testators.
1770	Roberts, Ann
„	Robinson, George
„	Reeves, Sarah
„	Ross, Sarah
„	Rudder, Richard
„	Rollins, Richard
1771	Robinson, Thomas
„	Robinson, William
„	Reece, Benjamin
„	Rosell, William
1772	Riddan, Ignatius
„	Roach, William
„	Rider, George
„	Rowe, John
„	Raven, John
„	Robinson, Alexander
1773	Rogers, Mary
„	Roberts, Nathanil
„	Robinson, John
„	Reed, Thomas
„	Roach, Elizabeth
„	Redman, George
1774	Reed, Rebecca
„	Rowe, Lawrance
1775	Rogers, Thomas
„	Rudder, Thomas
„	Reeves, John
„	Rice, Ambrose
„	Rollock, Mary
„	Ramsey, Susanna
1776	Robson, Sarah
„	Robinson, Daniel
„	Rycroft, William *alias* Wildey
„	Rock, Samuel
1777	Roach, Thomas
„	Rayne, John
„	Reece, Samuel
„	Rowe, Snr., Hilary
„	Rudder, William Francis
„	Robinson, Francis
„	Reed, Elizabeth
„	Reynolds, Nichols
1778	Roach, John
„	Rollstone, Samuel
„	Roach, Richard
1779	Rawlins, Elizabeth
„	Rowe, Hilary
1780	Rowe, Thomas
„	Reese, Elizabeth
„	Riley, Wooten
„	Ridgway, John Wheeler
„	Rollstone, Joseph Pickering
„	Ross, Francis
1781	Rock, Richard
„	Rice, Mary
„	Raily, Edmund
1781	Rudder, Richard
„	Ryley, Thomas
1782	Rawlins, Mary
„	Rawlins, Bevelia
„	Rowe, Sarah
„	Rose, James
„	Rycroft, Thomas
1783	Rice, Alice
„	Robinson, Benjamin
„	Robinson, Thomas
„	Reece, Snr., John
1784	Robinson, Ruth
„	Reece, Mary
„	Rose, Thomas
1785	Reece, Margaret
„	Robinson, Jacob
„	Rochford, Thomas
„	Reece, Richard
1786	Rawlins, Edward
„	Ruck, Thomas
„	Riches, John
„	Reed, John
„	Robinson, John
1787	Rouse, Samuel
„	Roberts, William
„	Rawlin, Elizabeth
„	Ramsey, John
„	Ross, Samuel
1788	Rachaell, Elizabeth
„	Richards, William
„	Rose, James
„	Rogers, Gertrude Aris
„	Roach, Nathaniel
1790	Rowe, Sarah
„	Robson, Nicholas
„	Rowe, Grishild
„	Raper, John
„	Riley, William
„	Richards, Richard
„	Roach, David
„	Robinson, Abigail
„	Rogers, James
„	Rose, Mary
1791	Russell, John
„	Robinson, Benjamin
„	Roach, Susannah
1792	Rawlins, Lewis
„	Richards, Samuel
„	Rosbotham, James
„	Rudder, Rawlins
„	Richardson, John
„	Reece, Mary
1794	Rice, Nicholas
„	Robinson, Ann
„	Robinson, Elizabeth Ann
„	Robinson, Margaret

Year.	Names of Testators.
1794	Rich, Elizabeth
"	Robinson, George
"	Rock, Martha
"	Rock, Thomas
"	Reeves, William
1795	Rowe, Catherin
1796	Reed, Elizabeth Hackett
1797	Rous, Elizabeth
"	Rudder, Charles Straghn
"	Ross, Benjamin
"	Reece, Francis
"	Rudder, Francis
"	Robinson, Samuel
1798	Roach, Richard
"	Russel, John Gill
"	Riley, Edward

Year.	Names of Testators.
1798	Rudder, Thomas Charles
"	Roberts, Mary
"	Richards, Edward
"	Riley, Francis
"	Rogers. Thomas
"	Rice, John
"	Ramsey, Sarah
"	Rock, James
"	Riley, Thomas
"	Ruck, Daniel Thomas Hooper
1799	Redwar, Richard
"	Rose, James
"	Russel, Samuel
"	Ross, Katherine
"	Redman, John Reed

(*To be continued.*)

Heming of Jamaica.

John Heming of J'ca. Will recorded there 1672—82.
Richard Heming of J., 1672. (*Ante*, II., 147.) Will recorded 1691—4.

Samuel Heming of St. Anne's, J. Will dated 3 June 1720; sworn 20 Dec. 1720; proved 17 April 1724 (85, Bolton). ═ . . . ., ? dau. of Mrs. Eliz. Rose.

- Richard Heming, 1st son and heir, under 20 in 1720; of St. Anne's. Will dated in London 23 Jan. 1753; proved 3 Nov. 1755 (283, Paul). ═
  - Samuel Heming, proved his father's will 9 Nov. 1763.
  - George Heming, under 15.
  - Francis Heming.
  - Eliz., under 18.
  - Rose, under 12.
- Samuel Heming, 2nd son, under 8 in 1720; ex'or 1753; of St. Cath. and of "Saville" in St. Anne's. Will dated 19 July 1773; sworn 24 Aug., proved 25 June 1781 (301, Webster). ═ Eliz. Amelia, youngest dau. of Sam. Long of J.; born 1740. (Burke's "Landed Gentry.")
  - Richard Samuel Edward Heming.
  - Sam. Scudamore Heming, cousin of his wife. ═ Mary Charlotte Long, dau. of Rob. Long of the Jamaican family.
    - Issue.
  - George Fra. Heming.
- Eliz., under 17.
- Mary, under 16.

Sam. Heming of the parish of St. Anne, J., Esq. Will dated 3 June 1720. My dau. Eliz. £2000 at 17 or M. and £100 a year till paid. My dau. Mary H. the like sum at 16. My yst. son Sam. my cowpenn in S[t] Annes called the little Thickets and all my lands within 2 miles round. My 1st son Rich[d] to settle a sugar work there before Sam. is 20 and clear 150 a. whereof 80 to be planted for canes, 20 for a plantin walk and 50 for pasturage, and 50 working slaves, 24 steers and 20 mules be put thereon. I give him also £1000 c. at 20 and £40 a year till 8 years of age, £50 till 15 and £150 a year till 20. My M.-in-law Eliz. Rose now residing in L. £20 a year. All residue to my s[d] eldest son, his G. to allow him £200 a year till 20. I appoint my couzen Thos. Rose, Esq., my bro. John Charnock, D[r] in Phy., and D[r] Tho. Price, all of J., and my bro. John Seracold, M[t] in L., G., together with my couzin Tho. Green of Kensington and my eldest son Rich[d], Ex'ors. In the presence of Edw[d] Charlton, John Scott, Jn[o] Humphry. On 20 Dec. 1720 Ed. C. was sworn before Nich. Lawes, R[t] Baillie, Sec[y]. Certified by Rob. Baillie, Esq., 9 June 1721 and by Sir Nich. Lawes, K[t], Gov[r]. Proved 17 April 1724 by John Serocold, one of the Ex'ors; power reserved to the others. (85, Bolton.)

Richard Heming of the parish of S[t] Ann, J., Esq., but now residing in L. Will dated 23 Jan. 1753. To my son Geo. £4000 at 21, £60 a year till 15, then £150 a year till 21. To my son Francis the like sum. To my 1st dau. Eliz. H. £2000 at 18 or m., and £100 a year till then. To my yst. dau. Rose H. the like sum and £60 a year till 12 and £100 a year till 18 or m. To R[d] Holmes £20 a year till 14, then £100 for apprenticeship and £300 at 21. To Margaret Hawksworth £5 a year for 3 years. All my plantations, real and personal estate to my eldest son Sam., my bro.-in-law Tho. Orby Hunter, Esq., and John Serocold of L., M[ts], G., they to allow my 1st son £200 a year till 20, and together with my bro. Sam. H., Sam. Whitehorne, Esq., M[r] Henry Tucker, M[r] Israel Clark and my 1st son, Ex'ors. L. 16 Oct. 1755. To M[rs] Lucretia Luxford, wife of M[r] Fra. L., £25 yearly. To my black servant £10 yearly. Proved 3 Nov. 1755 by John Serocold, Esq.; power reserved to the others. Proved 11 Nov. 1755 by T. O. H., Esq. Proved 9 Nov. 1763 by Sam. H., Esq., the son; power reserved to the others. (283, Paul.)

Sam. Heming of the parish of S[t] Cath., J., Esq. Will dated 19 July 1773. Weak in body. Affairs much unsettled owing to a Trust on my pl[n] in S[t] Ann called Saville. I bequeath all my estate to my friends John Dalling, Esq., L[t]-Gov. of this I., Sir Cha. Price, Bart., Scudamore Winde, Esq., and Ed. Long of L., Esq., on T. for the support of my wife Eliz. Amelia and apply the residue for my 3 sons Rich. Sam. Ed. H., Sam. Scudamore H. and Geo. Fra. H., and such child as my wife is now ensient with, and appoint them G. In the presence of F. Rigby Brodbelt, Benj. Lyon, Anthony Rosdew. On 24 Aug. 1773 was sworn B. Lyon before John Dalling, R[d] Lewing, Sec[y]. Certified by John Dalling, Esq., Gov[r], 4 April 1780, and R[d] Lewing, Esq. and Sec[y]. Proved 25 June 1781 by Ed. Long, Esq.; power reserved to J. D., Esq., and Sir Cha. Price, B[t], the other surviving Ex'ors. (301, Webster.)

1761, Nov. 21. Breach of promise. Freemantle v. Hemming of J. ("G.M.," 538.)

In 1764 Lord Adam Gordon met in J'ca Mr. Hemmings, a nephew-in-law to Tho[s] Orby Hunter. ("Genealogist," New S., xiv., 15.)

1769, Sept. 19. Geo. Hemming, Esq; of J. to Miss Bracebridge, of Weddington. ("G.M.," 462.)

Blenman of Barbados.

1654, Jan. Elianor Bliuman. On the 27th adm'on to Roger B. son of E. B. late of Stokewisey, co. Som. fo. 2.

Geo. Blynman l. of the citty of Bristoll linendraper but now resident within the I. of Barbadoes. Will dated 20 Nov. 1702, 1 Q. Anne. To my brothers John B. and Fra. B. my messuage called Buckmans in the town of Watchett. p. of S[t] Decumans, co. Som., given by my l. dec[d] father during my term. My sister Jane Steward wife of Tho. S. of S[t] Malla in France £100. Accounts depending between me and Mary Jones of this I., wid., f. Mary Didras, and bet. me and M[r] Sampson Wood of s[d] I., gent. I desire my friends Joseph Mole of Bridge Town M[t] and Tho. Denny of s[d] p. M[t] and M[r] Adam Shand of s[d] p. to receive all sums due and make them overseers. All residue to my said brothers whom I nominate Ex'ors. Wit. by Edw. Austen, Adam Shand, M: M[c] Kaskell. On 3 Feb. 1706/7 appeared Fra. B. of Williton in the p. of S[t] Decumans, co. Som., Esq., one of the brothers and Ex'ors of test. l. of B'oes, bach., dec[d], and this deponent having been abroad at the siege of Barcelona and in Spain and Portugal came to the city of Exon in Nov. last where lived M[rs] Phillips Salter wife of M[r] Tho. S., goldsmith, sister of dec[d], who gave him the copy of will delivered her by M[r] Hole M[t] of s[d] city, who received it from Joseph Hole of Bridgetown in s[d] I. M[t] his brother and was sworn. Proved 3 Feb. 1706 by F. B., J. B. the other Ex'or renouncing. (26, Poley.)
Will also recorded in B'os.

Edward Warner of Antigua, esq. Will dated 1732. Jonathan Blenman of Barbados, esq., a guardian.

Harry Slingsby of Barbados, esq. Will dated 1746. Hon. Jonathan Blenman of Barbados, an Ex'or.

Edward Blenman of Tempell in the city of Bristol. Will dated the 4th day of the 7th month 1752. To my dau. Rachel Willett 2 of my shares in the Brass Works. My grands. Jacob Post, gunner, 1 share. My grands. Edw. Post 1 share. My dau. Liddo Holwell 2 shares for her and her husband's life. My tenement in Debtford to my 2 grandsons Jacob Ager and Edw[d] Ager. My kinswomen Eliz. Godwin, Love Peters, Sarah Peters. W[m] Tilly. My dau. Drew, dec[d], without a will. Joseph Loscombe, Rob. Payn, W[m] Tilly and Rob. Peters, all merchants of Bl., to be Ex'ors. On 3 Jan. 1753 ad' to Rachell Willett, widow, the Ex'ors having renounced. (1, Searle.)

Margaret Bevilia Blenman l. of the I. of B'oes, now at Welbeck Str., S[t] Marylebone, spinster, sick. Will dated 29 May 1772. My debts and legacies to be paid by my brother W[m] B., Esq. To my Mother Mary B. the annual interest of what shall be due from my said brother, and after her death I give to my brother Wm., my brother Timothy and sister Caroline £500 each. My nephew Jonathan B. books, nephew W. B. my m. ring for my father, nephew Jos. B. a ring, nephew Timothy B. a ring. My 2 neices Eliz. and Ann B. wearing apparel. Friend Miss Mary Gibbes a ring. My friend the Hon. R[d] Salter, Esq., and Margaret his wife rings. Friend Geo. James of B'es, Esq., my negro woman. Friend W[m] Forbes. Remainder of money to Hon. R[d] Salter and his wife for a charitable purpose, and to be T. for this fund. My Mother and brother W[m] Ex'ors. Proved 23 Sept. 1774 by W. B. the brother p. r. to Mary B. the Mother. (330, Bargrave.)

ARMS.—*Per chevron engrailed Azure and Argent two lozenges in chief, a bee in base.*
CREST.—*A dexter arm holding a scroll.*

Thomas Blenman of Croscombe, co. Som.=

Jonathan Blenman of Barbados, Attorney-Gen. 1727; Judge of the Admiralty 1734; Grant of arms 1739; M. of C. 1746. W.I. Bookplate No. 168. = Mary, ..., living 1774. Arms: *Argent, three daggers.*

William Blenman of Bath. Will dated 13 May 1794; proved 13 Aug. 1800 (576, Adderley).	= Eliz., dau. of Joseph Dotin; born 1728; mar. 1748; died 10 Aug. 1763. M.I. at Clifton (*ante*, II., 371). Had four sons and two daus.	Timothy Blenman, born 1725; of Christ Church, Oxford, matric. 17 Dec. 1741, aged 16; of Gray's Inn 22 Jan. 1741-2; living 1744. ? Will recorded in 1799.	Margaret Bevilia Blenman of Welbeck Street. Will dated 29 May 1772; proved 23 Sept. 1774 (330, Bargrave).	Caroline Blenman of Welbeck Street. Will dated 23 Feb. and proved 23 Sept. 1774 (330, Bargrave).

Jonathan Blenman, born 1753; of Christ Coll., Camb., 18 Oct. 1769, aged 16; of Lincoln's Inn 24 Aug. 1771; Solicitor-Gen. and Judge of Vice-Admiralty, Barbados; bur. at St. George 14 Feb. 1807. Will (363, Ely).	= Anna Maria, born 1759; ? dau. of . . . . Cobham; died 16 Aug. 1817, aged 58. M.I. in crypt of St. Paul's Cathedral (*ante*, IV., 232).	Joseph Blenman, d.v.p. 1794—8. — Ann Blenman, mar. Tho., son of Alex. Graeme of Barbados; living 1804.	Rev. Timothy Blenman, ? 5th son, went to Barbados 1783. W.I. Bookplate No. 169, quartering arms of Dotin.	= . . . ., died at Clifton 27 Nov. 1820.	Wm. Blenman. — Eliz. Blenman.

Jonathan Blenman, born 1785; of Christ Church, Oxford, matric. 21 Feb. 1802, aged 17; B.A. 1806; Lincoln's Inn 1803; died at Penzance 22 July 1843, aged 58.	= Sarah Isabella . . . ., died at Tonbridge Wells 4 Sept. 1850.	Timothy Blenman, born 1795; died 28 Dec. 1829, aged 34. M.I. at St. Paul's Cathedral.	John Cobham Blenman, born 1798; died 12 April 1828, aged 30. M.I. in St. Paul's Cathedral.	Anna Maria Blenman, born 4 Feb. 1794; died 26 Aug. 1837. M.I. in St. Paul's Cathedral.

Caroline B. of Welbeck Str. Will dated 23 Feb. 1774. To my Mother £500 and all my slaves in the I. of B'oes. Cubbah to be free after her death. Romeo to be free immediately. Friend Mary Gibbes jewels, £300. Mr Farquhar 5 gns. My 2 neices Eliz. and Ann B., Mr Sam. Gibbes a ring. All res. to my bro. Wm B. My friend Mr Geo. James 10 gns. My Mother and Bro. Ex'ors in the p. of Philip Gibbes, jr, Sam. Osborne Gibbes. Proved 23 Sept., 1774 by W. B. Esq., p. r. to Mary B. (330, Bargrave.)

Wm. Dottin Battyn l. of B'os now of Bristol. Will dated 23 Oct. 1798. My relation Jonathan Blenman, Esq., £1000. (14, Howe.)

Ann Battyn l. of B'os now of Bristol, widow. Will dated 3 March 1799. My cousin Jonathan Blenman, Esq., £1000. (246, Howe.)

The will of Timothy B was recorded in 1799 in B'os.

Wm Blenman of Walcot Terr., Bath, Esq. Will dated 13 May 1794. My age. To my friend Mrs Fra. Jones, whose true name is Fyscot, who has lived in my house for 13 years, all my furniture, she paying my debts and funeral. Books on music to my s. Joseph, the rest of my books to my 1st s. Jonathan. Cod. To Mrs F. J. arrears of H.M. bounty and the salary of a little employment I hold in St Jas. Palace. Having agreed for the sale of a farm in N. Wootton in this Co. for £1000, and the books bequeathed to my s. Joseph lately decd to my 1st s. Jonathan. 17 Jan. 1798. Sworn 14 July 1800. On 13 Aug. 1800 ad. of all the est. of testr, widr, decd, gr. to Tho. Greene, Esq., atty of Jon. B., Esq., Fra. Fyscot *als.* Jones, spr., renouncing. (576, Adderley.)

Jonathan B. of St Mich., B'os, barrister. Will dated 9 June 1804. Wife Anna Maria my Duke's farm. All res. to her and my chn. My sister Ann Graeme. My brothers John and Rd Cobham and Tho. Graeme. Sworn 27 Feb. 1807. Proved 1808. (363, Ely.)

Susanna Christian Cobham late of B'os now of Bristol, widow. Will dated 3 Dec. 1801. My godson Jonathan Blenman £1500 c. My godson John Cobham Blenman £1000 c. (194, Pitt.)

1676, Apr. 3. Francis Blynman of Abbotsleigh and Penelope Payton of ditto. (Bristol Mar. Bonds and Alleg. Glouc. N. and Q., x., 84.)

Deed between Hugh Fortescue of Filleigh, in the co. of Devon, Esq., and Richard Blonman, of the co. of Somerset, clothier, relates to a fulling mill and the land belonging, in the co. of Somerset, with fine signature and *seal* of Hugh Fortiscue, dated 1700. (Dealer's Catalogue.)

1726-7, Mar. 5. Jonathan Planman (*sic*), Esq., appointed his Majesty's Attorney-General in the I. of B. (Hist. Reg., 13.)

1728, Mar. 19. Mr. Bloman (*sic*), Attorney-at-Law, appointed Attorney-General in the I. of B. (*Ibid.*, 18.)

1734, July. Jonathan Blenman, Esq., Attorney-General of B., made sole Judge of the Admiralty there. (*Ibid.*, 19, and "G.M.," 391.)

1741-2, Jan. 22. Timothy Blenman, 2nd s. of Jonathan B., Attorney-General of B'os. (Gray's Inn Admissions.)

Rev. T. Blenman went out to Barbados 27 June 1783. (Fothergill's "Emigrant Ministers.") He was licensed to St George's parish on the 24th inst.

Jonathan B. s. of Wm, arm., b. in B. School, Kensington, under Mr. Lally. Adm. fell. commoner under Dr Shipherd, 18 Oct. 1769. Age 16. Resided till Midsr 1773. Gave two large silver candlesticks as his plate. Adm. at Linc. Inn, 24 Aug. 1771, as s. of W. B. of Welbeck Str. (Christ's Coll., Camb., Regr. II., p. 289.)

1796. William Blenman. (Eton School List, p. 26.)

Grantees of Arms, &c., 1687—1898.

(Part I., A. to J., Harl. Soc. Pub.)

The following West Indian names have been abstracted. The Volumes mentioned refer to the Grant Books preserved in the Heralds' College:—

ABERDEIN to HARVEY, John, of Covent Garden, L., and Grenada, Match 17 . ., Vol. XVII, fo. 428.
ABINGER, James, Baron, of Surrey and Norwich, co. Norf., and his descendants. 1835, Vol. XL, fo. 334.
ADEY to WILLETT, John Willett, of Merley Place, co. Dorset, 1795, Vol. XIX, fo. 19.
AKERS before DOUGLAS, Aretas, of Chilston Park, Maidstone, co. Kent, and Baads, Edinburgh, 1875, Vol. LIX, fo. 110.
ARCEDECKNE, Chaloner, of Harley Str., L., 178 ., Vol. XVI, fo. 281.
AUSTIN, William Piercy, D.D., Oxf., Bp. of Guiana, 1842, Vol. XLVI, fo. 138.

BAILLIE late REID, John, of Jamaica, 17 . ., Vol. XVIII, fo. 85.
BAILLIE, John, of Roehampton, co. Surrey; St. James, co. Cornwall; Minard, par. of St. Anne, co. Middx., Jamaica, 181 ., Vol. XXIX, fo. 71.
BARRETT, Capt. Samuel (s. of Edmund*) of Cinnamon Hill, Jamaica, 17 . ., Vol. XVIII, fo. 121.
BARRETT-BARRETT, Edward and brother Samuel (late MOULTON), of Cinnamon Hill, Jamaica, and New York, 17 . ., Vol. XX, fo. 110; Ed. M. B. [Edward Moulton Barrett] of Hope End, [co. Hereford], 181 ., Vol. XXIX, fo. 25.
BARRITT, Thomas Hercy, of Jamaica, 28 Oct., 1768, Vol. XI, fo. 312.
BARROW, Simon, of Lansdown Grove, Bath, co. Som., 182 ., Vol. XXXVII, fo. 284.
BARUH-LOUSADA, Emanuel, of L., and Jamaica, 28 Jan. 1777, Vol. XIII, fo. 255.
BECKFORD (and GORDON, wife), William, of Fonthill-Gifford, Wilts, and Jamaica, Arms 1791, Vol. XVII, fo. 414.
BECKFORD, William, Quartering HERRING, Match 1793, Vol. XVIII, fo. 163.
BECKFORD and HAMILTON, William, Match and augmentation 1799, Vol. XX, fo. 283, Crest 180, Vol. XXV, fo. 387.
BECKFORD, William, of Fonthill-Gifford, Wilts, 2nd Crest, augmentation 20 March 1810, Vol. XXV, fo. 387. (Berry.)
BECKFORD to PITT-RIVERS, Baron Rivers, co. Dorset and Hampsh. [1828 ?], Vol. XXXVII, fo. 229.
BECKWITH, Lieut.-Gen. Sir George, K.B., [1809, G.C.B. 1815], Gov. of Barbados, ? Arms and Supporters 181 ., Vol. XXVII, fos. 438, 434, Crest of Augmentation 181 ., Vol. XXVIII, fo. 260.
BENDALL, Hopefor, of Mile End, co. Middx., [8 Feb.] 1692-3, Vol. IV, fo. 130. Harl. MS. 1085, fo. 57. (See Berry.)
BENSON, Moses, of Kingston, Jamaica, Liverpool and Ulverston, co. Lanc., 17 . ., Vol. XVII, fo. 11.
BERNAL, Ralph, of Lincoln's Inn, L., from Seville in Andalusia, Spain, 181 ., Vol. XXX, fo. 252.
BERNAL, Ralph Osborne, of Newton Anner, co. Tipperary, 184 ., Vol. XLVII, fo. 206.
BERTIE before GREATHEED, Anne Caroline, of co. Essex, and Guys Cliff, co. Warw., and St. Kitts. 181 ., Vol. XXXI, fos. 222, 224.
BERTIE (GREATHEED), before PERCIE (Hon. Charles) of Guys Cliff to Warw. (mar. Anne Caroline Bertie), 182 ., Vol. XXXV, fo. 392.

* Error for Edward.

Bertie-Mathew, Brownlow, 181 ., Vol. XXXI, fo. 296.
Bertrand late D'Anglebermes of Dominica, 182 ., Vol. XXXII, fo. 179.
Bethell late Codrington, Christopher, of Dodington, co. Glouc., 17 . ., Vol. XX, fo. 68.
Bethell late Codrington, of Swindon Hall, co. York, 17 . ., Vol. XX, fo. 125.
Bidgood late Sloane (? Stone), Henry Fisher, of Rockbeare, co. Devon, and Tobago, 1822, Vol. XXXIII, fo. 336. (See Burke.)
Biscoe, Anne, late Earle (widow of Timothy Hare Earle), of Holton Park, co. Oxf., and Swallowfield, co. Berks, 1829, Vol. XXXVIII, fos. 79, 80.
Bishop, Edward, of Essequibo in Guiana, and of Barbados, 181 ., Vol. XXXI, fo. 260.
Blackman to Harnage, George, Bart., of Shropsh., s. of John Lucie Blackman of L., 1821, Vol. XXXIII, fo. 88.
Blagrove late Bradshaw of Abshott, Hampsh ; Ankerwyke Ho., Bucks.; Lifton, co. Devon, and Woodmans, Kings Langley, co. Hertf., 1840, Vol. XLV, fo. 51.
Blagrove to Bradshaw of Abshott, etc., as above, 1856, Vol. LII, fo. 98.
Blagrove late Coare, Henry John, of Orange Valley, St. Anne's, Jamaica, and Ankerwyke Ho., co. Bucks, 184 ., Vol. XLVI, fo. 191.
Blenman, Jonathan, Attorney-Gen., of Barbados, and of Croscombe, co. Som., to descendants of his father Thomas, 10 Oct. 1739, Vol. VIII, fo. 260; Add. MS. 14,831, fo. 119.
Boucher late Crabb, of Shedfield, and Droxford Ho., Hampsh., and Marlboro' Mount, Middx., Jamaica, 183 ., Vol. XLII, fo. 195.
Branigan, Henry, of Jamaica and L., 181 ., Vol. XXIX, fo, 237.
Brockden, ..., of Barbados (Match with Heysham). 172 ., Vol. VII, fo. 158.
Brodbelt, Francis Rigby, M.D., of Bath Easton, co. Som., and Jamaica, 182 ., Vol. XXXIV, fo. 3.
Brouncker, ..., of Beveridge, co. Dorset, and St. Chr., 183 ., Vol. XLII, fo. 161.
Browne, before Mill, George Græni, of Bath, and Cariacou, W.I., 180 ., Vol. XXII, fo. 298.
Bruley, Joseph (s. of James), of Liverpool, co. Lanc., and Tortola, 180 ., Vol. XXIII, fo. 112.

Camm to Thornhill, Christopher, of Thornhill, co. Durham, and Antigua, 180 ., Vol. XXII, fo. 156.
Campbell late Mackinnon, ..., of Greenock, co. Renfrew; Kilmodan and Ormaig, co. Argyll, Scotland, and Tobago, 180 ., Vol. XXIII, fo. 430.
Carroll, Edward, of Kingston, Jamaica, 181 ., Vol. XXVI., fo. 163.
Clare, Michael Benignus, M.D., of Spanish Town, Jamaica (Ballyshandy, co. Tipperary, Ireland), 182 ., Vol. XXXII, fo. 221.
Clarke, Bart., with Haughton, of Oakhill, Barnet, co. Hertf., and Jamaica, 182 ., Vol. XXXIII, fo. 298.
Codrington, ..., of co. Glouc., 16 . ., Vol. II, fo. 533.
Codrington late Miller, Jane Charlotte, of Dodington, co. Glouc., nat. dau. of Sir William Codrington, Bart., 179 .. Vol. XVIII, fo. 33.
Codrington to Bethell, William and Christopher, of Dodington [1798], Vol. XX, fo. 68, and of Swindon Hall, co. York, 179 ., Vol. XX, fo. 125.
Codrington, Sir Edward, K.C.B., [1815], of co. Glouc., ? Arms for wife Jane Hall, 182 ., Vol. XXXIII, fo. 102. Also Jasper Taylor Hall of Sutton Park, co. Bedford, nephew of Jane.
Coleridge [Dr. William Hart, D.D., Bishop of Barbados, 1824 to 1841. 1824 (Her. and Geneal., V, p. 280)].
Colleton late Garth, Charles, of Hirst, co. Berks., and Haynes Hill, and Devizes, co. Wilts, 180 ., Vol. XXIII, fo. 177.

COLYEAR-DAWKINS, [James], of Over-Norton, co. Oxf.; Richmond, co. Surrey, [s. and h. of Henry Dawkins of] Standlinch, co. Wilts, [Collyear in the 2d quarter. 21 Jan. 1836], Vol. XXXI, fo. 188.
COOKE to FREEMAN, John & brother Stephen, of Fawley, co. Bucks, 17 . ., Vol. IX. fo. 361.
COWARD, ..., of Whitehall and Islington, Jamaica, ? L., 18 . ., Vol. XXXI, fo. 317.
CRISP (MOLINEUX before MONTGOMERIE) of Garboldisham, co. Norf., Quarterly Arms 18 . ., Vol. XXVII, fo. 392.

DAVY, George Thomas, of Sussex Sq., L., and Jamaica, 185 ., Vol. L, fo. 39.
DAWKINS to PENNANT, George Hay, of Penrhyn, co. Carnarvon, Wales; Standlynch, co. Wilts, and Jamaica, 180 ., Vol. XXIV, fo. 414.
DAWKINS, James, of Over-Norton, co. Oxf., etc., 31 Jan. 173¾, Vol. VIII, fo. 183b. (Berry.)
DAWKINS, Henry, of St. James', Westminster; Oxford, etc., 20 April 1761, Vol. X, fo. 352. (Berry.)
DELPRATT, ..., of Bristol, co. Som.; Jamaica; and Queen's Gardens, L., 180 ., Vol. LVI, fo. 316.
DILLON before TRANT, Henry, of Easingwold, co. York; Rathmile, co. Roscommon; & Belgrade Ho., co. Dublin, Quarterly Arms, 181 ., Vol. XXIX, fo. 364.
DONALD to HARVEY. of Medmar, co. Aberdeen, Scotland, and Grenada, Match 17 . ., Vol. XVII, fo. 426.
DOTTIN, Samuel Rouse, of English in Nuffield and Newnham Murren, co. Oxf., and Barbados, 17 March 1817, Vol. XXX, fo. 107. (Berry's Supp.)
DOUGLAS after MONTEATH, Col. Thomas, C.B., of Kepp, co. Perth, Scotland, and Kingston, Jamaica, Arms with design (Douglas suppor. and Monteath), 1851, Vol. XLIX, fo. 412.
DRAX, (ERLE-) after SAWBRIDGE, John, of Charborough, co. Dorset, 1828, Vol. XXXVII (? XXVII), fo. 364.

EAST, Sir Edward Hyde, Knt. (Bart. 1823), of L., Calcutta, and Jamaica, 182 ., Vol. XXXIV, fo. 29.
EGGINTON-ERNLE, J. Lloyd (s. of Rev. John C.) of Charboro' Park and Bere Regis, co. Dorset, and Ellerton Abbey, co. York, 1887, Vol. LXIV, fo. 71; 1888, Vol. LXIV, fo 193; and 1890, Vol. LXVI, fo. 17.
ELLIS, ..., of Sunning Hill, co. Berks, and Jamaica, 180 ., Vol. XXV, fo. 432.

FARLEY, ..., of Antigua, 17 . ., Vol. XVII, fo. 272.
FEUILLETEAU, William, s. of Lewis, s. of Jacob, of St. Chr., 20 Sept. 1774, Vol. XIII, fo. 7.
FORD,* Francis (Bart.) [22 Feb. 1793], of Thames Ditton, co. Surrey, and Lears, Barbados, 179 ., Vol. XVIII, fo. 187.
FOSTER, George, of par. of St. Joseph, Barbados, 3 May 1703, Vol. V, fo. 101; Add. MS. 14,831, fo. 184; Harl. MS. 6,834, fo. 112. (Genealogist XV.)
FRANCKLYN to WEBBE, ..., of Tonbridge Wells, co. Kent, and Nevis and Court of Scindia, 185 ., Vol. L, fo. 106.
FRANCO, Jacob (afterwards LOPEZ). of St. Catherine Coleman, L. (2nd s. of Moses Franco, late of Leghorn, decd.) [10 April] 1760, Vol. X, fo. 227 (Berry) [Trans. Jewish Hist. Soc. II, p. 166.]
FRANCO to LOPES, ... [4 May 1831] (Bart.), of co. Devon, 18 . ., Vol. XXXVIII, fo. 240.
FREEMAN after WILLIAMS, Adm. of Fawley Court, co. Bucks, and Hoddesdon, co. Hertf., 182 ., Vol. XXXIII, fos. 146, 148.

* See Grant, *ante* III, 367.

FREEMAN now THOMAS, Inigo, of Ratton, co. Sussex, Arms 1786, Vol. XV, fo. 161.
FREEMAN, ..., of Ratton, co. Sussex, Arms 17 . ., Vol. XVII, fo. 440.
FRYE late NEWTON, ..., of Wallington, co. Surrey, 180 ., Vol. XXI, fo. 152.
FULLERTON late DOWNING, George Alexander, of Ireland and St. Anne's, Jamaica (of Wadham Coll. Oxf.), 179 ., Vol. XVIII, fo. 404.

GALE, William, s. of John, of co. York and Jamaica, 178 ., Vol. XV, fo. 92.
GALE late MORANT, Edward Gregory, of Brockenhurst, Hampsh., co. York, and Jamaica, 179 ., Vol. XIX, fo. 189.
GALLIMORE (see HAMILTON), ..., of St. Anne's, co. Middx., Jamaica, Match 177 ., Vol. XIII, fo. 108.
GALLWEY after PAYNE [2 March 1814], Lieut.-Gen. [Sir William], Bart., of St. Chr., 181 .. Vol. XXVIII, fo. 61.
GALLWEY, Lieut.-Gen. Sir Thomas Lionel John, K.C.M.G. [1889] (s. of Major John), 189 ., Vol. LXXI, fo. . . .
GARBRAND, Joshua, of St. Thomas, Jamaica, Quarterly to BARRITT, 28 Oct. 1768, Vol. XI, fo. 312 (Berry).
GARDNER, John, of St. Olave's, Southwark, L. and Jamaica, 1 March 170⅔, Vol. VII, fo. 176.
GARRIQUES, ..., of Yarmouth Estate, Vere, and Kingston in Jamaica, 182 ., Vol. XXXVII, fo. 268.
GENT after THARP, of Chipperton Park, co. Camb., and Moyers Park, Steeple Bumpstead, co. Essex, 186 ., Vol. LIV, fo. 184.
GIBBES, Sir Philip, Bart., of Barbados, Escutcheon of pretence Agnes Osborne, 177 ., Vol. XIV, fo. 71.
GOMM, William, of Clerkenwell, L., 24 Jan. 1761, Vol. X, fo. 278 (Berry).
GOMM after Carr, ..., of L. [1878], Vol. LX, fo. 130.
GOMM, Gen. Sir William Maynard, G.C.B., of L., Supporters 10 Oct. 1859, Vol. LIII, fo. 226 (Misc. G. et H. New S. II, p. 184).
GORDON, ..., of Braes, Trelawney, Jamaica, 179 ., XVIII, fo. 308.
GRAEME after JONES, Thomas Valentine, Capt. Dragoon Guards, of Oldbury Court, co. Glouc.; Bailbrook Ho., co. Som.; and Barbados, 182 ., Vol. XXXIII, fo. 304. (Jamaica, in the entry under Jones.)
GRANT (Hon.), ..., of Jamaica and L., 17 . ., Vol. XVII, fo. 296.
GRANT, Charles, Col. of Horse, Jamaica (s. of Ludovic Grant, Bart., of Dalvey, Scotland), of Hopewell Estate, Jamaica, Crest, 182 ., Vol. XXXVIII, fo. 85.
GRANT, John, of Glenlochry, Jamaica, by J. H. Campbell, Lyon King of Arms, 6 Nov. 1783 (Burke's Commoners II, p. 613).
GREATHEED, see Bertie.
GREEN, Col. . . . ., Gov. of Grenada, of L., 180 ., Vol. XXII, fo. 81.
GROSETT-MUIRHEAD after STEUART, ... of Bredisholm, co. Lanark, Scotland, 186 ., Vol. LV, fo. 86.

HAIGH, Arthur S., of Bahamas, and Charles T. E., of Bradley and Huddersfield, co. York (sons of Thomas), 18 . ., Vol. LXXI, fo. . . .
HALE to RIGBY, Francis, M.P., of Mistley Hall, co. Essex, 178 ., Vol. XVII, fo. 29.
HALL, ..., wife of KING, of Bridgetown, Barbados, Arms for self and descendants (see also HALL DARE-), 181 ., Vol. XXIX, fos. 132, 133.
HALL, ..., of Trinidad, 182 ., Vol. XXXIII, fo. 333.
HALL-DARE, Robert Westley, of Ilford Lodge, co. Essex, and Wyefield, Cranbrook, co. Kent, 1823, Vol. XXXIV, fos. 94. 96, 100.
HALLIDAY to TOLLEMACHE, Rear-Adm., of Leasowes, Shroph., and Castlemains, co. Kirkcudbright, Scotland, 182 ., Vol. XXXII, fo. 351.
HAMILTON, George Robinson, of St. James, co. Cornwall, Jamaica, 13 July 1775, Vol. XIII, fo. 108.

HAMPDEN [Renn Dickson], Bp. of Hereford [1847-1868], of co. Hereford, 184 ., Vol. XLIX, fos. 3, 4.
HAREWOOD, Baron of [9 July 1790, Edwin Lascelles], of co. York, 17 . ., Vol. XVII, fo. 254.
HAREWOOD [Baron, 18 June 1796, Edward Lascelles], of co. York [1796], Vol. XIX, fo. 285.
HARRIS, George David, of the Bahamas, Castlebar, Christchurch, for Bishoprick of Nassau, New Providence. Bahamas, 186 ., Vol. LVII, fo. 123.
HARVEY, ..., of L.; Midmar, co. Aberdeen, Scotland; and Grenada, 179 ., Vol. XVII, fo. 242.
HARVEY late RAE, ..., of Grenada, 17 . ., Vol. XVII, fo. 424. See also under ABERDEIN and DONALD.

HERBERT after MORTON, ..., of Nevis, 182 ., Vol. XXXIII, fo. 208.
HEYSHAM, William, of E. Greenwich, co. Kent, M.P. for Lancaster.. To the descendants of his grandfather Giles, 9 or 3 Feb. 1722-3, Vol. VII, fo. 158 (Illustrated in Misc. G. et H. New S. IV, p. 375, and see Berry's Suppl.).
HIBBERT, ..., of Munden Ho., Mottram, co. Chester, 184 ., Vol. XLVIII, fo. 35.
HIBBERT after HOLLAND, Arthur Henry, of Watford, co. Hertf., 1876, Vol. LIX, fo. 234 (see Berry's Suppl.).
HOLLIGAN, James, of Barbados, 18 . ., Vol. XLIV, fo. 113.
HOPLEY, George Augustus, of Charlestown, S. Carolina, and Liverpool, co. Lanc., s. of Joseph, Gov. of St. Vincent [1863], Vol. LV, fo. 50.
HORSFORD, Lieut.-Gen. George, of Falmouth Estate, Antigua [1831], Vol. XXXVIII, fo. 199 (Berry's Suppl.).
HORSFORD, Sir Alfred Hastings, G.C.B. [29 May 1875], of L., Supporters 1875, Vol. LIX, fo. 147 (Berry's Suppl.).
HUNTER, ..., of Crowland Abbey, co. Linc. [1803], Vol. XXII, fo. 176.

JACKSON (Sir John, Bart. [1815]), of Jamaica, and Bury Arlsey, co. Bedf., "one of the Barons in the Parliament for Dover" [1810], Vol. XXVI, fo. 44.
JAMES, Montagu, of Haughton Hall, Hanover, Cornwall, Jamaica, 29 June 1772, Vol. XII, fo. 201 (Berry).
JARRATT, Herbert Newton J., of Trelawny, Jamaica, [1793], Vol. XVIII, fo. 218.
JERVIS late RICKETTS [10 June 1801, William Henry, Capt. R.N.], heir of Earl of ST. VINCENT, of co. Staff., 180 ., Vol. XXI, fo. 188. (There are other grants.)

King of Antigua.*

Peculiar of Wimborne Minster at Blandford. Bundle K., No. 13. 3 July 1683.

Joan King of Furschill, Wimborne Minster, widow, mentions will of husband John King, dated 16 Aug. 1677 and proved in Peculiar Court of Wimborne Minster, probate† whereof is in my custody.

My youngest son Benjamin King, living in the island of Antegoe; my daughter Joane Stevens, widow, living in the island of Antegoe.

Proved 29 July 1715.

The will of Wm. Stevens, husband of Joane, was recorded at Antigua in 1680. [ED.]

* Communicated by Mr. G. S. Fry.
† Note.—This is not in the existing Register of Wills. (G. S. F.)

Rawlins of St. Kitts and Nevis.[*]

The following additions and corrections have been supplied by Mr. John Bromley, who has collections of several old families of St. Kitts.—Ed.

(*Ante*, p. 98.)

Henry Rawlins who heads the pedigree was doubtless son of Henry Rawlins, whose will was dated 1709. He was buried 12 Aug. 1733, but his will has not been found. Eliz. his 1st wife was dau. of Tho. Dinsey, and his will was proved 26 March 1728-9. By her he had (besides Eliz.) 1, Thomas, 2, Frances, 3, Mary, mar. 21 Sept. 1738 Joseph Peets. Henry Rawlins, by his 2nd wife Ann, had: 1, Henry, bapt. 17 Oct. 1724, but delete the marriage with Mary Hill Brotherson; 4, Charles, bapt. 26 April 1729; add 5, Joseph, born 25 and bapt. 30 May 1730. (See Pedigree B.)

Ruth Rawlins, mar. 1stly . . . . Garner, and 2ndly Chas. Lowndes. She was bur. 22 July 1763.

Stedman Rawlins (will dated 1788) had nine children:—

I. Stedman, born 23 Feb. 1754; mar. 15 Jan. 1784 Eliz. Taylor Wharton, dau. of Wm. and Ann Wharton. She died 18 Nov. 1797.

II. John, mar. Sarah Hart in 1794, not 1784.

I. Mary, born 21 Nov. 1755; mar. 15 June 1777 John Satterthwaite.

II. Ann, born 15 Dec. 1758; died young.

Stedman R. the 2nd by Eliz. T. Wharton had another dau. Eliz. Stedman R., born posthumously 14 July 1794; mar. in L. 30 Sept. 1813 Worthington R. Stedman R. the 3rd by Gertrude Tyson had an eldest son Stedman, born 5 Sept. 1806. Delete John and add a 4th son Tho. Chas. Corry R., born 3 Feb. 1813 and bapt. 1 Jan. 1814. Anne Taylor R. mar. Capt. Stedman R., later a Colonel; she died 15 Feb. 1831. Wm. Wharton R. mar. a Miss Bayford.

John R. by Sarah Johnson Hart had another dau. Sarah Ann R., born 18 Oct. 1796; mar. Stedman R. She died 1 Nov. 1877. Delete on p. 99 the Rev. Wm. Henry R. Anthony Hart R., barrister, was born posthumously in 1800; mar. Rosina Caines, and was bur. s.p. 25 Oct. 1843. John Hart R., born 9 April 1795; bur. 5 June 1840, aged 45; had two other daus. and one son, viz.:—

I. Sarah Swanston R., born 26 March 1823; mar. 21 Aug. 1845 Henry Charles Newman.

II. Eliz. Martha, born 26 Dec. 1825.

III. John, born 2 July 1830.

Richard R. by Eliz. Vanderpool Maillard (born 1767; bur. 3 Sept. 1835) had six sons and five daus., viz.:—

I. Stedman, born 1789; mar. 20 Aug. 1816 Sarah Ann R., his first cousin, born 18 Oct. 1796. He was bur. s.p. 13 Dec. 1833. She left him in 1828, and died in L. 1 Nov. 1877.

II. John, born 1790, a doctor; mar. Louisa Morton Fahie. He was bur. 18 May 1850, and his will is given.

IV. Henry, born 22 Feb. 1791; died bach.; bur. 7 Dec. 1824.

V. Joseph, died bach.; bur. 29 March 1828.

VI. Adam Sprott, died bach.; bur. Nov. 1846.

II. Eliz., born 1 July 1795; mar. Rev. John Perry. She was bur. 9 May 1874.

[*] Continued from p. 103.

III. Ann-Akers, born 29 Oct. 1799; mar. 28 Nov. 1816 Capt. Geo. Molyneux Fahie Mercer.

IV. Frances, mar. 15 May 1828 Wm. Jasper Bryan. She was bur. 16 Nov. 1877.

V. Louisa-Johnson, mar. John Joseph Esdaile. She was bur. 12 May 1872.

(P. 100.)

Eliz. Wilkes was dau. of Wm. and Sarah Wilkes. Of her children:—

I. Stedman, born 1782, was a Colonel in the army; mar. at Eltham, co. Kent, 22 Aug. 1803, Ann Taylor Rawlins, first cousin. She died at Walke estate 15 Feb. 1831. They had three other sons: Henry, bapt. 7 April 1812; John James, bapt. 24 Feb. 1813; died 16 Oct. 1839; Wm., died Jan. 1840.

III. Wm. Henry, born 1788; entered the church; mar. 14 Nov. 1822 Eliz. Rawlins Maillard. He died 14 Jan. 1840, as given on p. 99, where his name was wrongly placed.

V. Worthington, mar. at St. James's, Blackfriars, 30 Sept. 1813, Eliz. Stedman R., a first cousin. He died 13 June 1868.

IV. Sarah, born 20 Nov. 1793; mar. 14 July 1812 Richard Drew of Bristol.

V. Caroline, mar. Francis John Galpin.

VI. Eliz. Frances, born 7 May 1795.

VII. Rebecca, mar. James Fitzpatrick. She was bur. 27 March 1830.

Stedman Akers R. had two children Anna and Stedman, both bapt. 7 Jan. 1839. The latter died 5 Feb. 1892, aged 56. M.I. at St. George's, Gingerland, Nevis.—Ed.

(P. 101.)

Joseph R., 5th son of Henry and Ann; born 25 and bapt. 30 May 1730; mar. at Sandy Point 29 Oct. 1751 Eliz., dau. of Geo. and Eliz. Linnington, and had issue:—

I. Henry, born 29 March 1756; mar. Mary Hill, dau. of Lewis Brotherson. She was born 24 Feb. and bapt. 11 March 1754. His will (149, Gostling). Their two children died young.

II. Joseph, mar. 1st . . . ., by whom he had a dau. Eliz., bapt. 6 Nov. 1791 and bur. 15 Jan. 1798, aged 7.

I. Ann, mar. 11 June 1776 her cousin John Hutchinson Wallwyn.

II. Mary, born 24 Feb. and bapt. 11 March 1754; she died 22 Dec. 1823.

III. Eliz., mar. Wm. van Wyck.

IV. Rebecca, mar. James Warner Thomas.

V. Frances, bapt. 6 Dec. 1767.

Henry Rawlins of Nevis, planter. Will dated 11 Jan. 1709. To my sister Eliz. Perry of London a diamond ring and £5 per annum. To my two grandchildren Edward and Eliz. Gardiner 10,000 lbs. of sugar between them. To my dau. Mary Rawlins one of my best gold rings, two of my silver spoons and £1000 st. at marriage or 21, and to continue in England under the care of Mr. Richard Meriwether,* but if she come to this island, a negro woman, a horse and a chamber. To my dau. Jane £500 at marriage or 21. To my dau. Bridget

* His will was dated 20 Dec. 1713. He refers to his moiety of Lady Bawdens and Sharlowes plantations in St. Tho. Lowland, Nevis. (9, Aston.)

Rice* my cornelian ring and my negro woman Betty. To my godson Geo. Pemberton a hhd. of sugar. To my godson Wm. Evans 1000 lbs. of sugar. All my plantations, slaves and all residue to my son Henry Rawlins and sole Ex'or, sufficient sugar to be shipped to Mr R. Meriwether to make up with the £1600 st. in his hands the portions for my daus. Mary and Jane. Mr. Azariah Pinney and Major Michael Smith of this island to be Guardians of my son and of my two daus. under 21. Signed with testator's mark. In the presence of Roger Pemberton, John Griffin, Wm. Peterson, Jeoffry Meriwether. (Public Record Office, C.O., 243, p. 279.)

Stedman Rawlins, S^r^, of St Chr., Esq. Will dated 27 May 1788. To my dau. Eliz. Young, wife of Anthony Young, the dwelling house in Irish Town where she resides and 7 slaves (named). To my grandson Stedman, s. of my s. Henry, at 21 £4000 st. To each other grandchild £50 st. To the children of Edward Gilliard of St Chr. £200 c. per annum during his life. To my dau. Mary wife of John Satterthwaite £500 in satisfaction of a parcel of negros left when she quitted the island. To my sons John, Henry, Richard and Joseph £200 st. yearly until 1 Aug. 1792, To Mrs. Eliz. Johnson, wife of Anthony Johnson, Esq., late President, the rents of property in Irish Town. I have lately contracted for the purchase of property with Benj. and Tho. Boddington of L., merchants. Estate called Hutchinsons. All residue to my brother Joseph Rawlins, my son Stedman Rawlins and my sons-in-law John Satterthwaite and James Akers till 1 Aug. 1792. I have already made provision for my eldest son Stedman, my daus. Mary Satterthwaite, Eliz. wife of Anthony Young and Ann Akers, wife of Jas. Akers, J^r^. Testator died 6 June, probate 11 June 1788. (St. Kitts Records.)

(*Ante*, p. 97.) In the will of Stedman Rawlins, dated 24 July 1793, add:— To my dau. Ann Taylor £5000 at 21, and to all my children the like sum. John Taylor, Esq., receiver of the late Wm. Wharton's estates. Probate 17 Feb. 1794.

1800, Aug. Letters of administration granted to Richard Rawlins of the estate of John Rawlins, lately deceased. Value of estate £21,397. (St. Kitts Records.)

John Rawlins of St Chr., practitioner in physic and surgery. Will dated 12 Jan. 1850. To my wife Louisa Morton all my estate for her life, and at her death to Cath. Louisa, wife of Henry James Schooles and dau. of Hugh Riley Semper of the said island, Esq., and at her death to her children equally. Wife sole Ex'trix. Witnessed by A. C. Fahie Mercer (now Wilson, wife of Robert W. of the said island), Aston Davoren. Earlier probate 6 May 1851. (*Ibid.*)

1635, May 21. To be transported to St Christophers, Jo. Rawlins, aged 18. (Hotten, 80.)

1635, Nov. 20. Henry Rawlins,† aged 25, for Barbadoes. (*Ibid.*, 139.)

1665. Giles Rawlins in Virginia.

1670. Edward Rawlins owned 120 acres in St. John's, Jamaica.

1673. John Rawlins, S^r^, M. of A. in the Somers Islands. (Hotten, 303.)

* See *ante*, II., 267, for Rice entries at St. George's, Nevis.

† Information wanted by the "Baltimore Sun" *re* Henry Rawlins, emigrant to America in 1635.

1676. Thomas Rawlins, gunner, Austins Bay, Barbados.

1677-8. Nevis. In Capt. Robert Chuppin's Company:—
Chr. Rawlings 6 m., 2 w., 1 ch., 11 slaves.

1677-8. Capt. Tho. Rawlings 40 a., 17 negros, St. Philips, Barbados.

1677-8. John Rawlins, M. of C., Somers Islands.

1679. John Rawlines, 15 a., Christ Church, Barbados.

1680. John Rawlings and wife 2 servants, 1 slave, S[t] Michaels, Barbados. (Hotten, 449.)

1680. Benjamin Rawlings and wife 2 slaves, S[t] Michaels, Barbados. (*Ibid.*, 443.)

1680-82. John Rawlins, a King's subject in Surinam, removed to Antigua.

1680. Cap[t] Rawlins in Col. Chr. Lynes' reg. of foot at Barbados.

1680. M[r] Wm. Rawlins 9 a. 4 slaves, S[t] Andrews, Barbados. (Hotten, 470.)

1693. Society of Apothecaries. List of members in or about London:—
Mr. Wm. Rawlins, retired, "have left off the trade."

1700. Wm. Rawlins, clerk of the A. in Barbados.

1700. John Rawlings, storekeeper powder magazine, etc.

1700. John Rawlings in Boston, Mass,

1700, Jan. 15. Attestation of John Rawlins, Dep. Marshal and Searcher at Bermuda. He was Marshal in 1702 and dead 1703.

1712. Nevis. Richard Rawlings, merchant of a Liverpool ship named in the will of Michael Nowell.

1713. Nevis. Deposition of Joan Symonds, widow, witnessed by Wm. Rollins, Rich[d] Rollins.

1713. St. Kitts. Henry Rawlins was taken into custody by the Provost Marshal *re* certain lands at Cayon he had taken possession of. (St. Kitts Records.)

1713, March 25. Barber Surgeons of L. M[r] John Rawlins.

1717, Aug. 22. London. Letter from John Smith to the Lords Commissioners for the Plantations "on behalf of Henry Rawlings now residing in St. Christopher and having no lands there I humbly propose to purchase a parcel of land in Basseterre quarter bounded at the N.E. with the Canada Hills and at the S.W. with a silk cotton tree marked with 3 cutts and at the head with an old Trench and at the foot with the common path leading to Basseterre Town containing about 70 acres paying for the same £5 per acre."

1719-20. London. John Rawlins, owner of the Mary galley 150 tons Cha. Burnham master, 8 guns and 16 men bound for Jamaica and other ports.

1727. Henry Rawlins named in Treasury accounts of S[t] Kitts.

1734, Jan. 2. Ann Rawlins, Ex'or of Henry Rawlins. On the previous March 13 a judgment was made against her for £154 and £6 costs at the suit of Tho. Pilkington, also for £300 and £6 costs at the suit of Jas. Verchild. Execution issued on 16 March. Slaves were sold in June and realized £815 and title vested in Francis Phipps.

1734-5, Feb. 17. Ann Rawlins, wid., conveys to Richard Wilson, Esq., land in Basseterre for £400.

1735, April 17. Ann Rawlins buys back the above slaves for £815.

1750, April 26. Ind're between Edward Phipps and Ann Rawlins, widow, for 5*s.* sale of 100 a. in St. Thomas, Middle Island, also a second deed consideration £2500.

1769, June 12. Joseph Rawlins and Eliz. his wife. The said Eliz. Rawlins, Ann Hutchinson Wallwyn wife of Wm. Wallwyn, and Mary Fraser wife of Simon Fraser are the nieces and heirs-at-law of John Hutchinson, Esq., deceased.

1794, April 4. Marriage Settlement between John Rawlins and Henry Hart, Henry Rawlins and John Garnett of St. Kitts *re* marriage between John Rawlins and Sarah Johnson Hart. He entitled to 20 negros and she to 6. Manning and Anderton of L. agents for him. . . . . Whitton, lawyer of King's Road, Bedford Row. Power of attorney from her.

1819. £5500 due to Anthony Hart on the estate of John Hart Rawlins

mortgage of Johnsons estate subject to a first one to Manning and Anderton for £6000.

In Chancery 1847 and 1864. Advertisement. Anthony Hart Rawlins of Boswell Court, Fleet Street, entitled under a deed dated 1847 to participate in a sum of £5396 forming part of the unclaimed funds of a club in London.

In the High Court of Chancery. Affidavit of trustees dated 10 April 1884 on the payment and transfer of funds into Court. Druces and Attlee, 10 Billiter Square. Filed by Roberts and Barlow of 49 Lime Street, solicitors. £701 consols and £62 cash, being the whole of the trust fund, after deducting £63 costs, subject to the marriage settlement dated 19 Aug. 1816 of Stedman Rawlins with Sarah Ann Rawlins. Trustees: Stedman R., Sarah A. R., John Hart R. and John R.

Ind're recited made 27 May 1839 between Sir John Rae Reid and Robert Chester of the one part and Sarah Ann R. of the other to invest £701 for her benefit and at her death for whomsoever would be entitled in reversion to the plantation and slaves. This money was eventually paid out to the heirs of Stedman R.

(*To be continued.*)

Monumental Inscriptions in England relating to West Indians.*

MARYLEBONE NEW PARISH CHURCH.†

Below the north gallery, west side. On a small white marble tablet:—

DAVID CLARK ESQ[RE]
late of Calcutta,
Born 20th November 1779,
Died 18th June 1838.
(11 lines. Also his brother)
JOHN CLARK ESQ[RE]
Late of Jamaica,
Born 16th November 1778
Died 14th February 1814
They are both interred in the same vault
Beneath this church.

1814, Feb. 16. John Clarke, esq. late of Jamaica. ("G.M.," 410.)

Below the west gallery near the font. A white marble tablet with cherub above raising a curtain:—

SACRED
TO THE MEMORY
OF
REBECCA PHIPPS
THE BELOVED WIFE OF

* Continued from p. 88.

† The following M.I. appeared in "Misc. Gen. et Her.," 3rd Series, Vols. IV. and V., but the editor has checked them with the originals and added notes and heraldry.

HENRY MORETON-DYER
ESQUIRE,
OF THIS PARISH;
WHO DIED
ON THE 12TH OF AUGUST 1830.
(19 lines follow.)

1830, Aug. 12. Rebecca Phipps, wife of H. Moreton Dyer, esq. of Devonshire-place House. ("G.M.," 188.)

Below the west gallery near the second window from the north end:—

SACRED TO THE MEMORY OF
SOLOMON FRANCO ESQR
WHO DEPARTED THIS LIFE
ON THE 27TH DAY OF MARCH 1825,
AGED 46 YEARS,
AND WHOSE REMAINS ARE DEPOSITED
IN A VAULT BENEATH THIS CHURCH.
ALSO OF HIS WIFE MARGARET FRANCES FRANCO
WHO DIED AT PARIS THE 7TH DAY OF FEBRUARY 1845
AGED 53 YEARS.
ALSO OF HIS SISTER SARAH FRANCO
WHO DIED THE 6TH AUGUST 1835, AGED 66 YEARS.
ALSO OF FRANCIS FRANCO ESQRE
HIS RELATIVE
WHO DIED ON THE FIRST OF FEBRUARY 1837
AGED 83 YEARS.

1811, June 13. Thursday was married at Queen-square chapel, by the Rev. Dr. Gardiner, S. Franco, esq; of Burlington-str. London, to Margaret-Frances, dau. of Francis Franco, esq. of Amwell, Herts. ("Bath Chronicle.")

1837, Feb. 1. In Great Portland-st. aged 83, Francis Franco, esq. ("G.M.," 329.)

1845, Feb. 7. At Paris, aged 53, Margaret Frances, relict of Solomon Franco, esq. and dau. of the late Francis Franco, esq. of Great Portland-st. (*Ibid.*, 678.)

Leah Franco of Bath, co. Som., wid. of Raphael F., late of L., Mt. Will dated 15 Sept. 1807. To be bur. in the grd of Port. Jews in L. Son Jacob F. £5 for a ring. Dau. Simha, now wife of Edwd Watts, a ring. Son Moses F. £5. Son Ephraim F. £5. Dau. Esther, now wife of Saul Bonfil, £5. Dau. Sarah F. jewels and furniture. Plate to daus. Sarah F., Reba, wid. of Jacob Lousada. Son Solomon F. Nephew Fra. F. My sister Abig. F. my F.'s picture. All residue to daus. S. F. and R. L. Dau. S. F. sole Ex'trix. 15 Sept. 1807. Sworn by Margt F. of Walcot, spr., 17 Nov. 1808. Proved 22 Nov. 1808 by S. F. (881, Ely.)

Joseph F. of Jamaica. Will dated 1 June 1792. My Mother Leah F. and sisters Simha F., Sarah F. and Rebecca F., all of L., £40 each. My brothers Jacob, Abr. and Solomon F. of L. £10 each. My sister Esther Bonfil of Leghorn. My bros. Ephraim F. of L. and Moses F. of J., merchants. My uncle Sam. D'Aguilar. Proved 8 Dec. 1808. (958, Ely.)

This family, of Portuguese Jewish origin, settled as merchants in Fenchurch Street, Leghorn and India. Wills, 110, Hutton; 96, Rushworth; 196, Hay; 308, Collier; 525, Webster also relate to them.

Below the west gallery near the fourth window from the north end:—

TO THE MEMORY OF
JAMES CRUIKSHANK ESQ[R]
OF BALLARDS VALLEY S[T] MARYS IN THE ISLAND OF JAMAICA
AND OF GLOUCESTER STREET PORTMAN SQUARE LONDON
(3 lines; erected by his widow)
HE DIED 25TH NOVEMBER 1831 AGED 30 YEARS
SACRED ALSO TO THE MEMORY OF
MARY DANSEY
(ONLY DAUGHTER OF JAMES CRUIKSHANK ESQ & MARY HIS WIFE)
THE WIFE OF CHARLES CORNWALLIS DANSEY
MAJOR IN HIS MAJESTYS ROYAL REGIMENT OF ARTILLERY
WHO DIED 14TH FEBRUARY 1830, AGED 33 YEARS
(3 lines follow.)

Above on a shield cut in marble.

CREST.—*A sprig of three thistles slipped and leaved.*
ARMS.—. . . . *three boars' heads erased within a bordure engrailed*; impaling: . . . . *A cross lozengy.*

1787, Nov. 2. In Percy-st. Jn. Cruikshank, esq; of Ballard's Valley, Jamaica. ("G.M.," 1127.)
1812, March 31. At Berry-hill, St Mary's Jamaica, J. Cruikshank, esq. of Ballards Valley. (*Ibid.*, 594.)
1818, May 22. In Suffolk-st. Geo. Cruikshank, esq. of Jamaica. (*Ibid.*, 640.)
1831, Nov. 25. In Gloucester-st. Portman-sq. aged 69, James Cruikshank, esq. of Jamaica. (*Ibid.*, 569.)
The will of James Cruikshank was recorded in J. in 1738.

John Cruikshank of S[t] Mary's, J'ca, Esq., now of Percy Str. Will dated 28 May 1785. Ballards Valley and Berryhill penn to my reputed son John C., a Capt. 36 Regt., and reputed son James C. To my reputed dau. Mary £10,000. Proved 1787. (537, Major.)

John Cruikshank of Devonshire pl., Esq. Will dated 3 Dec. 1801. My wife Frances £1000 a year. Brother James my moiety of Ballards Valley and all residue. Proved 1812. (448, Oxford.)

Below the west gallery opposite the pulpit on a white tablet surmounted by a draped urn:—

TO THE MEMORY OF TWO BROTHERS
THE ONLY SONS OF THE LATE STEPHEN HAVEN ESQUIRE,
AND OF LYDIA HIS WIFE,
WILLIAM GORDON
DEPARTED THIS LIFE ON THE FIRST OF NOVEMBER 1809,
AGED 8 YEARS AND NINE MONTHS
CHARLES MACKINEN
DIED ON THE FOURTEENTH OF APRIL 1824,
IN THE TWENTY-FIRST YEAR OF HIS AGE:
(5 lines; erected by their mother.)

(See *Ante*, IV., 241.)

Above the east gallery at the north end, on a marble tablet with figures of two angels:—

SACRED TO THE MEMORY OF
HENRY MORETON-DYER ESQ[RE]
WHO DIED ON THE 16TH OF MAY 1841, IN THE 66TH YEAR OF HIS AGE, AND WHOSE MORTAL REMAINS ARE DEPOSITED IN THE FAMILY VAULT UNDER THIS CHURCH.
(6 lines follow.)

Below is a shield of arms.

CREST.—Broken off (part of an animal's head).

ARMS.—Quarterly of six: I. *Or, a chief indented Gules* [DYER]. II. *Gules, three square buckles* [MORETON]. III. *Or, two lions passant Gules* [DUCIE]. IV. Quarterly, *Or and Ermine, the 1st and 4th quarters charged with three pales Gules* [KNIGHTLY]. V. *Argent, on a bend Gules, a crescent between two leopards' faces; on a chief Azure, three catharine wheels Or* [HARDY]. VI. *Or and Ermine, on a chevron Gules, a bezant between two leopards' faces; a chief charged with a lion (or ? wolf) passant between two fleur-de-lis* [PRESTWICH].

(Some of the tinctures of above are uncertain, the paint being old.)

MOTTO:—NEC ULLA INTERMISSIO OFFICIT.

He was son of Mark Dyer, M. of C. of Tortola, who d. at Alphington, co. Devon, in 1832, aged 83, by Ann Arabella Moreton his wife, dau. of Major the Hon. Chas. Moreton, younger son of the first Lord Ducie. He was b. 20 Oct. 1775, and bapt. 12 Feb. 1776 at S[t] George's Basseterre, S[t] Kitts, and was Judge of the Vice-Admiralty Court in the Bahamas in 1810. His grandfather John Dyer, chief justice of Montserrat in 1751, d. March 1781. His uncle Henry Dyer, also chief justice of Montserrat, d. 13 Jan. 1788.

Below the east gallery near the 1st window from the south end, on a small white marble monument with grey marble background, surmounted by a martyr's crown:—

SACRED
TO THE MEMORY OF
ANNA MARIA,
THE WIFE OF
GEORGE CARRINGTON ESQ[RE]
OF
MISSENDEN ABBEY
IN THE
COUNTY OF BUCKS.
OBIIT 19TH AUGUST,
1829.

1829, Bucks, Aug. 19. Anna Maria, wife of G. Carrington, esq., of Missenden Abbey. ("G.M.," 188.)

There is a window at Great Missenden to Geo. C., who d. 8 July 1862.

The late M[r] Geo. C., b. 1856, succeeded his father in 1862, was at Eton and Trinity Coll., Camb., and d. 6 June 1916. Carringtons, the family plantation in Barbados, is well known for its fine works, of which a view is in Sinckler's "Barbados Handbook." (See *ante*, III., 55.)

(*To be continued.*)

The humble Addresse and Petition

Most Gracious Soveraigne

Petition from Antigua in 1708-9

Documents in Public Library, St. John's Town, Antigua.

The above document hangs in the Public Library in St. John's Town, the photograph having been supplied by Mr. Josè Anjo.

Of its history the Editor knows nothing, but it is evidently a duplicate of the original, dated 8 Jan. 1708-9, which is in the P.R.O. in London.

The 17 names in the two columns to the right are those of Members of the Assembly who were returned on 15 April 1708. and whose Speaker was Nathaniel Crump. The 26 names in the two columns to the left are those of merchants and planters.

The following document, being the Queen's response to the above Address, also hangs in the Library. The Governor acted in a dilatory manner and did not send home his defence until about June 1710. His disputes with the Assembly culminated in his appearance in the Court House with a party of grenadiers. On 7 Dec. over 300 armed men requested him to carry out the royal command and quit the island. On his refusal his house was carried by assault, the total casualties on both sides being 75, including the Governor who was mortally wounded.

The humble Addresse and Petition of the Vnder Subscribeing Members of the Afsembly Gentlemen Freeholders Merchants and other Inhabitants of your Majestys Island of Antigua. [1708-9.]*

Wee your Maties most Loyall Dutyfull and Obedient Subjects the Vnder Subscribeing Petitioners, most humbly Beg Leave to Afsure your Majestie, That none of your Subjects can be more truly & Clearly Sensible what an Inestimable Blefsing your Majties most Auspitious Reign has bin and still is to all your Majesties Dominions In all the Parts of your most Just and Gracious Administration, our Joy and Satiffaction has bin alwayes Such as wee want words to Exprefse, Upon Every fresh Information of the Repeated great and Signall Victorys obtained by your Ma'ties Great Generalls and gallant Troops against the Com'on Enemy and of all the other great and glorious actions of your Reigne and more Especially the Accomplishment of that great and happy Union between your Kingdoms of England and Scotland [one line destroyed by the fold of paper] . . . . of your great Predecefsors But was Reserved for a further Ornament, and to adde fresh Lustre still to the Reigne of soe Gracious a Queene, who Esteems the Provideing for the Present and future happinefse of her People, her greatest Glory Wee very Vnwillingly take up your Maties Precious time, Wee (*sic*) the great affaires under your Consideration makes it highly Valuable, Wee are very well afsured that it must be very Vnpleasant and Difagreeable to your Matie who (through all your Adminiftration) have appeared an Indulgent mother of all your People, to heare that any Part of your Dominions has bin Opprefsed Insulted and Tyranized over, Yea such has bin the Case of your Maties good Subjects the Inhabitants of the Island of Antigua, and other of your Subjects Tradeing to and from the same Vnder the admini [a line destroyed by the fold of paper—"General Daniel Parke Esqr" can be just deciphered] . . . . It will be found that It has fared little better wth the Rest of the Islands under his Comand, Wee doe must humbly thinke it our Vnquestionable Duty to apply to your Matie for Reliefe against the said Collo Parke, our P'sent chiefe Govern': who since his first Arrivall in this Govermt: has bin Ever wanting in makeing Provifion for the Defence and Security of this Island against the Com'on Enemy, and whose Conduct in times of the most Imminent Danger, Look'd more like Designing to Surrender up than defend the same, and who in all his Adminiftra-

* The Editor's additions are within square brackets.

tion has Exercis'd the highest acts of Injustice . . . . and Violence and Dispensed with and Trampled on our Laws. Wee have drawne up and Signed Articles against him wch wee have Transmitted* [a line destroyed by the fold of paper] . . . . And wee hope at present to give such satisfaction . . . . to the truth of the Articles, as can be Reasonably Exp[ected] from us, whilst this Yoke of Oppression is still upon our necks, by which wee are Debarr'd of Severall Witnesses . . . . other Evidences (which wee shall be Masters of assoone as he shall be moved from the Governmt: as will Sufficiently Justify and Maintaine Every one of our Articles.

Most Gracious Soueraigne

Wee [half a line destroyed by fold] . . . . for such Reliefe as yor: Matie shall thinke fitt In your great Wisdom Justice and Clemency to afford us in these our Dismall Melancholy Curcumstancies,

And Wee shall Ever Pray to God Almighty to grant your Matie a Long & happy Reigne over your happy and Vnited Subjects.

The Gent' of the Assembly.

Row Williams.
Bar Tankerd.
Giles Watkins.
John Paynter.
Jn° Otto Baijer.
Bastiaen Otto Baijer.
H. Guichenot.
Richd Cochran.
Hen: Symes.
Gervas Turton,
Sam: ffrye.
Wm Lavington.
Thomas Trant.
Antho: Brown.

Sa: Watkins.
Th Oesterman.
Hopefor Bendall.
John [? Roe].
Jacob Morgan.
Allen Gilbert.
W. Glanvile.
Joshua Jones.
Jos Abrams.
Andrew Murray.
Robt Duning.
Will . . . .

Edwd Chester.
Charles Kallahane.
John Barnes.
Ja: Reade.
Thomas Wi[? Williams].
Isaac Horsford.
Charles Lloyd.

Nathl Crump.
W: Thomas.
Dan: Mackinen.
Fran Carlile.
John Lightfoot.
Bap: Looby.
[? John] Duer.
Samll: Phillips.
Edw [? Perrie].
Jn° ffrye.

(Signed) Anne R.

Trusty and Welbeloved We greet you well Whereas several Members of the Assembly Gentlemen, Freeholders, Merchants and other Inhabitants of that Our Island of Antigua in America have by their humble Petition and Address and Articles by them exhibited made Complaint against you of great Oppressions and Mal-Administration the same being humbly presented unto Us in Our Privy Council, We have thought fit with the Advice of Our said Council to Order Copys thereof to be transmitted to you and . . . .† and . . . . as We do by these Presents require & command you, as you will answer the contrary at your peril, forthwith upon Receipt hereof to leave those Islands and return into Our Presence prepared to make your Defence [end of first sheet] before Us in Council upon the said several Complaints and all such other Matters as shall be further charged against you provided the respective Complaints: do deliver unto you before your coming away Copys of such other Complaints for your Information the better to enable you to make your Defence and for the better discovery of the Truth of the respective Allegations in the several Complaints beforementioned and in your Defence thereupon it is Our further Will and Pleasure that the Complainants and all other Persons concerned have full and . . ee liberty to make or procure to be made Affidavits or Informations and Depositions upon Oath of what they know of these matters before any Judge or other Magistrate who is hereby authorised and directed upon the Request of the said Complainants or any one or more of them to summon before him such person or persons as the said Complainant or Complainants shall name without . . . .† expecting an . . . .

* The Impeachment, consisting of 25 articles, is in the P.R.O.
† A line destroyed by crease.

or Signification from you therein and that publick notice shall be given by a Writing affixed on the several Courthoufes of thofe Our Islands of the time and place of taking such Affidavits, Informations or Depositions [end of second sheet] three days before the doing thereof, to the end that yourself and the said Complainants or some perfon or perfons to be respectively appointed in that behalf by both partys may be prefent to crofs examine the perfon or perfons making the same We do alfo exprefsly charge and command you not (*sic*) give any hindrance or molestation whatfoever directly nor indirectly to any such Judge or Magistrate in his or their proceedings in this Affair, nor any ways hinder or molest the said Complainants or other Perfons concerned or that shall be summoned thereunto or any of them from making Affidavits or Informations and Depositions upon Oath as aforesaid before such Judge or Magistrate thereunto legally qualifyed, as the Complainants and other perfons concerned shall think fit for the maintaining their said Complaints nor to employ either the Civil or Military power to profecute at Law or otherwife to vex and opprefs in any manner whatfoever or to afsault the said Complainants or any other Perfon or Perfons by reafon or upon Account of the said Complaint or with intent to fupprefs the same or prevent the difcovery of the Truth thereof which it is Our Intention shall be examined and [end of the third sheet] enquired into with all pofsible Justice Fairness and Impartiality. As soon as thefe Examinations are finisht which it is Our Pleafure to have done with all pofsible dispatch, you are then without any further delay immediately to deliver to the said Complainants authentick Copys of all such Affidavits and other Proofs as shall have been taken on your behalf and to receive from them interchangably authentick Copys of such Affidavits and other Proofs as shall have been taken on their side relating to this matter to all which Depositions and other Papers and Instruments you are to caufe our Seal of thofe Our Islands to be affixt and the same to be forthwith transmitted unto one of Our Principal Secretarys of State that he may lay the same before Us. And lastly We do hereby strictly charge require and command you that so soon as you shall have performed and executed the several matters and things hereinbefore recited which We expect you to do with all pofsible Care Diligence and Exactnefs you embark in the first Man of War that shall be bound home and repair to Our Prefence to give Us in Council an Account of your [end of fourth sheet] Proceedings and hereof fail not for such is Our exprefs Will and Pleafure and so We bid you farewel. Given at Our Court at S[t] James's the Eleventh day of February $170\frac{9}{10}$ in the Eighth Year of Our Reign. By Her Majesty's Command,

(Signed) SUNDERLAND.

[On the back.] To Our Trusty and Welbeloved Daniel Parke Esq[r] . . r Captain General and Governor in Chief of Our Leward Charibbee Iflands in America and in his absence to the Comander in Chief or to the President of the . . ncil of Our Island of Nevis for the time . . . ing.

Bayly and Edwards of Jamaica.

22[d] March 1763 Pestell & ano[r] by Att[y] to the Hon'ble Zachary Bayly Esq[r]. Conveyance of the Rev'on of sev[l] Penns Lands Mefs'ges Tenem[ts] Slaves & real Est'e in Jamaica under the Will of Alger Pestell deceased.

1st March 1768 Daniel Wright & ano[r] by Att[y] to Zachary Bayly Esq[r]. Deed of Confirmation.

1st Novr 1770 Mary Bayly to Wm Reynolds. Duplicate Afsignmt of the £1000 charged by the Will of Zachary Bayly Esqr deceased on Nonsuch & Unity.
16th May 1774 Bryan Edwards Esqr to Nathaniel Bayly Esqr. Afsignmt of Annuity of £300 p' Ann'.
1st & 2d Novr 1776 Bryan Edwards Esqr to Mr Carleton. Ingrofsmt of Lease & Release not Executed.
3 & 4 Novr 1776 Mr Carleton to Bryan Edwards Esqr. Do.
24th & 25 Novr 1776 Bryan Edwards Esqr to Wm White Esqr. Do.
In Chancery. Bayley Esqr agst Edwards Esqr. Close Copy of Bill filed 3d Decr 1770.
Same. Office Copy of Amended Bill fo. 155 filed 31st Decr 1770.
22d Jan'ry 1776 Order for 6 Weeks time to Answer.
Instructions for Answer to Amended Bill.
Drt & Copy of Defts. Answer. Exceptions to Defts. Answer.

A Schedule of all Sums of Money rec'd or pofsefed by Mr Edwards on Acct of the Test'ors real & p'sonal Est'e & also of the proceed of the Serl plantations.

11 June 1776 Order to rejoin & for Comm'on to Examine Witnefses for the Plt.
12 July 1776 Copy Notice of Motion for Comm'on to Examine Witnefses in the Island of Jamaica.
15th July 1776 Order thereon.
Stia* to rejoin & join in Comm'on.
Copy of Interrogatories intended to be Exhibited to the Witnefses.
Dral of Bond of Arbitration.
22d Decr 1777 Bayly Esqr to Edwards Esqr. Bond of Arbitration.
Instructions for Council to move to make the Agreemt a Rule of Court—on behalf of Mr Edwards.
Thomas v. Sorocold & ors.
Apl 1775 Dral of Bill to revive & answer.
Fair Copy thereof.
Drt of Deft. Bryan Edwards's Ansr.
In Chancery. Jamaica Is.† Bayley v. Edwards & ors.
2 Copy's of Brief of Bill filed 17th April 1773 & Demurrer filed 16th Decr 1773.
The like. Brief of Affts to Support Petition for Appointmt of Receiver of the produce of the Plantations.
Copy of the Sevl Affts of Thos Holmes, Wm Williams Clerk, & Wm Jackson.
In the King's Bench. Bayley Esqr v. Edwards Esqr. Brief in this Cause Zachary Bayly Esqr Acct Current with Morse & Baily.
In Chancery. Edwards Esqr v. Bayley Esqr. Drt of Exceptions to Defts. Ansr.
Office Copy of Afft of the Deft.
Brief of Bill and Answer.
26th Apl 1777. A Recl for £3 9s from Mr Morgan to Mr Blake.
In Chancery. Bayly Esqr v. Mary Bayly & Elizth Edward. Stia* & Label.
Sundry L'res.

Endorsed: Easter Term 1783. Bryan Edwards Esq. Dral. Schedule of Deeds and papers delivered by John Blake Esqr to Morgan Thomas Esqr.

---

* Stia = Sententia. † Is = Insula.

Cunyngham and Roberdeau of St. Kitts.

(*Ante*, I., 101; III., 46.)

Robert Cunyngham of Cayon wrote the history of his family in 1740, in a notebook of 40 pages, still preserved by one of the Roberdeaus in U.S.A.

On an old silver tea caddy is a Jacobean shield with these arms:—

Quarterly: 1 and 4, *Argent, a shake fork Sable* (CUNYNGHAM); 2 and 3, *Or, a fess checky Azure and Argent* (STEWART).

On an inescutcheon Vert, a chevron Or, between 3 garbs Argent (CLOSE, DARBY, or GREENACRE. See Papworth, 430). *Around the whole a bordure Gules.*

CREST.—*An unicorn's head couped Argent, horned and maned Or.*

MOTTO.—VIRTUTE ET LABORE.

The arms of Rob. C. of St. Kitts are entered in Nisbet's "Heraldry."

Illustrations of the above shield and of a bookplate of "Roberdeau" (see W.I. Bookplates, No. 698), are given in the following work: "The Genealogy of the Roberdeau Family. By Roberdeau Buchanan. Printed for private circulation. Washington. Jos. L. Pearson, Printer. 1876. 8°, pp. 196."

A pedigree of another branch of the Roberdeaus has appeared in "Misc. Gen. et Her.," 5 S., I., 178.

1728. Recital of a patent of 22 Dec., 8 Geo., to Robert Cunyngham, Esq., of the estate of Eliz. Salenave of 398 acres. (St. Kitts' Records, Vol. A., No. 34.)

1749, July 10. Daniel Roberdeau of St Chr., gent., sells his Pelham River pl^n^ of 150 acres. (*Ibid.*, 4139.)

Close Roll, 6017.

This Ind're made 20 Oct. 32 Geo. 2^d^, 1758, Between Daniel Cunyngham, l. of the I. of St Chr., now of Clapton, Esq., and Eliz. his wife, and Rob. C., Esq., their 1st s. and h., of the one part, and Eliz. Fabie of St C., widow, of the other. Whereas D. C. by Ind're of Dec. 1755 for £8000 sold to E. F. all that pl^n^ in the p. of St John Capesterre of 136 a.. bounded N. with the sea and common path, E. with lands of Sam Okes Taylor, Esq., and lands l. of Tho. Buncombe, Esq., dec^d^, S. with lands of Wm Estridge, Esq., dec^d^, and of Wm Johnson, Esq., dec^d^, and Fra. Estridge, with the buildings mills they now confirm the same to her.

1753. Dan. Robertau. 1 plantation in Trinity Palmetto Point. (Baker's Map.)

1795, Feb. Daniel Roberdeau, Virginia. (European Mag., 215.)

ST. MARY CAYON, ST. KITTS.

1722	July 13	Ann Judith, D. of Isaac and Mary Roberdraw, bapt.	
1723	8ber 15	Robina Mary, „ „ „ „ „	
1725	8ber 15	Cuningham, „ „ „ „ „	
1727	Xber 5	Daniel, S. „ „ „ „	
1726	Xber 15	Cuningham, D. „ „ „ bur.	

(Will translated from the French.) Elizabeth de Salenave. By an Act of 13 April 1715 I have made a guift to my Niece Judith Elizabeth wife of Mr Robert Cunningham of my land in the Island of St. Christopher, charged with the payment of certain sums. To the poor French Refugees £42, viz., £12 for 6 poor widows of Bearn. To Judith Eliz. Bonnefont Cunningham my niece £100. To

ARMS.—*Sable, a chevron Or between two annulets in fess and a tower in base, on a chief Argent a cross-crosslet Gules* (ROBERDEAU).

CREST.—*A demi-greyhound erect couped reguardant, around its neck a cloth collar Sable, with a cross Argent on its end.*

MOTTO.—NE CEDE MALIS.

Richard Cunyngham, descended from C. of Craigends, purchased the Barony of Glengarnock; raised a troop of 100 horse in 1648 and 1651; was at the battle of Worcester; died 27 Oct. 1670. = Elizabeth, dau. of James Heriot of Trabroun, jeweller to K. Chas. I.; mar. 3 Oct. 1654; died 1672. Had twelve children.

William Cunyngham, 6th son, born 29 May 1662; bound to a merchant in Glasgow, then settled at St. Kitts.

Robert Cunyngham, 8th son, born 24 March 1669; served a year with a merchant at St. Kitts, then entered as a cadet the Duke of Bolton's Regt. at the Leeward Isles; Lieut. when the regt. was broke 1698-9; rented and then purchased a plantation at Cayon and became a large landowner; wrote an account of his family 1740; dead April 1749. Will dated 27 Oct. 1743, but lost. = 1. Judith Eliz., dau. of Daniel de Bonnefons by Mary de Barat of Morlaix, and sister to Chas. de Barat seigneur de Labadie, Gov. of Lisle; mar. 26 Sept. 1693. 1st wife. = 2. Mary Gaines, mar. late in her husband's life; brought an action in 1749 in the Court of Chancery to establish his will, by which she received an annuity of £200. She had an only child Susannah.

A

Elizabeth Cunyngham, born 14 Aug. 1694.

Richard Cunyngham, born 13 Feb. 1696.

Richard Cunyngham, born 29 July 1697.

Mary Cunyngham, 4th child, born 4 April 1699; mar. *circa* 1723; her father left her £2000; after her husband's death removed to Philadelphia; remar. .... Keighley, s.p. by him, and died 13 March 1771. = Isaac Roberdeau, from Rochelle, settled in 1685 at St. Kitts; dead 1743.

B

Mary Bostwick = Daniel Roberdeau, only son, bapt. at Cayon 5 Dec. 1727; a merchant; Gen. Com. Penna. Militia in the Revolution; M. of Continental Congress; died 5 Jan. 1795. = Jane Milligan, mar. 2 Dec. 1778.

Isaac Roberdeau, Lt.-Col. Top. Eng., U.S.A., and Chief of Bureau; died 1829. = Susan S. Blair.

Three daus.

James M. Roberdeau, mar. 1st M. L. Denny, and 2ndly M. L. Triplett. =

Two daus.

Three daus.

James D. Roberdeau = W. S. McCormick

Four daus.

Susanna Bonnefont, also my Niece, 200 crowns, payable at Bordeaux or Bayonne. Mr. Bernard de Vignan my relac'on £14 a year and £100, and at his death one moiety of the said £14 a year to Eliz. Cunningham my goddau., and the other moiety to Richard Cunningham her brother. I give her also £20 and a negro woman. Some years ago I gave a note for £100 to Mrs. de Stapleton for her

New Year gift, which I confirm. Madam Eliz. Helot de Lense my goddau. £10. Eliz. Anne Rufanne and Eliz. La Coste and Mary Anne Boinot my goddaus. £8 each. John Moses Rival Isaac Bataille my godson £8. Mr. Rival Minister £10. Mr. Lichigaray £6. Mr. Isaac Bataille £30. Henrietta Bataille £10. Ann Lafforcade £15. My Lady Stapleton. Mrs. Charron the Apothecary £8. Peter Passelaigne my servant 50 crowns for service when the English took my Estate at St. Christopher. Mr. Duport £8. All residue to my nephew Richard Cunningham. If I die in London to be buried in the Greek Church and £10. My annuity of £60. Messrs. Peter Rival Minister, B. de Vignan my relation and Isaac Bataille, Ex'ors. 25 June 1715. Witnessed by David de Passebon, J. Peter De Lose.

1st Codicil. 15 Dec. 1715. Mesdames de Pinsun, de Lense, La Coste and Larquier. Furniture to be returned to Lady Stapleton and Mrs. Stapleton. Ann Laforcade, M[rs] Catin Bournet, Demoiselles Mouchard, Dombidan, and Mary Colombier. Mr. Robert Cunningham's bill of £40 on Mr. Addison for two

A

Daniel Cunyngham, born 19 July 1701, 1st son and heir; in 1743 was renting his father's estate of Cayon at £2500 a year; of Clapton in 1758. = Eliz. ...., living 1758.	Charles Cunyngham, born 2 Oct. 1702.	Susanna Cunyngham, born 20 Feb. 1701; mar. Robt. McKennen (youngest son of Dr. Daniel McK. of Antigua). He died at Pensacola in Florida in 1765 intestate.	Heriot Cunyngham, born 11 Feb. 1705; mar. Clement Crooke of St. Kitts. (See Pedigree of C., *ante*, III., 194.) — Jourdine Cunyngham, living 1743; died unmar.

Robert Cunyngham, 1st son and heir, 1758.

B

Ann Judith Roberdeau, bapt. at Cayon 13 July 1722; mar. 19 Jan. 1742 Wm. Clymer. He died 1760.	Robina Mary Roberdeau, bapt. 15 Oct. 1723. — Elizabeth Roberdeau, died unmar. in 1799, aged 75.	Cuningham Roberdeau, (a dau.), bapt. 15 Oct. 1725; bur. 15 Dec. 1726.

horses sold years ago before my leaving the Islands. Mr. Hamilton, merchant in London. Messrs. Rowland and Tryaud,* merchants in London.

2nd Codicil. 28 Dec. 1715. Proved 28 March 1716 by the 3 Ex'ors. (57, Fox.)

A Mr. de Salnave was at Martinique in 1689. He was a confidential emissary of the Count de Blenac to Sir Nath. Johnson. (Col. Cal., p. 85.)

---

* Tryon.

Eliz. Philadelphia Pearce Hall of St James, Bristol, wid. Will dated 12 Nov. 1810. Whereas by an Ind're trip. dated 12 March 1766, between Daniel Cunnyngham of the 1st part, Chas. Pearce Hall (then C. P.) and me his then wife formerly E. P. C., spr., 1st dau. of the said D. C., of the 2^{d} part, and Andrew Thomson and John Townson, since dec^{d}, of the 3^{d} part, being a sett. made on my marriage, whereby D. C. for securing £5000, part of my fortune, demised to A. T. and J. T. a plantation in St Mary Cayon and all other his plantations and lands in Basseterre Town upon Trust to raise £5000, and at our deaths transfer the sum to our children, viz., Charles Pearce, Daniel P., Eliz. Phil^{a} P., then late the wife of Bedingfield Pogson, and Maria P., our 4 inf. ch^{n}, and every other child, and Danl C. covenanted that all that other pl^{n} purchased of Clement Crooke called the Spring, with the negroes and stock, and all other his estate in St Chr. and Scotland should also stand charged, and whereas the trustees raised £2500 in the lifetime of s^{d} D. C., and D. C. d. many years ago and the £2500 was invested in £2816 3 per cents. consol, and And. T. died, and whereas my late Brother Rob. C., Esq., eldest s. of s^{d} Dan. C., by his will dated 16 March 1761 devised the equity of redemption of the s^{d} pl^{s} to trustees and gave his sister Henrietta C. £2000, and by Ind'res of 28 and 29 Aug. 1765 a sett. made by s^{d} D. C. previous to the marriage of his dau. the s^{d} H^{ta}, then the wife of John Knight, Esq., D. C. released to J. K. the s^{d} pl^{n} in St Mary Cayon to secure the £2000 to her, and whereas by Ind're 1 and 2 July 1788 W^{m} McDowell Colhoun (a mortgagee of s^{d} est. for £10,646) did in consideration of £10,646 paid by J. K. conveyed est. to him (subject to the equity of redemption of Anthony C.), and there being then due to J. K. £18,551 with a large arrear of interest J. K. was to file a bill for the foreclosure, it was agreed betw. him and C. P. Hall on 1 June 1788 that £2000 sh^{d} be paid us and the interest accumulate. John K., J^{r}, Harriot K. and Tho. K., children of J. K. and Henrietta. Thomson Bonar, a trustee, and whereas by an Ind. of 4 parts, dated 21 Oct. 1796, made between Anthony C. and Edwd Knight (the parties named in the marr. sett. of J. K. and H^{ta} his widow) of the 1 p^{t}, John K., Esq., 1 s. and h. and sole adm'or of s^{d} J. K. and H. his wife the s^{d} Hen^{ta} K., Harriet K., spr., only dau. of J. K., dec^{d}, and Tho. K., only yr. son of the 2^{d} part, me then the widow of C. P. H., dec^{d}, Bedingfield Pogson, Esq., and Eliz. Phil^{a} his wife, Maria Cath. Antonia, Harriet Lucretia Pearce Hall and Tho. Whately, Surgeon, and Caroline his wife, the 6 only surviving ch^{n} of us, of the 3^{d} part, T. Bonar of the 4th part, reciting the deaths of C. P. Hall on 23 June 1795, of the s^{d} J. K. on 24 Dec. 1795, and that Caroline Whately, yst. dau. of us, had attained 21, as had Tho. K., yst. s. of J. K., dec^{d}, £2000 was assigned to T. Bonar and interest £763 paid, and John Townson died 3 March 1797 (will recited), and I am now entitled to £2846 consol. and £1100 consol. and whereas by an Ind're of 4 parts dated 20 March 1796 betw. John Stewart and Cha. James of the 1st part, myself of the 2^{d}, B. Pogson, Esq., and Eliz. Phil^{a} his wife, formerly E. P. P. Hall, spr., and Maria P. H., spr., Cath. Antonia P. H., spr., Harriet P. H., spr., and Lucretia P. H., spr., of the 3^{d} part, the £2846 was conveyed to trustees upon the trust of 12 Apr. 1766, and after a suit of Chan^{y} £2568 bal. was paid to the Court, and whereas my dau. Cath. A. P. H. hath married Mr John Lane I appoint that the £2568, £1490 and also £2000 shall be divided amongst my 4 daus. I appoint T. Bonar and T. B. the yr., Esquires, Exors.

On 10 Aug. 1816 adm'on with the will of test., living at Clifton, dec^{d}, was granted to Harriot Hall, spr., T. B. the yr., Esq., surviving Ex'or, not appearing. (438, Wynne.)

List of Wills recorded in Barbados down to the year 1800.*

Year.	Names of Testators.
1647	Salter, Richard
„	Sayers, Thomas
1650	Sturdivant, Roger
„	Stephens, Jonathan
„	Simple, William
1651	Starr, Peter
„	Starr, Clement
1652	Sweeteney, William
„	Smyth, Thomas
„	Smart, William
„	Smith, Nathaniel
„	Stanes, Thomas
„	Smyth, Thomas Knight
1653	Scott, Michael
„	Skering, Richard
„	Saunders, James
„	Summers, Thomas
„	Simons, Nicholas
1654	South, William
„	Smither, William
„	Skotch, Thomas
„	Smith, Edward
„	Stevens, Theodore
„	Suddal, Joane
1655	Sunderland, Hannibald
„	Strytholt, Conrad
1656	Skipwith, John
„	Symonds, Thomas
1658	Say, Thomas
„	Stevens, Henry
„	Standfast, George
„	Sprigge, Thomas
„	Smith, Thomas
„	Stone, Andrew
„	Smitt, John
„	Sevillesran, Teage
1659	Sevan, John
„	Sparkes, Robert
„	Sayre, Thomas
„	Saer, Jane
1660	Squibb, Lawrance
„	Smelling, William
„	Sprake, Richard
„	Scorey, George
„	Smite, Michael
1661	Symons, John
„	Skellham, Edward
„	Sims, Elizabeth
1661	Stephens, David
„	Studd, Abraham
„	Struton, Francis
1662	Sisnett, Cornelius
„	Smith, John
„	Stanford, John
1663	Smith, Walter
„	Soley, Elizabeth
„	Smith, John
1664	Sladden, John
1665	Sutton, John
„	Styles, Walter
„	Spicer, Stephen
„	Scooler, Anthony
„	Sutton, John
„	Stebbin, Rowland
1666	Simons, Richard
„	Sandeford, Thomas
„	Sinclere, Robert
1667	Smyth, John
„	Smith, Margaret
„	Saer, Habukuk
„	Seaward, Malachia
„	Skillearne, William
„	Shenton, William
„	Smith, Thomas
„	Scattergood, Christopher
„	Shorte, Henry
„	Sotherton, Nicholas
1668	Simon, James
„	Symons, Ann
„	Shepherd, Robert
„	Sellers, John and Elizabeth
1669	Stone, Thomas
„	Small, Walter
„	Simpson, George
„	Sheldrack, Martha
„	Sherrah, Abraham
1670	Smith, John
„	Scamoure, Thomas
„	Stokes, John
1671	Sainclemenor, John
„	Smith, Francis
„	Strange, Anthony
„	Stones, William
„	Sylvester, Constant
„	Settle, Richard
„	Stout, Nicholas

* Continued from p. 151.

Year.	Names of Testators.
1671	Snisses, Thomas
"	Saffold, Henry
1672	Stokes, Nicholas
"	Stevens, Elizabeth
"	Sturton, Edward
"	Scott, John
1673	Sealton, Joseph
"	Stewart, Thomas
"	Shaw, Margaret
"	Sermon, John
"	Skea, Daniel
"	Simpson, William
1674	Sheaperd, Roger
"	Scott, Margaret
"	Smith, Robert
"	Sharpe, John
"	Symonds, Dorothy
"	Scott, Roger
"	Sadler, Thomas
"	Sincklare, Patrick
"	Stanley, William
"	Skeett, Joseph
"	Symonds, Thomas
1675	Slocomb, Thomas
"	Stone, Margery
"	Sisters, Garrett
"	Shipton, George
"	Spellman, Francis
"	Sigley, John
1676	Smith, John
"	Sharpe, Thomas
"	Symonds, John
"	Sanders, Andrew
"	Shelford, John
"	Sweet, Henry
1677	Smith, Alexander
"	Snipe, Thomas
"	Sealy, William
"	Smith, William
"	Shunck, Valentine
"	Scotton, Miles
"	Settle, Francis
"	Sharp, James
1678	Small, William
"	Sayers, John
"	Stroud, Anthony
"	Selmore, Henry
"	Sparke, John
"	Stringer, John
"	Stewart, Daniel
"	Steward, William
"	Seaton, Francis
"	Smith, James
"	Steveman, George
1679	Seaton, John
"	Squires, John

Year.	Names of Testators.
1679	Stuff, John
"	Sandeford, Thomas
"	Stady, Thomas
"	Strahan, Daniel
"	Sellcom, William
"	Smith, Thomas
"	Sanders, Thomas
"	Spanswick, Joan
"	Smith, Thomas
1680	Shaw, Richard
"	Smith, John
"	Sergeant, John
"	Shelley, Thomas
"	Stanfast, John
"	Simes, William
1681	Smith, Sarah
"	Swayne, Peter
"	Sherman, Richard
"	Schenger, John
"	Smith, Michael
"	Shackmaple, Jeremiah
1682	Skare, William
"	Spiar, Thomas
"	Seale, John
1683	Sharpe, William
"	Sword, Nicholas
"	Stone, Sarah
"	Sharpe, John
"	Smith, Joshua
"	Swenho, Thomas
"	Stretch, John
"	Smith, Samuel
"	Saule, Patrick
"	Stever *or* Wallis, Thomas Cromo
1684	Smythe, Francis
"	Sedwick, Samuel
"	Stenans, Hector
"	Smith, Joseph
"	Spencer, John
"	Simes, Winnifred
"	Stonehouse, Elizabeth
"	Shachness, Daniel
"	Smith, Thomas
"	Scott, James
"	Segwick, Thomas
"	Scott, Benjamin
1685	Scantlebury, Robert
"	Stephens, Jnr., John
"	Sevenhoe, Joseph
"	Smith, Thomas
"	Sutton, John
"	Salmon, James
"	Smith, John
"	Stoakes, Capt. William
"	Smith, Thomas
1686	Swan, John

Year.	Names of Testators.
1686	Sparkes, Susanna
„	Simmons, Philip
„	Stevenson, Charles
„	Sober, Robert
„	Sober, Thomas
„	Strutt, John
„	Stantor, Thomas
„	Smith, Susannah
„	Stewart, Charles
„	Synon, John
„	Shepherd, Robert
„	Stroud, Henry
„	Salaun, Anthony
„	Scantlebury, Jacob
1687	Sanders, Thomas
„	Spencer, John
„	Sharpe, Jane
„	Steward, Daniel
„	Speer, Ann
„	Shunck, Valentine
„	Street, Michael
1688	Spicer, William
„	Seawell, Thomas
„	Senet, William
„	Sherron, George
1689	Spense, James
„	Stoakes, Nicholas
„	Sandiford, John
„	Sampson, John
„	Stonham, Jeremiah
„	Smith, Ann
„	Snoocke, George
„	Sharlott, Peter
1690	Smith, Byron
„	Sturt, Thomas
„	Steart, Gabriel
„	Somerhay, John
„	Spencer, John
„	Smithwick, William
„	Seddon, Nathaniel
1691	Shipley, Jonathan
„	Shattock, William
„	Smith, Thomas
1692	Snerling, Ann
„	Smith, Francis
„	Shahan, John
„	Shockness, William
„	Sesnett, Elizabeth
„	Sisnett, William
„	Stoker, Samuel
„	Stone, Mary
„	Stockdale, Elizabeth
„	Spratt, George
1693	Soulsby, Edward
„	Sturton, George
„	Shurland, John

Year.	Names of Testators.
1693	Scott, Philip
„	Skutt, William
„	Sturton, Ann
„	Swellivant, Tobias
„	Savory, Elizabeth
„	Scott, Robert
„	Spring, Thomas
„	Stoop, Mary
„	Scone, Abraham
„	Sandiford, Ruth
1694	Scrope, Edmond
„	Salmon, Snr., Joseph
„	Snookes, Ellinor
„	Spencer, Margaret
„	Southward, John
„	Sacr, Thomas
„	Stanton, Daniel
„	Stoakes, Edward
„	Smithy, John
„	Swan, John
„	Stillingfleet, Robert
„	Stephenson, Edward
„	Stoaks, John
„	Simon, Nicholas
„	Sutton, Richard
1695	Sherman, Thomas
„	Smith, Richard
„	Stewart, John
„	Sampson, John
„	Smith, Margaret
„	Shorey, John
1696	Stubbs, Katherine
„	Sturdimant, Roger
„	Snipe, John
„	Sober, John
1697	Smith, Zachariah
1698	Spring, John
„	Salter, Richard
„	Salwey, Posthumus
1700	Strelfield, John
„	Shatterden, Drax
„	Somers, Cornwall
„	Shipton, Elizabeth
„	Sullavan, Dermon
„	Sears, John
„	Stretton, John
„	Sargeant, John
„	Smith, Francis
„	Shurland, Charles
1701	Southron, Isaac
„	Spry, Francis
„	Springham, John
„	Snow, John
„	Sadler, Thomas
„	Shorey, Anthony
„	Smith, Ephraim

Year.	Names of Testators.
1701	Savage, Francis
„	Smith, Samuel
„	Seaward, Mallichy
1702	Sutton, Thomas
„	Smith, William
„	Slogrove, Richard
„	Steevens, John
„	Scott, Sarah
„	Scott, Edward
„	Stockdall, George
„	Southwood, Epaphraditus
„	Swimsted, John
1703	Stachely, Andrew
„	Swinhoe, George
„	Smith, Elizabeth
„	Sutton, John
„	Sampson, John
„	Sommers, Elizabeth
„	Sober, Thomas
„	Sherron, Edward
„	Smith, Richard
„	Sherard, Daniel
„	Smith, Robert
„	Slaughter, Joseph
„	Seaward, John
„	Sharpe, Richard
1704	Sherman, Elizabeth
„	Scantlebury, Jacob
„	Stratton, John
1705	Stady, Thomas
„	Sparke, John
„	Smith, Joseph
„	Shipton, William
„	Stede, Edwyn
1706	Snipes, Robert
„	Steward, John
„	Sturt, Lawrance
1709	Shene, Joseph
„	Smith, Judith
1710	Somers, John
„	Sadleir, Susanna
„	Saile, John
„	Sterrup, Joseph
„	Singleton, Edward
„	Strut, Robert
„	Stears, George
„	Strode, John
„	Sholl, Hannah
„	Stears, George
1711	Smith, Francis
„	Smith, John
1712	Skeete, Francis
„	Shipman, Alexander
„	Sutton, Susannah
„	Sharesmore, Elizabeth
1713	Saudiford, Thomas

Year.	Names of Testators.
1713	St. John, Elizabeth
„	Sweeney, William
„	Skreen, Parshena
1714	Staples, Mary
„	Strode, Mary
„	Simpson, Christopher
„	Spence, George
„	Stewart, Robert
„	Stewart, Elizabeth
„	Smith, Sarah
„	Sweaney, Katherine
1715	Sutton, Margaritt
„	Sober, Thomas
„	Shuller, William
„	Smethwicke, Stephen
„	Simson, Margaret
„	Swan, Robert
„	Spooner, John
„	Sealy, William
„	Seaward, Richard
„	Seaward, Mary
„	Sawyer, Elinor
„	Starkey, Roger
„	Slow, Elias
„	Stewart, James
„	Seawell, Davers
1716	Salmon, Joseph
„	Severs, Marmaduke
„	Stuart, Elizabeth
„	Stevens, Edwin
„	Stevens, John
„	Saunders, William
„	Southward, Richard
„	Savory, Mary
„	Sivers, Marmaduke
1717	Siston, William
„	Sayers, Nicholas
„	Spooner, Thomas
„	Stafford, Thomas
„	Skinner, Abraham
„	Scott, Robert
„	Stevens, Ellinor
„	Shephard, James
„	Smith, John
„	Seston, William
„	Spooner, Thomas
1718	Simons, Timothy
„	Smith, Elizabeth
„	Sanders, Ambrose
„	Steward, Thomas
„	Scott, William
„	Saywell, Alexander
„	Simons, John
„	Swan, Mary
„	Seymore, Thomas
1719	Seaward, Benjamin

Year.	Names of Testators.
1719	Shorey, Thomas
,,	Stuart, Thomas
,,	Smith, John
,,	Sparrock, James
,,	Scotr, Richard
1720	Spencer, William
,,	Skeete, Redman
,,	Sisnett, William
,,	Smith, John
,,	Shaw, Thomas
,,	Siston, Letitia
,,	Sandeford, Anne
,,	Sullevant, Dennis
,,	Somers, Thomas
1721	Stephens, Mary
,,	Stroud, Thomas
,,	Small, William
,,	Stoute, Francis
,,	Swan, John
,,	Sulton, John
,,	Swane, Joseph
,,	Sumers, John
,,	Santford, Jacob
,,	Skeete, Edward
,,	Strode, Judith
,,	Skeete, Reynold
,,	Sandeford, Anne
1722	Savage, John Moore
,,	Somers, Jane
,,	St. John, Barnett
,,	Square, Mary
,,	Salter, Margaret
,,	Smith, Adam
,,	Sparrock, John
,,	Sparrock, Mary
,,	Stewart, Thomas
1723	Senhouse, Thomas
,,	Scott, Andrew
,,	Shepherd, Elizabeth
,,	Smith, John
,,	Shovett, James
,,	Skrun, Parthena
,,	Smith, John
,,	Sienzae, John
1724	Sandiford, Thomas
,,	Spencer, William
,,	Smith, John
,,	Shepherd, William
,,	Salamon, Joseph
,,	St. John, Barnett
,,	Scott, Elizabeth
,,	Sampson, John
,,	Sullivant, Elizabeth
1725	Sadler, Ralph
,,	Sandiford, Martha
,,	Sharpe, Hannah

Year.	Names of Testators.
1725	Simmons, Phillip
,,	Spooner, William
,,	Snooke, Thomas
,,	Southward, Susanna
,,	Senior, Jacob
,,	Sandiford, William
1726	Sparrock, Sarah
,,	Smith, Benjamin
,,	Sober, John
,,	Stoute, John
,,	Shorey, John
,,	Scott, John
,,	Smith, Soloman
,,	Sandiford, Richard
,,	Stevens, John
1727	Sullevant, Benjamin
,,	Smethwicke, Francis
,,	Snow, John
,,	Smith, George
,,	Sinkler, Adam
1728	Skeete, Zacharias
,,	Shepherd, John
,,	Sandiford, Elizabeth
,,	Smith, John
,,	Shillingford, Benjamin
,,	Seawell, Elizabeth
,,	Scott, Robert
,,	Sutton, Edmund
,,	Shepherd. John
,,	Strying, George
,,	Sandiford, Elizabeth
,,	Sutton, Edmund
,,	Seawell, Elizabeth
,,	Scott, Robert
,,	Southward, Susannah
1729	Steward, Margaret
,,	Stewart, Charles
,,	Stocker, John
,,	Sinkler, Richard
,,	St. John, Honor
,,	Scott, Walter
,,	Sharpe, Johannis
,,	Smith, William Pool
1730	Smith. William
,,	Smith, John
,,	Scott, Alexander
,,	Shute, Weaver
,,	Smith, Ann
,,	Sisnett, William
,,	Salter, Timothy
,,	Sisnett. William
,,	Smalridge, John
,,	Somers, James
1731	Scales, Francis
,,	Sealy, Mary
,,	Shockness, John

Year.	Names of Testators.
1731	Smithwecke, Rachael
"	Stokes, Thomas
"	Stadey, Richard
"	Spencer, Hackett
1732	Sherren, Rebeccka
"	Smith, Avis
"	Sherrin, Rebecca
"	Stanford, Adam
"	Sayers, John
"	Southorn, Isaac
"	Sisnett, Ann
"	Sadlier, Elizabeth
"	Simson, James
1733	Sharpe, Mary
"	Spencer, Arthur
"	Stokes, Thomas
"	Shepherd, Hester
"	Smith, Elizabeth
"	Scott, John
"	Seymour, John
"	Smith, John
"	Slingsley, Arthur
"	Stroud, Richard
"	Stuard, John
1734	Scott, Phillip
"	Stretch, Jaspar
"	Smethwicke, John
"	Shae, William
"	Street, Thomas
"	Snow, Jane
"	Springham, William
"	Sullevant, Ann
"	Smith, Mary
"	Sutton, Henry
"	Smith, John
"	Speght, Thomas
1735	Sayers, Elizabeth
"	Sanders, George
"	Sanderson, Richard
1736	Sparrock, Thomas
"	Scott, John
"	Shurland, John
"	Sandeford, Thomas
"	Spencer, Thomas
1737	Sivers, John
"	Seawell, Robert
"	Shewell, Edward
"	Smith, Israel
"	Seaward, Samuel
"	Spencer, Dorothea
"	Sherrin, Henry
"	Sayers, Thomas
1738	Sisnett, Edward
"	Stewart, James
"	Sandeford, John
"	Spencer, William
1738	Stroud, John
1739	Scantlebury, Simon
"	Smith, John
"	Scott, Robert
"	Stewart, John
1740	Spooner, Rebecca
"	Sanders, George
"	Skeete, Francis
"	Smiton, Patrick
"	Scott, John
"	St. John, Charles
1741	Salmon, Samuel
"	Sargant, Charles
"	Shepherd, James
"	Stocker, Daddlestone
"	Seuvzae, John
1742	Sober, John
"	Stevens, John
"	Sanger, William
"	Strong, George
"	Silman, Henry
"	Stroud, Matthew
"	Shipley, Mary
1743	Simpson, Elizabeth
"	Settle, Anne
"	Sutton, Richard
"	Sanders, Mary
"	Smith, William
"	Seward, Thomas
"	Strode, Sarah
"	Skeete, Jean
"	Smith, John
"	Smirk, Sampson
"	Sayers, Jane
1744	Smith, Alice
"	Spencer, Anne
"	Skelton, Richard
"	Simmons, Philip
"	Stevens, Elizabeth
"	Sullivant, Daniel
1745	Sarjaint, Henry
"	Spencer, Ann
"	Stevens, Peter
"	Stapleton, Thomas
"	Scott, Elizabeth
1746	Sandeford, William
"	Salmon, Thomas
"	Stevens, George
"	Snow, Mary
"	Snow, John
"	Scale, Thomas
"	Smith, William
"	Santford, Sarah
"	Savery, Mary
1747	Stevenson, John
"	Slingsbury, Harry

Year.	Names of Testators.
1747	Smith, Dorothy
„	Sarjant, Robert
„	Stuart, William
„	Sinkler, Powel
„	Snarling, John
„	Skinner, Ann
1748	Suliven, John
„	Scott, John
„	Scantlebury, Joseph
„	Skeete, Margaret
„	Skeete, Edward
„	Sandeford, William
1749	Sandeford, Richard
„	Smethweek, Henry
„	Smith, John
„	Smith, Benonie
„	Stevens, William
„	Salter, Ann
„	Skeete, Elizabeth
„	Sedgwick, Samuel
1750	Seaward, Mary
„	Sutton, George
„	Smith, Alexander
„	Stuck, Ann
„	Smith, Margaret
„	Stanley, Mary
„	Stanton, Richard
1751	Scantlebury, Giles
„	Sherrin, William
„	Skeete, William Wheeler
„	Sealy, John
„	Smith, Samuel
„	Sandeford, Cornelia
1752	Smith, Henrietta
„	Smith, Barbara
„	Stewart, Mary
„	Sainthill, Margaret
„	Stewart, John
„	Stewart, Thomas
„	Southorn, Elizabeth
„	Skinner, Jacob
1753	Shield, William
„	Stroud, Matthew
„	Spencer, William
„	Stroud, Robert
„	Steel, Alexander
„	Scott, Jane
„	Smith, George
„	Shockness, Elizabeth
„	Sayers, Edward
„	Stanton, Richard
„	Smethweek, John
„	Stanford, Adam
1754	Starkey, Philip
„	St. John, Charles
„	Spencer, John
1754	Scott, John
„	Smith, William
„	Speed, Mary
„	Smith, William
1755	Shurland, Elizabeth
„	Spencer, Samuel
„	Sherrin, Elizabeth
„	Sober, John
„	Skinner, Isaac
„	Simpson, John
„	Sherewood, Elizabeth
1756	Scott, Walter
„	Sullivan, Patrick
„	Stewart, Francis
„	Smith, Benjamin
„	Snarling, Robert
„	Stuart, Bridget
„	Southward, John
„	Stroud, Mary
„	Snelling, Elizabeth
„	Seaward, Malachi
„	Stroud, Henry
1757	Smith, Tennison
„	Smith, Edith
„	Settle, Margaret
„	Sayers, Ann
„	Smith, John
„	Steart, Dymock
„	Smith, Robert
„	Steele, Sarah
„	Settle, William
1758	Sparrock, Eleanor
„	Shorey, Christopher
„	Sims, William
„	Shaw, John
1759	Spencer, Michael
„	Simmons, Rebecca
„	Skeete, Edward
„	Sair, Rose
„	Siddy, Robert
„	Skeete, Francis
„	Seward, William
„	Seward, Ann
„	Stroud, John
„	Scrutton, William
„	Shore, Margaret
1760	Seymore, John
„	Sellman, John
„	Sayer, John
„	Sayer, Elliott
„	Stanton, Daniel
„	Sesnett, James
„	Spencer, Ann
„	Sandeford, Mary
„	Sharpe, Richard
„	Salmon, Richard

Year.	Names of Testators.
1761	Simmons, Philip
,,	Savory, Samuel
,,	Sober, Sarah
,,	Saers, Benjamin
,,	Seymore, John
,,	Saer, Elizabeth
,,	Sturge, William
,,	Scott, James
,,	Shockness, William
,,	Simpson, Andrew
,,	Stroud, Elizabeth
1762	Salmon, Thomas
,,	Slacy, Edmund
,,	Sheilds, William
,,	Stede, Mary
,,	Settle, Ann
,,	Shehee, Roger
,,	Sandeford, John
,,	Stoute, Edward
,,	Spencer, John
,,	Saer, Jane
,,	Stewart, John
,,	Swan, John
1763	Skeen, Edward
,,	Skeete, Francis
,,	Seymore, Ann
,,	Smith, Elizabeth
,,	Sandeford, Sarah
,,	Swan, Samuel
,,	Spencer, Elizabeth
,,	Scott, Jane Wood
1764	Sharp, Ann
,,	Stevenson, Thomas
,,	Smith, John
,,	Stewart, Daniel
,,	Sutton, Richard
,,	Sadler, Michael Corner
1765	Smith, Alexander
,,	Simpson, Mary
,,	Stretch, George
,,	Sharp, Francis
,,	Shaw, Mary
,,	Smith, Sarah
,,	Sealy, William
,,	Smittin, Thomas
,,	Sedgweck, James
,,	Smith, John
,,	Scott, Elizabeth
,,	Searles, Catherine
1766	Skeete, Martin
,,	Seale, Jacob
,,	Smethweck, John
,,	Sharrett, Allen
,,	Sherren, Samuel William
1766	Shersone, Ralph
,,	Salmon, Joseph
1767	Stoute, George
,,	Serjeant, Harrison
,,	Smith, Margaret
,,	Salmon, William
,,	Smith, Elizabeth
,,	Scott, Edward
,,	Sayer, William
,,	Shepherd, William
,,	Swan, Margaret
,,	Salmon, Samuel
,,	Sanahan, John
1768	Shurland, William
,,	Smith, Samuel
,,	Sayers, Dorothy
,,	Scandritt, Christopher
,,	Smith, Margaret
,,	Smith, Henry
,,	Stanton, Anderson
,,	Skeete, Bridget
,,	Sullivan, James
1769	Sanford, Richard
,,	Shepherd, Rebecca
,,	Smith, Thomas
,,	Seale, John
,,	Sadler, Elizabeth
,,	Sober, Thomas
,,	Shurland, William
,,	Smith, Mary
1770	Skeete, Robert
,,	Seale, William
,,	Sims, Katherine
,,	Stoute, Thomas
,,	Smith, Mary
,,	Scott, Agness
,,	Saers, Elizabeth
,,	Stoute, Philip
,,	Strutton, John
,,	Sarjeant, Samuel
,,	Shepley, Revd. John
1771	Sherman, John
,,	Selman, Mercy
,,	Scott, Ann
,,	Standford, Mary
,,	Smith, Sarah
,,	Smith, Mary
,,	Slade, Elizabeth
,,	Spencer, Thomas
1772	Spry, Governor William
,,	Shepherd, Samuel
,,	Spooner, Guy
,,	Siddey, John
,,	Sturge, Jane

(To be continued.)

Walter of Barbados and South Carolina.

John Walter, Esq[r], of Woking, co. Surry. Will dated 30 Dec. 1731. I appoint my eldest son Abell W. sole Ex'or, and his Mother my wife G. to my young ch[n], and to my s[d] son Abell I devise all my manors and lands in G[t] Britain and I. of B'oes, and also my pers. estate in T., to sell to pay £400 a year to my wife for her life, but I give her and her heirs for ever my mansion house at Hoebridge and all else purchased by me of Jas. Feild, Esq., dec[d], and of R[d] Bird and Cath. his wife and all plate and furniture, coach and pair of best horses, and 100 gns. To my s. Henry W. the moiety of my lands purchased in Grenvill Co. in S. Carolina from Capt. Douglas with 20 negroes now on the same, also 1000 acres which I hold by grant from the Crown, being part of the Baroney lying at Days Creek in the said co. To my s. W[m] W. the other moiety of said lands, 20 negroes, 1000 a. part of s[d] baroney, and £1250. To my sons Jas. W., Alleyne W., and Meynell W. each 2000 a. in s[d] co., part of the Barony granted me by the Crown, and to each £2000. To my 2 daus. Lucy and Mary £2000 each at 18. My Ex'or to manage 1000 acres part of my said Baroney, with 20 negroes, for my s. John W. for his life. To my s. Rich[d] W., who has already rec[d] a fine fortune from me, 1000 a., part of said Baroney, and £500. To my grandson John W., the s. of Abell W., Esq[r], all my lands in Goose Creek, South Car., called Red Bank, and all the remainder of my Baroney, being 2000 acres. To my dau. Eliz. Dottin £500. My dau. Lucy W. £500 more at 21. If my s. Henry W. do not settle in S. C. I revoke the gift of land and give £1500 Barb. c. in lieu thereof, to be p[d] by M[r] W[m] Walker, and the moiety of Douglas' lands I give to my s. W[m] in lieu of the 1000 a. and the 2000 a. taken from my s. Henry and W[m]. I give to my yr. sons Jas., Alleyne and Meynell equally. Whereas I may have 100 negroes in Car. I w[d] have them valued and put on the land of Jas., Alleyne and Meynell, and the value deducted from their legacies. To my grandson John W. £2000 to stock his lands. Witnessed by Tho. Bunde Alleyne, Benj. Maynard.

Codicil, dated 18 March 1735. To my s. Henry W., if he shall settle in S. C., £1250. Sons Jas., Alleyne and Meynell £40 a year till 18. All residue to my s. Abel W. Proved 5 June 1736 by Abel W., Esq[r], the s. and sole Ex'or. (142, Derby.)

Edward Baron of Abergavenny. On 27 Oct. 1724 commission to Gideon Harvey, Esq., the Guardian of Lady Cath., dowager Baroness of Abergavenny, a minor, the widow and relict.

Abel Walter of Baddesley, co. S'ton, Esq. Will dated 13 Aug. 1767. Weak in body. Whereas I have by deed poll dated 12 of this present month of Aug. executed a power for raising portions for my younger sons and daus. I confirm it, and my wife Jane being entitled to a joynture of £800 a year, I give all my real and personal estate to my s. John W. of Farley Hill, co. Berks, Esq., in T. to sell and to pay to my wife £500, and as to certain plate and furniture for my wife, and to sell the remainder and divide proceeds into 6 parts for my dau. Ann 2-6th, my dau. Charlotte 1-6th, my s. Neville 1-6th, my s. George 1-6th. My s. John sole Ex'or. (Signed with a cross.) Proved 24 Oct. 1767 by John W., Esq., the son. (397, Legard.)

Jane Walter of Badsley in the p. of Bolder in Hampshire. Will dated 20 Sept. 1769. My dear children John W. and Anne W. to be trustees, and all real and personal estate. £20 for funeral. To my s. John all my family pictures.

A dau of Col. Lewis Morris of B'os is stated to have m. John Walter of Piercefield co. Mon.

ARMS.—*Or, guttée-de-sang, two swords in saltire Gules, over all a lion rampant Sable.*

Richard Walter of Barbados, merchant and planter 1678; Donor of the font in 1684 in St. James's; M. of C. 1698; bur. at St. James' 17 Aug. 1700. ═ [wife unnamed]

- John Walter of Barbados, then of Woking, co. Surrey, M.P. Surrey 1719 and 1722; bur. at Woking 5 May 1736. Will dated 30 Dec. 1734; proved 5 June 1736 (142, Derby). Owned a barony of 12,000 acres in S. Carolina. ═ Lucy, dau. of the Hon. Abell Alleyne of Barbados; died 1738. A.
  - Abel Walter, 1st son and heir, of Badsley in Boldre, co. Southampton; sold his manors in Surrey; bur. in Bath Abbey 15 Oct. 1767. Will dated 13 Aug., and proved 24 Oct. 1767 (397, Legard). ═ Hon. Jane Nevill, dau. and eventual heir of Geo., 11th Baron Abergavenny, who died 1720-1. She died 19 Mar. 1786. Will dated 20 Sep. 1769; proved 2 May 1786 (314, Norfolk). W.I. Bookplates, No. 744.
    - John Walter, 1st son and heir, of Farley Hill, co. Berks, 1767, later of S. Badsley in Boldre; owner of Mount Wilson and Apeshill, Barbados. Will dated 19 July 1806; proved 4 May 1811 (263, Crickitt). ═ Newton Walker, mar. at St. George's, Hanover Square, 17 Nov. 1757.
    - Rev. Neville Walter, born 1737; of Christ Church, Oxford; matric. 24 May 1753, aged 16; B.C.L. 1784; R. of Bergh Apton, co. Norfolk; died Dec. 1802.
    - George Walter.
    - Ann Walter.
    - Charlotte Walter, mar. 5 May 1768 at St. George's, Hanover Square, Ascanius Wm. Senior of Bray, co. Berks, where he died 24 Oct. 1789. M.I. Will (559, Macham). She was sole heir of her brother John. Her will (354, Crickitt). (*Ante*, IV., 281.)
  - Henry Walter, sold his lands at Woking in 1761.
  - William Walter of Wampee plantation of 1000 a. in Ashley Barony, S. Carolina. ═ [wife unnamed]
    - John Alleyne Walter, Lieut. in Col. Moultrie's regt.; succeeded to Wampee plantation. ═ Jane, dau. of Dr. David Oliphant of S. Carolina; mar. at Charles Town *circa* Feb. 1774.
    - Elizabeth Walter, mar. in England Wm. Haggatt of Haggatt Hall of 1300 a. in Ashley Barony, S. Carolina. He was born 1743, and died 1773. (*Ante*, IV., 168.)
    - Capt. John Abel Walter, cousin of John, 1806.
  - James Walter, Capt., under 18 in 1734. ═ Eliz. Hillman of Salisbury, co. Wilts, mar. at Woking 28 Oct. 1749 by lic.

The money I owe them. When the legacy of £500 left me by Mr Shirk is rec^d, I give my children Neville W. and Charlotte Senior £50 each. All residue to my dau. Ann W. Witnessed 19 June 1770. Proved 2 May 1786 by John W. the son and Ann W., spr., the dau. (314, Norfolk.)

John Walter of South Badsley in the p. of Boldre, co. S'ton, Esq. Will dated 19 July 1806. To M[rs] Helen Anstey wife of John Anstey, Esq., and dau. of the late Ascanius Wm. Senior, Esq., my gold watch. My cousin Capt. John Abel Walter £50. To Tho. Berkley of Lymington, co. S'ton, Esq., and Chas. Harbin of Ringwood, gent., my plantations in the I. of B'oes called *Mount Wilson* and *Apeshill*, with the negroes, and my dwelling house in Albemarle Street, St. George's, Hanover Square, now in the occupation of Wm. Erle on Trust to sell. I give them also my freehold and leasehold messuages in S. Badsley and Sharpurcks to sell to pay all interest to M[rs] Charlotte Senior of Bath, widow of Ascanius Wm. Senior, Esq., for her life, and at her death to pay the interest to Jane Long wife of the Rev. Rob. Churchman Long of Denston Hall, co. Norfolk,

A

Sarah, dau. and coheir of Rich. Bird of Woking; widow of Rich. Winch of Bray, co. Berks, whom she mar. 15 Feb. 1742; mar. lic. dated 7 Aug. 1754. 1st wife. =	Rev. Alleyne Walter, born 1724; of Christ Church, Oxford, matric. 24 Oct. 1740, aged 16; B.C.L. 1748; D.C.L. 1752; R. of Crowcombe, co. Som.; died April 1806, aged 82. =	Bridget Butler, mar. at Sunninghill, co. Berks, 24 Oct. 1759. 2nd wife.	John Walter. — Meynell Walter. — Richard Walter, bapt. 1 Sept. 1698 at St. James, Barbados.	Lucy Walter. — Mary Walter.	Elizabeth Walter, mar. Abel Dottin of English, co. Oxford, and of Barbados. His will was dated 19 Nov. 1759; proved 3 Jan. 1769 (9, Lynch). Their only son Abel was born 1737.

and at her death to divide the principal among her children. Trustees to be Ex'ors. Witnessed by Sarah Burrard of Lymington, etc. Proved 4 May 1811 by both Ex'ors. (263, Crickitt.)

1643, July 8. Tho. Walter, gent., sells 20 acres. (B'os Records, vol. i., p. 228.)

1678. The "Constant Warwick" returning to B'os as she came near the Island took an Interloper, commanded by one Capt. Golding, and bound to this I. with Negroes. The Ship belonged to Mr. Richard Walter, a Merchant there, and M[r] John Bowden, a Merchant in L. (Col. Cal., 36.)

1680. S[t] James. Richard Walters. 3 servants, 206 acres, 140 negroes. (Hotten, 506.)

1687-8. Mr. Rich[d] Walter, a considerable planter. (Col. Cal., 43.)

1697, Oct. 28. Mandates were given by the King in 1695 for the appointment of Rich[d] Walter (and others) to the Council of B'os, tho' owing to the miscarriage of the mandates by sea these gentlemen have never been admitted. (*Ibid.*, p. 2.)

1698. Rich[d] Walter, Esq., then a M. of C. (*Ibid.*, p. 60.)

1699, Jan. 25. Capt. John Walter appointed assistant to Judge Hooker. (*Ibid.*, p. 31.)

1720. John Walter, M.P. for Surrey, and M[r] Alleyne his brother in law, men of great interest in B'os, were heard by the Lords Justices in the complaints against Gov. Rob. Lowther. (Oldmixon, ii., 69.)

1736, May 12. John Walters, Woking, M.P. for Surrey. ("G.M.," 292.)

1745, April 14. John Walter, Esq., at Worcester Park, Surrey. (*Ibid.*, 220.)

1758. Hugh Hamersley by John Walter and Newton Walter his wife. (Close Roll.)

1780, March 19. In Hampshire. the hon. Mrs. Walter, dau., and at length sole heiress, of Geo. Nevill, Lord Abergavenny, first baron of England, wife of Abel W., esq. ("G.M.," 270.)

1802. Lately (Dec.). Rev. Neville Walter, rector of Bergh-Apton, and the moiety of Holveston, Norfolk, in the gift of Lord Abergavenny. He was of Christ Church, Oxford; B.C.L., 1784. (*Ibid.*, 1226.)

1806, April. At Crowcombe, co. Somerset, of which he was rector, in his 83rd year, the Rev. Alleyne Walter, LL.D. (*Ibid.*, 388.)

Duncan Grant, Lieut. R.N., wrote 21 Oct. 1913 from Australia that his grandmother was a Miss Mary Eliz. Walter of the Barbadian family.

ST. GEORGE'S, HANOVER SQUARE.

1768 May 5 Ascanius William Senior of Tewin Place, Herts, Esqr, W., and Charlotte Walter of this p., S. Married by Nevill Walter, Clerk, L.A.C. Witnessed by John Walter and Nassau Senior.

1757 Nov. 17 John Walter of this p., Esq., B., and Newton Walker of St Mary le Bowe. Lic.

BATH ABBEY, CO. SOMERSETSHIRE.

1767 Oct. 15 Abel Walter, Esq., buried.

ST. JAMES', HOLE TOWN, BARBADOS.

1679 July 4 Alice ye Wife of Thomas Walter; buried.
1698 Sep. 1 Richard the S. of Cap^tn^ John and Lucy W.; bap.
1700 Aug. 17 The Honb^le^ Richard W., Esqr; buried.

SUNNINGHILL, CO. BERKS.

The Reverend Alleyne Walter, D.L., of Woking in the county of Surrey, Clerk, and Mrs Bridget Butler of this parish were married by Licence, Oct. 24th, by me J. Thistlethwaite. 1759.

MARRIAGE LICENCES OF COMMISSARY COURT OF SURREY.

1740 Oct. 28 James Walter of Wokeing, captain, and Eliz. Hillman of Salisbury, co. Wilts, at Woking. Rev. Alleyne Walter of Chobham, clerk. (Vol. ii., 268.)

1754 Aug. 7 Alleyne Walter of Chobham, abode several years, LL.D., clerk, bach., 29, and Sarah Wynch of Woking, abode several years, wid., 29; at Woking. (*Ibid.*, p. 322.)

EXTRACTS FROM MANNING AND BRAY'S "SURREY."

Chobham.—The Duke of Cleveland sold the manor to John Walter, Esq. In 1748 this gentleman's son Abel Walter obtained an Act of Parliament enabling the Crown to sell him the Freehold of this, with Bisley and Woking (see Vol. I., p. 126), which was done accordingly. Of this family it was purchased, in 1752, by Lord Onslow's Trustees. (iii., 193.)

Bisley.—The Duchess of Cleveland died 9 Oct. 1709. In 1715 her interest was sold to John Walter, Esq. Mr. Walter died 12 May 1736, and was succeeded by his son Abel, who in 1748 obtained an Act of Parliament enabling the Crown to grant him the Freehold, which was done, and in 1752 he sold it to Lord Onslow's Trustees. (*Ibid.*, 189.)

The Manor of Fosters *alias* Windlesham.—In 1717 it became the property of John Walter, Esq. About 1744 it was bought of him by the Trustees of Lord Onslow. (*Ibid.*, 82.)

The Manor of Bagshot.—It came into the hands of John Walter, Esq., probably as purchaser of the Zouch Estate (see Woking). It was sold in 1748 to the Trustees of Lord Onslow. (*Ibid.*, 83.)

Woking.—In 1715 this estate was purchased by John Walter, Esq., of Busbridge in Godalming . . . . in 1719 was elected one of the Knights for this Shire in Parliament, for which also he was a second time returned at the General Election in 1722 . . . . the estate was sold in 1752 by Abel W. (*Ibid.*, i., 126.)

Manor of Brookwood.—Tenement called "The Hermitage." Mrs Cath. Wood inherited from Jas. Zouch. She, after Mr Wood's death in 1708, married Rd Bird of Woking, yeoman, by whom she had two daus. Cath. and Sarah. Cath. married Tho. Lambourn of Woking, yeoman. Sarah married (1) Rd Winch, gent., of Bray Wick, co. Berks; and (2) Rev. Alleyne Walter, LL.D., who purchased the other moiety and sold the whole. (*Ibid.*, i., 129.)

Hough Bridge in Woking.—Purchased in 1730 by John Walter, Esq. In 1735 he devised it to Lucy his wife, who in 1738 devised it to Abel and Henry her sons, who sold in 1761 to Alleyne W., LL.D., their brother. He sold in 1763.

Busbridge, a capital messuage in Eashing, a hamlet in Godelming.—Laurence Eliot sold it about 1710 to John Walter, Esq., of the Island of Barbadoes. (*Ibid.*, i., 618.)

John Walter married Lucy dau. of . . . . Alleyne, Esq., of Barbadoes, and left Abel his s. and heir, who sold this estate in 1737. (*Ibid.*, p. 620.)

WOKING, CO. SURREY.

1742 Feb. 15 Were married Mr Richard Winch of the parish of Braywick in the County of Berks, and Mrs Sarah Bird of this Parish.

1749 — Captain James Walter and Miss Elizabeth Hillman were married October 28th.

BURIAL.

1736 May 5 Was buried John Walter, Esqr, of Hobridge.

[There is no memorial in old Woking Church.—ED.]

ASHLEY BARONY, S. CAROLINA.

Alex. Skene, to whom Sam. Wragg sold 3000 a. in 1721, was also a man of prominence in the Province.

He had originally come from Barbados, and was a M. of C. with Sam Wragg in 1717 .... He early conveyed away a tract of 1000 a. from the southern part of his purchase to Wm. Douglas, who transferred it to John Walter of Woking Park or Tooting, County Surrey, England .... 1300 acres Skene continued to hold. He apparently called his plantation "New Skene," and at his death it passed to his son John Skene. John Skene died in 1768 .... His real and personal property he devised to his friend Wm. Wragg, Esq., who in 1770 sold the 1300 a. to Wm. Haggatt, who renamed it "Haggatt Hall." Wm. Haggatt was an Englishman, who married Eliz. Walter the dau. of Wm. Walter and granddau. of John Walter of Woking Park. She had been educated in England, where she married Haggatt.

After Haggatt's death the property was acquired by Sam. Wainwright, who further subdivided it .... The name "Haggatt Hall" still survives locally, but corrupted to "Hackett's Hill" ....

The 1000 a. acquired by John Walter was called "Wampee" plantation, and was devised to his son William. John Walter owned considerable real estate in S. Carolina, viz., a plantation called "Red Bank" on the Copper River, and a tract of 12,000 a. called Walter's Barony, on Day's Creek or New River in Granville, now Beaufort County. Wm. Walter devised the "Wampee" plantation to his son John Alleyne Walter, who was for a time a lieutenant in Col. Wm. Moultrie's regiment, and married Jane Oliphant the dau. of Dr David Oliphant, a member of the Council of Safety, a prominent figure in the Revolutionary councils. (S. Car. Hist. and Gen. Mag., vol. xi., p. 89—91. An excellent map accompanies the article.)

1774. Jno Allen Walter, Ash: River (married to) Jane Oliphant, S. C. Town. (*Ibid.*, 102.)

Rawlins of St. Kitts and Nevis.*

ST. JOHN'S CAPPISTERRE, ST. KITTS.

1754	Mar. 11	Mary Estridge d. of Joseph & Eliz^th Rawlins, b. 24 Feb.; bapt.
1756	Mar. 29	Henry s. of Joseph & Eliz^th Rawlins, ,,
1767	Dec. 6	Frances d. ,, ,, ,,
1794	Nov. 6	Jenet d. of J. Rawlins, ,,
1806	Mar. 20	Joseph Rawlins, Esq., Bach., & Eliz^th Caines, Spin., by Revd Wm Julius.
1813	Sept. 8	Thos Tyson, Bach., & Eliz^th Thomas Rawlins, widow of late Joseph Rawlins. St Johns.
1842	Jan. 21	Anthony Hart Rawlins & Rosina Louisa Farrell Caines, Spin.
1853	Jan. 28	John Hart Rawlins, aged 22. Stonecastle Estate. Burial.

ST. ANNE'S, SANDY POINT, ST. KITTS.

1799	Nov. 25	Ann Akers d. of Richard & Eliz^th Vanderpool Rawlins, b. 28 Oct. 1799; bapt.
1751	Oct. 29	Joseph Rawlins & Elizabeth Linnington.
1776	—	John Hutchinson Wallwin & Ann Hutchinson Rawlins.
1778	—	Isaac Hardtman & Mary Rawlins.

* Continued from p. 165.

ST. PETER'S, BASSETERRE, ST. KITTS.

1856 June 28 Eliz[th] Martha Rawlins, aged 30. Millikens Estate. Burial.

ST. GEORGE'S, BASSETERRE, ST. KITTS.

1789 Mar. 23 Stedman s. of Stedman & Eliz[th] Rawlins, b. 20 July 1788, bapt.
1798 Jan. 15 Elizabeth d. of Joseph Rawlins, Esq., & wife, aged 7 years, bur.
1846 May 26 Thomas Berkeley Hardtman & Alice Hart Rawlins.

ST. THOMAS, MIDDLE ISLAND, ST. KITTS.

Baptisms.

1821 Jan. 4 Theodore, aged 7, s. of Hon. W[m] Wharton Rawlins & Marg[t] his wife.
1822 Nov. 30 Gertrude Amelia dau. of Hon. W[m] Wharton Rawlins & Marg[t] his wife.
1838 — W[m] Wharton Rawlins, b. at Walk estate 10 Nov. 1838.

[The two following baptisms were also given by Mr. Bromley under this parish, but they are not in the printed volume:—]

1794 — posthumous Elizabeth Stedman dau. of Stedman & Eliz[th] Rawlins, b. 14 July in London.
1795 May 2 John Hart s. of John & Sarah Johnson Rawlins, b. 9 April.

TRINITY, PALMETTO POINT, ST. KITTS.

Baptisms.

1754 April 11 Stedman s. of M[r] Stedman Rawlins & Mary h. w., b. 23 Feb.
1754 Nov. 30 Mary d. of " " b. 21 .
1757 May 15 John s. of " " b. 5 April.
1759 July 1 Ann d. of " " b. 15 Dec. 1758.
1787 June 22 Stedman s. of Stedman & Eliz[th] Rawlins.
1787 June 22 Ann Taylor s. of Stedman & Eliz[th] Rawlins.
1787 June 22 Sarah Worthington d. of Stedman & Eliz[th] Rawlins.
1787 June 22 Mary Johnson d. of Stedman & Eliz[th] Rawlins.
1797 Feb. 7 Sarah Ann d. of John & Sarah Johnson Rawlins, b. 18 Oct. 1796.
1807 Feb. 3 Stedman s. of Hon. Stedman & Gertrude Rawlins, b. 5 Sept. 1806.
1812 April 9 Henry s. of Stedman Rawlins, Sen[r], & wife Ann Taylor.
1813 Feb. 24 John James s. of Stedman Rawlins, Sen[r], & wife Ann Taylor.
1814 Jan. 1 James Tyson s. of Hon. Stedman & Gertrude Rawlins, b. 30 July 1811.
1814 Jan. 1 W[m] Wharton s. of Hon. Stedman & Gertrude Rawlins.
1814 Jan. 1 Tho[s] Charles Corry s. of Hon. Stedman & Gertrude Rawlins, b. 3 Feb. 1813.
1823 Aug. 9 Sarah Swanston d. of John Hart Rawlins & Martha Hart h. w.
1826 Jan. 22 Eliz[th] Martha d. of John Hart Rawlins, b. 26 Dec. 1825.
1826 Nov. 20 Gertrude Amelia d. of W[m] Wharton Rawlins, Esq., & Margaret h. w.

BURIALS.

1784 July 3 Henry inft. son of Henry & Eliz[th] Rawlins.
1788 June 6 Hon. Stedman Rawlins.
1789 Mar. 24 John inft. s. of Stedman & Eliz[th] Rawlins. Mornes Estate.
1791 Jan. 7 Mary inft. d. of " "
1791 Mar. 2 Henry s. of " " Walk Estate.
1811 April 5 Joseph Rawlins, Esq.
1833 Feb. 18 Martha Rawlins, aged 30. Johnsons Estate.
1837 Aug. 12 M[rs] S. J. Rawlins, aged 76. Johnsons Estate.
1840 June 5 John Hart Rawlins, aged 45. Johnsons Estate.
1843 Oct. 25 Anthony Hart Rawlins, aged 44. Johnsons Estate.

MARRIAGES.

1752 Dec. 21 M[r] Stedman Rawlins, Planter, and Mary Johnson dau. of Elizabeth Johnson, widow.
1784 Jan. 15 Stedman Rawlins and Miss Eliz[th] Wharton.
1787 June 21 Capt[n] Anthony Young and Eliz[th] Rawlins, Spin. Lic.
1794 April 5 John Rawlins and Sarah Johnson Hart, Spin. Lic.
1805 Mar. 28 Stedman Rawlins and Gertrude Tyson, Spin. Lic.
1816 Aug. 20 Stedman Rawlins, Esq., and Sarah Ann Rawlins.
1845 Aug. 21 Henry Charles Newman and Sarah Swanston Rawlins.

CAYON DIARY, ST. KITTS.

1788 June 6 Stedman R., aged 63, gout.
1792 May or June M[rs] Joseph R. d. in America.
1793 Dec. 12 Stedman R. d. in England.
1795 Jan. 31 Joseph R., Sen[r], d. in America.
1797 Nov. 18 M[rs] Stedman R. d. in England.
1800 May 25 John R. d. in England.

ST. GEORGE'S, NEVIS.

1812 July 14 At Henry Rawlins, Esq., Richard Drew, Esq., to Miss Sarah Rawlins.

The following baptisms were probably noted in Nevis, but Mr. Bromley omitted the name of the parish:—

1830 Dec. 28 Rich[d] Ed. W[m] s. of Henry and Eliz[th] Rawlins.
1830 Dec. 28 James Davoren " " " "
1830 Dec. 28 Henry John " " " "
1832 — Francis Galpin " " " "
1833 — Elizabeth dau. of " " "
1839 Jan. 7 Anna dau. of Stedman Akers and Eliz[th] Rawlins of Gingerland Est.
— Stedman s. of " " " " "
by Rev[d] Pemberton.

The following are from newspapers, almanacs, etc.:—

1824 Nov. 6 H. R., Esq, d. at Sandy Point. S[t] Kitt's Gazette.
1826 Aug. .. Eliz. widow of Henry R., aged 65.
1827 — John R., on passage to America.
1830 Mar. 27 Rebecca Fitzpatrick *née* R., aged 25.

1830	—	Stedman R., at Halifax, aged 46.
1831	Feb. 15	Ann Taylor R. wife of Col. R., at Walk Estate.
1831	Sept. 18	James R. of Stoney Hill.
1833	Sept. 18	Eliz. Mary R. of Montpelier, Nevis.
1833	Dec. 13	Stedman R., at New Guinea Estate, aged 44.
1834	Jan. 5	Miss Worthington R. of Fothergills.
1834	Apr. 14	Eliza R., at Symonds Estate.
1835	Sept. 3	Mrs Richd R., at Rev. Parry's, Sandy Point, aged 68.
1839	Oct. 16	John James s. of Stedman R., S^r, at Eliza Brown's.
1850	—	Stedman Akers R., at Hendricksens.
—	Aug. 28	" " " d. suddenly at Nevis, aged 48.
1850	May 18	Dr John R., at Burkes, aged 59.
1868	June 13	Worthington R., aged 77.
1877	Nov. 1	Sarah Ann R., at Castlemain Road, Camberwell, London.

CAMBERWELL, CO. SURREY.

1828 May 7 Alice Hart dau. of John Hart Rawlins and Martha; bapt.

SHEPPERTON, CO. MIDDLESEX.

1830 Nov. 1 John Hart Rawlins s. of John H. and Martha A. R., b. 2 July; bapt.

ST. JAMES', BLACKFRIARS, LONDON.

1813 Sept. 30 Worthington Rawlins and Elizabeth Stedman Rawlins.

Monumental Inscriptions in England relating to West Indians.*

MARYLEBONE OLD PARISH CHURCH.

N.W. wall above the gallery:—

Sacred to the Memory
of STEPHEN HAVEN Efquire;
who departed this Life, the 17th of March 1805;
aged 44.
He was a Native of IRELAND
But paffed the greater Part of his Life in AMERICA
and the BAHAMAS; in which last Place
he filled many Offices of Truft and Honour.
(6 lines omitted.)
He has left a Widow and three Children.

See his will, *ante*, IV., 241.

* Continued from p. 168.

1819, Dec. 19. At Brighton, aged 87, John Gordon Haven, esq., formerly Major of the 50th Regiment. ("G.M," 220.)

The above M.I. appeared in "Mis. Gen. et Her.," 3 Series, I., 202, but the Editor has checked it with the original.

BATTERSEA, CO. SURREY.

North gallery. On a stone tablet surmounted by an urn:—

SACRED TO THE MEMORY
OF
WILLIAM VASSALL Esq^RE WHO DIED ON THE 8TH OF MAY 1800
IN THE 85TH YEAR OF HIS AGE AND WAS BURIED IN A VAULT IN THIS CHURCH
AND OF
MARGARET WIFE OF THE ABOVE SAID WILLIAM VASSALL
WHO DIED ON THE 6TH OF FEBRUARY 1794
ALSO OF
M^RS ANN HUBBARD SISTER OF THE SAID MARGARET VASSALL
WHO DIED ON THE 13TH OF DECEMBER 1785
AND OF
LEONARD SAMUEL THE INFANT GRANDSON OF THE ABOVE NAMED
WILLIAM AND MARGARET VASSALL
AND OF
MARGARET VASSALL DAUGHTER OF THE SAID WILLIAM AND [MARGARET VASSAL
WHO DIED ON THE 17TH OF DECEMBER 1819
THIS MONUMENT TO THE MEMORY OF HER BELOVED AND AFFECTIONATE PARENTS
IS ERECTED AGREEABLY TO THE DIRECTIONS CONTAINED IN THE WILL OF THE SAID
MARGARET VASSALL.

Below on a plain shield: *Azure, in chief a sun in its glory, in base a cup* [VASSALL]; impaling, *Gules, on a bend Or three lions rampant* [HUBBARD].

1800, May 18. After a short illness, in his 85th year, Wm. Vassall Esq. of Battersea Rise, Surrey. ("G.M.," 491.)

He was a son of Leonard Vassall of Jamaica and Boston, Mass., by Ruth Gale; b. 23 Nov. 1715; m. 1st, Ann Davis, who d. 26 Jan. 1760, and 2ndly, Margaret Hubbard. He was a M. of C. of Mass. in 1774, and was banished in 1778. In his will, dated 2 May 1794 [630, Adderley], he refers to his Green River plantation in Jamaica. See "The Vassalls of N.E.," by E. D. Harris, and *Ante*, p. 107, for Col. Henry Vassall, his younger brother.

On a coffin-plate in the crypt:—

William
Philip Holder
Esqr
Died 17th Oct^r:
1797
In his 25th Year.

William Thorpe Holder, formerly of Barbados then of Grosvenor Place, was also buried in the crypt in 1787, but I could not find any memorial of him. His

will was dated 4 Oct. 1785 and proved 5 Sept. 1787 [411, Major]. By Philippa Elliot his wife—will dated at Bath 7 Aug. 1813, proved 1813, "To be buried at Battersea near my husband" [501, Heathfield]—he had issue: 1. Wm. Philip Holder above mentioned, will [647, Exeter]; 2. John Hooper Holder, m. twice and left issue; 1. Philippa Harbin Holder, d. young, bur. at Battersea; 2. Margaret Dehany Holder, will dated 16 April 1804, proved 10 Nov. 1809 [824, Loveday], bur. at Battersea.

ST. MARY'S, MELCOMBE REGIS, CO. DORSET.

On the west wall of the nave, north side, on a plain grey marble tablet:—

Underth: lies ye Body of
Chrifr: Brooks Efqr: of Jamaica
Who depard: this Life 4th: Sepr: *1769*
Aged 38 Years ; one of ye Worst: of Men
Friend to ye Diftreft:
truly Affectd: & kind hufband
tender Part: & a Sincr: Friend.

(Transcribed 24 April 1917.)

See his pedigree, *Ante*, II., 50, and his will, III., 171.

On the east wall of the north gallery, on a white marble sarcophagus-shaped tablet on black:—

SACRED
TO THE MEMORY OF
GENERAL GORE BROWNE,
COLONEL OF H.M. 44TH REGT,
WHO DIED AT WEYMOUTH, ON THE 12TH OF JANUARY,
1843, AGED 79.
ALSO OF
JENNETTA, HIS WIFE, WHO DIED AT WEYMOUTH,
ON THE 25TH OF MAY, 1838, AGED 76.
ALSO
OF HIS DAUGHTER, JULIA ANNA, WHO DIED
AT WEYMOUTH, ON THE 10TH OF JANUARY 1831.

1843, Jan. 12. At Weymouth, aged 79, General Gore Browne, Colonel of the 44th regiment. He married Miss Bannister, dau. of the President of the Island of St. Vincent. ("G.M.," 534.)

See pedigree of Browne of Nevis with note of James Browne of Weymouth in 1777. (*Ante*, I., 35.)

1787, Aug. 9. Gore Browne an Ensign of the 25th foot & Janetta his wife (sister and heir-at-law of Robert Bannister late of St Vincent, gent., who d. a bach. & under age) sell a plot in Church Street, St John's, Antigua, for £165 *c.* She was single on 5 April 1785. ("Antigua," I., 33.)

St. George's, Hanover Square.

1834, Jan. 30. Thomas Gore Browne, Esq., W. of St Martin's in the Fields, & Mary Ann Benyon, S. Lic.

On the east wall of the south gallery, the tablet a duplicate of the preceding:—

SACRED
TO THE MEMORY OF
MARY BECKWITH
WIFE OF LIEUTENANT-COLONEL R. F. MELVILLE BROWNE,
AND TWO OF THEIR CHILDREN: LOUISA WHO DIED ON THE
21ST OF NOVEMBER 1835, AGED 13 YEARS,
AND VILLIERS GORE, WHO DIED ON THE 26TH OF MARCH 1831,
AGED 15 MONTHS.

On the south wall of the nave, on a white marble sarcophagus-shaped tablet surmounted by an urn:—

SACRED
to the memory of
WILLIAM HENRY HAMILTON ESQR.
of the County of Monaghan Ireland;
who departed this life at Weymouth,
June the 10th 1830, Aged 69.
His remains are deposited near this Spot
and by his affectionate Wife
this Monument has been Erected.
ALSO TO THE MEMORY OF
ANN HAMILTON WIFE OF THE ABOVE
WILLIAM HENRY HAMILTON ESQR AND DAUGHTER
OF THE LATE NICHOLAS GARNER ESQR.
NASSAU NEW PROVIDENCE WHO DEPARTED THIS
LIFE AT WEYMOUTH THE 14TH MARCH 1837
AGED 66.

Below is the crest of the ducal house of Hamilton surmounted by the motto.

In the pedigree in Burke's "L.G." he is given as eldest s. and h. of Sir James Hamilton of Cornacassa, co. Monaghan, Knt., was a Capt. in the Army, m. Miss Gardner and d. s.p.

CHIPPENHAM, CO. WILTS.

On a floor stone in the south aisle of nave, opposite to the fourth bay from the west, the inscription somewhat indistinct:—

FRANCES HILL VERCHILD
wife of
LEWIS BROTHERSON VERCHILD
(of the Island of
Saint Christopher
in the West Indies)
Departed this life
20 Septr 1810.

(Copied Aug. 1913. See this also in the "Genealogist," New Series, vol. vii., 53.)

She was probably a dau. of Benjamin Markham Brotherson of the same island, and was m. at St. George's, Hanover Square, 5 July 1804. Her husband, a clergyman, was at Eton in 1793, then Rector of St. Ann, Sandy Point, for eight years till his death by fever about 1818. His three orphan children, two boys and one girl, were in 1822 in the care of Miss Markham, his estate in debt and the produce only half its former value.

CORSHAM, CO. WILTS.

On a white marble shield-shaped tablet on the south wall of south transept:—

IN MEMORY OF
WILLIAM SINCLAIR CATHCART MACKIE, ESQ[RE].
BREVET MAJOR
AND CAPTAIN 88TH REGIMENT,
ELDEST SON OF THE LATE
MAJOR GENERAL MACKIE, C.B.
AND OF CATHERINE CEELY HIS WIFE,
HE DIED OF CHOLERA NEAR VARNA,
WHILE SERVING
WITH THE ARMY IN TURKEY
AUGUST 29TH 1854,
AGED 44 YEARS.
ALSO OF
CATHERINE CEELY HIS MOTHER,
WHO DIED MAY 7TH 1867.

In the south transept:*—

In memory of | ELIZA FRANCES, | CATHERINE MARGARET MASSY, | and JAMES FRANCIS, | children of the late | Major General MACKIE, C.B. | and CATHERINE CEELY his wife, | they died of decline | A D. 1840, 1841, 1842, | aged 26, 21 and 18 years. | The remains of | ELIZA | are interred at Stoke Damaral, Devon; | CATHERINE and JAMES | repose in the adjoining churchyard.

On the east wall of the south transept:—

ALSO
IN MEMORY OF
OTTO BAÏJER MACKIE ESQ[RE]
LIEUTENANT ROYAL ARTILLERY
5TH SON OF THE ABOVE
GEORGE AND CATHERINE CEELY MACKIE
HE DIED AT TOBAGO WEST INDIES AUGUST 3RD 1846,
AGED 27 YEARS.
SO GREATLY WAS HE BELOVED AND RESPECTED THAT
A SUBSCRIPTION WAS RAISED
BY THE PRINCIPAL INHABITANTS OF THAT ISLAND
TO ERECT A TABLET TO HIS MEMORY IN THE PARISH CHURCH
OF THAT COLONY.
AND ALSO
TO THE MEMORY OF
GEORGINA JANE, HIS SISTER
WHO DIED
ON THE 27TH OF AUGUST 1814, AGED 18 YEARS;
HER REMAINS ARE INTERRED IN THE ADJOINING
CHURCHYARD.

See a close-roll relating to the above in Antigua I., 28. In 1815 Geo. Mackie the father, L[t] Col. of the 60th Foot, was residing in Cheltenham. His wife Catherine

* I did not notice this M.I. when visiting the church April 1913; it was probably high up.

Ceely Edwards, whom he married 19 Jan. 1809 at St. John's, Antigua, was a dau. of Zacchary Bayley Edwards of Dove Hall, St. Thomas in the Vale, Jamaica, by Catherine his wife, dau. of Rowland Otto-Baijer of Antigua. Bryan Edwards Mackie their third son was of Dove Hall and d. 21 Feb. 1880. M.I. in St. Thomas in the Vale.

WALTHAMSTOW, CO. ESSEX.*

In the west portion of the churchyard, on a stone altar-tomb within rusty iron railing. On the south face:—

Adjoining this Tomb are interred the Remains of
JAMES INGLIS Esqre late of Kingston in Jamaica
who died the 5th of November 1815
Aged 41 Years.

On the north face:—

REBECCA Second Wife of JOHN INGLIS
of this Parish
and of Mark Lane London Merchant
Died 5th of September 1818 Aged 49 Years
Deeply Lamented
Also the Body of MARY HELEN INGLIS
Daughter of JOHN B. INGLIS Esqr
who died 2nd Feby 1820 aged 5 months.

1818, Sept. 5. At Walthamstow, the wife of John Inglis, esq. of Mark-lane. ("G.M.," 470.)

On a black marble floor slab finely polished and in perfect condition lying within the altar rails:—

Here Lyeth the Body of
Mr ARCHER MARTIN late of
the ISLAND of IAMAICA Merch^t:
Obijt the 14TH of Iune 1707.

See his will, *ante*, 88.

ST. LUKE'S, CHELSEA.*

In the churchyard. On a slab over a brick vault, near the south boundary wall:—

SACRED TO THE MEMORY OF
MR HENRY HEATLY,
A NATIVE OF KINGSTON, *JAMAICA*,
WHO DIED 17TH OCT^R 1824,
IN THE 17TH YEAR OF HIS AGE
HE WAS THE ONLY DARLING AND AFFEC
-TIONATE CHILD OF HIS DISCONSOLATE
MOTHER, WHO IS LEFT TO DEPLORE
HIS IRREPARABLE LOSS.

* Transcribed 15 Aug. 1917.

In the churchyard. On a head-stone near the east boundary wall:—

In Memory of
JOHN GRANT Efq[r].
of Wallibou,
in the Ifland of S[t] Vincent,
who died 3rd March 1820,
Aged 42 Years.

1820, March 3. In Cadogan-terrace, aged 42, John Grant, esq. of Wallebow, in the Island of St. Vincent. ("G.M.," 284.)
See *ante*, III., 93.

HIGHGATE CEMETERY, CO. MIDDLESEX.

Sacred
To the Memory of
CHARLES MILNER RICKETTS, F.R.S.
Member of the Supreme Council of India,
And sometime His Majesty's Consul General in Peru,
Died 7th September, 1867, aged 91 years.
Sacred to the Memory of
MORDAUNT RICKETTS, Esq[re].,
Bengal Civil Service,
Born 5th June, 1786, Obit. 29th July, 1862,
(3 lines.) [Cansick, p. 150.]

George Poyntz Ricketts of Jamaica, b. 1750, Gov. of Barbados 1794, d. 8 April 1800. He had married 13 Dec. 1772 Sophia dau. of Gov. Watts, by whom he had: I. Geo Poyntz Ricketts, Jr., of the Bengal C. S., m. at Calcutta 20 Feb. 1800, Sophia dau. of Capt. Peirce, E.I.C.S., and d. at Benares April 1816. II. ? Chas. Milner Ricketts, b. 1776. III. Mordaunt Ricketts, who m. 1. in Bengal 21 Feb. 1812 Maria Eliz. dau. of C. R. Crommelin, and 2 at Lucknow 1 Nov. 1824 Mrs. Charlotte N. Ravenscroft, dau. of Col. Martin Fitzgerald of the Bengal Cavalry.

Sacred to the Memory of
ELIZA
Born in ye year of our Lord 1777, died 21st Dec. 1859;
daughter of James Mapp Esq[re],
and of Kitty his wife;
Adopted and taught by her aunt, Sarah Rous,
and by her grandmother, Eliz. Rous,
widow of the Hon. Samuel Rous, many years
member of the Legislative Council of Barbadoes,
and twice President of that island.
(2 lines.) [Cansick, p. 100.]

The Hon. Sam. Rous of Clifton Hall plantation was acting Govr. in 1766 and 1772, and d. in 1784. His widow Eliz. d. 19 Nov. 1796 and they were both buried in a vault on Haltons, formerly Haughtons, in St. Philip's parish. In 1654 Tho. Rous, Esq., for £6500 c. sold to Geo. Pasfield a plantation in the above parish of 217 acres. His elder son John Rous m. Margt. Fell (whose mother remar. Geo. Fox the Quaker), and in his will dated 1692 devised his plantation in the above parish to his son Nath[l]. (103, Irby.) There was also a Capt. Anthony

Rous of Barbados in 1656. The first settler appears to have come from Wootton-under-Edge, co. Glouc. Arms: *Or, an eagle displayed Azure.*

In St. Philip's churchyard, Barbados, was a stone inscribed: "James Mapp Esq. died 1757."

James son of Jas. Mapp of Barbados was at Eton 1763—65, and matriculated at Oxford from Christ Church 9 May 1766, aged 16.

(*To be continued.*)

Letter from the Hon. W. Mackinnen of Antigua.

Monmouth, Septr the 3^d 1782.

Sir,

Being obliged to go out of Town sooner than I expected, your obliging Note of august the 31st reached me at this Place; it was not therefore posible for me to have the Honour of waiting on you on Tuesday according to the appointment you were so good as to make.

The principal reason for which I desired to have the Honour of speaking to you, was respecting the suspension of Mr Jeffreason a Member of the Council of Antigua. I find by Mr Nepean, with whom I had some Conversation on the Busines, that the governor had sent his Reasons for so doing. You certainly are the best judge of the Validity of those Reasons. This step was taken without the advice of the Council, the major Part of which declared to Mr Jeffreason, they would not have advised it, had they been consulted. Mr Jeffreason is a gentleman of very good Character, a Man of considerable Estate in Antigua, and has had the best Education *this* Country affords. He at present fills the seat of an asistant Judge in the Court of Common pleas; and upon his suspension from the Council, having expressed his Intention to resign his seat on the Bench, most of the Barristers addresed a joint letter to him, expresing their satisfaction with his Conduct as a judge, and desiring him not to resign his Seat, as they thought it would be a Detriment to the publick.

There was another Matter I wished to have the Honour of mentioning to you. Upon Mr Shirleys going to his Government of the Leeward Islands, he carried with him a Mandamus for one Mr Winstone, who had been a practising Lawyer in Dominica, to be of the Council of Antigua. Mr Winstone has no Property whatever in Antigua. You certainly know, Sir, that the Councils in the old Colonies are composed of gentlemen of the best Fortunes and Families in the Colony; that the Council of Antigua constitutes the Court of Chancery and Court of Error in that Island. Not long before my Departure, Mr Winstone appeared as advocate at the Chancery Bar, tho' a judge of the Court. I confes I was a good deal surprized at the Inconsistency of a gentleman's sitting one Day as Judge and the next appearing as advocate at the Bar of the same Court; I therefore moved that he should make his Election, either to be judge, or Counsel, and not act in both Capacities in the Court of Chancery, which was carried without opposition. The Governor, I have reason to imagine, will endeavour, if he has not already done it, to support Mr Winstone, but I am confident, when you consider the evil Tendency of a Man's being judge and advocate in the same Court, you cannot approve of it; for such a Person might receive a large Fee in a Cause, draw the Pleadings, conduct the Proces to a hearing, then give his Brief to another to argue it, and sit as judge in the Cause, the Inconsistency and evil Tendency of which is too glaring to be dwelt upon. I have not the least variance with the governor or Mr Winstone, on the contrary am upon Terms of Civility with the former, whom I look upon as a well-meaning Man. There are

some other Matters, I should be glad to converse with you upon, which I shall reserve till I have the Honour of a personal Interview upon my return to Town. In the mean time, if you please to favour me with a Line addressed to me at this Place I shall esteem it an Honour done to

Sir
with great Respect
your most obedient humble Servant
WILLIAM MACKINNEN.

(Notes on the preceding letter.)

Governor-Col. Tho. Shirley wrote home on 2 May 1782, that he had suspended Mr. Jeaffreson of the Council for saying: "The King could do what he pleased with his Privy Council, and that he had a corrupt Parliament to give him a sanction for it, or Words to that Effect," and on my calling him to order said: "Why, you yourself think so too, don't you?" Later in the year the Governor was ordered to re-instate Mr. Jeaffreson and not to act so hastily for the future. This Robert Jeaffreson matriculated from St. Mary's Hall, Oxford, in 1766, aged 17. He eventually sold his estate and died in England about 1807.

In a list of the Council of July 1783 W. Mackinnen was noted as absent. Col. Shirley had been Lieut.-Governor of Dominica, before being appointed, about 4 April 1781, to succeed the late Wm. Mathew Burt as Governor of the Leeward Islands. Chas. Winstone on 4 Oct. 1780 took the oaths as Solicitor-General, and the mandamus appointing him a M. of. C. was dated 30 April 1781. He returned to Dominica in 1783, where he continued to reside for many years.

Letter from W. Woodley, Esq., of St. Kitts.

MY LORD,

Ever since I had the Honour of being seen by your Lordship at S[t] James's, I have been prevented paying my personal Respects to you by the Gout which is only now leaving me; and I shall be happy if your Lordship will afford me an early opportunity of waiting upon you on a Business which some of my Friends have already made known to you by their Sollicitation in my Behalf to succeed S[r] Thomas Shirley in the Government of the Leeward Islands. The Governor's public Declaration for two years together of his intending to return to England was the Reason of my making the early Application I have done, as I shall be able to explain to your Lordship when I have the Honour of waiting upon you.

I am, with my great Esteem and Regard
your Lordships very obedient
humble Servant
W[M] WOODLEY.

Stratford Place, Dec[r] 21st 1787.

(Notes to Woodley letter.)

On 6 Jan. 1787 Governor Shirley was granted six months' leave of absence, but did not apparently sail until 18 June 1788. This is confirmed by the letter. On 22 Nov. 1789 he wrote from Barbados that he had arrived the previous day, 28 days out from Falmouth. On 18 May 1791 the King accepted his resignation, and on 21 Sept. it was announced that Wm. Woodley, then at St. Kitts, was to succeed him. Woodley did not long survive, but died at St. Kitts on 2 June 1793.

Administrations (P.C.C.) relating to West Indians.*

Abbreviations.

B. = Barbadoes. J. = Jamaica. W.I. = West Indies. ba. = batchelor. G. = Guardian. S.S. = States Service. P^r C^r = principal creditor.

1656.

folio.

Jan. Rob. Scott. †23, to Eliz. S. ye rel. of R. S., l. of ye p. of St Geo. in ye B., but dying at Burton upon Trent, co. Stafford. 1

April. Wm. Marshall. 5, to Wm M. the f. of W. M., l. of Bristoll, but at Mevis. 70

April. Jas. Fockett. 12, to Eme F., wid., ye rel. of J. F., l. in ye W.I. 70

April. Wm King. 21, to Judith K., wid., ye rel. of W. K., l. of Wapping, but at Antigoa. 71

May. Tho. Bayliff. 6, to Mary B., wid., ye rel. of T. B., l. of Kingston upon Hull, but in ye W. I. 104

May. Sam. Hawkes. 8, to Dorcas H., wid., ye rel. of S. H., l. in the W. I. 104

May. Capt Nath. Rockwell. 19, to Tho. R., the brother of N. R., l. in ye W. I. 105

May. Benj. Williams. 9, to Anne W., wid., ye relict of B. W., late in ye ship ye Phillipp of London at sea going to ye B. 105

May. Tho. Hole al's Howell. 13, to Wm H., l. in ye W. I., ba. 105

May. Tho. Hill. 16, to Alice Hill, cozen jerman by ye father's side of T. H., l. in ye B., ba. 105

May. Richd Bamford, Esq. 13, to Anne B., wid., ye relict of R. B., Esq., l. Major-Gen. in ye W. I. 106

May. Rob. Tirrell. 15, to Eliz. T., wid., ye Mother of R. T., l. in ye shipp ye Guift in ye S.S. at J., ba. 106

June. Chr. Codrington.‡ 15, to Mary C., the relict of C.C., l. of Bathe, co. Som. 121

June. Wm. Paise. 23, to Tho. P., the brother of W. P., l. of Chatham, but at J. 133

June. Rob. Nore. 24, to Tho. N., father of R. N., l. at J. in ye Gloucester frigott, ba. 133

July. Wm Alder. 1. to Tho. A., bro. of W. A., l. in ye S.S. at J., ba. 161

July. Tho. Edwards. 3, to Mary E., rel. of T. E. the elder, l. of Tudnam in Sufl., but at J. 162

July. Tho. Edwards. 10, to Mary E., M. of T. E. ye yr, l. in ye S.S. at J. 162

Aug. John Talbott. 12, to Walter T., only bro. of J. T., l. of Gt Yarmouth, Norf., but at J. 202

Aug. Edwd Talbott. 12, to Walter T., only bro. of Edwd T., l. of Southwould in Suff., but in ye ship ye Gt Charity at J. 202

Sept. Tho. Fisher. 24, to Dorothy F., rel. of T. F., l. in ye Glr frigott S.S. at J., ba. 221

Sept. Tho. Falkiner. 30, to Martha F., rel. of T. F., l. of Plimouth, but at J. 221

* Continued from p. 86.

† The words "Adm'on on the" at the beginning, and "deceased" at the end of each entry for the saving of space I omit.

‡ It has been thought by some that this was the first settler from Barbados, but there is no evidence of identity.

folio.

Sept. Major Rob. Sedgwick. 30, to Johanna S., rel. of Major R. S., l. in pts. Esq. 221

Sept. Rachell Yeamans. 3, to Sus^n Close, y^e sister of R. Y., l. of St Peter's, Paul's Wharf, l. wid., dec^d, for ye use of Geo. Y.* and Edw. Y., ye sons, in pts. 222

Sept. Briant Hagan. 23, to John Ward, ye coz. Jerman by ye mother's side of B. H., l. at J., ba. 224

Sept. John Jones. 23, to Kath. J., rel. J. J., l. of Stepney, but at J. 224

Oct. Rowland Ridge. 31, to Row. Butcher, cozen german to R. R., l. of Plym., ba. 251

Oct. Arthur Dansey, 1, to Anne D., wid., the M. of A. D., l. at J., ba. 251

Oct. Henry Lane. 16, to Anne L., rel. H. L., l. in ye ship ye Success at J. 252

Oct. John Palmer. 16, to Anne P., rel. of J. P., l. in ye ship ye Success at J. 252

Oct. Tho. Salkeild. 17, to John S., Esq., F. of T. S., at J. 253

Oct. Wm Spencer. 28, to Wilmott S., rel. of W. S., l. in ye ship ye Sampson in ye B. 253

Oct. John Roafe. 28, to Mary R., rel. of J. R., l. at J. 253

Oct. Tho. Barker. 28, to Bryan Harrison, the uncle by ye m's side of T. B., at J., John B. ye father and John and Ellinor B., ye bro. and sist., renouncing. 253

Oct. Tho. Bishopp. 28, to R^d B., uncle of T. B., l. of I. of Wight, but at J. 253

Nov. John Roades. 18, to Rachell R., rel. of J. R., l. in ye W. I. 274

Nov. Tho. Coppin. 4, to Daniel Webb, cozen Jerman of T. C., l. of Armton in Cornwall, but in ye Portl^d frigott at J. 279

Nov. Tho. Barnes, 11, to Sarah B., rel. of T. B., l. in the W. I. 280

Nov. Tho. Rowe. 11, to Mary R., rel. of T. R., l. at J. 280

Nov. Soloman Griffen. 18, to John G., bro. of S. G., at J., ba. 280

Nov. Josias Hopkins. 18, to Eliz. H., mother of J. H., at J. 281

Nov. Wm Broughton. 18, to R^d B., only bro. of W. B., at J. 281

Nov. Wm Hider. 20, to Henry H., f. of W. H., at J. 281

Nov. Mathew Dancy. 25, to Mary D. al's Morris, wid., Moth. of M. D., at J. 281

Nov. Wm Amy. 25, to Eliz. A., wid., M. of W. A., l. a soldier at J., ba. 281

Nov. Tho. Bird. 6, to Jonath. B., bro., n. in t. will nunc. of T. B., l. in ye Torrington frigott, S.S., at J. 283

Nov. John Halde. 28, to Doro. H., ye M. and univ. leg. in will of J. H., l. soldier, at J. 284

Nov. Geo. Watts. 13, was p. ye will of G. W., l. at J., by oath of R^d W. and Humph. W., bros. 285

Nov. Wm Soward. 28, to R^d S., Fath. of W. S., l. soldier at J., ba. 298

Nov. Isaack Nattris. 29, to Wm N., ye F. of I. N., at J., ba. 298

Dec. Wm Snelling. 2, to Martyn S., ye F. of W. S., soldier at J. 314

Dec. John Bishopp. 4, to Rob. B., ye F. of J. B., soldier at J. 314

Dec. Gilbert Bixtith. 4, to Marg^t B., wid., ye M. of G. B., l. of Liverpool, at J., ba. 314

Dec. Apharah Brigham. 24, to Cha. B., bro. of A. B., in ye I. of B. 315

Dec. John Spencer. 30, to Anne Filliol, spr., sister by ye M's side of J. S., at J., ba., Pen. S., y^e M., Tho. S., y^e bro., and Rachell S., the sister, renouncing. 316

Dec. Michael Kenrick. 15, to Mich. Jones, y^e uncle of M. K., l. at J., ba. 316

* Geo. was at Barbados. See his will proved 2 March 1656 (106, Ruthen).

folio.

Dec. Sam. Broadstreete. 12, to Rich. Alworth, y^e G. of Sam. and Mary B., minors, y^e ch^n of S. B., late at J. 317

Dec. Joseph Hall. 22, to Anne Sayer al's Symonds, wife of John S., creditor of J. H., late in ye S.S. at J. 317

1657.

Jan. Wm. Pedder. 27, to Eliz. P. al's Oliver, wife of John O., the M. of W. P., late in ye S.S. at J., paup. 11

Jan. Edw. Hunt. 29, to Randall Hunt, ye uncle of E. H., late in ye S.S. at J., ba. 11

Jan. Wm. Buck. 29, to Eliz. Tymms al's Buck, ye only sister of W. B., late in ye S.S. at J., ba. 11

Jan. Gerrard Hawtayne. 29, to Mary H., spr., ye dau. of G. H, l. of B., Mercht. 11

Feb. Tho. Boylston. 27, to Sam. Cock, pr. creditor of T. B., l. in ye I of B. 31

Feb. John King. 3, to Rebecca K., wid., ye relict of J. K., l. of Wapping, but at J. 32

Feb. Henry Little. 10, to Mary Taylor al's L., now wife of Wm. T., ye only sister of H. L., l. in ye S.S. at J., ba. 32

Feb. Tho Johnson. 10, to Rob. J., ye brother of T. J., in B. 32

Feb. Tho. Ridley. 10, to Edw. R., ye father of T. R., at ye B., ba. 32

Feb. John Groome. 12, to Geo. G., ye father of J. G., l. of St Andrewes, Holbourne, but at J., ba. 32

Feb. Gabriell Huntley. 19, to Henry H., ye brother of G. H., at J., ba. 32

Feb. Rich. Crane. 19, to Priscilla C., wid., ye M. of R. C., at J. 32

Feb. Henry Fanting. 19, to Jeremy F., ye onely bro. of H. F., at J. 32

Feb. Tho. Fanting. 19, to Jeremy F., at Constantinople, ba. 32

Feb. Job. Syar. 24, to Sarah S., ye M. of J. S., at J., ba. 32

Feb. Wm Syar. 24, to Sarah S., ye M. of J. S., at J., ba. 33

Feb. Mathew Smith. 24, to Rose S., spr., ye onely child of M. S., l. of Aldburgh, co. Suffolk, but at J., widdower. 33

March. Peter Roseman. 2, to Ame Salter al's R., wife of James S., ye onely sister of P. R., l. in ye Sarah of L., at ye B., ba. 62

March. James Mills. 6, to Edmond M., ye brother of J. M., l. a souldier in Capt. Moult's Co., at J., ba. 63

March. John Grover. 11, to Tho. G., ye F. of J. G., l. in ye S. S., a souldier, at J., ba. 63

March. Isack Rycroft. 11, to W. R., ye F. of I. R., l. in ye S. S., at J., ba. 63

March. Timothy Hix. 13, to Cicily H., wid., ye relict of T. H., l. in ye S. S., at J., ba. 63

March. David Knowles. 14, to Joane K., wid., ye rel. of D. K., l. in ye S. S., at J., ba. 63

March. Wm. Webb. 16, to Ellen Smith al's Webb, wife of Wm Smith, ye sister of W. W., l. M^r of ye Trayne, at J., widdower. 63

March. Geo. Sympson. 25, to Jane Moody al's S., ye sister and only next of kin of G. S., at J., ba. 64

March. John Plumer. 25, to Richd P., ye brother of J. P., at J., ba. 64

March. Tho. Tinckham. 26, to Joane T., wid., ye rel. of T. T., l. of Plimouth, but at J. 64

April. Jonathan Bowell. 16, to Bridgett B., wid., y^e M. of J. B., l. drummer in y^e S. S., at J., ba. 77

April. Rich. Tucker. 21, to Mercy T., wid., y^e relict of R. T., l. of y^e I. of Wight, but at J. 77

April. Elias Cox. 21, to Mary C., y^e M. of E. C., at J., ba. 78

Folio.

April. James Picroft. 23, to Judith Falkner, ye Aunt and G. of Sarah P., a minor, ye sister of J. P., a souldier, at J. 78

April. Arthur Keeler. 28, to John K., ye F. of A. K., l. of Corkshall, co. Essex, at J., ba. 79

April. Wm. Tracy. 28, to Mary T., wid., ye rel. of W. T., l. of Framingham, co. Suff., at J., in ye S. S. 79

April. Tho. Willoughby. 15, to Tho. Midleton, Esq., nephew of T. W., l. of Virginia, but in Alhalowes Barking, to the use of Tho. and Eliz. W., ye children now beyond sea. 81

May. Henry Middleton. 14, to Ralph Allen,, ye Master, and pr. cr. of H. M., l. in ye B. Further Ad. 8 Aug. 1660. 115

May. Coll. Richard ffortescue, Esq. 1, to Mary ff., wid,, the relict of the hon. Col. R. ff., late of Hickfeild, co. Southton, but at J., Esq., decd. 29 July 1657. Cancelled and a will proved. 116

May. Geo. Dudley. 5, to Rd D., ye onely brother of G. D., l. at J. 116

May. John Barnam. 5, to Margt Skinner al's B., wife of John S., ye onely sister of J. B., l. att J. 116

May. Richard Elford. 7, to Nehemiah E., ye uncle and G. of Mary and Rd Elford, minors, ye children of R. E., l. of Plimouth, but at J. 116

May. Nich. Nash. 7, to James N. the Elder, ye brother of N. N., l. at J., ba. 117

May. John Barker. 14, to W. B., ye father of J. B., in B., ba. 117

May. Henry Rigby. 14, to Gilbert R., ye father of H. R., a souldier, at J., ba. 117

May. Eliza Bland. 14, to Bridgett B., onely dau. of E. B., in ye B., wid. 117

May. Wm. Wickham. 21, to Anne Lee al's W., wid., ye M. of W. W., at J., ba. 117

May. W. Blanch. 29, to Mary Hilton, cozen german of W. B., at J., paup. 118

May. Rob. Twittee. 29, to W. T., ye F. of R. T., at J., paup. 118

May. John Hamblyn. 29, to W. Stafford, ye brother by ye mother's side of J. H., at J., ba., Mary Mainwaring, ye mother of Humfrey S. ye half-brother, renouncing. 118

June. Roger Gates. 10, to Dorothy Palmer, al's G. the M. of R. G., at J., ba. 150

June. Sam. ffirebrass. 10, to Jane Arpe, wid., ye M. of S. F., at J., ba. 150

June. Wm. Smallwood. 11, to Erasmus S., ye brother of W. S,, at J., ba. 150

June. Wm Ward. 11, to Rd W., ye onely brother of W. W., in ye S. S., at J. 150

June. Wm Huntley. 15, to Henry H., ye onely bro. of W. H., l. one of ye fellows of New Collidge, Oxford, at J., ba. 150

June. Wm Cunstable. 15, to Mary C., wid., ye rel. of W. C., at J.

June. Capt. John Cooke. 22, to Wm C., ye nephew of Capt. J. C., in the S. S., at J. 151

June. Edmond Walter. 26, to Henry W., ye eldest Bro. of E. W., l. of Ashbury, co. Devon, but in B., ba. 151

June. John Walter. 26, to Henry W., ye eldest Bro. of J. W., l. of Achbury, co. Devon, but in Ireland, decd. 151

July. Garrett Horonson. 2, to Geo. Cobden, pr. Cr of G. H. in theB., ba. 171

July. Geo. White. 4, to Tho. Hogg, pr. Cr of G. W. l. Leiftt to Capt. Blunt in Collo Carter's Reg. at J., ba. 172

July. Richd Hawkins. 7, to Rd H., ye F. of R. H., l. of Cockshall in Essex, but a souldier in ye S. S. at J., ba. 172

July. Garrett Pellatory. 20, to Hannah P., wid., ye M. of G. P. at J., ba. 174

folio.

July. John Beckford. 20, to Tho. B., ye F. of J. B. at J., ba. 174

July. Tho. Judd. 21, to Tho. J., ye F. of T. J. at J., ba. 174

July. Rob. Jacob. 20, to Wm. J., ye onely Brother of R. J. at J., ba. 174

July. John Sores. 27, to John Sores, ye F. of J. S., l. a souldier in Capt. Handcock's Co. at J., ba. 174

Aug. Wm Bowe. 4, to Eliz. B., wid., ye rel. of W. B., l. belonging to ye Shipp ye Lyon, in ye S. S. at J. 191

Aug. Tho. Wood. 17, to Rob. W., ye F. of T. W. at J., in ye shipp ye Beare. 192

Aug. John Philpott. 18, to Eliz. P., wid., ye M. of J. P., l. a souldier at J., ba. 192

Sept. Mathew Child. 11, to Jas. Thompson, pr. Cr of M. C. at J. 216

Sept. Abr. ffinicher. 2, to Rd ff., ye Bro. of A. ff, at J., ba. 216

Sept. Sampson Jenkins. 5, to John J., ye F. of S. J., at J., ba. 216

Sept. Geo. Normondy. 7, to Fra. N., ye F. of G. N., l. a souldier at J. in Collo Bullwer's Reg., paup. 217

Sept. Rd Stanning. 10, to Jane S., wid., ye rel. of R. S., l. of Limehouse, but at J., in ye S. S. 217

Sept. Peter Raven. 14, to Wm. R., ye F. of P. R., l. a souldier at J. in Collo Bulwer's Reg, ba. 217

Sept. Dorothy Dyton. 14, to Jane Ellerton, spr., ye dau. of D. D., l. at J., wid. 217

Sept. Tho. Cornish. 14, to Dyana Davies al's C., ye M. of T. C., l. in ye shipp the Lyon, at J., ba. 217

Sept. Tho. Williams. 16, to Eliz. Harding, wid., ye Aunt and next of kin of T. W., in ye B. 217

Sept. Wm. Sessions. 16, to Emelyn S., wid., ye M. of W. S., of J., ba. 218

Sept. John Leison. 17, to Mathew L., ye onely Bro. of J. L., at J., ba. 218

Sept. John Palmer. 21, to John P., ye F. of J. P., l. a souldier at Ja. in General Venables Reg., ba. 218

Sept. Geo. Browne. 28, to Anne B., spr., ye Aunt of G. B., a souldier at J., ba. 218

Sept. Wm Hudson. 29, to Daniel H., ye only Bro. of W. H., at J., ba. 218

Oct. Nich. Bowden. 27, to Tho. B., the uncle & G. of Nich. B., a minor, ye only child of N. B., at J. 239

Oct. Edward Lee. 7, to Grace Jones, wife of Alex. J., ye only child of E. L., at J. 240

Oct. Wm Hurlestone. 7, to Anne H., wid., ye M. of W. H., at J., ba. 240

Oct. John Lawless. 15, to Eliz. Moone al's L., ye Sister of J. L., l. of Gravesend, but at J. 240

Oct. Rowland Barker. 27, to John B., ye Bro. of R. B., in ye S. S., at J., ba. 241

Oct. Henry Colléton. 30, to Eliz. C., rel. of H. C., l. of B., but in Shoe Lane, L. 247

Nov. John Towne. 10, to Eliz. T., wid., ye rel. of J. T., l. of St Sepulchers, L., but at J., in ye S. S. in Capt. . . . . co., paup. 281

Nov. John Langdon. 17, to Rob. L., ye uncle of J. L., in ye B., ba., Ellen L., ye M., renouncing. A 2d entry gives Ellen L., ye Relict. 282

Nov. Rob. Langdon. 17, to Rob. L, ye Uncle of Rob. L., in ye B., ba., Ellen L., ye M., ren. 282

Nov. John Wilson. 20, to John W., ye F. of J. W., at J., ba. 283

Nov. John Edwards. 24, to Eliz. Crowder, ye wife of Rob. C., ye sister of J. E., l. in ye Marston Moore frigott at J., in the S. S., ba. 283

Nov. Tho. Holmes. 24, to Mary H, spr., ye sister of T. H., in ye W.I., ba. 283

Dec. Roger Manners. 3, to Roger M., the F. of R. M., at J., ba. 315

Dec. Edward Cason. 7, to Peter Stockton, pr. Cr of E. C., at J., ba. 315

folio.

Dec. Henry Bull. 8, to Anne B., ye rel. of H. B., l. of Defford, co. Kent, but in ye ship ye Convertyne, at J. 315

Dec. Sam. Wright. 17, to Eliz. Jones al's W., then wife of Tho. J. ye Sister of S. W., at J., ba. 315

Dec. Rob. Lane. 21, to Alice L., wid., ye rel. of R. L., late slayne at sea in ye Lyme frigott, in ye S. S., at Saucta Cruze, paup. 315

Dec. William Stapleton. 21, to Sarah S., wid., ye rel., etc., as above. 315

Dec. John Belton. 14, to Tho. Vigures the Grandfather & G. of Eliz. B., a minor, ye only child of J. B., in the B. 317

1658.

Jan. John Kendall. 13, to James K., ye Father of J. K., in ye ship ye Gilbert, in ye B., ba. 8

Jan. Tho. Knapton. 15, to Eliz. K., wid., ye rel. of T. K., l. of New Sarum, co. Wilts, but in the I. of B. 9

Jan. Tho. Younge. 25, to John Y., ye Father of T. Y., l. in ye S. S., in Capt. Hancock's Co., at J., ba. 9

Jan. Jerrard Gates. 26, to Tho. G., ye F. of J. G., l. in ye ship ye Convertyne, at J., in ye S. S., ba. 10

Feb. Wm. Ayscough. 4, to Sr George A., Knt, ye Bro. of W. A., l. Lieut. of ye Laurell frigott, in ye S. S., att J., gent. 51

Feb. Cap. Geo. Parsons. 8, to Eliz. Pope, ye Sister of Capt. G. P., l. in ye S. S., in Gen. Venables Reg., att J., ba. 51

Feb. John Segnoir. 5, to Geo. S., ye F. of J. S., l. in ye B., ba. Further Admon. Jan. 1670. 51

Feb. Richard Ellis. 12, to Alice Westill al's Ellis, wid., ye M. of R. E., in ye B., ba. 51

Feb. Symon Foulk. 19, to Eliz. Hills al's F., wife of Capt. Wm Hill, ye onely sister of S. F., l. souldier, at J., in Coll. Haynes' Reg., in ye S. S., ba. 53

Feb. Tho. Jenkes. 23, to John Lyddall, ye Bro. by ye half blood of T. J., l. in ye S. S. at J., ba. 54

Feb. Richard Lydall. 20, to John L., ye Bro. of Rd L., l. in ye S. S., at J., ba. 54

March. Edward Willier. 3, to John W., ye Bro. of E. W., l. a souldier in ye S. S. at J., paup. 69

April. Anthony Moorecroft. 20, to Anne M., wid., ye rel. of A. M., l. of B. 87

April. Robert Jacob. 26, to Tho. J. and Eliz. J. his wife ye F. and M. of R. J., l. of ye Minories, L., but at J., a souldier under Capt. Allen, ba. 87

April. Edward Craufeild. 10, to Eliz C., wid., ye relict of E. C., l. in B., of goods left unad. by Mary Peasley ye M. and also by Tho. Payne. The 1st ad. to Mary Peisley was in Dec. 1649, ye other in April 1653. Revoked in July 1663. 87

May. Tho. Saxby. 18, to Tho. S., ye F. of T. S., in ye ship ye Indian in ye S. S. at J., ba. 117

May. John Pagett. 21, to Amy P., wid., ye rel. of J. P., l. of Southwark, but in ye ship ye Indian in ye S. S., at J., paup. 127

May. Fra. Clifford. 21, to John C., ye F. of F. C., l. of Barkin in Essex, but at J., ba. 127

May. Henry Towers. 21, to Rd Maydman, ye cozen german of H. T., l. of Algate, but at J., ba. 127

May. Geo. Mawborne. 21, to Eliz. M., wid., ye rel. of G. M. in ye ship ye Indian in ye S. S., at J., paup. 127

May. James Martin. 21, to Mergery Payne, ye M. of J. M., at J., ba. 127

folio

May. Jacob Frost. 24, to Eliz, F., y[e] Sister of J. F. in y[e] ship y[e] Indian, at J., ba. 127

May. Richard Beaman. 25, to John B., y[e] Bro. of R. B., l. of B. 127

June. John Alkin and Henrey Alkin. 4, to Tho. A. y[e] elder, y[e] F. of J. A., l. of Uttoxeter, co. Staff., but at J., ba. 129

June. Richard Beane. 4, to Effata B., wid., y[e] rel. of R. B. in y[e] ship Paul in y[e] S. S., at J., paup. 129

June. Geo. Lander. 22, to Joane L., wid., y[e] rel. of G. L., at J. 130

June. Wm. Harvey. 11, to Tobiah H., y[e] Bro. of W. H. in the B. 136

July. Enoch Ditty. 1, to Eliz. Pyott al's D., wife of Edw. Pyott, y[e] M. of E. D., l. of Bristol, but at sea, ba. 196

July. John Swift. 6, to Tho. S., y[e] Bro. of J. S., l. in y[e] B., ba. 196

July. Rob. Cradock. 15, to Peter C., the Uncle of R. C., l. at sea in y[e] ship Odwell coming from y[e] B., ba. 197

July. Edw. Warbreake. 15, to Tho. W., y[e] Bro. of E. W., at J., ba. 197

July. Jas. Buttery. 16, to Barbarah B., y[e] rel. of J. B., at J. 197

July. Edward Madox. 24, to Eliz. M., spr., y[e] Sister of E. M., l. of the ship the Convertine, at J., ba. 199

Aug. Geo. Ellyott. 3, to Sam. Hill, pr. C[r] of Geo. E., l. in parts beyond the seas, outward bound to the B. 225

Aug. W[m] Gartford. 4, to Sarah G., wid., y[e] rel. of W[m] G., l. of L., but in the B. 225

Aug. John Morrice. 3, to Frances Morris, the rel. of J. M., l. of J., in the S. S., mariner, paup. 227

Aug. Tho. Bemister. 20, to Joanna B., y[e] rel. of T. B., l. of the ship the John and Kath., in y[e] B. 227

Aug. James Buttler. 23, to Eliz. B., wid., y[e] rel. of J. B., l. Adjutant Gen., at J. 229

Sept. None.

Oct. Arthur Stuart. 6, to W. S., Esq., the F. of A. S., l. at J. 255

Oct. W[m] Phillipps. 8, to Anne P., wid., the rel. of W. P., in the B. 255

Oct. W[m] Trattle. 12, to Ralphe T., the uncle and G. of Anne, Ralph, Kath., and W[m] T., the ch[n] of W. T.. l. in the B., widd. 256

Oct. John Day. 27, to Kath. Miller al's D., the only Sister of J. D., in the B., ba. 256

Nov. Jas. Abney. 15, to John Croakelyn, pr. C[r] of J. A., l. of S[t] Mary Aldermanbury, at J., ba. 295

Dec. Rob. Atkinson. 15, to R[d] Hutchinson, pr. C[r] of R. A., in B., widd[r]. 336

Dec. R[d] Walker. 1, to Tho. W., the Bro. of R. W., in J., ba. 344

Dec. Cap[t] Wm. Wiseman. 3, to Mary Bockingham al's W., the sister of Capt. W. W., at J. 344

Dec. Emanuell Sandys. 14, to Eliz. S., wid., the M. of E. S., in J., in the Service of the Army, ba. 344

St. Nicholas Abbey, Barbados

St. Nicholas Abbey, Barbados.

This ancient stone mansion stands in the parish of St. Peter in the northern part of the Island. Very little seems to be known about its history or date of erection. In appearance it resembles an English manor house of the end of the 17th century.

Captain Charles J. P. Cave of Ditcham Park, Hampshire, its present owner, writes that the estate belonged to Abraham Cumberbatch, who died in 1785, from whom it passed to his son Edward Carlton Cumberbatch, whose daughter married Charles Cave, the writer's grandfather.

An earlier owner may have been Abraham Cumberbatch who died in 1750, leaving two daughters, of whom one married John Sober, and the other Ann, in 1726, Edward Carleton. Their son Abraham Carleton, as sole heir to his grandfather, assumed the surname of Cumberbatch, and died as already stated in 1785. (See *Ante*, II., 84.)

Without an examination of the title deeds and other records it is impossible to give the early descent of the estate, as although testator in 1750 desired that his plantation should be kept stocked with 250 slaves and 100 head of cattle he does not name the estate.

From inquiries just made by my friend Mr. E. G. Sinckler, who resides in the parish, it appears that the flooring of the ground floor rooms was relaid in 1813 by an English workman named Thomas Shilstone, and the house repaired. In 1913 Mr. Thaddeus Deane, the Manager, renewed the flooring, and as the previous one had thus lasted 100 years we may reasonably assume that the one worn out in 1813 (supposing it to have been of equally lasting wood) dated from about 1713.

An old man named James Chandler states that in 1831 after the hurricane, the house, being the only undamaged one in the neighbourhood, was occupied by several families. The drawing-room, dining-room and parlour have been comparatively recently panelled with cedar grown on the estate.

There is a flue for a fire-place in the corner of one of the bedrooms, but I saw no signs of a grate having ever been fixed, and the chimneys are only an ornamental feature of the design. There are also a very old bedstead and grandfather's clock, but these were not shewn me. A very beautiful arbor vitæ tree grows near the entrance, rather filling up the fore-court. The mansion with its setting of trees and shrubs is a very charming bit of old-time building, and the only example of this style in the Island. Further information is desired.

Bridgwater of Nevis.

1677-8. Census of Nevis. Col. Edw. Bridgwater's Company. (*Ante*, III., 29, 70.)

1707-8. Census of Nevis. Charles Bridgwater. 3 whites, 60 blacks. Thomas Bridgwater. 3 whites, 28 blacks. (*Ibid.*, 174, 177.)

1710. Charles Bridgwater, a M. of Council. Tho. B., a M. of Assembly. (French, 75. Oldmixon, ii., 257.)

1715. Hon. Tho. Bridgwater, then Chief Justice. (Nevis Records, p. 151.)

1718. Harvard College Graduates: Edward Bridgwater from the Island of Nevis. Judge there. Supposed death 1782. (New Eng. Reg., xxxii., 232.)

1727. Edward Bridgewater, Treasurer, signs the levy. (C. O., 152.)

1727. Tho. and Margaret Bridgwater, then holding lands in St. Kitts.

Col. Edward Bridgwater = (? Eliz., party to deed of Nevis, 1677. | of 1738.)

Hon. Col. Charles Bridgwater, Sen.; M. of C., 1710; deed of 1728. = Eliz. . . . ., widow, 1738. 2nd wife.

Hon. Thomas Bridgwater of St. Peter's, St. Kitts; M. of A., Nevis, 1710; Chief Justice, 1715; bur. at St. George's, 9 July 1744. Will dated 23 June, sworn 12 July 1744. = Eliz. . . . ., died 16 May 1739, aged 63; M.I. at St. Peter's, Basseterre.

A

Charles Bridgwater, Jun., son and heir; owned Hog Valley of 90 acres in St. James, which decended to his 2 daus. = Elizabeth dau. of Walter Tobin; mar. sett. dated 21 Nov. 1728. She re-married . . . . Thomson. Her will dated 3 Jan., and sworn 1 March 1765. (*Ante*, IV., 289.)

Thadeus Bridgwater, living 1744. =

Hon. Richard Bridgwater of St. Peter's, 1753; died 27 June 1761.

B

Chas. Bartlet Bridgwater, born and bapt. 30 Apr. 1734 at St. Thos.

Mary, coheiress, mar. Wm. Smith, 1st son and heir of Mich. Smith. He sold his moiety of Hog Valley in 1764. (*Ante*, IV., 294.) m. at St Geo. B'Terre 1753.

Eliz., coheiress, mar. 20 Oct. 1748 Rev. Edwin Thomas, M.A., Rector of St. John's, Figtree, 1750—64, and of Basseterre 1764 until his death, 19 Jan. 1789, aged 69.

Thadeus Macarty Bridgwater. living 1778 = Hannah Smith, mar. 21 July 1763. dead 1778

Chas. Bridgwater, bapt. 30 Nov. 1744.

—

Bridget Bridgwater, bapt. 7 Sept. 1740; mar. before 1763 Rob. Pemberton.

1728, Nov. 21. Ind're between the Hon. Charles Bridgewater, Senior, Esq., and Elizabeth his now wife, Charles B. his s. and h. by Eliz. his wife, and Eliz. Tobin dau. of Walter Tobin, planter, deceased, and John Tobin, planter, and Sarah Tobin, widow and relict of Walter Tobin. A marriage to be solemnized between Charles Bridgewater, Jun[r], and Eliz. Tobin. Walter Tobin by his will made 10 April 1719 gave his dau. Eliz. £200 st. and £500 c. (Nevis Records, ii., 65.)

1733, June 29. Tho. Bridgwater of the Inner Temple, gent., Ex'or of the will of Susanna Cole, appoint Daniel Brodbelt of the I. of Jamaica, gent., my attorney. (*Ibid.*, p. 185.)

1738, May 23. Eliz. Bridgwater of Nevis, widow, and Chas. B., Esq., her s. and h., convey 100 acres on mortgage for a debt of £554. (*Ibid.*, vol. I. & J., p. 117.)

1750. Tho. Abbott, for £1200, sold Hog Valley of 100 acres to Walter Nisbet.

1759. College of Chemistry, Scotland. Edw. Bridgwater. America. (*Ante*, III., 384.)

1761. Tho. Bridgwater, a witness. (*Ibid.*, 226.)

1778. Bridgewaters, then owned by James Smith.

1780. Tho. Bridgwater, a witness to the will of John Welch of St. Kitts. (*Ante*, III., 144.)

1797. Dr. Swanston m. Miss Bridgwater, 25 Sept. Cayon Diary. (*Ibid.*, 165.)

1811, Sept. 5. In Charlotte-st., Portland-pl., E. Bridgewater, esq., many years a medical practitioner in the island of St. Christopher. ("G.M.," 203.)

Sus^a Cole, late of the I. of St Chr., now of St Paul's Churchyard, London, widow. Will dated 1 Dec. 1732. All estate in G. B. and St C. and negroes to my nephew Tho. Bridgwater, and sole Ex'or. Wit.: Dan. Brodbelt, Mary Taylor. Proved 22 Feb. 1732 by T. B. (35, Price.)

Thos. Bridgwater of the p. of St Peter in the island of St Chr. Will dated 23 June 1744. My s. Thadeus £50. Son Richard £100. My 2 grandsons Thadeus Macarty B. and Roger Pemberton B., sons of my son Thadeus B., £100

A

- Thomas Bridgwater, ? of Inner Temple, 1733, and Executor of his aunt Mrs Sus^a Cole.
- Edward Bridgwater, Graduate of Harvard, 1718. Treasurer of Nevis, 1727. ? died 1782. = Sarah ....
- Margaret Bridgwater, mar. Rich. Rowland, Esq. His will dated 1761. (265, Cheslyn.)
- Susannah Bridgwater, mar. Dr. Geo. Irwin.

B

- Roger Pemberton Bridgwater, Esq., bur. at Charlestown 20 July 1816. [handwritten: under 14 in 1778]
- [handwritten: Bridget Pemberton B. liv. 1778]

Children of Edward Bridgwater and Sarah:

- Thos. Bridgwater, ? bapt. 8 Aug. 1730. = Mary Paris sister of Edward Paris, mar. 10 May 1764.
  - Mary Bridgwater, born 30 July and bapt. 27 Aug. 1765; living 1770.
  - Eliz. Bridgwater.
- Edward Bridgwater, of a Scotch University, 1759; M.D., practised in St. Kitts; died in London 5 Sept. 1811. Will dated 1810, proved 1811. (433, Crickitt.) = Harriot .... s.p.
- Joseph Bridgwater.
- Sarah Bridgwater.
- Eliz. Bridgwater, ? mar. 12 Feb. 1771 Roger Gardner. He was bapt. 4 Dec. 1744.

each. My estate in Nevis to my s. Edward, his ch^n Tho., Edwd, Joseph, Sarah and Eliz. My dau. Margaret Rowland wife of Mr Richd Rowland. My dau. Susannah. Dau. Eliz. Thomas £400. My s. Thos. My s.-in-l. Mr Tho. Bowry. Sworn 12 July 1744. (Nevis Records, No. 3321.)

Richard Rowland, late of St. Chr., Esq. Will dated 10 June 1761. My moiety of the plantation in St. Peter's p., St. Chr., which I purchased of Dr. George Irwin and Susannah his wife, and a parcel of land in Basseterre, also the other moiety of the said pl^n which belonged to my late wife Margaret, which were formerly the entire estate of Tho. Bridgewater, Esq., I give in trust for my dau. Margaret.

Edwd Parris of Nevis, Esq. Will dated 6 March 1770. My sister Mary Bridgwater. Her dau. Polly B. £300, and Polly's sister Eliz. £300.

Sarah Pemberton of St George's, Nevis, sp^r. Will dated 4 Sept. 1773. My brother Robt P. and Bridget his wife (formerly Bridget Bridgwater). A ring to Mr John B. of Nevis.

James Smith of St Tho. Lowland Esq. Will dat. 29 Oct. 1778. To Roger Pemberton Bridgwater s of Thadeus McCarty B. by his late decd wife Hannah £800 at 14 Bridget Pemberton B. his sister £600. [323 Warburton]

Edw. Bridgwater, late of St Chr., now of London. Wife Harriot all estate. My friend Eumenes Moore, Esq., late of St Chr., now at Coleshill, Bucks. 1810. Proved 1811. (433, Crickitt.)

ST. GEORGE'S, BASSETERRE, ST. KITTS.

1744 July 9 Thoms. Bridgewater, Esqr, buried. (*Ante*, I., 355.)
1752 May 23 Francis Hamm to . . . . es Bridgwater; by L.
?1753 — . . . . m Smith to Mary Bridgwater; by Lic.
1755 July 6 Richd Bridgw . . . ., free mulatto, to Susannah Hildin, mulatto, belonging to Mrs . . . . N. B. Mrs Gerald . . . . me she would give her her freedom by her last will.
1757 — John s. of Richd & Susannah Bridgwater, b. 20 Nov. 1756; bapt.
[handwritten:] .. Dec. 1. Sarah Bridgwater bur.
1765 Aug. 27 Mary dau. of Thos & Mary Bridgwater, b. 30 July.
1776 Sept. 23 Edward s. of „ „ „ b. 30 June.
1783 June 3 Almeria dau. of „ „ „ b. 3 Dec. 1780.
[handwritten:] 1762 Nov. 3. Richd s. of Richd & Susan B. / „ Susannah B. b. 11 June ult.
[handwritten:] .. 3 Aug. 17. Henrietta, d. of

ST. THOMAS, NEVIS.

1733 Nov. 25 John s. of Colo Charles Bridgewater, buried.
1734 April 30 Charles Bartlett s. of Charles Bridgewater, Esqr, & Eliz. his Wife, Born & Bap. this day; bapt. (*Ibid.*, 233, 234.)
1782 Nov. 15 Thomas Bridgwater, aged 42 years, buried.
1784 Dec. 18 Joseph Symonds Bridgwater, aged 43 years, buried.

ST. JAMES, NEVIS.

1740 Sept. 7 Bridt Bridgwater dau. of Thadus Bridgwater; bapt.
1744 Nov. 30 Charles „ s. of „ „ „ (*Ibid.*, 235.)

ST. PAUL'S, NEVIS.

1816 July 20 Roger Pemberton Bridgwater, Esqr, buried.

ST. JOHN'S, NEVIS.

1748 Oct. 20 Rev. Edwin Thomas & Eliz. Bridgwater. (*Ante*, I., 324.)
1763 July 21 Thaddeus McCarty Bridgewater & Hannah Smith. (*Ibid.*, I., 378.)
1764 May 10 Thomas Bridgewater & Mary Paris.
1771 Feb. 12 Roger Gardiner to Elisabeth Bridgewater, spinster. (*Ibid.*, II., 324.)

ST. GEORGE'S, NEVIS.

1730 Aug. 8 Thomas s. of Edward Bridgewater & Sarah his W.; bapt. (*Ibid.*, III., 218.)

ST. GEORGE'S, HANOVER SQUARE, CO. MIDDX.

1836 Sept. 3 Roger Pemberton Bridgewater & Susan Matilda Adams.

Higinbotham of Barbados.

The following records were forwarded by Mr. William M. Sweeny of the Custom House, New York City. The Editor has made abstracts of the wills to save space. The entries from the parish register are unfortunately not in full:—

17 Sept. 1649. I, Otwell Higginbotham, in the Barbadoes, being bound in a voyage for England. The £250 I am to receive by bill of exchange I bestow as follows: To my father Oliver Higginbotham and Anne my mother £20. To my brother William £10. Brother John £20. Brother Oliver £5. To William Higginbotham, son and heir of my body, £50. My daughter Anne £25. My cosen Capt. John Higginbotham in the Barbadoes £5. Cosens John, Joan, Martha, Alice, Sara and Priscilla, children of the said Capt. John Higginbotham, £30 amongst them. Cosen Mary Higginbotham, daughter to said Capt. John, £20. Katherine, wife of John Bunce, and her children, £20. Alice Zeale £5. For my funeral £20. All other my estate in England or elsewhere, land or otherwise, I give unto my son and heir William Higginbotham, and I make Nicholas Higginbotham of Cheshire in England, and Capt. John Higginbotham in the Barbadoes, who is my attorney, my executors. Witnesses: Tho. Higginbotham, Tho. Zealell. Proved 30 Jan. 1651-2 by Nicholas Higginbotham, power being reserved to the other executor. (P.C.C. Bowyer, 6.)

John Higinbotham of S[t] Philip's, Barbados, Sen[r]. Will dated 19 Sept. 1672. To my son Cap[t] John H. 2000 lbs. of sugar, besides the 70 acres I settled him in, and acquit him of all accounts when I sold unto him and Lef[t] Sam. Tweney the work and 60 acres or for his voyage to Jamaica and New England. I also give him 60 feet square of land on Carlisle Bay between M[rs] Griffin's house and the sea. To Chas. H, my grandson 1000 lbs., and to his two sisters Jane and Millicent 500 lbs. each at the age of 15. To my dau. Joane Waitte, widow, 2000 lbs., and to her four children Tho. Gibbs, John Gibbs, Higinbotham Gibbs and Jane Gibbs 1000 lbs. each at 21 the two sons, and 15 the two daus., and quitclaim to her the plantation whereon she now lives, being 50 acres, she giving equal portions to them at 21 only to Tho. Gibbs her eldest son to have 4000 lbs. more. To my dau. Martha Knightly 3000 lbs., and to her three children Shedon K., John K., and Martha K. all my plantation in the Thicketts where they live, about 25 acres, with the housing built when the eldest son Shedon attains 21, and I give them the negroes Sampson and his wife Mingo, Winbar and his child Pefoe. My dau. to have the management or 6000 lbs. apiece. To my dau. Mary Townsend wife of Lieut. Richard T. 2000 lbs., and to him 500 lbs., and to my three grandchildren Tho. T., Alice T., and John T. 500 lbs. each at 15, and to the child wherewith my dau. now goeth 500 lbs. To Nicholas Buckerfield late husband to my deceased Goddau. (*sic*) Alice 200 lbs., and to his two sons my grandchildren Nicholas and Higinbotham B. 1000 lbs. each at 12. To my dau. Sarah H. 14 acres next to M[r] Francis Dethickshire from Exors long gully square over to D[r] Tho. Parkins, but my wife to enjoy one half the crop of ginger, cane or corn, and I give her one negro woman Nen Judy, and one wench Ocain, and a girl Black Jane, one bedsted of Bully tree and a cedar tester and 4000 lbs. and one year's maintenance. To my dau. Prisilla Long 3000 lbs., and to her two daus. Merandila Clenen and Mellicent Clenen 500 lbs. each at 18. To my granddau. Jane Beleffe 1000 lbs. at 21, and have her stock of cattle and sheep. To my natural brother L[t] Tho. Higinbotham 2000 lbs., and my sister his wife 100 lbs., and to Marg[t] Jones 500 lbs., and to his two children Nicholas and Eliz. each 500 lbs. at 21. To my nephews Sam. Finny and Joseph Higinbotham 500 lbs. each, and to coz. Finney's wife Mary 500 lbs., and to their son Jeffrey my graud (*sic*, but ? god) son 500 lbs. at 16. To my dau. Sarah H. the house and lands rented to M[rs] Griffin at the Bay for which she pays 50*s*. by the year.

I give my dau. Priscilla Long my tenement at the Carlisle Bay wherein Mr Hampton lives and pays 50s. rent. To my son Capt. John H. my tenement on Carlisle Bay rented to Mr Robert Gibson in lieu of the 60 feet square, and the latter I give to my two daus. Joane Waite and Martha Knightly. To my wife Alice all the rest of my estate, she paying my debts and legacies, and leave her sole Ex'trix.

Codicil, 21 Feb. 1672. If wife die suddenly the Ordinary to appoint a trustee. In the presence of Tho. Parkins, David Evans, Sibbell Powell, Tho. Wormbarton. By his Excellency, the 13 Oct. 1673, Dr Tho. Parkins, David Evans and Tho. Wormbaton made oath that they did see Lt Coll. John H. seal and publish his will. Signed "R. Colleton." Entered 27 Nov. 1673.

John Higinbotham of Barbados, bound off for the recovery of my health. Will dated 21 March 1682. To my wife Jane all my estate, and Ex'trix. To my kinsmen Mr John H. and Mr Joseph H. 15s. apiece for a ring. To my good friends Major John Johnson and Mr Geo. Mason each £10 st., and to be overseers. In the presence of Will. Tusson, Edw. Cutler. By the Rt Hon. the Lt Gov., Mr Edw. Cutler appeared and was sworn. Given at Fontabelle 7 Nov. 1687. Signed "Edwyn Stede." Entered 9 Nov. 1687.

Tho. Higinbotham of Barbados and p. of St Philip. Will dated 13 July 1679. Small estate. To my son Nicholas and dau. Eliz. all my estate equally at 19, if both die then to my kinsman Sam. Finney and his three children John, Samuel and Mary, he to be sole Ex'or, and I give him and his wife a gold ring. In the presence of John Gibbs, Wm. Lewis. By L. E. appeared both witnesses and were sworn this 16 March 1679. Signed "J. Atkins." Entered 16 March 1679.

Joseph Higinbotham of Barbados and p. of St Philip, merchant. Will dated 6 April 1693. To my wife Eliz. H. all my estate, and sole Ex'trix. In the presence of Willburring Merrey, Tho. Gibbs, Sam. Finney, Jr, John Frizell, Jr, Sam. Smith. By L. E. John Frizell, Jr, appeared and was sworn 9 May 1693. Signed "Kendall." Entered 17 Aug. 1693.

Charles Hegenbotham of the p. of St Philip and I. of Barbados, gent. Will dated 17 Aug. 1732. To my wife Ann H. the negro women Folly, Cubba and Accamema, Violet and Quashebah girls, and Benn, Cuffey and Bemass boys, and all my household goods and cow. To my son Cleavor H. the reversion of the above. To my granddau. Ann Reddin a negro girl Sarah. My granddaus. Hepsibah H. and Ann H. All residue to my son John H. My wife to be sole Ex'trix. In the presence of Rd Sandford, Tho. Heggenbotham. By his Excellency Mr Tho. H. appeared and was sworn. At Pilgrim 20 May 1734. Signed "Howe." Entered 28 May 1734.

Ann Heggenbotham of St Philips, Barbados. Will dated 29 March 1740. To my son John H. 5s. as a bar against any demand. To my son Chas. H. 5s. in like manner. To my three sons Tho., Joseph and Cleavor H. £3 c. each annually for 4 years. To my son Tho. H. a negro Robinson. To my grandson John Redan at 21 £20 c. To my granddau. Ann Redan at 21 a negro woman and the land and building wherein I dwell, being 10 a., also goods and furniture, and to be Ex'trix. My friend Sam. Lashley and Roger Weeks Ex'ors in trust and Guardians. In the presence of John Irondall, Wm Peckerin. By his Excellency Mr John Irondall appeared and was sworn. At Pilgrim 28 Aug. 1740. Signed "Robert Byng."

Wm. Higginbotham of St Philip's, Barbados. Will dated 22 Sept. 1748. To my cozen Joseph Waith one negro Jack and a woman Sesley, and sole Ex'or. Signed with his mark. By his Excellency Jos. Bayley appeared and was sworn. At Pilgrim 7 April 1749. Signed "H. Grenville."

John Higinbotham of the p. of St Thomas in the East, Jamaica. Will dated 5 Feb. 1739. To my son Tho. Higinbotham Alice Nusum, 4 negro boys (*sic*). To my friend Dorothy Nusum 2 negro boys. To my son Chas. H. my riding horse. All residue to my son Tho. Higinbotham Alice Nusum. My son John H. now residing in Barbados. Dorothy Nusum to be sole Ex'trix. Signed by his mark. In the presence of John Plimly, Peter Bascom. On 26 July 1744 appeared John Plimley and made oath. Signed "Edwd Trelawny." Dorothy Nusum renounced 26 July 1744, in the presence of Tho. Mascall. Entered 26 July 1744 in Lib. 24, fo. 135. Jamaica.

1638. John Higinbotham, owner of 10 acres or more.

1666. Barbadoes. Gentlemen of the country: Lieut.-Col. Higginbottom, a stout man and fit for command. (Col. Cal., p. 413.)

John Higginbotham was clerk of the Assembly from 1670—1682. His salary was £100 or 20,000 lbs. His last letter was dated Jan. 4, 24, 1682, and at the new election of 25 April his name disappeared. The Election of his kinsman Sam. Finney for St Philip's was voided.

Census of 1680. St. Michael's. Jno Higginbotham and wife, 5 acres, 2 servants, 3 slaves. (Hotten, 441 and 455.)

Chr. Codrington II. leased on Feb. 1683 for 11 years at the rent of £2200 st. all those 2 plantations called Didmarton and Consett of 750 acres in the p. of St. John to Capt. John Higginbotham. (See Close Roll of 1690, "Antigua," i., 153.)

EXTRACT FROM BAPTISMAL REGISTERS, 1637—1750.

Year.	Name.		Parish.
1650	Higginbotham, Bridget		St. Philip.
1655	Heginbotham (Child of)		„
1657	Higinbotham, Joane		„
1661	„	John	„
1664	„	Charles	„
1667	„	Jane	„
1673	„	Hepzibah	„
1677	„	John	„
1678	„	Elizabeth	„
1678	„	Bula	„
1679	„	Joseph	„
1684	„	Rebekah	„
1686	„	Joseph	„
1686	„	Elizabeth	„
1689	„	Sarah	„
1695	„	John	„
1696	„	Charles	„
1699	„	Thomas	„
1701	„	Ann	„

Year.	Name.	Parish.
1701	Higinbotham, William	St. Philip.
1703	„ Joseph	„
1718	„ Charles	Christ Church.
1722	Higginbotham, Sarah	St. Michael.
1722	Higinbotham, Hephzibah	St. Philip.
1724	Higginbotham, Melicent	Christ Church.
1724	Higinbotham (Son of John)	St. Philip.
1726	Higginbotham, Benjamin	Christ Church.
1726	Higenbotham (Son of Thomas)	St. Philip.
1728	Higginbotham, Susanna	Christ Church.
1729	„ Roebuck	St. Michael.
1736	„ Elizabeth	Christ Church.
1736	„ John	St. Philip.
1738	Higinbotham, Mary	„
1738	„ John	„
1739	Higginbotham, Benjamin	Christ Church.
1739	Higinbotham, Cleaver	St. Philip.
1742	Higginbotham, Esther	Christ Church.
1745	„ John	„
1747	„ Esther	„
1747	„ John	„

EXTRACT FROM MARRIAGE REGISTERS, 1643—1768.

Year.	Name.	Parish.
1674	Higinbotham, Sarah	St. Philip.
1676	„ Joseph	„
1677	„ Jno.	St. Michael.
1682	Higginbotham, Rebecca	„
1685	Higinbotham, Martha	„
1685	„ Mary	„
1688	Higginbotham, Charles	St. Philip.
1695	„ Sarah	St. Michael.
1706	„ Elizabeth	St. Philip.
1714, Jan. 11	Higinbotham, Joh[n] and Henry Dewick	„
1715	Higginbotham, Thomas	St. Michael.
1717, Apr. 5	Higinbotham, John and Susanna Walker	Christ Church.
1717	„ Mary	St. Philip.
1721	Higginbotham, Thomas	„
1732	„ Cleaver	„
1754	„ Elizabeth	St. Michael.
1755	„ Susanna	Christ Church.
1763	„ Benjamin	St. Philip.

EXTRACT FROM BURIAL REGISTERS, 1644—1755.

Year.	Name.	Parish.
1674	Higinbotham, Mary	St. Philip.
1679	„ Hepzibah	„
1684	Higginbotham, Joseph	„
1684	„ John	St. Michael.

Year.	Name.	Parish.
1687	Higginbotham, John	St. Michael.
1693	Higinbotham, Jane	"
1693	" (Son of Joseph)	St. Philip.
1700	Higginbotham, Jno.	St. Michael.
1701	" Mary	"
1705	" Henry	Christ Church.
1724	" Margaret	St. Michael.
1726	" Benjamin	Christ Church.
1726	" Millicent	"
1732	" Elizabeth	St. Michael.
1754	" Esther	"
1755	" John	"
1755	" Jonathon	Christ Church.

Administrations (P.C.C.) relating to West Indians.*

Abbreviations.

B. = Barbadoes. J. = Jamaica. W.I. = West Indies. ba. = batchelor. G. = Guardian. S.S. = States Service. Pr Cr = principal creditor.

A. A Book. 1659.

[It begins Jan. 1658. English style.]

folio.

Jan. 1658-9. Payton Meeres. 3, to Bridgett Banckworth al's M., ye Sister of P. M., at J., widr. 18

Jan. Rob. Brookstead. 4, to Anne Greenaway al's B., ye rel. of R. B, at J. 18

Jan. Tho. Iddenden. 19, to Rd I. ye Bro. of T. I., at J., ba. 19

Feb. Tho. Wilberfors. 4, to Hester W., spr., ye onely Sister of T. W., l. in ye ship ye Rose Pinch at J. 55

Feb. Rd Starling. 11, to Rob. S., ye onely Bro. of R. S., of Mildenhall, co. Suff., but a souldier at J., ba. 55

Feb. Fra. Marler. 19, to John M., Humfrey M. & Jane M., ye Bros. & Sister of F. M., of L., but at J., ba. 56

Feb. Rob. Dangerfeild. 11, to Rd Floyd, Cr of R. D., l. of ye p. of Allhallowes, Hony Lane, L., but in B. 57

March. John Adams. 10, to Susan A., wid., ye rel. of J. A., l. of Stepney, but at J. 92

April 1659. Wm Husband. 14, to Wm H., ye F. of W. H., l. of Palmeto Hill in ye p. of St Lucy in ye I. of B., Merchl, but at sea, ba. 141

April Luke Blacklock. 19, to Mary B., wid., ye Rel. of L. B., l. of Brumley next Bow, but at ye B. in ye ship the Seaven Brothers. 141

May. Margery Rawdon. 6, to Marmaduke Jaques, gent., the grandchild of M. R., l. of Crux p. within the city of York. 177

June. Arthur Clayton. 8, to Eliz. Cotton, ye Cozen Jerman of A. C., at J., ba. 232

June. Abr. Wistlake. 10, to Joane Fox, wife of Tho. F., ye Sister of A. W., l. of Limehouse, co. Middx., but in ye W. I. 232

* Continued from p. 208.

folio.

June. Chr. Barrett. 13, to Rebecca Cluff al's Hall, the neece of C. B., l. of Limehouse, in y^e W. I. Mary Hall, y^e Sister of dec^d, renounced. 233

June. Wm Fetherston. 16, to Tho. F., the only Bro. of W. F., in ye W. I., ba. 233

July. No W. I. ones.

Aug. Tho. Edwards. 13, to Mary Clough al's E., wid., ye only dau. of T. E., at J., of goods left unad. by Mary E. his l. rel., since also dec^d. 296

Sept. Marke Saxby. 3, to Anthony S., ye uncle & G. of Ambrose & James S., minors, y^r ch^r of M. S., at J. 301

Sept. Wm Roberts. 16, to Geo. Thorogood, ye uncle by ye M's side of W. R., l. in the S.S., at J., ba. 302

Sept. John Woodward. 22, to Mary W. al's Head, wife of Edward Head, ye Rel. of J. W., l. of Stepney, but at J. 302

Sept. Tho. Eastridge. 29, to R^d E., ye F. of T. E., at J., ba. 303

Sept. John Richardson. 29, to Martha R., wid., the Rel. of J. R., at B. 303

Oct. Geo. Stevenson. 3, to Susan S., wid., ye Rel. of G. S., at Mevis in ye W. I. 338

There are no adm'ons at all for Nov^r.

Dec. Jas. Carter. 12, to Joanna Beamister, wid., ye only child of J. C. in B. 370

Dec. Tho. Rowe. 22, to Eliz. R., wid., ye Rel. of T. R., l. of Wapping, in ye B. 371

1660.

[It commences with March 1659, and the entries are again in Latin.]

March 1659-60. Chr. Dawson. 27, to John D., the Bro. of C. D., l. of B. 4

April 1660. Sam. Bobyer. 9, to Mary B., the Rel. of S. B., l. of Bristoll, but in the B. 15

[The top of fo. 23 for the first time is marked "Transmarine"]

April. Elliott Sheares. 3, to Sarah S., wid., ye Rel. of E. S., l. of Stepney, but at J. 23

April. John Skelen. 10, to Alex. S., ye onely Bro. of J. S., at J., ba. 23

July. Henry Boucher. 20, to Frances Davy, y^e Grandm. & G. of Humphrey B., a minor, y^e s. of H. B., late of Serenam, in America. 89

July. Wm. Akers. 14, to Isabell A., y^e rel. of W. A., l. dyeing in y^e B. 94

July. Rob. Peasley. 23, to Wm P., the s. of R. P., in y^e I. of Bermodus, $widd^r$. 94

Aug. Nich. Swan. 7, to Mary S., the sister of R. S., ba., in J. 108

Sept. John Poore. 5, to Joan P., rel. of J. P., in the W. I. 133

Nov. Wm Dickonson. 8, to John Winder, C^r of W. D., in B. 170

1661.

Jan. 1660-1. Wm Dickenson. 21, to Sara D., nep. & n. of k. of W. D., of B., ba. 3

Jan. Tobias Holden. Last day, to Hester Billington, wife of John B., the sister of T. H., of B., ba. 5

May 1661. Sir $Rich^d$ Peers. 18, to Dame Mary P., wid., the rel. of Sir R. P., of B., Knt. 47

May. Andrew Smith. 24, to James S., the F. of A. S., ba., in B. 49

July. Jenkin Gammon. 1, to Anthony Tutchen, C^r of J. G., l. of Poplar, but in B. 68

[There are very many entries of "in partibus ultramarinis" with no place named.]

folio.

Oct. Cha. Moore. 9, to Joyce M., wid., the rel. of C. M., l. of B. 99

Nov. Sir Marmaduke Roydon al's Rawdon, Knt. 18, to Ambrose Bennet & Rich. Walcott, Crs of Sir M. R., l. of L., merch^t, but at Wallingford, co. Berks, dec^d, resident of Hoddesdon, co. Hertf.

[1662 is missing.]

1663.

March. John Segnior. 10, to Mary S., the M. of J. S., ba., in B. 33

May. John Lea. 6, to Judith Lea, wid., the M., & Joan Brockett, consobrinus of J. L., in B., ba. 57

July. Tho. Andrews. 22, to Jonathan A., the F. of T. A., of B., ba. 80

July. Edward Cranfield. 10, to Edw. C., the son of E. C., l. of B., left unad. by Mary Peasley al's C., the M. Previous adm'ons in Ap. 1658, Ap. 1653 & Dec. 1649. 83

Sept. Jas. Young. 25, to Rich. Devon, Cr of J. Y., of J. 93

Oct. Sam. Thompson. 24, to Sir Tho. Gonne, Knt, Cr of S. T., in the B. 108

1664.

[Folios not numbered in this vol.]

Jan. Edward Tomes. 13, to W. T., the Bro. of E. T., of J., ba.

March. John Kippax. 21, to Rob. Andrewes, consobrinus & next of kin of J. K., at the Barbathoes, ba., Egbert K. & Edward K., the brothers dying.

March. Egbert Kippax. 21, to Rob. Andrewes, etc., of E. K., of St. Olave's, Hart Str.

March. Simon Gostlin. 21, to Mary G., rel. of S. G., at the B.

April. James Larkin. 18, to Alice L., rel. of J. L., l. of St Botolph without Aldgate, but at J.

April. Will. Culvyn. 21, to Nich. C., the Bro. of W. C., l. at Mevis, ba.

April. Will. Pardoe. 26, to Sarah P., wid., the rel. of W. P., at Mevis.

May. Rich. Sheffeild. 26, to Rich. S., cousin german of R. S., s. of Wm. S., cit. & tallow chaundler of L., l. in J., ba.

June. Mathew Yate. 2, to John Y., the F. of M. Y., l. of B., at sea.

July. Arthur Towne. 5, to John T., the Bro. of A. T., at J., ba.

July. John Drowne. 19, to Shem Turner, Cr of J. D., at le B.

Nov. Tho. Edson. 24, to Ellen E., paternal aunt & next of kin of T. E., l. of B., ba.

1665.

May. Robert Stampe. 30, to Wm Clarke, Cr of R. S., at B. 74

July. John Foster. 7, to Tho. F., the Bro. of J. F., l. of the ship called Mevis and Antego, at sea. 96

1666.*

Aug. Fabian Hill. Last day, to John Clements, Cr of F. H., l. of L., but at J. 157

Nov. Tho. Calverley. 27, to Wm Skynner, Cr of T. C., l. of Kingston on Hull, but in B. 205

Dec. Wm Leeds. 4, to Lambert Leeds, maternal uncle of W. L., "nuper in Insula St Christopheri, London" (*sic*). 228

---

* In this vol. there are names of many ships and mariners, but not of places.

Welch of Jamaica.

ARMS.—*Azure, three mullets Or.*

Richard Welch, barr.-at-l., Chief Justice of J'ca 1779, of Hyde and Georgia; died 15 Oct. 1782, aged 49; bur. in Bath Abbey (*ante*, II., 230). Will dated 23 March 1781, then of Upper Wimple Str.; proved 29 Oct. 1782 (525, Gostling). = Lucretia Mary Favel, eldest dau. of Geo. Dehany by Mary Gregory his wife; bapt. 21 March 1751; mar. 23 Jan. 1769; died July 1813. W.I. Bookplates, No. 562.

A

Richard Welch, born 1770, s. and h., barr.-at-l., of Hyde estate; matric. from Christ Ch., Oxf., 7 Oct. 1786, aged 16; B.A. 1790; died 1809; bur. at Swainston. Will dated 2 Oct. 1806; proved 2 May 1809 (417, Loveday). = Alice Anne, dau. of Rev. Nath. Preston of Swainstone, co. Meath; died at Exmouth 10 Oct. 1847.

John Gregory Welch, born 1776; of Arle House, Cheltenham; died 12 Jan. 1854, aged 78. = Frances Asser, dau. of Tho. White of Alstone, co. Glouc.

Children of Richard Welch and Alice Anne: Arthur. — Rob. Gregory. | Mary Eliz., named 1802 in the will of her great-grandmother Mrs. Dehany. | Geraldine. — Anne Louisa.

Geo. Asser White Welch, born 1800, of Arle House, J.P., D.L. Essex, J.P. Glouc.; matric. from Magd. Coll., Oxf., 8 Feb. 1821, aged 21: died 8 Feb. 1874. = Anne Cath. Gardiner, dau. and h. of Lt.-Col. Mannooch; mar. 1828.

Geo. Asser White Welch, born 1829, Capt. R.N., of Arle House, J.P. Glouc.; living 1901 (*v.* Walford). = Mary Cath., youngest dau. of Major England; mar. 1864.

Geo. Asser White Welch, born 1865.

The above pedigree has been taken from Add. MS. 27,968, fo. 196, to which additions have been now made.

Richard Welch of Upper Wimpole str., Esq. Will dated 23 March 1780-1. All my estate to Philip Dehany of this Kingdom. Jas. Pinnock of J'ca, John Allen of Berners str., Rob. Cooper Lee of Bedford sq. and John Grant of J'ca, Esq[rs], to pay my wife Lucretia Mary £500 st. yearly and £3,000 c. out of the bonds granted me by Rich[d] Brissett, Esq., for the purchase of Georgia est. and the remainder of the bonds to my children equally Richard my eldest son included. My trustees out of the annual produce of my Hyde est. and all other my est. in J'ca to maintain them and they to have the use of my leasehold house I now live in. To each of my four daus. Mary Eliz. Lucretia Favel Jane and Georgia* £2,500 st. at age or marriage. All residue to my s. Rich[d]. To a reputed son in J'ca named John Welch £100 c. My trustees and my wife Ex'ors and G.

* Owing to the wording and absence of punctuation it is difficult to sort the names.

Proved 29 Oct. 1782 by J. A., R. C. L., Esq^{res}, and L. M. W. the relict. Power reserved to P. D., J. P. and J. G. Proved 29 Nov. 1782 by P. D., Esq. (525, Gostling.)

Richd Welch of Marylebone, Esq. Will dated 2 Oct. 1806. My wife Alice Anne and ch^n all my personal estate in J. Philip Dehany of Hayes Pl., Kent, Esq., etc., all real est. on trust for my 1st s. Arthur, 2^d s. Rob. Gregory W., daus. Mary Eliz. W., Geraldine W. and Anne Louisa W. Estate of Hyde in St Tho. in the Vale. Proved 2 May 1809. (417, Loveday.)

Robert Gregory, died infant. — Mary, 1st dau.; mar. Tho. Reignold of the Scots Greys. He was killed at Waterloo in 1815.	Eliz. Lucretia, born 1774; mar. 1815, at Dorchester, Sir Wm. L. G. Thomas, 4th Bart., of Dale Park, co. Sussex. He was born 1778 and died 24 Aug. 1850 She died 21 Jan. 1848, aged 74. Both bur. and M.I. at Radipole, Dorset (*ante*, IV., 182).	Favel, died spr. 1798. — Jane, 4th dau.; mar., Aug 1800, Sir Rob. Lewis Fitzgerald, K.C.H., Vice-Adm. R.N. He died at Bath 17 Jan. 1844, aged 68.	Georgina, 5th dau.; died spr. Oct. 1816 at East Cowes.

1816, Oct. 24. At Sir Geo. Thomas's bart. East Cowes, Miss Welsh, sister of Lady Thomas. ("G.M.," 470.)

Jamaica, St. Tho. in the Vale, 1823:—

Richard Welch, Hill Side 142 slaves 38 stock.
" " Hyde 150 " 141 "

1844, Jan. 17. At Bath, aged 68, Vice-Admiral Sir Robert Lewis Fitzgerald, K.C.H. Served at J'ca .... m. in Aug. 1800, Jane, a dau. of Richd Welch, esq. f. Chief Justice of the island of J'ca & sister to the lady of Sir Geo. Thomas, Bart. &c. ("G.M.," 319.)

1847, Oct. 10. At Exmouth, at an advanced age. Alice Anne, relict of Rd. Welsh of Hyde J. esq. & dau. of the Rev. Nath. Preston of Swainstone, co. Meath. (*Ibid.*, 554.)

1854, Jan. 12. At Cheltenham, aged 78, John Gregory Welch, esq. l. of Arle House, a magistrate of the co. of Glouc. (*Ibid.*, 331.)

Mary Dehany of Devonshire Str., wid. 23 Oct. 1802. Whereas I have paid my s. Geo. ¼ of the proceeds of sale of the moiety of Swansea pl. in J'ca, the other ¾ to be paid to those entitled to the same. To my grandch^n Mary Reynolds, Eliz. Lucretia Thomas, Jane Fitzgerald and Georgina Welch 50 g^{ns} each. To my great-grand-dau. Mary Eliz. Welch 20 g^{ns}. To my grand-daus. Mary Scott, Eliz. Favell Pinnock and Lucretia Pinnock 50 gns. ea. To my great-grand-dau. Mary Pinnock Scott 20 g^{ns}. My grandsons John Lee Allen and Jas. Allen 50 g^{ns} ea. My s. Geo. 100 g^{ns} and to my grandch^n Wm Knight Delany, Eliz. Whitehorne D. and Mary Favell D. 50 g^{ns} ea. Of residue ½ to my dau. Luc^a Mary Welch and sole Ex'trix, and ½ to my dau. Eliz. Pinnock.

Codicil. The ¾ of proceeds of sale of Swansea pl. I have laid out in the purch. of £8,500 4 per cent. ann. for my 3 other ch^n in names of myself and of Geo. Scott and Lestock Wilson. 17 March 1808.

2nd Codicil. 22 Jan. 1811. Linen to my dau. L. M. Welch, dau.-in-l. Sarah D., grandson Wm K^t^ D., great-grandson John Jas. Scott, great-grand-dau. Mary Pinnock Scott, great-grandson Matthew Rob. Scott.

3rd Codicil. 17 Feb. 1811. My dau. Luc. M. W. is indebted to me in £500 and £200.

4th Codicil. 15 Sept. 1811. Great-grand-dau. Sophia Thomas, dau.-in-l. Sarah D.

5th Codicil. Dau. Eliz. Pinnock to be also Ex'trix. Grand-dau. Luc. P. 5 July 1812.

Proved 20 Aug. 1813 by Eliz. P., the dau. and surv. Ex'trix. Testatrix l. of Cumberland Str. (411, Heathfield.)

See pedigree *Ante*, III., 290, to which this is an addition.

Rawlins of St. Kitts and Nevis.

(*Ante*, p. 191.)

TRINITY, PALMETTO POINT.

It is obvious that in the second entry of 30 Nov. 1754 the year should read 1755. Mr. Bromley having been pressed for time did not make all his extracts verbatim, but having now lent me his transcript of the Register I repeat some of the entries in their fuller form wth the names of sponsors:—

1787	June 22	Stedman & Ann Taylor s. & dau. of Stedman & Eliz^th^ Rawlins from Middle Island.
		Also Sarah Worthington & Mary Johnson daus. of Henry & Eliz^th^ Rawlins from M. Isl^d^.
1795	May 2	John Hart s. of John & Sarah Johnson Rawlins, b. Apr. 9, 1795. Godfathers: Henry Hart, Henry Rawlins & Richard Rawlins, Esquires. Godmothers: Miss Henrietta Hart, Mrs Eliz^th^ Young & Mrs Ann Akers.
1797	Feb. 7	Sarah Ann dau. of John & Sarah Johnson Rawlins, b. Oct. 18, 1796. Godfathers: Edward Gilliard, Esq., Joseph Rawlins, Esq., by his friend John Rawlins, Esq., & Anthony Hart, Esq, by his friend Anthony Young, Esq. Godmothers: Mrs Mary Sprott, Mrs Margaret Richards & Mrs Ann Hart.
1807	Feb. 3	Stedman inf^t^ s. of the Honble Stedman & Gertrude Rawlins, b. Sept. 5, 1806. Godfathers: Henry Rawlins & the Honble James Tyson, Esq. Godmothers: Mrs Eliz^th^ Rawlins & Margaret Tyson.
1812	April 7	Henry inf^t^ s. of Stedman Rawlins, Senr, Esq., & his wife Ann Taylor.
1813	Feb. 3	(Privately) Thos Charles Corry (b. Sept. 11, 1812), s of the Hon. Stedman Rawlins & his wife Gertrude.
1813	Feb. 24	John James s. of Stedman Rawlins, Senr, Esq., & his wife Ann Taylor.
1823	Aug. 9	Sarah Swanston dau. of John Hart Rawlins, Esq., & Martha Hart his wife. Godfathers: Hon. S. Rawlins, Hon. Ja^s^ Davoren & Thos Swanston, Esq. Godmothers: .... Rawlins, Junr, Mrs Swanston, Miss Rebecca Young.
1826	Jan. 22	Eliz^th^ Martha, b. Dec. 26, 1825, dau. of John Hart Rawlins, Esq., & Martha Hart his wife. Sponsors: Eliz^th^ Hart, Mrs Henry Hart and Henry Wilson, Esq.

The entries of 1814, Jan. 1, and 1826, Nov. 20, do not appear in the transcript.

Herbert of Nevis.

Mountserat. Edward Herbert of Bristoll, merch[t], now upon the Island aforesaid. Will dated fift July 1684. To my wife Anne all goods in her hands in Bristoll, with one eight part of the ship "Mary" of Bristoll, M[r] W[m] Whetstone, com[r], also 50,000 lbs. of sugar from here. To my natural brother Abram Herbert, mariner, my fourth part of the ship "Patience" of Bristoll. To Edmund Ellis my new tenement in the possession of M[r] Broome. To John Atwood the next and lower tenement, with my black horse. E. Ellis to continue in my plantacon and storehouse business until his apprenticeship be expired. To M[rs] Mary Liddell my new feather bed, etc., in my storehouse. Further to E. E. 10,000 lbs. of muscovada sugar. To my natural sister Eliz. Pumfret £50, to be paid her by Cap[t] Humphry South of London. My son Tho. H. to be sole Ex'or and all my estate real and personal to him, viz., all my goods in the hands of Capt. H. South, my plantacon, viz., my part thereof, a storehouse at Plymouth in M., and negroes, my other houses and lands here and debts due in the W. I., proceeds to be sent to Capt. South to invest for my son at 18, he to be sent to school if Capt. South die, then my wife Anne to have full possession of my son and estate, she to then give good security to M[r] Sam Wood of Bristoll, sugar baker, but if my son die under 18 said estate to my nephew Edward H. son of my brother Wm. H., he paying to each of his brothers and sisters £30, and to my sister Eliz. Pumfrett £30. Capt. Tho. Ellis, John Bramley and L[t] Geo. Liddell to be overseers. To my loving friends Capt. H. South, Capt. T. Ellis, M[r] S. Wood, J. Bramley, M[r] G. Liddell and M[rs] Mary wife of s[d] Geo. Liddell £5 each. In the p. of Phil. Brome, John Attwood, London, y[e] 2 of Oct. 1684, lately arrived from M., sick and weak. To my brother Abr. H. £100 and a debt of £30 due from Walter Rumzey, chyrurgeon. Commission 15 July 1685 to Ann H. the mother and guardian of Tho. H., a minor, the son and ex'or. On 4 Jan[y] 1699 proved by Tho. H. the son and ex'or. (88, Cann.)

Tho. Harvey of Bristol, gent. Will dated .... To my dau.-in-law Martha Parsons £200. My friend Tho. Tovy of Nevis £100. All residue to my wife Mary and son Thomas H. Proved 1691. (192, Vere.)

James Lytton of Nevis, and Camberwell, co. Surrey. Will dated 1718. My niece Sarah Herbert and nephews Tho. H. and Joseph H., dau. and sons of my brother-in-law. Tho. H. and my sister Dorothy his wife. Niece Sarah Browne. Nephew W[m] Carpenter. (51, Browning.)

Wm. Fenton, late of S[t] Chr., now of Northaw, co. Herts, Esq. Will dated 1 July 1753. All estate to my dau. Jane and her heirs, and in default to Joseph Herbert, Esq., Judge of Nevis. His son Horatio Herbert. (131, Pinfold.)

Robert Thompson of S[t] Chr., gent. Will dated .... 1753. My son-in-law George Herbert and Mary my dau. his wife. Adm'on 8 Jan. 1776 to her, a widow. (41, Bellas.)

Tho. Williams of Nevis, Esq. Will dated 20 Sept. 1766. To my niece Eliz. wife of the Hon. John Richardson Herbert 5 negros, and to Martha Williams Herbert their dau. £1500 c. at 21. One moiety of my plantation in Antigua to the said Mrs. Eliz. Herbert. Proved 8 July 1767. (290, Legard.)

Joseph Herbert, esq. Will dated 8 Aug. 1767. My s. Horatio, s. Tyrrell £500, dau. Mary H. £700, dau. Sarah H. £500. dau. Ann H. £500, dau. Fra. Campbell £500, dau. Lucretia Pemberton £500, dau. Amillia Brodbelt £20. My grandchⁿ the sons and daus. of my s. George in England £100 each. My granddau. Sally H. 10,000 lbs.; her sister Emma. All residue to my s. Edwᵈ H. Sworn 16 Dec. 1767. (Nevis Book of Wills, p. 184.)

Eliz. Hulberd late of Nevis now of Bath, co. Somerset, widow. Will dated 23 Nov. 1769. To my brother Horatio Herbert £350 c. To my sisters Mary Herbert, Sarah Herbert, Amelia Brodbelt, Frances Campbell and Lucretia Pemberton £235 c. each. To Sarah and Emma Herbert daus. of my brother Joseph Herbert, deceased, £235 c. equally. To Mary, Lucretia, Harriot, Eliza and Joseph Herbert the children of my brother George Herbert, deceased, £235 c. equally. To Mary Amelia Nisbet dau. of Walter Nisbet of Nevis, Esq., a mulatto girl. To my friends John Mills the Younger, of Great Sᵗ Helen's, merchant, Edward Parris and John Ward of Nevis, Esquires, all my plantations, negros, cattle, etc., for my brothers Edward and Tyrrell Herbert equally. Trustees to be Ex'ors. Witnessed by Arthur Hele, Mary Clapp, R. Brigden Fowell.

Codicil, dated 1 April 1770. Mʳ and Mʳˢ Hele of Bath my tea-table. My 2 nephews George and Richard Brodbelt suits of mourning. My sister Brodbelt 2 pairs of silver candlesticks. Witnessed by John Jarman, Richᵈ Brodbelt. Proved 10 April 1770 by John Mills, power reserved to the others. (147, Jenner.) (Recorded in Nevis Book of Wills, p. 584.)

Tho. Neale late of Sᵗ Vincent now of Nevis, esq. Will dated 19 June 1773. My wife Henrietta, my sister Ann Herbert, my sister Henrietta wife of John H., nephew John H., £5000. Sworn 16 Sept. 1773. (Nevis Book of Wills, p. 333.)

Ann Herbert, spr. Will dated 20 Sept. 1779. My sister Frances Iles, widow, ⅓ of Old Herberts. Sworn 22 Sept. 1783. (Nevis Book of Wills, p. 578.)

John Richardson Herbert, President of Nevis, now residing in Cavendish Sq. Will dated 24 Dec. 1788. To John Lane and Tho. Fraser of Nicholas Lane, L., Mᵗˢ, Evan Baillie of Bristol, Mᵗ, James Stevens of Sᵗ Chr., Esq., bar.-at-law, now residing in L., and James Huggins of N., Esq., Ex'ors, and £50 each. To Aves Cocker of Little Stanhope Str., May Fair, spr., £100 for a ring. My niece Sarah wife of Wᵐ Kelly of Plymouth, Capt. R.N., £1500, and my goddau., her only chᵈ £500 at 16. My dau. Martha Williams Hamilton wife of Wᵐ* H. of Henrietta Str., Covent Garden, now gone to the W.I., the use of all my furniture and plate, in trust after her death for her 1ˢᵗ s. Whereas I have allowed my niece Frances wife of Horatio Nelson, Capt. R.N. £100 a year. I give her £3000, and to Josiah Nesbitt s. of sᵈ F. N. by a former husbᵈ £500 at 21. To James Huggins £50 c. a year on trust for Martha wife of Mʳ Tho. Winham of N. To a free mulatto woman called Maria 3 slaves, and at her death to a free mustee called John Herbert, my reputed natural s. by her, now living at Bˡ, also to her £200 c. a year, and to him £1500. To a free mulatto man called Tho. Herbert, my reputed natural s., £300 c. My mulatto slave John Mintas his freedom and £30 a year. Whereas I have pᵈ to the Rᵗ Hon. Lord Cranstown £3000 due to him from my late brother-in-law Magnus Morton, Esq., decᵈ, upon a mortgage of an estate at N., and wishing to discharge a further £4180 due from M. M. to Wᵐ Tuckett of Bridgewater, Esq., on a mortgage of

* ? an error for Andrew.

his estate at N. I give the s[d] £3000 and £4180 to my nephew Magnus Morton the Younger of N., Esq. All residue to Trustee for my dau. to receive rents intail.

A. *Codicil.* 5 Dec. 1792. To my dau. £500 a year till legacies are paid. My niece Sarah Kelly £1000. Niece Frances Nelson £1000. Nephew M. Morton to be also an Ex'or. Witnessed by Sholto Archbald, John Williamson, Joseph Webbe Stanley,

B. *Codicil.* Of Nevis, Esq. 13 Jan. 1793. My son-in-law Andrew Hamilton, Esq., £500 a year if he survive my dau. My nephew M. M as much more as will make up his legacy to £10,000, and to be p[d] £320 c. a year for management of my estate. To John Dasent the Elder s. of John D., late of N., Esq., dec[d], £100 and £150 a year for 4 years, and to the daus. and s. of s[d] J. D., dec[d], who usually reside on this Island in the house of the estate late of their Father, £20 c. a year each for 4 years, then £250 c. each. To George D, one other s. of s[d] J. D. the elder, now in England, £10 a year till 21. My lease under Lord Le Despencer to be renewed. If my nephew Magnus Morton sh[d] inherit he shall take the name and arms of Herbert. My friend John Stanley, Esq., of N., also a Trustee and Ex'or. Witnessed by Robert Robertson Jones, John Williamson, Tho. Slaider . ., Sam. Hicks. Dep[n] of Evan Baillie that he rec[d] from John Stanley s[d] Codicils sent on 27 Jan. 1793. Proved 23 March 1793. (151, Dodwell.)

Wm. Priddie of St. Chr., Esq. Will dated 1 Dec. 1792. To Joseph Herbert, Esq., of Montserrat, and his sisters M[rs] Sconce, M[rs] Henderson and Miss Herbert £50 each, as a token of the early friendship I received of their father Capt. George Herbert. (109, Exeter.)

W[m] Mead of Nevis, Esq., petitioned on 18 Dec. 1701 that he and his wife had owned the lease of a plantation there called Harveys, now claimed by a low fellow one Tho. Herbert.

In the Col. Cal., p. 685, is also the petition of Wm. Shipman and Mary his wife and Tho. Harvey, a minor, by W. S., his guardian, to the King. Pet[rs] thro' their ancestors claiming for 15 years have possessed 2 plantations in Nevis called Harveys, to which they are jointly entitled during the life of Mary, and after her death the other moiety descends to Tho. Harvey. Tho. Herbert pretending some title, encouraged by Gov[r] Codrington, ejected (Wm.) Mead, their tenant. An appeal was allowed, yet Mead's crop, worth £3000, was seized.

Archibald Hutcheson, Att[y] Gen. of the Leeward Isles, reported on this 31 Dec. 1701 that John Mountstephen formerly owned the estate, whose widow married Barth. Harvey, who had issue Tho. Harvey, who was father to Tho. Harvey the petitioner, a minor. Adm'on of the goods of the widow of Mountstephen was granted to her 2[d] husband. Tho. Herbert is nephew and heir of the said Mountstephen. Jone wife of John Barnes was sister of John Mountstephen, since dead, s.p., and Herbert is the son of another sister. Tho. Herbert has for 15 years been endeavouring to recover his right. Tho. Harvey was living on 6 March 1688. Tho. Harvey, a minor, now or late of Bristol, gent.

This plantation was formerly rented at £100 per annum to one M[r] Eddy, and since to the pet[r] Mead, who married Eddy's widow. (The result of the appeal does not appear.)

1677-8. Census of Nevis. Thomas Herbert.

1707-8. Census of St. Kitts. Joseph Herbert, Jun[r], aged 25: 1 white man, 1 woman, 1 boy, 1 girl and 1 negro.

Census of Nevis. Tho. Herbert: 1 white male, 3 females, 4 negro males and 6 females. Anne Herbert: 3 white males, 2 females, 4 negro males and 6 females.

Arms.—*Per pale Azure and Gules, three lions rampant.* (Seal of J. R. Herbert.)

Note.—It is uncertain whether Dorothy Lytton married Thomas son of Edward Herbert or Thomas son of Thomas Herbert. There are other doubtful points in the pedigree.

Bartholomew Harvey, ad'mor of his wife's estate. 2nd husband. = ..., died intestate. = John Mountstephen of Nevis, planter, 1655; dead 1688, leaving his nephew Tho. Herbert, his heir.

Anne Mountstephen, living in Bristol 1684. = Edward Herbert of Bristol, merchant. Will dated in Montserrat 5 July 1684, codicil 2 Oct. 1684 in L.; proved 15 July 1685 (88, Cann).

Thomas Harvey of Harveys in Nevis and of Bristol, gent. Will dated at Nevis; proved 1691 (192, Vere). = Mary . . . ., remar. Wm. Shipman.

Thomas Herbert of Nevis, born 1678; only son and heir and a schoolboy 1684, aged 21 in 1699; claimant 1701; (? in census of 1707-8; M. of C. 1738, and died 1750). = Dorothy Lytton, dau. of Major Henry Lytton; born 1682-3; mar. 1699; died 16 Jan. 1721, aged 41. Had ten sons and seven daus. M.I.

A

Frances . . . ., bur. 28 June 1736. 1st wife. = Thos. Herbert of Nevis, Esq. = Ann Williams, spr., mar. 31 Jan. 1741-2. 2nd wife.

Joseph Herbert, living 1718; bur. 19 April 1731.

Wm. Litton Herbert, bapt. 9 Sept. 1716.

Charles Herbert, bapt. 30 Nov. 1718.

B

Hon. John Richardson Herbert, bapt. 21 Dec. 1732; M. of C. 1757, President 25 years; died 18 and bur. 19 Jan. 1793 at Figtree. Will (151, Dodwell). = Eliz., dau. of Col. John Williams of Antigua; bapt. 1 Feb. 1734; mar. 1752; died 29 Sept. 1769, aged 35. M.I.

. . . . = Magnus Morton, Esq., dead 1788.

Martha Williams Herbert, only child and heiress, mar. 18 May 1787. = Andrew Hamilton, Esq., President of Gen. Council of Leeward Islands 1798; died 3 April 1808. M.I. s.p.

Magnus Morton-Herbert, nephew and heir of J. R. Herbert, whose surname and arms he took; died at Brussels 31 Oct. 1834. = Christiana Forbes, mar. 6 April 1792; died 3 Mar. 1835 in London.

1715. No. 79. Private. An Act to settle the estate of Tho. Herbert, eldest s. of Mr Tho. H., deceased, on him and his heirs and assigns for ever. (Printed Book of Acts, p. 75.)

1718. Jos. Herbert then a Member of the Assembly of Nevis

1721. No. 87. Private. An Act for the settling an Estate in fee-simple of and in the lands and tenements, negroes and other the appurtenances which were of Tho. Herbert, late of this Island, decd, in his 3 sons John, Wm. and Jos.

H., and for the confirming the estate of John Richardson, Esq., and John Smith, planter, purchasers of part of the s[d] estate from and under the s[d] John H. (Book of Acts, p. 90.)

1727. Tho. Herbert, S[r], then an inhabitant of Nevis.

1738, Oct. 21. Tho. Herbert, Esq., sworn in as a Member of Council. (B. T., Leeward Islands, vol. 26.)

1741. Jan. 27. Tho. Herbert of N., esq., about to marry Ann Williams, spr., covenants to settle 10,000 lbs. a year. Recorded 3 June 1749. (Nevis Deeds, iii., p. 272.)

Horatio Herbert. Notary public and Dep. Secretary. 1749. (*Ibid.*)

1749. A mandamus for Joseph Herbert to be of the C[l] was signed at Kensington. (America and W.I., vol. 103.)

Thomas Herbert of Nevis 1677, dead 1715.=

John Herbert.	Will. Herbert.	Joseph Herbert.	Thomas Herbert, 1st son and heir of Thos.; his paternal estate settled on him by Act of 1715.

All three named in Act of 1721.

A

John Herbert, Esq., of Nevis, bapt. 20 Aug. 1719; sold 115 acres in 1752. = Henrietta . . . ., ? sister of Tho. Neale 1773; died at Bath 10 July 1813.	Henrietta Herbert, bapt. 19 Jan. 1720-1. — James Herbert, bapt. 12 June 1722.	Henry Herbert, Esq., bapt. 1 Dec. 1723; ? died intestate 1762—7. = Ann . . . ., ? of St. Kitts.	Frances Herbert. Adm'on 20 May 1762 to her brother Henry. — Sarah Herbert.

John Herbert, living 1773.

B

Thomas Herbert, bur. 23 July 1734.	Sarah Herbert, died 5 Sept. 1785, aged 53. M.I.	Mary Herbert, mar. Wm. Woolward, Esq. He died 18 Feb. 1779. M.I. Parents of Lady Nelson.

. . . . Herbert, Capt. 48th regiment=

Magnus Will. Morton-Herbert, born 1859; at Charterhouse 1872, later army student.

1751, Sep. 27. Joseph Herbert of Nevis, Jun[r], enters into bond of £2000 with Roger Pemberton to abide by arbitration. J. H. was administrator of the estate of Simon Brown, Esq. His (J. H.'s) wife's name was Sarah. In 1767 the Hon J. H., Esq., was President and Ordinary of Nevis, and in 1762 Horatio H. and Lucretia Pemberton were appointed guardians of her s. Jos. Herbert P., and by petition of 23 Aug. 1767 the minor stated Horatio H. was residing beyond the sea and asked that Walter Nisbet and Ed. Herbert, Esq[res], might be his guardians.

Hon. Joseph Herbert, born 1689; Chief Justice 1754, President; bur. at St. John's 7 Oct. 1767, aged 78 (?). Will dated 8 Aug. and sworn 16 1767; recorded in Nevis. = Elizabeth . . . ., bur. 26 Jan. 1763, aged 64.

A

Edward Herbert, 1st son and heir, born 13 and bapt. 26 April 1731; insolvent 1775.

Tyrrell Herbert, born 4 March and bapt. 2 April 1733; bur. 9 Nov. 1791 at St. Geo., Antigua, intestate; inv. £2080.

George Herbert, a Captain, dead 1769. = Mary, dau. of Rob. Thompson of St. Kitts and his ad'trix 1776.

Joseph Herbert, ad'mor 1751 of Simon Browne, Esq. = Sarah, widow of Simon Browne; mar. 30 Aug. 1741; living 1751. (*Ante*, I., 269.)

Hon. Joseph Herbert, born 1758; President of Montserrat forty years; of 3 Devonshire St. and Agent for Nevis 1779; died 20 Dec. 1836, aged 78. M.I. at Dover. = ..., died at Montserrat 3 Dec. 1795.

Mary Herbert.
—
Lucretia Herbert.
—
Harriet Herbert.
—
Eliza Herbert.

Eliz. Herbert, bur. 26 July 1745.
—
Sarah Herbert.
—
Emma Herbert.

Mary Ellis Herbert, eldest dau., mar. at Leyton, co. Essex, 22 Nov. 1808 Rev. E. Repton.

1752, Dec. 1. John Herbert of Nevis, Esq., sells to Jer. Browne of S[t] Chr., Esq., 2 pl[ns] of 69 a. and 48 a. (Nevis Deeds, vol. v., p. 34.)

1754, June 21. At the Court of Kensington Jos. Herbert was appointed Chief Justice *vice* John Dasent, Esq., dec[d].

1757, Dec. 6. A mandamus appointing John Richardson Herbert to the C[l] was signed at the Court of S[t] James.

1760. Memorial of Joseph Herbert, Chief Justice, who has been impeached by the Assembly. Received Jan. 24.

Pet[n] of Ann Herbert of S[t] Chr., widow, that Henry H., your petitioner's late husband, obtained adm'on on 20 May 1762 of the estate of his sister Frances H. Hen. H. has died intestate. (Nevis Deeds, p. 173.)

Petition of the Hon. John Richardson Herbert that adm'on of the will of Frances H. was granted to her brother Henry H., esq., now dead. Adm'on now granted 10 July 1767. (Nevis Book of Wills, p. 170.)

1768, Jan. Lately. Hon. Joseph Herbert, Esq., president of the Island of Nevis. ("G.M.," 47.)

1775. Edward Herbert, an insolvent debtor, eldest s. of the late President, from whom he inherited a very considerable patrimony, has had great misfortune.

1799. Tyrrell Herbert and Jos. H. were witnesses to the will of Arthur Freeman, Esq., of Antigua.

1785. The seal on a letter written by the Hon. John Richardson Herbert, President, bears: *Per pale Azure and Gules 3 lions rampant.* (B.T., Leeward Islands, vol. 39.)

1793, Jan. 18. In the island of Nevis, John Richardson Herbert, esq., president of his Majesty's council in that island. ("G.M.," 373.)

Ind're of 1793 between Joseph Herbert of Montserratt, Esq., and Tyrrell H. of the Island of Antigua, Esq. (Antigua Records Lib., x., vol. 5.)

1795, Dec. 3. At Montserrat, in the W.I., Mrs. Herbert, the lady of the Hon. Joseph H., esq., of that island. ("G.M.," 1796, 168.)

1797. Leave of absence given to President Jos. Herbert.

1799. Jos. Herbert was then of 3 Devonshire Str., and acting as Agent for Nevis.

1808, Nov. 22. At Layton, Essex, the Rev. E. Repton to Mary Ellis, eldest

A

Horatio Herbert, Dep. Sec. 1749; not in Nevis 1767. =Sarah .... Peter Matthew Mills Herbert, bapt. 29 July 1764 at St. George Basseterre.	Eliz. Herbert, mar. 19 July 1747 Nath. Hulberd.* Her will dated at Bath 23 Nov. 1769; proved 19 April 1770 (147, Jenner). — Mary Herbert. — Sarah Herbert.	Ann Herbert, bur. 7 March 1769, aged 41. — Amelia Herbert, born 25 and bapt. 31 Aug. 1729; mar. 1 Jan. 1755 James Brodbelt.	Frances Herbert, mar. 10 June 1760 Geo. Campbell. — Lucretia Herbert, mar. 1 Jan. 1760 Sam. Clarke Pemberton. He was bur. 30 Nov. 1761 at St. George.

dau. of the Hon. Joseph Herbert, president of H.M. Council of the island of Montserratt. ("G.M.," 1039.)

1813, July 10. At Bath, Mrs. Henrietta Herbert, widow of the late John H., Esq., of Nevis. (*Ibid.*, 93.)

1813, Oct. 21, Sat., was mar. Archibald Paul, esq., of St. Christopher's, to Miss E. Herbert of Bath-Hampton. (Bath Chronicle.)

1830, March 17. At Jamaica, aged 29, John Cottle Herbert, 5th s. of the late R. M. H. of Bristol. (*Ibid.*, 651.)

1834, Oct. 31. At Brussels, Magnus Morton Herbert, esq., of the I. of Nevis. ("G.M.," 1835, 446.)

1835, April. On the 3rd ult. in Montagu Street, Portland Square, Christiana, relict of the late Magnus Morton Herbert of the I. of Nevis, Esq. (Court Mag.)

1836, Dec. 20. At Dover, aged 78, Joseph Herbert, esq., late President of the island of Montserrat. ("G.M.," 1837, 220.)

1847, Oct. 12. In Oxford-terr., aged 57, Horatio Herbert. ("G.M.," 553.)

ST. JOHN'S FIGTREE, NEVIS.†

Baptisms.

1729	Aug. 31	Amelia dau. of Joseph Herbert, Esq., & Elizabeth his wife. Born ye 25th ins. & Baptized this day.
1731	April 26	Edward s. of Joseph Herbert, Esq., & Elizabeth his wife. Born ye 13 instant & Baptized this day.
1733	April 2	Tyrrell s. of Joseph Herbert, Esq., & Elizabeth his wife. Born Mar. 4 last past and Baptized this day.
1751	Dec. 29	William & Mary, Mulattoe children of William Herbert, baptized.
1773	June 20	Ann White, a natural dau. of Joseph Brown Herbert by Sarah, a negro woman belonging to Miss Sally Pemberton, and her mother were baptized.
1784	Dec. 26	James & Elizabeth s. & dau. of Joseph Brown Herbert.
1787	Sep. 8	Walter s. of Joseph Brown Herbert.

* 1727 May 7 Nathaniel s. of Edward Hulbird. Bapt. (Bath Abbey).

† See *ante*, Vol. I.

MARRIAGES.

1745 April 7 Robte Pemberton & Ann Herbert.
1747 July 19 Nathl Hulburd & Eliz. Herbert.
1755 Jan. 1 James Brodbelt & Emilia Herbert.
1760 Jan. 1 Samuel Clarke Pemberton & Lucretia Herbert.
1769 June 10 George Campbell & Frances Herbert.
1787 May 18 Andrew Hamilton, Esquire, to Martha Herbert, Spinster.
1792 Apr. 6 Magnus Morton, Esquire, and Christiana Forbes, Spinster.

BURIALS.

1749 June 7 Joanna Herbert.
1759 June 17 Anne Herbert. 58.
1763 Jan. 26 Elizabeth wife of the Honble Joseph Herbert, Esq., President, 64.
1767 Oct. 7 The Honble Joseph Herbert, Esqr. Aged 7 . . (? 78).
1769 Mar. 7 Anne Herbert, Spinster, aged 41 y.
1769 Sept. 30 Mrs Elizabeth Herbert, aged 34 years.
1789 Nov. 12 Joseph Browne Herbert, Mulatto.
1793 Jan. 19 J. R. Herbert.

ST. JAMES', NEVIS.

1745 July 26 Elizth Herbert daugr of Jos. Herbert, buried.

ST. GEORGE'S GINGERLAND, NEVIS.*

MARRIAGES.

1741 Aug. 30 Joseph Herbert & Sarah Browne. Lic.
1741-2 Jan. 31 Thomas Herbert & Ann Williams.

BURIALS.

1731 April 19 Joseph S. of Thomas Herbert, Senr, and Dorothy his Wife.
1734 July 23 Thomas S. of " " Junr, and Frances his Wife.
1736 June 28 Frances wife of Thos. Herbert, junr.
1738 Sept. 9 Anne Herbert wife of Thomas Herbert.
1795 Mar. 28 Jane Herbert.

BAPTISMS.

1716 Sept. 9 William Litton S. of Thomas Herbert by Dorothy his wife.
1718 Nov. 30 Charles s. of Mr Thomas Herbert, Senr, by Dorothy his wife.
1719 Aug. 20 John the S. of " " Senr, " "
1720-1 Jan. 19 Henrietta dau. of " " Senr, " "
1722 June 12 James the S. of " " " "
1723 Dec. 1 Henry the S. of " " " "
1730 Jan. 28 Sarah D. of " " Junr, and Frances his wife.
1732 Dec. 21 John Richardson S. of Thomas Herbert, Junr, and Frances his wife.

ST. GEORGE'S BASSETERRE, ST. KITTS.

1764 July 29 Peter Matthew Mills s. of Horatio & Sarah Herbert, bapt.

ST. JOHN'S, ANTIGUA.

1774 July 29 Edward Herbert, buried.

* *Ante*, Vol. II.

ST. GEORGE'S, ANTIGUA.

1794 Nov. 9 Tyrrel Herbert, from Blackmans Estate, buried.

CAYON DIARY,* ST. KITTS.

Henry Herbert, d. in July or Aug. 1768; decline.
Miss Eliz. Herbert, born in Sept. '82.
Reid Peter Herbert, d. 18 Sept. 1787; decline.
Will. Henry Herbert, d. at sea 11 Dec. 1787; decline.
Mrs Jane Herbert, d. 1 Feb. 1790, aged 63; decline.
Miss Ann Herbert, d. 25 Mar. 1791, abt 29; decline.
Joseph Herbert, d. at St. Croix in Oct. or Nov. 1791; decline.
John Richardson Herbert, d. at Nevis 17 Jan. 1793; fever.
John Herbert, d. 5 Feb. 1793; leaprousy.†
Jos. Herbert (Montst), mar. to Miss Ann Tucket 8 Jan. '97; separated the same year.
Charles Herbert, d. 22 Oct. '3.

ST. JOHN'S FIGTREE, NEVIS.

Blue marble ledger:—

Sacred to the Memory
of
SARAH HERBERT
Daughter of THOMAS & FRANCES *HERBERT*
and Sister
To the Honble the PRESIDENT of this ISLAND.
who departed this Life *Septr* 5th 1785
Aged 53.
(20 lines omitted.)

White marble ledger with two cherubs' heads at top corners:—

Under this Stone
is Depofited
the Mortal part of
MRS ELIZABETH HERBERT,
Wife of the *Hon.ble*
JOHN RICHARDSON HERBERT *Efqr*;
Prefident of this *Ifland*.
She Died univerfally lamented
Sepr; 29th; 1769, in the 34th; Year of her
Age, & the 17th; of her Marriage.
(10 lines omitted.)

White stone:—

Sacred to the Memory of
ANDREW HAMILTON Esqr
who died on the 3d of April 1808
in the . . Year of his Age
(several lines worn away)
by his wife MARTHA WILLIAMS HAMILTON.

* *Ante*, Vol. III. † It was very rarely that whites became lepers.

ST. GEORGE'S GINGERLAND, NEVIS.

A blue marble ledger cracked across. In sunk oval a Jacobean shield blank:—

Here lieth Entomb'd M[RS] DOROTHY HERBERT, wife
of M[R] THOMAS HERBERT, of this Ifland Gen[t]: & Daughter
of Major HENRY LYTTON, of the fame Place deceafed
When living she was an Ornament to y[e] Marriage state
in which she Virtuously liv'd Twenty five years & Ten
Months, and had Iffue . . . . Sons & Seven Daughters
But to the Irreparable lofs of her Afflicted Family
Died in Childbed with her tenth Son
(6 lines)
She changed this Life for A Better JAN[RY] 16TH 1724
In the 42[d] Year of Her Age.

The late Rector, Dr. L. B. Thomas (*Ante*, II., 315), gave the arms as "Three lions rampant," but did not state they were on the stone. I took great interest in the heraldry, and would not have written "blank" had there been even traces of arms.

ST. MARY THE VIRGIN, DOVER.*

In the churchyard (copied 27 July 1901):—

IN MEMORY OF
JOSEPH HERBERT ESQ[R]
WHO WAS MORE THAN
40 YEARS PRESIDENT OF
THE ISLAND OF MONTSERRAT,
HONOURED, AND RESPECTED
DIED 20TH DECEMBER, 1836,
AGED 78 YEARS.

Halsted of Jamaica.

Mathias Halsted of London, merch[t]. Will dated 3 Aug. 1677, 29 Ch. II. "Bound out to the parts beyond the seas." All residue to Frances my wife, and make my brothers Abra. H. of Woodham Feryes, co. Essex, gent., and Chas. H. of L., grocer, Ex'ors. Proved 8 July 1679 by Cha. H; power reserved to Abr. H. Proved 4 March 1679 by Abr. H. (85, King.)

The following wills are on record in Jamaica:—

Lawrence Halstead, 1691—4, Lawr. H., Jr., 1694—7, Eliz. H., 1733, and Eliz. H., 1746.

Matthew Halsted of Jamaica, now of the Inner Temple, Esq. Will dated 8 Sept. 12 Geo. 1725. To my sister-in-law Barbara Ermin Halsted of Chelsea, widow of my late brother Gerrard H., £200 a year. My plantations called *Mowdenhall, Ducks*, and lands in the mountains called *Murmuring Brook* and *Pimento Grove*, Savanna lands to my nephew Gerrard Halsted, son of my late brother Gerrard H., remainder to my cousin Lawrance H. of J'ca, Esq. All

* Communicated July 1910 by Mr. F. Cundall, F.S.A., of Jamaica, who received it from a correspondent.

residue to my said nephew at 21. The Hon. Tho. Bernard of J'ca, Esq., Ex'or for that Island, and Mr Sam. Bernard of London, merchant, Ex'or for G. B., and £200 each and to be T. and G. Sealed (early armorial seal).

ARMS.—*Gules, an eagle displayed, a chief checky . . . .*
CREST.—*Out of a coronet a demi-eagle Ermine displayed.*

[This will, the original one, is on five folio sheets of paper in the Editor's possession.]

. . . . Halsted of Jamaica=[Mrs. H., aged 40 in 1688 (Sloane MSS.).]

[Laurence= Halsted,* M. of A. 1694 and 1716.]

John Halsted of St. Dorothy's, M. of A. for St. John=Eliz. . . . . 1706—9, St. Dorothy's 1719, St. Mary 1721. Will dated 6 Jan. 1721 (Livingston).

Lawrence= Halsted of J., Esq., cousin of Mathew H. 1720; dead 1768.

Gerrard=Barbara Ermin of Chelsea, widow, 1726. Gerrard Halsted of Chelsea, Esq., dead 1725.

Mathew Halsted, Esq., M. of A. 1726, and of the Inner Temple. Will dated 7 Mar. 1726; sworn 31 Aug. 1728.

Richd. Halsted, M. of A. 1735.

Priscilla, mar. 1729 Denis Kelly, Chf. J. 1725—47. Their only child Eliz. mar. the 1st Earl of Altamont.

Edwd. Halsted, heir 1726 to his cousin Mathew, and then in England; died 25 Dec. 1744, æt. 26, s.p. intestate. M.I. St. Cath.

Tho. Halsted, died 1745, a minor, intestate.

Sarah Grace, wife 1768 of Rd. Lewing of St. Cath., Esq.

Wm. Halsted, M. of A. 1769-70; died 1774.

Gerrard John Halsted, born 1721; matric. from Q. Coll., Oxf., 17 Dec. 1740, aged 19.

Matthew Halsted of Jamaica, gent. Will dated 7 March 13 Geo. 1726. My lands may be sold. To my nephew Gerrard H., son of my late brother Gerrard H., £3000 c. at 21, and in default to my three cousins Eliz. H., Mary Emily H. and Maximelia Emily H. My Pen in the p. of St Dorothy called the Savana Pen and my land on the Black River to Favel Peeke, Esq., of J., now in England. My *Mowden Hall* plantation in the p. of St John, and *Ducks* plantation and lands known as *Murmuring Brook* and all other lands in St Johns, lands called *Pimento Grove* in St Dorothy and all residue to my cousin Lawrence Halsted's eldest son now in England and his heirs, in default to my nephew Gerrard H. Tho. Bernard and Wm. Nedham, Esquires, to be Ex'ors for J., Mr Sam. Bernard of London, merchant, Ex'or for G. B. and £50 apiece. Sworn 31 Aug. 1728. Signed by the Secy Jos. Maxwell and Governor Robert Hunter. [From an ancient certified copy.] Endorsed: "Stephen Richard Redwood, Esqr, in Spanish Town."

Tho. Fuller of St Dorothy, J'ca, Esq. Will dated 19 Aug. 1768. Names Richd Lewing of St Cath., Esq., and his wife Sarah Grace, one of the daus. of Laurence Halsted, Esq., decd. (88, Bogg.)

* Connected with the family of Whitgift Aylmer (Archer).

1661-2, Jan. 28. William Halsted of S[t] Bride's, L., grocer, Bach., ab[t] 28, and Eliz. Bickerton of S[t] Andrews, Holborn, Sp[r], ab[t] 26; consent of father—Bickerton, of Beeby, co. Leic., Gent.; at the Temple Ch., L. (Lic. Vic. Gen. of Archb. of C.)

1669, July 14. Lawrence Halsted of the Mid. T., Gent., Bach., 28, & Alice Barcroft, Sp[r], 21, dau. of John B. of S[t] Martin in the F., Esq., who consents, at S[t] Dunstan in the E., S[t] Jas., Garlick Hithe, or S[t] Bot., Bishopsgate, L., or Wickham, co. Glouc. (Fac. Off. of Arch. of C.)

1670, April 1. Richard Halsted of S[t] Andrew's, Holborn, Gent., Bach., ab[t] 24, & Rebecca Gregory of Cornhill near the Old Exchange, L., Sp[r], ab[t] 20; her f's consent; at S[t] Dunstan's in the East. (Lic. Vic. Gen. of Archb. of C.)

1667, 9 of 10th month. Barbadoes. Church-dues demanded by Laurence Halstead. (Besse's Quakers, ii., 283.)

1674, June 10. Patent to Anthony Westgarth for 300 a. in the p. of S[t] Thomas bounded E. on Henery Halsteed. (On one skin, p. the Editor.)

1688. Mrs. Halstead of Jamaica, then aged about 40. (Sir Hans Sloane's Voyage I., cxxiii.)

1678. Edw[d] H., M[t], v. Price. (*Ante*, III., 272.)

ST. CATHERINE'S CATHEDRAL, JAMAICA.

M.I. to Edward Halstead, Esq[r], Lieut. of y[e] Troop, son of Lawrence, died 25th Dec. 1744, aged 26. (Archer, 50; Roby, 18.)

Laurence Halsted, lord of the manor of Sunning, co. Berks, Esq., 2nd son of John H. of Rowley, co. Lanc., a merchant of L., entered his pedigree in the Visitation of London 1634, when he had the following sons living: (1) Laurence, aged 12, (2) Abraham, (3) John, (4) Oliver, (5) James, (6) Mathias, and (7) William. An exemplification of arms and grant of crest made to him in 1628 is given in the Visitation of Berks (Harl. Soc. Pub., ii., 136). It is probably from one of the above sons that the Halsteds of Jamaica derive their descent.

1652, May. James Halsted. On the 5th adm'on to Laurence H., the brother to J. H., in foreign parts, bach., deceased. fo. 82.

Laurence Halsted, Dep. to Dr. Brady, Keeper of Records, Tower of London, had a grant of arms in 1688. (Grantees of Arms, p. 111, Harl. Soc. Pub.)

Sir Humfrey Forster, Bart., d. 1663, had a dau. Sophia, late wife to Laurence Halsted of . . . ., by whom she had three daus., Sophia, Anne and Mary. (Visit. of Berks 1664—6, p. 36.)

Chas. H. s. of Laurence of L., arm. of Bras. Coll., Oxf., matric. 23 March 1690-1, a. 16; d. 1732; his f. keeper of the records in the Tower.

Matthias H., gt., of Bras. Coll., Oxf., matric. 27 July 1652, stud. of the Inner T. 1664.

Gerard John H. s. of Gerard of Chelsea, arm. of Q. Coll., matric. 17 Dec. 1740, a. 19. (Foster.)

1636. Laurence Halsted of Burnely, Lancashire, s. of John H., yeoman, bred at Burneley (Mr. Aspden) for 10 years; adm. pensioner, tutor and surety Mr Fogg, 8 Nov., æt. past 18. (St. John's Coll., Camb., p. 130.)

Adm. Sir Lawrence Wm Halsted, G.C.B., C. in C. on the Jamaica station 1824—7, was son of Capt. W. A. Halsted, R.N., died 1778, and was born 2 April 1764. Died 22 April 1841. (O'Byrne's Naval Biog. Dict.)

List of Wills recorded in Barbados down to the year 1800.*

Year.	Names of Testators.
1772	Sealy, John
"	Saint Hill, Thomas
"	Swan, Sarah
"	Sanders, William
"	Stewart, John
"	Snaile, Mary
"	Shurland, Joseph Sharrett
"	Spry, Gov., William
"	Smith, John
"	Sargeant, Thomas
"	Scott, Judith
"	Shepherd, Jnr., James
1773	Sober, Abraham
"	Saer, David
"	Smith, Elizabeth
"	Sharp, Thomas
"	Settle, Richard
"	Stuart, John
"	Shaw, John
"	Stevens, John
1774	Skute, Elizabeth
"	Smethweek, William
"	Sesnett, William
"	Squires, Deborah
"	Sergeant, Richard
"	Stoute, Jane
"	Sherson, Elizabeth Mary
"	Sandeford, Richard
"	Speght, Grant
"	Stevenson, Alexander
1775	Snooke, Margaret
"	Smith, Margaret
"	Steward, Sarah
"	Southwell, Benjamin
"	Smith, John
"	Sandeford, Alexander
"	Sandeford, William
1776	Staples, Mary
"	Smith, Mary
"	Shepherd, Thomas
"	Skeete, Rebecca
"	Smith, Mary
"	Skeett, Benjamin
"	Stewart, James
"	Searle, Jacob
"	Stoute, Thomas
"	Simmons, James
1777	Salter, Richard
1777	Smith, Richard
"	Straker, James
"	Skinner, Isaac
"	Scott, Elizabeth
"	Springer, William
1778	Sutton, Ann
"	Scott, Alexander
"	Straghan, Abel
"	Swane, Joseph
"	Singleton, William
"	Squires, Sarah
1779	Steele, George
"	Sheafe, John
"	Siddey, Mary
"	Sandeford, William
"	Scott, Mary Ann
"	Sinkler, Alice
1780	Smitten, Martha
"	Smethwick, Francis
"	Simmons, Henry Peter
"	Smith, John
"	Smith, Thomas
"	Shuffler, William Hoyte
"	Saer, Mary
1781	Smith, Mary
"	Springer, Richard
"	Stewart, Rebecca
"	Skeete, Ann
"	Shaw, William
"	Seymore, Edward
"	Scott, Mary
"	Smith, Henry Sacheverell
"	Smith, Margaret
1782	Swan, Joseph
"	Smith, John Harrison
"	Sharp, Joseph
"	Sandeford, Mary
"	Sheldon, Richard Cure
1783	Sparrock, James Akerman
"	Singleton, Jane
"	Smart, Martin
"	Seale, Benjamin
"	Seale, John
"	Seymore, Christian
"	Sherley, James
"	Standards, Adam
"	Skeete, Rynold
"	Springer, Jacob

* Continued from p. 184.

Year.	Names of Testators.
1784	Scott, Jacob
,,	Smith, Elizabeth
,,	Sharrett, Anthony
,,	Salmon, John
1785	Smethweck, Francis
,,	Selman, Thomas
,,	Spence, Douglas
,,	Straker, William
,,	Straghan, Charles
,,	Stroud, Robert
,,	Skeete, Reynold
,,	Sim, Robert
,,	Smith, Sir John
1786	Stoute, Snr., Benjamin
,,	Springer, William
,,	Storey, William
,,	Sharp, Jnr., William
,,	Sieuzac, John
,,	Sander, William
,,	Scott, Sarah
,,	Senior, Nassau Thomas
,,	Smith, Henry
,,	Skeete, Edward
1787	Sainthill, Thomas
,,	Savery, Samuel
,,	Stoute, Thomas
,,	Stewart, Julian
,,	Sober, John
,,	Straghan, Francis
,,	Sealy, George
1788	Sealy, Thomas
,,	Sinckler, James
,,	Shepherd, William
,,	Stewart, James
,,	Skeete, Elizabeth
1789	Simpson, Elizabeth
,,	Springer, William
,,	Sandeford, Sarah Judith
,,	Sharp, William Michael
1790	Simmons, Mary
,,	Savery, Sarah
,,	Sainthill, Rebecca
,,	Smith, Samuel
,,	Southern, Mary Ann
,,	Scott, John
1791	Stanton, Mary Hall
,,	Stewart, Elizabeth
,,	Smith, Joseph
,,	Straghan, Charles
,,	Spencer, Priscella
,,	Scale, Rebecca
,,	Straker, James
,,	Stacey, Edmund
,,	Stammers, Sarah
1792	Shockness, Jemott
,,	Sealy, Henry
1792	Stewart, Robert
,,	Snarling, Elizabeth
,,	Spencer, John
1793	Scott, Henry
,,	Scott, Mary
,,	Snow, Franklin Jonathan
,,	Sisk, John
,,	Simpson, John
,,	Sherley, Thomas
,,	Skeete, John Brathwaite
1794	Stephen, Zachariah
,,	Springer, Ann
,,	Sesnett, Mary
,,	Strong, Benjamin
,,	Skinner, Edmund
,,	Stewart, John
,,	Skeete, Elizabeth
,,	Skinner, Alice
,,	Sinclair, Priscella
,,	Scott, Samuel
,,	Stewart, John
,,	Scott, Edward Wiggings
,,	Straghan, Francis
,,	Spellos, John
1795	Sober, Philip
,,	Shaw, Mary
,,	Sharp, George
,,	Sainthill, Jane
,,	Shepherd, Hon. James
,,	Scott, Sarah Elizabeth
,,	Smith, John
,,	Salmon, Sarah
,,	Shepherd, Thomas
1796	Sisk, John
,,	Smith, Mary
,,	Salmon, John
,,	Springer, William
,,	Smith, Elizabeth
,,	Stanford, John
,,	Spellin, John
,,	Storey, Mary
,,	Skeete, William Edward
,,	Standards, Richards
,,	Scutt, John
,,	Steele, Joshua
,,	Stewart, Mary
,,	Stoute, Robert James
1797	Sanders, Elizabeth
,,	Sober Martha Bersheba
,,	Shutt, Shechaniah
,,	Steele, Samuel
1798	Swan, Philip
,,	Scott, Nathaniel
,,	Smith, Jnr., Thomas
,,	Smetten, Jeremiah
,,	Savery, Francis

Year.	Names of Testators.
1798	Simpson, William
1799	Summers, George
„	Sandiford William
„	Sarjeant, Hamson
„	Sulivan, Thomas

Year.	Names of Testators.
1650	Terry, Basil
„	Terrie, Richard
„	Turner, John
1651	Turner, Arthur
„	Turner, John
1653	Towell, Philip
„	Turner, John
„	Toownsend, William
1654	Thorne, Stephen
„	Tue, Richard
„	Thode, Steven
„	Thode, Ellinor
1657	Thorneton, Katherine
„	Terrill, Edward
„	Thomas, William
„	Taylor, William
1658	Tristram, Robert
„	Thody, Stephen
„	Trott, Fulluetby
1659	Turner, James
„	Thompson, Edward
1660	Townsend, Walter
„	Thomas, William
„	Thomas, Johanna
„	Tharlo, Henry
„	Thurston, Thomas
„	Thomas, William
1661	Tibotts, Robert
„	Taylor, Ricard
„	Thomson, Christopher
„	Terrill, Michael
„	Townes, Brian
„	Tappin,* John
„	Trewman, Edward
„	Thomas, Mary
1662	Thompson, George
1663	Tibballs, Nicholas
1664	Thawyer, Richard
1665	Thawyer, John
„	Tauener, Henry
„	Terry, Thomas
„	Tench, Rowland
1666	Taylor, Richard
1667	Thomas, Josias
„	Thompson, John
„	Thompson, Edward
1668	Thorne, Thomas
„	Talbott, Richard
„	Tucker, William

Year.	Names of Testators.
1668	Tothill, Robert
„	Tudor, James
„	Tilley, Nicholas
1669	Thorne, James
1670	Tixtover, John
„	Tarry, Stephen
1671	Tennent, Edward
„	Tyler, John
„	Taylor, John
1672	Taylor, William
„	Tristune, Nicholas
„	Torkington, George Gilbert
1673	Thorn, Joseph
„	Thomson, Katherin
„	Tompkins, Roger
„	Townes, Francis
1674	Tyler, Susanna
1675	Taylor, Arthur
„	Turner, John
„	Tiggley, John
1676	Thickpenny, Thomas
„	Taylor, Francis
„	Thweat, James
„	Tibbott, John
„	Turbile, Hercules
1678	Trattle, William
„	Tresteene, Nicholas
1679	Tuff, Thomas
„	Thornburgh, George
„	Teyler, Robert
„	Turpin, Henry
„	Taylor, John
„	Thompson, Samuel
1680	Taylor, Robert
„	Turvill, Edward
„	Therry, James
1681	Taylor, John
„	Thornburgh, Ann
„	Travers, Robert
„	Thornhill, Timothy
„	Townes, Edward
„	Travers, Philip
„	Triston, Nicholas
„	Taylor, Florvris
„	Trindar, John
„	Tate, Mary
1682	Titchborne, Francis
„	Turpin, Anne
„	Tate, Marry
„	Turney, Robert
„	Tuckar, Martin
„	Thompson, John
„	Trindar, John
1683	Toppin, John
„	Torvill, Philip
„	Traversie, Alexander

* Probably Toppin.

Year.	Names of Testators.
1683	Turneham, Robert
1684	Taylor, Jonathan
"	Tindall, Richard
"	Taggart, James
"	Tubbs, Edward
1685	Townes, James
"	Townes, Thomas
"	Tyson, James
"	Trimble, Walter
"	Turton, Francis
"	Thornburgh, Edmond
"	Trefusis, Bridget
"	Taylor, Robert
1686	Tixtover, William
"	Travers, James
"	Turton, Edward
"	Turney, Henry
1687	Turner, John
"	Temple, John
"	Todd, Thomas
"	Todd, John
"	Thurston, Edward
"	Toyn, Katherine
"	Tickle, Samuel
1688	Thomas, John
1689	Tucker, Walter
1690	Topling, Paul
"	Terrill, Michael
"	Tyron, Edward
1692	Taprell, Alexander
"	Trevanion, Nathaniel
"	Teague, Phyladelphia
1693	Tidcombe, Samuel
"	Terry, John
"	Tysoe, William
"	Taggart, Alexander
"	Taylor, Mary
"	Trent, Lawrence
"	Thomby, Jone
1694	Terry, Christopher, "Deponant"
"	Triscott, Mary
"	Taylor, John
"	Taylor, Edith
"	Thorne, John
"	Taylor, Ezekiel
"	Tuke, Valentine
1695	Thomas, John
"	Twerton, Elizabeth
"	Thorp, James
1696	Thompson, Joseph
"	Taylor, Jennett
"	Thorpe, Robert
"	Thorne, William
"	Taggart, Alexander
1697	Tongue, William
"	Tuder, Cap. Richard
1698	Tate, John
"	Tyler, Joseph
1700	Tolley, Thomas
"	Taylor, John
1701	Townesend, Richard
"	Taylor, Philip
"	Tyrwhitt, Francis
"	Tabbott, Joane
1703	Trefusis, Bridget
"	Thurbarne, James
"	Turpin, Susannah
1704	Thurgar, Thomasin
"	Turpin, Henry
1705	Trant, Richard
"	Thomas, Charles
"	Tubbs, Edward
1706	Tirrill, Michael
"	Travors, Philip
"	Taylor, George
"	Trant, Richard
1709	Taylor, John
"	Toose, Ann
1710	Townsend, George
1711	Tatem, Nathaniel
"	Tull, Thomas
1712	Tildesley, Henry
"	Thomas, Ann
1713	Toyer, Jonathan
"	Thomas, Charles
"	Thomas, John
"	Tull, Rowland
1714	Toppin, Percival
"	Thorne, James
"	Thorne, Anne
"	Taylor, John
"	Thompson, Benjamin
1715	Thompson, Sarah
"	Thomas, Hopkin
"	Todd, Joseph
"	Terrill, Thomas
"	Teage, Jane
"	Thomas, Roger
"	Trywhitt, Charles
"	Tonstall, William
"	Thompson, George
"	Thomson, Andrew
"	Taylor, Andrew
1717	Terrill, Charles
"	Taylor, John
"	Turpin, John
1718	Toppin, Thomas
"	Thwaite, Thomas
"	Taylor, Amy
"	Thorne, Mary
"	Terry, Francis
"	Taylor, Margaret

Year.	Names of Testators.
1719	Turpin, Susan
„	Tull, John
„	Taylor, Samuel
„	Thomson, Mary
„	Tyler, Anthony
„	Turner, John
1720	Taylor, Roger
„	Thomas, John
„	Tennill, Edward
„	Thriscott, Nicholas
1721	Thomas, John
„	Tapas, Margaret
„	Thomas, Stephen
„	Thorpe, Alice
„	Tysoe, William
„	Tyrwhite, George
„	Taylor John
„	Thwaite, Katherine
„	Toppin, Deborah
1722	Tomkins, John
1723	Toppin, John
„	Toppin, Thomas
„	Taitt, Henry
„	Tiake, John
1724	Thwiat, Thomas
„	Towsend, John
„	Tacey, Joseph
„	Thompson, George
1725	Trott, George
„	Turner, John
„	Thweat, Thomas
„	Townes, John
1726	Thomas, Alice
„	Tebling, Sarah
„	Tudor, Thomas
„	Thomas, John
„	Thornhill, Timothy
„	Taylor, Isaac
1727	Turner, Susannah
1728	Trannell, Thomas
„	Thomson, John
„	Toppin, Edward
„	Treasure, John
„	Terrill, Thomas
1729	Trotman, Thomas
„	Toppin, Joseph
1730	Timbrell, Thomas
„	Toppin, Mary
„	Thomas, Edward
„	Thornhill, Thomas
1731	Taitt, Thomas
„	Taylor, John
1732	Thorpe, Isaac
„	Tull, John
„	Taitt, Elizabeth
„	Thornhill, Dowding

Year.	Names of Testators.
1732	Towne, Richard
1733	Terrill, Martha
„	Thomas, Richard
„	Thomas, William
1734	Thornhill, Phillippa
„	Thurbarne, Benjamin
„	Tappin, John
1735	Trent, John
„	Tresse, Joshua
„	Terrill, William
1736	Thomas, William
„	Tappin, Elizabeth
„	Trent, Andrew
„	Taitt, Robert
„	Towill, Christopher
„	Taylor, Patience
1737	Treasure, Thomas
„	Taylor, John
1738	Treasure, Antipass
„	Tuder, Elizabeth
„	Toyer, Benjamin
„	Taylor, John
„	Tucker, Timothy
1739	Taylor, Bryan
„	Thornhill, Jane
„	Thweat, Priscilla
„	Toppin, Mary
„	Triscoatt, Elizabeth
„	Terrill, Jean
„	Taylor, Elizabeth
1740	Triscoatt, Nicholas
„	Taverner, Henry
„	Tysoe, Margaret
1741	Thomas, Edward
„	Thomas, Mary
1742	Taylor, Anne
„	Tirrill, Martha
„	Trendell, John
„	Tyldesley, Robert
„	Toppin, Ann
„	Toppin, Catlin Thomas
„	Thweat, James
„	Thompson, Katherine
1743	Toppin, Robert
„	Timbrill, William
„	Trent, Lawrence
„	Thomas, John
„	Toppin, Joseph
1744	Terrill, William
1746	Tuxeira, Samuel
„	Terrill, Jane
„	Taylor, Henry
„	Thomas, William
„	Terrill, Ann
„	Toppin, Ann
„	Turner, William

Year.	Names of Testators.
1747	Tull, Martin
"	Terrill, Mary
"	Townsend, Kingstown
"	Tryon, Sarah
1748	Taylor, John
"	Toppin, Jonathan
"	Tipling, Dorothy
1749	Turton, Robert
"	Thornton, William
"	Thornburgh, Alicia
"	Turton, Francis
"	Tanner, John
"	Townsend, Sarah
1750	Thomas, William
"	Taylor, Robert
"	Toney, John
1751	Thomas, John
"	Taylor, Patience
"	Taylor, James
"	Thorpe, Mary
"	Thomas, Gabriel
"	Thorp, Deborah
1752	Toppin, James
"	Taylor, Dorothy
"	Tappin, Thomas
"	Taylor, William
"	Tempro, John
1753	Teap, Isabell
"	Terrill, Michael
"	Thorne, Daniel Greaves
1754	Thorne, William
"	Thorne, James
"	Terrill, Joseph
"	Thompson, James
1755	Terrill, Joseph
"	Thornton, Thomas
"	Taylor, John
1756	Teale, Peter
"	Thomas, George
"	Thomas, Jane
"	Triscott, David
"	Trottman, Thomas
1757	Terrill, Michael
"	Thorne, Benjamin
"	Trotman, William
"	Taitt, Robert
"	Teague, Andrew
"	Turney, Thomas
"	Tylsbury, Robert
1758	Taylor, John
"	Taylor, Stephen
"	Thomas, Thomas
"	Traverse, Judith

Year.	Names of Testators.
1758	Thomas, Deane
1759	Thornhill, Timothy
"	Tunckes, Thomas
1760	Todd, Samuel
"	Thompson, Eatrick
"	Turney, Robert
"	Thorp, Joseph
1761	Thody, John
"	Thomas, Dorcas
"	Thomas, John
1762	Thornton, John
"	Turton, Thomas
"	Thompson, William
"	Thorne, Benoni
"	Thorne, John
"	Toppin, Sarah
"	Trywhitt, Francis
1763	Taylor, Robert
"	Taitt, Henry
1764	Triscoat, Susanna
"	Thorne, Sarah
1765	Thorne, James
"	Twentymen, Thomas
"	Turton, William
"	Thomas, Fitt
1766	Thorne, Joseph
"	Taitt, Abel
"	Thomas, John
1767	Taylor, Martha
"	Tull, William
"	Thorne, Ann
"	Thomas, George
"	Turner, Richard
"	Tull, William
"	Taylor, Martha
1768	Taylor, Thomas Estwick
"	Thorne, Mary
1769	Tempro, Sarah
"	Tapshire, Jane
1770	Turton, Samuel
"	Tubbs, Joseph
"	Thornhill, Dowding
"	Trute, Mary
"	Tempro, William
"	Thornhill, Hon. Henry
"	Teague, Thomas
1771	Thomas, Elizabeth
1772	Tyldesley, Henry
"	Turpin, Francis
1773	Tapers, John
"	Thoney, Thomas
1774	Taylor, John
"	Thomas, Philip

(*To be continued.*)

Losack of St. Kitts.

Richard Hawkshaw Losack of Suffolk Street, St. Marylebone, Esq. To my wife Christiana furniture, china, linen, and use of plate. The property bequeathed to her by her Mother. To my s. Henry £10. I confirm the bond for £1,000 to my s. Richard at his marriage. My s. Wm. £30. My s. Woodley, now a post capt., £1,000. Confirm the bond to my dau. Eliz. White on her marriage for £1,000. My son-in-law Dr John W. £10 for a ring. To my s. Geo., an admiral, my plantation in the I. of St. Chr. charged with an annuity of £150 I give to my wife, which is more than one-third of the net proceeds of sd estate, and to pay my s. Richd £800 and s. Woodley £500, discharged of my note for £600 I owe my s. Geo. and of bills of exchange for £1,420, and the paymt to Messrs. Manning and Anderdon of the balance of my acct. To be interred in the parish church of St Anne, Westmr. Sam. Bilke of Stamford Str. and Geo. Hyde of Old Burlington Str., apothecary, Ex'ors. 22 June 1813. + (Signed with his mark.)

Codicil. To Jane Eliz. Eliner Watson, spr., otherwise called Eliz. Jackson, wid., of Upper Tichfield Str., an annuity of £150 charged on my plantation for her care and attention, and after the death of my wife a further £50 a year, and I also give her the lease of my house I now inhabit, No 9 Titchfield Str., with all its contents and 1 pair of silver candlesticks in my house in Suffolk Str., my bank long annuities and arrears of my pay as Lt.-Gov. of the Leeward I. 22 June 1813. His +.

2nd codicil. 26 July 1813. Estate to Ex'ors in trust. £24 a year for the nat. s. of my s. Col. Losack.

Proved at London 18 Nov. 1813. (Long will and codicils.) (553, Heathfield.)

Matilda Losack. Will dated 20 Feb. 1815. All property to my dear Mother. My brother Beckford and Mary his wife. My child Charles, his father Capt. Losack.

On 1 Dec. 1815 appeared Eumenes Moore of Charlotte Str., Portland Pl., and Ann Clarke of Barner Str., Spr., and swore that they knew testx, wife of Woodley L., late of Burner Str., Oxford Str. On 4 Dec. adm'on was granted to Patience Gordon, wid. (615, Pakenham.)

1685-6, March 5. To be a free denizen: Lewis de Lausac (*sic*), but probably Lausac. (Cooper's List of Aliens, 44.)

1727. Deposition with signature of James Losack, clerk in the Secretary's Office, 3 Oct. (C. O., 152.)

1728, Oct. Mr James Losack, then Dep. Sec. (*Ibid.*, 241-2 and 211-3. Noted by Major Phipps.)

Ind're of 8 May 1739 between Rebecca Hawkshaw, widow, James Losack, Esq., and Mary his wife as to the remainders to Margaret Heron, Dorothy Fletcher and Juliana Hawkshaw (now Gladwin) created by the will of Richd Hawkshaw, mercht. Richd Hawkshaw his son and Sarah Hawkshaw one of his daus. dying within age, and Mary Hawkshaw the other dau. mar. James Losack. Settlement of the estate. (St. Kitts Records, No. 1,965.)

Antoine de Lussac, Comte d' Eran, supposed to have emigrated from France to St. Kitts soon after the Revocation of the Edict of Nantes in 1685.

Richard Hawkshaw of St. Kitts, merchant; dead 1739. = Rebecca . . . ., settled her estate in 1739.

James Losack of St. Kitts, Esq., Dep. Sec. 1728; Speaker 1744; M. of C. and of St. John's, Cappesterre, 1733; Judge of Vice-Admiralty Court 1754; bur. at St. Geo. 30 Nov. 1756. = Mary Hawkshaw, dau. and h.; bur. 25 Feb. 1762 at St. Geo., Basseterre.

Richard Hawkshaw, died a minor.

Sarah Hawkshaw, died a minor.

Richard Hawkshaw Losack, b. c. 1730; admitted to Westminster School Oct. 1744, aged 12; Lieut.-General of Leeward Isles 1769; President of St. Kitts 1770; died 2 Nov. 1813, aged 83. M.I. in St. Anne's, Soho. Will dated 22 June and proved 18 Nov. 1813 (553, Heathfield). = Christiana Maclure, mar. at St. George's, Hanover Square, 17 March 1753; died 26 March 1818, aged 87, in Nassau Street, Cavendish Sq. M.I. in Marylebone Old Parish Church.

James Losack, admitted to Westminster School May 1746, aged 11.

George Losack, Admiral R.N.; died 22 Aug. 1829 at Milan. = ..., dau. of George Story; mar. 1796 in H.M.S. Jupiter at the Cape of Good Hope.

James Henry William Losack, born 4 March and bapt. 12 June 1755 at Basseterre; died 21 Jan. 1810, aged 54, in John Street, Fitzroy Square. Lt.-Col. 23rd Regt. M.I. in Marylebone Old Church. = ..., dau. of . . . . Zouch; mar. 21 Sept. 1789.

Richard Ottley Losack of West Malling Abbey, co. Kent, which was sold about 1800; a stock-broker; born 1766; died 27 Jan. 1839, aged 73. = Anne . . . ., died 5 June 1849 at Tunbridge Wells.

Augustus Losack, Lt.-Col., only son; died 21 Oct. 1854 at the Bridge of Allan near Stirling. = Grace Grant Spalding, widow of Melville Losack; mar. at All Soul's, Langham Place, 14 Aug. 1840.

A dau., born 1806; died 14 March 1863, aged 57, in the Harrow Rd.

James Losack, bapt. Dec. 1790.

William Losack, born and bapt. 3 March 1795 at Basseterre.

Ind're of 9 May 1739 between James Losack of Basseterre, gent., and Mary his wife and Edwd Bourryau of the same place, gent. (*Ibid.*, No. 1,851.)

1744, March 18. "Jas. Losack, Speaker," signs the Address of the Assembly.
Richard Laussac, admitted Oct. 1744, aged 12.
James Lusack, admitted May 1746, aged 11, to Westminster School. ("Notes and Queries," 11 S., xii., 380.)

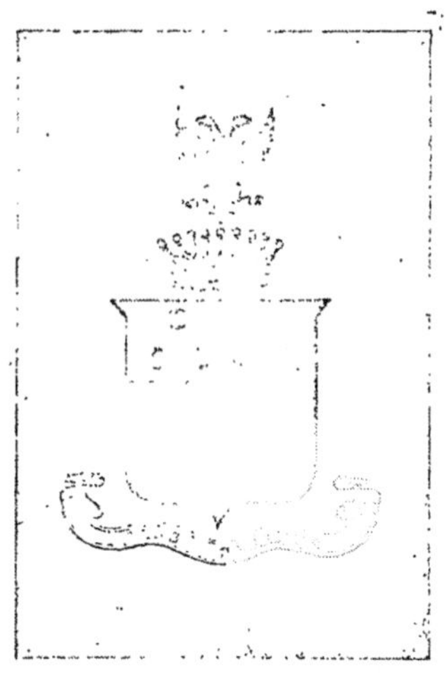

A

Woodley Francis Losack, born 5 Oct. and bapt. 20 Nov. 1769 at Basseterre; Capt. R.N. 1806; mar. 23 Aug. 1823 the widow of Capt. E. L. Crofton, R.N.; died May 1838 in Florence. ═ Matilda, dau. of Mrs. Patience Gordon; died at Putney 13 Aug. 1815. Will (615, Pakenham).

Elizabeth, only dau., mar. 22 Feb. 1796 Dr. John White, R.N. She died in Torrington Square 3 Dec. 1837.

Henry Losack.

William ═ Losack.

Melville Charles Losack, R.A., died 1837-8. ═ Grace Grant Spalding, mar. 2ndly Lieut.-Col. Augustus Losack.

George Losack, Capt. 69th Regt., died 20 March 1848 at Cape Coast Castle. ═ Anne Hatley, remar. 18 April 1850, at St. Mary's, Bryanston Sq., Rob. B. Boyd of 1st Royal Dragoons.

. . . . ═ Losack.

C. M. Losack, 1 month old at her father's death; now, 1915, of Findhorn House, Forres, N.B. ═ Major Chadwick of Binsness, Findhorn Bay; purchased the estate 1871; died 12 Dec. 1908.

Helena Woodley Losack, born 18 June 1805; mar. William Henry Fryer. He was born 1800 and died 1842. She died 23 Jan. 1893. M.I. in Church of Farleigh Hungerford, co. Wilts.

Only son.

Grace, mar. George Wynter Blathwayt of Melksham House, Wilts.

Two daus.

The above plate is from a photograph of the Arms used by Admiral George Losack, forwarded by Mrs. Chadwick. It may have been from a book-plate.

1753. Hon. James Losack, one plantation in S[t] John's, Cappesterre. (Baker's Map.)

1754, Nov. James Losack is Judge of the Court of Vice-Admiralty.

1769, July 23. Governor Woodley announces the arrival at the Leeward Islands of "Mr. Losack, H.M. Lieut.-General." (Colonial Correspondence, vol. iv.) Mr. Losack (Richard Hawkshaw Losack) was also President of St. Christopher 1770, and used a seal to his official papers bearing:—Crest: A double-headed eagle displayed over a French coronet of seven points. Arms: [Azure] A double-headed eagle displayed, on a chief party per pale [Argent and Gules] on the dexter side three crescents, on the sinister as many mullets. (*Ibid.*, vol. v.)

Richard Ottley Losack owned Malling Abbey, Kent, which was sold about 1800 to the Akers family, who were also from St. Kitts.

ENTRIES FROM THE "GENTLEMAN'S MAGAZINE."

1796, Feb. 22. John White, esq. of the royal navy, to Miss Losack, only daughter of Richard H. L. esq. of St. Kitts, and lieutenant-general of the Leeward Islands. (p. 253.)

1796, lately. At the Cape of Good Hope, Capt. Losack, of the Jupiter man of war, to Miss Story, daughter of George S. esq. (p. 1054.)

1810, Jan. 21. In John-street, Fitzroy-square, James Losack, esq. late lieutenant-colonel of the 23d Regiment of Foot. (p. 184.)

1813, Nov. 2. Aged 83, Rich. Hawkshaw Losack, esq. of the Island of St. Christopher, and lieut.-general of the Leeward Islands. (p. 622.)

1815, Aug. 13. At Putney, the wife of Capt. Losack, R.N. (p. 279.)

1818, March 26. In Nassau-street, Cavendish-square, in her 88th year, Christiana, widow of R. H. Losack, esq. late Lieut.-gen. of the Leeward Islands. (p. 473.)

1823, Aug. 23. Capt. Woodley Losack, R.N., to widow of Capt. E. L. Crofton, R.N. (p. 552.)

1829, Aug. 22. At Milan, George Losack, Esq. Admiral of the Blue. . . . . He was son of Richard Hawkshaw Losack, Esq. of St. Kitts . . . . was married on board the Jupiter in 1796 . . . . and had several children. He has left a brother in the Navy, Woodley Losack, esq. who attained the rank of Post-Captain in 1806. James, another brother, died Lieut.-Colonel of the 23d foot, Jan. 21, 1810. (p. 465, long notice.)

1831, Aug. 13. At St. Paul's Covent-garden, Mr. George Robins, of the Piazza, to Miss Marian Losack, of Alfred-place, Bedford-sq. (p. 171.)

1837, Dec. 3. In Torrington-sq. in her 45th year, Eliza, wife of John White, esq. (1838, p. 106.) The age must be wrong.

1839, Jan. 27. In Northumberland-court Strand, from the rupture of a blood vessel of the heart, aged 73, Richard Losack, esq. of the Abbey, West Malling, Kent; & a member of the Stock Exchange. His brother, a Captain in the Navy, d. suddenly at Florence, in May last. His sister also d. suddenly in Conduit-st. a few months since. (p. 328.)

1840, Aug. 14. At All Soul's Langham-pl., Lt. Col. L., B.A.L. s: of the l. Adm. L. to Grace-Grant, widow of M. C. Losack, R.A. (p. 423.)

1848, March 20. At Cape Coast Castle, Capt. George Losack, of the 1st West India Reg. (p. 334.)

1849, June 5. At Tonbridge-wells, at an advanced age, Anne, widow of R. Losack, esq. formerly of West Malling Abbey. (p. 107.)

1850, Ap. 18. At St. Mary's Bryanston sq. Robert B. Boyd, esq. 1st Royal Dragoons, to Anne-Hatley, widow of Capt. George Losack, 69th Regt. (p. 87.)

1854. Oct. 21. At the Bridge of Allan, near Stirling, N.B. Lieut.-Col. Augustus Losack K.S.F. only son of the late Admiral Losack. (p. 643.)

1863, Mar. 14. In Harrow-road, aged 57, Miss Losack, dau. of the late Adm. George Losack, and granddau. of R. Hawkshaw Losack, Lieut.-Gen. and Gov. of the Leeward Islands. (p. 667.)

The Rev. Arthur Robins, Chaplain to the Queen and Rector of Windsor since 1873, died Dec. 1899. He was born 24 Jan. 1834, the second son of the late Geo. Henry Robins, auctioneer, by Marian Amelia, dau. of Fra. Losack, in direct descent from Admiral Losack and the Marquess de Lussac. Mr. Geo. R. died in 1846, and his wife in 1819. The late Rector entered Magdalene Hall and Hertford College, Oxford, in 1865; M.A. 1866. A widow and several sons and daus. survive. (Abstract from obituary in the "Standard" of 25 Dec. 1899.)

Mr. N. Bosanquet has kindly searched the Huguenot Society's publications for Losack but found nothing, so they probably emigrated straight from France to the W.I.

TRINITY, PALMETTO POINT, ST. KITTS.

Burials.

1738, Nov. 30. Sarah Hawkshaw of Basseterre.
1738, Dec. 11. Mr Richard Hawkshaw of Basseterre.
1751, July 28. Mrs Rebecca Hawkshaw.

ST. GEORGE'S, BASSETERRE, ST. KITTS.

Burials.

1756 Nov. 30 James Losack, Esqr.
1762 Feb. 25 Mary Losack (Vidua).

Baptisms.

1755 June 12 James Henry William, S. of Richard Hawkshaw & Christiana Losack, b. 4th March 1755.
1769 Nov. 20 Woodley Francis, s. of Richard Hawkshaw & Christiana Losack, b. 5 Octr 1769.
1790 Dec. (13 to 23) James, s. of James .... Losack ....
1795 Mar. 3 William Losack, the s. of James L. & Sarah his wife, b. 3 March.

ST. GEORGE'S, HANOVER SQUARE.

1753 Mar. 17 Richard Losack of this p., B., & Christiana Maclure of St Ann's, Westminster, Spr. L.B.L.

ST. PAUL'S, COVENT GARDEN.

1831 Aug. 13 George Henry Robins of this P., Wid., and Amelia Marian Losack of the P. of St Giles in the fields, in the Co. of Mid., Spr.; by L. Wit. by M. D'Almaine, F. C. Losack.

ST. ANNE'S, SOHO.

"In 1897 rubbings were taken of all the legible inscriptions upon the tombstones in the aisle passages previous to their being covered with Mosaic pavement." Among these was one to "R. H. Losack, Nov. 2, 1813." ("Misc. Gen. et Her.," 4th S., vol. i., 305.)

MARYLEBONE OLD CHURCH.

On a flat stone in the floor of the south passage. The stone has flaked in places and a few words are mutilated :—

JAMES LOSA . K Es . . . .
Island of St Chr . . . . ph . .
late Lieutenant Colonel of
the 23rd Regiment of Foot
who died January the 21st, 1810
Aged 54 Years.
Deeply lamented by all his
Family and Friends.
ALSO
. . MOTHER CHRISTIAN
WIDOW OF
RICHARD HAWKESHAW LOSACK
late LIEUTENANT GENERAL
of the LEEWARD ISLANDS
who departed this Life
on the 26th of March . . . .
in the 88th Year of her . . . .
ALSO
THE BODY OF ELIZABETH . . . .
WIFE OF DOCTOR W . . . .
ONLY DAUGHTER OF
RICHD LOSACK, ESQ.
DIED . . . .

The above M.I., but incorrectly copied, appeared in "Misc. Gen. et Her.," 3rd Series, vol. i., p. 241. I have checked it in the church this 27 Aug. 1917.

FARLEIGH, HUNGERFORD, CO. WILTS.

Brass to Wm. Hen. Fryer, born 1800; died 1842.

Helena Woodley Losack Fryer his wife, born 18 June 1805; died 23 Jan. 1893.

Arms (which I omitted to take).

Monumental Inscriptions in England relating to West Indians.*

ST. JOHN'S, WITHYCOMBE RALEGH, CO. DEVON.

On the south wall of the north aisle, the only remaining portion of the church, are these two tablets. (Transcribed 23 May 1917) :—

Sacred to the Memory
of
JANE PETERS BOURKE
Daughter of
EDMUND FEARON BOURKE, *Esq*[r]
late of *Exmouth*.
She died April 8th 1815,
Aged 22.

1815, April 13. Sat. d. at Exmouth, Miss Jane Bourke, dau. of the late Edmund F. Bourke, esq; formerly of Summerhill house near this city. ("Bath Chronicle.")

SACRED
to ANNE LYDIA, the wife
of RALPH RICE, *Esq*,
She died on the 29th day of Dec[r] 1816,
after a long and painful illness
in the 31st year of her age,
and lies in the same tomb with her sister,
JANE PETERS BOURKE.
Her afflicted Husband placed this memorial
of his love and of his sorrow.

Mr. E. F. Bourke left Jamaica about 1790, resided for seven years at Cromhall, co. Glouc., where his wife died in 1800, then removed to Bath and Exmouth, at which latter place he died in 1812, but was buried at Cromhall. (See *ante*, III., 23.)

There is in the churchyard a vault with inscriptions on the top slab to :—

John Teschemaker LL.D. died 20 March 1867 aged 71; also two of his children.

As son of John of Essequibo, Esq., he matriculated from Exeter Coll., Oxf., in 1813, aged 19. (See W.I. Bookplates, No. 281.)

Another vault records the death of :—

Frederick Thomas Emanuel Teschemaker 26 Sept. 1853 aged 52.

1853, July 20. At Exmouth, Eliza-Ann, eldest dau. of J. Teschemaker, esq. D.C.L. ("G.M.," 323.)
1853, Sept. 26. At Exmouth, aged 52, Thos. Teschemaker, esq. (*Ibid.*, 540.)

---

* Continued from p. 200.

ST. ANNE'S, SOHO, CO. MIDDLESEX.

West side of the churchyard:—

Sacred | to the Memory of | BENJAMIN PEREIRA, Esq[r] | of Kingston, Jamaica | Late of Marylebone, London, | who departed this life | November 8th, 1828, Aged 56.

Also to | M[rs] MARGARET CARROLL | the beloved mother in law | to the above | who departed this life | Jan[y] 12th 1826, Aged 72.

("Misc. Gen. et Her.," 4th S., I., 244.)

(To be continued.)

Review.

"Notes on Colonel Henry Vassall (1721—1769), his wife Penelope Royall, his house at Cambridge, and his slaves Tony and Darby." By Samuel Francis Batchelder. Cambridge, Massachusetts, 1917. 8vo, pp. 85. Reprinted from the Cambridge Historical Society's Proceedings, Vol. X.

The subject of this interesting memoir was born in Jamaica on Xmas Day 1721, the fourteenth child of Major Leonard Vassall of that island, grandson of Col. John Vassall who removed there from Virginia in 1672, and great-grandson of William Vassall, Esq., of Stepney, then of Scituate in New Plymouth, but last of Sion Hill, Barbados, at his death in 1657.

Henry's wife Penelope was the only daughter of Isaac Royal of Royalls in Popeshead, Antigua, who late in life removed to Charlestown, New England. Another relative who joined in this migration was Col. Robert Oliver of St. Philip's parish, Willoughby Bay, whose wife was a daughter of Mrs. Royall.

These West Indians formed a coterie of men of wealth, good education and cultured leisure. They erected superior houses and filled them with fine mahogany furniture, pictures, books, plate and china. They planted ornamental trees and laid out charming gardens. They kept full stables, and one of them, Col. Oliver, had his pack of hounds. With the advent of the rebellion, being loyalists, they were forced to quit their elegant homes, which were unjustly seized and confiscated by the rebels. Those who had plantations in the Islands continued to draw ample incomes, but others less fortunately situated retired to England to live out a miserable existence, dependent on the charity of the Government.

As an example of colonial life of the period this little book is highly instructive, for it contains much original information derived from letters and diaries, being also well illustrated with portraits and views, including a practically unknown Chippendale armorial book-plate by N. Hurd. A tabular pedigree of six generations serves to straighten out the intricate intermarriages.

Antiguan Bookplates.*

James Athill.

No. 7.

Arch.d Gloster
Middle Temple

No. 755.

Sir James Laroche Bart.

No. 756.

William Salmond Esq.
Seaforth, Antigua.

No. 758.

* Contributed by Mr. FREDERIC CATTLE of Heanor.

Sober of Barbados.

Robert Sober of St Andrew Overhills. Will dated 31 Oct. 1685. My wife Mary. Proved 1686. (Recorded at Barbados.)

Lawrence Trent of St Peters, Barbados, Esq. Will dated 2 July 1742. To the children of my nephew John Sober, Esq., £100 each. (278, Edmunds.)

John Sober, late of the p. of St Peter in the I. of B'es, now of Little Bursted, co. Essex, Esq. Will dated 12 Oct. 1751. My father-in-law Nich. Wilcox of B'es, Esq., Edwd Clark Parish of L., Esq., Abr. Carleton Cumberbatch and Joseph Lindsey, both of B'es, Esq^res, on T. all my sugar work plantations and personal estate. 200 negroes, 100 cattle and 10 horses to be kept on my estate, 60 a. to be planted in provisions, negroes to be well fed and clothed, and casks to be made. My s^d father-in-law Nich. Wilcox and Mother-in-law Marg^t Wilcox, Ed. C. Parish, A. C. Cumberbatch, J. Lindsey and my brother-in-law Nich. Wilcox £50 each. My nephew and niece W^m and Sarah Timbrill, ch^n of my late sister Eliz. T., wife of Wm. T., dec^d, £500 each at 21 and £40 a year each till then. My friend Rob. Wadeson £10. My wife Mary S., late Mary Wilcox, dau. of s^d Nich. W., Esq., £1500, our mar. sett. dated 25 Oct. 1743, and £100 for mourning, all my plate with the coat of arms of her father, her riding horse, jewels, use of my house in B'es until my eldest son be 21. My father-in-law Abr. Cumberbatch has by his will lately made broke his contract in regard to four of my ch^n, Sarah S., Abr. S., Mary S. and Cumberbatch S. I give them each £3000 c. at 21. My cousin Joseph Pickering, now in L., £10. My eldest son John at 21 all my real estate and residue of personal estate; power to heir to charge estate with joynture of £200 c. Son John to go to Oxford at 17. T. to be Ex'ors.

Codicil. Late of G. B., now of B'es. My father-in-law Nich. Wilcox has died. To my wife my coach and 6 horses, the use of my house called the Castle on my pl^n in St Peters and use of house-negroes and £150 a year if she do not dwell there. My aunt Mrs Reb^a Almond of St Lucy £50 c. To poor of St Peter £10 a year for 10 years. My wife, my bro.-in-law N. W. and friends Hon. Ph. Gibbes of St Jas., Esq^res, and Rev. Jonathan Dennis, Fellow of Q. Coll., Oxf., with Edw. C. Parish and Jos. Lindsay Ex'ors and T. and G. of my 5 ch^n. Revoke app. of A. C. Cumberbatch. Jon. Dennis £100 for his care of my 3 sons and £50 for mourning. Ph. Gibbes £50. Dated 16 Nov. 1755 in the presence of Geo. Lavine, Edw. Willson, Ph. Lovell. B'es by the Presid^t Ph. Lovell was sworn at Pilgrim 2 Dec. 1755, Ralph Weekes. A true copy 28 May 1762. Rich. Husbands, D. Sec^y. Proved 3 March 1763 by Mary S., widow, the relict, and Nich. Wilcox, Esq.; power reserved to E. C. P. and J. L., Esq^res, surviving Ex'ors, and Hon. Ph. G. and Rev. J. D. (152, Cæsar.)

Abraham Sober of Kensington, Esq. Will dated 30 March 1772. My Mother-in-law Mrs Mary Sober £300. My sister Sarah Sandiford, wife of Dr S. of B., £1000. All residue to my sister Mary Sober and my brothers John Sober and Cumberbatch Sober, Ex'ors. Proved 16 June 1772 by Mary S., spr., power reserved to the others. (234, Taverner.)

Mary Sober. Will dated 28 July 1792. To be buried at St Faiths under St Pauls with my dear Mother Mrs Mary S. To my sister Mrs Sarah Frewin £30. Mrs Judith S. £30. Mary Cumberbatch Cumberbatch £25 a year. Sarah S. £500. Johannes S. £500. Elletson S., now in the E. I., £2000. Penelope

Arms.—*Ermine, a saltire Gules, on a chief Sable three crescents Or.*

Crest.—*Out of a crescent Or a lion's head Gules.* (Book-plate of John Sober.)

John Sober of Barbados 1638. Tho. Sober of Barbados 1638.

Robert Sober of St. Andrew's. Will dated 31 Oct. 1685; proved 1686. = Mary ....

Abr. Cumberbatch of St. Andrew's, Esq. Will dated 22 Nov. 1750; proved 1753 (8, Searle). (*Ante*, II., 84.) Names his grandchildren Sober.

John Sober of Barbados, gent. =

Lawrence Trent of St. Peters, Esq. Will dated 2 July 1742; proved 1 Sept. 1746 (278, Edmunds). Uncle of John Sober.

A

1. .... Cumberbatch. = John Sober of The Castle in St. Peter's, Esq., and of Little Bursted, co. Essex, born 1715; of Q. Coll., Oxf., matric 24 Aug. 1731, æt. 16; died in B'os 1755. Will dated 12 Oct. 1751; cod. 16 Nov. 1755; sworn 2 Dec. 1755 (152, Cæsar). = 2. Mary Wilcox, dau. of Nich. W., Esq., and Margt. (he died 1751—55); mar. sett. made 25 Oct. 1743; of Welbeck Str.; bur. in St. Paul's crypt. Will dated 27 July 1789; proved 21 June 1791 (302, Bevor). s.p.

Eliz. Sober, mar. Wm. Timbrill of St. Michael's Town, Barbados, merchant. His will dated 25 July 1743; proved 1743 (530, St. Eloy).

Penelope Blake, dau. of Maj. Martin B. of A.; mar. 6 Nov. 1760; died 29 Jan. and bur. 2 Feb. 1774 in Bath Abbey. M.I. (*Ante*, II., 231.) 1st wife. = John Sober, 1st son and heir, of Sober Castle, born 1739; of Q. Coll., Oxf., matric. 8 Apr. 1756, æt. 17: n.; presented font to St. Peter's in 1767; named in 1772 in the will of his brother Abr.; dead 1795; bur. in St. Faith's under St. Paul's Cath. = Martha Bersheba. Will dated 26 Apr. 1795; proved 7 Jan. 1797 (49, Exeter). 2nd wife. s.p.

Hope Elletson Sober, in the E. I. in 1789; ? left natural children by an Indian woman.

John Sober of Latheron near Dunbeath, Scotland. =

John Middleton Sober.

Abr. Cumberbatch Sober, born 1771; Capt. Dragoon Guards; died in L. 7 Dec. 1813, æt. 42. (248, Bridport.) = Ann, dau. of Tho. Kemp, M.P. for Lewes, who died 3 May 1811. She died in 1855. ("G.M.," i., 331.)

Mary Esther Sober, died in L. 16 Oct. 1832, æt. 18.

Abr. C. Sober the younger, 1791.

Penelope Wentworth Sober.

W.I. Bookplates, No. 235 (reduced).

A

Abr. Sober, bur. in crypt of St. Paul's Cath. Will dated 30 Mar. and proved 16 June 1772 (234, Taverner.)

Cumberbatch Sober, born 1742; of Barbados 1772; heir 1792 to his sister Mary; of U. Geo. Str., Marylebone; died 13 Jan. 1827, æt. 85. = Judith ....

Sarah Sober, wife of Dr. Sandford of Barbados in 1772; wife of .... Frewen 1792.

Mary Sober, died 24 Aug. 1793; bur. in St. Paul's Cathedral crypt. Will dated 28 July 1792; proved 6 Sept. 1793 (478, Dodwell.)

Sampson Wood Sober of the Polygon, Southampton, later of St. Peter's, Barbados, only son and heir, died 4 March 1811 v.p. in U. Geo. Str. Will dated 18 April 1799; proved 22 April 1811 (198, Crickitt.) = Jennett, niece to Tho. Walke of Barbados; died in L. 1 Dec. 1815, æt. 42. Will dated 22 Nov. and proved 15 Dec. 1815 (624, Pakenham).

John Sober, ? died 1816. M.I. St. Peter's Font, Barbados.

Mary Cumberbatch Sober, mar. Abr. Cumberbatch, who was born 1754 and died 16 June 1796. She re-mar. 20 Aug. 1797 Wm. Smith Forth of King's Dragoon Guards.

Sarah Sober, mar. Samson Wood, Jr. He was at Eton 1762—8; adm. to Mid. Temple 1768.

Harrison Walke Sober, heir 1800 to his great-uncle Tho. Walke, then under 16; at Eton 1811; of 14th Hussars; died shortly before 1863.

Judith Sober, born 18 March 1794; mar. 19 Feb. 1818 at St. George, Hanover Square; died 1871. = Francis Onslow Trent, Lieut. 14th Light Dragoons; died 10 April 1846.

Eliz. Jennett Sober, died 26 Dec. 1795, aged 18 months and 19 days. M.I. at St. Peter's.

Harrison Walke John Trent-Stoughton, Col. of 68th L. I., great-nephew of John Sober, who died 1816; mar. 1889; of Ashton Hall plantation 1891; died 1899. = Rose, youngest dau. of Wm. Plunkett and widow of Tho. Anthony Stoughton of Owlpen, co. Glouc., and Ballyhorgan, co. Kerry, who died 1885.

Wentworth S. £3000, plate, linen, furniture. To John S., now in Scotland, £20 a year. Abr. Cumberbatch S. £20 a year. All residue in money, land or negroes to my brother Cumberbatch S. and his son Sampson Wood S. equally and Ex'ors. On 5 Sept. 1793 appeared Daniel Coxe of John Str., S[t] Geo., Han. Sq., Esq., Cumberbatch Sober of Welbeck Str., Esq., and Judith Sober his wife, and Penelope Wentworth Sober of the same place, spr. P. W. S. swore her aunt died 24 of last month and sealed the will with her arms. Cumb. S. is the brother of dec[d]. Testx. of S[t] Mary le bone, sp[r]. Proved 6 Sept. 1793 by C. S., Esq., the brother; power reserved to S. W. S., Esq. (478, Dodwell.)

Martha Bersheba Sober. Will dated at Margate in y[e] Isle of Thanet 26 Apr. 1795. All my freehold and personal estate in the I. of B'oes which came to me by the will of my late husband unto Hope Elletson S. for his life, he paying to his next brother Abr. Cumberbatch S. and his sister Penelope Wentworth S. £100 per annum each, and at the decease of H. E. S. I give my estate to his next brother John S. and his heirs male, he then paying to Abr. C. S. £200 a year and to his sister P. W. S. £150 a year, remainder to his younger brother Abr. C. S., then to my dau.-in-law Pen. W. S. I appoint Sir John Gay Alleyne, Bart., Speaker of the Assembly, and W[m] Bishopp, Esq., of Spring Hall, Trustees and Ex'ors, with Tho. King, Esq., of Chiswick Mall, co. Middx., Ex'or for Eng. To be bur. at S[t] Peters.

Codicil, 26 April 1795. Lord Harewood's mortgage on Sober Castle estate not quite liquidated all sugars must be consigned to Messrs. Elliott Adams and Whalley in Hylords Court, Crutched Friars. If any Ex'or be dead Nath[l] Elliott, Esq., Merch[t], Crutched Friars, to be Ex'or for W. I. affairs. I have left my estate to Hope Elletson Sober for his life only, as I believe his attachment to the Indian is not legal and his ch[n] are illegitimate in justice to the rest of my husband's family. His handsome legacy from his grandmother and aunt. Ex'ors £100 each.

Codicil, 27 April 1795. My own £5000 in the 4 per cents. £2800 for M[r] Sober's private debts the estate has cleared. The legacy of my father. To M[rs] Eliz. Middleton of Kensington Palace £1000 for life and at her death to my cousin John Gowan, Esq., of Chichester, and the portrait of my father by Gainsborough, then to J. G. To M[rs] Gowan an enamelled miniature of my father and to J. G. a crayon portrait of our relation Sir Jas. Napier. To Sir J. N. a ring. My carriage to my sister-in-law Juliana King. To Sir J. N. the gold medal of H.M. given my F. when he was P. of Wales. My late husband's ch[n] as follows: To Hope E. S. £500 for his little Eliza. To John S. his next brother £100 and to his son John Middleton S. also £100. To Abr. C. S. £100 and Pen. W. S. £100 and £1000. M[rs] John S. a silver pencil. M[rs] Grace Marler of Starpoint Ho., Powderham in Devonshire, £50 and the portrait of my mother and miniature picture of our dear sister Reading with one of M[rs] Middleton. Rob. Ladbroke, J[r], Esq., £200. My sister-in-law M[rs] Juliana King £100 the locket of her brother (? Edw. Gascoigne), and the ring left me by her mother. My bro.-in-law Tho. King, Esq., of Chiswick Mall my Ex'or for Eng. If I die in L. to be bur. in the chapel of S[t] Faiths under S[t] Pauls n[r] my late husb[d] M[r] Sober. At West Horsley Place, Surrey, are two chests of mine to be sold for the poor there. The things I left at Kensington Palace. Account of leg. John S. of Scotland and his wife Ann. Latheron n[r] Dunbeath. Sworn by Abr. C. S. of Baker Str. 16 Jan. 1797. Test. l. of Kensington Palace, after of Margate, but late of Pall Mall, widow. Proved 7 Jan. 1797 by Abr. C. S. the residuary legatee. (49, Exeter.)

Mary Sober of Welbeck Str., Cav. Sq., co. Middx., widow. Will dated 27 July 1789. To be bur. in S[t] Faith's Church under S[t] Paul's Cath. in or near the grave of my son Abraham S., Esq. Funeral £50. My dau.-in-law Sarah

Frewen £50. My son-in-law Cumberbath (*sic*) S., Esq., now in the I. of B'oes, £100. My friend and pastor the Rev. Jacob Duch'. c of Sloan Str. £50. My friend Mr John Pedder of Chatham Place £100, if he die to his four chn Sarah Ainslie, John P., W. P. and Mary P. To my dau.-in-law Mrs Judith S. of B'oes £25 and to her daus. Mary Cumberbatch Cumberbatch, Sarah Sober and Johannas Sober £25 each. To my great-grandson Abr. Cumberbatch the yr £25 for a ring. My friends Mrs Barbara Kennedy 5 gas. Mrs Mary Ashley 5 gas. and the silver bread basket she gave me when with me in St James Place. Mrs Sarah Knight 10 gas. Miss Eliz. Redwar, now living at Sir Philip Gibbes's, 10 gas. Mrs Ringston 5 gas. Mrs Alicia Wilcox, widow of my decd brother, 10 gas. My goddau. Mrs Mary Pringle £20. My godson Wm Sturge Moore, Esq., £30. My grandson Elliston Sober, now in the E. Indies, £1000, if he die then £500 to his sister Penelope, £250 to his brother John S. and £250 to his brother Abr. S. To my Ex'or £1000 on Trust for my granddau. Pen. S. at 25. My grandson John S. £500. My grandson Abr. S. £200. To the ch. wardens of Christ Ch., B'os, £10 c., also of St Peters £10 for poor widows. My grandson Samson Wood Sober £100. My friend Sir Philip Gibbes, Bart., 10 gas., and John Brathwaite, Esq., 10 gas. Release my dau. Mary Sober and granddau. Pen. Sober from all sums owing for their board and lodging with me. All residue to my dau.-in-law Mary Sober. My sd dau. and Sir Ph. Gibbes, John Brathwaite, Esq., and my grandson Samson Wood Sober, Ex'ors. Proved 21 June 1791 by Mary S., spr., the dau. On 18 Feb. 1791 proved by John Brathwaite, Esq.; power reserved to Sir Ph. Gibbes and S. W. Sober. (302, Bevor.)

Samson Wood Sober of the p. of St Peter and I. of B'os. Will dated 18 April 1799. My wife Jennett S. £1000 and plate. My dau. Judith S. at 18 £3000. My dau. Eliz. Jennett S. £3000 at 18. To my son Harrison Walke S. my sugar work plantation in St Peter with the slaves, and all residue remr to my 2 daus. My wife, my father Cumberbatch S., Esq., my wife's uncle Tho. Walke, Esq., Ex'ors and G. In the presence of Jno Howell, P. W. Sandiford, Wm Cadogan. Proved 22 April 1811 by Jennett S., wid., and C. S., Esq., the father. (198, Crickitt.)

Tho. Walke of the I. of B'os, Esq. Will dated 5 April 1800. To my wife Eliz. Jennett W. £1200 a year from my bank annuities in lieu of dower, to reside on my plantation of Ashton Hall, power to bequeath £8000, if she marry then only £800 a year. My niece Jennett Sober £1000 a year for her support and the education of her son Harrison Walke S. (not 16). To Judith S. and Eliz. Jennett S., daus. of my sd niece, £5000 each at 21. My niece Abigail Jane Thomas, wife of Mr Wm Carter, T. formerly A. J. Dunckley, spr., the follg sums due to my late brother Harrison W., Esq., viz.: £3090 due from Cumberbatch Sober, Esq., on judgment dated 15 May 1793; £1852 due from Mr Jacob Goodridge on judgment dated 26 Aug. 1795, and £1300 due from Mr Eyare Pile on judgment dated 26 Aug. 1795, making £6242 c. To Eliz. Jennett T. and Mary Jane T., daus. of sd W. C. T. and Abig. Jane T., £3000 each at 21. My niece Mary Harrison Dunckley £12,000 annuities. I remit to Miss Dorothy Lisle and Miss Margt Warren Lisle all sums due including £310 secured by their late Mother's note, and to Doro. L. £200 a year, and to bequeath by her will £4000. To Margt W. L. £409 a year with power by her will to dispose of £4000. My godson Tho. Harrison Walke Wharton, son of Mrs Mary W., wid., £150 a year until 18, £200 a year till 23, then £1000. To his M. £50 a year. Mrs Mary Walke, wid. of my late brother John W., decd, £50 a year. My godson Tho. Walke Lemar Wood, son of Samson Wood, Jr, and Sarah his wife, formerly Sarah Sober, £500 at 21. My godson Edwd Beaufoy, son of Wm Henry B. and Agnes his wife, formerly Agnes Payne, £200 at 21. Godson Tho. Daniel the Yr of Bristol, Mt, £1000. My godson Tho. Daniel, son of sd Tho. D. the Yr, £1000

at 21. My goddau. Maria Daniel, d. of s[d] Tho. Daniel the Y[r], £500 at 21. John Daniel of Mincing Lane, M[t], £1000. M[rs] Ann Cave, wife of M[r] Stephen C., £100. John Cave, son of s[d] Stephen C. by Ann his wife, £500 at 21. M[rs] Eleanor Belfield, wife of Rev. Finney B., £200. M[rs] Eleanor Gell £100 and her sons John G. and W[m] G., Edw. Gell and Tho. G. and Chas. G. £100 each at 21. To Miss Joan Worrell, dau. of Edw. W., Esq., dec[d], £250. To my wife Eliz. J. W., Tho. Daniel the Elder of Mincing Lane, M[t], Tho. Daniel the Y[r], John Daniel and W[m] Carter, Thomas and W[m] Prescod of B'os. Esq., my sugar work pl[n] in the p. of S[t] Tho. heretofore belonging to the Hon. Jas. Carter, Esq., dec[d], also my Ashton Hall pl[n] in S[t] Peter, my pl[n] of Overhill in S[t] Andrew with the houses, mills and slaves to the use of Harrison Walke Sober, the eldest son of my niece Jennett S., at 23, remainder to the sons of my nieces Abig. J. Thomas, and Mary H. Dunckley, etc., 130 slaves to be kept on Carters, 130 on Ashton Hall and 115 on Overhill. To each child of my s[d] 3 nieces £3000. All sums in the hands of Messrs. Tho. Daniel and Co. of L. or Tho. D. and Son of Bristol, and all residue to T. for H. W. S. Trustees to be Ex'ors. In the presence of Tho. M[c]Intosh, Renn Hamden, W[m] Welch, Sam. Moore. Proved 3 Nov. 1800 by E. J. W., wid., Tho. Daniel the Elder, Tho. D. the Y[r] and John Daniel; power reserved to the others. (826, Adderley.)

Abraham Cumberbatch Sober. (Will very short and not dated.) My wife Ann the dau. of the late Tho. Kemp, M.P. for Lewes, co Sussex, all my estate and sole Ex'trix, she paying to each of my brothers and sister 100 gas. Proved 7 April 1814 by Ann S. (248, Bridport.)

Jennett Sober. Will dated 22 Nov. 1815. All sums due from the £1000 left me by my husband, the £1000 annuity left me by my uncle Tho. Walke, the £800 c. annuity left me by my uncle Harrison Walke and my jointure of £600 st. to my mother M[rs] Mary Walke. £100 to my father-in-law Cumberbatch Sober, Esq., for Eliza Rice, late Allison, for the support of Emily Allison her child. Plate equally to my three ch[n] Harrison Walke Sober, Judith Sober and Eliza Jennett Sober. My father-in-law sole Ex'or. In the presence of Jennett Sober, Eliza Brauthwayt, Joan Trent. Proved 15 Dec. 1815 by C. S., Esq. (624, Pakenham.)

ST. JOHN'S, BARBADOS.

1734-5 Feb. 18 Thomas Sober to Jane Redman.

ST. JOSEPH'S, BARBADOS.

1738-9 Mar. 2 John Sobers to Margaret Ceeley.

ST. GEORGE'S, HANOVER SQUARE.

1818 Feb. 19 Francis Onslow Trent, Esq., B., of this parish. & Judith Sober, S., of St. Marylebone. Lic.

1638. John Sober and Tho. Sober, owners of more than 10 acres. (Memoirs of the First Settlement, p. 82.)

1760, Nov. 6. John Sober, Esq., of Barbadoes, to Miss Pen. Blake of Sevenoak, Kent. ("G.M.," 542.)

1774, Feb. 2. Bath. Sat. died at her lodgings in this City, the lady of John Sober, Esq., of the island of Barbados. ("Bath Chronicle.")

1802, Feb. 15. At her father's house, the wife of A. C. Sober, esq. a still-born dau. ("G.M.," 181.)

1805, July 6. Mrs. Hannah Sober, St. Michaels. ("Barbados Mercury.")

1805, Dec. 24. Mr. Aaron Sober to Miss Sarah Elizabeth Wilkie, St. Michael's. (*Ibid.*)

1811, March 7. In Upper George-street, Portman-sq. Sampson Wood Sober, esq. of the Polygon, Southampton, only son of Cumberbatch Sober, esq. ("G.M.," 397.)

1811, Apr. 23. On the 4th ulto. at his father's house, London, Sampson Wood Sober, Esq., of this island. ("Barbados Mercury.")

1813, Dec. 7. Aged 42, Abraham Cumberbatch Sober, esq. ("G.M.," 700.)

1815, Dec. 1. In Blandford-st. aged 42, Mrs. Jennett Sober, relict of the late S. W. Sober, esq. of the Polygon, Southampton. (*Ibid.*, 642.)

1827, Jan. 13, In Upper George-st. Bryanston-sq. aged 85, Cumberbatch Sober, esq. (*Ibid.*, 92.)

1832, Oct. 16. In Torrington-sq. aged 18, Mary-Esther, youngest dau. of late Abraham Cumberbatch Sober, esq. (*Ibid.*, 482.)

Tho. Kemp of Lewes Castle and Hurstmonceaux Park, co. Sussex, M.P., left a son Tho. R. Kemp, born 1782, and a dau. Anne, who mar. 1, Rev. Geo. Bythesea, R. of Ightham, co. Kent, and 2, Capt. A. C. Sober of the Dragoon Guards. (Burkes "Landed Gentry.")

Eton, 1811. Harrison Walke Sober, formerly of the 14th Hussars, died lately. (Eton School Lists, published in 1863, p. 73.)

Grantees of Arms, &c., 1687–1898.*

(Part II., K. to Z., Harl. Soc. Pub.)

ADDITIONS AND CORRECTIONS, Vol. II., Part. I.

Aberdein to Harvey, *for* "17 . ." *read* "[1791]."
Bethell late Codrington, Christopher, ? *for* "late" *read* "before; Roy. Lic., 17 Nov. 1797."
Colyear-Dawkins, *add* "[Crisp., Fragm. Geneal., XIII, p. 23]."
Drax, (Erle-), *after* "1828" *add* "[1829]."
Ellis, of Sunning Hill, *for* "180 ." *read* "[1810]."
Grant, Charles, *for* "182 ." *read* "[1830]."

KENNEDY before LAURIE, ..., of Jamaica and London, Quarterly Arms, [1802], Vol. XXI, fo. 425.
KENNION, ..., of Finsbury Square, London, [1809], Vol. XXV, fo. 118.

LAFOREY, John (s. of John), afterwards a Baronet, of Plymouth, co. Devon, 1789, Vol. XVII, fo. 160.
LAMEGO, ..., of London, Match with BARUH-LOUSADA, [1777], Vol. XIII, fo. 255.
LAROCHE, ..., Post-Capt., R.N., of Totnes, co. Devon, [1803], Vol. XXII, fo. 220.

* Continued from p. 160.

LASCELLES, ..., Baron Harewood, [1790], of co. York, Supporters [1790], Vol. XIX, [XVII ?], fo. 285.

LAVINGTON (Ralph PAYNE), Baron, [1795], grant to William PAYNE, his brother of half-blood [who assumed the Surname and Arms of GALLWEY, 1814; Bart. 1812], [1813], Vol. XXVII, fo. 454.

LEMAN late ORGILL, M.A., Naunton Thomas, of Brampton and Worlingham, co. Suff., 1808, Vol. XXIV, fo. 372.

LETTSOM, ..., of London, [1802 ?], Vol. XXI, fo. 289.

LEVY, ..., of Porchester Gate, London, and Jamaica [1872], Vol. XVIII, fo. 162.

LEYBORNE before POPHAM, [Brig.-Gen. Edward William Leyborne ?], of Littlecot, Wilts, [Gov. of the ?] Isle of Grenada, etc., Quarterly Arms, [1804], Vol. XXIII, fo. 107, Quarterly Arms, fo. 109.

LEYBOURNE, ..., of London and Barbados, [1809], Vol. XXV, fo. 200.

LINDO, ..., of Devonshire Square, London, [1819 ?], Vol. XXXI, fo. 177.

LONG, Edward, of Aldermaston House, Berks; Tredudwell, St. Blaze, co. Cornwall; Saxmundham, co. Suffolk; and the Island of Jamaica, 1797, Vol. XIX, fo. 423; 1795 [in pencil].

LONG now NORTH, Dudley, of Glemham Hall and Saxmundham, co. Suffolk, [1797], Vol. XIX, fo. 440.

LONG, Edward, Charles and Samuel, of Saxmundham, co. Suffolk, and Carshalton, co. Surrey, 1800, [1801 ?], Vol. XXII, fo. 247.

LONG, Sir Charles, G.C.B., [1820], Paym.-Gen. to H.M. Forces, Supporters, 1820, Vol. XXXII, fo. 377 [?].

LOPES, Manasseh Masseh, of Clapham, co. Surrey, (Bart., died s.p.), [1782], Vol. XV, fo. 14.

LOPES late FRANCO, Sir Ralph, of co. Devon, [1831], Vol. XXXVIII, fo. 240.

LOUSADA, Emanuel Baruh, of London and Jamaica (*see* Dav. E. CARDONELL), 28 Jan. 1777, Vol. XIII, fo. 255.

LYONS, Sir Edmond, Knt., K.C.H., [1835], and Bart., [1840], Minister Plenipotentiary to Greece, Capt. R.N., of Lyons, Isle of Antigua, and St. Austin, Hampshire, [1841], Vol. XLV, fo. 150, augmentation [1843], Vol. XLVI, fo. 360, G.C.B., [1844], Supporters, [1844], Vol. XLVII, fo. 233.

MAITLAND, Maj.-Genl. Sir Peregrine, K.C.B., [1815], of Shrub's Hill near Lyndhurst, Hampshire, 1818, Vol. XXX, [? XXVIII, 1815], fo. 369.

MARTIN, ..., of St. Kitts, [1810], Vol. XXVII, fo. 123.

MATHEW (and NAYLOR), H. E., of co. Cornwall, and Shrub's Hill and Clanville Lodge, Hampshire, [1819], Vol. XXXI, fo. 293.

MATHEW to BERTIE, Brownlow Bertie, of Shrub's Hill and Clanville Lodge, Hampshire, [1819], Vol. XXXI, fo. 296.

MAY, ..., (Spr.), of Bath and Jamaica, [1838], Vol. XLVIII, fo. 187.

MAYER, ..., of London, Quartering with WICKHAM, [1785], Vol. XVI, fo. 45.

MILL, George G., [? David], of Bath, co. Som., and Carriacou, W.I., [16 July 1803], Vol. XXII, fo. 294, [Crisp, Fragm. Gen., V, p. 60].

MILLER to CODDRINGTON, James, of Dodington, co. Glouc., nat. s. of Sir William Codrington, of Dodington, [1792], Vol. XVIII, fo. 33.

MINTO, Capt. of Mil., of Water Valley, par. of Trelawney, co. Cornw., and Jamaica, [1815], Vol. XXVIII, fo. 332.

MOLINEUX before MONTGOMERIE, George, Capt. Norfolk Mil., Quartering [1782], Vol. XV, fo. 32.

MOLINEUX (CRISP) before MONTGOMERIE, George, of Garboldisham, co. Norf., Quarterly Arms, [1813], Vol. XXVII, fo. 392.

MOORE, ..., of St. Michael, Barbados, [1781], Vol. XV, fo. 367.

MORANT to GALE, Edward G., of Hampsh., [1796 ?], Vol. XIX, fo. 189.

MORSE, ..., of London and Jamaica, (*see* GRIFFITHS), [1810], Vol. XXVI, fo. 108.

MORTON-HERBERT, ..., of the Isle of Nevis, Arms of Herbert, [1822], Vol. XXXIII, fo. 208.
Moss, Samuel, Capt. of Artillery, of Kingston, Jamaica, [1845], Vol. XLVIII, fo. 87.
MOULTON to (? after) BARRETT, Edward Barrett, of New York, and Cinnamon Hill, Island of Jamaica, and his brother Samuel, [1797], Vol. XX, fo. 110.
MOULTON, Edward (wife BARRETT), of Wakefield, Island of Jamaica, [1815], Vol. XXIX, fo. 25
MUNT, ..., of Cheshunt, co. Hertf., and Kingston, Island of Jamaica, [1832 ?], Vol. XXXIX, fo. 170.

NEAVE, Richard, of St. Mary-at-Hill, London, 1763, Vol. X, fo. 467. (Berry.)
NEAVE, ..., of Dagnam Park, co. Essex, [1795], Vol. XIX, fo. 175.
NELSON, Viscountess, (WOOLWARD), widow, Escutcheon of pretence, [1805], Vol. XXIII, fo. 250.
NEVELL, Mary, relict of Vice-Adm. John, of the West Indies, to descendants of the Admiral, 15 Dec. 1697, Vol. IV, fo. 239.
NEWTON, (Jarratt), of Trelawney, Island of Jamaica, [1793], Vol. XVIII, fo. 218.
NEWTON to FRYE, ..., of co. Surrey, Quarterly Arms, [1801], Vol. XXI, fo. 152.
NIBBS, James LANGFORD-, of Antigua, and co. Som.; of St. John's Coll., Oxf., 13 Oct. 1759, Vol. X, fo. 188. (Berry.)

OGILVIE late PERRY, ... (Arms for CLARKE, his wife), of Stanwell, co. Middx.; Langley Park, co. Forfar, Scotland; and of St. Mary, Jamaica, 1801, Vol. XXI, fo. 162.
OSBORNE late BERNAL, Ralph, of co. Middx., and Ireland, 1844, Vol. XLVII, fo. 206.
OTTLEY, ..., of York Terrace, Regent's Park; Stanwell, co. Middx.; Delaford, co. Dublin; and St. Vincent, [1848], Vol. XLIX, fo. 32
OTTLEY late HOOKER, John, of Hampsh.; co. Suff.; Sussex; and Oriel Coll., Oxf., [1820], Vol. XXXII, fo. 123.
OUGHTON, [Lieut.-Gen.], Sir James Adolphus, K.B., [1773], Gov. of Antigua, Arms, [1773], Vol. XII, fo. 234; Supporters, 1773, Vol. XII, fo. 236.

PALMER, ..., of St. James' Cornwall, and Island of Jamaica, [1791], Vol. XVII, fo. 408.
PAYNE, Ralph, of Marylebone, co. Middx. and St. Christopher's, West Indies, Quartering CARLISLE, 1770 [1771 ?], Vol. XII, fo. 49 (Berry). Sir Ralph [K.B., 18 Feb. 1771], Supporters, 1771, Vol. XII, fo. 75, [afterwards, 1795, Baron Lavington].
PAYNE, Col. William (half-brother to Baron Lavington), of co. York, London, and St. Kitts, [1813], Vol. XXVII, fo. 454.
PAYNE before GALLWEY [7 Mar. 1814], Lieut.-Gen. Sir William, Bart., of co. York, London, and St. Kitts, [1814], Vol. XXVIII, fo. 61.
PAYNE-FRANKLAND, Lady, [widow of Sir William PAYNE-GALLWEY, 2nd Bart.], of co. York, [2 Oct.] 1882, Vol. LXII, fo. 1.
PENNANT after DAWKINS, George Hay [Dawkins], of Wales, and co. Wilts, Quarterly Arms, 1806, Vol. XXIV, fo. 114.
PENNANT after DAWKINS, ..., of Wales, 1841, Vol. XLV, fo. 57.
PENNANT after DOUGLAS, Hon. Edward Gordon Douglas, of Wales, [Arms and Surname of Pennant], 1841, Vol. XLV, fo. 55.
PENNANT after DOUGLAS-, [Edward Gordon Douglas-Pennant], Baron PENRHYN, [3 Aug. 1866], Supporters, 1866, Vol. LVI, fo. 148.

PERCY (GREATHEED-BERTIE), Lord Charles, of co. Warw. [s. of the 5th Duke of Northumberland], [Surname and Arms of Greatheed-Bertie, 1 April 1826], Vol. XXXV, fo. 392.

PERRY, Micajah, of the City of London, 23 July 1701, Vol. V, fo. 45 (*see* Harl. MS., 6834, fo. 121; and Add. MS., 14,831, fo. 46, has Micajah), (8 Mar. 1700, Berry).

PINNEY late PRETOR, John, of Bettiscombe, co. Dorset, and Isle of Nevis, N. America, 18 April 1776, Vol. XIII, fo. 181. [Burke's Suppl.].

PINNEY now PRETOR, John Pinney; Rev. John Charles, of Somerton Erley, The Grange, Somerton, Carey Rivel, Burton Pinsent, [all ?], co. Som., 1877, Vol. LX, fo. 56. I. Frederick Wake, etc., of co. Som., 1877, Vol. LX, fo. 58, [*see* Burke's Suppl.]

PINNOCK, ..., of London and Jamaica, [1790], Vol. XX, fo. 385.

PITT-RIVERS late BECKFORD, [26 Nov. 1828, William Horace, 3rd Baron], RIVERS, of co. Dorset, Glouc., and Hampsh., Vol. XXXVII, fo. 229.

PLUES, Samuel Swire, of Ripon, co. York, Attorney-Gen. Brit. Honduras, [1871], Vol. LVIII., fo. 6.

PLUM(M)ER, ..., of Frome, co. Som., and Jamaica, [1805], Vol. XXIII, fo. 209.

POPE, Edward, D.D., of London, Archdeacon of Jamaica, [1842], Vol. XLVI, fo. 222.

PREVOST, Maj.-Gen. [George], of Greenhill Grove, co. Hertf., and Governor Isle of Jamaica [?], [1805], Vol. XXIII, fo. 272.

PREVOST, Lieut-Gen. [Sir George], Bart, [6 Dec. 1805], (decd. [1816]), Supporters to widow and son, [1817], Vol. XXX, fo. 124.

PRICE, Charles, of Rose Hall, Jamaica, 13 Aug. 1766, Vol. XI, fo. 182. (Berry.)

RAE to HARVEY, ..., of the Island of Grenada (Match), [1791], Vol. XVII, fo. 424.

RAE to HARVEY, ..., (reputed dau.), wife of LEE, now Harvey, of Scotland, [1820]. Vol. XXXII, fo. 235.

REID to BAILLIE, ..., of Jamaica, [1792], Vol. XVIII, fo. 85.

RICKETTS, William Henry, of Ridgland, co. Westmorland; Longwood, Hampsh; Jamaica; and the Jerseys, N. America, 3 Nov. 1773, Vol. XII, fo. 271.

RICKETTS to JERVIS (Earl ST. VINCENT), co. Staff., (Match), [1801], Vol. XXI, fo. 188.

RICKETTS to JERVIS, Viscount ST. VINCENT, of co. Staff., [1823], Vol. XXXIV, fo. 62.

RIGBY late HALE, of co. Essex, [1788], Vol. XVII, fo. 29.

RIVERS, Baron, [20 May 1776, George], Pitt, Supporters, with the consent of his brother, [1776], Vol. XIII, fo. 217.

RIVERS, [? George (PITT) 2nd], Baron, [1792], Vol. XVIII, fo. 100.

RIVERS, [3rd] Baron, [assumed the Surname of] PITT-RIVERS, 26 Nov. 1828, of co. Dorset, late BECKFORD (of co. Dorset), of co. Glouc., and Hampsh., [1828], Vol. XXXVII, fo. 227.

ROBERTS, ..., FENTON, wife of, of London, Escutcheon of pretence, [1802 ?], Vol. XXII, fo. 30.

ROGERMAN to CHAMBERS, John, of Kingston and St. Elizabeth, Jamaica, [1795], Vol. XVIII, fo. 437.

CHAMBERS,* Edward Hanover, of co. Corn., and Jamaica, 1771, Vol. XII, fo. 106. (Berry.)

ST. VINCENT, [Earl, 1797; Viscount, 1801], Adm. [Sir John JERVIS], K.B., [1782], Supporters, [1797], Vol. XIX, fo. 455.

* This entry should have appeared *ante*, p. 157.

St. Vincent, Viscount, Jervis, of co. Staff., Arms [1823], Vol. XXXIV, fo. 62. [Edward Jervis Ricketts, 2nd Viscount, assumed Roy Lic. in 1823, the Surname of Jervis only.]
St. Vincent to Parker before Jervis, ..., of co. Staff., [1861], Vol. LIV, fo. 140; 2 S[urviving] s[on].
Sandiland, ..., of Speight's Town, Island of Barbados, [1798], Vol. XX, fo. 225.
Sawbridge-Erle-Drax, John Samuel W. [Sawbridge to], of Charborough Park, co. Dorset, and Olantegh, co. Kent, [1829], Vol. XXXVII, fo. 344.
Sawbridge-Erle-Drax, Wanley E., [Sawbridge to], of Holnest Place, co. Dorset, and Olantegh Towers, co. Kent, 1887, Vol. LXIV. fo. 102.
Scarlett, [Sir] James, [Knt., 1827], Baron Abinger, [12 Jan. 1835], of co. Surrey, Supporters, [1835], Vol. XL, fos. 334 and 336.
Scarlett, [Lieut.-Gen.], Sir James Yorke, G.C.B., [2 June 1869], of co. Surrey, Supporters, [1870], Vol. LVII, fo. 276.
Seaford, Baron, [15 July 1826], [Charles Augustus], Ellis, [Baron Howard de Walden], of co. Sussex, [1826], Vol. XXXVI, fo. 27.
Senior, Ascanius William, of Tewin, co. Hertf., 26 Mar. 1767, Vol. XI, fo. 204. ([26 May], Berry.)
Senior, ..., of Musquito Cove and Shafton, co. Corn., Jamaica, [1792], Vol. XVIII, fo. 89.
Shickle, ..., of Clarendon, Island of Jamaica, [1793], Vol. XVIII. fo. 181.
Simpson, ..., of Fairlawn, Wrotham, co. Kent; Tileston, co. Chester; and Bounty Hall, Trelawney, Jamaica, [1799], Vol. XX, fo. 306.
Swete, Adrian, of Train, co. Devon, and to the descendants of his father, 13 Feb. 171⅞, Vol. VI, fo. 85; Add. MS., 14,830, fo. 86.

Tarleton-Fothergill, Dame, of Hensol Castle, co. Glamorgan, Wales, (widow of Sir Rose L. Price, Bart.) ? this, 1888, Vol. LXIV, fo. 138.
Taylor after Watson, George, of Wilts and Jamaica, Quarterly Arms, 1815, Vol. XXIX, fo. 93.
Tharp, John, of Good Hope, Island of Jamaica, 11 Oct. 1776, Vol. XIII, fo. 239.
Tharp-Gent, Lieut., of cos. Camb. and Essex, [1861], Vol. LIV, fo. 184.
Thomas late White, George, of Chichester, co. Sussex, [1777-78], Vol. XIV, fo. 12.
Thomas late Freeman, Inigo, of co. Sussex, and Antigua, 1786, Vol. XVI, fo. 161; (Match), [1791], Vol. XVII, fo. 410. (Berry.)
Tobin, ..., Capt. in Army, (Match), [1810], Vol. XXV, fo. 398.
Tollemache late Halliday, Rear-Adm. John Richard Delap, of Leasowes, Shroph., and Castlemains, co. Kircud., Scotland, [1821], Vol. XXXII, fo. 351.
Tollemache, Baron, [17 Jan. 1786], John [formerly Halliday, of Peckforton Castle, co. Chester, (*see* Halliday), and Helmington, co. Suff.], Supporters, 1876, Vol. LIX, fo. 192.
Trant after Dillon [Trant to Dillon-Trant], Henry, of co. York, and Ireland, Quarterly Arms, [1816], Vol. XXIX, fo. 361.
Trent-Stoughton, H. W. J., of Saltwood, Hythe, co. Kent. 1889, Vol. LXV, fo. 76.
Trower, ..., of Lincoln's Inn, London, and Jamaica, [1823 ?], Vol. XXXIII, fo. 352.

Vassall, Lieut.-Col. [Spencer Thomas], K. at Monte Video, [7 Feb. 1807], Arms to widow, 1808—10, Vol. XXV, fo. . . . .
Virgin, ..., of London, and Hope Park, Clarendon, Jamaica, [1810], Vol. XXVI, fo. 15.

WALKER, Major-Gen. Sir Geo. Townsend, K.C.B., [1815], Lieut.-Gov. of Grenada, [1815]; of Bushey, co. Hertf., Allusions, [1815], Vol. XXVI, fo. 294; G.C.B., Supporters, [1817], Vol. XXX, fo. 161; Lieut.-Gen. and Bart., [1835], Vol. XL, fo. 359.

WALKER, Thomas, s. of James, of Bow, co. Middx., descendants of his father James, 28 Jan. 1713-14, Vol. VI, fo. 128 (*see* Add. MS., 14,830, fo. 53).

WHITE before WILLIAMS, ..., of Duckworth Plantation, co. Surrey, Island of Jamaica, Quartering, [1809 ?], Vol. XXV, fo. 72.

WILDMAN, Thomas and James, of Hornby, co. Lanc.; Jamaica; and Lincoln's Inn, London, 9 Dec. 1776, Vol. XIII, fo. 247.

WILDMAN, Capt., of co. (Kent ?), and Arms of OLIVAR (his wife), reputed dau. of Sir H. Oakes, Bart. impaled, [1818], Vol. XXXI, fo. 55.

WILDMAN, Lieut.-Col. . . . ., of co. Kent ?, and Arms of PREISIG (his wife) impaled. [1824], Vol. XXXIV, fo. 321.

WILDMAN-LUSHINGTON, ..., of co. Kent, [1870], Vol. LVII, fo. 234.

WILKIE, Patrick, of St. Vincent, W.I., 15 Sept. 1770, Vol. XII, fo. 30. (Berry.)

WILLETT late ADYE, John Willett, of Merley Place, co. Dorset, (Match), 11 Mar. 1795, Vol. XIX, fo. 19.

WILLOCK to DAWES, ..., of cos. Kent and Sussex, [1870], Vol. LVII, fo. 258.

WILLOCK, Henry C. and Col. George W., of Marine Parade, Brighton, 1893, Vol. LXVII, fo. 156.

Monumental Inscriptions in England relating to West Indians.*

CROMHALL, CO. GLOUC.

The following four inscriptions are from Glouc. N. and Q., iv., 645.

In the church:—

Sacred
to the memory
of MARY the wife
of EDMUND FEARON BOURKE,
of the Island of Jamaica,
who resided at Wood End, in this Parish,
for more than seven years.
Her remains are placed in a vault purchas'd,
by a faculty from the Diocese of Gloucester, by the
said EDMUND FEARON BOURKE in the chancel of
this Church for the interment of his family.
She died the 30th July, 1800,
and in the 38th year of her age.

In the church:—

Sacred to the memory | of | Edmund Fearon Bourke, Esq., | of | the Island of Jamaica, | who | departed this life | at Exmouth, | in the County of Devon, | on Tuesday, Jan. 14th, | 1812, | aged 57 | whose remains are deposited | in the family vault | underneath.

"1772, Feb. Nicholas Bourke, Esq; Jamaica." ("G.M.," 151.)

* Continued from p. 248.

Nicholas Burke of Clarendon, Esq., d. 11 Dec. 1771. Will dated 13 May 1771, of which his brother John B. of L., Esq., was a trustee. By Eliz. his wife (party to mortgage of 1765) he had: 1. Tho. B. of St. Mary, Esq., 1791; 2. Edmund Fearon B., late of Clarendon. but of Gt. B., 1791: and 3. A dau., wife of Cha. Pallmer of St. Tho. in the Vale, Esq , in 1771. See Livingstone's Sketch Pedigree (which gives the year of death of Nich. as 1774 instead of 1771) and a deed of conveyance of Bourke's of 192 acres in the parish of St. Dorothy dated 1791. (*Ante*, III., 23.)

Nicholas B. was cousin of Rob. Arcedeckne, and both families were from Ireland. He was M. of A. for Kingston 1754, '55, Portland 1761, Clarendon 1757, '66, '68, '70; Speaker 1770, but resigned shortly after.

Lord Adam Gordon met in 1764 at Jamaica "Nich[s] Bourke, Esq[r], a Counsellor, son in law to C. J. Fearon." Footnote says: m. Eliz. dau. of Tho. Fearon, Chief Justice. His dau. Fra. m. Geo. Crawford Ricketts, Atty. Gen. and Advocate Gen., and of Combe, co. Hereford. (Genealogist, New S., xiv., 16.)

Tho. B. was M. for St. Mary 1773, '76, '81, Clarendon 1790.

Edm. F. B. was M. for Clarendon 1779. (Feurtado.)

See W.I. Bookplates, No. 311.

1812, Jan. 23. On the 14th inst. died at Exmouth, Edmund Fearon Bourke, esq; late a resident of this city; a gentleman of most benevolent disposition, and held in the highest esteem in the first circles of society; an affectionate and kind relative, a sincere and valuable friend. ("Bath Chronicle.")

1814, July 7. Sat. was m. at Topham, the Rev. J. C. Glascott, of Exmouth, to Georgiana, dau. of the l. E. F. Bourke, esq; of Exmouth. (*Ibid.*)

Edmund Fearon Bourke of Exmouth, Esq. Will dated 30 May 1808. My dau. Mary Judith wife of Henry Fellowes, clerk. My dau. Eliz. Ann Kath. wife of Chas. Freeman, Esq. All my plantations in J. to T. to sell for my 5 ch[n] Ann Lydia B., Georgina Goodin B., Jane Peters B., Charlotte Woollery B. and George Rob. Goodin B. My eldest son Edm[d] F. B. to have the option of purchase of plantations for £25,000. Proved 1 Feb. 1812. (55, Oxford.) (See *ante*, III., 23.)

See the M.I. to his dau. Jane at Withycombe Ralegh, co. Devon.

In the church:—

Under this place
(in the vault belonging to
Edmund Fearon Bourke, Esq[r])
are deposited the remains
of
Agnes Chisholme,
daughter of
James and Susanna Chisholme,
who departed this life
April 23rd, 1798,
in the twelfth year of her age.

In the vault underneath are deposited the remains of—

Susanna Chisholme wife of
James Chisholme, Esq[r], of Stonedge.
in Roxburghshire, North Britain,
who died December, 31st, 1801,
aged 59.
Also the remains of
the said James Chisholme, Esq[r],
who died December 31st, 1812,
aged 68,

1801, Dec. 31. In Portland-place, the wife of James Chisholme esq. of Stonedge, co. Roxburgh. ("G.M.," 1217.)

1802, Feb. 13. In Portland-place, Lord Sinclair, to Miss Chisholme, only dau. of James C. esq. (*Ibid.*, 181.)

1812, Dec. 31. In Portland-place, aged 68, Jas. Chisholme, esq. of Chisholme & Stonedge co. Roxburgh. N.B. (*Ibid.*, 674.)

1814, July 16. At Nisbet-house, co. Berwick, N.B. R[t] Hon. Lady Sinclair. She was the only dau. of James Chisholme, of Chisholme esq. & was married to the R[t] Hon. Charles Lord Sinclair Feb. 13, 1802. (*Ibid.*, 292.)

Will. Chisholme of Queen Ann Street, Marylebone, Esq. Will dated 25 June 1801. To be buried in Selkirk. Sister Margaret Scott of Edinburgh £500 a year. My one fourth share of Trout Hall and Green River sugar plantations in Clarendon, Jamaica, and two penns, one called Iveys and the other at Mammee Valley, to my brother James Chisholme of Portland place. My reputed son Charles, a waiter at Bengal, £20,000. My sugar plantations and penns in Clarendon called Thomas's River and North Hall, Health Crawl and Broadland Penn to be sold for the 8 children of my sister Margaret Scott, Miss Agnes Chisholme (the dau. of my brother James) and my reputed son Charles equally. Proved 29 Nov. 1802. (812, Kenyon.)

James Chisholme of Portland-place, Esq. Will dated 21 Jan. 1803. My leasehold house No. 5 Portland-place for my dau. Mary Agnes Lady Sinclair. My house at Green River, co. Roxburgh, and all other real estate in G. B. and Jamaica to be sold and proceeds in trust for her. To be buried in the vault over the grave of my late wife in the church-yard of Cromhall near the village of Wickwar, co. Glouc. Proved 1 Feb. 1813. (62, Heathfield.)

OLD WOKING, CO. SURREY.

A tablet on the south wall of the chancel:—

In the Chancel
Near the Remains of his Father and Mother
MAXIMILIAN and JANE EMILY,
and of his Brothers and Sister
THOMAS, FRANCES, MORGAN and GEORGE EMILY,
and those of his Neice MARY JAMES
Daughter of RANDYLL EMILY who died at Jamaica,
reſt alſo the Remains
of EDWARD EMILY
of Weſt-Clandon, in this County Eſquire
who on the thirteenth day of May 1760
and on the ſeventy third Year of his Age
Exchanged this Life for a better.
(Five verses of four lines omitted.)

Haughton James of Jamaica, Esq., married Mary Emily, and in the codicil to his will dated 17 Oct. 1740 bequeathed to his sister-in-law Mrs. Maximillia Emily £100 c. See the bookplate of testator's son with the quartered coat of Emily: *Sable, a man Argent, in the dexter hand a club.* (Illustrated, *ante*, II., 1.)

Edward Emily of New Inn, gent., made his will 4 Feb. 1760. He owned the manor of Woking which descended to his eldest son Charles, two farms in Hemdon, co. N'ton, and a leasehold house in Henrietta Street, Covent Garden. He named also his wife Joyce, his younger son Edward, his dau. Emelia and brother-in-law Chr. Blanchard. (192, Lynch.) A pedigree of Emyly of Helmedon was entered in the Visitation of Northamptonshire of 1618.

TOPSHAM, CO. DEVON.

Mural tablet north side:—

SAMUEL MITCHELL, of Hope Vale, Grenada, W.I. President of the Council of that Island, and Colonel of the Colonial Militia (for thirty years a resident in the W.I.) born 5 Oct. 1750, died at Newport near Topsham 4 Feb. 1805. He married Mary, daughter of Daniel Floud, of Exeter, who was born 6 April 1773 and died 12 March 1861.

ARMS.—*Gules, on a chevron between three birds' wings erect Or, as many griffins' heads erased of the first*; impaling: *Vert, a chevron between three wolves' heads erased Argent.* (FLOUD.)
CREST.—*A dragon's head erased Gules, holding in the mouth a cross-fitchée Or.*

The arms of Floud as above described were confirmed in the time of Q. Eliz. to Sir Tho. Fludd in the county of Kent, and are now borne by the Irish family, of which Henry Flood the orator was a distinguished ornament. ("Devon Notes and Gleanings," iv., 159.)

1805, Feb. 4. At Newport, near Exeter, the Hon. Samuel Mitchell, president of his Majesty's Council at Grenada. He had spent the greatest part of his useful life in that island, which, during a period of dangerous revolt, the wisdom of his measures, & the promptitude with which they were executed, prevented from falling into the hands of the French.
For this conduct so highly honourable to his character, he received a vote of thanks from the Council, & the grateful tribute of all those who were interested in this important event. In private life he was a man whose mild virtues eminently endeared him to his family & his friends, & whose active benevolence diffused happiness through a widely-extended circle. ("G.M.," 189.)
In his will dated 26 Nov. 1804 he confirmed his wife's joynture of £500 a year and gave her £12,000 and the use of his estate of Newport. He desired to be interred in the midst of the clump of firs on the mount overlooking the marsh. All his estate passed to his dau. Mary Eliz. Stewart, who in 1836 as wife of Wm. Jas. D'Urban, together with her mother, consented to the further proving of the will. (531, Nelson.)

(To be continued.)

Sanders of Nevis.

Jacob Williams of Nevis, planter. Will dated 10 Dec. 1736. My sister Eliz. Saunders £2 for a ring. To Eliz., dau. of George Saunders, a negro. My nephew Jacob Williams Saunders £25. ("Antigua," iii., 233.)

Tho. Williams of Nevis, Esq. Will dated 20 Sept. 1766. To Eliz. Sanders, spinster, my housekeeper £100 c. a year, my dwelling house at Saddle Hill and the use of the S. chamber. To my great-niece Eliz. Sanders, dau. of my late nephew Francis Sanders, Esq., £1000 c. at 21, to forfeit it if she marry Roger Pemberton before her age of 21. My great-nephew John Williams Sanders, son of my said nephew Francis S., Esq., deceased, my plantation in the p'sh of St Tho. and my plantn in Nevis at 21. Jacob Williams Sanders, Esq., deceased. Proved 8 July 1767. (290, Legard.)

Edward Paris of Nevis, Esq. Will dated 6 March 1770. Francis Sanders, s. of my sister Sanders £300.

Francis Sanders of Nevis, 1677-8.

Francis Sanders, Sen., planter. Will dated 17 June 1739. = Anne . . . ., bur. 4 June 1720 at St. George's.

A

George Sanders = Elizabeth . . . ., born 1693; sister 1736 of Jacob Williams; bur. 22 Oct. 1764, aged 71, at St. John's.

Jacob Williams Sanders, born 1729; nephew 1736 of his uncle Jacob Williams. Will dated 22 Sept. 1753; bur. 6 Jan. 1756, aged 27, at St. John's.

Elizabeth Sanders, 1736.

Francis Sanders, Jun., nephew 1766 of Tho. Williams; died intestate. = Martha, dau. of Col. John Williams of Antigua; bapt. 28 Oct. 1729 at St. John's, Antigua; mar. *circa* 1748; remar. 24 Oct. 1756 Tho. Wenham, Sen.

John Williams Sanders, only son and heir, great-nephew and heir 1766 of Tho. Williams; a minor 1768; bur. 1791 at St. John's. = Elizabeth . . . ., ? sister 1770 of Edward Paris, Esq.

Eliz. Sanders, only dau., mar. 1 Jan. 1767 Roger Pemberton. She was bur. in 1783.

Francis Williams Sanders, Esq., bapt. about 1769 at St. Tho. Lowland; of Lincoln's Inn. (See W.I. Bookplate No. 602, engraved about 1820.)

1748. Petition of John Le Sprainger Spencer Rossington and Eliz. Stephens his wife, one of the daus. of Sarah Saunders, late of Nevis, last of A., widow, dec^{d}, who d. intestate 22 Dec. 1748 and left 3 daus., pet^{r} her eldest dau. Ann wife of Walter Rossington; and Frances wife of John Butler. Filed 11 Jan. 1748. (Court of Ordinary, Antigua.)

1763, March 25. Ind're trip. betw. Wm. Woolward of N. gent. of the 1st part; Tho. Wenham of N. gent. and Martha his wife l. widow of Fra. Sanders l. of N. gent. and Tho. Williams esq. which said Martha Wenham and Tho. Williams are adm'ors of Fra. Sanders of the 2^{d} part; John Williams Sanders esq. and Eliz. Sanders spr. only ch^{n} of the said Fra. S. by the said Martha of the 3^{d} part; Whereas Wm. Woolward the Elder gent. by his will dated 10 March 1744 bequeathed to his wife Martha ½ his est. and ½ to her for life and after her death to his nephew Wm. Woolward party to this, his nephew Thos. and sister and Wm. Woolward party to this sold his ½ to Fra. Sanders for £1000. (Nevis Deeds, L., p. 15.)

1768, June 28. Petition of John Williams Sanders, a minor, that your petitioner's father d. intestate and your petitioner's uncle Jacob Williams S., esq., by his will made 22 Sept. 1753 left all his est. to yor pet^{r}. As to Guardians. (Nevis Book of Wills, p. 188.)

I have the signature of "John Williams Sanders, 1768," which I discovered beneath a bookplate of John Pinney.

1772, Dec. 22. Petition of Margt. Gardner, aged 19½, for her brothers-in-law David Gardner and Wm. Sanders, Esquires, who m. her two sisters, to be her Guardians. (*Ibid.*, p. 319.)

See *Ante*, II., 22, for schedule of deeds of Stony Hill, the estate of Fra. Sanders, Esq.

See *Ante*, Vols. I. and II., for several entries from the registers of St. John's and St. George's.

A

Francis Sanders, Jun., born 1691; died 18 July 1742, aged 51. M.I. at St. Geo. Will dated 2 April 1742. = Sarah Choppin, mar. 7 Sept. 1718 at St. Geo.; died intestate 22 Dec. 1748 at Antigua. Her sister Fra. mar. John Williams and Eliz. mar. Tho. Stevens of A.

John Sanders. = Henrietta, dau. and coh. of Jas. Bevon, Speaker of Nevis 1696; bur. 30 Dec. 1746, and M.I. at St. John's. See his will, *Ante*, III., 410.

Eliz. Stephens Sanders, 1st dau. and coh., bapt. 9 Nov. 1722; mar. John Le Spranger Rossington of Antigua. His will dated 1759. She was bur. 18 April 1770.

Ann Sanders, 2nd dau. and coh., mar. *circa* 1748 Walter Rossington of Nevis, Esq.

—

Frances Sanders, marr. sett. 1746—8 with John Butler of Nevis, merchant; a widow in 1772.

Jas. Bevon Sanders, born 21 July, bapt. 29 Aug., and bur. 11 Nov. 1733 at St. John's.

Santa Cruz or St. Croix.

This island, one of the group of the Virgin Islands, recently purchased from Denmark by the U S.A., attracted during past years many settlers from the Leeward Islands. British merchants were also drawn thither by the large profits derived in war-time from the sales of cargoes. These men were often smugglers and sometimes traitors, as proved by correspondence seized by Lord Rodney at the capture of St. Eustatius.

There is an early map of 1671, with the names of plantations, in Du Tertre, iii., 114. The following list gives one a good idea of the status of the British planters, as there are Members of Council and Officers of Militia among them; evidence of their fair treatment by the Danish Government. A few notes have been added as a guide to the origin of some of the families:—

A Treatise on Planting, by Joshua Peterkin, 1790.

A List of Subscribers in St. Croix.

Anderson, John, Esq.
„ James, Esq.
Armstrong[0], Edward, Esq.
Armstrong, Thomas T., Esq.
„ Thomas, Sen., Esq.
Avery, Christopher, Esq.

Baker, George, Esq.
Barnes[1], John, Esq.
„ John, Jun., Esq.
„ John, M.D.
Benners, Isaac S., Esq.
Bladwell, Thomas M., Esq.
Bourke[2], M. L., Esq.
„ William, Esq.
Brakle[3], John Van, Esq.
Bretton[4], Baron Paulus Van
Buchanan, J. S., Esq.
Burd, Robert, Esq.
Byam[5], William, Esq.

Carden, John, Esq.
Castle, Henry, Esq.
Chabert, Charles, Jun., Esq.
Clark, Mr. William
Coakley[6], Major
Colbiörnsen, Hon. Edward, Esq.
Conoran, Patrick, Esq.
Constable, Jacob, Esq.
Coppinger, Peter. Esq.

Daly[7], Charles, Esq.
Davies, Rowland, Esq., Captain
Delaney[8], John William, Esq.
De Windt[9], Jan, Esq.
„ Lucas, Esq.
Dogherty, Felix, Esq.
Dunlop, John, Esq.

Ellis, Charles, Esq.
England, Francis, Esq.

Farrington, William, Esq.
Ferrall[10], Peter, Esq.
„ Richard, Esq.
Finlay, Thomas, Esq.
Fitzpatrick, James, Esq.
Flanagan, Christopher, Esq., Captain of Kings-Quarter
Forster, Richard S., Esq.
Fraser, James, Esq.
„ Mr. John
Fullerton, Archibald, Esq., Lieut. in the Militia of West-End Quarter

Gerairdt, J. P., Esq.
Gordon, Alexander, Esq.
„ George, Esq.
„ [11] John, Esq.
Gordon, Robert Melville, Esq.
„ William, Esq.
Grant[12], Alexander, Sen., Esq.
„ Colin, Esq.
Gumbs[13], Jacob, Esq.

Hartwell, Mr. Garrett
Hatchet, Mr. John, Jun.
Heitmann, Henry, Esq.
„ „ Sen., Esq.
Hendricksen, Cornels. Farrington, Esq.
Henderson, James, Esq.
Hern, . . ., Esq., for self and the estate of Sion-Hill
Heyliger, Mrs. Catherine, Widow of B. P. de Neilly, Esq.
Heyliger[14], John De Windt, Esq.
„ Hon. Chamberlain Major Martin Meyer, Captain of Frederickstœd Company
Higgins, Æneas, Esq.
Huyghue[15], Samuel, Esq.
„ William, Esq.

James, John, Esq.
Johnson, Christopher Robert, Esq.
„ Dr. Christopher
„ Dr. J.

Kipnorse, Mrs. Catherine
Kortright[16], C. H., Esq.
Krause, John, Esq., Lieut. in the Town of Christianstæd

Lang, Robert, Esq,
„ William, Esq.
Love, James, Esq.

McBean. William, Esq.
McEvoy[17], Christopher, Esq.
„ Michael, Esq.
McFarlane, Daniel, Esq.
„ David, Esq.
Mardenbrough[18], George, Esq.
Markhoe[19], Abraham, Jun., Esq.
„ William, Esq.
Maynard, John, Esq.
Meyer, Hon. John, Esq., Member of the Burgher Council
Millar, Mr. Robert
Montgomery, Duncan, Esq.
Morton, John, Esq.

Navin, John, Esq.
Newton, Samuel, Esq.
„ [20], William, Esq.
Nugent, Hon. Christopher, Esq., Member of the Burgher Council

O'Connor, John, Esq.
O'Neil, Hon. Tully, Esq., Member of the Burgher Council
Osborn[21], Robert Weir, Esq.
Oxholm, Hon. P. L., Esq., Staadt-Hauptman of the Militia

Parson[22], Jasper, Esq.
Pentheny[23], Augustine, Esq.
„ Estate of Peter, Esq.

Rayn, Cornelius, Esq.
Reid, Giles, Esq.
Robertson, James, Esq.
Rodgers, James, Esq.

Ryane[24], John, Esq., F.R.S.
Sempill, John, Esq.
Söbötker, Adam, Esq.
Steedman[25], Dr. William
Strideron, John, Esq.

Thompson, Robert, Esq.
„ [26], Hon. Samuel, Esq.
Todd, James, Esq.
Tuite[27], Hon. Chamberlain
„ Richard, Jun., Esq.

Vaughan, Paul, Esq.

Walsh, Thomas, Esq.
Walterstorff, his Excellen. Ernest Frederick von, Esq., Major-General, Chamberlain to the King, Governor-General, and President
West[28], Rector
Wyse, Mr. Peter

[0] 1817, Oct. 30. At St. Croix, in her 20th year, Eliza, eldest dau. of Edmund Armstrong, esq., of St. Croix. ("G.M." for 1818, 87.)

[1] 1807, Jan. 12. At St. Croix, John Barker Barnes. ("G.M.," 376.)

[2] 1791, Oct. 15. At St. Croix, Jas. B. Thomason, son of the Hon. Tho. Thomason, one of h.M. counsel in Tortola, to Miss Maria Bourke, dau. of .... Bourke Esq. of the former island. ("G.M.," 1157.)
Theobald Bourke of St. Croix. Will proved 1783 [602, Cornwallis].

[3] 1848, June 2. At Paris, Mary Elizabeth, wife of John Van Brakle, esq. of the island of St. Croix. ("G.M.," 611.) Grace Franklyn Van Brakle m. 18 May 1835 Isidore P. L. Dyett, M.D. (*Ante*, IV., 148.)

[4] 1811, Aug. Lately. At Guadaloupe, Lieut. Cumming, to Baroness Judith De Bretton, eldest dau. of Baron Frederick De B. of St. Croix. ("G.M.," 188.)

[5] Of the well-known Antigua family. ("Antigua," I., 99.)

[6] 1790. At St. Croix, Major John Coakley, a relation of Dr. J. Coakley Lettsom, of London, besides sugar estates and negroes, he is said to have died worth 200,000 pieces of eight. ("G.M.," 859.)

[7] Daly of Montserrat. (*Ante*, I., 115.)

[8] Perhaps of the well-known family in St. Kitts.

[9] Cha. Pym Burt of St. Kitts, who m. Petronella, dau. of John Heyliger, Gov. of St. Eustatius, in his will dated 1772, refers to his moiety of a plantation called St. John's, in St. Croix, and cancels the will he left in 1770 with his brother-in-law John Jacob de Windt at St. Eustatius. Mrs. Adriana Gibbons (*née* de Windt) m. at St. Kitts, 15 Nov. 1770, Wm. Mills.
Will dated 24 June 1796. I, Jan de Windt, planter, of St. Croix, with my wife Sarah, born Roosevelt, by our contract of marriage of 6 July 1790, appoint her Extrix., and my brothers Peter, Wm. and James De Windt, with Peter Heyliger Robinson, Sen[r], Exors. My children Peter, Henry, Adolphus and Elizabeth. On 24 Dec. 1803 appeared James De Windt of Piccadilly, Esq., the brother. Testator, late of St. Croix, died last March. Proved 29 Dec. 1803 by Wm. and James De Windt [962, Marriott].

[10] 1787, Aug. 13. Ed. Cary, of Exeter, to Miss Bridget Farrell of the Island of St. Croix. ("G.M.," 739.) There were Farrells in Montserrat.

[11] See *ante*, i., 77, for M.I. in Bath Abbey to John Gordon, M.D., of St. Croix, who died 30 Jan. 1807, aged 53.

[12] 1835, June. On the 22nd March, in the Danish Island of St. Croix, the Lady of R. J. Grant, of a dau. ("Court Mag.")

[13] 1829, Jan. 21. At Clifton, aged 68, Sarah, relict of Wm· Gumba, esq. of the island of St. Martin. ("G.M.," 188.)

[14] John Heyliger was Gov. of St. Eustatius. John Heyliger of St. Croix graduated 29 Sept. 1763 at Leyden. There were some in St. Kitts. See also Foster, the Register of the Dutch Church, and L. Archer.

[15] See Pedigree in "Antigua," ii.

[16] 1850, April 9. At St. Leonards, aged 32, Wm. Alex. Kortright, esq. 3d son of Cornelius K. esq. late of Porto Rico. ("G.M.," 553.)

[17] He died 11 July 1792. M.I. at St. Pancras.

[18] Of a well-known family in St. Kitts.

[19] Philip Markoe was Dep. Gov., and Peter a M. of C. of Spanish Town, Virgin Islands, in 1737. Peter Markoe, son of Abraham of St. Croix, Kings Quarter, gent., matriculated from Pembroke College, Oxford. 17 Feb. 1767, aged 16. (Foster.) Wm. Markoe of St. Croix died 9 Oct. 1797, aged 34; M.I. at St. Olave's, Jewry, London. The family intermarried with the Hartmans of this island and of St. Kitts. A descendant, Francis Harman Markoe, M.D., of New York, died in 1912.

[20] Probably of St. Kitts, and died 12 May 1794, aged 78.

[21] See his Pedigree in "Antigua," ii., 369.

[22] Jasper Parson, 5th son of Edw. P. of St. Kitts, was living 1771.

[23] Augustine Pentheny of Dublin, Esq. Will dated 12 March 1802. My brother Dr. Peter P., late of St. Croix, left two daus., Mary and Ellen P. The eldest mar. Geo. B. Kelly, Esq., of the said island, and the second mar. Wm. Bourke, Esq., of Springfield in the said island; their issue to be my heirs. [191, Oxford.] Testator, a native of Longwood, co. Meath, died in Dublin, 23 Nov. 1811, aged 82; was a miser, formerly a cooper, and amassed £300,000 in Antigua and St. Croix. (See "G.M.," 187.) Geo. Bourke O'Kelly of Acton House, co. Middx., and of St. Croix, mar., 1799, Maria, dau. and coheir of Peter Pentheny. (Burke's "L.G.")

[24] See *ante*, i., 293, for note of John Ryan of St. Kitts, who owned Negro Bay estate in St. Croix.

[25] 1841, March 1. At Portobello, near Edinburgh, Lucretia Gordon, eldest dau. of Wm. Stedman, M.D., of the island of St. Croix. ("G.M.," 669.)

1813, Sept. 20. At St. Croix, Eliz. wife of Wm. Stedman, M.D., K.D. (*Ibid*, 670.)

1844. Apr. 7. At the Danish Island of St. Croix, aged 80, Wm. Stedman, M.D., Knight of Dannebrog. (*Ibid.*, .)

[26] He married.

[27] Nicholas Tuite, died 16 Nov. 1772, aged 66; M.I. in St. Pancras. (*Ante*, iii., 127.) He owned estates in Montserrat and St. Croix. His only son and heir Robert, Chamberlain to the King of Denmark, d. at Baltimore in 1813. Richard Tuite, first cousin of Robert, died in 1803.

[28] Presumably Chaplain of the English Church. It would be interesting to know if there are any English registers existing.

List of Wills recorded in Barbados down to the year 1800.*

Year.	Names of Testators.
1775	Thorne, William
„	Treasure, Jane
„	Taylor, Sarah
„	Todd, Margaret
„	Thomas, Tabitha
„	Thoyts, John
„	Turton, Francis
1776	Thompson, Ann
„	Trump, Levi
„	Thorne, Ann
„	Thomas, William
„	Thomson, Charles
„	Trotman, Henry
„	Trotman, Ann
1777	Taverner, Mary
„	Thorne, John
„	Thorpe, Mary
1778	Thomas, Benjamin
„	Triscott, Samuel
„	Thomas, Margaret
„	Thomas, John
1779	Thorne, James
„	Tunckes, Katherine
1780	Tempro, Mary
„	Triscott, John
„	Thompson, William
„	Thurbane, James
„	Thorne, William
1781	Tucker, Elizabeth
„	Turney, Henry
„	Thornhill, Henry
1782	Taylor, John
„	Thomas, Edward
„	Taylor, George House
1783	Taylor, Abigail
1785	Thomas, Mary
„	Toppin, William
„	Trusler, Jacob
1786	Tull, John
„	Turney, Henry
„	Trent, John
1787	Tull, Beaver
„	Thomas, Benjamin
„	Tapin, Thomas
„	Thorne, Jun., Joseph
1788	Turton, Edward
„	Turton, Sarah
„	Thomas, Mary
1788	Thomas, Mary
1789	Turner, John
„	Thomas, Prudence
1790	Turney, Francis
„	Thompson, Mary
„	Thomson, Christian
„	Thorne, James
1791	Terrill, Edward Brace
„	Taitt, John
„	Thornhill, Alexander
1792	Thornton, Susanna
„	Tucker, John
„	Thoney, Thomas
„	Thornton, David Aubin
„	Twine, Richard
1793	Taylor, William
„	Trewin, Sarah
„	Taylor, John Sutton
„	Thornborrow, Giles
1794	Tubbs, Thomas
„	Thompson, Susannah
„	Turner, Retta Emblin
„	Thompson, Dorothy
„	Trotman, Susanna
„	Tubbs, Hall
1795	Tapers, Robert
„	Turney, Mary
„	Tull, John Thomas
„	Tasker, Thomas
1796	Trotman, Robert
„	Tempro, Sarah
„	Thomas, Jane
„	Trent, John. (Recorded in Power of Attorney Book No. 46.)
1797	Terrill, William
„	Taitt, Mary
„	Todd, John
1798	Turton, Henry
1799	Thorp, Mary
„	Turpin, William
1684	Usher, Cuthbury
1686	Umphrey, Edward
1688	Usher, Nicholas
1695	Ufford, John
1704	Umphrey, Henry

* Continued from p. 240.

Year.	Names of Testators.
1713	Ulloa, Daniel
1714	Umphrey, Jonathan
1720	Ufford, John
1731	Usher, Nicholas
1739	Ulloa, Solomon
1744	Ulloa, Esther
1749	Umphrey, James
1751	Underwood, Francis
1751	Umphrey, Martha
1755	Umphrey, James
1772	Usher, James
1775	Umphrey, Isaac
1781	Upton, Philip
1785	Umphry, Edward
1791	Ulloa, Daniel
1791	Umphry, Edward Downes
1651	Vines, Richard
1652	Vaughan, Roland
1658	Vines, Richard
„	Villacott, Walter
1660	Vines, Edward
„	Vassall, William
1667	Virty, Richard
„	Vodry, George
1671	Vincent, Richard
1675	Vines, Joane
1678	Vrisbie, Thomas
1686	Vale, Isaac
1688	Vanderwherest, Francis
1691	Vaughan, Henry
1694	Valkurb, Isak, *or* Faulconborough, Isaack
1695	Veford, John
„	Veren, Joshua
„	Vestin, James
1697	Veryer, William
1702	Vawdrey, Sarah
„	Vaughan, Margaret
1703	Vanderwarfin, Margaret
1712	Voss, John
1714	Vaughan, James
1718	Viguers, Emanuel
„	Vaughan, James
1719	Viguers, Thomas
1723	Vaughan, John
1725	Vonlengerken, Herman
„	Valvirdee, Eleezer
1726	Vegars, Emanuel
„	Vonlengerken, George
„	Vaughan, Margaret
1729	Vaughan, Robert
„	Valverdee, Jacob
1733	Vieguers, Emanuel
„	Viguers, Mary
1735	Vaughan, Richard
1736	Vonlengerken, Eleanor
1739	Valverdee, Elias
„	Vaughton, John
1740	Valverdee, Moses
1741	Vaughan, Ann
1743	Valverdee, Isaac
1745	Valverde, Jnr., David
1746	Valverde, Aaron
„	Valverde, Abraham
1752	Vaughan, Benjamin
„	Verhulst, Stanford
„	Vaughan, Robert
1753	Valverde, David
1755	Valverde, Hester
1756	Valverde, Lunah
„	Valverde, Jacob
1757	Vaughan, Francis
1759	Vaughan, Francis
„	Vaughan, James
1766	Vaughan, Mary
1767	Vaughan, James
1781	Verhulst, Richard
1782	Valverde, David
1784	Vallance, Roger
1793	Valverde, Jacob
„	Vaughan, Francis
1795	Vaughan, Mary
1796	Vaughan, John
1648	Wight, Daniel
„	Whitlock, Thomas
1649	Williams, Thomas
1650	Wiscombe, George
„	Webb, Archupus
1651	White, William
„	Williams, Thomas
„	White, Thomas
1652	Wolfe, Gabriel
„	Wilkinson, John
„	Ward, William
„	Whitaker, William
„	Weston, William
„	Wateredge, William
„	Weston, Grace
„	Webster, Richard
„	Watson, James
1654	Watson, Louis
„	Williams, Francis
„	Wildgoose, John
„	Wood, Edward
„	Woodcock, Robert
„	Williamson, William Ganes
„	Woodwell, Patrick
„	Weekes, Thomas

Year.	Names of Testators.
1655	Whitehead, Thomas
1656	Weawell, Thomas
„	Walker, William
1657	Walis, Richard
„	Walters, William
„	Winde, Arthur
1658	Woolcott, Philip
„	Winnmill, Edward
1659	Wilkins *alias* Macbbye, John
„	Wolfe, Thomas
„	Williams, John
„	Webster, Nicholas
„	Williamson, Nathaniel
„	Willcox, Robert
„	Warde, Richard
„	Williams, Owen
„	Webster, Richard
„	Williams, Ezekiell
„	West, Dorothy
„	Wilshire, Robert
1660	Whittikar, John
„	Wood, Thomas
„	Waad, Thomas
„	Wyne, Edward
„	Woodley, Thomas
„	Weekes, John
„	Weekes, Elizabeth
„	Williams, Francis
„	Ware, Thomas
„	Willis, Nicholas
„	Wass, William
1661	Waterland, John
„	Woodward, Anthony
1662	Williams, John
„	Watson, William
„	Webb, Robert
„	Waterer, Jervis
1663	Worrill, Ralph
„	Wolverstone, John
„	Whitehead, Thomas
„	Weston, William
„	Watkins, Philip
„	Wheeler, William
1664	Wilson, Joane
1665	Wattson, Nicholas
„	Welsh, Philip
1666	Witting, Rubes
„	Ware, William
„	Waterman, Humphry
1667	Wall, Richard
„	Williams, Theophilus
„	Williams, Rice
„	Wood, Lockland
1668	Walker, William
„	Willoughby, Francis
„	Williams, William

Year.	Names of Testators.
1668	White, James
„	Wythers, Ann
„	Watson, Francis
„	Williams, Robert
1669	Worson, John
„	Webster, John
„	Warner, John
„	Wothersall, Thomas
1670	Webster, John
„	Williams, Thomas
1671	Walcott, Eyare
„	Webb, Robert
„	Welsh, William
„	Welch, Margaret
„	Whiston, George
„	Williams, John
„	Wills, William
„	Walford, John
1672	Webb, Roger
„	Walker, Peter
„	Withington, William
„	Walters, James
„	Woodhouse, Wllliam
„	Willoughby, William Lord
1673	Whitehead, Samuel
„	Wood, Thomas
„	Waterland, William
„	Williamsongraft, William
„	Walcott, Ayre
„	White, William
„	Weese, James
1674	Wilson, John
„	Wichham, Abraham
„	Wade, Dorothy
„	Wade, Richard
„	Worsey, Robert
„	Watson, George
„	Walmesley, Andrew
„	Williams, David
„	Weston, Henry
„	Williams, John
1676	Wood, Thomas
„	Wollaston, John
1677	Williams, Thomas
„	Willett, Jacob
„	White, Patrick
„	White, William
1678	Walker, Joseph
„	Woodcock, David
„	Wood, Andrew
„	Williams, George
„	Wilshire, Thomas
„	Winn, Daniel
1679	Weekes, John
„	Wyse, John
„	Willoughby, John Lord

Year.	Names of Testators.
1679	Watkins, Daniel
"	Williams, Elizabeth
"	Williams, Anthony
"	Whytin, Richard
"	Whitehead, Thomas
"	Ware, Thomas
"	Wolfe, Emanuel
1680	Watson, William
"	Williams, Richard
"	Williams, Jane
"	Walrond, Alexander
"	Williams, Evan
"	Withers, Jacob
"	Waters, John
1681	Willson, William
"	West, James
"	Wallcott, Nicholas
"	Worsam, John
"	Wilson, John
1682	Warren, Thomas
"	Warren, Garrett
"	Watkins, John
"	Warde, Henry
1683	Willoughby, Ann
"	Wallis, Thomas Cromc *alias* Thomas Stever
"	Wood, James
"	Walke, Robert
"	Wege, Christopher
"	Wake, John
1684	Wood, John
"	Watty, Henry
"	Watt, Alexander
"	Webster, Patrick
"	Wallace, Archibald
"	Warren, Richard
"	Woodward, John
"	Williamson, Nathaniel
"	Walrond, Henry
1685	Wagg, Nicholas
"	Welch, Edward
"	Whearby, Henry
"	Wheelock, William
1686	Waterlayne, William
"	Wayett, Daniel
"	Watkins, Jean
"	Warner, John
"	Wilshire, Ralph
"	Wright, Benjamin
"	Wooldfoll, John
"	White, Nathaniel
"	Wade, Thomas
"	Windsor, John
1687	Watson, Mary
"	Walcott, Eyare
"	Williams, Richard
1687	Wright, William
"	Warren, Joseph
"	Withers, John
1688	Withington, William
"	Wilson, William
"	Whitney, Richard
"	White, Anthony
"	Wheeler, John
"	Williams, William
"	Whitock, Thomas
"	Walrond, George
1689	Wethinson, Peter
"	Watt, David
"	Wilson, Thomas
"	Williams, Katherine
"	Ward, William
"	Watson, Walter
"	Webb, Robert
1690	Waters, Roger
"	Williams, John
"	Wynne, Richard
"	Wright, Edward
"	Wiltshire, Mary
"	Ward, Robert
"	Wilson, John
"	Wickham, Alice
"	Wildgoose, Jacob
1691	Watson, Robert
"	Watts, Edmond
1692	Waite, William
"	Williams, Elizabeth
"	Wisher, Ann
"	Wilson, John
"	Walrond, Henry
"	Wight, Rice
"	Willoughbie, Richard
1693	Walsall, Francis
"	Williams, John
"	Weale, John
"	Walton, Ellinor
"	Webb, Ellinor
"	Weddington, William
"	Weddington, Elizabeth
"	Wilson, Hugh
"	Walford, Musco
"	Wiltshire, John
"	Williams, Robert
"	Willie *or* Millie, Raleigh
"	Williams, Henry
1694	Whitstone, John
"	Woodward, Samuel
"	Winder, William
"	Walrond, Thomas
"	Wilson, George
"	Webber, John
"	Wilson, Richard

Year.	Names of Testators.
1694	Walrond, Henry
1695	Wait, John
"	Watkins, Francis
"	Watkins, David
"	Wake, Ann
1696	Woodroofe, Jonas
"	Willis, Richard
"	Wagg, Looe
"	Walrond, Grace
"	Wills, Micajah
"	Watchett, Katherine
1697	Warner, Stephen
"	Whaley, Zachariah
1698	Warren, John
"	Welbourne, —
1699	Wait, Priscilla
1700	Wilkinson, John
"	Weale, Benjamin
"	Walen, Mary
"	Wells, Jonathan
"	Wright, Thomas
"	Weale, Jnr., John
"	Williams, Hugh
"	Weekes, Ralph
"	Walter, Richard
"	Wilson, Mary
"	Wilse, Hope
"	Will, John
"	Willoughby, Nicholas
1701	Wethingtun, Mary
"	Wackley, Thomas
"	Wheeler, Edmund
"	Wheeler, Joane
"	Wells, Thomas
"	Wilkinson, Thomas
"	Williams, Thomas
"	Watson, Thomas
"	Waterman, John
"	Williamson, John
1702	Willy, Edward and Jane
"	Webb, William
"	Whitaker, Benjamin
"	Walford, Elizabeth
"	Woodhouse, William
"	Whilliker, Samuel
"	Wahup, William
"	Weale, Mary
"	Weaver, Thomas
"	Walcott, John
"	Waterman, Jacob
"	Willis, Richard
"	Williams, Roger
1703	Whitney, John
"	Weale, Robert
"	White, John
"	Waters, John

Year.	Names of Testators.
1703	Weller, Bryan
"	White, Roger
"	White, Edward
"	Willshire, Richard
"	Webb, Samuel
"	Wilson, James
"	Wells, Sarah
1704	Waterman, Snr., John
"	Williams, Michael
"	White, William
"	Wrong, Jacob
"	Walker, Robert
"	Webster, John
1705	Walrond, Alexander
"	Waite, John
"	Wright, Edward
"	Walter, Edward
"	Wright, Dorothy
"	Wise, John
"	Williams, Thomas
1706	Wright, John
"	Williams, John
"	Weltshire, George
"	Walrond, Theodore
"	Weaver, William
"	Walwyne, James
"	Wright, Elizabeth
1708	Wilcon, Edward
"	Webb, Nathaniel
1709	Walter, Henry
"	Wilkinson, Richard
"	Wheeler, William
"	Waters, Roger
"	Wrenfford, John
"	Wilson, Henry
1710	Willson, Susannah
"	Walters, Elizabeth
"	Wallesalle, Ann
"	Williams, Thomas
"	Waite, Thomas
"	Wilson, Ann
"	Wood, Dorothy
"	Webber, John
1712	Watts, David
"	Willson, James
"	Watts, Ann
"	Watson, Benjamin
1713	Welch, Edward
"	Water, John
1714	Watkins, Abraham
"	Wright, William
"	Wilkins, Margaret
"	Walcott, Richard
"	Williams, Ann
"	Watson, John
1715	Wood, William

Year.	Names of Testators.
1715	Waterman, Humphy
„	Wells, Jeremiah
1716	Wilson, Mary
„	Wells, Nicholas
„	Warner, Matthew
„	Watkins, Richard
„	Walker, Elizabeth
„	Willoughby, Darkins
„	Welch, Elizabeth
1717	Ward, John
„	Wheeler, Ann
„	Webb, Christopher
„	Waite, Thomas
„	Wake, John
„	Waite, Robert
„	Walrond, Deborah
1718	Wheeler, Thomas
„	Webb, Demaris
„	Whitehead, Elizabeth
„	Wilson, James
„	Woodard, Joanas
„	Williams. Elizabeth
„	Whitfoot, Amos
„	Wyer, Thomas
„	Williams, Esther
„	Weut, Ann
„	Worrell, John
„	Walcott, Richard
„	Watson, Ralph
1719	Wiltshire, Richard
„	Walters, Daniel
„	Woodcock, William
„	Whiteside, Robert
„	Webb, Roger
1720	Woodbridge, Dudley
„	Wicke, Mary
„	Wallsalle, Anne
1721	Wadsworth, John
„	Wilson, Thomas
„	Waters, Mary
„	West, William
„	Wiggins, Elizabeth
„	Walrond, Bridget
„	Webb, Roger
„	Wye, Robert
„	Whaley, Thomas
1722	Waterman, Mary
„	Wright, Thomas
„	Walrond, Charles
„	Waterman, Elizabeth
„	Whitaker, Benjamin
„	Wright, Jacob
„	Woodrooffe, John
„	Wallsall, Ann
„	Wallace, Daniel
1723	Walker, George

Year.	Names of Testators.
1723	White, Richard
„	Wilson, Hannah
„	Wright, Robert
„	Wilcoop, William
1724	Willett, Richard
„	Wooding, Walter
„	Wright, John
„	Webber, Elizabeth
„	Wells, Ann
1725	Wilde, John
„	Warriner, William
„	Wiltshire, Elizabeth
„	Ward, John
„	Williams, John
„	Walter, Margaret
„	Worsam, Richard
1726	Wheelwright, John
„	Walker, William
„	Webb, Nicholas
„	Wilward, William
„	Webb, Susanna
1727	Weekes, Agness
„	Waterland, Tomazin
„	White, Francis
„	Webley, John
„	Williams, Ann
„	Wright, Miller
„	Wall, John
„	West, Jane
„	Weare, John
1728	Wardell, Thomas
„	Ward, Thomas
„	Westwood, John
„	Wilcox, Jane
„	Worsam, Mary
„	Wilson, William
„	Watkins, William
„	Whitebread, Nicholas
„	Walronde, Jeane
„	Webb, Jane
„	Walker, William
1729	White, Ann
„	Williams, Thomas
„	Walker, Alexander
„	Wharton, Gilbert
„	Willshire, Richard
„	Wharton, Ann
„	Willshire, Margaret
„	Walrond, Henry
„	Williams, Henry
„	Welch, Richard
„	Walter, John
„	Walker, John
„	Walter, John
1730	Williams, John
„	Wall, James

Year.	Names of Testators.
1730	Webster, Robert
1731	Waterman, John
"	Williams, William
"	Waters, Mark
"	Ward, William
"	Wilson, Thomas
"	Williams, Richard
"	Wright, Elizabeth
"	Whyte, Archibald
1732	Wilson Joseph
"	Woodroofe, Charles
"	Wright, Benjamin
"	Wood, John
"	Wheeler, Thomas
1733	Wilkie, Thomas
"	Warner, Edward
"	Wright, Thomas
"	Willson, Edward
"	Whielock, William
"	Wynnell, Francis
"	Wiles, Daniel
"	Webster, William
"	Walker, Richard
1734	Williams, Thomas
"	Williams, Ann
"	Waters, George
"	Williams, Martha
"	Waterman, Benony
"	West, Thomas
"	Whitehead, John
1735	Woodward, Godfrey
"	Wheeler, Thomas
"	Wrong, Henry
"	Williams, Hugh
"	Waters, Christianna
"	White, Dorothy
"	Warren, Robert
"	Wadsworth, Robert
"	Wildey, Daniel
"	Wier, James
"	Warren, Timothy
1736	Watt, Alexander
"	Watson, John
"	Whitewood, Edward
"	Welloughby, John
"	Wright, Susannah
"	Wiltshire, James
"	Whyte, Elnor
"	Wilson, Henry
"	Waterman, Jchue
1737	Walter, John
"	Worrell, William
"	Warden, Mary
"	Wheeler, William
1737	Wroug, John
"	Wright, William
1738	Wilde, John
"	Walcott, Eayre
"	West, John
"	Walker, Jacob
"	Wadsworth, Robert
"	Waith, John
"	Waterman, Arthur
"	White, William
1739	Wiltshire, Richard
"	Whittaker, Ambrose
"	White, Edward
"	Wallace, Elizabeth
"	Wadeson, Samuel
"	Willy, Ralph
"	Walters, Thomas
1740	Webber, John
"	Woodrofe, Jonas
"	Ward, Thomas
"	Wilson, Elizabeth
"	Warren, James
"	Walker, Samuel
"	Warner, Henry
"	Worsley, Henry
"	Willshire, Elizabeth
1741	West, Thomas
"	Whittaker, Benjamin
"	Whittaker, John
"	Weekes, Elizabeth
"	Warren, John
"	Wiltshire, Thomas
1742	Willoughby, Turpin
"	Waterman, William
"	West, Barbara
"	Watkins, George
1743	Wilkinson, Richard
"	Wharton, Henry
"	Ward, Thomas
"	Willshire, Mary
"	Wright, Thomas
"	Ward, John
"	Worrell, Richard
"	Waterman, Joseph
"	Walrond, George
"	Waters, Martha
1744	Walrond, Bridgett
"	Wade, Ruth
"	Wransford, Elizabeth
"	Wilkinson, John
"	Washington, Richard
"	Wye, Richard
1745	Ward, Robert
"	Wilson, William

(To be continued.)

Hals of Jamaica.

Arms.—*A fess between three griffins' heads erased.*

John Halse or Halsey of Efford near Plymouth.=

Sir Nicholas Halse of Venlon Collum, co. Cornwall, knighted by K. Jas. 22 May 1605; Gov. of Pendennis Castle; inventor of kilns for drying malt; died 1636. ("D.N.B.") Will, as of St. Bride, Fleet Street, not registered, proved 19 Dec. 1636 by Anne Maddox. = Grace, dau. of Sir John Arundell of Tolverne; had four sons; mar. 43 Eliz. 1601.

A

1. John Hals, ? went to Ireland in 1630, and thence to Barbados with his only son. = Jane, dau. of Tho. Arundell.

William Hals, Capt. R.N., served at La Rochelle 1628.

Richd. Hals, purser of the King's ship "S. Claude."

Major Thos. Halse of Clarendon, born 1634; went to J. in 1655 with Venables; owner of 466 a. in 1670; died 27 Feb. 1701-2, aged 67; bur. at Halse Hall. M.I. with arms (Archer, 303). = Eliz., dau. of Tho. Canning; ? remar. .... Webber, and living 1702.

Tho. Halse, born 1676; died 24 Aug. 1702, aged 26. M.I. with arms at Halse Hall. Styled grt.-grds. of Sir Nich. H. Will dated 21 Aug. 1702; proved 20 April 1703 (69, Degge). = Mary, dau. of John Rose of L.; mar. T. H. 18 Dec. 1697; living 1720. = Lt.-Col. Chas. Sadler, M. for St. Jas. 1688 and Port R. 1698; M. of C. 1701. 2nd husband.

B

Hon. Tho. Hals, born 1699; died 20 Nov. 1737, aged 38. Arms, impaling Hening. = Eliz., dau. of Sam. Hening, Esq.; remar. Benj. Hume, M. for Port R. 1735-6, M. of C. 1745, Recr.-Gen. 1746, but dismissed 1753.

Tho. Richd. Hals, born 1724; died 1743-4 in Guernsey, bach., a lunatic.

Eliz. Hals, born 1726; died 1739.

Tho. Hals, Esq., of the parish of Clarendon, Island of Jamaica. Will dated 21 Aug. 1702. To my wife Mary all my household goods, plate, jewels, coaches and 8 horses, and £400 st. 12 months after my decease. My aunt Grace Moseley £20 st. yearly. My mother Eliz. Webber £20. Capt Jno Rose and his wife £20 each. Geo. Osborne £20. Eliz. Hem'ings £20. John Carver £20. Philemon Dun £10. Rich. Thomas £10. All residue to my s. Thos. Hals, the care and education of whom I leave to my wife. If he die without issue then to my cousin Greenvill Hals the s. of James H. of Merthar, co. Corn., paying yearly £100 st. to Tho. Rose, s. of Capt. John Rose of L., Mt. My wife Mary, Emanuel Morton, Esq., John Peeke, Esq., Dr Daniel Webber and Joshua Smith, Ex'ors and £20 each. Witnessed by Nath. Hale, Tho. Morrison, John Burrell, Rich. Osbourne. Proved 20 April 1703 by Joshua Smith, power reserved to the others. On

22 Dec. 1729 comⁿ to Tho. Hals, Esq., the son and residuary legatee, Joshua Smith being dead, as also E. Morton, J. Peeke and D. Webber and Mary Sadler al's Hals the widow, the surviving Ex'trix renouncing. (69, Degge.)

1700. Gov. Sir Wm. Beeston writes of the following who has been recommended for the Council:—

"Major Halse not long since kept a tavern: his wife now keeps a retail shop: he is old, lives 30 miles from town & is of very indifferent parts." (Colon. Cal., p. 51.)

There is a view of Halse Hall in Clarendon in Cundall's Historic J., p. 396.

A

James Hals of Fentongollan in St. Michael, Penkivel, co. Corn., served at Rochelle in 1628 and later in the W. I.; ? some time Gov. of Montserrat and sided with the Parliament. = Anne, dau. of John Martin of Hurston, co. Devon.

Grenville Hals (cousin of Thos. of Jamaica, 1702).

William Hals [1655—1737], 2nd son, compiler of the Parochial Hist. of Corn.; born at Tresawsen Merther; died at Tregury St. Wenn; mar. thrice, but s.p. ("D. N. B.")

James Guthrie of Westmoreland, Jamaica, died 10 July 1728. M.I. (Archer, 336); Left three daus. and coh. =

B

Capt. Francis Sadler-Hals, assumed name of Hals by Act of 15 May 1746; settled Montpelier 1739; M. for St. Jas. 1745-6 and 1749; died 1750. = Jannet Guthrie, 1st dau. and coh., inherited Halse Hall from her husband. = 1. John Hynes of Westmoreland. 1st husband.

s.p.

Helen Guthrie, 2nd dau. and coh., mar. Tho. Storer, Esq., of Westmoreland.

—

Eliz. Guthrie, 3rd dau. and coh., born 1711; mar. 1, Col. Rd. Haughton of Westmoreland, who died 15 Jan. 1740, aged 49, and 2, Major Edw. Clarke. She died 14 Oct. 1764, aged 53.

Eliz. Hynes, 1st dau. and coh., mar. Goudin Elletson, ? died in N. Carolina 10 Nov. 1789; died 31 Aug. 1760; bur. at Halse Hall. M.I.

Helen Hynes, 2nd dau. and coh., mar. Tho. Beach, Chief J.; bur. 1771 at Halse Hall. He died 29 June 1774. M.I. at Chapleton in Clarendon (Archer, 302).

From a pedigree in the British Museum, Add. MS. 27,968, fo. 34, to which I have added.

Abstracts of Nevis Wills in the P.C.C.*

Sir Francis Morton of Nevis, now in London, Knt. Will dated 26 June 1679. To poor of p'ish of St Thomas in Island Nevis 15,000 lbs. of muscava sugar. To p'ish church of St Thomas afsd. 5,000 lbs. of sugar to purchase Communion plate. To Mrs Susanna Bressy daur. to worshipful Ralph B., merchant, of Dort in Holland, lately dec., a pearl necklace of £50 value. To my neice Mrs Adriana Reymes of Dort afsd, daur. to Col. Charles R., formerly of St Christopher's Island in America, a like necklace and 2 silver tankards and 2 silver salts with her arms, which tankards and salts I had made at Barbados at my being there. To my mother in law Mrs Jane Dering £300. To my brother in law Capt. Joseph Crispe £20 for a sword and belt. To the 2 children of my sd. brother Capt. J. Crisp which he had by my sister in law Sybella Jordan his late wife £50 a piece, to be paid when they are 8 to their sd. father, who shall pay them at 21 or marriage. To Mr John Lawson, Minister of God's Word in Nevis, 6,000 lbs. of sugar. To the honourable Madam Adriana Bressy of Dort afsd. a £10 diamond ring. To Madam Sarah Castelee, Mr John Sikes, merchant, and the worshipful Richard Bressy of town of Dort a £5 diamond ring each. To Madam Bressy (wife of sd. Richard B.) a 12*s.* mourning ring. To Mr Randolphus Bressy, Mrs Anna Bressy, and to Mr Barney Sikes, Mr Bressy Sikes (sons to sd. Mr John S.), and to his 4 daurs. a 12*s.* ring each. 3 negroes now on my Plantation at Nevis named Daniel Betya and Marean Rebell, and one negro man lent my mother in law Mrs Jane Dering, by name Mathias, to be put on plantation of my sd. neice Mrs Adriana Reymes. Overseers to ship 9,000 lbs. of sugar and consign same to Mr George Morris of Bristol, who is to convert it into money, which I leave as follows, viz.: 12*s.* mourning ring a piece for sd. Geo. Morris, his wife, my cousin Robert Legg, his wife and children, and my uncle Richard Morton, and the rest for my father's sister [*blank*] in Worcestershire, or, if dead, to her children equally. To Edward Billingsly 6,000 lbs. of muscavado sugar and 2 other of my negroes and clothes, etc. My godson George Littman to be kept to school till 15, and then to be bound apprentice to a good trade, and at 18 to have 4,000 lbs. of muscavado sugar. To John Billingly 2 cows, etc., To my friends Mrs Parnall Mills, Capt Ansell, his wife, Capt William Manning, Mr Claudias Gidds, his wife and her daur. Parnall Lusigne, John Smith, Lieut. John Sackvell, Mr John Griffen, Michael Nowell and Anne Greene, widow, a 12*s.* ring each. To Edward Howsman of Nevis and Frances his wife 2 other of my negroes. To Mr William Wilkins a good horse for care he takes of my plantation. Rest of estate, real and personal, as follows, viz.: ½ to sd. Mrs Susanna Bressy in fee, the other ½ to my sd. neice Mrs Adriana Reymes in fee, and these two to be ex'trices. Mr William Wilkins, Capt. John Ansell and Lieut.-Col. John Sotridge of St Christopher's Island to be overseers, and to each a silver hilted sword and belt of £5, and they to be Trustees for Edward Johnson an orphan, he being recommended by his dec. father to my care, and also Trustees of my sd. neice Adriana Reymes' interest in St Christopher's Island. Wits.: Jane Dering, Geor. Gay, Edward Billingsley, Robt. Hodson, scr. Prob. 16 July 1679, by Susanna Bressy and Adriano Reymes the ex'trices. (88, King.)

Henry Michell, planter. Will dated Insula Nevis 15 Dec. 1679. To my brother Thomas M., now residing in the county of Cornwall in old England, the whole of my estate both here in the Island of Nevis and also the £120 according to tenour of the 3 Bills left in his wife's hands, being one from my brother-in-law Wm. Simmons ninety being the contents of one ten the other one, and the third Bill being one from my sister Joan whose contents is £20. To my wife's sister

* Continued from Vol. IV., p. 112.

dwelling in Ifford Come £10 to be paid by my brother Thomas, but if dead to her children if any issue. If my sd. brother (who is to be ex'or) be dead, whole of my estate to his children equally. My friends M[r] Solomon Baylie and Samuel Jeffery to be overseers. Testator made his mark. Witnesses: George Chapell, Wm. Chedcey, Owen Camwell, John Wall.

Adm'on c.t.a. 5 Sep. 1681 to John Juell, guardian of Joanna Michell, a minor, daur. of a brother and legatee named in will of H. M. of Island of Nevis, bach., dec., during her minority, Thomas M. the brother and ex'or having died before taking ex'orship.

Adm'on c.t.a. 14 April 1683 to William Doubt (husband and guardian of Joanna D. *als.* M., daur. of a brother and legatee named in will of dec. during her minority and to her use), Thomas M., brother and ex'or, having died before taking ex'orship, the grant to John Juell having expired by his death.

Adm'on c.t.a. 5 Feb. 1683[-4] to Joanna Doubt *als.* Mitchell (wife of William D.) nep'ti ex soror' (*sic*) and legatee named in sd. will, the grant to John Juell in Sep 1681 during minority to sd. Joanna being cancelled by reason of death of sd. John Juell, and also grant to William Doubt (husband to sd. Joanna D. *als.* M.) in April 1683 having ended by reason of full age of sd. Joanna. (131, North.)

Henry Sedgwick, of the Island of Nevis, chyrurgion. Will dated 30 May 1682. To M[r] Samuel Horne my silver hilt rapier at present in custody of M[r] John Cecill. My wife Mary S. to be ex'or and to her all my estate both here and elsewhere. Friend M[r] Thomas Fenton and M[r] Tho. Wall and M[r] John Cecill to be overseers. Witnesses: John Chinn, James Cecill.

Nevis, 21 June 1682. Appeared before Sir William Stapleton, Bt., Capt. General and Chief Governor of the Caribe Leward Islands in America, John Chinn and James Cecill, witnesses to above and vouch for sd. will. Recorded in books for inheritance, fo. 15, per Laut. Stepney, Dept. Secr.

Adm'on c.t.a. 3 Apr. 1685 to Toby S., brother and principal creditor of dec. Mary S., the relict and ex'trix having renounced probate. (49, Cann.)

Thomas Wale, of this Island, merchant. Will dated at Nevis 10 Mar. 37 Chas. II. 1684-5. To be bur. at discretion of M[r] Thomas Belchamber my trustee. To the children of my sister Mary Akerodge, the wife of Samuel A., £200 to be paid to their parents to their use. To my sd. sister all that is due to me from my uncle John Cooke, his heirs, etc. To the children of my sister Sarah Hughes, wife of James H., £200 to be paid to their parents to their use. To the eldest child of my sister Hughes a silver tankard which I left in my sd. sister's custody. M[r] John Cary of Bristoll, merchant, to be ex'or and to him in fee rest of my estate real and personal. If he will not perform my will my sd. two sisters to be ex'trices, and they and their children to have sd. residue. M[r] Thomas Belchamber, merchant, to be overseer and trustee for legatees and ex'ors and to manage my whole estate in these Island until other orders from ex'ors from England. John Hughes that now lives with me to settle my books, etc., and he to have 8000 lbs. of sugar to be paid him by my sd. Trustee. Witnesses: Aaron Chapman, Jos. Loyde and John Conant, Wal. Burchell, Eben[r] Kirtland.

Probate 20 June 1685 by John Cary the ex'or. (79, Cann.)

Elizabeth Combes, the now wife of John C. of the city of Bristol, merchant, and formerly the wife of Thomas Ayson, gent., dec. Will dated 28 Nov. 1685. Being by Articles of Agreement before my marriage with sd. J. Combes sufficiently improved thereto (*i.e.*, to make her will). To my sd. husband J. Combes for life my plantations on the Island of Nevis in America which were

formerly those of my sd. former husband T. Ayson. I release my sd. husband J. Combes the 20,000 lbs. of sugar a year which by the sd. Articles I had liberty to raise and dispose of. The ex'ors or adm'ors of sd. husband J. Combes to take from sd. plantations all improvements by him made. Sd. plantations after sd. husband J. Combes' dec. to my kinsman Walter Symonds in fee subject to following legacies: To my kinsman William Williams for putting him apprentice £30. To my kinswoman Elizabeth Symonds, daur. of my brother John S., 100,0000 lbs. of good cured Muscavado sugar. To sd. husband J. Combes messuage in Lewins meade in parish of S[t] James in Bristol for life if my interest so long continue, remainder to sd. kinswoman Elizabeth Symonds. To friend William Foxall of Barton Regis and his wife £20 for mourning. Sd. husband J. Combes to be ex'or. Witnesses: Fran. Yeamans, Wm. Jenkins, Susanna Combes, Andr. Shirley.

Probate 7 Dec. 1685 by John Combes, husband and ex'or. (148, Cann.)

Richard Watts. Auditis . . . meritis cuiusdam negotii probationis per testes Testamenti Richardi Watts nuper de Nevis in partibus transmarinis sed apud Dover in Comitatu Cantii defuncti . . inter Saram Page consobrinam in gradu Semel removo dicti defuncti partem dictum negotium promoventem ex una et Carolum Watts executorem in testamento dicti defuncti nominatum, necnon Richardum Woodford, Hannam Collins et Juditham Cradock etiam consobrinos in gradu semel removo dicti defuncti ad videndum processum fieri in hoc negotio usque ad prolationem Sententiæ definitivæ inclusive rite . . . citatos . . . partes contra quos idem negotium promovetur partibus ex altera vertitur: Dictis Richardo Woodford, Hannah Collins et Juditha Cradock . . . citatis . . . trina vice . . . nullo modo comparentibus . . . Nos Judex . . . deliberavimus . . . præfatum Richardum Watts defunctum . . . mentis compotum . . . testamentum suum . . . ex parte dicti Caroli Watts . . . exhibitum . . . condidisse . . . ac in eodem præfatum Carolum Watts, executorem nominasse . . . die Jovis 6 . . Maii 1686. (176, Lloyd.)

Rich. Gilman, of this Island, merchant. Will dated 7 May 1686. To my partner Mr William Davies of St Christophers, merchant, and his heirs 20,000 lbs. of good Muscovado sugar. To my sister Eliza G. and her heirs the same. To William Ling who now lives with me 10,000 lbs. of the same. My cousin M[r] John Cary of Bristol, merchant, and his heirs to be ex'ors, to whom remainder of estate real and personal. M[r] William Davies of S[t] Christophers afsd. to be overseers. Witnesses: John Hughes, Rich[d] Ailay, Jn[o] Maning. Wm. Ling.

Probate 18 Jan. 1686[-7] by John Cary the ex'or. (6, Foot.)

Phillip Tyler, of the city of Bristol, merchant. Will dated 18 Sept. 1686 To be bur. in S[t] Philip's churchyard near my late father. To my wife Elizabeth £300, she to release her dower of my lands in England or beyond the seas excepting house hereinafter mentioned. For her life the house wherein I now dwell she paying yearly to my ex'ors 40s. To my mother Mary Haines, widow, for life, if my term so long continue, the rents of my 2 houses in Winestreet in p'ish of Christ Church *als.* Holy Trinity, city of Bristol, now in tenures of George Bryant, buttonmaker, and John Harris, cutler. To sd. mother £100, also benefit of my contract lately made with Mayor and Corporation of Bristol, for reversion or fee of my sd. now dwelling house and certain other tenements in precincts of late demolished Castle of Bristol in fee. To my brother-in-law George Heath of London, plumber, £200. To each of the children of John

Haskins of Bussleton, co. Somers., mariner, and to each of the children of John Bilby of city of Bristol, bridle cutter, £10. To my late servant John Whitson £40. To James Bisse, merchant, now resident in Island of Nevis, my part of ship Europa and her cargo as now at sea, also all my houses and lands in Island of Nevis. To churchwardens and overseers of Christchurch afsd. £10 for poor in bread. To sd. brother-in-law George Heath, the sd. George Briant and Henry Lloyd, merchant, £40 each and they to be ex'ors and to take to their assistance Francis Yeamans of city of Bristol, my friend and attorney usually employed in my concerns, to whom £10. To churchwardens of S[t] Philip afsd. £10 for poor of in parish there. Rest of goods to sd. mother that she may consider her and my relations. Witnesses: Nico Barnord, Rich[d] Yeamans, Andr. Shirley.

Probate 8 Jan. 1686[-7] by George Heath, George Briant and Henry Lloyd the ex'ors. (14, Foot.)

NATHANIEL KING, now resident upon the Island of Nevis. Will dated 25 Jan. 1686-7. To be bur. in S[t] John's Churchyard of the p'ish I now live in. £200 Nevis* out of my refining-house for maintaining a free school that is in building this time whereof the parish books of S[t] John make mention to be free only for poor children of sd. p'ish which shall be so adjudged by my Trustees, viz.: M[r] Thomas Salt, minister, Lieut. Col. John Netheway, Capt. Philip Lee, esq., and M[r] Joseph Loyd, merchant. £200 Nevis out of same refining house for maintenance of 2 or more poor children. To all the poor of sd. p'ish that receive alms 20s. each. To my brother Richard K. and my sister Mary Chaunceyes children moneys I have in hands of M[r] Henry Loyd in Bristol equally, survivors of each family to have an equal part of those that die under 16. To Richard Hawke silver tankard marked B.O.B., gun marked H.C., etc. To William Bould his freedom, a sword, gun and wages as if he had served out his time. To M[r] Joseph Loyd what may buy him a mourning suit. To M[r] Jn[o] Covant a mourning ring marked G.K. To Richard Hawke, jun., £20 for a negro for him in the first ship that comes after my decease. To M[r] Thomas Solt those boards and shingles I bought for him of Capt. Timothy Clarke and also £5 for a hat. I remit to M[r] Robert Needs the £30 paid his wife formerly in England by Bill of Exchange, also what he owes me by book here for his care during my sickness. To Mary Bray a double double doonet† of gold for her care during my sickness. All the interest of my refining house as negroes, lands, etc., to be equally divided into four (but not to be parted), one fourth for the children of my brother Richard K. between them, one fourth to children of my sister Chauncey between them, one fourth to my cousin Nathaniell King son of my uncle Fulk K., and the remaining fourth to Richard Hawke, all in fee. My kinsman Nathaniel King and my friend Richard Hawke to manage affairs of sd. refining house and also the land lately purchased of M[r] John Coker. Debts which I have in this Island which are in partnership between me and M[r] Henry Loyd I leave to him, and he to be ex'or. Because of his absence I leave my friends Lieut. Col. John Netheway, Philip Lee, esq., M[r] Joseph Loyd and Richard Hawke to be ex'ors in trust. Witnesses: John Covant, Leon[d] Hancock, John Lewis, Tobias Pender, Tho. Fenton, scr.

Probate 12 Nov. 1687 by Henry Lloyd the ex'or. (139, Foot.)

SIR JAMES RUSSELL, Knight, of Nevis. Will dated 16 July 1687. To my daurs. Elizabeth R., Penelope R. and Frances R. half of my estate in Nevis, the other half to my wife Penelope R. during widowhood, remainder between my 3 daurs. afsd. in fee. To my brother Randall R. £5 to cut him off and debar him of all claims. To sd. 3 daurs. all money in hands of my correspondent or factor in England equally between them, also half my estate in Antigua. The other

* Currency. † ? doubloon.

half to my wife on same conditions, and she to be ex'trix. Will dat. in Nevis. Witnesses: Tho. Hill, Ush. Tyrrell, John Smargin, Martin Madan.

Probate 4 July 1688 by Dame Penelope R., relict and sole ex'trix. (99, Exton.)

Samuel Cole, of city of Bristol, marriner. Will dated 30 March 1688. The 2 rings now on my finger to the 2 sons of my brother-in-law Debrow Bridger, viz., one to Theophilus and the other to Samuel B. Rest of estate real and p'sonal to my wife Sarah C. in fee and she to be ex'trix. If I die in this Island Mr Richard Saunders to take goods, beef, shoes, etc., I have here into his hands and account to my ex'trix. Because I am to appoint a Master in case of my death here I do, with consent of sd. Mr R. Sanders, appoint Mr Thomas Lugg to be Master of the Ship Nathaniel. Witnesses: John Bankes, Richd Saunders, Jno Chinn, Ebenezr Kyrtland.

Probate 8 Oct. 1688 by Sarah C., widow, the relict and ex'trix. (134, Exton.)

Sir John Bawdon, of London, marchant. Will dated 30 June 1688. To be bur. either at Newington, Middx., or at Bridgwater, Somers., as my ex'trix intends to be bur. herself. Whereas by Articles of Agreement dat. 22 Feb. 1669 made before marriage with my now wife Lettitia B. between me of the 1st part, the sd. Lettitia then L. Popham sole daur. of Edward P., esq., dec., 2 part, and William Carr of All Souls Coll., Oxon, esq., and Edmond White of London, merchant, 3 part, I covenanted that if I died in my wife's lifetime before an actual settlement of lands of £500 annual value for sd. wife's life, sd. wife should have full third of all my personal estate in England, Barbados, New England, Nevis or elsewhere, and a third of all my real estate in same places. No such settlement having been made, I hereby give to sd. wife a full third of all personal and real estate as aforesaid in fee. To Mr John Gardner who is at present partner with me in my Commission £20 a year out of my plantation in Barbados during life of my sister Elizabeth Jones, wife of Moses J., upon trust for appointment of my sd. sister, her said husband having wasted and spent much of my money already and undone her. To Moses Jones son of Moses J. and my sister Elizabeth £50 at 21. I forgive my sister Elnor Oldmixon half of £100 and interest which she owes me by bond, the other half I give to her daughter Mrs Elnor Coleman, wife of William C. To my cousin Ann Gardner for mourning £10. To my cousin Elizabeth Myles £10. To my cousin Hannah Legg, wife of Ri: L, £10. To my cousin Sarah Oldmixon £10. To my cousin John Oldmixon £10. To poor of town of Bridgwater £40 as my ex'trix and my sister Oldmixon think fit. To such of my Barbados friends that were my Cor'espondents 20s. rings. To Francis Gwin, esq., 20 gu'as and to Mr John Gardner my present partner 20 guas. Rest of estate real and personal to my 2 daurs. Ann B. and Lettitia B. equally, if either die under 21 or unmarried survivor to take all, if both so die then to sd. sister Elnor Oldmixon £200, to sd. Elnor Coleman £100, to sd. Elizabeth Myles £100, to sd. Hannah Legg £100, to sd. Sarah Oldmixon £100, to sd. John Oldmixon £100 and to sd. Ann Gardner £100, and to sd. sister Elizabeth Jones £200, and to her sd. son Moses J. £100. Sd. wife Lettitia to be ex'trix. Sd. Francis Gwyn, esq., and John Gardner, merchant, my present partner in commission, to be overseers. Witnesses: Nicholas Battersby, George Hughes, William Parkhurst.

Probate 8 Jan. 1688[-9] by Dame Lettitia B., relict and ex'trix.

Adm'on c.t.a. 8 Nov. 1720 to Robert Thornhill, esq., guardian of Letitia Thornhill, minor, daur. of a daur. and n. of k. of Sir J. B., late of All Hallows the Great, London, knight, *d.b.n.a.* by Dame Lettitia B., relict and ex'trix, also dec., during minority of sd. minor. Sir Robert Thornhill, adm'or of Dame Lettitia Thornhill, surviving resid. legatee, renouncing. (1, Ent.)

CAPTAINE THOMAS BUTLER,* of this Island, Planter. Will dated 2 Dec. 1687. To my daurs. Sarah Rowland, Anne Oysterman and Mary Smith £5 each. To my 2 daurs. Carolina and Frances B. 60,000 lbs. of sugar apiece at 21 or marriage, and meanwhile to have their diet, etc., or 8000 lbs. sugar a year at their discretion. To my 4 sons William, Duke, Thomas and James B. rest of estate real and personal equally in tail with survivors' clause, the estate not to be divided until my youngest son be of full age. My sd. 4 sons to be ex'ors. My friends Capt. Phillip Lee, Lt. Henry Litton, Mr Thomas Tovey, junr, and Ebenezer Kyrtland to be overseers and guardians of my 2 youngest sons Thomas and James till they be 21 or choose other guardians. Signed, Thomas Buttler. Witnesses: Phillip Lee, Henry Litton, Michael Webber, Phillip Payne, Ebenezer Kyrtland.

Adm'on c.t.a. 17 Oct. 1689 to Joseph Martin, attorney of William Buttler, Duke Buttler, Thomas Butler and James Butler, sons and ex'ors of will of Capt. Thomas Butler, late of Island of Nevis, during absence of sd. ex'ors now dwelling in Nevis afsd. (134, Ent.)

(To be continued.)

Devereux and Gage of Montserrat.

Sir Wm. Gage of Firle, co. Sussex, Barronet and K.B. Will dated 13 July 1737. To Mary Gage of Firle, widow, £3000. All real estate to the Rt. Hon. Henry Pelham of Esher, co. Surrey, Esq., on T. to the use of Tho. Visct Gage for life, then to the Hon. Wm. Gage his eldest son. Tho. Gage his 2d son. Joseph Gage, Esq., brother of said Visct Gage. Sir Tho. Gage of Hengrave, co. Suffolk, Bart.

Codicil, 20 Jan. 1737. Proved 10 May 1744. (122, Anstis.)

Sir Tho. Gage of Hengrave, co, Suffolk, Bart. Will dated 31 Aug. 1741. To my mother Delariviere Gage, widow, my manor of Harlston, co. Suffolk, and all my personal estate, and appoint her sole Ex'trix. Proved 16 Jan. 1741 by D. G. (14, Trenley.)

1650, Jan. Nich. Devereux. Ad. on — to Mathew Edwards, creditor of N. D., in parts, decd. fo 1.

1671, Dec. 7. John Devereux, late an inhabitant of Montserrat, and Lieut. of a Company in the King's service, has petitioned that on 10 June last he killed Capt. Daniel Jones in self-defence and fled the island. The King orders that petitioner shall have a fair trial. (Col. Cal., Addenda, p. 149.)

1677-8. Cap. Juo Devereaux's Division. Census. (*Ante*, II., 318.)

1681, Sept. 24. Deed of John Devereux. (Montserrat Records, A. fos. 79-80 in old volume since destroyed. Recorded again 1772, No. 1880, p. 335.)

1684, June. John Devereux, a Member of Council of Montserrat. (Col. Cal., p. 648.)

1685, Dec. 30. Lieut.-Col. John Devereux, a Member of Council of Montserrat. (*Ibid.*, 132.)

1687, Nov. 23. Col. John Devereux, Marshal of Montserrat. (*Ibid.*, 470.)

1785, June. Essex Devereaux. On the 7th adm'on of goods of E. D., a Lieut. in H.M. 67 regt of foot, Esq., a batch., granted to Edwd Reddish the cousin german.

* See pedigree *ante*, II., 59.

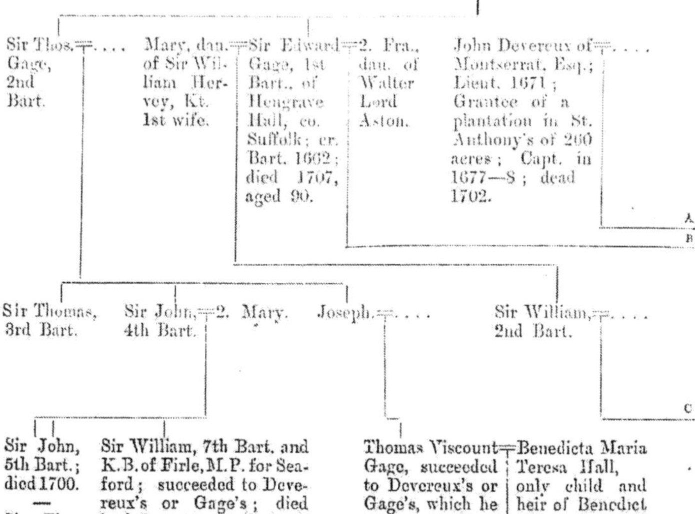

Their mother settled "Gages" on them in 1747.

This Indenture made the 2 Nov. 1 Anne 1702 Between Francis Gage of London, Esq., and Elizabeth his wife late Elizabeth Devereux sole daughter and heir of John Devereux Esq. late of the Isle of Mountserrat one of the Caribbee Islands in America of the one part, George Carleton and Richard James both of Symond's Inn London gentlemen of the other part Witnesseth that in consideration of a marriage already had between the said Francis Gage and Elizabeth they have agreed that a fine shall be levied upon all that plantation of 260 acres in the parish of St. Anthony bounded with the Great Indian Garden on the South side and with Col. Reid, Col. — and Capt. — (names difficult to read). (Close Roll, 4898, skin 37.)

This Indenture of lease made the 15 May 1730 3 George III. Between Devereux Gage of the parish of St George-the-Martyr Esq. of the one part and William Goosetree of St Clement Danes gentleman of the other Witnesseth that for 5s. Devereux Gage hath sold all that plantation of 260 acres in the parish of St Anthony Isle of Mountserrat bounded East with Thomas Lee Esq. North with

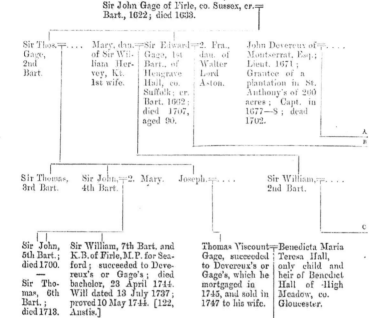

Samuel Cole and West with Samuel Cole and John Cockram Esq. deceased South with Grace Parson widow and Martin ffrench deceased with the waste lands that lye between the top of St George's Hill and the top of the mountains that lye East-South-East sugar works negroe slaves horses mules cattle houses for one year paying 1 peppercorn.

This Indenture tripartite made the 16 May 1730 between Devereux Gage only surviving son and heir of Francis Gage late in the parish of S[t] James Westminster Esq. deceased of the 1st part; William Goosetree of the 2[d] part; and James Travers of S[t] Andrew Holborn gentleman of the 3[d] part Witnesseth that for docking all estate and 10*s.* Devereux Gage hath released to William Goosetree all that plantation a recovery to be executed to the only use of Devereux Gage. (Close Roll 5412, skins 24 and 25.)

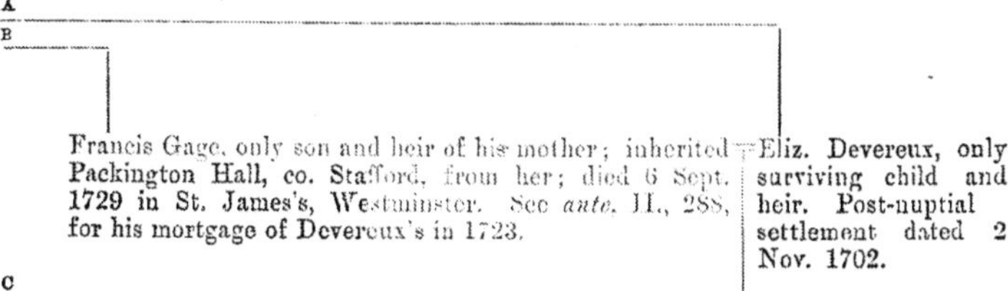

A

B

Francis Gage, only son and heir of his mother; inherited Packington Hall, co. Stafford, from her; died 6 Sept. 1729 in St. James's, Westminster. See *ante*, II., 288, for his mortgage of Devereux's in 1723. ═ Eliz. Devereux, only surviving child and heir. Post-nuptial settlement dated 2 Nov. 1702.

C

John, 2nd son. ═ . . , .

Devereux Gage, only son and heir, of St. Giles-in-the-Fields, Esq., 1741; of Devereux's or Gage's of 200 acres, which he leased in 1741 to Tho. Meade; d.s.p. before 1744.

Sir Thomas Rookwood Gage of Hengrave, succeeded as 5th Baronet in 1767; died 1795. ═ Mary, dau. of Dr. Patrick Fergus of Montserrat; mar. 30 July 1782, 2nd wife; died 15 April 1820.

s.p.

This Indenture made 28 Feb. 14 George 2[d] 1740 Between Devereux Gage late of the parish of S[t] George-the-Martyr but now of S[t] Andrew Holborn Esq. (only son and heir as well of Francis Gage late of S[t] James Westminster Esq. deceased as of Elizabeth his wife also deceased which said Elizabeth was the sole daughter and heir of John Devereux Esq. long since deceased formerly of the Isle of Mountserat) of the one part and Philip Bennett of Widcombe county Somerset Esq. and James Travers of S[t] Andrew Holborn gentleman of the other Witnesseth that for barring all estate tail and for 10*s.* Devereux Gage sells to them all that plantation of 260 acres in the parish of S[t] Anthony bounded with the lands of Thomas Lee Esq. East; the lands of Dame Cole to the North; the lands of said Dame Cole and of John Cockran Esq. dec[d] to the West and the lands of Grace Parsons widow and of Martin French deceased to the South with lands now or late in the tenure of John Farrill Esq. with the waste lands lying between the top of S[t] George's Hill and the top of the mountains that lye East-South-East with the buildings mill sugar worke the negroe slaves horses mules and cattle coppers stills in Trust for Devereux Gage for ever. (Close Roll 5433.)

This Indenture tripartite made the 11 Dec. 19 George II. 1745 Between the Right Hon. Thomas Lord Viscount Gage in Ireland cousin and heir-at-law of the Right Hon. Sir William Gage Bart. K.B. lately deceased who was cousin and heir-at-law of Devereux Gage of the parish of S[t] Giles-in-the-Fields Esq. lately deceased who was the eldest son and heir-at-law of Francis Gage of the parish of S[t] James Westminster Esq. lately deceased and of Elizabeth Devereux wife of the said Francis Gage also lately deceased which said Elizabeth was the sole surviving child and issue and heir-at-law of her father John Devereux heretofore of the Island of Montserrat Esq. long since deceased which said John Devereux was the original grantee of the plantation hereafter mentioned of the 1st part; Thomas Meade of Montserrat gentleman now residing there of the 2[d] part; and Nicholas Tuite of Lime Street London merchant and Peter Hussey of Mark Lane London merchant (being 2 trustees of Thomas Meade) of the 3[d] part Whereas Thomas Lord Viscount Gage is seized of the plantation descended to him etc. now in the tenure of Thomas Meade by a lease dated 17 Nov. 1741 for 15 years from the 2 July 1743 granted by Devereux Gage and Thomas Meade erected a new stone windmill and is entitled to an allowance for it agreed at £1200 currency and Thomas Meade placed several negroes Thomas Lord Gage has agreed to purchase for £1363 currency conveyed them by Indenture of 9 inst. Dec. and Thomas Lord Gage hath applied to Thomas Meade for a loan £1700 currency besides the above 2 sums total £4263 to be secured by a mortgage and Thomas Meade hath remitted to Nicholas Tuite and Peter Hussey the said £1700 now this Indenture Witnesseth that in consideration of £1700 currency or £1000 sterling and in consideration of the £1200 and £1363 owing Thomas Lord Gage doth sell to Nicholas Tuite and Peter Hussey all that plantation demised on 17 Nov. 1741 by Devereux Gage containing 200 acres bounded East with lands of Thomas Lee Esq.; North with lands of Dame Cole; West with Dame Cole and lands late of John Cockran Esq. deceased; South with lands of Grace Parson widow and lands late of Martin French deceased with the buildings slaves as per Inventory taken by John Davis Molineux and John Chilcott on 1 July 1743 (names and values given) 22 negroes valued at £918 9s. mules at £40 each 16 draft cattle at £16 each £616, buildings £1950. Total £1566 currency £2563 of which was placed there by Thomas Meade now agreed to and included in trust for Thomas Meade legal interest of 8 per cent., plantation to be insured during the war at 7 per cent. In the presence of Ferd: John Paris, H. Weston. (Close Roll, 5745.)

This Indenture tripartite made the 31 July 21 George II. 1747 Between the Right Hon. Benedicta Maria Teresa Viscountess Gage daughter and only child of Benedict Hall late of High Meadow county Gloucester Esq. deceased and wife of Thomas Lord Gage Baron of Castle Barr and Viscount Castle Island in the Kingdom of Ireland of the 1st part, the Right Hon. George Henry Earl of Litchfield and the Hon. William Murray of Lincoln's Inn Esq. H.M. Solicitor-General of the 2[d] part; and James Rook of Clanny county Gloucestershire Esq. of the 3[d] part Whereas the said Benedict Hall by his will dated 7 Aug. 1719 gave to George Henry late Earl of Litchfield and James Rooke of Pinbury county Gloucestershire Esq. all his lands in trust to sell for the use of his said daughter then wife of Thomas Gage Esq. and testator being seized of several messuages in county Oxford and a reversion on the death of Sir Francis Fortescue Bart. s.p.m. of a moiety of several manors in county Bucks and Sir Francis Fortescue after the death of Benedict Hall died s.p.m. recites deed of 13 Nov. 1730 re sale of lands and by deed poll of 16 June last indorsed an Indenture of 17 Dec. 1744 Viscountess Gage called in £10,000 lent on mortgage to the Duchess Dowager of Norfolk and to lay out in the purchase of plantation which Lord Gage was seized of in the Isle of Montserrat and it was paid to her and her Trustees have agreed for the purchase of the said plantation for £5000 out of which £2131

should on 2 July be paid to Nicholas Tuite of Lime Street merchant and Peter Hussey of Mark Lane merchant in discharge of a mortgage dated 11 Dec. 1745 and Lord Gage therefore sold all that plantation late of Devereux Gage of S[t] Giles-in-the-Fields Esq. deceased which by an Indenture of 17 Nov. 1741 was demised by Devereux Gage to Thomas Meade for 15 years with the slaves as by Inventory taken by John Davis Molineux and John Chilcott on 1 July 1743 and the Trustees are to hold this £10,000 for her for life and at her death the plantation for her children William Hall Gage, Thomas Gage and £5000 to her daughter Teresa Gage. Signed in the presence of Charles Pym Burt. (A very long deed of settlement of her father's property.) (Close Roll, 5787.)

ST. GEORGE'S, BASSETERRE, ST. KITTS.

1745 June 2 Esex Devereaux, a Surgeon, by Cap[t] Maxwell and pall.
1760 April 11 John Hall Devereux, buried.

Vernons Plantation, Antigua.

This Indenture made 26 Jan. 38 Geo. III. 1798 Between John Joseph James Vernon of Whitehall co. York* Esq. of the one part and Justinian Casamajor of Potterells in the parish of North Mimms co. Hertford and of St. Mary Axe London merchant of the other Whereas by a lease made 13 Sept. 1755 between Slingsby Bethell Esq. of the one part and Duncan Grant Esq. of the other Slingsby Bethell leased to Duncan Grant all that plantation in the parish of St. Peter and Division of New North Sound together with 212 slaves from the 1st of August then last past for the term of 15 years at the rent of £1500 st. a year and Slingsby Bethell died having by his will devised the said plantation to John Vernon Esq. and by an agreement dated 13 April 1763 between John Vernon of the one part and Duncan Grant of the other reciting that Duncan Grant's tenancy would expire on 1 Aug. 1770 John Vernon agreed to give a new lease for 14 years and John Vernon died having by his will devised the said plantation to his son James Vernon for his life in tail male and in default to his son John Joseph James Vernon and James Vernon died without male issue and Duncan Grant also died having by his will appointed Lydia Grant his widow and others Ex'ors and appointed his estate to his said wife Lydia and to his dau. Mary the wife of Justinian Casamajor and J. Casamajor became entitled to the said lease and Whereas by indenture of demise dated 30 Oct. 1771 Between J. J. J. Vernon s. and h. of John Vernon deceased of the first part, Tho. Warner and Ashton Warner Byam of the second part and J. Casamajor of the third part, J. J. J. Vernon leased to J. Casamajor the said plantation from 1 Aug. 1770 for 14 years at the rent of £1500 st. a year and Whereas by a lease dated 31 Jan. 1785 from the 1 Aug. then last past for 14 years at the rent of £1350 a year and by a lease dated 1 and 2 Sept. 1794 between J. J. J. Vernon of the first part, John Vernon of Peterhouse Coll. Camb. Esq. eldest s. and h. of J. J. J. Vernon of the second part, the Rev. Randle Andrews, M.A. Vicar of Ormskirk and Tho. Wilson of Preston co. Lanc. gent. of the third part, and Will. Cross of Lincolns Inn Esq. and John Sauter of New Inn gent. of the fourth part the plantation was conveyed to W[m] Cross and John Sauter that John Vernon during the lives of

* Apparently error for Whitehall in Clitheroe, Lancashire, as noted in a rough pedigree in my possession.

him and of his father J. J. J. Vernon should receive £250 a year now in consideration of the surrender of the lease of 31 Jan. 1783 J. J. J. Vernon leases to J. Casamajor the said plantation of 400 acres bounded East with the high road West with Edward Byam Esq. North with Parham Harbour S. with the late John Wickham Esq. from the 1st Aug. last past for 14 years at the rent of £1600 st. a year and they appoint Henry Benscombe [recte Benskin.—Ed.] Lightfoot, Daniel Hill Senr and . . . . Scholes Esquires as their attornies.

Indorsed: Lease of plantn and slaves in Antigua from 1st Aug. 1797. John Joseph James Vernon, Esq., to Justinian Casamajor, Esq. Recorded in the Registers Office lib. Q., Paul Horsford, Dep. Regr, Hon. H. B. Lightfoot. Before the Hon. James Athill, an Assistant Justice of the Court of C. P., appeared Samuel Oliver, now of Antigua, master mariner, and swore to the signatures of J. J. J. Vernon and J. Casamajor 21 June 1798. Signed by "Saml Oliver of the Ceres." On ten large skins in the Editor's possession. Noted *ante*, I., 32.

The Great House of Vernons occupies a delightful position on a steep hill overlooking Parham Harbour.

When visiting in 1914 the Hon. John Foote, who as attorney resides at the adjoining estate of Parham, I was informed that Mr. Tudway, the owner of the latter, had recently purchased Vernons, the works of which were then being "scrapped," as the canes grown on both estates were being crushed at the great central factory at Gunthorpes.

Carib Remains.

On land adjoining the high road near here Dr. Cook of Cedar Hill discovered many Carib implements. He took me to the spot and we soon found several Indian conch shell scrapers by turning up the loose soil with our sticks, but no regular digging was attempted. The same day, in company with Mr. Foote and a guide, we explored a neighbouring wooded hill, the supposed site of an Indian castle; but beyond a low bank of stones, which might have been an estate boundary, there were no signs of foundations, intrenchments or other earthworks.

The proximity to the harbour, where there would be good shelter for their canoes, would lead one to suppose that there was probably a large Indian settlement in this locality. A few miles to windward is "Indian Town Creek," and there are various caves which, if explored might possibly give evidence of early Carib occupation.

In several islands I examined small private collections of Indian relics, and one of the largest and most representative ones found its way several years ago to the Blackmore Museum in Salisbury.

An article by Mr. Branch, from an American magazine which was lent to me in Barbados, treats of the Carib remains.

Now that there is in every island a public library or institute, I would suggest that all objects of antiquarian interest should be there deposited so as to form a local collection. In that charming Carnegie library at Roseau in Dominica I noticed that a start had been made in this direction.

Holborn (or Fontabelle) House, Bridgetown, Barbados.
Built in 1650. (See p. 289.)

Holborn [or Fontabelle] House, Bridgetown, Barbados.

To the Editor.

H.M.S. Marlborough,
First Battle Squadron,
13 *Sept. and* 5 *Oct.* 1915

I thought possibly you might like to have the enclosed photographs (of paintings) of Holborn House, Barbados, in view of the article in your July number (*ante*, IV., 113).

The paintings were water-colours, and were painted from photographs which were taken when my father was living there.

They were cleverly done by a young artist in London, whose name I do not know.

The house and estate were in the possession of my family from about 1850 until about 1904, and it was my father's seat in the W.I. during that time . . . .

During the Pope Hennesy riots [in 1876] my father, who was at that time Speaker, put up some 60 guests at Holborn for over a week, until it was safe for them to return to their homes in the country. The trees meeting overhead near the entrance were bamboos, and this was arranged by my father. The large tree in front is what was called out there an "ever-green," and the one at the back, with a trunk some 16 feet in circumference, I think was a cotton tree. I cannot, however, remember very well, as the last time I visited the Island was 27 years ago.

Percy Grant,
(Capt. R.N.)

The Editor confirms Capt. Grant's interesting description. The two small dome-like structures just inside the entrance gates are stated to be the original sentry shelters, and they are still standing. The magnificent old cotton tree is now much broken and decayed.

Lygon wrote: "I drew out at least twenty plots when I came first [1647] into the Islands which they all lik'd well enough, and yet but two of them us'd, one by Capt. Midleton and one by Capt. Standfast, and those were the two best houses I left finish'd in the Island when I came away [1650]." I have lately found an earlier will than those given *ante*, IV., 113, viz., that of George Stanfast of Bristol, merchant, "now resident in the Island of Barbadoes," dated 23 Feb. 1657.—"My son John to take charge of the deed of sale of the Indian River Plantations made by Col. Humphrey Walrond to me for securing the payment of £2936 st." In Mayo's Survey of 1717 are marked "Fentabell Fort" and "Fontabell river," and as this latter was an old Indian creek, where Carib remains have been found ("Schomburgk," p. 219), it seems likely that the Indian River plantation must be what was later known as Fontabell. Col. John Stanfast, the son, owned in 1680 the Mount Stanfast plantation near Hole Town (N. of Porters), but his father settled that on him at his marriage previous to 1657, and I do not think it was near the creek.

The earliest reference to the mansion in the Colonial Calendar of State Papers is in 1668, when the Council ordered on 30 Dec. that 200 barrels of powder be put into Fontabell House. The preceding April William Lord Willoughby wrote of the terrible fire that burnt three parts of the town and blew up the magazine. On 19 Aug. 1669 Major William Bate was ordered to remove the powder from the new church to Fontabell House. On 8 July 1675 the Treasurer was ordered to pay Col. John Stanfast the rent of Fontabel plantation leased to his Excellency.

Adams, Maxwell and Walker of Barbados.*

In looking over an old Law Book, entitled "Cases with opinions of eminent Counsel in matters of Law Equity and Conveyancing," I came across the following two items:—

Vol. I., p. 358. Elizabeth Maxwell, widow, late of the Island of Barbadoes, deceased, by her will disposed of the residue of her Estate, which she left to her "grand nephew Thomas Maxwell Adams, an infant son of my nephew Thomas Adams, Esq.," in tail general, whom failing to "Frances Adams, sister to the said T. M. Adams," whom failing to my brother in law George Graeme and his heirs and assigns for ever."

The said T. M. Adams was living in 1768, and had issue a son and a dau., infants of tender years. The said Frances Maxwell was also living but sans issue.

Vol. I., p. 314. Alexander Walker, Esq., being then (*i.e.*, 19 May 1742) in Barbadoes, made his will whereby he bequeathed to his dau. and only child Newton Walker all his estate in the Island and elsewhere in the world, to be delivered to his said dau. on attaining 21 years of age or on marriage, whichever should first happen, but should she die s.p. then to his brother William Walker, but should William Walker die s.p. living at his death then to his brother in law Captain Thomas Walker, but should he also die s.p. surviving, then to his cousin George Walker. Alexander Walker died in 1759, and soon after his death Newton Walker married John Walter, Esq., and died in 1772 without ever having had issue. [This corrects the pedigree *ante*, p. 186.] William Walker predeceased his brother Alex. Walker. Thomas Walker was apparently living at the date of Newton's death in 1772.

Notes by the Editor.

"*Maxwells*" is a well-known plantation in the parish of Christ Church, close to the high road running from Hastings to Oistins.

In 1680 Tho. Maxwell owned 24 acres, 2 white servants and 30 negroes.

In 1715 the Hon. Lt.-Gen. Tho. Maxwell, Eliz. his lady, one son and five daughters were entered in the census.

Thomas son of Tho. Maxwell of Christ Church, Barbadoes, Esq., matriculated from Christ Church, Oxford, 23 Aug. 1717, aged 14. "*Graemes*" was an adjoining estate.

The family of Adams was also an old one in the parish.

Williams Adams, who had recently purchased a very considerable estate, was in 1701 recommended for the Council. He is stated to have married Frances, only child and heir of Col. Tho. Walrond by Frances his wife daughter of Sir Jonathan Atkins, Knt. (Burke's "L.G.")

The Hon. Tho. Adams of *Adams Castle* was buried at St. Michael's, 4 Sept. 1764. Margaret his wife died 30 June 1743 (?), aged 38, and was also buried there with several of her children, in the McNemara vault.

Their son, Tho. Maxwell Adams, entered Eton School 24 Jan. 1760; was admitted a student of Lincoln's Inn 21 Jan. 1762, and matriculated from Merton Coll., Oxford, 13 Aug. 1764, aged 19. This would give his birth about 1745, two years after his mother's death, so the year 1743 on her tombstone must be wrong. He married in 1770 Anne Foublanque, and she died his widow at Brompton, 27 March 1812. See his book-plate No. 160. Mr. Austen-Leigh in his MS. list of Etonians has a note of an earlier Adams, who entered Eton in Jan. 1753; perhaps William, elder brother of Tho. Maxwell Adams.

* Contributed by Mr. Erskine E. West of Dublin.

A will of Eliz. Maxwell, probably the one in question, was recorded in 1750.

Alex. Walker was son of Alex. W. of St. Peter's, a Judge, and grandson of the Rev. Wm. W., the Bishop of London's Commissary in this Island. He and his brother Wm. matriculated at Oxford on 17 Dec. 1715, aged respectively 18 and 17, but he did not graduate. He died 23 May, and was buried in Westminster Abbey 2 June 1757, aged 60, the date of 1759 in the legal case being therefore incorrect. His will was proved 21 Feb. 1758 by his daughter, then wife of John Walter, Esq. (59, Hutton.)

Will of Ralph Parkinson, Esq., of Jamaica.

Ralph Parkinson of the parish of St. James in the County of Cornwall and Island of Jamaica. Will dated 12 June 1805. If I die in this parish I desire to be buried in the churchyard near to my nephew and nieces, and that an elegant tomb* of marble be sent for and put over my grave with my age and place of nativity. I was born at Pickton in the North Riding of Yorkshire on the 14 Aug. 1762, and came to this Island on the 12 April 1778. Not one of the name of Scarlett to be asked to my funeral, and if I should die in the parish of Westmoreland I desire to be buried at White Hall* my Pen, near to my brother Robert, and that my tomb be placed there with an iron railing. To my four quadroon children which I have had by a mulatto woman, Betty Grant, that I purchased from Tryall Estate in Hanover and set free—the names are Richard, Jane, John and Robert Parkinson—£2000 st. each. They are to be educated in England and never return to Jamaica. My negroes Rose, Lilly and Minerva and wench Sally to serve them, and upon the said children going off the island I give these negroes to Betty Grant, together with Moggy and her two daus. Nancy and Mary, and Nancy and her children may be sold to Mr. Wm. Tonkin for £100 each. I give her also £50 a year, and at her death the negroes to my goddau. Ann Watson, to whom I also give my beaufet with all my china therein, to be handed to her father and mother, and if she die to her sister Ruth. To Betty Grant also my liquors and the furniture of my bedchamber. To Mrs. Eliz. Cunningham† my sett of mahogany tables containing eleven leaves, and at her death to her dau. Ann. To Mr. Wm. Tonkin my bookcase, and all the rest of my furniture to my nephew Matthew Parkinson, and my watch, gold buttons and rings to my son Richard. To my brother Leonard Parkinson a house and land in the New Town called Folly, purchased of John Perry, Esq. To my nephews, sons of my brother Leonard, viz., Leonard and Richard P., 20 guineas each for a ring, also the like to my niece Mary P. The large fortune my brother possesses. To my eldest sister Mrs. Johannah Bennett £50 a year, and at her death one half the principal to her dau. Mrs. Johannah Games, and the other half to the dau. of the said Johannah Games—the name is Jamina Wilkins by her former husband. To my sister Jane Games £50 st. a year, and at her death the principal to her children and grandchildren. To my brother John P. 200 guineas, if he die to his son Chr. P. To my nephew Isaac Games £300 st. in England. To my niece Johannah Games the wife of Isaac Games £50 st., as she comes in with her dau. for half of what I leave to her mother. To my niece Lucretia Games £100 st. in England.

* There is no M.I. in Archer.

† Wife of the Hon. John Cunningham; she died 1806. (Archer, 319.)

To my niece Johannah Dinsdale £100 st. in England. To my niece Jane Games £300 st. at 21. To my nephew Chr. P. £300 st. To my nephew Mathew P. £500 st. All residue to my brother Chr. Parkinson's children equally, and if he does not come to this island to be remitted to him in America. To each of my Ex'ors 20 guineas for a ring. I appoint as Trustees and Ex'ors my brother Chr. P., my nephew Mathew P. and my friends George Watson, Wm. Appleton and Henry Parry, Esquires, with power to sell all my estate. Witnessed by William Plummer, William Allen, William Tonkin

Codicil. 23 May 1806. I give to my nephew Ralph Parkinson Games son of Isaac G. of London £2000 st. at 21. My Ex'ors to purchase for Betty Grant for £700 c. a house in the town of Montego Bay. To my friend Mr. John Pender of the parish of St. James 20 guineas for a ring. In case Mr Wm. Tonkin my clerk shall settle my books and accounts I bequeath him £200 c. Witnessed by James Irving, William Boyd, William Allen.

Endorsed "The Will of Ralph Parkinson, Esq." Mr. Cardale, Bedford Row. And in pencil, "Mr Games, No. 5 Pear Tree Row, Lambeth M." [? Marsh]. [Abstracted from an old copy in the Editor's possession.]

Testator's brother Leonard P., formerly of the parish of St. James in Jamaica, purchased the estate of Kinnersley Castle in Herefordshire, where he died 11 July 1817, and a pedigree of his descendants appeared in Burke's "L.G." In a deed relating to Belvidere Estate in Hanover it is recited that Leonard Parkinson, Esq., as surviving partner of George Goodin Barrett, Esq. (who died 8 Oct. 1795), recovered judgment against Tho. Reid, Esq., for £28,000 and £31,657 and costs, on payment of which sums he signed a release.

Amory of St. Kitts.*

[From a bible printed by Baskerville in 1769.]

Benj. Amory Senr was born Augt 13th in the year 1739.
Mary Amory wife of Benjamin Amory Senr was born November the 22d 1744.
Benjamin Amory Senr departed this Life September the 21st 1806, on Sunday Evening, nine minutes of nine o'clock in the 67th year of his age.
Mary Amory, wife of the above Benjamin Amory Senr departed this Life August the 1st 1808 on Monday evening at half past ten o'clock in the 64th year of her age.
Isabella Amory Daughter of Benj. Amory Senr was Born Sept. 4th 1764.
Ann Amory Daughtr of the above B & Mary was Born July 30th 1768.
Benj. Amory Son of the above B. & Mary was Born 19th Octr 1769.
Frances Amory Daughtr of the above B. & Mary was Born 2d Jany 1777.
Susanna Amory Daughtr of the above B. & Mary was Born 6th Feby 1778.
Mary Amory Daughtr of the above B. & Mary was Born Sept. 1st 1781.
William Benj. Amory, son of B. Amory 3d was Born 8th Decr 1790.
Frances Amory Daughter of B. & Mary departed this life, on Wednesday morng the 27th December 1815 in the 39th year of her age much lamented.
Benjamin Amory 3d son of Benjamin & Mary Amory departed this life October 11th 1817 on Saturday morning at one o'clock in the 48th year of his age.

---

* Communicated by Mr. John Bromley.

List of Wills recorded in Barbados down to the year 1800.*

Year.	Names of Testators.
1745	Washington, Elizabeth
„	Whittaker, Mary
„	Whitehead, Samuel
„	Willoughby, Dorcas
„	Wilkinson, Anna
„	Whetstone, John
„	Waddington, Samuel
„	Wright, Jacob
„	Walcott, John
1746	Waters, Anthony
„	Wackley, James
„	Went, John
„	Warren, Henry
„	Wakefield, Lucy
1747	Watts, Samuel
„	Wildey, Elizabeth
„	Ward, Peter
„	Wall, Richard
„	Waterman, Humphry
„	White, George
„	Wittell, James
„	Warren, Francis
„	Wilson, Mary Ann
„	White, John
„	Waterman, Mary
„	Whitehouse, William
„	White, David
1748	Walcott, Thomas
„	Webb, Nathaniel
„	Wayles, William
„	Woodbridge, Dudley
„	Whitehead, Pope Ashford
„	Wheeler, Thomas
1749	Woodbridge, Ruth
„	Wrong, Jacob
„	Weeks, Henry
„	Wall, Andrews
„	Wiltshire, Margaret
1750	Wilson, Charles
„	Wallace, James
„	Withers, Thomas
„	Wentworth, William
„	Walters, Ann
„	Widdington, Oswall
„	Walrond, Anthony
1751	Walcott, John
„	Whitaker, Alexander
„	Whiteside, Elizabeth
1751	Williams, Thomas
„	Walcott, Evare
1752	Walcott, William
„	Whitaker, Alexander
„	Whitaker, Snr., Samuel
„	Walrond, Elizabeth
„	Williams, Hugh
„	Wood, John
„	Watkins, Abraham
„	Whitney, Richard
„	Woolford, Thomas
1753	Walter, John
„	Welch, Joseph
„	Watts, Samuel
„	Wiles, Daniel
„	Wiltshire, Richard
„	Westerman, Elizabeth
„	Webster, Peter
„	Weaver, William
„	Worrell, Jonathan
1754	Woodroffe, John
„	Wood, Samson
„	Welch, Mary
„	Waite, Honor
1755	Wiles, Margaret
„	Wilcox, Nicholas
„	Warren, Robert
1756	Williams, Robert
„	Willoughby, Turpin
„	Welch, William
„	Wharton, Devonish
1757	Whitaker, Thomas
„	Waterman, John Thomas
„	Worrell, Mary
„	Welch, William
„	Walters, Joseph
„	Walker, Alexander
„	Walker, Catherine
„	Wilkinson, Constance
„	Wood, William
„	Wilson, Sarah
„	Whitehall, William
„	Woodin, Samuel
1758	Worrell, Sarah
„	Welch, Edward
„	Williams, John
„	Warren, Mary
„	Wheelwright, Henry

* Continued from p. 275.

Year.	Names of Testators.
1758	Wallis, Sarah
„	Walker, William
1759	White William
„	Webb, Samuel
„	Walker, Mary
„	Wilson, John
„	Ward, Mary
„	Whitaker, William
1760	Wright, Arthur Rainer
„	White, Francis
„	Webster, Ann
„	Whittaker, William
„	White, Thomas
„	Walker, Mary
„	Wilson, Edward
„	Webb, Nathaniel
„	Warren, William Henry
„	Whittaker, Henry
„	Welch, Elizabeth
„	Webber, Ann
1761	Wilson, Barbara
„	Wiltshire, Alleyne.
„	Whaley, William
„	Wiggins, William
„	Wiltshire, Joseph Jordan
„	Whitewood, Henry
1762	Walcott, Mary
„	Wilson, John
„	Wrong, Ann
„	Webber, John
„	Worrell, Elizabeth
„	Worrell, Nathaniel
„	Williams, Thomas
1763	Wilson, Nicholas
„	Walrond, George
„	Webster, Isabella
„	Welch, Valentine
„	Wilson, Stephen
„	Wrong, Katherine
„	Warren, Elizabeth
„	Watson, John
1764	Wharton, Elizabeth
„	Watt, Thomas
„	Willoughby, Sarah
„	Weekes, Thomas
„	Weekes, Roger
„	Weekes, Mary
„	Woodin, Thomas
1765	Weekes, John
„	Walcott, Samuel
„	Walrond, Prudence
„	Wilse, Francis
„	Walcott, Robert
„	Wilson, Richard
„	Wilson, John
„	Weekes, Nathaniel

Year.	Names of Testators.
1766	Webster, William
„	Woodroffe, Charles
„	Whitney, Elizabeth
„	Walker, Jane
„	White, George
1767	White, Elizabeth
„	Whitstone, Sarah
„	Williamson, Isaac
„	Wayles, Bathsheba
„	Wane, Thomas
„	Watt, Margery
„	Webb, Charles
„	Walcott, William
„	Williams, Richard
„	Wales, Bathsheba
„	Whitstone, Sarah
„	White, Elizabeth
1768	Wadeson, Robert
„	Watson, Thomas
„	White, Thomas
„	Winter, Abigail
„	Webb, William
„	Wilcox, Margaret
„	Watts, Jones
„	Wilkey, William
„	Waller, Isaac
1769	Wilkinson, Christopher
„	Williams, Mary
„	Washington, George
„	Waterman, John
„	Walrond, Theodore
„	Wilkinson, Joseph
„	Walter, James
„	Walter, Abel
„	Williams, Rebecca
1770	Williams, William
„	Woodbridge, William
„	Wiles, William
„	Weatherhead, John
„	Walker, Margaret
„	Williams, John
„	Wobble, Jonas
„	Wheeler, John
„	Woodbridge, William
„	Wiltshire, Ralph
„	Watkins, Prudence
„	Waite, Lucretia
1771	Whittaker, Eyare
„	Willoughby, Elizabeth
„	Woodin, Mary
„	West, Jacob
„	White, William
„	Williams, Alexander
„	Williams, Mary
1772	Woodroffe, Mary
„	Walpole, Victoria Arrabella

Year.	Names of Testators.	Year.	Names of Testators.
1772	Welch, John	1778	Welch, James
,,	Wallace, William	,,	Wake, George
,,	Wrong, Isaac	,,	Whitaker, Sarah
1773	West, Thomas	,,	Wiltshire, John
,,	Walter, Newton	1779	Whitney, Richard
,,	Whealer, Ambrose	,,	Whitfoot, Ann
,,	Williams, Benjamin	,,	Wells, John
,,	Williams, Mary	,,	Williams, John
,,	Webb, Sarah	,,	Webster, John
,,	Wheeler, William	,,	Wheelwright, William
,,	Williams, William	,,	Wickham, John
,,	Williams, Thomas	,,	Wells, William Arnool
1774	Williams, Henry Jones	,,	Wiltshire, Ralph
,,	Williams, William	,,	Whitfoot, James
,,	Ward, Robert	1780	West, Edward
,,	Wood, Samson	,,	Worrell, Bathsheba
,,	Walcott, Richard	,,	West, Sarah
,,	Walrond, Henry	1781	Whittaker, Mary
,,	White, Snr., John	,,	Walcott, Thomas
,,	Waith, James	,,	Watt, Alexander
,,	Welch, William	,,	Wilson, Henry
,,	Wood, John	,,	Walcott, Stephen
1775	Williams, John	,,	Walker, Margaret
,,	Wignall, Jonas Bailey	,,	Williams, Mary
,,	Walcott, Mary	1782	White, Thomas
,,	Whitehall, William	,,	Wall, Ann
,,	Watts, Rebecca	,,	Webb, Samuel
,,	Warren, Robert Warren	,,	Walker, Thomas
,,	White, Burgess	,,	Watt, William
1776	Wilson, John	,,	Walrond, Thomas
,,	Walker, Ann	,,	Walcott, Mary
,,	Williams, Elizabeth	,,	Worrell, Sarah
,,	Wilkinson, Jonas	,,	Wrong, John
,,	Waith, Thomas	,,	Watt, Elizabeth
,,	Wildey, William *alias* Pycroft	1783	Willoughby, William
1777	Weatherhead, Mary	,,	Walrond, Anthony
,,	Wall, Snr., John	,,	Webster, Joseph
,,	Whiteside, William	,,	Williams, Rebecca
,,	Walcott, Benjamin	,,	Waith, Pearce
,,	Ward, Thomas	,,	Whitefoot, Elizabeth
,,	Walrond, Jane	,,	Williams, Wiltshire, Hoopers
,,	Woolford, Thomas	,,	Wilson, Grace Barnsted
,,	Williams, Mercy	,,	Ward, Robert
,,	Watts, William	,,	Walker, Robert
,,	Webb, Henry	,,	Williams, Thomas
1778	Webb, John	,,	Walcott, Margaret
,,	Williams, Elizabeth	1784	Wake, Dorothy
,,	Wood, Mary	,,	Wilcox, Nicholas
,,	Warner, Henry	,,	Workman, Thomas
,,	Whitaker, Elizabeth	,,	Walter, Thomas
,,	Welch, Samuel	,,	Whalley, Joseph
,,	Walker, Margaret	,,	Waterman, Thomas
,,	Whitehouse, Elizabeth	,,	Walker, Katherine
,,	Woodin, Martha	,,	Wilson, Susanna
,,	Williams, Thomas William	,,	Wheeler, Elizabeth
,,	Wingood, Ann	,,	Walker, Thomas

Year.	Names of Testators.
1784	Wheeler, Mary
"	Wood, Jane
1785	Wiles, Ann
"	Walrond, Francis
"	Williamson, John
"	Walcott, John
"	Woodman, William
"	Wharton, Samuel
"	Worrell, John
"	Worrell, William
"	Walker, George
1786	Workman, Elizabeth
"	Woodin, Ann
"	Walcott, John
"	White, Isaac
"	Wood, William
"	Watt, Richard
"	Willshire, Eleanor
"	Witaker, Jnr., Henry
"	Wiggins, Edward
1787	Wall, John
"	Wilson, Mercy
"	Waith, Joseph
"	Willson, Edward
"	Wilson, Benjamin
"	West, Thomas
"	Whaly, Ann
"	Waterman, Henrietta
1788	Williams, James
"	Watt, Nathaniel
"	Wildey, Alice
"	Woodroffe, Benjamin
"	Woodroffe, Charles
"	Watson, George
"	Woodroffe, Benjamin
"	Warren, Christian
"	Wiles, William
"	Wightman, Rebecca
1789	Waddington, Mary
"	Wood, James
"	Ward, Daniel, *alias* Rasbotham
"	Walcott, Eyare
"	Wooding, Elizabeth
"	Wickham, John
"	Whitfoot, Charles
"	Whitehall, Ann
"	Warner, Ashton, Dr.
"	Willing, Charles
1790	Walton, Robert
"	Ward, Austin
"	Weekes, Ralph
"	Walcott, Love
"	Welch, Samuel
"	Wilson, Richard
"	Wharton, Rev. Thomas
"	Waterman, Jnr., Benony

Year.	Names of Testators
1790	Workman, Ann
"	Waterman, Thomas
"	Walrond, Ann
"	Wells, Elizabeth
1791	Wright, Francis
"	Wilson, Nicholas
"	Warriner, Henry
"	Woolford, Thomas
"	Walcott, Dorothy Carrington
1792	Walcott, John
"	Williams, John
"	White, Mary
"	Whitfoot, William
"	Welch, Mary
"	Wharton, John
"	Welch, Edward
"	Wiltshire, Elizabeth
"	Waterman, Jane
"	Willey, Ralph Oxnard
1793	Webster, Joseph
"	Wood, Ursula
"	Waterman, Thomas
"	Wood, Barnard
"	Williams, Lewis
"	Woodward, George
"	Wright, John
"	Williams, John
"	Wall, John
"	Williamson, Richard
"	Williams, Robert
"	Walker, George
"	Walter, William
"	Webber, Lt. John Incledon
"	Waterman, Thomas
"	Weekes, Mary
1794	Waterman, Thomas
"	Walter, James
"	Willoughby, Edward
"	Williams, William Wiltshire
"	Welch, Daniel
"	White, Henry
"	Watson, Robert
"	Went, James King
"	White, William
"	Wilson, William
"	Whitfoot, Burnett
"	Wilson, James
"	Whitney, Thomas
"	Workman, Hamlet
1795	Westbrooke, George
"	Whitewood, Mathew
"	Williams, John Archibald
"	Wharton, William Henry
"	Wiles, Daniel Thomas
"	Walke, Harrison
1796	Wildey, Sarah

Year.	Names of Testators.
1796	Walcott, John
„	Willing, Elizabeth Hannah
„	Williams, Thomas
„	Walton, Robert
„	Wheeler, Stephen
„	Webster, Anthony
„	Whitfoot, Thomas
„	Wheelwright, James
„	Williams, Richard
„	West, William
„	Walters, Deliverance
1797	Whitfoot, Willoughby
„	Warner, Thomas
„	Webb, Roger
„	Williams, William Brinton
„	Worrell, Mary
„	Wentworth, William
„	Wilson, Jennett
„	Ward, Margaret
1798	Welch, Elizabeth
„	Webb, Charles
„	Whitaker, Margaret Ann
„	Walrond, Nathaniel
„	Watson, William
„	Wills, Nicholas
1799	Walke, Francis
„	Webb, William Thomas
„	Wood, William
„	Wilkinson, John
„	Walcott, Samuel
„	Way, William
„	Waterman, Ann
„	Walcott, Martha
„	Wharton, Mary
1652	Yate, Thomas
1654	Young, John
1655	Yeo, Abraham
1660	Yeoman, Robert
1667	Yeoman, John
1672	Younge, Robert
„	Young, Robert
1674	Yeamans, John
1682	Yate, Mary
1687	Yearwood, William
„	Yard, John
1689	Yeomans. Elizabeth
1695	Yearwood, John
1698	Young, John
1710	Young, Eleanor
„	Yeldhall, William
1719	Young, James
1721	Yeamans, John
1725	Yeamans, Sarah
1726	Young, Mary
1726	Yearwood, Samuel
1727	Yelling, John
1728	Yeaman, Margaret
1731	Yeamans, Margaret
1739	Yearwood, William
„	Yearwood, Snr., William
1742	Young, Henry
„	Yeats, Daniel
1743	Yearwood, Benjamin
1744	Yearwood, Joseph
„	Young, Joseph
1745	Young, William
1746	Young, William
„	Yearwood, Richard
„	Young, Joseph
1748	Yearwood, Samuel
1751	Young, Francis
1752	Young, John
1754	Young, John
„	Yeats, Cornelius
1756	Yearwood, Samuel
„	Yard, John
1760	Yard, Ratliff
1762	Young, James
1766	Yard, Thomas
1768	Yearwood, Joseph
1769	Yearwood, Israel
1770	Yeamans, Philip
1772	Young, William
1776	Yearwood, Matthew
1778	Yearwood, Benjamin
1779	Yearwood, William Sandiford
„	Yearwood, Mary
1780	Yard, Edward
1781	Yard, Thomas
„	Yearwood, Benjamin
1782	Young, James
1783	Yard, Ann
1784	Yeamans, John
1785	Yearwood, Elizabeth
1786	Yard, Adams
1787	Young, Elizabeth
„	Young, Francis
1788	Yearwood, Mary
1790	Young, William
1792	Yard, John
1794	Yard, Mary Elvira
„	Young, Thomas Moore
„	Young, Thomas
1797	Yearwood, Elizabeth
1799	Yearwood, Mary

The above list of testators was copied in 1914 by Henry Waite, a clerk in the Registrar's Office, Barbados.

Beckles of Barbados.*

25 Chas. II., 1672, Feb. 15. Robert Beckles, Complainant, states that a letter was sent to Barbadoes by defendant Timothy Whittingham, Esq., of Holmside, co. Durham, to Complainant to the effect that if the said Complainant would redeem Wm. Whittingham son of Defendant from slavery in Barbadoes and send him over into England he would pay to Complainant what he should lay out.

Richard Beckles, father of Complainant, was on a visit to his son in B. and brought back the said Wm. W. to England Dec[r] 1670.

Redemption, transportation and other necessary expenses cost £62.

1672, March 11. Rich. Beckles of Crosgate in or nigh the City of Durham, dyer, 52, is father of complt. Says he lent to sd. W[m] at Barbadoes and in England £62 at least, and confesses that he did cause the sd. Wm W. to be arrested and imprisoned at London for part of the sd. money so by him pd.

Timothy W. had complained that his son had not been brought to Durham as had been specified.

Rich. B. again deposes. Was in Barbadoes when the letter of Timothy W. arrived. He pd. to Thos. Bérisford in B., with whom the sd. Wm W. was then bound by indent as servant or apprentice (to serve in any imployment the sd. Thos. B. might think fit to imploy him in for the space of 3 yrs.) for releasing him, and some small necessary apparell, £20. Wm W. after the time of his being bound by the sd. indent. committed some misdemeanour to his sd. master Berisford for wh. he was committed to prison, and was then sold by his said master for a slave to go to Jamaica for £18, of wh. the sd. B. upon satisfaction of the sum of £20 to him as aforesd. did likewise acquit the said W[m] W., and delivered up the indent. dated 1669, July 23. Deponent laid out more for other necessaries of apparel and for moneys lent unto the sd. W[m] W., and more other money paid and laid out in and about the transporting of the sd. W[m] W. into England £12, for this dep. and W[m] W. were a great while at sea at a great charge there and in much danger of suffering shipwrack in their voyage from the Barbadoes. Their vessel the W[m] and J[s] of London did spring a leak and break in pieces by violence of weather and this dep. and the sd. W[m] W. with some danger escaped near Fayall within the King of Portugall's territorye where this dep. was at much charge and was constrayned to stay by the space of a month, and then was at a second charge to contract for the sd. W[m] W.'s passage into England with a master of a Dutch vessell there, wh. likewise fayling at sea he, this dep., was again at a greater charge, enforced to engage another vessel called by the name of the Fortune of Dover, whereof one W[m] Hare was then master, and this dep. sometime after landed safe at Dover in England about the month of Dec. 1670.

"R. B."

D. 2/68/119 and 181; D. 7/51.

The reference is Durham 7/51, i.e., bundle 51 of Durham Chancery Depositions, the suits in which are not numbered.

Durham 2/68, 119 and 181 the corresponding B. and A. in bundle 68 of Durham Chancery Proceedings.

Capt. Robert Beckles mentioned in the above suit d. 19 July 1682, aged 32. M.I. at St. Michael's, Barbados. His wife Susannah Povey d. 8 Sept. 1683, aged 27, and with two children was buried with her husband. She was a dau. of Capt. Wm. Povey, Provost Marshal of B'os 1662, by Ann his wife, which Ann d. 22 Feb. 1700 and was buried in the Beckles vault. The Poveys were very much interested in the Plantations. Wm. Povey's father Justinian was a commissioner in the

* Communicated by the Rev. T. C. Dale of Croydon.

Caribbees in 1637 for the Earl of Carlisle. William's brother Thomas Povey, M.P., was clerk to the Council for Plantations (see "D.N.B."). Another brother Major Richard Povey was Sec. of Jamaica 1661—71, and a nephew Wm. Blathwayt, M.P., was a commissioner for the Plantations and clerk to the Privy Council.

Mr. Thomas Beckles, perhaps a brother of Robert, was buried at St. Michael's 10 Jan. 1677-8. From one of these probably descended Henry Beckles, Attorney Gen. of B'os, who d. 26 Feb. 1772.

Edward Hyndman Beckles was Bishop of Sierra Leone in 1860.

Who is the present representative of the family?—[Editor.]

Abstracts of Nevis Wills in the P.C.C.*

Michael Perry. Ex'ors to Capt. Perry's will. According to his desire that Mr John Hine to be one, Mr Joseph Earle to be second, Mr Wm. Jones the third, Capt. Wm. Daves the fourth, and that it is his desire that these Gentlemen should make up the account that depends between him and Mr Thomas Walden which have been of long standing between them at that time, he the sd. Pery had moneys in Sr Wm. Cann's hand, and that the sd. Waldin would not let him alone before sd. Pery gave a noat on the sd. Sr. Wm. Cann for about £30 odd and upon giving that noates promised to refer the Acct. to any 2 men, therefore it tis my desire that those Articles shall be inspected into by those desired to be my ex'ors, for never a one of his articles dated after his receipt which my wife have am I any ways liable two knowing that after that we contracted no account between us for there was £50 that was in the Owners Endeavours book in Mr Hind's hand that I know not how it was answered. Mr Walden was purser two voyages ago and makes the sd. Pery Dept for the outlying frayt for which there is a great deal yt have not been gotherd in as the Ships book will make appear in Sr. Wm. Cann's hand as Mr Burges frayt for his sons sugar Mr Jacob Beales frayt and Sr. Wm. Cans frayt, and whereas the sd. Pery paid damage to several other men his pt. although that he had damage himself as appears by Acct. that his wife have, he could not be allowed any now her requireth his part of damage answerable to the other, likewise there was £50 which was to be received from Mr Cary which everyone received his part but myself, but Mr Cann could not get his part from Mr Cary but stopt it from me the sd. Pery, and if anything should be lost I ought to lose no more, but my part likewise they cut of my Commissions which was due to me at Jamaica which was about £12 not allowing me anything for my expences." Mr Rogers now my Chief Mate to succeed me as Master and Commander of Ship Owners Endeavour, Mr Leach to be Chief Mate, "and likewise the last voyage to Nevis in my absence at sea the owners of the ship Owners Endeavour passing the ships book makes me debtor for £3 odd moneys frayt for sugar that was not in the ship as Mr Walden well knownes." I have left in hands of Mr William Minor resident in Nevis 30 pipes of Madarro wine for which I was to pay him half Commissions and the effects he was to ship home at 12 months ago. Likewise £205 in hands of Mr William Dane, also my quarter part of ship Owners Endeavour with the value about £200 or £300 aboard sd. ship as will appear by the Inventory, all which goods here mentioned and what herself is privy to I leave to my dear and espoused wife, but if she die before it come to her hands to John Papwell £100 and £100 to parish of Temple in Bristol, to my father £100, and to overseers of my will £50 between them and the rest to the 2 daurs. of Mr Guilham whose names are Mary and the other sister unmarried. Witnesses: John Papwell, John Rogers, Joseph Leach.

* Continued from p. 283.

John Papwell of city of Bristol, mariner, swears that on 10 Sep. 1689 he, at request of Michael Perry, late of sd. city, since dec., wrote his will (as above) which was duly executed in the harbour of London Derry in the Kingdom of Ireland where sd. M. Perry was Commander of the Ship Owners Endeavour of Bristol in Service of their Majesties, this Deponent being then and there Commander of the Ship Jerusalem in the same service, and there afterwards in London Derry afsd. on Sunday 15 Sep. the sd. M. Perry died. Sworn 24 Dec. 1689.

Adm'on c.t.a. 4 Jan. 1689 to Sarah Perry, widow, relict of Michael Perry, late of city of Bristol, but at London Derry, Irel., dec., John Hine, Joseph Earle, esquires, William Jones and William Davies the ex'ors renouncing. (9, Dyke.)

William Davies, of this Island, merchant. Will dated 20 Aug. 1689. To be bur. at discretion of Mr John Whitson and Mr William Minor my Trustees hereinafter mentioned. To sd. J. Whitson and W. Minor of this Island, merchants, a beaver hat to each. To poor of parish of Charles Town in this Island 5000 lbs. of Muscovado sugar to buy bread for poor. To William Ling who now lives with me 5000 lbs. of Muscovado sugar. Mr John Cary of Bristol, merchant, to be ex'or and residuary devisee and legatee. Sd. J. Whitson and W. Minor to be overseers and trustees for my ex'or, etc. Witnesses: Ebenezar Kyrtland, Thomas Harney, John Chinn, William Linge.

Probate 16 May 1690 by John Cary the ex'or. (68, Dyke.)

Sarah Helmes,* of Island of Nevis, sole ex'trix of Robert H. of same, dec. Will dated 4 Oct. 1687. The £500 left by my dec. husband to my sister Christian Helmes, for which Capt. Philip Lee hath at my request entered into obligation to pay, to be pd. to sd. Capt. P. Lee out of money due to me in hands of Mr John Maryon of Breuntree, co. Essex. To my sister Elizabeth the wife of Capt. William Freeman, clothes, etc. £200, for which I have entered into bond this day to Mr Joseph Little of Island of Mountserrat, to be paid him. To Silvanus Tayler of Island of Nevis, merchant, £20. To my 3 servants Humphery Edwards, Elizabeth Hughes and Elizabeth Latchfeild £10 each. To my very good friend Capt. Philip Lee afsd. large silver tankard. To friends Mrs Jane Masculine of city of London my wrought bed being now in England. To Mrs Mary Maryon, daur. of sd. Mr John M., silver basin. To my 2 aunts Mrs Mary Baxter of London and Mrs Mary Little of Alsebury, Bucks, £25 apiece. To sd. Elizabeth Latchfeild £20, also £10 more, last being so much due for wages. To my bro. Capt. William Freeman £100. £50 to Mr Henry Freeman, bro. of sd. William. Residue to neice Mrs Elizabeth Baxter of London, only daur. and sole heir of my brother William B. of London, lately dec., and she to be ex'trix. James Houblin, esq., and sd. bro. Capt. W. Freeman of London and Philip Lee and Henry Carpenter, esquires, of Nevis, to be overseers. To sd. J. Houblin and H. Carpenter, esquires, a hhd. claret. Witnesses: Arch. Hutcheson, Ra. Lomax, Silvanus Taylor, William Harrington.

Adm'on c.t.a. 17 May 1690 to James Houblon, esq., lawful guardian of Elizabeth Baxter, a minor, daur. of a bro., ex'trix and resid. legatee during her minority.

Probate 25 June 1701 by Elizabeth Baxter afsd., she being of full age. (72, Dyke.)

Joseph Loyd, of Island of Nevis, merchant. Will dated in Nevis 16 Nov. 1689. To my kinsman John Lewis who now lives with me £150 at expiration of his apprenticeship. To my kinswoman Sarah Duffield £50. To Mr Richard

* See pedigree, *ante*, V., 40.

Meriwether £5 in full for what he can claim of my estate in partnership. Rest of es'te to my bro. Mr Henry L. of Bristol, merchant, in fee and he to be ex'or. Col. John Nethway and Capt. Philip Lee to be overseers. Witnesses: Ebenezer Kyrtland, Francis Simonds, Richard Mercer, David Thomas +.

15 Jan. 1689-90 before Honble Col. John Netheway, Deputy Governor, appeared Ebenezer Kyrtland, Richard Messer (*sic*), Francis Simons and David Thomas, all of full age, and swore they saw testator execute the will.

Probate 13 May 1690 by Henry L., bro. and ex'or. (74, Dyke.)

THOMAS HARVEY, of city of Bristol, gent., now resident in this Island (Nevis). Will dated 12 Dec. 1689. To my daur.-in-law Martha Parsons £200 at 16 or marr'e. To friend Thomas Tovy of this Island £100. Rest equally to my wife Mary H. and my son Thomas and they to be ex'trix and ex'or. Friends Mr John Freeke and Mr Thomas Hicks of city of Bristol, and Mr John Streater and Tho. Tovy of this Island to be overseers, and to each £10. Witnesses: Jn° Chinn, Ja. Browne, Tho. Bisse, Jun., Law. Brome.

23 Dec. 1690. Appeared Mr John Chinn, Capt. Ja. Browne and Mr Law. Brome, witnesses, and vouched for sd. will.

Probate 2 Nov. 1691 by Mary H., widow, relict and one of the ex'ors. Power reserved for Thomas H. the son and or. ex'or. (192, Vere.)

WILLIAM WRAXALL, of city of Bristol, mariner, now resident in Island of Nevis. Will dated 29 Jan. 1690-1. To my son William W. my 2 houses and land in North Street, Bedminster, co. Somers., in fee and £50 in my wife's hands, but if ship Sea Flower, now in this Road, arive with her cargo safe in England, I give him £50 more to be paid him at expiration of his apprenticeship. To my daur. Mary W. £200 and her own mother's wedding ring and £50, if sd. ship arive, at 21 or marr'e. To Mr John Streater and William Minor, merchants in Nevis, Mr Abraham Elton and my bro. Peter W., merchant and mariner of Bristol, £5 each. To Mrs Penelope Harris for care of me in my sickness £10. To my 6 sons Peter, Andrew, Nathaniel, John, Samuel and Joseph W. two third parts of all the remainder of est. equally at 21 or marr'e. If child my wife now goeth withal live, he or she to have equal share. To my wife Mary W. rest of este. in fee, and she to be ex'trix. My sd. friends Mr John Streater and Mr William Minor, Mr Abraham Elton and my bro. Peter W. to be ex'ors and overseers in trust and guardians of sd. children. Witnesses: Azariah Penny, Leon^d Hancock, Nico. Downing, Jn° Richardson, William Godman, Wm. Bates.

Probate 18 Feb. 1691[-2] by Mary W., relict and ex'trix. (38, Fane.)

WILLIAM WATERS, late of city of Bristol, but at present of Island of Nevis, merchant. Will dated 6 Nov. 1690. To St Thomas parish 1000 lbs. of sugar to be laid out in a piece of plate. To Mr Thos. Goar my beam, scales and weights. To Mrs Kath. Manning my negro woman Vendah. To Eleanor Murphy my negro boy named Nevis. To Thomas Ayres £10. To Mrs Penelope Harris 3 negro women and a child I purchd. of John Hendy. The £50 I am indebted to Mr James Gallop to be paid out of goods shipped home in partnership with Mr William Worgan. To Mr Thomas Tovy £50 out of rents of es'te in England. To Mr William Worgan £30. To my honoured mother Mrs Anne Harris all my es'te for life, remr. to my 2 nephews Thomas Harris and William Wilkins in fee in common. Wh'as there is mine and my mother's life in house known as Ralph Grant's House in Ratcliff Street, Bristol., my mother and Mr William Worgan to purchase same for life of my sister Anne Harris, and after mother's death I

bequeath same to sd. sister. Mother Mrs Ann Harris and friend William Worgan to be ex'ors in England and Mr Thomas Tovy to be ex'or here. My bro. John Wilkins to be discharged any debts he may owe me. Witnesses: Theoph Moses Levermore, John Isaacks, John Streater, Ebenezr Kyrtland.

26 Nov. 1690 Appeared Dr Theophilus Moses Levermore and Ebenezer Kyrtland and vouch for will.

Probate 18 March 1691[-2] by Ann Harris and William Worgan, two of the ex'ors. (60, Fane.)

ADAM COMBES, the now husband of Joanna C., of city of Bristol, mariner. Will dated 13 Sept. 1691. To my daur. Elizabeth C., the daur. of my former wife Elizabeth C., 100,000 lbs. of sugar, to be paid by Mr. Walter Symonds, planter in Nevis. To her the Westrage or tenmt. in Lewinsmead, p'ish of St James, Bristol. All goods equally between my wife Joanna and my 2 children Elizabeth and Susannah C., sd. wife Joanna C. and my 2 children to be ex'trices. Witnesses: Phillip Skrine, Nathaniel Coates, Ralph Barrow, Thomas Sampson, Jonah Jackson, Edward Darville.

Probate 6 Apr. 1692 by Joanna C., relict and one of the ex'trices. Power reserved for Elizabeth C. and Susanna C. the daurs. and other ex'trices. (64, Fane.)

COLL. JOHN NETHEWAY,* of this Island (Nevis) Governour. Will dated 25 July 1691. To my sister-in-law Anne Hanscombe, widow, living in London £300, she to clear my es'te from all debts of her former husband, Mr. Matthew H. dec. To my sister-in-law Elizabeth Smith in London £300. To my mother-in-law Mrs. Margt Netheway, widow, living in Bristol £100. To my kinswoman, Mrs. Sarah Gurney's first child 8,000 lbs. of sugar at age of 14. To my cousin John Richardson 8,000 lbs. of sugar at 18. To my wife's kinsman ['s] son, Phillip Dewitt, son of Phillip D., 40,000 lbs. of sugar at 18. To godson John Huffam 5,000 lbs. of sugar at 18. To godson William Chisurs 3,000 of sugar at 18. To godson Simon Brown son of Simon B., dec., 3,000 lbs. of sugar at 18 to buy him a young negro boy or girl. To Mary Thompson 4,000 lbs. of sugar and to Elizabeth Tompson 2,000 lbs. of sugar both at 14 or marr'e. To Thomas Thorne 2,000 lbs. of sugar for writing my Will. Rest of es'te to my wife Mrs. Mary N. for life and to kinsman Mr. Jonathan Netheway of London, gent., in tail male in deft. to next of blood of the name if any, otherwise to the heiresses of sd. Jonathan Netheway. Sd. wife and kinsman to be ex'ors. Capt. Walter Simonds, esq., Capt. William Helmes, Capt. John Standley, Danl Smith and Lieut. Phillip Dewitt to be overseers, to each 1,000 lbs. of sugar to buy them beaver hats. Witnesses: John Smargin, Tho. Belman, Tho. Thorne, Wm. Marden, James Rawleigh.

Probate 17 Sept. 1692 by Jonathan Netheway one of the ex'ors. Power reserved for Mary N. the relict and other ex'ors. The Governor died 12 Feb. last.

17 Sept. 1692. Appeared Jonathan Netheway, of city of London, gent., and swore that on 27 June last he received a letter by the Post from Nevis dated 16 Apr. 1692 signed John Stanley, Phil. Dewitt, Daniell Smith enclosing a copy of Will of deceased and believes copy to be written by sd. Phillip Dewitt, who is a man of good reputation and es'te in Nevis. 15 Sept. 1692. Appeared Joseph Martin, of city of London, merchant and vouches for letter and copy of will as being in hand of Phillip Dewitt who had formerly been his servant. (171, Fane.)

THOMAS BELCHAMBER, of Island of Nevis, Esq. Will dated 9 Feb. 1692-3. To my sister Elizabeth Pennington's children £50 each, they having greatest occasion thereof to be paid immediately. To my sister Meriam Shelberrie's children £10 each. To my sister Augustin's children £10 each. To my god-daur,

* See pedigree, *ante*, V., 36.

Elizabeth Rolt 1,000 of muscova lb sugar a year until she be 21 or married, off our Antegua Plantation. To my friend Col. Charles Pym, riding horse. etc. To Charles Town Parish of this island £20 piece of plate for service of Communion Table. To friends Silvanus Taylor and Henry Bolton of this island £100 between them to settle accounts in partnership with Henry Carpenter, etc. dec., as we were concerned for the Customs and the Royal African Co., they also having regard to our debts to Mr. Cary and myself. Col. Rowland Williams, Capt. Samuel Horne and Mr. Alexander Crafford to have managem't of our Antigua plantation and to ship home sugar to Richard Cary. To each a beaver hat. Richard Cary, merchant in London to be heir and sole ex'or, Col. Charles Pym, Aaron Chapman. esq., Mr. Phillip Brome and Silvanus Taylor to be overseers and to each a beaver hat. Witnesses: Thornton Jones, Bridget Rogers, Dinah Munde, Martha Moore, Hen. Bolton.

Probate 5 Sept. 1693 by Richard Cary the ex'or. Brought in and later will proved Nov. following. (136, Coker.)

Thomas Belchamber of Island of Nevis, esq. Will dated 23 May 1693. Same as foregoing except Silvanus Taylor is not joined with Henry Bolton to settle testators acc'ts, and Mr. William Ling is substituted for him as an overseer. Witnesses: Charles Rowland, Geo. Richardson, Geo. Littman, Henry Boulton.

Nevis 12 Aug. 1693 appeared before Hon[ble] Col. Samuel Gardner, Lieut. Governor, Doctor Charles Rowland, Mr. Geo. Richardson and Mr. Geo. Littman who vouched for will.

Probate 21 Nov. 1693 by Richard Cary the ex'or. Probate of an earlier will made 5 Sept. last having been brought in and declared void. (176, Coker.)

John Streater, of Island of Nevis, merchant. Will dated 12 Nov. 1691. To poor Quakers of this Island £10 to the Men's Meeting. To poor of Charles Town parish £10. To my bro. Henry S. £5 for a piece of plate and to each of his children 20*s*. To my bro. Samuel S. £5 for plate. To my sister Waller £3 and to each of her children 20*s*. To my sister Eliza Barnard £3 and to each of her children 20*s*. To my sister Mary Holden £3. To my partner Capt. Edmond Scroope £10 for piece of plate and 20*s*. each to his children. To Aza Pinney £5. If I have a child by my wife Sarah S. then half of residue of es'te and what I have as ex'or to my bro. William Minor, to him or her when of age and the other half to him or her after my wife's death in fee, but if I have no child my whole es'te to my wife Sarah in tail in deft. to my 2 brothers. Henry S. and Samuel S. in fee in common. Sd. wife to be ex'trix. Friends Capt. William Meade, Ebenezer Kyrtland, Sylvanus Taylor and Aza Penney to be overseers in Nevis and my brothers Henry and Samuel S. in England, and to each a beaver hat. Witnesses: Wm. Burt, Law[r] Brome, Tho. Bridgwater, Wm. Ling. Adm'on c.t.a. 20 June 1694 to Henry Streater and Samuel Streater ex'ors and resid. legatees in will of Sarah Streater, dec., relict and ex'trix of will of John S., late of Island of Nevis, merchant, dec., the sd. Sarah S. having died before taking Probate. (140, Box.)

Sarah Streater, relict and ex'trix of John S., late of this Island (Nevis), merchant, dec. Will dated 9 Mar. 1692-3. To my mother Sarah Minor of Bristol, widow, all money, etc., now in my possession, also dwelling house in Marsh Street in Bristol, bequeathed to me by John Minor of Bristol, mariner, for life, also £50 anny. out of my sd. late husband's estate for her life, to be paid by my brothers Henry Streater and Samuel Streater, whom I appoint ex'ors. To them all rest of estate in fee. To my negro woman Baly for her fidelity and care towards me her

freedom. Friends Aaron Chapman, William Meade and Silvanus Taylor to be ex'ors in trust in absence of my ex'ors afsd., and to each a beaver hat. Wits.: Wm. Ling, Tho. Evans, Hugh Gurney, Sarah Cammell ×.

Probate 20 June 1694 by Henry Streater and Samuel Streater the ex'ors. (140, Box.)

EDMOND SCROPE of sd. Island (Barbados), esq. Will dated 21 Aug. 1694. Mr. Robert Yate of Bristol, merchant, and Mr. Robert Henly of London, merchant, to be trustees of my will and guardians of my 3 daurs. Ann, Mary and Elizabeth S, whom I appoint ex'trices. Mr James Aynsworth, Mr William Godman, both of the sd Island, merchants, to be ex'ors in trust for sd. daurs. of all goods in sd. Island. To my sister Ann Castle £100. To my niece Ann Adams £50. To my daur. Mary all the gold in my little East India Escritoire. To Rev. Mr Francis Makenny £10. To sd. R. Yate and R. Henly £10 each. To sd. ex'ors in trust £10 each. To George Massey in lieu of all wages £30. To Mr Jonathan Wills a mourning ring. To my sd. daurs. ½ of house and land in Charles Town in Island of Nevis, which was between Mr Streets and myself, in fee. To my neice Elizabeth Castle £50. Wits.: James Lewis, Cicelia Lewis, Jane Jope, Nich. King.

Adm'on c.t.a. 16 Feb. 1694[-5] to Robert Yate and Robert Henley, overseers and guardians, during minority of Anne, Mary and Elizabeth S., minors, daurs. of dec. and ex'trices. (32, Irby.)

JOHN LLOYD of London, mariner. Will dated 27 Jan., Wm. and M., 1693. Bound on a voyage to East Indies. To my wife Hannah Ll. all estate in fee, and she to be ex'trix. Wits.: Nath Unwin, J. Wilmers, Zach. Hallings.

Codicil, dated at Nevis 10 Mar. 1695. To be bur. at discretion of Mr Pereman Basse, Mr John Conway and Mr Samuel Cooper. I confirm Will left with my wife before leaving England. As to Goods on board ship "Nassau," to ex'trix Hannah Lloyd 6800 jembe canes, 1200 canes that was Mr Cooper's, 190 bundles of rattans, and everything else of mine on board the "Nassau." £20 to Col. Gardener, Governor of the Island, £20 among company of ship "Nassau, and £80 for my enterment, and £1200 due to me per Mr Cooper's accounts to my ex'trix to be paid by my owners. Jeremiah Basse and Benninham West to take into custody all things belonging to me on board ship "Nassau," and John Valentine, they to manage all affairs till they get to England. Wits.: Samuell Gardner, Jos. Jordan, Ro. Stewart.

Probate 27 May 1696 by Hannah Lloyd, widow, the relict and ex'trix. (73, Bond.)

WILLIAM MINOR of this Island (Nevis), merchant. Will dated 12 Oct. 1691. To my mother Sarah M. of Bristol £100. To William Ling 5000 lbs. of muscavado sugar. To William Christophers 5000 lbs. of same. Rest to my brother John Streater in fee, and he to be ex'or. My friend Charles Jones of Bristol and Silvanus Taylor of Nevis to be overseers, and to each a beaver hat. Wits.: Walter Hamilton, Jno Lewis, Lawrence Broome, Arthur Plomer.

Adm'on c.t.a. 4 July 1696 to John Cary, principal creditor of testator (a bachelor), John Streater the ex'or having also died before taking Probate. *Vacat quia net sigillat'.* (162, Bond.)

Will apparently identical with above.

Adm'on c.t.a. 4 Sept. 1696 to Henry Streater and Samuel Streater, brothers and adm'ors c.t.a. of John Streater, dec. ex'or and residuary legatee of William Minor, junior, late of city of Bristol but at Nevis, a bachelor, dec., by the declaration of sd. H. and S. Streater. (188, Bond.)

THOMAS DITTIE of city of Bristol, merchant. Will dated 22 Jan. 1696, 8 Wm. III. To Master Thomas Attwood, merchant, on Island of Mountserrat, my moiety of young Negro man Jonny, he to make up all accounts of our partnership of factorage and merchandice. My mother Elizabeth D. to be ex'trix, and she to have all personal estate of sd. partnership and also of partnership with sd. T. Attwood on Island of Nevis, Barbadoes, or in Colony of New England. Friends Lieut. Col. Anthony Hodges, Capt. John Davis, merchant, of Mountserrat, and Mr Edward Foy, chyrurgeon, of Bristol, to be ex'ors in trust, and to each 3 gu'as for a beaver hat. Witnesses: Thomas Read, Sarah Berrow.

Probate 22 Feb. 1696[-7] by Elizabeth Ditty, mother and ex'trix. (28, Pyne.)

HUMPHRY LEWIS, Commander of the ship "Scarborough. Will dated at Nevis 8 Oct. 1696. To my sister Sarah a gold ring. To my sister Elizabeth the like. My father and mother Roger and Hannah L. to be ex'ors, and to them all due to me from the owners of said ship, also silver-headed cane and what is mine on board sd. ship, viz., 3 tierces of muscavado sugar marked H.W. one to three, and 12 barrels of sugar, a bag of cotton wool and a bag cotton in partnership with George Mills, and also 2 hhds. and a tierce of tobacco. Witnesses: Joseph Chapman, Hugo Parker, Charles Trecton, James Allison.

Probate 5 Aug. 1697 by Roger L., the father and one of the ex'ors. Power reserved for Hannah L. the mother and o'r ex'or. (163, Pyne.)

TIMOTHY MORESBY of the ship "Scarbrow," now riding in Nevis, under the command of Hugh Tucker. Will dated at Nevis 13 Oct. 1696. To my sister Cate 40*s*. To Thomas Martin 20*s*. Rest of wages to Thomas Teap, mariner, belonging to said ship, and he to be ex'or. Witnesses: Elias Richards, John Welsh.

Probate 6 Aug. 1697 by Thomas Teap the ex'or. (165, Pyne.)

JOHN BREWETT of Island of Nevis, planter. Will dated 19 June 1690. Bound off this Island. Wife Anne B., now living in Lambeth, co. Surrey, England, and my daur. Anne B. living with her to be ex'trices. Friends Mr John Streater and Mr Christopher Clifton, sen. to be overseers and feoffees in trust (for estate in Nevis), together with my brother in law Mr Walter Gore of parish of St George, Southwark (for estate in England). My sd. daur. not to enjoy my estate until 17 or married. To sd. 2 (Nevis) overseers 600 lbs. of sugar each for a hat, and to my other overseer W. Goar £6. Witnesses: Tho. Fenton, ser., Francis Franklyn, Margret Fenton, Anne Franklyn ×.

Adm'on c.t.a. 21 July 1699 to Walter Gore, uncle and guardian of Anne B., minor, daur. and surviving ex'trix of J. B., late of Lambeth, co. Surrey, but at Nevis, dec., during her minority. Adm'on of sd. dec. as intestate 7 July 1691 to Anne Schoolar *als.* Brewett (then wife of Isaac S.), relict of sd. dec., having been revoked.

Adm'on c.t.a. 8 Feb. 1699[-1700] to John Stone, husband and guardian of Anne S. *als.* Brewett, minor, daur. and surviving ex'trix of sd. dec., during her minority. Adm'on c.t.a. of July last to Walter Goare, uncle and guardian of sd. minor, having expired by reason of the marriage of sd. Anne with sd. J. Stone. (108, Pett.)

JOHN WHITSON of Nevis, merchant. Will dated 27 Aug. 1690. To the poor of Charles Town parish 5000 lbs. of sugar. To my eldest sister Mary £100. To

my sister Elizabeth £100. To my wife Elizabeth the rest of my estate in fee, and she to be ex'trix. Friends Mr John Streater, Mr Wm. Minor and Ebenezer Kyrtland to be ex'ors in trust. Witnesses: Wm. Tucker, Ebenezer Kyrtland, John Smith, Willm. Ling, Jeriah Wall.

Adm'on c.t.a. 12 Aug. 1699 to Thomas W., father of dec., Elizabeth W. the relict and ex'trix having also died before taking Probate. (140, Pett.)

Alexander Strennou, now resident in sd. Island (Nevis), chyrurgeon. Will dated 27 Feb. 1699, 12 Wm. III. All este. real and personal to the children of my brother-in-law John Hall of Peckham in Kent, England, by my sister Jone, now living at full age. Ex'or Mr Thomas Wych of London, merchant. Joseph Jewell, Commander of the ship the John and Roger now in sd. Island, to be ex'or in trust of goods in the Island. Ex'or in trust to pay Dugall Grey, Dr Semple's apprentice, 10 pieces of eight = £3, my nurse Katherine Weston 10 pieces of eight. Wits.: John Morrison, Ja. Taylor.

Probate 2 July 1700 by Thomas Wych, the ex'or. (105, Noel.)

Bernard White, now resident in Island of Nevis, merchant. Will dated 2 Oct. 1699. To Mr Thomas Bridgewater horse, clothes, etc. To his wife £10. To my brother Mr Samuel W., merchant in London, all este. in this Island, etc., in fee and to be ex'or. Mr Solomon Israel of Island of Nevis, merchant, and Mr Azariah Pinney, merchant, to be my ex'ors in trust for concerns in this Island and in all parts of America. Wits.: Ja. Taylor, Jo. Shank, James Ingles, Josa Borrow, Caleb Peirce.

Cod. undated. To sd. Mr T. Bridgewater a horse, to Mrs Bridgewater 2 small silver cups. To my sister Hannah Jenkinson £20. Same witns., omitting Jo. Shank.

Probate 16 May 1701 by Samuel W., brother and ex'or. (74, Dyer.)

John Lewis, of the Island afsd. (Nevis), merchant. Will dated 21 Dec. 1699. To my sister Elizabeth L. a three pint silver tankard, etc. To my father Thomas L. £40. To my kinswoman Grizell Lloyd, daur. of James Ll. of New England, £10. To Mary Gurney, daur. of John G., £5. To Sarah Morris, daur. of John M., formerly my overseer, £5. To James Taylor silver hilted sword. Friends Arthur Plomer and William Ling, both of Nevis, merchants, to be ex'ors in trust for my concerns in this Island and to each £10. Rest of este. to Mr Henry Lloyd, merchant of Bristol, in fee and he to be ex'or. Wits.: Richard Johnson, Richard Cooper, Thomas Nowell.

Probate 9 July 1701 by Henry Lloyd the ex'or. (99, Dyer.)

Jonathan Netheway, citizen and draper of London. Will dated 16 Aug. 1701. To be bur. with my mother and children in my burial ground at Bunhill, expences not more than £40, of which £10 to be expended in a stone. To my cousin George Netheway, his wife and children, my cousin Warren, his wife and children, my cousin Lawrence, his wife and children, my cousin Denby, his wife and children, my cousin Edith Seward, my cousin Thomas Atwood, his wife and children, my cousins Mary and Charles Richardson, my cousin John Richardson, his wife and children, to Madam Netheway, the widow of my late cousin Col. John N., dec., to my cousin Wm. Ward, his wife and children, and to my cousin Dorington Adams, his wife and children, 20s. each for rings. To my mother

Clarke £5 for mourning and to my brothers Samuel and Joseph Clarke 20s. a piece for rings. To my brother Cudsden, his wife and children, 20s. a piece for rings. To my brother Waxham, his wife and children. to my cousin Mary Notal, and to my aunt Sarah Clarke, the like. To my wife Mary N. my 4 houses in New Court, Throgmorton St., London, in tenures of Wm. Stubbs, Nathaniel Gifford, [*blank*] Bertram and Edmund Day, for her life if my term so long continue, also my 2 houses in Throgmorton Street afsd. in tenures of John Hitchcock and Wm. Smith, for life, they being already settled on her upon marriage, she paying ground rent. All este. in Island of Nevis, one of the Caribbee Leeward Islands in English Plantations in America, viz.: my plantation there, negroes and other servants to my sd. brother John Waxham and my 2 friends Mr John Skinner the elder and John Skinner the younger, his son, apothecaries in Whitechapel, in fee upon trust for sale. Residue of purchase money for my son Jonathan N. My este. in New West Jersey in America and my 35 shares in West Jersey Co. to my sd. son Jonathan N. in fee. My 6 black slaves in hands of widow Symonds of Charles Town in Carolina in America to my sd. son. My 11 shares in the Blue Paper Co. and my one share in the Greenland Co., my 4½ shares in the Royal African Co. and my one share in the old East India Co. to my sd. son. My copyhold lands held of Reeconden Manor, co. Essex, to sd. son in fee. My 2 leaseh. mess'es held for 2000 years at a peppercorn in Bell Alley in Coleman St., London, in tenures of John Gladwin and Nathaniel Winchester, to sd. son. My 2 freeh. messes. in tenures of John Hitchcocke and Wm. Smith, after sd. wife's death, to sd. son in fee, and to him freeh. mess'e in River St. or Savage Garden near Tower Hill. My sd. 4 mess'es in New Court and Throckmorton St. in p'ish of S. Bartholomew Exchange, now in tenures of sd. Wm. Stubbs, Nathaniel Gifford, [*blank*] Bertram and Edmund Day, after death of wife, to sd. son, and to him 2 mess'es in Shorters Court in Throckmorton St. in sd. pish. in tenures of Benjamin Gladman and John Blanch, and my 3 mess'es in the Little Minories in p'ish of Trinity Minories, in tenures of Jonathan Matson, Nathaniel Clement [*blank*], and my 2 mess'es in Buttolph Lane in p'ish of St Geo., Botolph Lane near Billingsgate, the one in tenures of Henry Marten, Dr William Bedford, and the cellar under Mr Marten, the Grocers Shop in my own hands, and the other in the occupation of Robert Dodd, and my mess'e in Little Thames Street called the Flying Horse, in p'ish of St Magnus, London, in tenure of Sir Bartholomew Gracedue, my mess'e in Threadneedle St. in p'ish of St Christophers, in tenure of Wm. Peepys, and my 2 mess'es in St Mary Ax in p'ish of St Andrew Undershaft, in tenures of Joseph Jacob and Thomas Dashwood, my 6 mess'es in Lamb Court in Abchurch Lane near Lumbard St. in p'ish of St Mary Abchurch, in tenures of Elizabeth Smith, Anne Waterman, Thomas Chadwell [*blank*], Wm. Cheeseman and Bridget [*blank*], my 3 mess'es in Clements Lane near Lumbard St. in p'ish of St Clement's, East Cheap, in tenures of Thomas Hackley, [*blank*] Townsend and Thomas Trayton, and my mess'es in Shoe Lane in occupation of John Call. To my sd. son my library, about 1,600 books. To my wife Mary N. all household goods, etc. To sd. son, bed which his grandmother Netheway wrought a little before her death. The house I now dwell in and hold of Esqre Austin to be disposed [of]. Sd. son to be put out to board to a pious and good schoolmaster at £30 a year until he be 12, then £40; from 14 to 16 £60, that is, if he shall for the last 2 years be bred up at the University, otherwise but £40, at which age he is to be put forth to an Attorney for 7 years. Upon his articling he to be entered into one of the Inns of Court so that he may the sooner come to the Bar. During such service he to have £40 a year. Rest of goods to my sd. son, ex'ors to manage same until he be 22. My sd. brother John Waxham and 2 friends John Skinner, senior and junior, to be ex'ors until my sd. son be 22, and to each £10, also £30 on surrendering their trust, when my sd. son is to be ex'or. Wits.: Samuel Layfield, Jno Hancock, Edm. Wood, Thomas Seth, servant to Mr. John Garrett Scr.

Adm'on c.t.a. 12 Sept. 1701 to Mary N., widow, mother and guardian of Jonathan N., son and substituted ex'or of will of J. N., late of St Leonard,

Shoreditch, co. Middx., until sd. ex'or be 22 or sd. Mary N. be married; John Skinner, sen., and John Skinner, jun., 2 of the ex'ors in trust, having renounced, John Waxham, the other ex'or in trust, being at present in the Indies and consenting.

Probate 21 Jan. 1702[-3] by John Waxham, one of the ex'ors. Adm'on c.t.a. of Sept. 1701 having expired by reason of death of sd. Mary N., widow.

Probate 18 July 1716 by Jonathan N., son and ex'or. Probate of Jan. 1702[-3] having ceased by reason of sd. Jonathan N. being 22. (129, Dyer.)

Martin Madan, late of Nevis in America and now of London, esq. Will dated 17 March 1703, 3 Anne. To my eldest son Martin M., over and above the plantation called *Russells* with negroes which I and my wife have settled on him by deed lately made in England, £2000 at 21. To my daur. Penelope M., in addition to her provision under sd. deed, £3000 at 21 or marriage. To my son James Russell M. £2000 at 21 in addition to the 2 plantations in Nevis settled under sd. deed. To my yst. son Richard M., in addition to his provision under sd. deed, £2500 at 21. To my wife Penelope M., on whom the plantations in Nevis are settled for life, all household goods, etc., £500. To my mother-in-law Dame Penelope Russell £20 for mourning, also £20 annuity for life. To my sister Giraldine in Dublin £50. To my brother Robert M. £50. To my sister Margaret (whose surname I do not know) £30. To my sister Dame Frances Stapleton £25 for mourning. To my friend Col. Wm. Ling of Nevis 20 French pistolls. To my maidservant Margaret Wroth £10. Friends Mr Joseph Martyn of London, merchant, and his 2 sons-in-law, Mr Wm. Fellowes and Mr Thomas Andrews to be ex'ors, and to each mourning and £20 for a diamond ring. Rest of est'e to sd. ex'ors in trust for my sd. 4 children equally at 21. Wits.: W. Cockburne, P. Allix, Wm Bolton.

Probate 20 Mar. 1703[-4] by Joseph Martyn, William Fellowes, esq., and Thomas Andrews, the ex'ors. (69, Ash.)

(*To be continued.*)

Christian of Antigua.

This Ind're of four parts made the 15 Nov., 39 Geo. III., 1798 Between James Taylor of Wanstead co. Essex Esq. of the 1st part; Tho. Rodie late of the town of Liverpool but now of the island of Antigua merchant and Geo. MacIntosh of the Royal Exchange insurance broker of the 2d part; the said Geo. MacIntosh and Richard Thornton of the borough of Southwark, co. Surry merchant creditors of the said James Taylor and trustees of the 3d part; and several other creditors of the 4th part. Whereas by an Ind're dated the 12 Sept. 1781 made between John Rose Esq. dep. provost marshall of Antigua of the 1st part, Boyce Ledwell and Alexr Scott of the same island merchants of the 2d part, Nath. Evanson of the same island, Esq. of the 3d part, reciting that sundry judgments were obtained in the court of C.P. in 1778 against Matthew Christian for several considerable sums upon which executions were levied upon his plantations which were also charged with divers mortgages annuities it was agreed between the heirs at law and execution creditors that his right and title and equity of redemption should be sold in one lot and on the 10 July 1781 Boyce Ledwell and Alex. Scott purchased the same at auction for £5200 and he John Rose with their consent sold to Nath. Evanson all the said plantations and slaves upon trust to permit Boyce Ledwell and Alex. Scott to take the rents and profits and Whereas Alex. Scott died the

13 Jan. 1787 in the said island having made his will on the 10 Aug. 1786 whereby he gave the residue of his estate to Wm. Butler, Tho. Rodie, John Scott and Henry Pearson for several trusts and appointed them his executors which will was recorded in Antigua and Whereas by Ind're dated the 27 Jan. 1790 made between Boyce Ledwell, Wm. Butler, Tho. Rodie and John Scott of the one part and James Taylor of the other part Reciting that the joint est. and co-partnership of Boyce Ledwell and Alex. Scott was then indebted in considerable sums and that Tho. Rodie had borrowed of James Taylor £10,000 st. for the said joint estate with interest at 6 per cent. by a mortgage it is now witnessed that they sell to him All that plantation formerly of Matthew Christian deceased and afterwards purchased by Ledwell and Scott called *Red Hill* in the division of Falmouth and parish of St. Paul containing 410 acres bounded E. with the sea, S. with the plantation of Edward Byam and Godschall Johnson Esq. called the Savannah, W. with the plantation of Archibald Cockran Esq., N. with the plantation of Sam. Rodhead Esq. called ffryes with the slaves, also all that other plantation formerly of the said Matthew Christian and also purchased by Ledwell and Scott called *Biffins* or Bevans lying in New and Old Road divisions and parish of St. Mary containing 200 acres bounded E. with another plantation formerly belonging to Matthew Christian called Huyghes, S. with lands of Sir Wm. Young Bart, W. with lands of the heirs of Foster deceased and another plantation formerly of Matthew Christian called the Valley, N. with lands of Wm. Allan Esq. with the slaves, and also all that other plantation formerly of the said Matthew Christian and also purchased by Ledwell and Scott called the *Valley* lying in New division and parish of St. Mary containing 350 acres bounded E. with lands of Wm. Allan, S. with Biffins, S.W. with lands of the heirs of John Foster, W. with lands of John Bott Esq., N. with lands of Robert Pearce deceased called Blubber Valley and with lands of Wm. Allan with the slaves, also all that other plantation formerly of the said Matthew Christian and also purchased by Ledwell and Scott called *Huyghes* lying in the division of Old Road and parish of St. Mary containing 200 acres bounded S.E. and E. with lands of Stephen Lynch Esq. deceased called Tom Moores, N.E. with lands late of John Gilchrist Esq., N. with lands of Fra. Farley, W. with other lands late of the said Matthew Christian, S. with lands of Sir Wm. Young B[t] called the River estate with the slaves, also all that other plantation formerly of the said Matthew Christian and also lately purchased by Ledwell and Scott called *Elmes Creek* estate lying in the division of Nonsuch and parish of St. Philip containing 149 acres bounded N. with lands partly of Stephen Lynch deceased and John Lavicount Esq. and late of Rob. Gray Esq. S. with lands of John Nibbs gent. and country lands of John Jackson and Stephen Norden, E. with lands of Sir Geo. Colebrooke B[t] and late of Stephen Lynch, W. with other lands of John Lyons Esq. and John Lavicount, also all that other plantation etc. called *Elmes Windward* lying in the division of Nonsuch and parish of St. Philip containing 180 acres bounded N. with lands of Alex. Willock Esq., Sir Geo. Colebrooke and Nich. Lynch Esq. deceased, S. with lands late of said Nich. Lynch E. with lands in the possession of persons to whom grants have been made of 10 acres with the slaves and the dwelling houses, still houses, windmills and cattle mills, cattle mules and other stock utensils, also all that parcel of land in Newgate Street in the town of St. John bounded E. with Leslie's Wharf and lands late of Wm. Garratt Hillhouse deceased and then of John Taylor, W. with lands of John Payne, N. with Newgate Street, S. with the sea late of Sam. Brown and sold by Ind're dated 15 June 1782 by him and Ph. Hicks of A. Esq. in trust for Ledwell and Scott, also the messuage built thereon, also that parcel of land in the parish of St. John and division of Dickenson's Bay containing 15 acres bounded N. and E. with lands of Wm. McKinnen S. with lands of John Taylor and W. with the sea, also all those 20 negro men slaves all which said plantations and slaves are to the use of Jas. Taylor his heirs subject to a proviso for redemption and Whereas by a deed poll dated the 28 Feb. 1795 after reciting that £2000 part of the above £10,000 was the money of Tho. Rodie. Jas. Taylor declared he would stand as trustee for that sum and by another deed poll dated the 9 Dec. 1795 it was declared

that £2000 was money of Geo. MacIntosh and Whereas the whole of the £10,000 remains owing and Jas. Taylor is indebted to Geo. MacIntosh and Richard Thornton and to the other parties of the 4th part in the sums opposite their names in the schedule annexed Jas. Taylor hath agreed to assign and convey the plantations to Geo. MacIntosh and Richard Thornton upon Trust that they may call in the £10,000 and apply £6000 in discharge of his debts, &c. and Tho. Scotland and Anthony Browne Esquires are appointed attornies. Signed and Sealed (plain seals) by James Taylor, George MacIntosh, and Richd Thornton. Signed also by 21 creditors for a total of about £2000 in various sums.

(On eleven wide skins—purchased May 1917 from a dealer by the Editor).

By Ind're of 28 Jan. 1779 Wm. Gunthorpe the Yr. and Margt. his wife only sister and h. at l. of Matthew Christian decd conveyed all the above plantations to Godschall Johnson in trust for the use of W. G. (Antigua I., 135).

List of Wills proved in the P.C.C. from 1813 to 1816 inclusive.*

ANTIGUA.

Mary Langford	31	Heathfield.	Sam. Turner	163	Pakenham.
Tho. Foot	132	,,	Joseph L. Walrond	286	,,
Barbara Nibbs	468	,,	Sir Geo. Thomas, Bt	344	,,
Joseph G. Buckley	534	,,	Clement Tudway	480	,,
Andrew Lessley	22	Bridport.	Ann Jones	613	,,
Sir Rich. Neave, Bt	161	,,	Cath. Potter	620	,,
John Dewar	282	,,	John Lyons	206	Wynne.
Archd Cochran	342	,,	Cha. Young	229	,,
Edward Rigg	439	,,	Tho. L. Brooke	298	,,
Rob. Mathews, Lt-Gov.	484	,,	John Duer	359	,,
Anthony J. P. Molloy	485	,,	Louisa MacKinnon	628	,,
Ann C. Duer	18	Pakenham.	Richd Donovan	650	,,

BARBADOS.

Jane Baroness Dow. Harewood			Will. Prescod	41	Pakenham.
	252	Heathfield.	Sir Wm. Gibbons, Bt	135	,,
Clement Horton	303	,,	George James	571	,,
Philippa Elliot Holder	501	,,	Edw. Rob. Lascelles	574	,,
James Maxwell	157	Bridport.	Jennett Sober	624	,,
Jonathan Worrell	191	,,	Sir Ph. Gibbes, Bt	22	Wynne.
Abr. C. Sober	248	,,	Will. Cadogan	422	,,
Sarah Barrow	550	,,	Dorothy Bruce	505	,,
John Lane Payne	578	,,	Eliz. F. E. Wiltshire	552	,,

BRITISH GUIANA.

Hugh L. Carmichael	12	Bridport.	Edward Ellaway	16	Wynne.
John Ettles	62	,,	Robert Kingston	31	,,
James Wollen	545	,,	John F. Kendall	378	,,
Robert Gibbons	606	,,	Tempest Coulthurst	479	,,
James Austice	217	Pakenham.			

* Continued from Vol. III.

JAMAICA.

1813. "Heathfield."

Anna Eliza Duchess of Chandos	1	Mary Dehany	411
Charles Long	32	Thomas Aspinall	447
Daniel Crokatt	65	William Dick	454
Smart Aldred	113	Simon Taylor	477
Alice Kennion	143	William Dwarris	493
Alexander Lindo	146	Charles Joshua Manning	507
Charles Goodhall	195	Thomas Alexander Beach	536
Elizabeth Lythgow	202	Susanna Coppell	540
Henry Shirley	215	Thomas Sutton	570
Sarah Whetcombe	227	John Borrows	579
Edward Long	257	William Green	595
David Patrick Molony	259	George Udney M^c^Kenzie	611
Benjamin D'Aguilar	410		

1814. "Bridport."

John Scott	37	Henry Dawkins	402
Tho. Fullarton Warren	43	Richard Crewe	458
Rev. Tho. Warren	43	John Clark	556
Edward Martin Whitehead	46	Joshua Hughes	565
Fyff Elletson King	76	George Hobkirk	566
Rice Davis	212	Richard Latimer	570
Joseph Royall	373	John Orr	577
Joseph Wilson	383	John Bourke	595

1815. "Pakenham."

George Atkinson	1	Cath. Knowles Evans	308
John Willey	58	John M^c^Lean	328
Zachary Hume Edwards	77	Sir Simon R. B. Taylor, B^t^	351, 409
Henry Hough	85	Daniel Rodrigues *als.* Cardozo	498
William Nasmyth	96	Adam Smith	517
William Parke	98	Samuel Queneborough	581
William Shackerley	153	Isaac Dias Fernandes	602
Samuel Virgin	164	George Phillips	619
George Ellis	235		

1816. "Wynne."

Sir Simon R. B. Taylor, B^t^	49	Nathaniel Gray	369
Henry Wildman	52	Esther Lindo	447
Sarah Cosens	70	Thomas Prince	454
Robert Ingram	145	James Worsfold	470
Lachlan M^c^Gillivray	154	Stephen Hill	484
Martha Countess of St Vincent	164	Tho. Garland Murray	490
Samuel Mainley	213	James Walker	501
James Wildman	229	Michael Collman	506
Ann Sus^a^ Baroness Dow. of Penrhyn	276	James Robertson	539
David Lopes Torres	341	Mary Louisa Arcedeckne	663
Thomas Winder	346	Mary Powell Royall	638

ST. KITTS.

Eliz. Mathew	33 Heathfield.	Lucas Garvey	503 Pakenham.
Robert Claxton	63 ,,	John Julius	572 ,,
Andrew Perrott	154 ,,	Will. Ottley	578 ,,
Frances Woodley	277 ,,	Matilda Losack	615 ,,
Rd H. Losack	553 ,,	John W. Willett	629 ,,
John Julius	604 ,,	Mich. O'Loughlin	157 Wynne.
Joseph Estridge	347 Bridport.	Cath. Stapleton	394 ,,
Will. Armstrong	546 ,,	Anne S. Blake	416 ,,
Mary Mathew	619 ,,	Eliz. P. P. Hall	438 ,,
Benj. Archer	170 Pakenham.	Aretas Akers	602 ,,

VARIOUS.

James Jordan. Dominica. 30 Heathfield.
John Wardrobe. ,, 49 ,,
Andrew Whiteman. Grenada. 108 Heathfield.
James Rouayne. Hayti. 160 Heathfield.
Walter Sheen. Tortola. 162 ,,
Justin McCarthy. St. Croix. 205 Heathfield.
Dominique Pechier. Martinique. 377 Heathfield.
Ackey Lawrence. St. Lucia. 554 Heathfield.
Robert Tuite. St. Croix. Vol. XI. Heathfield.
Francis Tucker. Bermuda. 40 Bridport.
John Corlet. Dominica. 344 ,,
Robert Smith. Tobago. 374 ,,
Alexander Begbie. Bahamas. 393 ,,
Samuel Chollet. Trinidad. 459 ,,
Ann Wyke. Montserrat. 501 ,,
Isaac Hartman. St. Croix. 610 ,,
John Clark. St. Vincent. 12 Pakenham.
George Morison. Tobago. 94 ,,
Duncan Campbell. Dom. Tob. Gren. 125 Pakenham.
William Alexander. St. Vincent. 170 Pakenham.
James Bruce. St. Vincent. 226 Pakenham.
John Tate. Grenada. 285 Pakenham.
John Reid. ,, 336 ,,
Thomas S. Gore. Bahamas. 372 Pakenham.
Helena, Bridget and Tho. Meade. Montserrat. 455 Pakenham.
James Menzies. Bahamas. 458 Pakenham.
John Ward. Nevis. 486 Pakenham.
James Gordon. Honduras 504 Pakenham.
Mary and Sarah Meade. Montserrat. 510 Pakenham.
George Godwin. Domca St. Vincent. 567 Pakenham.
William Akid. Tobago. 576 Pakenham.
Charles K. Du Vernet. St. Lucia. 15 Wynne.
John Norris. St. Croix. 38 ,,
John Ker. Grenada. 85 ,,
John C. Lettsom. Tortola. 148 ,,
Sir C. Shipley. Grenada. 335 ,,
John Miller. Bahamas. 386 ,,
Stephen Castor. Curacoa. 509 ,,
Andrew De Vaux. Bahamas. 511 Wynne.

Notes and Queries.

AKERS. (*Ante*, IV., 97.)

St. George's, Basseterre, St. Kitts.

Baptisms.

1765	Oct. 16	John s. of James and Jane Akers; b. 2 April.
1766	Aug. 21	Isaac Dupuy s. of James and Jane Akers; b. 11 June.
1768	May 12	Isabella dau. of Aretas and Jane Akers; b. 7 May.
1785	Aug. 11	Mary Rawlins dau. of James and Ann Akers; b. 16 July.

MARRIAGES.

(? 1752, 1753 Jan.) 4 Aretas Akers to Jane Douglas.
1760 . . . . es Akers to Jane Abbot, Widow.
1775 July 20 Robert Houston and Mary Douglas Akers.

BURIALS.

1769 June 11 Jane wife of Aretas Akers.
1780 May 18 Edmund Akers, aged 38.
1785 Sept. 30 Mary Rawlins dau. of James, jun[r], and Ann Akers, aged 2¼ m[s].
1786 May 28 Hugh Vance Akers. 37.
1791 Jan. 24 James Akers. 67.
1793 Oct. 17 John Akers, Barrister at Law, aged 27.

(*Ante*, IV., 98.)

Aretas Akers now of Holles Street, Esq. Will dated 9 June 1814. Whereas in March 1795 I intermarried with my wife Jane, and I have issue by her two sons, Aretas A. my eldest son and Jas. Ramsay A. my youngest and only other son, and two daus. Mary A. and Caroline A., and I secured by my bond £400 a year to my wife during her widowhood and her fortune was vested in trustees for our lives and then for our children. I appoint my said wife and Geo. Douglas of Tunbridge Wells, co. Kent, Esq., and the Rev. Rich[d] Warde of Yalding, clerk, Ex'ors, they and Rob. Houston of G[t] Cumberland Street, Esq., G., a suit in Chancery to be instituted, Government securities to be purchased which shall yield £1000 a year, my wife to have the income. I bequeath her all furniture, etc., £10,000 apiece for each of my daus. at 21. £15,000 for my son Jas. Ramsay A. at 21, £25,000 for my eldest son Aretas A. at 21. All residue of personal estate to my said eldest son in tail, and on death of all issue to the children of my brothers Edmund Fleming A. and John Houston A., and of my late sister Isabel Morson. To my wife £200 immediately. I give my 100 acres of uncultivated land in S[t] Vincent to my eldest son, and all my books, watches, seals and family portraits. To my dau. Mary the small bedstead which her sister Jane used. My son Aretas not to be educated at a public school except to a University. My wife to give up all control over my nephew Henry Morson the son of my sister Isabel M. A black marble to be put over the grave of my two children who were interred in Margate church and a small monument near it, and a monument to be placed over the grave of my son buried in Yalding church. Proved 24 Dec. 1816 by Jane Akers, widow, the relict, and the Rev. Richard Warde, p.r. to G.D., Esq. (602, Wynne.)

AUDAIN. (*Ante*, IV., 214.)

ST. ANNE'S, SANDY POINT, ST. KITTS.

BAPTISMS.

1726 July 14 Peter s. of Andrew Audain. 11 July 1725.
1727 June 4 Maria Alluisia Audain dau. of Andrew Audain.
1730 Feb. 8 Gorges Andrea s. of Andrew Audain. April 10, 1729.
1738-9 Jan. 10 . . . . dau. of Abraham Audain.
1746 July 6 Lucy (b. July 4, '46), dau. of Abraham and Tabitha Audain.
1747 Aug. 27 Susanna (b. Aug. 24, '47), dau. of John and Mary Audain.
1748 Jan. 12 Isaac Peter Audain (b. Jan. 5, '48), s. of Abraham and Tabitha.
1751 Nov. 11 Mary Elizabeth dau. of John and Mary Audain.
1751 July 4 Isaac Peter (b. July 4, 1751), s. of John and Mary Audain.

Burials.

1725 July 11 Doctor Peter Audain.
1729 April 10 Francis s. of Andrew Audain.
1752 Nov. 9 Dr Isaac Peter Audain.
1751 Dec. 26 Tabitha wife of Abraham Audain.
1751 Nov. 28 Lucy Audain, aged 5 years, 4 months and 24 days.

Marriage.

1736 Oct. 3 Abraham Audain and Tabitha Manning.

St. George's, Basseterre, St. Kitts.

Burials.

1781 Nov. 28 Ann dau. of Philip Audain. 4 years.
1799 Aug. 2 Thomas Audain, Gentleman, aged 19 years.

BUNCOMBE OF MONTSERRAT.

Edward Buncombe late of the Island of Mountseratt but now of Bristol, Esq. Will dated 26 Aug. 11 Q. Anne, 1712. Whereas I have conveyed to my eldest son John my share of the Manor of Goathurst, co. Som., and in consideration thereof he gave me a bond dated 16 Aug. of £800 conditioned for the payment of £400 I confirm the same. My son Wm B. £200, and my two sons Charles and Joseph B. £100 each at 21. If they die the said bond to my sons and dau. Edward, Tho., George and Ann B. equally at 21. My dau. Mary Molineux wife of John M. of the I. of Mountseratt, planter, £10. To each of my grand children John Davis Molineux and his sister Mary Molineux 3000 lbs. of Muscovado sugar at 18. My son Tho. B. 60,000 lbs. at 21, and during his minority 4000 lbs. yearly with meat, lodging, and permission to keep stock. My dau. Ann B. 60,000 lbs. at 18 and 4000 lbs. yearly, etc. My sons Charles, Joseph and Geo. B. 30.000 lbs. each at 21 with "sufficient Apparell, Meat, Drink, Washing, Lodging and Schoolling;" if they die their shares to my s. George. My wife Ann B. ⅓ of the produce of and liberty to live on my plantation with the use of a horse and boy and 2 negro women and their children and furniture of her chamber. My friend Edward Hackett of Bristol, Merchant, £5. My plantation, negros, horses, plate and all residue to my s. Ed. B. and Ex'or for the Leeward Islands, and Ed. Hackett Ex'or for Great Britain.

Witnessed by Eliz. Stayner, ffra. ffreeman, Rd Higgins.

Proved 30 Oct. 1712 by Ed. Hackett, power reserved to Ed. B. the son. (P.C.C., 182, Barnes.)

On the E. wall of the chancel of St. Nicholas Church, Bristol, was formerly a tablet to him recording his death on 11 Sept. 1712, aged 53. (*Ante*, II., 275.) He was Speaker *c.* 1710. (Oldmixon, ii., 233.)

1693, Oct. 17. Govr. Codrington writes: About 10 days ago a French privateer in the night carried off one Capt. B. and 40 negroes from Montserrat. (W.I. Cal., p. 183.)

1738, April 10. Edward Buncombe, Esq. Gift of a slave to Benjamin Estridge his father in law. (St. Kitts Records, No. 1823.)

Edward Buncombe, Esq. Will dated 1 Aug. 1741. My father Benjamin Estridge, Esq. My brothers Thomas, George and Charles B., etc. Sworn 1 Sept. 1741. (*Ibid.*, No. 2209.)

Cath. Estridge Buncombe, spr., of St Chr., now residing in St Marylebone. Will dated 6 June 1772. To my valuable friend Mr John Calfe of St Mary Rotherhithe £200. Mrs Cath. Hammond, spr, of M'bone, £250. To my goddau.

Miss Eliz[th] Caines, dau. of Cha. C., Esq., and Judith his wife, £50 at 21. To every one of that amiable family a m. ring apiece. To John Estridge, Esq., now residing in S[t] Geo, Hanover Sq., and his 4 children a ring apiece as a mark of my tender love, in particular my dearest girl Polly—her ample fortune. To my friend M[rs] Marg[t] Willson (once Halliday) £50 for a ring, being second in my affections. To my more than mother M[rs] Leigh, to her mother, her husband and her father a ring each. To my sister M[rs] Ann Cath. Perreau £100. To my sister M[rs] Mary Wylly* £100, her husband M[r] Tho. W. My negro women Fildry and Bemba their freedom. To little Geo., s. of Nelly, dec[d], his freedom, £50, and to be in the care of Capt. Calfe. 5 gns. to Mary Leigh the negro woman serving her mistress M[rs] A. M. Leigh. Dresses to Miss Mary Estridge, Miss Harriot Caines, Miss Fanny Caines, and my goddau. Miss Betsey Caines. M[rs] Halliday the mother of my dear M[rs] Willson. My watch chain to Master Geo. Leigh, s. of Cha. L., Esq. To s[d] Cha. Leigh, Esq., and his wife £100 for 2 rings as a mark of my sisterly love. To poor old M[rs] Jones and her dau. £10. To Miss Otto and Miss Wills a 25*s.* ring. All residue to my good and tender parent (for she has been all that but the name) M[rs] Anna Maria Leigh, widow, of S[t] Chr., now of Great Q. Ann Str., M'bone, and sole Ex'trix. Cod.: To my gods. Geo. Bryan s. of M[rs] Mary Buncombe Bryan of S[t] Chr. and my goddau. Miss Ann Caines dau. of Cha. C., Esq., of S[t] Chr., £25 each. Proved 2 Dec. 1772 by A. M. Leigh. (130, Taverner.)

BURT OF ST. KITTS. (*Ante*, 89.)

St. Anne's, Sandy Point, St. Kitts.

Baptisms.

1725	Jan. 6	Anne Mathew dau. of Colonel William Pim and Louisa Burt.
1726	Nov. 22	Charles Pym Burt s. of Colonel William Pim Burt and Louisa.
1728—1729	Jan. or Feb. 15	Abednego Van Lempit s. of Col. W[m] Burt.
1733	May 10	Mary (b. May 7, '33) dau. of W[m] Pym Burt by his wife Louisa.
1738	April 15	Margaret (b. Ap[l] 15, 1736) dau. of W[m] Pym Burt by his wife Louisa.
1735	Jan. 19	Edward Blake B. (b. Dec. 6, 1734) s. of William Pym B. by his wife Louisa.
1738	Aug. ..	Mathew dau. of .... Pym and Louisa Burt.
1751	April 29	Charles Pym Burt (b. Ap. 29, '51) s of Charles Pym and Catherine.

Burials.

1730	June 29	Abednego Van Lempit Burt.
1750	April 6	The Honourable William Pym Burt, Esq.
1751	April 30	Charles Pym Burt, aged 1 day.
1738-39	Jan. ..	.. odrington Burt.
1738	May 25	Margaret Burt.
1738	May 27	Edward Blake Burt.

Marriages.

1730	April 19	W[m] Markham and M[rs] Elizabeth Burt.
1730	Aug. 28	Benjamin Markham and M[rs] Burt (Frances).
1735	June 26	James Verchild and Penelope Burt.
1744	Feb. 1	Alexander Fraser and Louisa Burt.
1745	Nov. 1	Francis Phipps and Susanna Burt.
1740	May 15	Dan[l] Everard Guilben and Mary Burt.
1741	May 8	James Emra and Catherine Burt.

* B. 1733, a dau. of John Estridge by Eliz. Phipps his wife.

St. George's, Basseterre, St. Kitts.

1753 Dec. 2 Jane Wood dau. of Charles-Pym and Catherine Burt; b. 20 Nov., bapt.

COTTLE OF ST. KITTS. (*Ante*, IV., 210.)

St. George's, Basseterre, St. Kitts.

Baptisms.

1756 July 24 Sarah Grace Bell, dau. of Thomas & Grace C., b. 29 Dec. 1754.
1759 June 10 John Durandt, s. of Thos & Grace Cottle, b. 15 May.
1762 April 23 Elizabeth, dau. of Thos & Grace Cottle, b. 29 March.
1763 Mar. 27 John Mark, s. of Thos & Grace Cottle, b. ye 14 March.

Burials.

1760 May 16 John Durant Cottle, an infant.
1765 Nov. 19 Thos Cottle. 40 years.

CROOKE OF ST. KITTS. (*Ante*, III., 193.)

Trinity, Palmetto Point, St. Kitts.

Baptisms.

1749 Feb. 26 Clement, s. of Ensign Thos Crooke & Mary his wife, b. Nov. 14.
1754 Mar. 31 Henrietta Garnett, dau. of Captn Thos Peter Crooke & Henrietta his wife.
1757 Feb. 27 Elizth Assily, dau. of Thos Peter Crook, a Lieut., & Henrietta his wife, b. Nov. 10, 1756.
1805 July 7 John Kerie, inft s. of Wm Greatheed & Christina Crooke, b. Ap. 15, 1804, etc.
1810 May 14 Wm Phipps, inft s. of Wm Greatheed & Christina Crooke, b. Jan. 16, 1807, etc.
1811 May 2 Christina, dau. of Wm Greatheed Crooke & Christina his wife, b. Aug. 31, 1805, etc.
1811 May 2 Milward Pickwood, s. of Wm Greatheed Crooke & Christina his wife, b. July 14, 1809, etc.

Burials.

1751 Dec. 21 Clement, s. of Ensign Thos Crooke & Mary his wife.
1797 Dec. 28 Mrs Henrietta Crooke from Basseterre.
1811 Jan. 24 Henrietta Crooke, aged 20 years, from Basseterre.

Marriage.

1753 Feb. 26 Peter Thomas Crooke, Esq., & Henrietta Gibbons, dau. of Mrs Henrietta G., widow.

St. George's, Basseterre, St. Kitts.

1771 Aug. 21 Milward Crooke & Anne Smith Clarke.
1772 Mar. 31 The Honourable Samuel Crooke & Mary Duport.
1797 Dec. 28 Henrietta Crooke, spinster, aged [*blank*], card to Palmetto Point.

St. Anne's, Sandy Point, St. Kitts.

1725 May 24 John Crooke & Mrs Martha Assalie.
1737 Dec. — Saml Crooke & Sarah Milward.

Baptism.

1750 May 3 Elizabeth Assailly Crooke (b. Ap. 25, 1750), dau. of Assailly & Frances of the p. of St John.

Burials.

1725 June 1 John Crooke.
1726 Dec. 31 Dowson Crooke.

Wm. Crooke, late of the Island of St Chr., now of Nottingham Place, Marylebone, Esq. Will dated 17 July 1805. My house and lands in the Town of Sandy Point which I inherit from my decd uncle Henry Bennett which he purchased from Stephen Payne to my sister Parker Francken wife of Parker Bennett F. of S. Pt and the land called Old Fort with the buildings also from my sd uncle to my neph. Wm Crooke Wood and the land formerly Rev. John Baldrick's, decd, and since inherited from my uncle and lying between the land I have given to my sister P. F. and land late of Stafford Somarsall, decd, and Jonath. Clarke to my servt Tho. Phipps. To my friends Jedediah Kerie of St C., Esq., Cornelius Hendrickson Kortright, late of St Croix, now of Hylands, co. Essex, Esq., £5000 to pay the interest to my sister and her husband. I give her all my plate, linen and china. My nephew Wm Henry F. at 21 £1000 and £80 a year until then. My niece Jane F. at 21 £1000 and £80 a year. Nephews Wm Crooke Wood, Henry Bennett Wood, Jas. W., Edw. W., Decimus W., £1000 each. To sd Trustees £1000 for my niece Ann Henville wife of Fra. Phipps H. of St C. and dau. of my sister Mary Wood. My niece Mary Crooke Deeble, wife of John D. of St C. and dau. of my sister Mary W., £1000. My niece Jane Baldrick Wood £1000. Niece Eliz. Sprott, wife of Henry S. of St C. and dau. of sd sister, £1000. £4000 for my niece Mary Nesbitt, wife of Dr W. N. and dau. of my decd sister Jane Hewson. My niece Jane Hewson, dau. of my sd sister Jane Howison and half-sister of Mary Nesbitt, £500. To the 2 daus. of my decd nephew Archibald Henry Esdaile and Rebecca his wife £300 between them, servt Tho. Phipps £100, housekeeper Eliz. Spree £100, servt Wm Clarke £200. My goddau. Eliz. Kerie, dau. of Jedediah K. and Mary his wife, £100. Goddau. Mary Kerie Walrond, dau. of Cha. Wills W., £100. Gods. Wm Kortright £100. My mulatto Wm. s. of a mulatto girl Polly Audian (*sic*) and reputed dau. of Abr. A., decd, by a negro w. Nancy, £100. Friend Mrs. Fra. Caines £100. Ex'ors £100 each. All my plantations and lands in G. B. and the W. I. to sd trustees and all leasehold est., goods and money to sell and residue for my sister Parker F., nephew Wm H. F., niece Jane F., sd g. nephews and nieces chn of sist. Mary Wood and the chn of my niece Ann Henville in equal shares. T. to be Ex'ors. Proved 20 March 1817 by C. H. K., Esq., power reserved to J. K. On 23 Oct. 1818 adm'on of est. left unad. by C. H. K., Esq., decd, gr. to Henry Bennett Wood, Esq., J. K. having renounced.

On 15 Dec. 1827 adm'on to John Stewart Wood, Esq., the atty of Patrick Woodley Henville, Esq., a child of Ann H. wife of Fra. P. H., now residing in St Chr. (117, Effingham.)

DALY OF MONTSERRAT. (*Ante*, I., 114.)

1675-6. Daniel Daly, aged 60, his deposition. ("Antigua," I., lii.)
1677-8. Lieut. Edmond Daly.
1702, Aug. 8. Major John Daly, in the army many years and served in all the expeditions in the late wars in those parts, is recommended for a seat in the Council. (Col. Cal., p. 512.)
1710. John Daly, Esq., and Dennis Daly, Esq., Member of the Council or Assembly. (Oldmixon, ii., 233.)
Rees Daly, s. of John Daly of M., esq., Exeter Coll., matric. 13 July 1731; aged 18. (Foster);
1735, Dec. 18. He went out as a minister. (Fothergill.)
1779. Tho. Oliver and Richard Oliver then owned the Bugby Hole plantation in the parish of St George, which included John Daly Fitz Dennys 100 acres. ("Antigua," II., 328.)
1785, Jan. 6. Nath. Bass Daly of the parish of St Peter, planter. My son Wm. Collins Daly, a infant, gift of a cow, foal and negro woman; and to my dau. Mary Alice Daly a negro woman. (M. Records, No. 3848.)
M.I. at Carrs Bay in the parish of St John to Eliz. wife of Nath. Bass Daly, Esq.; born 31 Jan. 1762; died 10 Jan. 1793. Also to Barbara wife of Mr Justin Daly; died 26 Aug. 1829; aged 46.
Anna Daly mar. Joshua Dyet. He died in 1827 at Antigua.

St. Michael's, Barbados.

1754, Dec. 28. Rich. Bass Daly and Marg. Crips.

ESTWICK OF BARBADOS. (*Ante*, III., 60; IV., 44.)

Abstracts from the Island Records.

1640, May 2. Edward Estwick for 34,000 lbs. of cotton and tobacco sells 100 acres and 6 men servants. On pp. 853 and 866 his name is written "Elswicke." (Vol. I., 734.) As there is no Edward in the Estwick pedigree, the entry probably refers to the former name.
1640, Dec. 12. Richard Estwick lets his 100 acres in the parish of St. John, below the cliff, for 21 years at 1000 lbs. of cotton yearly rent. (*Ibid.*, p. 926.)
1641, Feb. 21. Richard Estwick sells 8 acres under the cliff in St. John's parish. (Vol. II, 340, 401.)
1642, Aug. 25. Richard Estwicke sells 100 acres on the Windward side of the island. (*Ibid.*, 115.)
1643, Apr. 18. Mr Henry Estwicke owes the church of St. George 445 lbs. of cotton. (Vol. I., 168.)
1647, March 29. Richard Estwicke and Francis Estwicke, gent^n, sell 100 acres in St. George's. (Vol. II., 104.)

Henry Estwick of the parish of St. George. Will dated 20 Jan. 1679. To my son Thomas one moiety of all my estate and to my son Richard the other moiety. My cousin Francis E., son of my brother Francis E. Sworn 25 Feb. 1679 (Vol. xiv. of Wills, p. 32.)

FAHIE OF ST. KITTS. (*Ante*, IV., 266.)

St. Anne's, Sandy Point, St. Kitts.

Baptisms.

1720 Mar. 20 Antony s. of Antony Fahie.
1727 May 28 George s. of Colonel Antony Fahie.
1733 Aug. 12 Molineux (b. Aug. 6, 1733) s. of Antony & Eliz^th Fahie.
1734 June 30 Sarah Fahie (b. Aug. 10, 1733) dau. of Thos Fahie & Eliz^th Richards.
1752 Jan. 24 Antony George F. (b. Dec. 22, 1751) s. of John Davis Fahie & Sarah.
1753 Oct. 14 Mary (b. June 18, 1753) dau. of George & Marg^t Fahie.
1752 May 14 Antony (b. May 14, 1752) s. of George & Marg^t Fahie.

Marriages.

1730 July 24 Colonel Antony Fahie, Widower, & Mrs Eliz^th Molineux.
1734 Jan. 30 Richard Crispin & Sarah Fahie, by Lic.
1751 Sept. 15 John Deeble & Sarah Fahie, spr.

Burials.

1737 or 8 Mar. 22 Anthony Fahie.
1752 May 29 Antony Fahie, aged 15 days.

St. George's, Basseterre, St. Kitts.

1757 — — . . . . r Fahie to Julian Dexter.

Mary Bourryau, widow [or ? wife] of Anthony Fahie, was buried at Blyborough, Lincolnshire, in 1751 in the vault of Zachariah Bourryau of St. Kitts.

PHIPPS TO FAHIE, SALE OF A MESSUAGE FOR £350.

This Ind're of lease made the 17 Feb. 31 Geo. II., 1758 Between Fra. Phipps of Temsford, co. Bedf., Esq., of the one part and Geo. Fahie of the I. of St Chr., Esq., of the other Wit. that for 5s. by G. F. paid F. P. sells him all that messuage and land in the p'ish of St Ann, Sandy P^t bounded E. with the common road, S. with lands of Mr John Nolan, W. with the street, N. with lands of Capt. Philip Brotherson for one year. Release. This Ind're trip. made the 18 Feb. 1758 Between Fra. P. and Eliz. his wife of the 1st part, Sir Gillies Payne of Roxton, co. Bedf., Bart., Constantine Phipps of Upper Brook St^r, St Geo., Han. Sq., Esq., and Jas. Geo. Douglas of Broad St^r, L., merch^t of the 2^d part, and Geo. Fahie of the 3^d part. Whereas Joseph Phipps l. of St Chr., Esq., dec^d by his will* dated 3 Jan. 1744-5, gave to his dau. Ann £1000 st., to his dau. Mary £1000, his dau. Alletta La Cousay £1000, all at 21 or m., and after providing for his wife Ann gave to his s. Fra. all the residue of his estate and died and his will was p. before his E. Wm. Mathew and Whereas by an Ind're dated 26 May 1756 made between Fra. P. and J. G. Douglas for paying the said legacies F. P. sold to Sir G. P. and C. P. and J. G. D. his p^tn in T. and whereas Geo. F. hath agreed for the purchase of the messuage for £350 c., they release it to him, and Fra. P. and Eliz. his wife app^t Rob. Colham (*sic*) and Fra. Philips of St C., Esq^es, their att^y. (Close Roll, 6025.)

* See *Ante* II., 359.

GEORGES OF ST. KITTS. (*Ante*, III., 305.)

St. Anne's, Sandy Point, St. Kitts.

Baptisms.

1726 Oct. 10 Sarah, dau. of Theodore Georges & Sarah.
1730 Dec. 28 Catherine, dau. of Captain Georges & Sarah.
1732 Dec. 24 Sarah (b. Dec. 19, 1732), dau. of Theodore van Elburgh & Sarah Georges.
1737 May 14 Anne, dau. to Theodore van Georges & Martha his wife.
1738 Aug. 24 Wm Payne, s. to Theodore . . . . Martha Georges.

Marriage.

1748 Oct. 10 The Honourable Charles Morton, Esq., & Anne Louisa Georges.

Burials.

1729 Sept. 6 . . . . s. of Captain George.
1732 Sept. 17 Sarah, dau. of Theodore van Elburgh & Sarah Georges.
1735 May 10 Sarah, wife of Theodore van Elburgh Georges.
1775 — Anne, wife of the Honble Wm Payne Georges, Esq.

St. George's, Basseterre, St. Kitts.

Baptisms.

1772 Nov. 25 Caroline Louisa, dau. of Wm Payne & Ann Georges, b. 12 July 1772.
1793 Jan. 18 Caroline, dau. . . . . Georges & . . . . his wife, about 3 weeks old, at Trinity P. Pt.
1794 Dec. 27 Henry St John, s. of Wm Payne Georges & Ruth his wife, b. 11 Sept.

These two notices from newspapers probably relate to descendants:—

1915, Feb. Georges.—On the 21st inst., at 24 South-parade, Southsea, Mary Jane, the widow of Colonel Theodore Clayton Georges, Indian Army, aged eighty-five. Funeral at Highland-road Cemetery, Southsea, Feb. 24th, at 12.30.

Carter : Georges.—On the 14th Oct., at St. Mary's, Aberdeen, by the Lord Bishop of Aberdeen and Orkney, assisted by the Rev. Canon Christie, Rector, Captain John Fillis Carré Carter, I.A., General Staff, War Office, only son of the late Captain Charles Carré Carter, Royal Engineers, and Mrs. Cummings, to Gwendolyn Marjorie, only surviving child of the late Lieut.-Colonel William Payne Georges, Royal Artillery, and Mrs. Georges, of Albyn Lodge, Aberdeen.

GREATHEED OF ST. KITTS. (*Ante*, 49.)

St. George's, Basseterre, St. Kitts.

Baptisms.

1749 Dec. 16 Frances dau. of Craister and Mary Greatheed; b. 25 May.
1750 Dec. 11 Anne dau. of Marmaduke and Anne Greatheed; b. 30 Nov.
1750-1 . . . . . John s. of Craister and Mary Greatheed; b. 1 Jan.
1753 Oct. 30 Mary Bertie dau. of Marmaduke and Anne Greatheed; b. 22 Oct.
1755 July 3 Jane dau. of Marmaduke and Anne Greatheed; b. 8 June.
1756 April 18 William s. of Craister and Mary Greatheed; b. 18 May 1755.

BURIALS.

1747 Dec. 18 Anne Greatheed.
1748 July 18 Frances Greatheed, a child.
1757 May 23 Jane Greathheed, a child.
1758 Aug. 4 John Greatheed, a child.
1781 June 25 William Greatheed.

ST. THOMAS, MIDDLE ISLAND, ST. KITTS.

1762 Nov. 12 Richard Greatheed and Priscilla Morphy, widow.

There is a mezzotint portrait of Samuel Greatheed (1732—1829) by Houston after Hoare.

JACKSON OF ST. VINCENT. (*Ante*, III., 98.)

ST. GEORGE'S BASSETERRE, ST. KITTS.

Baptisms.

1765 June 15 John Mills s. of Josias & Eliz[th] Gerrald Jackson.
1767 Jan. 18 Eliz[th] Gerald dau. of Josias & Eliz[th] Gerald Jackson, b. 4 Aug. 1762.
— John Mills s. of the said parents, b. 10 June 1764.
— Josias s. „ „ b. 28 June 1765.
— Mary dau. „ „ b. 7 Dec. 1766.

I cannot discover any entry of marriage, but the register at this period is very defective.

LETTSOM OF TORTOLA. (*Ante*, III., 306.)

ST. ANNE'S, SANDY POINT, ST. KITTS.

1732 Jan. 19 Robert (b. Dec. 11, 1730) s. of Robert & Mary Letsom of the Island of Tortola, bapt.
1733 July 1 John (b. April 20, 1733) s. of Robert & Mary Letsom of the Island of Tortola, bapt.

LICENCE TO PRACTISE MEDICINE AND SURGERY.

Before any physicians or surgeons were allowed to practise their profession, they were compelled by the island laws to produce their certificates or diplomas and satisfy some of their deputed brethren as to their competence and skill. The following I copied from an old volume at Nevis containing the Minutes of the Council:—

"1763, Aug. 18. Then came into Council M[r] John Benton and produced his Honour's Warrant to Doctor Onslow Barret for his Examination in Physick and Surgery with Doctor Barret's report thereon of his capacity and abilities therein which was read at this board and he took all the Oaths prescribed by Act of Parliament and repeated and subscribed the Test."

MARKHAM OF ST. KITTS. (*Ante*, IV., 73.)

St. Anne's, Sandy Point, St. Kitts.

Baptisms.

1731 Aug. 9 Mary (b. Aug. 4, 1731) dau. of Benjamin & Frances Markham.
1733 Mar. 21 Benjamin Pym (b. March 18, 1733) s. of W^m^ & Eliz^th^ Markham.
1734 July 21 Anne Burt Markham (b. July 12, 1734) dau. of William Elrington Markham by his wife Elizabeth.
1736 July 9 Mary Elrington Markham (b. July 9, 1736) dau. of W^m^ & Elizabeth.
1745 Oct. 25 Benjamin Gibbons Markham (b. Aug. 22, 1745) s. of Benjamin.

Marriages.

1730 April 19 Wm Markham & Mrs Eliz^th^ Burt.
1730 Aug. 28 Benjamin Markham & Mrs Burt (Frances).
1748 Nov. 25 Lewis Brotherson & Frances Hill Markham.
1752 May 27 Saml Harris & Anne Markham.

Burials.

1726 Dec. 10 Jacob Markham.
1737 or 8 Oct. 13 William Markham's child.
1745 June 28 Benjamin Markham.
1746 May 17 Benjamin Markham.
1747 May 5 Mary Markham.
1747 Feb. 11 Vesey Markham.
1747 Sept. 13 Benjamin Markham.

1771 Aug. 21 Benjamin Pym Markham a Coun . . . .

MOLINEUX OF MONTSERRAT. (*Ante*, III., 1.)

This Ind're made the 7 Oct., 15 Geo. III., 1775 Between John Davis Molineux of Montserrat, now in the City of London, Esq., s. and h. of John Davis Molineux late of the said island, Esq., deceased of the one part and Tho. Meade, Henry Parsons and Charles O'Garra all of the said island Esquires of the other part, Witnesseth that for docking all estate tail John Davis Molineux for 10s. hath conveyed to them all that plantation in the parish of St. Peter called the Water Work containing 250 acres with the mansion house mills works, negroes stock and a messuage in the town of Plymouth as per schedule on trust to sell and pay all debts and legacies of the said John Davis Molineux, deceased, and pay the residue to John Davis Molineux and he appoints Tho. Daniel and Joseph Hamer, both of the said island Esquires his attornies. Total valuation (all set out in detail) £21,583. (Close Roll 6405.)

SMITHER OF ANTIGUA. (Antigua I., xxiii.)

Mr. J. Challenor Smith forwards the following note:—

John Smither, citizen and scrivener, of St. Fayths, London. Will dated 6 Aug. 1652 "Whereas my sonne Robert Smither is safely arrived at the island of Antego in America and there hath purchased all or parte of a plantation to whome at his goeing oute of England I gave £200," give him £200 more. Proved 8 Dec. 1654. [35 Aylett.]

STERNE IN JAMAICA.

In "Familiæ Minorum Gentium," vol. ii., 516 (Harl. Soc. Pub.), is a pedigree of Sterne, by which it appears that Roger Sterne, Lieut. in Handasydes Regt., died at Port Antonio in Jamaica, March 1731. He married Agnes, widow of Captain Herbert, dau. or dau.-in-law of .... Nuttle, a suttler following the Army in Flanders. They had issue a dau. and one son, Laurence Sterne, "The Author," born at Clonmel, 24 Nov. 1713; died 1768.

TOBIN OF NEVIS. (*Ante*, I.)

James Tobin of the I. of Nevis, planter, at present residing in Bristol. Will dated 11 Nov. 1811. To my wife Eliz. an annuity of £500 charged on my plantations all furniture, plate, jewells, china, pictures, linen. I confirm the settlements made on my two daurs. Eliz. Cobham and Fanny Bush at their marriage. To each of my sons except the eldest £1000. To my sister Eliz. Crosse, widow £100. To my brother-in-law Geo. Webbe, Esq., a r. of 10 gs. My s. in l. Rob. Bush my gold watch and r. of 10 gs. To Edw. Parson, Esq. the husbd of my wife's sister a r. of 10 gs. To the Rt Hon. the Earl Manvers and the Hon. Vice Adm. Berkeley r. of 10 gs. for their kind attentions. All my plantations, mills, negroes in Nevis with the stock to my eldest son, all books and engravings and all residue. I appoint the eldest of my sons, my s. in l. Rob. Bush, Esq. and my wife Ex'ors. Cod. Whereas my eldest son Jas. Webbe T. hath died leaving a wife and several infant children and my s. Geo. a Capt. R.N., will now become entitled to my plantations I charge the same with £2000 for Mrs Jane T. the widow of my said late son. 15 March 1815.

Probate 20 Oct. 1817 by Geo. T., Esq., p.r. to the others. On 6 Aug. 1824 Rob. Bush, Esq., renounced. (549, Ellingham.)

TURNER OF ANTIGUA.

Petition of Rowland Oliver late of Antigua now of G. B., Esq. that by Ind're of 12 Aug. 1751 made between Tho. Turner* of A., planter of the one part and your petitioner and John Watkins, Esq., and John Wise, merchant of the other Tho. Turner conveyed a plantation in Popeshead Division of 80 acres to Trustees to pay himself £100 a year and Eliz. his wife £100 a year and to pay debts. Your petitioner went to G B. in June 1762 and John Watkins d. 5 Aug. 1762. John Wise d. long ago. Asks for the appointment of a new Trustee. By a decree of the Court Tho. Burton is to act. (Antigua Record Office.)

FOX OF MONTSERRAT.

Charles Pym of St Kitts, Esq. Will dated 1739. My niece Mrs Eliz. Fox, widow, of M., £300 c. (*Ante*, III., 50.)

---

* Nephew of the Petitioner. He was a spendthrift and living in 1775 in New London, N. America.

Wm. Fox of Montserrat, gent. Will dated 22 Dec. 1749. My wife Eliz. Burt Fox. My daus. Anne, Eliz., Mary and Sarah Fox. My dau. Polenah. My sisters Eliz. Wyke, Jane Fox and Blanche Burt Fox. Sworn 18 April 1750. (Vol. i. of Deeds, p. 53.)

1681, April 15. Mr. Wm. Fox, a M. of C. of M. (A., lxiv.) And again in March 1691. In 1700 Cap. Wm. Fox of the C., aged and indisposed, declines as senior M. to take on the gov^{t} at the death of Col. Tho. Delavall the Lt Govr. (*Ibid.*, lxxii.)

1700. Col. Edwd Fox, acting Gov. Genl. (*Ibid.*, lxxii.)

1710-11, Feb. 22. Capt Anthony Fox, a M. of the Genl A. for M. (*Ibid.*, lxxxii.)

SIDNEY COLLEGE, CAMBRIDGE.*

Ashton Warner Byam, 3rd son of Rev. Francis, Rector of St. John, Antigua; born there; educated at Tonbridge and Charterhouse; admitted 1759, May 15, aged 15; migrated to St. Peter's Coll.

Henry William Coulthurst, 1st son of Henry, merchant, of St. Michael's, Barbadoes; born there 28 June 1753; school—Hipperholme, Halifax, Yorkshire; M.A. of St. John's Coll., and in Priests Orders; migrated 27 April 1781; Fellow bo 1 Oct. 1781.

William Coulthurst, 3rd son of above; born there; school—Shipton, Yorkshire; admitted pensioner May 22, 1782.

[Matthew, born 30 Sept. 1757; died 24 June 1833; aged 76; M.I. in St. Michael's; was probably a brother of the above. Mathew son of Henry was articled a solicitor in 1770.—Ed.]

WEST INDIAN CHANCERY SUITS IN P.R.O.*

The enclosed slips represent the only W.I. items in vol. iv., P—Z, Bridges Chanc. Proc. before 1714 that I noticed in the printed calendar:—

1693. Parish of St. Philip in Barbadoes. Edw. Witheridge *v.* Mary Evans, widow. 196/21.

1915. Parish of Vere in Jamaica. Personal estate of Eleanor Bradway, widow. Jn. Scrimshire and Ruth his wife et al. *v.* Sam. Philp et al. 629/83.

1702. Antigua. Personal estate af George Turney. Geo. Turney, Sancta his wife, Sarah Turney, widow, and Anthony Turney *v.* Tho. Saunders et al. 273/37.

---

* Communicated by the Rev. T. C. Dale of Croydon.

Memoirs of William Hickey.

Edited by ALFRED SPENCER, 1918. Vol. II. (1775—1782).

[Pages 13 to 62 relate to a voyage to Jamaica in the ship "New Shoreham," Capt. Paul Surman.]

After calling at Barbados on 18 Oct. 1775 the author landed at Grenada, then a scene of desolation, a fire a fortnight previously having utterly destroyed the town of St. George. The fort was then garrisoned by two regiments of Infantry (one of them Highlanders), and two companies of Artillery. He was entertained by a Mr. Irwin, an old merchant residing in a melancholy, dirty house at the Careenage, a neat little town of some 50 wooden houses. Mr. Young, the Lieut.-Gov., lived a mile up the mountain. Several of the finest sugar plantations were being ruined by the ravages of small red ants*, for whose destruction rewards of £30,000 had been unavailingly offered. The same pest for 3 years had been destroying the canes in Martinique. A week after their arrival his fellow-passenger Mr. Theophilus Byers, a young Scotch clerk, died of fever. This loss and his uncomfortable surroundings induced Hickey to leave in a small schooner for Antigua, where he spent 10 pleasant days with a family named Mathison. The "New Shoreham" calling for him, they sailed for Jamaica, anchoring on 27 Nov. at Kingston. Here he boarded at a famous lodging-house in the High Street, where at two p m. 25 of them sat down to a plentiful board, having turtle and madeira. He was surprized to see the windows sashed, glazed, and no larger than at home, the heat and smell being most oppressive. The town abounded with noble public and private buildings, European in style and ill-calculated for such a climate. The most celebrated tavern was kept by Jack Baggs, brother to the sporting and well-known Major Baggs. After in 10 years amassing a fortune of £25,000, Baggs had squandered it in 4 years in England, but had then just returned to Jamaica, where in 3 years he again made £8000 and then died of fever.

Hickey's friend Mr. Robert Richards† placed rooms in his house at his disposal, and other persons on whom he called included the Chief Justice, Mr. Harrison, Mr. Welch‡, Mr. Baker, Mr. Webley, Mr. Colcborne, Messrs. Lyon and Ridge§, eminent attorneys and old friends of Mr. Edmund and Mr. Richard Burke (? of London). He was informed that there was no opening for practice in the Courts, the Judges having limited the number of attorneys. Mr. Richards, who had been at the Bar and filled the office of Attorney-General, and other friends all advised him to return to England. He accompanied this friend in his chariot and four to his other house in Spanish Town, where they called on the Gov. Sir Basil Keith‖, who looked dreadfully ill and emaciated. Next evening they attended a splendid ball, given in compliment to Col. Dalling¶, the Lieut.-Gov., on his arrival from Europe. Here he met the only son of Dr. Bonynge, a physician who had amassed considerable wealth, besides inheriting a large property from an elder brother.

* These ants had first appeared in Antigua in 1771, and were supposed to have been brought from Dominica.

† ? Will proved in 1798. [677, Walpole].

‡ Richard Welsh, Chief Justice in 1779. See *ante*, III., 290, and II., 230.

§ Benjamin Lyon of St. Jago Park near the town of St. Jago de la Vega, in his will dated 12 Aug. 1776, names his friend James Ridge, Esq. Sir Simon Clarke, Bart., in his will dated 29 Oct. 1777, bequeathed to Mrs. Mary Willikin Ridge, wife of James Ridge, Esq., £50, and to her husband 20 guineas.

‖ Keith died 15 June 1777, after 3 years and 4 months of office, and a public monument to him was erected in the chancel of St. Catherine's, Spanish Town.

¶ Eliz., wife of Lt.-Col. John Dalling, died 6 July 1768, aged 21. (Archer, 247.) He was appointed Lt.-Gov. in 1771. General Sir John Dalling, K.B. and Bart., died at Clifton, Jan. 1798.

This young man having lost his mother when he was only 10, had spent 4 years at a school in Paris, and 3 at the College of Geneva. He kept a phaeton, a stylish "Tim Whiskey*," and half a dozen blood horses. With him Hickey went to the theatre to see the performance of a company of actors recently arrived from New York, which they left owing to the impending hostilities.

On 7 Dec. a large party started for a tour of the island, including a French Colonel, Mr. Richards, Mr. Jasper Hall† and Mr. Harrison in Mr. Richards' coach and four; the Colonel's A.D.C. and Secretary with Major Butter in Mr. Harrison's coach and four; young Mr. Bonynge and Hickey in his phaeton. In the rear was Mr. Richards' phaeton, two whiskeys and saddle horses, etc. Proceeding along the coast on the S. side, they dined upon an estate of the great Beckford‡, an Alderman of London.

In the afternoon they passed on their left, within 10 miles of Bushy Park, the residence of Dr. Bonynge§, and that night slept at the house of Alderman Kirkman, whose nephew entertained them and next day shewed them the works, which were the finest on the island. The third day they reached Savanna La Mar, visiting 2 noble estates, one belonging to the Forrest family, the other to Mr. Thellasso. There being scarcely an inn in 100 miles it was customary to stop at gentlemen's plantations. The French Colonel being suddenly recalled the party broke up, and Hickey then visited Bushy Park, an estate abounding with immense timber, the house having a noble portico at the head of a large flight of stone steps. A neighbour, Mr. Armstrong‖, a strong, hale man of 60, dined with them. He had been at a school in the North of Ireland, was badly educated and indolent. At the age of 20 was sent for by his father to Jamaica, who dying in 5 years left him an estate of £1500—£2000 a year. Dr. Bonynge was also nearly 60, thin and plain, likewise from Ireland, and nearly related to the noble family of Belvidere. He possessed 3 estates, which together yielded full £12,000 a year, but should have cleared £16,000. On 30 Dec. the writer returned to town, and on New Year's Day 1776 set off with Mr. Richards and party to Mr. Tho. Wallings at Cold Spring, a few miles from Kingston. They ascended Grand Legance Mountain full 4 miles, when they came upon a romantic spot where stood a house of 15 spacious rooms, with magnificent views over the town and harbour. Owing to the height above the sea the nights were cold, and 2 blankets and a coal fire were necessary.

Mr. Richards about 14 years previously had married a widow of large property, but she dying after 2 years bequeathed all to him, part of which was a noble estate in the parish of St. Ann, on the N. side of the island, yielding upwards of £3000 a year. In 18 months he married another wealthy widow, and she dying after 10 years left him a plantation in St. Mary's, at the E. end of the island, worth at least £6000 a year. Thus, with his own private fortune, he possessed between 11 and £12,000 a year.

On 3 Feb. Hickey set out with Mr. Richards to visit the latter's estate in St. Mary's and travelling in a phaeton for 18 miles dined at a gentleman's house, completing their journey of as many more miles on horseback. Two miles from the mansion they were met by the slaves who danced and shouted for joy. Mr. Richards treated them with such kindness that they worked better, and the birth-rate was so high that he had not bought 20 the last 10 years. An opportunity was afforded of seeing the effect of the trade wind and current for they watched the "Augustus Cæsar,¶" commanded by Capt. Duffell, take 8 days before she

* Luffman writing from Antigua in 1787 mentions persons "riding in wiskys" (*sic*).

† Jasper Hall, Receiver-Gen., 1760; M. of A. for Kingston, 1764—70: Speaker at his death, Nov. 1778. He built in 1756 Constantine House, a famous mansion. His eldest son was also named Jasper.

‡ Lord Mayor William Beckford had died in 1770.

§ George Bonynge of St. Dorothy, Esq., party to Deed of 1783. (*Ante*, II., 127.)

‖ A will of John Armstrong was proved in 1752. [82, Bettesworth.]

¶ Sir Wm. Young in his Tour described a similar scene.

succeeded in beating up 3 leagues to Port Morant*. On leaving after an 18 days stay they drove the longer half or 21 miles to a pretty penn for breakfast, where they partook of Johnny (? Journey) cakes, and then rode to Kingston.

Capt. Surman having invited Hickey to Old Harbour (about 35 miles from Kingston) where the New Shoreham lay, for the 17th March, St. Patrick's Day, they proceeded on the 15th to Dr. Bonynge's at Bushy Park, which was in the road to Old Harbour and only 6 miles from it. On his return he went with Mr. Richards to Spanish Town and they then set out on a visit to his estate in St. Ann's. After riding 8 miles they reached sixteen-mile-walk, the road passing through grand rocky scenery and past several waterfalls. Beyond they ascended and crossed the central mountain range. In all his travels the writer stated that he never beheld any scenes equal to those in this altogether beautiful Island. On descending the other side they rested for the night at an Inn, the only country one he saw. Next morning they got into the phaeton and reached the house to a late breakfast. This mansion of the best masonry and of 2 stories situated at the very edge of the surf had been erected by Mr. R's first lady.

Inland the view extended over a delightful plain several miles in extent, containing many fine sugar estates. 500 slaves joyfully greeted them on their arrival. There were no other residents within a dozen miles. Next day they rode 9 miles to the estate belonging to Mr. Fitzherbert Richards, brother of his host. The annual produce of this until the last 5 years having been 500 hhds. of sugar and 400 puncheons of rum. The overseer here being guilty of great cruelty to the slaves, Mr. Richards signed a warrant and sent him under military escort to Kingston prison, but attempting escape on the roadway he was shot. On inquiry it was discovered that the slaves were addicted to dirt eating, of which practice 200 had thus destroyed themselves.

On the 7 April, Hickey sailed for England, from Old Harbour in the "New Shoreham," the only other passengers being Capt. Dobbins of the 36th regiment, who had served 16 years in the W. I., and a little boy of 9, son of a wealthy gentleman, who was going to England to be educated.

Hickey left the island with regret for it was the finest country he ever beheld, and from its inhabitants he had experienced extraordinary civilities and acts of kindness. During a residence of 5 months he had lived extremely free in point of wine, kept late hours, exposed himself to heats and damps, but never had the slightest fever. After returning to England Hickey went twice to India and while waiting for a ship at Falmouth in Feb. 1782 "a packet arrived from the W. I., in which came young Georges,† a smart boy, at that time a midshipman belonging to the Admiral's ship on the Jamaica station, he having been obliged to return to Europe from bad health. His father was brother-in-law to Sir Ralph Payne and his family were upon the most intimate terms with mine."

This journal of Hickey is very interesting and entertaining, giving a vivid picture of the social life of the period, as entered into by a gay young man fond of pleasure and amusement. The editor possesses a MS. journal, written in 1774, one year previously, by Miss Schaw, describing her visit to Antigua and St. Kitts from which he hopes to quote in a future issue.

---

* See view of Morant Bay, 31 miles from Kingston (*Ante* III., 81.)

† See *Ante* III., 305. Mrs. Anne Georges was probably Anne Payne, born 28 Nov. 1718, half-sister to Sir Ralph Payne, later Lord Lavington. (*Ante* II., 98.)

The midshipman may have been Henry Theodore Georges, her younger son.

West Indian Bookplates.

Mr. F. Cattle has recently discovered the two following plates :—

803. "RALPH WILLETT PAYNE" Festoon arm, plain spade shield.
1780—90. Arms and Crest of Payne as in No. 691.
Son of Willett Payne of St. Kitts by Elizabeth his wife, he was b. 27 Sept. and baptized 30 Nov. 1749 at St. George's Basseterre; matriculated from Oriel Coll., Oxf., 14 Feb. 1767, aged 17; B.A. 1770; M.A. 1773.

804. "JAMES SCARLETT, ESQ^R." Arm.
Arms.—*Checky Or and Gules, a lion rampant Ermine, a canton Azure* [SCARLETT]; *impaling, Gyronny of eight Or and Sable* [CAMPBELL].
CREST.—*A Tuscan column supported on either side by a lions jamb erased Ermine.*
Second s. of Robert Scarlett of Duckett's Spring, Jamaica; born 1769; Attorney-Genl.; knighted 30 April 1827; created Lord Abinger 12 Jan. 1835; married, 22 Aug. 1792, Louisa Henrietta dau. of Peter Campbell of Kilmory, co. Argyll, and of Jamaica. She died 8 March 1829.

---

805. "HENRY VASSALL. *N: Hurd fec:*" Chip. arm.
Arms (without tinctures) and Crest of Vassall.
A very scarce plate, almost unknown to collectors; discovered in a rare book, printed in 1748, in the Library of Christ Church, Boston. Illustrated in "Notes on Col. H. V.," by Sam. F. Batchelder of Cambridge, Mass., 1917.
He was 14th child of Leonard Vassall of Jamaica and Boston, Mass.; born Xmas Day, 1721, in the West Indies; removed about 1741 to Cambridge, Mass.; married, 28 Jan. 1742, Penelope only dau. of Isaac Royall of Antigua and Medford, Mass. (W.I. Plate, No. 111); Lt.-Col. of Militia, 1763; and died at Camb. 17 March 1769, in his 48th year.

806. "PETER TRAILLE OF SABA, ESQ^R, MEMBER OF THE ACADEMYS OF ROME AND FLORENCE, CAP^T IN THE R. REG^T OF ARTILL^Y." Festoon, garlands at sides of shield. MOTTO.—DISCRIMINE SALUS. (F. 29,737.) See List of Festoon plates in E. L. Journal, xviii, 94.
Saba is a very small rocky island N.W. of St. Eustatius, both belonging to Holland.

End of Volume V.

INDEX.

Pedigrees are printed in SMALL CAPITALS; Arms in *italics*.

A

C

E

F

G

H

I

J

K

L

M

N

O

P

Q

R

S

T.

U

V

W

INDEX TO ADDITIONS AND CORRECTIONS.

London: Mitchell Hughes and Clarke, 11-13 Bream's Buildings, E.C. 4.

Lightning Source UK Ltd.
Milton Keynes UK
UKHW052145150123
415295UK00021B/898